Rick Steves®

BEST OF
ENGLAND

with EDINBURGH

Contents

Post-Pandemic Travels: Expect a Warm Welcome...and a Few Changes
Research for this guidebook was limited by the COVID-19 outbreak, and the long-term impact of the crisis on our recommended destinations is unclear. Some details in this book will change for post-pandemic travelers. Now more than ever, it's smart to reconfirm specifics as you plan and travel. As always, you can find major updates at RickSteves.com/update.

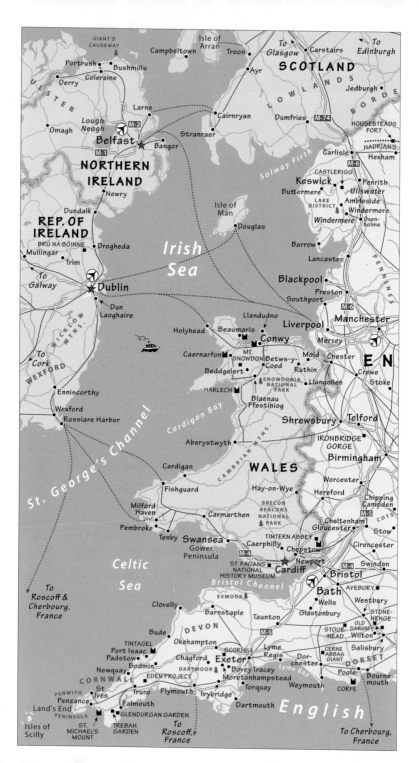

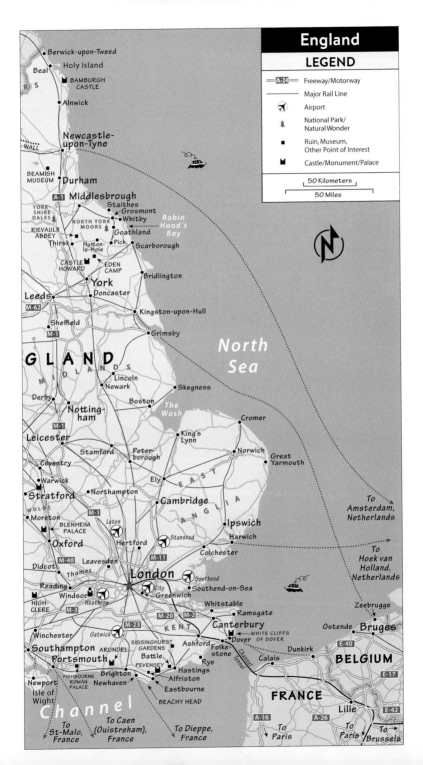

Introduction

Climb the dome of St. Paul's Cathedral and marvel at the pageantry of the guards at Buckingham Palace. Strike up a conversation just to hear the Queen's English. Ponder an ancient stone circle and wander the windswept hills that inspired Wordsworth. See a Shakespeare play or the latest splashy West End musical. Bite into a scone smothered with clotted cream, sip a cup of tea, and wave your pinky as if it's a Union Jack. From appealing towns to the grandeur of London, England delights.

England is the center of the United Kingdom in every way: home to four out of five UK citizens, the seat of government, the economic powerhouse, and the cultural heart. Regardless of the revolution we had centuries ago, many American travelers feel that they "go home" when they visit England.

The English people have a worldwide reputation for being cheery, courteous, and well-mannered. And like in days past, Brits flock to the pub to be social. No matter what time of day, a visit to a historic pub is an enriching experience—and you'll likely make a new friend or two.

Even as England races forward as a leading global player, it preserves its rich history. This means stone circles, ruined abbeys, cathedrals, castles, and palaces are still yours to explore.

Britannia rules—enjoy it royally.

THE BEST OF ENGLAND

This book focuses on England's top destinations, offering a mix of exciting cities and irresistible villages.

London is one of the grandest cities in the world. The town of Bath has attracted visitors since the time of ancient Rome. Quaint Cotswolds towns offer an endearing contrast to the modern-day world. The serene Lake District—crisscrossed with trails, ridges, and lakes—has enough pubs to keep hikers watered and fed. York, with its colorful old town and ghost walks, is a popular haunt for travelers. Across the northern border, Edinburgh is too convenient to pass up—adding a wee bit of Scotland to your trip.

When there are interesting sights or towns near my top destinations, I cover these briefly (as "Near" sights), to help you fill out a free day or a longer stay.

Beyond the major destinations, I'll cover the Best of the Rest—great destinations that don't quite make my top cut, but are worth seeing if you have more time or specific interests: the historic college town of Oxford, majestic Blenheim Palace, Shakespeare's hometown of Stratford-upon-Avon, rejuvenated Liverpool, small Durham with its big cathedral, and ancient Hadrian's Wall.

To help you link the top sights, I've designed a two-week itinerary (on page 26), with tips for tailoring it to your interests.

THE BEST OF LONDON

This thriving, teeming metropolis packs in all things British with a cosmopolitan flair: royal palaces, soaring churches, world-class museums, captivating theater, and people-friendly parks. Come prepared to celebrate the tradition and fanfare of yesterday while catching the buzz of a trend-setting city forging its future.

❶ *London's many grand* **parks** *provide a peaceful respite from the big city.*

❷ *Plays at* **Shakespeare's Globe** *attract modern-day Juliets and Romeos.*

❸ *Spanning the Thames, the pedestrian-only* **Millennium Bridge** *connects St. Paul's Cathedral and Tate Modern.*

❹ *The pomp and pageantry of the* **Changing of the Guard** *entertains onlookers.*

❺ *It's easy to* **eat well** *and affordably in cosmopolitan London.*

❻ *A statue of Churchill overlooks historic* **Parliament Square.**

❼ *The* **London Eye** *Ferris wheel, a fun addition to the cityscape, offers stunning views to riders.*

❽ **Street performers** *give London a lively vibe.*

THE BEST OF BATH

This genteel Georgian showcase city, built around the remains of an ancient Roman bath, hosts an abbey, museums, a spa, walking tours, and graceful architecture that was part of Jane Austen's world.

Proud locals remind visitors that the town is routinely banned from the "Britain in Bloom" contest to give other towns a chance to win.

❶ Bath's glorious **abbey** takes center stage in town.

❷ **Jane Austen** lived—and set two of her novels—in Bath.

❸ The **baths** that gave the town its unusual name date to Roman times.

❹ The **Pump Room** has tea, goodies, and samples of "curative" spa water to drink.

❺ The fanciful **Parade Gardens,** worth a stroll, are near the shop-lined Pulteney Bridge.

❻ The **Bizarre Bath walking tour** makes any evening enjoyable.

❼ The **Thermae Bath Spa** taps the thermal springs burbling under Bath.

❽ The lawn in front of the **Royal Crescent** offers a royal place to relax.

THE BEST OF THE COTSWOLDS

Scattered over this hilly countryside are fragrant fields, peaceful sheep, and dear villages. My favorites are cozy Chipping Campden and popular Stow-on-the-Wold—each with pubs, hikes, and charm to spare. All the Cotswold towns run on slow clocks and yellowed calendars. If the 21st century has come, they don't care.

1 *Lovely little* **Chipping Campden** *invites and rewards exploration.*

2 **Sheep** *are as much a part of the Cotswolds as the people.*

3 *Visitors cool off at* **Bourton-on-the-Water.**

4 *The lodgings in* **Stow-on-the-Wold** *can be as quaint as the village itself.*

5 *In* **Broadway,** *the buildings—made of local limestone—give off a warm glow.*

6 *At* **Cotswold Farm Park,** *it's easy to make new friends.*

7 **Pubs** *throughout the Cotswolds provide an atmospheric destination for hikers, bikers, and drivers.*

THE BEST OF THE LAKE DISTRICT

The Lake District, about 30 miles long and 30 miles wide, is nature's lush, green playground. This idyllic region of rugged ridges and tranquil lakes offers scenic hikes, cruises, joyrides, timeless vistas, and William Wordsworth and Beatrix Potter sights, plus an ancient stone circle perfect for pondering it all.

❶ *Keswick, the best home base, has an appealing main square, fine eateries, and a lovely lake.*

❷ *Ullswater is one of the many lakes that give the district its name.*

❸ *At Dove Cottage, William Wordsworth wrote his finest poetry, inspired by the wonders of nature.*

❹ *Old-time signs mark old-time pubs.*

❺ *Castlerigg Stone Circle, just outside Keswick, is 5,000 years old— as old as Stonehenge.*

❻ *B&Bs provide a welcome home away from home.*

❼ *An easy loop trail around Buttermere Lake rewards hikers with serene views.*

THE BEST OF YORK

Encircled by medieval walls, compact York has a glorious Gothic cathedral, a ruined abbey, and modern museums (on Vikings and more). Classy restaurants hide out in the atmospheric old center, with its "snickelway" passages and colorful Shambles shopping lane.

1 York's massive **Minster** offers up a divine evensong and magnificent, medieval stained glass.

2 The **National Railway Museum**'s models range from early "stagecoaches on rails" to the sleek Eurostar.

3 Gurkha soldiers in the **British Army** march past the Minster.

4 A Viking amusement ride or a museum? **Jorvik** **Viking Centre** is a bit of both.

5 Breaking from the pope, Henry VIII closed all monasteries, leaving many—like **St. Mary's Abbey**—in ruins.

6 Along the **Shambles** street, shops hang old-fashioned signs from old, tilting buildings.

7 At **Bettys Café Tea Rooms,** window seats offer the best people-watching.

THE BEST OF EDINBURGH

Just north of England's border is Scotland's showpiece city. Nestled by craggy bluffs, photogenic Edinburgh is studded with a prickly skyline of spires, towers, and domes. Its Royal Mile, lined with medieval buildings, connects the castle and palace in an attraction-studded stroll through Scottish history. Edinburgh's proximity and exuberance (nonstop during August's festivals) bring a Scottish flair to an England trip.

❶ Edinburgh's famous street, the **Royal Mile,** offers a pleasing array of attractions, pubs, shops, and historic churches.

❷ **Highland dancers** stepping over crossed swords practice the Sword Dance.

❸ Some shops make **custom kilts** using woven (not cheaply printed) tartan material.

❹ A **bagpiper** in full regalia plays Scotland's national instrument.

❺ **Shops and pubs,** fueled by Scotland's many whisky distilleries, sell the national drink.

❻ Try a few drams of **whisky** at a tasting.

❼ Edinburgh's **formidable castle** repelled foes long ago and attracts visitors today.

THE BEST OF THE REST

With extra time, splice any of these destinations into your trip. **Oxford** has revered colleges and illustrious alumni, and nearby **Blenheim Palace** is good enough for Churchill. All the world's a stage, but if you want Shakespeare, **Stratford-upon-Avon** is the top venue. The lively port of **Liverpool** launched The Beatles. **Durham,** with a cavernous cathedral, makes a good stop before or after **Hadrian's Wall,** near the Scottish border.

❶ *Durham's cathedral has Europe's tallest bell tower and memorials for saints, scholars, and coal miners.*

❷ *In Oxford, rental **punts** await unsuspecting novices who think punting looks easy.*

❸ *The dining hall at **Oxford**'s Christ Church College puts most college cafeterias to shame.*

❹ *Near Oxford, **Blenheim Palace** attracts historians and garden lovers.*

❺ *In Liverpool, **John Lennon** hangs out at the Cavern Club, named after the original club (now gone) where The Beatles played.*

❻ *Through his work, Stratford-born **Shake-speare** explored the sweet sorrow of the human condition.*

❼ *Built by Romans, the now-ruined **Hadrian's Wall** blocked out invaders from what is Scotland today.*

❽ *Liverpool's **Albert Dock** is awash with attractions—museums, restaurants, and nighttime fun.*

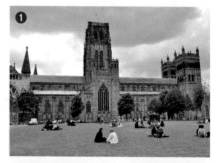

TRAVEL SMART

Approach England like a veteran traveler, even if it's your first trip. Design your itinerary, get a handle on your budget, make advance arrangements, and follow my travel strategies on the road.

For my best advice on sightseeing, accommodations, restaurants, and transportation, see the Practicalities chapter.

Designing Your Itinerary

Decide when to go. July and August are peak season in England, with long days, the best weather, and a busy schedule of tourist fun. May and June can be lovely anywhere. Spring and fall offer decent weather and smaller crowds.

Winter travelers face few crowds and soft room prices (except in London), but sightseeing hours are shorter and the weather is reliably bad. In the countryside, some attractions open only on weekends or close entirely (Nov-Feb). While rural charm falls with the leaves, city sightseeing is fine in winter.

Choose your top destinations. My itinerary (on page 26) gives you an idea of how much you can reasonably see in 14 days, but it's easy to adapt it to fit your interests and time frame.

London offers an amazing variety of sights, food, markets, and the most entertainment. Many travelers could spend a week here (and make easy day trips, if desired). Edinburgh offers similar big-city excitement, especially during its festivals in August. If you prefer midsize towns, Bath and York have much to offer.

Historians can choose among sights prehistoric (Stonehenge), Roman (Bath and Hadrian's Wall), medieval (York and Warwick), royal (Tower of London, Windsor, and Blenheim), and many more.

Nature lovers linger in the Lake District (offering a range of easy-to-challenging hikes in a lakes-and-hills setting) and the Cotswolds (with easier hikes through villages, meadows, and rolling hills).

Literary fans make a pilgrimage to Stratford (Shakespeare), Oxford (Tolkien, Lewis, Woolf, Wilde, and more), Bath (Austen), the Lake District (Wordsworth and Potter), and Edinburgh (Burns, Stevenson, Scott, and more). Beatles fans from here, there, and everywhere head to Liverpool.

Draft a rough itinerary. Figure out how many destinations you can comfortably fit in the time you have. Don't overdo it—few travelers wish they'd hurried more. Allow enough days per stop: Figure on at least

two days for most destinations and four or more for London. Staying in a home base—like London or Bath—and making day trips can be more time-efficient than changing locations and hotels. Minimize one-night stands, especially consecutive ones; it can be worth taking a late-afternoon train ride or drive to get settled into a town for two nights.

Connect the dots. Link your destinations into a logical route. Determine which cities you'll fly into and out of; begin your search for transatlantic flights at Kayak.com.

Instead of spending the first few days of your trip in busy London, I'd recommend a gentler small-town start in Bath and saving London for the grand finale. Going from Heathrow Airport to Bath takes just two hours by train. You'll be more rested and ready to tackle England's greatest city at the end of your trip.

Decide if you'll travel by car, take public transportation, or use a combination. A car is particularly helpful for exploring the Cotswolds and the Lake District (where public transportation can be time-consuming), but is useless in big cities. Some travelers rent a car on site for a day or two, and use public transportation for the rest of their trip.

Shakespeare fans visit Stratford-upon-Avon.

If relying on public transportation, you'll likely use a mix of trains and buses. Trains are faster and more expensive than buses (which don't run as often on Sundays). Also, for efficient regional sightseeing, consider minibus tours (offered from London, Bath, the Lake District, York, and Edinburgh).

Allot sufficient time for transportation in your itinerary. Whether you travel by train, bus, or car, it'll take a half-day to get between most destinations. To determine approximate transportation times between your destinations, study the driving chart on page 407 or check Google Maps; visit NationalRail.co.uk for train schedules or Traveline.info (a route-planning site that includes train and bus options). If traveling beyond England, consider taking the Eurostar train (to the Continent) or a flight; check Skyscanner.com for intra-European flights.

Plan your days. Fine-tune your itinerary; write out a day-by-day plan of where you'll be and what you want to see. To help you make the most of your time, I've suggested day plans for each major destination. But take sight closures into account: Avoid visiting a town on the one day a week that its must-see sights are closed. Check if any holidays or festivals fall during your trip—these attract crowds and can close sights (for the latest, visit England's tourist website, www.visitbritain.com).

Give yourself some slack. Every trip, and every traveler, needs downtime for doing laundry, picnic shopping, relaxing, people-watching, and so on. Pace yourself. Assume you will return.

Ready, set... You've designed the perfect itinerary for the trip of a lifetime.

Trip Costs

Run a reality check on your dream trip. You'll have major transportation costs in addition to daily expenses.

Flight: A round-trip flight from the US to London costs about $900-1,500,

BEST OF ENGLAND IN 2 WEEKS

This unforgettable trip will show you the very best that England has to offer, with a little help from Scotland. You can use public transit, rent a car, or use a combination. Renting a car for just a day or two is most fun in the Cotswolds and the Lake District.

DAY	PLAN	SLEEP
	Arrive in London, head to Bath (2 hours by train from Heathrow, transfer at London's Paddington Station)	Bath
1	Bath	Bath
2	Bath (could add day for Stonehenge, Wells, and/or Glastonbury)	Bath
3	To Cotswolds (2 hours by train to Moreton-in-Marsh, then 45-minute bus ride)	Chipping Campden
4	Cotswolds	Chipping Campden
5	To Lake District (a minimum of 6 hours by bus, with transfers in Stratford-upon-Avon and Penrith)	Keswick
6	Lake District (hikers could add another day here)	Keswick
7	To Edinburgh, Scotland (allow 3 hours: bus to Penrith, then train to Edinburgh)	Edinburgh
8	Edinburgh	Edinburgh
9	To York later in day (2.5 hours by train)	York
10	York	York
11	To London (2 hours by train)	London
12	London	London
13	London	London
14	London	London
	Fly home	

Adding Best of the Rest Destinations: Visit Oxford and Blenheim Palace after Bath and before the Cotswolds. Stratford and/or Liverpool fall logically between the Cotswolds and the Lake District. Hadrian's Wall (easier for drivers) and Durham (on the main train line) can be added between Edinburgh and York.

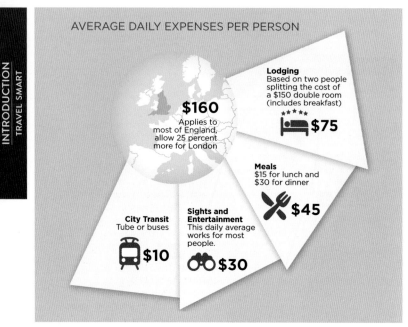

AVERAGE DAILY EXPENSES PER PERSON

$160
Applies to most of England, allow 25 percent more for London

Lodging
Based on two people splitting the cost of a $150 double room (includes breakfast)
★★★★ $75

Meals
$15 for lunch and $30 for dinner
$45

City Transit
Tube or buses
$10

Sights and Entertainment
This daily average works for most people.
$30

depending on where you fly from and when.

Car Rental: Allow roughly $250 per week, not including tolls, gas, parking, and insurance. Rentals are cheapest if arranged from the US.

Public Transportation: For a two-week trip, allow about $500 for second-class trains and buses, including Tube fare in London. You'll usually save money by buying a Britrail England pass that matches your train travel days ("standard" class is cheaper than first class, buy in US before you go); for specifics, see page 403.

By purchasing individual train tickets online, you can get advance-purchase discounts, though you'll be locked into the travel time you choose; a rail pass gives you more flexibility if your plans change.

Budget Tips: You can cut your daily expenses by taking advantage of the deals you'll find throughout England and mentioned in this book.

City transit passes (for multiple rides or all-day use) decrease your cost per ride. For example, it's smart to get an Oyster card in London to cover your Tube and bus travel affordably.

Avid sightseers buy combo-tickets or passes that cover multiple museums. (For country-wide passes, see page 390.) If a town doesn't offer deals, visit only the sights you most want to see, and seek out free sights and experiences (offered even in London—see page 54).

Some businesses—especially hotels and walking-tour companies—offer discounts to my readers (look for the RS% symbol in the listings in this book).

Book your rooms directly with the hotel. Some hotels offer discounts if you pay in cash and/or stay three or more nights (it pays to check online or ask). Rooms cost less outside of peak-season (July and August). And even seniors can stay in hostels (some have double rooms) for about $30 per person. Or check Airbnb-type sites for deals.

It's no hardship to eat inexpensively in England. You can get tasty, affordable meals at pubs, cafeterias, chain restaurants, street food joints, and fish-and-chips stands. Some upscale restaurants offer early-bird dinner specials. Groceries sell ready-made sandwiches; cultivate the art of picnicking in atmospheric settings.

When you splurge, choose an experience you'll always remember, such as an elegant high tea or a splashy London musical. Minimize souvenir shopping; focus instead on collecting wonderful memories.

Before You Go

You'll have a smoother trip if you tackle a few things ahead of time. For more info on these topics, see the Practicalities chapter and RickSteves.com, which has helpful travel tips and talks .

Make sure your passport is valid. If your passport is due to expire within six months of your ticketed date of return, you need to renew it. Allow up to six weeks to renew or get a passport (www.travel.state.gov).

Arrange your transportation. Book your international flights early. It's worth thinking about buying essential train tickets in advance, getting a rail pass, renting a car, or booking cheap British flights. (You can wing it once you're there, but it may cost more.)

Book rooms well in advance, especially if your trip falls during peak season or any major holidays or festivals.

Reserve or buy tickets ahead for must-see plays, special tours, or sights. If there's a particular play or musical you're set on seeing, you can buy tickets before you go. When you're in London, you can save time in line by buying Fast Track tickets for some popular sights. At Stonehenge, most visitors are happy to view the stones from a distance, but to go inside the circle, you'll need reservations. To tour the interior of Lennon and McCartney homes in Liverpool, reserve ahead.

Edinburgh's festivals in August are popular; book ahead for any events you must see (theater, dance, and the Military Tattoo). It's also smart to book online for Edinburgh Castle. Specifics on booking tickets and reservations are in the individual chapters.

Consider travel insurance. Compare the cost of the insurance to the cost of your potential loss. Check whether your

Rick's Free Video Clips and Audio Tours

Rick Steves Classroom Europe, a powerful tool for teachers, is also useful for travelers. This video library contains over 400 short clips excerpted from my public television series. Enjoy these videos as you sort through options for your trip and to better understand what you'll see in Europe. Check it out at Classroom.RickSteves.com (just enter a topic to find everything I've filmed on a subject).

Rick Steves Audio Europe, a free app, makes it easy to download my audio tours and listen to them offline as you travel. For this book (look for the 🎧), these audio tours cover sights and neighborhoods in London, plus Edinburgh's Royal Mile. The app also offers insightful interviews from my public radio show with experts from Europe and around the globe. Find it in your app store or at RickSteves.com/AudioEurope.

existing insurance (health, homeowners, or renters) covers you and your possessions overseas.

Call your bank. Alert your bank that you'll be using your debit and credit cards in Europe. Ask about transaction fees, and get the PIN number for your credit card. You won't need to bring along pounds; you can withdraw currency from cash machines while traveling.

Use your smartphone smartly. Sign up for an international service plan to reduce your costs, or rely on Wi-Fi in Europe instead. Download any apps you'll want on the road, such as maps, transit schedules, and Rick Steves Audio Europe (see sidebar, earlier).

Pack light. You'll walk with your luggage more than you think. I travel for weeks with a single carry-on bag and a daypack. Use the packing checklist in Practicalities as a guide.

Travel Strategies on the Road

If you have a positive attitude, equip yourself with good information, and expect to travel smart, you will.

Read—and reread—this book. To have an "A" trip, be an "A" student. As you study up on sights, note opening hours, closed days, crowd-beating tips, and whether reservations are required or advisable. Check the latest at RickSteves. com/update.

Be your own tour guide. As you travel, get up-to-date info on sights, reserve tickets and tours, reconfirm hotels and travel arrangements, and check transit connections. Visit local tourist information offices. Upon arrival in a new town, lay the groundwork for a smooth departure; confirm the road, train, or bus you'll take when you leave.

Give local tours a spin. Your appreciation of a place and its history can increase dramatically if you take a walking tour in any big city (try London Walks) or at a museum (some offer live or audio

tours), or even hire a private guide (some will drive you around). If you want to learn more about any aspect of England, experts are happy to teach you.

Plan for rain. No matter when you go, the weather can change several times in a day, but rarely is it extreme. Bring a jacket and dress in layers. Just keep traveling and enjoy the "bright spells." A bout of rain is the perfect excuse to go into a pub and make a new friend.

Outsmart thieves. Although pickpocketing isn't a major problem outside of bigger cities, it's still smart to keep your cash, credit cards, and passport secure in a money belt tucked under your clothes. Carry only a day's spending money in your front pocket or wallet. Don't set valuable items down on counters or café tabletops, where they can be quickly stolen or easily forgotten.

Minimize potential loss. Keep expensive gear to a minimum. Bring photocopies or take photos of important documents (passport and cards) to aid in replacement if they're lost or stolen. Back

Welcome to Rick Steves' Europe

Travel is intensified living—maximum thrills per minute and one of the last great sources of legal adventure. Travel is freedom. It's recess, and we need it.

I discovered a passion for European travel as a teen and have been sharing it ever since—through my bus tours, public television and radio shows, and travel guidebooks. Over the years, I've taught millions of travelers how to best enjoy Europe's blockbuster sights—and experience "Back Door" discoveries that most tourists miss.

This book offers you a balanced mix of England's biggies (such as Big Ben and Stonehenge) and more intimate locales (windswept Roman lookouts and nearly edible Cotswold villages). It's selective: There are dozens of hikes in the Lake District; I recommend only the best ones. It's in-depth: My self-guided museum tours and city walks give insight into the country's vibrant history and today's living, breathing culture. And for a Scottish fling, I've added Edinburgh, because it's close and refreshing.

I advocate traveling simply and smartly. Take advantage of my money- and time-saving tips on sightseeing, transportation, and more. Try local, characteristic alternatives to expensive hotels and restaurants. In many ways, spending more money only builds a thicker wall between you and what you traveled so far to see.

We visit England to experience it—to become temporary locals. Thoughtful travel engages us with the world, as we learn to appreciate other cultures and new ways to measure quality of life.

Judging from the positive feedback I receive from readers, this book will help you enjoy a fun, affordable, and rewarding vacation—whether it's your first trip or your tenth.

Have a brilliant holiday! Happy travels!

Rick Steves

up photos and files frequently.

Guard your time and energy. Taking a taxi can be a good value if it saves you a long wait for a bus or an exhausting walk across town. To avoid long lines, follow my crowd-beating tips (such as making advance reservations, or sightseeing early or late).

Be flexible. Even if you have a well-planned itinerary, expect changes, closures, sore feet, drizzly days, and so on. Your Plan B could turn out to be even better.

Connect with the culture. Interacting with locals carbonates your experience. Enjoy the friendliness of the English people; most exchanges come with an ample side-helping of fun banter. Ask questions—most locals are happy to point you in their idea of the right direction. Slow down, step out of your comfort zone, and be open to unexpected experiences. Set up your own quest for the friendliest pub, grandest cathedral, or best musical. When an unexpected opportunity pops up, say "yes."

Ready for a spot of tea and a freshly baked scone? Hear the friendly buzz from the corner pub?

Your next stop...England!

London

A longtime tourist destination, London seems perpetually at your service, with an impressive slate of sights and entertainment. Blow through this urban jungle on the open deck of a double-decker bus and take a pinch-me-I'm-here walk through the West End. Hear the chimes of Big Ben and ogle the crown jewels at the Tower of London. Cruise the Thames River and take a spin on the London Eye. Hobnob with poets' tombstones in Westminster Abbey and rummage through civilization's attic at the British Museum.

London is also more than its museums and landmarks, it's a living, breathing, thriving organism...a coral reef of humanity. The city has changed dramatically in recent years: Many visitors are surprised to find how diverse and cosmopolitan it is. Chinese takeouts outnumber fish-and-chips shops. Eastern Europeans pull pints in British pubs, and Italians express your espresso. Outlying suburbs are home to huge communities of Indians and Pakistanis. This city of 10 million separate dreams is learning—sometimes fitfully—to live as a microcosm of its formerly vast empire.

LONDON IN 4 DAYS

Day 1: Get oriented by taking my Westminster Walk from Big Ben to Trafalgar Square (stop in Westminster Abbey and the Churchill War Rooms on the way). Grab lunch near Trafalgar Square (maybe at the café at St. Martin-in-the-Fields Church), then visit the nearby National Gallery or National Portrait Gallery.

On any evening: Have an early-bird dinner and take in a play in the West End or at Shakespeare's Globe. Choose from a concert, walking tour, or nighttime bus tour. Extend your sightseeing into the evening hours; some attractions stay open late. Settle in at a pub, or do some shopping at any of London's elegant department stores (generally open until 20:00 or 21:00). Stroll any of the main squares, fine parks, or the Jubilee Walkway for people-watching. Ride the London Eye Ferris wheel for grand city views.

Day 2: Early in the morning, take a double-decker hop-on, hop-off sightseeing bus tour from Victoria Station, and hop off for the Changing of the Guard at Buckingham Palace. After lunch, tour the British Museum and/or the nearby British Library.

Day 3: At the Tower of London, see the crown jewels and take the Beefeater tour. Then grab a picnic, catch a boat at Tower Pier, and have lunch on the Thames while cruising to Blackfriars Pier.

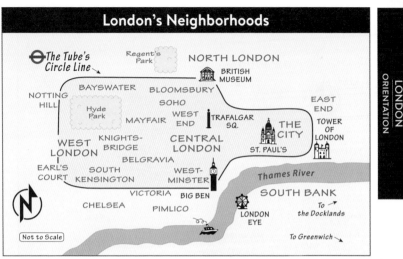

London's Neighborhoods

The Tube's Circle Line

Regent's Park

NORTH LONDON

BRITISH MUSEUM

BAYSWATER

BLOOMSBURY

NOTTING HILL

Hyde Park

SOHO

EAST END

MAYFAIR

WEST END

TRAFALGAR SQ.

THE CITY

TOWER OF LONDON

WEST LONDON

KNIGHTS-BRIDGE

CENTRAL LONDON

ST. PAUL'S

BELGRAVIA

EARL'S COURT

SOUTH KENSINGTON

WEST-MINSTER

Thames River

VICTORIA

BIG BEN

SOUTH BANK

CHELSEA

PIMLICO

LONDON EYE

To the Docklands

Not to Scale

To Greenwich

Tour St. Paul's Cathedral and climb its dome for views, then walk across Millennium Bridge to the South Bank to visit the Tate Modern, tour Shakespeare's Globe, or stroll the Jubilee Walkway.

Day 4: Take your pick of the Victoria and Albert Museum, Tate Britain, Imperial War Museum, or Houses of Parliament. Hit one of London's many lively open-air markets. Or cruise to Greenwich or Kew Gardens.

THE CROWN JEWELS

ORIENTATION

To grasp London more comfortably, see it as the old town in the city center without the modern, congested sprawl.

The Thames River (pron. "tems") runs roughly west to east through the city, with most sights on the North Bank. Mentally, maybe even physically, trim down your map to include only the area between the Tower of London (to the east), Hyde Park (west), Regent's Park (north), and the South Bank (south). This is roughly the area bordered by the Tube's Circle Line. This four-mile stretch between the Tower and Hyde Park (about a 1.5-hour walk) looks like a milk bottle on its side (see map), and holds most of the sights mentioned in this chapter.

The sprawling city becomes much more manageable if you think of it as a collection of neighborhoods.

Central London: This area contains the Westminster district, which includes Big Ben, Parliament, Westminster Abbey, Buckingham Palace, and Trafalgar Square, with its many major museums. The West End is the center of London's cultural life, with bustling squares: Piccadilly Circus and Leicester Square host cinemas, tour-

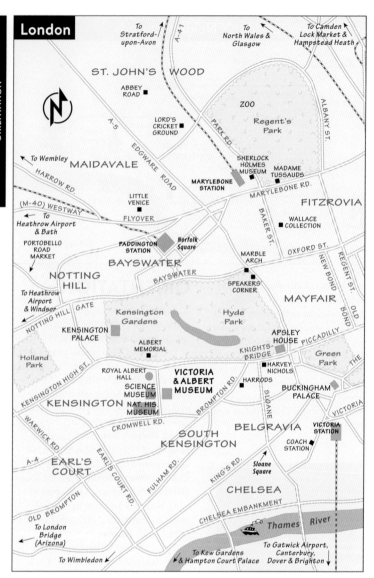

ist traps, and nighttime glitz. Soho and Covent Garden are thriving people zones with theaters, restaurants, pubs, and boutiques. And Regent and Oxford streets are the city's main shopping zones.

North London: Neighborhoods in this part of town—including Bloomsbury, Fitzrovia, and Marylebone—contain such major sights as the British Museum and the overhyped Madame Tussauds Waxworks. Nearby, along busy Euston Road, is the British Library.

The City: Today's modern financial district, called simply "The City," was a walled town in Roman times. Gleaming skyscrapers are interspersed with histori-

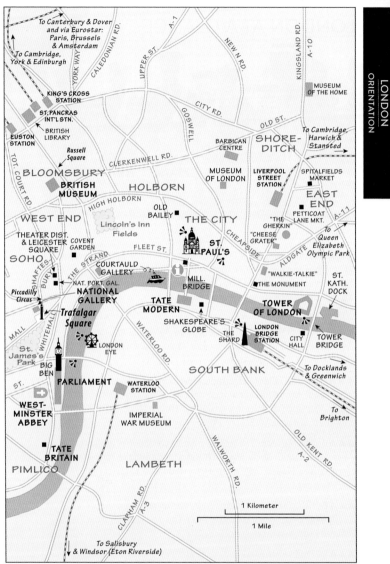

To Canterbury & Dover
and via Eurostar:
Paris, Brussels
& Amsterdam

To Cambridge,
York & Edinburgh

YORK WAY

CALEDONIAN RD.

UPPER ST.

A-1

NEW N RD.

KINGSLAND RD.

A-10

KING'S CROSS
STATION

ST. PANCRAS
INT'L STN.

BRITISH
LIBRARY

EUSTON
STATION

TOT. COURT RD.

Russell
Square

CITY RD.

GOSWELL

OLD ST.

MUSEUM
OF THE HOME

BARBICAN
CENTRE

SHORE-
DITCH

To Cambridge,
Harwich &
Stansted

CLERKENWELL RD.

BLOOMSBURY

BRITISH
MUSEUM

HOLBORN

MUSEUM
OF LONDON

LIVERPOOL
STREET
STATION

SPITALFIELDS
MARKET

HIGH HOLBORN

WEST END

OLD
BAILEY

THE CITY

EAST
END

PETTICOAT
LANE MKT.

A-11

"THE
GHERKIN"

THEATER DIST.
& LEICESTER
SQUARE

Lincoln's Inn
Fields

COVENT
GARDEN

CHEAPSIDE

ST.
PAUL'S

"CHEESE
GRATER"

To
Queen
Elizabeth
Olympic Park

SOHO

SHAFTES-
BURY

THE STRAND

FLEET ST.

COURTAULD
GALLERY

ALDGATE

NAT. PORT. GAL.

Piccadilly
Circus

NATIONAL
GALLERY

MILL.
BRIDGE

"WALKIE-TALKIE"

THE MONUMENT

ST.
KATH.
DOCK

MALL

WHITEHALL

Trafalgar
Square

TATE
MODERN

TOWER
OF LONDON

St.
James's
Park

London
Eye

SHAKESPEARE'S
GLOBE

THE
SHARD

LONDON
BRIDGE
STATION

CITY
HALL

TOWER
BRIDGE

BIG
BEN

WATERLOO RD.

SOUTH BANK

To Docklands
& Greenwich

ST.

PARLIAMENT

WATERLOO
STATION

WEST-
MINSTER
ABBEY

IMPERIAL
WAR MUSEUM

To
Brighton

TATE
BRITAIN

PIMLICO

LAMBETH

WALWORTH RD.

OLD KENT RD.

A-2

CLAPHAM RD.

A-3

1 Kilometer

1 Mile

To Salisbury
& Windsor (Eton Riverside)

cal landmarks such as St. Paul's Cathedral and the Museum of London. The Tower of London and Tower Bridge lie at The City's eastern border.

East London: Just east of The City is the East End—the former stomping ground of Cockney ragamuffins and Jack the Ripper, and now an increasingly gen- trified neighborhood of hipsters, "pop-up" shops, and an emerging food scene.

The South Bank: The South Bank of the Thames River offers major sights (Tate Modern, Shakespeare's Globe, London Eye, Imperial War Museum) linked by a riverside walkway. Within this area, Southwark (SUTH-uck) stretches

LONDON AT A GLANCE

▲▲▲**Westminster Abbey** Britain's finest church and the site of royal coronations and burials since 1066. **Hours:** Abbey—Mon-Fri 9:30-16:30, Wed until 19:00, Sat 9:00-16:00 (Sept-April until 14:00); Diamond Jubilee Galleries—Mon-Fri 10:00-16:00, Sat 9:30-15:30; closed Sun except for worship. See page 47.

▲▲▲**Churchill War Rooms** Underground WWII headquarters of Churchill's war effort. **Hours:** Daily 9:30-18:00, July-Aug until 19:00. See page 56.

▲▲▲**National Gallery** Remarkable collection of European paintings (1250-1900), including Leonardo, Botticelli, Velázquez, Rembrandt, Turner, Van Gogh, and the Impressionists. **Hours:** Daily 10:00-18:00, Fri until 21:00. See page 56.

▲▲▲**British Museum** The world's greatest collection of artifacts of Western civilization, including the Rosetta Stone and the Parthenon's Elgin Marbles. **Hours:** Daily 10:00-17:30, Fri until 20:30 (select galleries only). See page 66.

▲▲▲**British Library** Fascinating collection of important literary treasures of the Western world. **Hours:** Mon-Thu 9:30-20:00, Fri until 18:00, Sat until 17:00, Sun 11:00-17:00. See page 71.

▲▲▲**St. Paul's Cathedral** The main cathedral of the Anglican Church, designed by Christopher Wren, with a climbable dome and daily evensong services. **Hours:** Mon-Sat 8:30-16:30, closed Sun except for worship. See page 75.

▲▲▲**Tower of London** Historic castle, palace, and prison housing the crown jewels and a witty band of Beefeaters. **Hours:** Tue-Sat 9:00-17:30, Sun-Mon from 10:00; Nov-Feb closes one hour earlier. See page 80.

▲▲▲**Victoria and Albert Museum** The best collection of decorative arts anywhere. **Hours:** Daily 10:00-17:45, Fri until 22:00 (select galleries only). See page 93.

▲▲**Houses of Parliament** Famous for Big Ben and occupied by the Houses of Lords and Commons. **Hours:** When Parliament is in session, generally open Oct-late July Mon-Thu, closed Fri-Sun and during recess late July-Sept. Guided tours offered year-round on Sat and most weekdays during recess. See page 51.

▲▲**Trafalgar Square** The heart of London, where Westminster, The City, and the West End meet. See page 56.

▲▲**National Portrait Gallery** A *Who's Who* of British history, featuring portraits of this nation's most important historical figures. **Hours:** Daily 10:00-18:00, Fri until 21:00. See page 61.

▲▲**Covent Garden** Vibrant people-watching zone with shops, cafés, and street musicians. See page 64.

▲▲**Changing of the Guard at Buckingham Palace** Hour-long spectacle at Britain's royal residence. **Hours:** May-July daily at 11:00, Aug-April Sun-Mon, Wed, and Fri. See page 65.

▲▲**London Eye** Enormous observation wheel, dominating—and offering commanding views over—London's skyline. **Hours:** Daily 10:00-20:30 or later, Sept-May 11:00-18:00. See page 86.

▲▲**Imperial War Museum** Exhibits examining military conflicts from the early 20th century to today. **Hours:** Daily 10:00-18:00. See page 86.

▲▲**Tate Modern** Works by Monet, Matisse, Dalí, Picasso, and Warhol displayed in a converted powerhouse complex. **Hours:** Daily 10:00-18:00, Fri-Sat until 22:00. See page 88.

▲▲**Shakespeare's Globe** Timbered, thatched-roof reconstruction of the Bard's original "wooden O." **Hours:** Theater complex, museum, and tours generally daily 9:00-17:30; April-Oct generally morning theater tours only. Plays are also staged here. See page 89.

▲▲**Tate Britain** Collection of British painting from the 16th century through modern times. **Hours:** Daily 10:00-18:00. See page 90.

▲▲**Natural History Museum** Packed with engaging exhibits and enthralled kids. **Hours:** Daily 10:00-18:00. See page 95.

from the Tate Modern to London Bridge. Pedestrian bridges connect the South Bank with The City and Trafalgar Square.

Rick's Tip: *You'll find pedestrian-focused maps around town—especially handy when exiting Tube stations. In this sprawling city—where predictable grid-planned streets are relatively rare—it's also smart to buy a good map.*

West London: This area contains neighborhoods such as Mayfair, Belgravia, Pimlico, Chelsea, South Kensington, and Notting Hill. It's home to London's wealthy and has many trendy shops and enticing restaurants. Here you'll find a range of museums (Victoria and Albert Museum, Tate Britain, and more), lively Victoria Station, and the vast green expanses of Hyde Park and Kensington Gardens.

Tourist Information

It's amazing how hard it can be to find unbiased sightseeing information and advice in London. You'll see "Tourist Information" offices advertised everywhere, but most are private agencies that make a big profit selling tours and advance sightseeing and/or theater tickets.

The City of London Information Centre, on the street just below St. Paul's Cathedral, is the only publicly funded—and impartial—"real" TI. It sells Oyster cards, London Passes, and advance "Fast Track" sightseeing tickets (all described later). It also stocks various free publications: *London Planner* (a monthly that lists all the sights, events, and hours), walking-tour brochures, the biweekly *Official London Theatre Guide,* a free Tube and bus map, and the *Guide to River Thames Boat Services.* The TI gives out a free map of The City and sells several citywide maps; ask if they have a free map with coupons for discounts on sights (Mon-Sat 9:30-17:30, Sun 10:00-16:00; Tube: St. Paul's, tel. 020/7606-3030, www.visitthecity.co.uk).

Visit London, which serves the greater London area, doesn't have an office you can visit in person—but does have an information-packed website (www.visitlondon.com).

Fast Track Tickets: To skip the ticket-buying queues at certain London sights, you can buy Fast Track tickets (sometimes called "priority pass" tickets) in advance—and they're typically cheaper than tickets sold right at the sight. These are smart for the Tower of London and Madame Tussauds Waxworks in high season. They're available through various sales outlets (including the City of London TI, souvenir stands, and faux TIs scattered throughout touristy areas).

Rick's Tip: *The Artful Dodger is alive and well in London.* **Beware of pickpockets,** *particularly on public transportation, among tourist crowds, and at street markets.*

London Pass: This pass, which covers many big sights and lets you skip some lines, is expensive but potentially worth the investment for extremely busy sightseers (£75/1 day, multi-day options available, sold at City of London TI, major train

stations, and airports, tel. 020/7293-0972, www.londonpass.com).

Helpful Hints

Laundry: Pimlico Launderette near Victoria Station has self-service and same-day full-service (daily 8:00-19:00, last wash at 17:30; 3 Westmoreland Terrace; tel. 020/7821-8692).

Rick's Tip: *Buying* **tickets online in advance** *is smart—you'll generally save a few pounds per sight and can skip the ticket-buying line once you arrive—though you may need to wait in a security line or pick up your ticket at the sight.*

Useful Apps: Mapway's free **Tube Map London Underground** and **Bus Times London** (www.mapway.com) apps show the easiest way to connect Tube stations and provide bus stops and route information. The handy **Citymapper** app for London covers every mode of public transit in the city. And **Time Out London**'s free app has reviews and listings for theater, museums, and movies.

Baggage Storage: Train stations have left-luggage counters, where each bag is

scanned (just like at the airport); expect up to 45-minute waits (£12.50/24 hours per item, most stations open daily 7:00-23:00). You can also store bags at the airports (similar rates and hours, www.left-baggage.co.uk).

Tours

HOP-ON, HOP-OFF DOUBLE-DECKER BUS TOURS

London is full of hop-on, hop-off bus companies competing for your tourist pound. I've focused on the two companies I like the most: **Original** and **Big Bus.** Both offer essentially the same tours of the city's sightseeing highlights—an experience rated ▲▲▲.

Each company offers at least one route with live guides, and a second (sometimes different route) with recorded narration.

Buses run daily about every 10-15 minutes in summer and every 10-20 minutes in winter, starting at about 8:30. The last full loop usually leaves Victoria Station at around 20:00 in summer, and 17:00 in winter.

You can buy tickets online in advance, from drivers, or from staff at street kiosks (credit cards accepted at kiosks at major stops such as Victoria Station).

Original: City Sampler—£29, 24 hours—£34, RS%—£6 discount with this book, limit four discounts per book, they'll rip off the corner of this page, www.theoriginaltour.com.

Big Bus: £39 (cheaper online), tel. 020/7808-6753, www.bigbustours.com.

Rick's Tip: *For an efficient intro to London, catch an 8:30 departure of a* **hop-on, hop-off overview bus tour,** *riding most of the loop (which takes just over 1.5 hours, depending on traffic). Hop off just before 10:00 at Trafalgar Square (Cockspur Street, stop "S"), then walk briskly to Buckingham Palace to find a spot to watch the* **Changing of the Guard ceremony** *at 11:00.*

NIGHT BUS TOURS

Various companies offer a lower-priced, after-hours sightseeing circuit (1-2 hours). **Golden Tours** buses depart at 19:00 and 20:00 from their offices on Buckingham Palace Road (£28, tel. 020/7630-2028; www.goldentours.com). **See London By Night** buses offer live guides and frequent evening departures from Green Park (next to the Ritz Hotel); Oct-March at 19:30 and 21:20 only (£28.50, tel. 020/7183-4744, www.seelondonbynight.com).

WALKING TOURS

Top-notch local guides lead (sometimes big) groups on walking tours—worth ▲▲—through specific slices of London's past. **London Walks'** extensive daily schedule is online, as well as in a white brochure (most reliably found in the Café in the Crypt, below Trafalgar Square's St. Martin-in-the-Fields church). Their two-hour walks are led by top-quality professional guides (£12, cash only, private tours available, tel. 020/7624-3978, www.walks.com).

London Walks also offers day trips into the countryside (£20 plus £15-70 for transportation and admission costs, cash only: Stonehenge/Salisbury, Oxford/Cots-

wolds, Bath, and so on).

LOCAL GUIDES AND DRIVERS

Rates for London's registered Blue Badge guides are standard (about £165-200 for four hours and £270 or more for nine hours). I know and like these fine local guides: **Sean Kelleher** (tel. 020/8673-1624, mobile 07764-612-770, sean@seanlondonguide.com); **Britt Lonsdale** (£265/half-day, £365/day, tel. 020/7386-9907, mobile 07813-278-077, brittl@btinternet.com); **Joel Reid** (mobile 07887-955-720, joelyreid@gmail.com); **Tom Hooper** (mobile 07986-048-047, tomh1@btinternet.com); and **Gillian Chadwick** (£300/day, mobile 07889-976-598, gillychad@hotmail.co.uk). If you have a particular interest, London Walks (see earlier) can book one for your exact focus (£215/half-day).

Rick's Tip: *If you're taking a bus tour mainly to get oriented,* **save time and money** *by taking a night tour. You can munch a memorable picnic dinner while riding on the top deck.*

These guides have cars or a mini-bus for day trips, and also offer walk-

Thames Boat Piers

While Westminster Pier is the most popular, it's not the only dock in town. Consider all the options (listed from west to east, as the Thames flows).

Millbank Pier (North Bank): At the Tate Britain museum, used primarily by the Tate Boat ferry service (express connection to Tate Modern at Bankside Pier).

Westminster Pier (North Bank): Near the base of Big Ben, offers round-trip sightseeing cruises and lots of departures in both directions (though the Thames Clippers boats don't stop here). Nearby sights include Parliament and Westminster Abbey.

London Eye Pier (a.k.a. **Waterloo Pier,** South Bank): At the base of the London Eye; good, less-crowded alternative to Westminster, with many of the same cruise options (Waterloo Station is nearby).

Embankment Pier (North Bank): Near Covent Garden, Trafalgar Square, and Cleopatra's Needle (the obelisk on the Thames). This pier is used mostly for special boat trips, such as some RIB (rigid inflatable boats) and lunch and dinner cruises.

Festival Pier (South Bank): Next to the Royal Festival Hall, just downstream from the London Eye.

Blackfriars Pier (North Bank): In The City, not far from St. Paul's.

Bankside Pier (South Bank): Directly in front of the Tate Modern and Shakespeare's Globe.

London Bridge Pier (a.k.a. **London Bridge City Pier,** South Bank): Near the HMS Belfast.

Tower Pier (North Bank): At the Tower of London, at the east edge of The City and near the East End.

St. Katharine's Pier (North Bank): Just downstream from the Tower of London.

ing-only tours: **Janine Barton** (£390/half-day, £575/day, day tours outside of London start at £625 depending on the distance, tel. 020/7402-4600, www.seeitinstyle.synthasite.com, jbsiis@aol.com); **Mike Dickson** (£345/half-day, £535/day, mobile 07769/905-811, michael.dickson5@btinternet.com); and **David Stubbs** (£375 for 1-3 people, £395 for 4-6 people, mobile 07775-888-534, www.londoncountrytours.co.uk, info@londoncountrytours.co.uk).

CRUISE BOAT TOURS
London offers many made-for-tourist cruises, most on slow-moving, open-top boats accompanied by entertaining commentary (an experience worth ▲▲). Take a **short city-center cruise** by riding a boat 30 minutes from Westminster Pier to Tower Pier (particularly handy if you're visiting the Tower of London anyway), or choose a **longer cruise** that includes a peek at the East End, riding from Westminster all the way to Greenwich (save time by taking the Tube back).

Each company runs cruises daily, about twice hourly, from morning until dark; many reduce frequency off-season. Boats come and go from various docks in the city center. The most popular places to embark are Westminster Pier (at the base of Westminster Bridge across the street from Big Ben) and London Eye Pier (also known as Waterloo Pier, across the river on the South Bank).

A one-way trip within the city center costs about £11. With a Travelcard, you get a 33 percent discount off most cruises; the Oyster card can often be used as payment but nets you a discount only on Thames Clippers.

The three dominant companies are **City Cruises** (handy 45-minute cruise from Westminster Pier to Tower Pier; www.citycruises.com), **Thames River Services** (fewer stops, classic boats, friendlier and more old-fashioned feel; www.thamesriverservices.co.uk), and **Circular Cruise** (full cruise takes about an hour, operated by Crown River Services, www.circularcruise.london).

Cruising Downstream, to Greenwich: Both **City Cruises** and **Thames River Services** head from Westminster Pier to Greenwich. The cruises are usually narrated by the captain, with most commentary given on the way to Greenwich. To maximize both efficiency and sightseeing, take a narrated cruise to Greenwich one way, and take the DLR back to avoid late-afternoon boat crowds.

Rick's Tip: *Zipping through London every 20-30 minutes, the* **Thames Clippers are designed for commuters.** *With no open deck and no commentary, they're* **not the best option for sightseeing.**

Cruising Upstream, to Kew Gardens: **Thames River Boats** leave for Kew Gardens from Westminster Pier (£15 one-way, £22 round-trip, discounts with Travelcard, 2-4/day depending on season, 1.5 hours, boats sail April-Oct, about half the trip is narrated, www.thamesriverboats.co.uk).

WESTMINSTER WALK

Just about every visitor to London strolls along historic Whitehall from Big Ben to Trafalgar Square. This walk is a whirlwind tour as well as a practical orientation to London. Most of the sights you'll see are described in more detail later in this chapter.

🎧 You can download a free, extended audio version of this walk.

Rick's Tip: Cars drive on the left side of the road—*confusing for foreign pedestrians and for foreign drivers. Always look right, look left, then look right again just to be sure.* **Jaywalking is treacherous** *when you're disoriented about which direction traffic is coming from.*

○ Self-Guided Walk

Start halfway across ❶ **Westminster Bridge** for that "Wow, I'm really in London!" feeling. Get a close-up view of the **Houses of Parliament** and **Big Ben.** Downstream you'll see the **London Eye,** the city's giant Ferris wheel. Down the stairs to Westminster Pier are boats to the Tower of London and Greenwich (downstream) or Kew Gardens (upstream).

En route to Parliament Square, you'll pass a ❷ **statue of Boadicea,** the Celtic queen who unsuccessfully resisted Roman invaders in AD 60. Julius Caesar was the first Roman general to cross the Channel, but even he was weirded out by the island's strange inhabitants, who worshipped trees, sacrificed virgins, and went to war painted blue. Later, Romans subdued and civilized them, building roads and making this spot on the Thames—"Londinium"—a major urban center.

You'll find four red phone booths lining the north side of ❸ **Parliament Square** along Great George Street—great for a

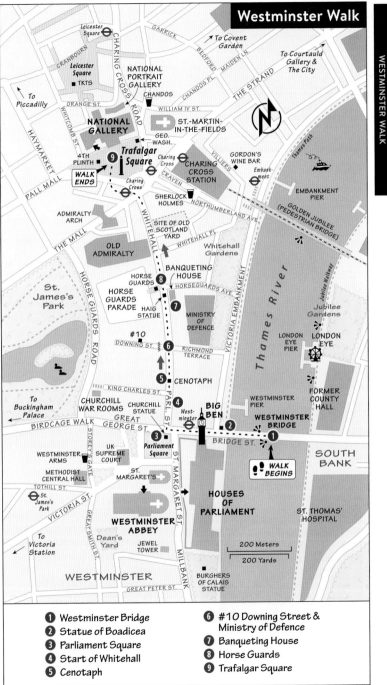

Westminster Walk

1. Westminster Bridge
2. Statue of Boadicea
3. Parliament Square
4. Start of Whitehall
5. Cenotaph
6. #10 Downing Street & Ministry of Defence
7. Banqueting House
8. Horse Guards
9. Trafalgar Square

A *Boadicea statue*

B *Churchill statue in Parliament Square*

C *Horse Guards*

phone-box-and-Big-Ben photo op.

Wave hello to Winston Churchill and Nelson Mandela in Parliament Square. To Churchill's right is the historic **Westminster Abbey,** with its two stubby, elegant towers. The white building (flying the Union Jack) at the far end of the square houses Britain's **Supreme Court.**

Head north up Parliament Street, which turns into ❹ **Whitehall,** and walk toward Trafalgar Square. You'll see the thought-provoking ❺ **Cenotaph** in the middle of the boulevard, reminding passersby of the many Brits who died in the last century's world wars. To visit the **Churchill War Rooms,** take a left before the Cenotaph, on King Charles Street.

Continuing on Whitehall, stop at the barricaded and guarded ❻ **#10 Downing Street** to see the British "White House," the traditional home of the prime minister since the position was created in the early 18th century. Break the bobby's boredom and ask him a question. The huge building across Whitehall from Downing Street is the **Ministry of Defence** (MOD), the "British Pentagon."

Nearing Trafalgar Square, look for the 17th-century ❼ **Banqueting House** across the street, which is just about all that remains of what was once the biggest palace in Europe—Whitehall Palace. If you visit, you can enjoy its ceiling paintings by Peter Paul Rubens, and the exquisite hall itself. Also take a look at the ❽ **Horse Guards** behind the gated fence. For 200 years, soldiers in cavalry uniforms have guarded this arched entrance that leads to Buckingham Palace. These elite troops constitute the Queen's personal bodyguard.

The column topped by Lord Nelson marks ❾ **Trafalgar Square,** London's central meeting point. The stately domed building on the far side of the square is the **National Gallery,** which is filled with the national collection of European paintings, and has a classy café in the Sainsbury Wing. To the right of the National Gal-

Trafalgar Square and St. Martin-in-the-Fields

lery is the 1722 **St. Martin-in-the-Fields Church** and its Café in the Crypt.

• *Our Westminster walk is over. But if you want to keep going, walk up Cockspur Street to Haymarket, then take a short left on Coventry Street to colorful* **Piccadilly Circus.** *Near here, you'll find several theaters and* **Leicester Square** *with its half-price TKTS booth for plays (see page 101). Walk through trendy* **Soho** *(north of Shaftesbury Avenue) for its fun pubs.*

SIGHTS

Central London
Westminster

These sights are listed in roughly geographical order from Westminster Abbey to Trafalgar Square, and are linked in my self-guided Westminster Walk (earlier) and 🎧 my free audio tour.

▲▲▲WESTMINSTER ABBEY

The greatest church in the English-speaking world, Westminster Abbey is where England's kings and queens have been crowned and buried since 1066. Like a stony refugee camp huddled outside St.

Peter's Pearly Gates, Westminster Abbey has many stories to tell. To experience the church more vividly, take a live tour, or attend evensong or an organ concert.

Rick's Tip: *Many of London's great museums don't charge admission—though they do suggest a donation (typically £5). All such contributions are completely optional.*

Cost and Hours: £24, £5 more for timed-entry ticket to worthwhile Queen's Diamond Jubilee Galleries, family ticket available, cheaper online; Abbey—Mon-Fri 9:30-16:30, Wed until 19:00 (main church only), Sat 9:00-16:00 (Sept-April until 14:00), guided tours available; Queen's Galleries—Mon-Fri 10:00-16:00, Sat 9:30-15:30; Cloister—Mon-Sat 9:30-17:30; closed Sun to sightseers but open for services; last entry one hour before closing; Tube: Westminster or St. James's Park, tel. 020/7222-5152, www.westminster-abbey.org.

Rick's Tip: *Westminster Abbey is most crowded at midmorning and all day Saturdays and Mondays.* **Visit early, during lunch, or late.** *Weekdays after 14:30 are less congested; come late and stay for the 17:00 evensong. Skip the line by booking tickets in advance via the Abbey's website at www.westminster-abbey.org.*

Church Services and Music: Mon-Fri at 7:30 (prayer), 8:00 and 12:30 (communion), 17:00 evensong (on Wed it's spoken, not sung); Sat at 8:00 (communion), 9:00 (prayer), 15:00 (evensong; May-Aug it's at 17:00); Sun services generally come with more music: at 8:00 (communion), 10:00 (sung Matins), 11:15 (sung Eucharist), 15:00 (evensong), 18:30 (evening service). Services are free to anyone, though visitors who haven't paid church admission aren't allowed to linger afterward. Free organ recitals are usually held Sun at 17:45 (30 minutes).

Westminster Abbey Tour

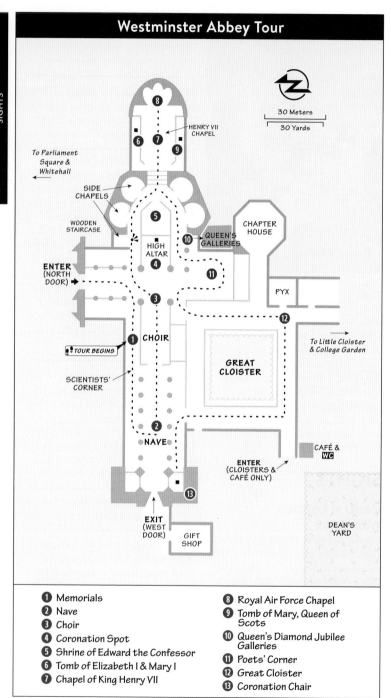

30 Meters
30 Yards

HENRY VII CHAPEL

To Parliament Square & Whitehall

SIDE CHAPELS

WOODEN STAIRCASE

CHAPTER HOUSE

ENTER (NORTH DOOR)

HIGH ALTAR

QUEEN'S GALLERIES

PYX

TOUR BEGINS

CHOIR

SCIENTISTS' CORNER

GREAT CLOISTER

To Little Cloister & College Garden

NAVE

CAFÉ & WC

ENTER (CLOISTERS & CAFÉ ONLY)

EXIT (WEST DOOR)

GIFT SHOP

DEAN'S YARD

① Memorials
② Nave
③ Choir
④ Coronation Spot
⑤ Shrine of Edward the Confessor
⑥ Tomb of Elizabeth I & Mary I
⑦ Chapel of King Henry VII
⑧ Royal Air Force Chapel
⑨ Tomb of Mary, Queen of Scots
⑩ Queen's Diamond Jubilee Galleries
⑪ Poets' Corner
⑫ Great Cloister
⑬ Coronation Chair

Tours: The included **multimedia guide** is excellent. Vergers (docents) give informative 90-minute **guided tours** (£7, schedule posted outside and inside entry, up to 5/day April-Sept, 2-4/day Oct-March).

➡ SELF-GUIDED TOUR

• *Walk straight through the north transept. Follow the crowd flow to the right, passing through a number of...*

❶ Memorials: You'll pass statues on tombs, stained glass on walls, and plaques in the floor, all honoring illustrious Brits, both famous and not so famous.

• *Now enter the spacious nave and take it all in.*

❷ Nave: The Abbey's 10-story nave is the tallest in England. With saints in stained glass, heroes in carved stone, and the bodies of England's greatest citizens under the floor stones, Westminster Abbey is the religious heart of England.

The king who built the Abbey was Edward the Confessor. Find him in the stained glass windows on the left side of the nave (as you face the altar). He's in the third bay from the end (marked *S: Edwardus rex...*), dressed in white and blue,

with his crown, scepter, and ring.

On the floor near the west entrance of the Abbey is the flower-lined Grave of the Unknown Warrior, one ordinary WWI soldier buried in soil from France with lettering made from melted-down weapons from that war. Contemplate the 800,000 men from the British Empire who gave their lives. Their memory is so revered that, when Kate Middleton walked up the aisle on her wedding day, by tradition she had to step around the tomb.

• *Now walk straight up the nave toward the altar. This is the same route every future monarch walks on the way to being crowned. Midway up the nave, you pass through the colorful screen of an enclosure known as the...*

❸ Choir: These elaborately carved wood and gilded seats are where monks once chanted their services in the "quire"—as it's known in British church-speak. Today, it's where the Abbey's boys choir sings the evensong. Up ahead, the "high" (main) altar—which usually has a cross and candlesticks atop it—sits on the platform up the five stairs.

❹ Coronation Spot: The area immedi-

The west facade of Westminster Abbey

ately before the high altar is where every English coronation since 1066 has taken place. Royalty are also given funerals here, and it's where most of the last century's royal weddings have taken place, including the unions of Queen Elizabeth II and Prince Philip (1947) and Prince William and Kate Middleton (2011).

• *Now veer left and follow the crowd. Pause at the wooden staircase on your right. This is the royal tomb that started it all.*

❺ **Shrine of Edward the Confessor:** Step back and peek over the dark coffin of Edward I to see the tippy-top of the green-and-gold wedding-cake tomb of King Edward the Confessor—the man who built Westminster Abbey. It was finished just in time to bury Edward and to crown his foreign successor, William the Conqueror, in 1066. After Edward's death, people prayed at his tomb, and, after getting good results, he was made a saint. Edward's tall, central tomb (which unfortunately lost some of its luster when Henry VIII melted down the gold coffin case) is surrounded by the tombs of eight other kings and queens.

• *At the top of the stone staircase, veer left into the private burial chapel of Queen Elizabeth I.*

❻ **Tomb of Queens Elizabeth I and Mary I:** Although only one effigy is on the tomb (Elizabeth's), there are actually two queens buried beneath it, both daughters of Henry VIII (by different mothers). Bloody Mary—meek, pious, sickly, and Catholic—enforced Catholicism during

her short reign (1553-1558) by burning "heretics" at the stake.

Elizabeth—strong, clever, and Protestant—steered England on an Anglican course. She holds a royal orb symbolizing that she's queen of the whole globe. When 26-year-old Elizabeth was crowned in the Abbey, her right to rule was questioned (especially by her Catholic subjects) because she was considered the bastard seed of Henry VIII's unsanctioned marriage to Anne Boleyn. But Elizabeth's long reign (1559-1603) was one of the greatest in English history, a time when England ruled the seas and Shakespeare explored human emotions. When she died, thousands turned out for her funeral in the Abbey. Elizabeth's face on the tomb, modeled after her death mask, is considered a very accurate take on this hook-nosed, imperious "Virgin Queen" (she never married).

• *Continue into the ornate, flag-draped room up a few more stairs (directly behind the main altar).*

❼ **Chapel of King Henry VII** (the Lady Chapel): The light from the stained-glass windows; the colorful banners overhead; and the elaborate tracery in stone, wood, and glass give this room the festive air of a medieval tournament. The prestigious Knights of the Bath meet here, under the magnificent ceiling studded with gold pendants. The ceiling—of carved stone, not plaster (1519)—is the finest English Perpendicular Gothic and fan vaulting you'll see (unless you're going to King's College Chapel in Cambridge). The ceiling was sculpted on the floor in pieces, then jigsaw-puzzled into place. It capped the Gothic period and signaled the vitality of the coming Renaissance.

• *Go to the far end of the chapel and stand at the banister in front of the modern set of stained-glass windows.*

❽ **Royal Air Force Chapel:** Saints in robes and halos mingle with pilots in parachutes and bomber jackets. This tribute to WWII flyers is for those who earned their

Tomb of Elizabeth I (and Mary I)

angel wings in the Battle of Britain (July-Oct 1940). A bit of bomb damage has been preserved—the little glassed-over hole in the wall below the windows in the lower left-hand corner.

• *Exit the Chapel of Henry VII. Turn left into a side chapel with the tomb (the central one of three in the chapel).*

❾ Tomb of Mary, Queen of Scots: The beautiful, French-educated queen (1542-1587) was held under house arrest for 19 years by Queen Elizabeth I, who considered her a threat to her sovereignty. Elizabeth got wind of an assassination plot, suspected Mary was behind it, and had her first cousin (once removed) beheaded. When Elizabeth died childless, Mary's son—James VI, King of Scots—also became King James I of England and Ireland. James buried his mum here (with her head sewn back on) in the Abbey's most sumptuous tomb.

• *Exit Mary's chapel. Continue on, until you emerge in the south transept. Look for the doorway that leads to a stairway and elevator to the...*

❿ Queen's Diamond Jubilee Galleries: In 2018, the Abbey opened a space that had been closed off for 700 years—an internal gallery 70 feet above the main floor known as the triforium. This balcony—with stunning views over the nave—now houses a small museum of interesting objects related to the Abbey's construction, the monarchs who worshipped here, royal coronations, and more from its 1,000-year history. (Because of limited space, a timed-entry ticket is required.)

• *After touring the Queen's Galleries, return to the main floor. You're in...*

⓫ Poets' Corner: England's greatest artistic contributions are in the written word. Many writers (including Chaucer, Lewis Carroll, T. S. Eliot, and Charles Dickens) are honored with plaques and monuments; relatively few are actually buried here. Shakespeare is commemorated by a fine statue that stands near the end of the transept, overlooking the others.

Poets' Corner

• *Exit the church (temporarily) at the south door, which leads to the...*

⓬ Great Cloister: You're entering the inner sanctum of the Abbey's monastery. The buildings that adjoin the church housed the monks. Cloistered courtyards like this gave them a place to stroll in peace while meditating on God's creations.

• *Go back into the church for the last stop.*

⓭ Coronation Chair: A gold-painted oak chair waits here under a regal canopy for the next coronation. For every English coronation since 1308 (except two), it's been moved to its spot before the high altar to receive the royal buttocks. The chair's legs rest on lions, England's symbol.

▲▲HOUSES OF PARLIAMENT (PALACE OF WESTMINSTER)

This Neo-Gothic icon of London, the site of the royal residence from 1042 to 1547, is now the meeting place of the legislative branch of government. Like the US Capitol in Washington, DC, the complex is open to visitors, though the exterior may be under scaffolding for restoration. You can view parliamentary sessions in either the bickering House of Commons or the sleepy House of Lords. Or you can simply wander on your own (through a few closely monitored rooms) to appreciate the historic building itself.

The Palace of Westminster has been the center of political power in England for nearly a thousand years. In 1834, a horrendous fire gutted the Palace. It was

LONDON SIGHTS

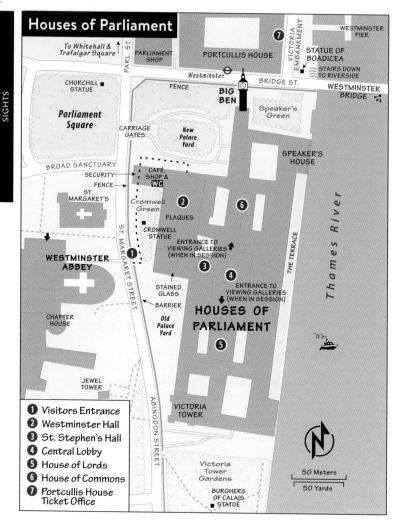

Houses of Parliament

To Whitehall &
Trafalgar Square

PARL. ST.

PARLIAMENT
SHOP

PORTCULLIS HOUSE

VICTORIA EMBANKMENT

WESTMINSTER
PIER

STATUE OF
BOADICEA

❼

Westminster ⊖   BRIDGE ST.

STAIRS DOWN
TO RIVERSIDE

WESTMINSTER
BRIDGE

CHURCHILL
STATUE

FENCE

**BIG
BEN**

Speaker's
Green

**Parliament
Square**

CARRIAGE
GATES

*New
Palace
Yard*

SPEAKER'S
HOUSE

BROAD SANCTUARY

SECURITY
FENCE

CAFÉ,
SHOP &
WC

St.
MARGARET'S

*Cromwell
Green*

❷

❻

PLAQUES

**WESTMINSTER
ABBEY**

CROMWELL
STATUE

ENTRANCE TO
VIEWING GALLERIES
(WHEN IN SESSION) ⬆

❸

ST. MARGARET STREET

STAINED
GLASS

❹

ENTRANCE TO
VIEWING GALLERIES
(WHEN IN SESSION)

THE TERRACE

Thames River

BARRIER

*Old
Palace
Yard*

**HOUSES OF
PARLIAMENT**

CHAPTER
HOUSE

❺

JEWEL
TOWER

ABINGDON STREET

VICTORIA
TOWER

❶ Visitors Entrance
❷ Westminster Hall
❸ St. Stephen's Hall
❹ Central Lobby
❺ House of Lords
❻ House of Commons
❼ Portcullis House
   Ticket Office

*Victoria
Tower
Gardens*

BURGHERS
OF CALAIS
STATUE

N

50 Meters
50 Yards

rebuilt in a retro, Neo-Gothic style that recalled England's medieval Christian roots—pointed arches, stained-glass windows, spires, and saint-like statues. At the same time, Britain was also retooling its government. Democracy was on the rise, the queen became a constitutional monarch, and Parliament emerged as the nation's ruling body. The Palace of Westminster became a symbol—a kind of cathedral—of democracy. A visit here offers a chance to tour a piece of living history and see the British government in action.

Cost and Hours: Free when Parliament is in session, otherwise must visit with a paid tour; nonticketed entry generally Oct-late July, House of Commons—Mon 14:30-22:30, Tue-Wed 11:30-19:30, Thu 9:30-17:30; House of Lords—Mon-Tue 14:30-22:00, Wed 15:00-22:00, Thu 11:00-19:30; last entry depends on debates; exact day-by-day schedule at www.parliament.uk.

Tours: Audioguide-£19.50, guided tour-£26.50, tours available Sat year-round 9:00-16:30 and most weekdays during recess (late July-Sept), 1.5 hours. Confirm the tour schedule and book ahead at www.parliament.uk or by calling 020/7219-4114. The ticket office also sells tour tickets, but there's no guarantee same-day spaces will be available (ticket office open Mon-Fri 10:00-16:00, Sat 9:00-16:30, closed Sun, in Portcullis House next to Westminster Tube Station, entrance on Victoria Embankment). For either a guided tour or an audioguide, arrive at the visitors entrance on Cromwell Green 20 minutes before your tour time to clear security.

Choosing a House: The House of Lords is less important politically, but they meet in a more ornate room, and the wait time is shorter (likely less than 30 minutes). The House of Commons is where major policy is made, but the room is sparse, and wait times are longer (30-60 minutes or more).

Rick's Tip: *For the* **public galleries** *in either House,* **lines are longest** *at the start of each session, particularly on Wednesdays. For the shortest wait, try to show up* **later in the afternoon** *(but don't push it, as things sometimes close down early).*

➲ SELF-GUIDED TOUR

Enter midway along the west side of the building (across the street from Westminster Abbey), where a tourist ramp leads to the ❶ **visitors entrance.** Line up for the airport-style security check. You'll be given a visitor badge. If you have questions, the attendants are helpful.

• *First, take in the cavernous...*

❷ **Westminster Hall:** This vast hall—covering 16,000 square feet—survived the 1834 fire, and is one of the oldest and most important buildings in England. England's vaunted legal system was invented in this hall, as this was the major court of the land for 700 years. King Charles I was tried and sentenced to death here. Guy Fawkes

The history of the Houses of Parliament spans more than 900 years.

Affording London's Sights

London is one of Europe's most expensive cities, but with its many free museums and affordable plays, it offers days of sightseeing thrills without requiring you to pinch your pennies (or your pounds).

Free Museums: Free sights include the British Museum, British Library, National Gallery, National Portrait Gallery, Tate Britain, Tate Modern, Imperial War Museum, Victoria and Albert Museum, Natural History Museum, and the Museum of London. Some of these museums request a donation of about £5, but whether you contribute is up to you.

Free Churches: Smaller churches let worshippers (and tourists) in free, although they may ask for a donation. The big sightseeing churches—Westminster Abbey and St. Paul's—charge higher admission fees, but offer free evensong services nearly daily (though you can't stick around afterward to sightsee). Westminster Abbey also offers free organ recitals most Sundays.

Other Freebies: London has plenty of free performances, such as lunch concerts at St. Martin-in-the-Fields. There's no charge to enjoy the pageantry of the Changing of the Guard, rants at Speakers' Corner in Hyde Park (on Sun afternoon), displays at Harrods, the people-watching scene at Covent Garden, and the colorful streets of the East End. It's free to view the legislature at work in the Houses of Parliament. You can get into the chapel at the Tower of London by attending Sunday services. And, Greenwich is an inexpensive outing.

Good-Value Tours: The London Walks tours with professional guides (£12) are one of the best deals you can get. Hop-on, hop-off big-bus tours, while expensive (around £30-40), provide a great overview and include free boat tours as well as city walks. (Or, for the price of a transit ticket, you could get similar views from the top of a double-decker public bus.) A one-hour Thames ride to Greenwich costs about £12 one-way, but most boats come with entertaining commentary.

Buy Tickets Online: Tickets for many popular and expensive sights can be purchased online in advance, which will usually save you a few pounds per ticket.

Theater: Compared with Broadway's prices, London's theater can be a bargain. Seek out the freestanding TKTS booth at Leicester Square to get discounts from 25 to 50 percent on good seats (and full-price tickets to the hottest shows with no service charges). Buying directly at the theater box office can score you a great deal on same-day tickets. A £5 "groundling" ticket for a play at Shakespeare's Globe is the best theater deal in town.

was condemned for plotting to blow up the Halls of Parliament in 1605.

• *Continue up the stairs, and enter...*

❸ **St. Stephen's Hall:** This long, beautifully lit room (which may be under renovation) was the original House of Commons. Members of Parliament (MPs) sat in church pews on either side of the hall—the ruling faction on one side, the opposition on the other.

• *Continue into the...*

❹ **Central Lobby:** This ornate, octagonal, high-vaulted room is often called the "heart of British government," because it sits midway between the House of Commons (to the left) and the House of Lords (right). Video monitors list the schedule of meetings and events going on in this 1,100-room governmental hive. This is the best place to admire the Palace's interior decoration—carved wood, chandeliers, statues, and floor tiles.

• *This lobby marks the end of the public space where you can wander freely. From here, you'll visit the House of Lords or the House of Commons. If either house is in session, you'll go through a series of narrow halls and staircases to reach the upper viewing galleries.*

❺ **House of Lords:** When you're called, you'll walk to the Lords Chamber by way of the long Peers' Corridor—referring to the House's 800 unelected members, called "Peers." Paintings on the corridor walls depict the antiauthoritarian spirit brewing under the reign of Charles I. When you reach the House of Lords Chamber, you'll watch the proceedings from the upper-level visitors gallery. Debate may occur among the few Lords who show up at any given time, but these days, their role is largely advisory—they have no real power to pass laws on their own.

The Lords Chamber is church-like and impressive, with stained glass and intricately carved walls. At the far end is the Queen's gilded throne, where she sits once a year to give a speech to open Parliament. In front of the throne sits the woolsack—a cushion stuffed with wool. Here the Lord Speaker presides, with a ceremonial mace behind the backrest. To the Lord Speaker's right are the members of the ruling party (a.k.a. "government") and to his left are the members of the opposition (the Labour Party). Unaffiliated Crossbenchers sit in between.

❻ **House of Commons:** The Commons Chamber may be much less grandiose than the Lords', but this is where the sausage gets made. The House of Commons is as powerful as the Lords, prime minister, and Queen combined. When the prime minister visits, his ministers (or cabinet) join him on the front bench,

Big Ben

while lesser MPs (the "backbenchers") sit behind. It's often a fiery spectacle, as the prime minister defends his policies, while the opposition grumbles and harrumphs in displeasure. It's not unheard-of for MPs to get out of line and be escorted out by the Serjeant at Arms and his Parliamentary bouncers.

Nearby: Across the street from the Parliament building's St. Stephen's Gate, the **Jewel Tower** is a rare remnant of the old Palace of Westminster, used by kings until Henry VIII. The crude stone tower (1365-1366) was a guard tower in the palace wall, overlooking a moat. It contains an exhibit on the medieval Westminster Palace and the tower (£5.70, daily 10:00-18:00, shorter hours and closed Mon-Fri in off-season; tel. 020/7222-2219). Next to the tower is a quiet courtyard with picnic-friendly benches.

Big Ben, the 315-foot-high clock tower at the north end of the Palace of Westminster, is named for its 13-ton bell, Ben. Currently covered in scaffolding for renovation, the light above the clock is lit when Parliament is in session. The face of the clock is huge—you can actually see the minute hand moving (best view from halfway over Westminster Bridge).

▲▲▲CHURCHILL WAR ROOMS

This excellent sight offers a fascinating walk through the underground headquarters of the British government's WWII fight against the Nazis in the darkest days of the Battle of Britain. It has two parts: the war rooms themselves, and a top-notch museum dedicated to the man who steered the war from here, Winston Churchill. Allow 1-2 hours for your visit.

Cost and Hours: £22 for timed-entry ticket (buy online in advance), includes essential audioguide; daily 9:30-18:00, July-Aug until 19:00, last entry one hour before closing; on King Charles Street, 200 yards off Whitehall—follow signs, Tube: Westminster; tel. 020/7930-6961, www.iwm.org.uk/churchill-war-rooms.

Advance Tickets Recommended: While you can buy a ticket on-site, ticket-buying lines can be long (1-2 hours), so it's smart to buy a timed-entry ticket online in advance. You still may have to wait up to 30 minutes in the security line. Note: London Pass holders do not get to skip the line here—they wait along with ticket buyers.

Cabinet War Rooms: The 27-room, heavily fortified nerve center of the British war effort was used from 1939 to 1945. Churchill's room, the map room, and other rooms are just as they were in 1945. As you follow the one-way route, the audioguide explains each room and offers first-person accounts of wartime happenings here. While the rooms are spartan, you'll see how British gentility survived even as the city was bombarded—posted signs informed those working underground what the weather was like outside, and a cheery notice reminded them to turn off the lights to conserve electricity.

Churchill Museum: Don't bypass this museum, which occupies a large hall amid the war rooms. It dissects every aspect of the man behind the famous cigar, bowler hat, and V-for-victory sign. Artifacts, quotes, political cartoons, clear explanations, and interactive exhibits bring the colorful statesman to life. Many of the items on display—such as a European map divvied up in permanent marker, which Churchill brought to England from the postwar Potsdam Conference—drive home the remarkable span of history this man influenced.

On Trafalgar Square

Trafalgar Square, London's central square, worth ▲▲, is at the intersection of Westminster, The City, and the West End. It's the climax of most marches and demonstrations, and is a thrilling place to simply hang out. At the top of Trafalgar Square (north) sits the domed National Gallery with its grand staircase, and to the right, the steeple of St. Martin-in-the-Fields, built in 1722. In the center of the square, Lord Nelson stands atop his 185-foot-tall fluted granite column, gazing out toward Trafalgar, where he lost his life but defeated the French fleet. Part of this 1842 memorial is made from his victims' melted-down cannons. He's surrounded by spraying fountains, giant lions, and hordes of people (Tube: Charing Cross).

▲▲▲NATIONAL GALLERY

Displaying an unsurpassed collection of European paintings from 1250 to 1900—including works by Leonardo, Botticelli,

Churchill War Rooms

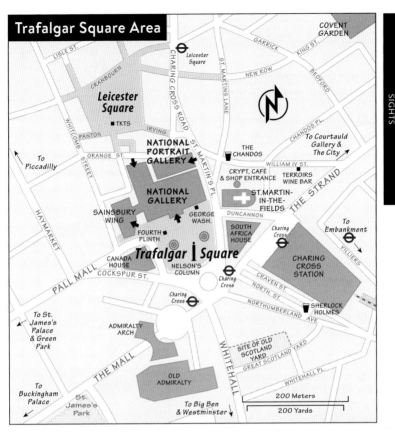

Trafalgar Square Area

Velázquez, Rembrandt, Turner, Van Gogh, and the Impressionists—this is one of Europe's great galleries. Use the map in this book to find specific examples of the art styles described here.

Cost and Hours: Free, £5 suggested donation, special exhibits extra; daily 10:00-18:00, Fri until 21:00, last entry to special exhibits 45 minutes before closing; floor plan-£2; on Trafalgar Square, Tube: Charing Cross or Leicester Square, tel. 020/7747-2885, www.nationalgallery.org.uk.

Tours: Free one-hour overview tours leave from the Sainsbury Wing info desk Mon-Fri at 14:00 (no tours Sat-Sun); excellent £5 audioguides—choose from one-hour highlights tour, several theme tours, or an option that lets you dial up

info on any painting in the museum.

Eating: Consider splitting afternoon tea at the **$$$ National Dining Rooms,** on the first floor of the Sainsbury Wing. The **$$$ National Café,** located near the Getty Entrance, has a table-service restaurant and café. Seek out the **$ Espresso Bar,** near the Portico and Getty entrances, for sandwiches and pastries.

Visiting the Museum: Enter through the Sainsbury Entrance (facing Trafalgar Square), in the modern annex to the left of the classic building, and climb the stairs.

Medieval: In Room 51 (and nearby rooms), shiny gold paintings of saints, angels, Madonnas, and crucifixions float in an ethereal gold never-never land. Art in the Middle Ages was religious, domi-

MEDIEVAL
1 ANONYMOUS – The Wilton Diptych

EARLY ITALIAN RENAISSANCE
2 UCCELLO – Battle of San Romano
3 BOTTICELLI – Venus and Mars
4 CRIVELLI – The Annunciation, with Saint Emidius
5 LEONARDO – The Virgin of the Rocks
6 LEONARDO – Virgin and Child with St. Anne and St. John the Baptist
7 VAN EYCK – The Arnolfini Portrait

HIGH RENAISSANCE
8 MICHELANGELO – The Entombment
9 RAPHAEL – Pope Julius II

MANNERISM
10 BRONZINO – An Allegory with Venus and Cupid
11 TINTORETTO – The Origin of the Milky Way

NORTHERN PROTESTANT ART
12 VERMEER – A Young Woman Standing at a Virginal

BAROQUE
13 RUBENS – The Judgment of Paris
14 REMBRANDT – Self-Portrait at the Age of 63
15 REMBRANDT – Belshazzar's Feast
16 VELÁZQUEZ – The Rokeby Venus
17 VAN DYCK – Equestrian Portrait of Charles I
18 CARAVAGGIO –The Supper at Emmaus

FRENCH ROCOCO
19 BOUCHER – Pan and Syrinx

BRITISH ROMANTIC ART
20 CONSTABLE – The Hay Wain
21 TURNER – The Fighting Téméraire

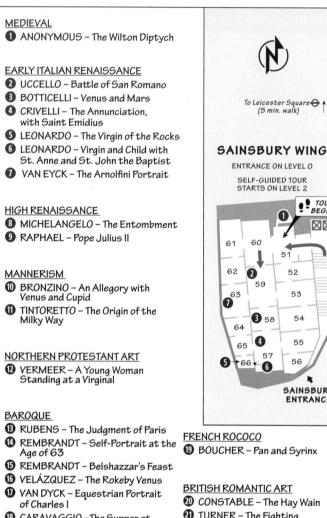

To Leicester Square (5 min. walk)

SAINSBURY WING

ENTRANCE ON LEVEL 0

SELF-GUIDED TOUR
STARTS ON LEVEL 2

TOUR BEGINS

SAINSBURY ENTRANCE

nated by the Church. The illiterate faithful could meditate on an altarpiece and visualize heaven. It's as though they couldn't imagine saints and angels inhabiting the dreary world of rocks, trees, and sky they lived in. One of the finest medieval altarpieces, *The Wilton Diptych*, is tucked in the small alcove in Room 51.

Italian Renaissance: In painting, the Renaissance meant realism. Artists rediscovered the beauty of nature and the human body. In Room 63, find Van Eyck's *The Arnolfini Portrait* (1434), once thought to depict a wedding ceremony forced by the lady's swelling belly. Today it's understood as a portrait of a solemn, well-dressed, well-heeled couple, the Arnolfinis of Bruges, Belgium (the fashion

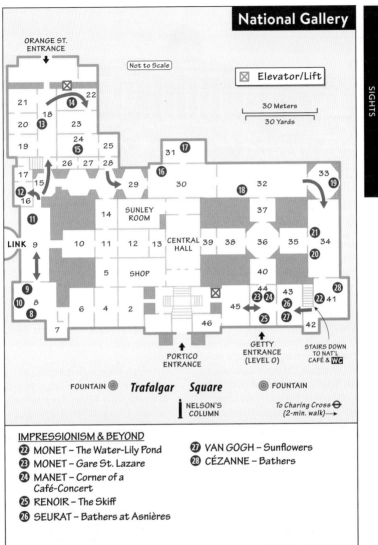

National Gallery

ORANGE ST.
ENTRANCE

Not to Scale

⊠ Elevator/Lift

30 Meters
30 Yards

LINK

SUNLEY
ROOM

CENTRAL
HALL

SHOP

PORTICO
ENTRANCE

GETTY
ENTRANCE
(LEVEL 0)

STAIRS DOWN
TO NAT'L
CAFÉ & WC

FOUNTAIN ◉ *Trafalgar Square* ◉ FOUNTAIN

NELSON'S
COLUMN

To Charing Cross ⊖
(2-min. walk)→

IMPRESSIONISM & BEYOND

㉒ MONET – The Water-Lily Pond
㉓ MONET – Gare St. Lazare
㉔ MANET – Corner of a Café-Concert
㉕ RENOIR – The Skiff
㉖ SEURAT – Bathers at Asnières

㉗ VAN GOGH – Sunflowers
㉘ CÉZANNE – Bathers

of the day was to gather up the folds of one's extremely full-skirted dress).

Michelangelo's (unfinished) *The Entombment* is inspired by ancient statues of balanced, anatomically perfect, nude Greek gods. Renaissance balance and symmetry reign. Raphael's *Pope Julius II* gives a behind-the-scenes look at this complex leader. The pope's dress indi-cates wealth and success. But at the same time, he's a bent and broken man, with an expression that seems to say, "Is this all there is?"

Mannerism: Developed in reaction to the High Renaissance, Mannerism subverts the balanced, harmonious ideal of the previous era with exaggerated proportions, asymmetrical compositions,

The massive National Gallery is one of the world's great art museums.

and decorative color. In *The Origin of the Milky Way* by Venetian painter Tintoretto, the god Jupiter places his illegitimate son, baby Hercules, at his wife's breast. Juno says, "Wait a minute. That's not my baby!" Her milk spurts upward, becoming the Milky Way.

Northern Protestant Art: While Italy had wealthy aristocrats and the powerful Catholic Church to purchase art, the North's patrons were middle-class, hardworking, Protestant merchants. They wanted simple, cheap, no-nonsense pictures to decorate their homes and offices. Greek gods and Virgin Marys were out, hometown folks and hometown places were in—portraits, landscapes, still lifes, and slice-of-life scenes.

Look for Vermeer's *A Young Woman Standing at a Virginal*. By framing off such a small world to look at—from the blue chair in the foreground to the wall in back—Vermeer forces us to appreciate the tiniest details, the beauty of everyday things.

Baroque: While artists in Protestant and democratic Europe painted simple scenes, those in Catholic and aristocratic countries turned to the style called Baroque. Baroque art took what was flashy in Venetian art and made it flashier, what was gaudy and made it gaudier, what

was dramatic and made it shocking.

In Velázquez's *The Rokeby Venus,* Venus lounges diagonally across the canvas, admiring herself, with flaring red, white, and gray fabrics to highlight her rosy white skin and inflame our passion. This work by the king's personal court painter is a rare Spanish nude from that ultra-Catholic country.

French Rococo: As Europe's political and economic center shifted from Italy to France, Louis XIV's court at Versailles became its cultural hub. The Rococo art

Van Eyck, The Arnolfini Portrait

of Louis' successors was as frilly, sensual, and suggestive as the decadent French court. We see their rosy-cheeked portraits and their fantasies: lords and ladies at play in classical gardens, where mortals and gods cavort together. One of the finest examples is the tiny *Pan and Syrinx* by Boucher.

British Romantic Art: The reserved British were more comfortable cavorting with nature than with the lofty gods. John Constable set up his easel out-of-doors, making quick sketches to capture the simple majesty of billowing clouds, spreading trees, and everyday rural life. The simple style of Constable's *The Hay Wain*—believe it or not—was considered shocking in its day.

Impressionism and Beyond: At the end of the 19th century, a new breed of artists burst out of the stuffy confines of the studio. They donned scarves and berets and set up their canvases in farmers' fields or carried their notebooks into crowded cafés, dashing off quick sketches in order to catch a momentary... impression. Check out Impressionist and Post-Impressionist masterpieces such as Van Gogh's *Sunflowers*.

Princess Diana's portrait at the National Portrait Gallery

Cézanne's *Bathers* are arranged in strict triangles. He uses the Impressionist technique of building a figure with dabs of paint (though his "dabs" are often larger-sized "cube" shapes) to make solid, 3-D geometrical figures in the style of the Renaissance. In the process, his cube shapes helped inspire a radical new style—Cubism—bringing art into the 20th century.

▲▲NATIONAL PORTRAIT GALLERY
A selective walk through this 500-year-long *Who's Who* of British history is quick and free, and puts faces on the story of England. The collection is well-described, not huge, and in historical sequence, from the 16th century on the second floor to today's royal family, usually housed on the ground floor. Some highlights: Henry VIII and wives; portraits of the "Virgin Queen" Elizabeth I, Sir Francis Drake, and Sir Walter Raleigh; the only real-life portrait of William Shakespeare; Oliver Cromwell and Charles I with his head on; portraits by Gainsborough and Reynolds; the Romantics (William Blake, Lord Byron, William Wordsworth, and company); Queen Victoria and her era; and the present royal family, including the late Princess Diana and the current Duchess of Cambridge—Kate.

Cost and Hours: Free, £5 suggested donation, special exhibits extra; daily 10:00-18:00, Fri until 21:00; excellent audioguide-£3, floor plan-£2; entry 100 yards off Trafalgar Square (around the corner from National Gallery, opposite Church of St. Martin-in-the-Fields), Tube: Charing Cross or Leicester Square, tel. 020/7306-0055, www.npg.org.uk.

▲ST. MARTIN-IN-THE-FIELDS
The church, built in the 1720s with a Gothic spire atop a Greek-type temple, is an oasis of peace on wild and noisy Trafalgar Square. St. Martin cared for the poor. "In the fields" was where the first church stood on this spot (in the 13th century), between Westminster and The City. Stepping inside, you still feel a compassion for

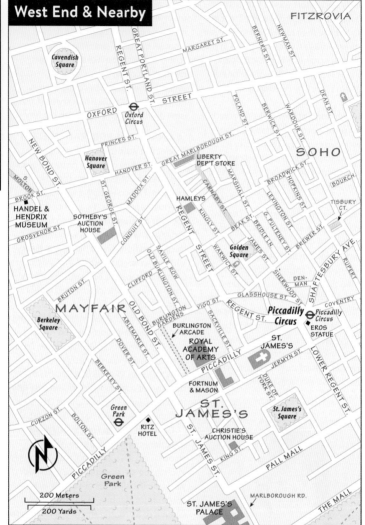

West End & Nearby

FITZROVIA

Cavendish Square

REGENT STREET

GREAT PORTLAND ST.

MARGARET ST.

BERNERS ST.

NEWMAN ST.

OXFORD STREET

Oxford Circus

POLAND ST.

BERWICK ST.

WARDOUR ST.

DEAN ST.

SOHO

PRINCES ST.

NEW BOND ST.

Hanover Square

HANOVER ST.

GREAT MARLBOROUGH ST.

LIBERTY DEP'T STORE

MARSHALL ST.

BROADWICK ST.

HOPKINS ST.

LEXINGTON ST.

BOURCH.

TISBURY CT.

S MOLTON ST.

BROOK ST.

HANDEL & HENDRIX MUSEUM

GROSVENOR ST.

SOTHEBY'S AUCTION HOUSE

ST. GEORGE ST.

MADDOX ST.

CONDUIT ST.

HAMLEYS

CARNABY ST.

KINGLY ST.

REGENT STREET

WARWICK ST.

Golden Square

BEAK ST.

BRIDLE LN.

JAMES ST.

G. PULTENEY ST.

BREWER ST.

SHAFTESBURY AVE.

RUPERT

SAVILE ROW

OLD BURLINGTON ST.

SHERWOOD ST.

DEN-MAN

GLASSHOUSE ST.

COVENTRY

MAYFAIR

BRUTON ST.

Berkeley Square

CLIFFORD ST.

OLD BOND ST.

BURLINGTON GARDENS

VIGO ST.

REGENT ST.

Piccadilly Circus

Piccadilly Circus

ALBEMARLE ST.

DOVER ST.

BURLINGTON ARCADE

ROYAL ACADEMY OF ARTS

SACKVILLE ST.

ST. JAMES'S

EROS STATUE

LOWER REGENT ST.

BERKELEY ST.

PICCADILLY

FORTNUM & MASON

JERMYN ST.

DUKE OF YORK ST.

CURZON ST.

BOLTON ST.

Green Park

RITZ HOTEL

ST. JAMES'S

CHRISTIE'S AUCTION HOUSE

St. James's Square

PICCADILLY

KING ST.

PALL MALL

Green Park

200 Meters

200 Yards

ST. JAMES'S PALACE

MARLBOROUGH RD.

THE MALL

the needs of the people in this neighborhood—the church serves the homeless and houses a Chinese community center. The modern east window—with grillwork bent into the shape of a warped cross—was installed in 2008 to replace one damaged in World War II.

A freestanding glass pavilion to the left of the church serves as the entrance to the church's underground areas. There you'll find the concert ticket office, a gift shop, brass-rubbing center, and the recommended support-the-church Café in the Crypt.

Cost and Hours: Free, donations welcome; Mon-Fri 8:30-18:00, Sat-Sun from 9:00, closed to visitors during services—listed at the entrance and on the website; Tube: Charing Cross, tel. 020/7766-1100, www.stmartin-in-the-fields.org.

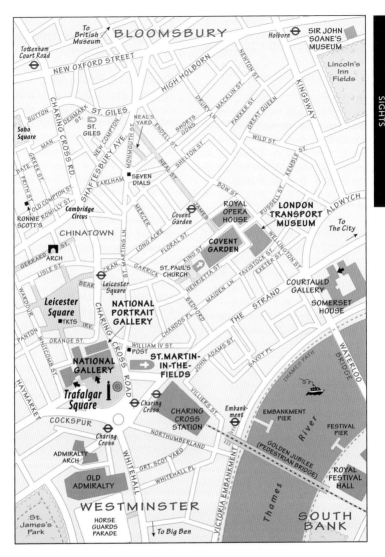

Rick's Tip: St. Martin-in-the-Fields *is famous for its* **concerts.** *Consider a free lunchtime concert (£3.50 suggested donation; Mon, Tue, and Fri at 13:00), an evening concert (£9-29, several nights a week at 19:30), or* **Wednesday night jazz** *(£8-15, at 20:00). See www.stmartin-in-the-fields.org for the schedule.*

The West End and Nearby
▲PICCADILLY CIRCUS

Although this square is slathered with neon billboards and tacky attractions (think of it as the Times Square of London), the surrounding streets are packed with great shopping opportunities. Nearby Shaftesbury Avenue and Leicester Square teem with fun-seekers, theaters, Chinese restaurants, and street singers. To the northeast is London's Chinatown and, beyond that, the funky Soho neighborhood. And curling to the northwest from Piccadilly Circus is genteel Regent Street, lined with exclusive shops.

▲SOHO

North of Piccadilly, once-seedy Soho has become trendy—with many recommended restaurants—and is well worth a gawk. It's the epicenter of London's thriving, colorful youth scene, a fun and funky *Sesame Street* of urban diversity.

▲▲COVENT GARDEN

This large square is filled with people and street performers—jugglers, sword swallowers, magicians, and guitar players. London's buskers (including those in the Tube) are auditioned, licensed, and assigned times and places where they are allowed to perform.

The square's centerpiece is a covered marketplace. A market has been here since medieval times, when it was the "convent" garden owned by Westminster Abbey. In the 1600s, it became a housing development with this courtyard as its center, done in the Palladian style by Inigo Jones. Today's fine iron-and-glass structure was built in 1830 to house the stalls of what became London's chief produce market. In 1973, its venerable arcades were converted to boutiques, cafés, and antique shops. A tourist market thrives here today.

Better Covent Garden lunch deals can be found by walking a block or two away from the eye of this touristic hurricane (check out the places north of the Tube station, along Endell and Neal Streets).

Buckingham Palace Area

The working headquarters of the British monarchy, Buckingham Palace is where the Queen carries out her official duties as the head of state. She and other members of the royal family also maintain apartments here.

Combo-Tickets: A £45 "Royal Day Out" combo-ticket covers the three palace sights that charge admission: the State Rooms, the Queen's Gallery, and the Royal Mews. You can also pay to enter each sight separately (prices listed later; www.royalcollection.org.uk).

▲STATE ROOMS AT BUCKINGHAM PALACE

This lavish home has been Britain's royal residence since 1837, when the newly ascended Queen Victoria moved in. When today's Queen is at home, the royal standard flies (a red, yellow, and blue flag); otherwise, the Union Jack flaps in the wind. The Queen opens her palace to the public—but only for a couple of months in summer, when she's out of town.

Cost and Hours: £25 timed-entry to State Rooms and throne room, includes audioguide; late July-Sept only, daily 9:30-19:30, Sept until 18:30, last entry 75 minutes before closing; limited to 8,000 visitors/day; Tube: Victoria, tel. 0303/123-7300—but Her Majesty rarely answers.

Piccadilly Circus

Covent Garden

The Changing of the Guard is all about pomp and ceremony.

QUEEN'S GALLERY AT BUCKINGHAM PALACE

A small sampling of Queen Elizabeth's personal collection of art is on display in five rooms in a wing adjoining the palace. The exhibits change two or three times a year and are lovingly described by the included audioguide. The gallery is small and security is tight (involving lines): Visit only if you're a patient art lover interested in the current exhibit.

Cost and Hours: £12, daily 10:00-17:30, from 9:30 late July-Sept, last entry 75 minutes before closing, tel. 0303/123-7301.

ROYAL MEWS

A visit to the Queen's working stables is likely to be disappointing unless you follow the included audioguide or the hourly guided tour (April-Oct only, 45 minutes), in which case it's fairly entertaining—especially if you're interested in horses and/or royalty. You'll see a few of the Queen's 30 horses, a fancy car, and a bunch of old carriages, finishing with the Gold State Coach (c. 1760, 4 tons, 4 mph).

Cost and Hours: £12; daily 10:00-17:00, off-season until 16:00; closed Sun in Feb, March, and Nov, plus all of Dec-Jan; last entry 45 minutes before closing, busiest immediately after Changing of the Guard, guided tours on the hour in summer, tel. 0303/123-7302.

Rick's Tip: *Want to go inside* **Buckingham Palace?** *It's* **open to the public only in late July through September,** *when the Queen is out of town.*

▲▲CHANGING OF THE GUARD AT BUCKINGHAM PALACE

This is the spectacle every London visitor has to see at least once: stone-faced, bearskin-hatted guards changing posts with much fanfare, accompanied by a brass band. The most famous part takes place right in front of Buckingham Palace most days at 11:00 (check www.householddivision.org.uk for schedule). Many tourists just show up and get lost in the crowds, but you can catch a satisfying glimpse from less crowded locations

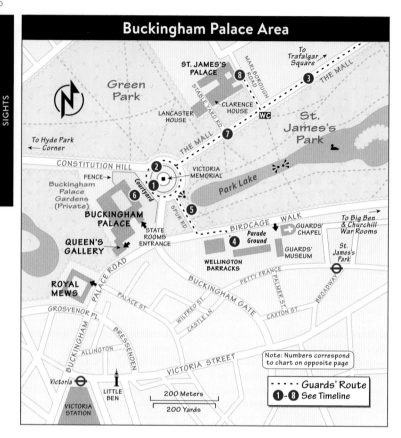

Buckingham Palace Area

Green Park

ST. JAMES'S PALACE

To Trafalgar Square

THE MALL

MARLBOROUGH ROAD

STABLE YARD RD.

CLARENCE HOUSE

LANCASTER HOUSE

WC

St. James's Park

To Hyde Park Corner

THE MALL

CONSTITUTION HILL

FENCE→

Buckingham Palace Gardens (Private)

Courtyard

VICTORIA MEMORIAL

Park Lake

BUCKINGHAM PALACE

SPUR RD.

STATE ROOMS ENTRANCE

BIRDCAGE WALK

Parade Ground

GUARDS' CHAPEL

To Big Ben & Churchill War Rooms

QUEEN'S GALLERY

WELLINGTON BARRACKS

GUARDS' MUSEUM

St. James's Park

ROYAL MEWS

PALACE ROAD

PALACE ST.

BUCKINGHAM GATE

PETTY FRANCE

PALMER ST.

BROADWAY

GROSVENOR PL.

WILFRED ST.

CASTLE LN.

CAXTON ST.

BUCKINGHAM

BRESSENDEN

ALLINGTON

VICTORIA STREET

Note: Numbers correspond to chart on opposite page

Victoria

LITTLE BEN

VICTORIA STATION

200 Meters

200 Yards

- - - - Guards' Route
1 - 8 See Timeline

within a few hundred yards of the palace. To plan your sightseeing strategy (and understand what's going on), see the "Changing of the Guard Timeline."

Join a Tour: Local tour companies such as **Fun London Tours** more or less follow the guards' route but add in history and facts to their already entertaining march. These walks add color and good value to what can otherwise seem like a stressful mess of tourists (£17, Changing of the Guard tour starts at Piccadilly Circus at 9:40, must book online in advance, www.funlondontours.com).

North London

▲▲▲BRITISH MUSEUM

Simply put, this is the greatest chronicle of civilization...anywhere. A visit here is like taking a long hike through *Encyclopedia Britannica* National Park. The vast British Museum wraps around its Great Court (the huge entrance hall), with the most popular sections filling the ground floor: Egyptian, Assyrian, and ancient Greek, with the famous frieze sculptures from the Parthenon in Athens. The museum's stately Reading Room sometimes hosts special exhibits.

Cost and Hours: Free, £5 donation requested, special exhibits usually extra (and with timed ticket); daily 10:00-17:30, Fri until 20:30 (select galleries only), least

Changing of the Guard Timeline

When	What
10:00	Tourists gather by the ❶ fence outside Buckingham Palace and the ❷ Victoria Memorial.
10:45	Cavalry guards, headed up ❸ The Mall back from their Green Park barracks, pass Buckingham Palace en route to the Horse Guards (except on Sundays).
10:57	❹ The New Guard, led by a band, marches in a short procession from Wellington Barracks down ❺ Spur Road to Buckingham Palace.
11:00	Guards converge around the Victoria Memorial before entering the ❻ fenced courtyard of Buckingham Palace for the main Changing of the Guard ceremony. (Meanwhile, farther away along Whitehall, the Horse Guard changes guard—except on Sundays, when it's at 10:00.)
11:10	Relief guards leave from Buckingham Palace along The Mall to Clarence House, via ❼ Stable Yard Road.
11:25	The remaining Old Guard leaves St. James's Palace for Buckingham Palace.
11:37	Cavalry guards, headed down The Mall back to their Green Park barracks from Horse Guards, pass Buckingham Palace.
11:40	The entire Old Guard, led by a band, leaves Buckingham Palace and heads up Spur Road for Wellington Barracks, while a detachment of the New Guard leaves Buckingham Palace to march up The Mall to take over at ❽ St. James's Palace (arriving around 11:45).

crowded late on weekday afternoons, especially Fri; free guided tours offered, multimedia guide-£7; Great Russell Street, Tube: Tottenham Court Road, ticket desk tel. 020/7323-8181, www.britishmuseum.org.

Tours: Free 40-minute EyeOpener tours by volunteers focus on select rooms (daily 11:00-15:45, generally every 15 minutes). More in-depth 90-minute tours are offered Fri-Sun at 11:30 and 14:00. Ask about other specialty tours and lectures. The £7 multimedia guide offers dial-up audio commentary and video on 200 objects, as well as several substantial and cerebral theme tours (must leave photo ID). There's also a fun family multimedia guide offering various themed routes.

🎧 Download my free British Museum audio tour.

Visiting the Museum: From the Great Court, doorways lead to all wings. To the left are the exhibits on Egypt, Assyria, and Greece—the highlights of your visit.

Egypt: Start with the Egyptian Gallery. Egypt was one of the world's first "civilizations"—a group of people with a government, religion, art, free time, and a written language. The Egypt we think of— pyramids, mummies, pharaohs, and guys who walk funny—lasted from 3000 to 1000 BC with hardly any change in the government, religion, or arts.

The first thing you'll see in the Egypt section is the **Rosetta Stone.** When this rock was unearthed in the Egyptian desert in 1799, it was a sensation in Europe. This black slab, dating from 196 BC, caused

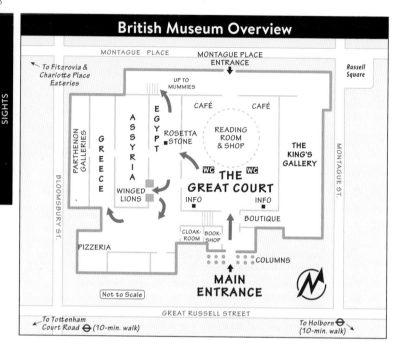

British Museum Overview

MONTAGUE PLACE

MONTAGUE PLACE ENTRANCE

To Fitzrovia & Charlotte Place Eateries

Russell Square

UP TO MUMMIES

CAFÉ   CAFÉ

A S S Y R I A

E G Y P T

ROSETTA STONE

READING ROOM & SHOP

THE KING'S GALLERY

PARTHENON GALLERIES

G R E E C E

WINGED LIONS

WC **THE GREAT COURT** WC

INFO   INFO

BOUTIQUE

BLOOMSBURY ST.

MONTAGUE ST.

CLOAK-ROOM   BOOK-SHOP

PIZZERIA

COLUMNS

Not to Scale

MAIN ENTRANCE

GREAT RUSSELL STREET

To Tottenham Court Road (10-min. walk)

To Holborn (10-min. walk)

a quantum leap in the study of ancient history. Finally, Egyptian writing could be decoded.

Next, wander past the many **statues,** including a seven-ton Ramesses, with the traditional features of a pharaoh (goatee, cloth headdress, and cobra diadem on his forehead). When Moses told the king of Egypt, "Let my people go!" this was the stony-faced look he got. You'll also see the Egyptian gods as animals—these include Amun, king of the gods, as a ram, and Horus, the god of the living, as a falcon.

At the end of the hall, climb the stairs or take the elevator to **mummy** land. Mummifying a body is much like following a recipe. First, disembowel it (but leave the heart inside), then pack the cavities with pitch, and dry it with natron, a natural form of sodium carbonate (and, I believe, the active ingredient in Twinkies). Then carefully bandage it head to toe with hundreds of yards of linen strips. Let it sit 2,000 years, and...voilà! The mummy

was placed in a wooden coffin, which was put in a stone coffin, which was placed in a tomb. The result is that we now have Egyptian bodies that are as well preserved as Larry King. Many of the mummies here are from the time of the Roman occupa-

A mummy case

Two human-headed winged stone lions guarded an Assyrian palace (11th-8th century BC). With the strength of a lion, the wings of an eagle, the brain of a man, and the beard of an ancient hipster, they protected the king from evil spirits and scared the heck out of foreign ambassadors and left-wing newspaper reporters. (What has five legs and flies? Take a close look. These winged quintupeds, which appear complete from both the front and the side, could guard both directions at once.)

Carved into the stone between the bearded lions' loins, you can see one of civilization's most impressive achievements—writing. This wedge-shaped **(cuneiform)** script is the world's first written language, invented 5,000 years ago by the Sumerians (of southern Iraq) and passed down to their less-civilized descendants, the Assyrians.

The **Nimrud Gallery** is a mini version of the throne room and royal apartments of King Ashurnasirpal II's Northwest Palace at Nimrud (9th century BC). It's filled with royal propaganda reliefs, 30-ton marble bulls, and panels depicting wounded lions (lion-hunting was Assyria's sport of kings).

Greece: During its Golden Age (500-430 BC), Greece set the tone for all of Western civilization to follow. Democracy, theater, literature, mathematics, philosophy, science, gyros, art, and architecture as we know them, were virtually all invented by a single generation of Greeks in a small town of maybe 80,000 citizens.

Your walk through Greek history starts with pottery—from the earliest, with geometric patterns (8th century BC), to painted black silhouettes on the natural orange clay, and then a few crudely done red human figures on black backgrounds. Later, find a vase painted with frisky figures **(Wine Cooler Signed by Douris as Painter),** which shows a culture really into partying, as well as an evolution into more realistic and three-dimensional figures.

The highlight is the **Parthenon Sculptures**—taken from the temple dedi-

Assyrian human-headed lions

tion, when fine memorial portraits painted in wax became popular. X-ray photos in the display cases tell us more about these people.

Don't miss the animal mummies. Cats (near the entrance to Room 62) were popular pets. They were also considered incarnations of the cat-headed goddess Bastet. Worshipped in life as the sun god's allies, preserved in death, and memorialized with statues, cats were given the adulation they've come to expect ever since.

Assyria: Iraq has long been home to palace-building, iron-fisted rulers. The Assyrians conquered their southern neighbors and dominated the Middle East for 300 years (c. 900-600 BC). Their strength came from a superb army (chariots, mounted cavalry, and siege engines), a policy of terrorism against enemies ("I tied their heads to tree trunks all around the city," reads a royal inscription), ethnic cleansing and mass deportations of the vanquished, and efficient administration (roads and express postal service). They have been called the "Romans of the East."

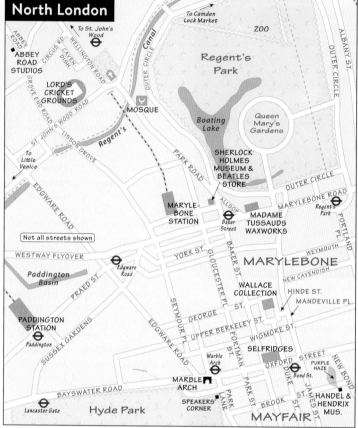

North London

To St. John's Wood
ABBEY ROAD
STUDIOS
LORD'S CRICKET GROUNDS
ABBEY ROAD
CIRCUS RD.
WELLINGTON ROAD
CAVEN-DISH
GROVE END ROAD
ST. JOHN'S
LISSON GROVE
MOSQUE
Regent's
To Little Venice
EDGWARE ROAD
Canal
OUTER CIRCLE
To Camden Lock Market
ZOO
Regent's Park
Boating Lake
Queen Mary's Gardens
PARK ROAD
SHERLOCK HOLMES MUSEUM & BEATLES STORE
OUTER CIRCLE
ALBANY ST.
OUTER CIRCLE
MARYLEBONE ROAD
Regent's Park
ALLSOP
MARYLE-BONE STATION
Baker Street
MADAME TUSSAUDS WAXWORKS
PORTLAND PL.

Not all streets shown

WESTWAY FLYOVER
Paddington Basin
PRAED ST.
PADDINGTON STATION
Paddington
SUSSEX GARDENS
EDGWARE ROAD
Edgware Road
YORK ST.
GLOUCESTER PL.
BAKER ST.
MARYLEBONE
NEW CAVENDISH
WEYMOUTH
WALLACE COLLECTION
HINDE ST.
MANDEVILLE PL.
SEYMOUR PL.
GEORGE ST.
UPPER BERKELEY ST.
PORTMAN ST.
WIGMORE ST.
SELFRIDGES
Marble Arch
OXFORD STREET
PURPLE HAZE
Bond St.
NEW BOND ST.
DUKE ST.
MARBLE ARCH
BAYSWATER ROAD
Lancaster Gate
Hyde Park
SPEAKERS CORNER
PARK LANE
BROOK ST.
ST. JAMES ST.
HANDEL & HENDRIX MUS.
MAYFAIR

cated to Athena, the crowning glory of an enormous urban-renewal plan during Greece's Golden Age. While the building itself remains in Athens, many of the Parthenon's best sculptures are right here in the British Museum—the so-called Elgin Marbles, named for the shrewd British ambassador who had his men hammer, chisel, and saw them off the Parthenon in the early 1800s.

These much-wrangled-over bits of the Parthenon (from about 450 BC) are indeed impressive. The marble panels you see lining the walls of this large hall are part of the frieze that originally ran around the exterior of the Parthenon, under the eaves. The statues at either

A reconstructed Greek temple

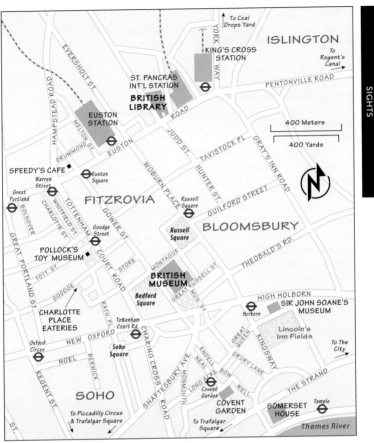

end of the hall once filled the Parthenon's triangular-shaped pediments and showed the birth of Athena. The relief panels known as metopes tell the story of the struggle between the forces of human civilization and animal-like barbarism.

Rest of the Museum: Be sure to venture upstairs to see artifacts from Roman Britain that surpass anything you'll see at Hadrian's Wall or elsewhere in the country. Also look for the Sutton Hoo Ship Burial artifacts from a seventh-century royal burial on the east coast of England (Room 41). A rare Michelangelo cartoon (preliminary sketch) is in Room 90 (level 4).

▲▲▲ BRITISH LIBRARY

Here, in just two rooms, are the literary treasures of Western civilization, from early Bibles to Shakespeare's *Hamlet* to Lewis Carroll's *Alice's Adventures in Wonderland* to the *Magna Carta*. The British Empire built its greatest monuments out of paper; it's through literature that England made her most lasting and significant contribution to civilization and the arts.

Cost and Hours: Free, £5 suggested donation, admission charged for special exhibits; Mon-Thu 9:30-20:00, Fri until 18:00, Sat until 17:00, Sun 11:00-17:00; 96 Euston Road, Tube: King's Cross St. Pancras or Euston, tel. 033/0333-1144, www.bl.uk.

Tours: Two £10 one-hour tours are offered daily—a Treasures Tour (generally at 11:00) and a building tour (generally at 14:00); book online or call 019/3754-6546. There are no audioguides for the permanent collection. Touch-screen computers in the permanent collection let you page virtually through some of the rare books.

🎧 Download my free British Library audio tour.

Visiting the Library: Everything that matters for your visit is in a tiny but exciting area variously called "The Sir John Ritblat Gallery," "Treasures of the British Library," or just "The Treasures." We'll concentrate on a handful of documents—literary and historical—that changed the course of history. Note that exhibits change often, and many of the museum's old, fragile manuscripts need to "rest" periodically in order to stay well-preserved.

Upon entering the Ritblat Gallery, start at the far side of the room with the display case showing historic ❶ **maps and views,** illustrating humans' shifting perspective of the world. Next, move into the area dedicated to ❷ **sacred texts and early Bibles,** including the Codex Sinaiticus (or the Codex Alexandrinus that may be on display instead). This bound book from around AD 350 is one of the oldest complete Bibles in existence—one of the first attempts to collect various books by different authors into one authoritative anthology. In the display cases called ❸ **Art of the Book,** you'll find various medieval-era books, some beautifully illustrated or "illuminated." The lettering is immaculate, but all are penned by hand. The most magnificent of these medieval British "monkuscripts" is the **Lindisfarne Gospels,** from AD 698.

In the glass cases featuring early ❹ **printing,** you'll see the Gutenberg Bible—the first book printed in Europe using movable type (c. 1455). Suddenly, the Bible was available for anyone to read, fueling the Protestant Reformation.

Through a doorway is a small room with the ❺ **Magna Carta.** Though historians talk about *the* Magna Carta, several

The British Library is filled with treasures ranging from the Magna Carta to Beatles song sheets.

British Library Tour

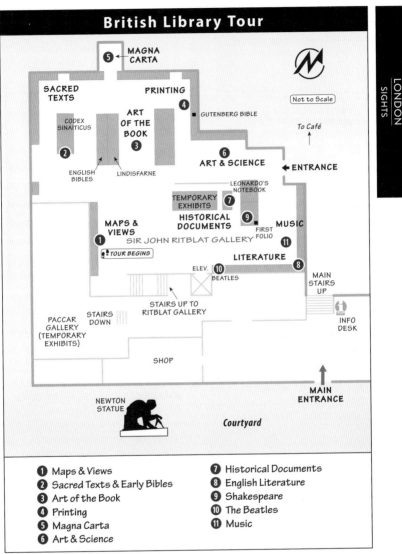

5 ← MAGNA CARTA

SACRED TEXTS

PRINTING

4

Not to Scale

CODEX SINAITICUS

ART OF THE BOOK

3

■ GUTENBERG BIBLE

To Café

2

ENGLISH BIBLES   LINDISFARNE

6
ART & SCIENCE

← ENTRANCE

LEONARDO'S NOTEBOOK

TEMPORARY EXHIBITS

7

HISTORICAL DOCUMENTS

9

MUSIC

MAPS & VIEWS

1

SIR JOHN RITBLAT GALLERY

FIRST FOLIO

11

TOUR BEGINS

LITERATURE

8

ELEV. **10**

BEATLES

MAIN STAIRS UP

STAIRS UP TO RITBLAT GALLERY

PACCAR GALLERY (TEMPORARY EXHIBITS)

STAIRS DOWN

INFO DESK

SHOP

MAIN ENTRANCE

NEWTON STATUE

Courtyard

1 Maps & Views
2 Sacred Texts & Early Bibles
3 Art of the Book
4 Printing
5 Magna Carta
6 Art & Science
7 Historical Documents
8 English Literature
9 Shakespeare
10 The Beatles
11 Music

different versions of the document exist, some of which are kept in this room. The basis for England's constitutional system of government, this "Great Charter" listing rules about mundane administrative issues was radical because of the simple fact that the king had agreed to abide by them as law.

Return to the main room to find display cases featuring trailblazing **6** **art and science** documents by early scientists such as Galileo, Isaac Newton, and many more. Pages from Leonardo da Vinci's notebook show his powerful curiosity, his genius for invention, and his famous backward and inside-out handwriting. Nearby are many more **7** **historical documents.** You may see letters by Henry VIII, Queen Elizabeth I,

The only known manuscript of the epic saga Beowulf

Lewis Carroll's manuscript for Alice's Adventures in Wonderland

Darwin, Freud, Gandhi, and others.

Next, trace the evolution of ❽ **English literature.** Check out the AD 1000 manuscript of Beowulf, the first English literary masterpiece, and *The Canterbury Tales* (c. 1410), Geoffrey Chaucer's bawdy collection of stories. This display is often a greatest-hits sampling of literature in English, from Brontë to Kipling to Woolf to Joyce to Dickens. The most famous of England's writers—❾ **Shakespeare**—generally gets his own display case. Look for the First Folio—one of the 750 copies of 36 of the 37 known Shakespeare plays, published in 1623. If the First Folio is not out for viewing, the library should have other Shakespeare items on display.

Now fast-forward a few centuries to ❿ **The Beatles.** Look for photos of John Lennon, Paul McCartney, George Harrison, and Ringo Starr. Among the displays, you may find manuscripts of song lyrics written by Lennon and McCartney. In the ⓫ **music** section, there are manuscripts by Mozart, Beethoven, Chopin, and others (kind of an anticlimax after the Fab Four, I know). George Frideric Handel's famous oratorio, the *Messiah* (1741), is often on display and marks the end of our tour. Hallelujah.

▲**MADAME TUSSAUDS WAXWORKS**

This waxtravaganza is gimmicky, crass, and crazy expensive, but dang fun...a hit with the kind of tourists who skip the British Museum. The original Madame Tussaud did wax casts of heads lopped off during the French Revolution (such as Marie-Antoinette's). She took her show on the road and ended up in London in 1835. Now it's all about singing with Lady Gaga, and partying with The Beatles. In addition to posing with all the eerily realistic wax dummies—from the Queen and Will and Kate to the Beckhams—you'll have the chance to learn how they created this waxy army; hop on a people-mover and cruise through a kid-pleasing "Spirit of London" time trip; and visit with Marvel superheroes. A nine-minute "4-D" show features a 3-D movie heightened by wind, "back ticklers," and other special effects.

The Beatles at Madame Tussauds

Rick's Tip: *To skip* **Madame Tussauds' ticket-buying line** *(which can be an hour or more), book a* **Priority Entrance** *ticket and reserve a time slot at least a day in advance. Or, pay royally for a Fast Track ticket in advance (available from souvenir shops or at the TI). The place is less crowded if you arrive after 15:00.*

Cost and Hours: £35, kids–£30 (free for kids under 3), up to 25 percent cheaper online; combo-deal with the London Eye. Very flexible hours (check online), but roughly July-Aug and school holidays daily 8:30-18:00, Sept-June Mon-Fri 10:00-16:00, Sat-Sun 9:00-17:00, these are last entry times—it stays open roughly two hours later; Marylebone Road, Tube: Baker Street, tel. 0871-894-3000, www.madametussauds.com.

The City

When Londoners say "The City," they mean the one-square-mile business center in East London that 2,000 years ago was Roman Londinium. The outline of the Roman city walls can still be seen in the arc of roads from Blackfriars Bridge to Tower Bridge. It's a fascinating district to wander on weekdays, but since almost nobody actually lives there, it's dull in the evening and on Saturday and Sunday.

You can 🎧 download my free audio tour of The City, which peels back the many layers of history in this oldest part of London.

▲▲▲ST. PAUL'S CATHEDRAL

Sir Christopher Wren's most famous church is the great St. Paul's, its elaborate interior capped by a 365-foot dome. Since World War II, St. Paul's has been Britain's symbol of resilience. Despite 57 nights of bombing, the Nazis failed to destroy the cathedral, thanks to St. Paul's volunteer fire watchmen, who stayed on the dome. Today you can climb the dome for a great city view. The crypt is a world of historic bones and memorials, including Admiral Nelson's tomb and interesting cathedral models.

Cost and Hours: £20, cheaper online,

includes church entry, dome climb, crypt, tour, and audioguide; Mon-Sat 8:30-16:30 (dome opens at 9:30), closed Sun except for worship; Tube: St. Paul's, tel. 020/7246-8350, www.stpauls.co.uk.

Avoiding Lines: Purchasing tickets in advance online saves a little time (and a little money); otherwise the wait can be 15-45 minutes in summer and on weekends. To avoid crowds in general, arrive first thing in the morning.

Rick's Tip: *If you come to St. Paul's 20 minutes* **early for evensong worship** *(under the dome), you may be able to grab a big wooden stall in the choir, next to the singers.*

Music and Church Services: Worship times are available on the church's website. Communion is generally Mon-Sat at 8:00 and 12:30. On Sunday, services are held at 8:00, 10:15 (Matins), 11:30 (sung Eucharist), 15:15 (evensong), and 18:00. The rest of the week, evensong is at 17:00 (Mon evensong is occasionally spoken, not sung). On some Sundays, there's a free organ recital at 16:45.

Tours: There are 1.5-hour **guided tours** Mon-Sat at 10:00, 11:00, 13:00, and 14:00 (call to confirm or ask at church). Free 15-minute **"highlights" tours** are offered throughout the day. The **audioguide** (included with admission) contains video clips that show the church in action.

🎧 Download my free St. Paul's Cathedral **audio tour.**

Visiting the Cathedral: Start at the far back of the ❶ **nave,** behind the font. This big church feels big. At 515 feet long and 250 feet wide, it's Europe's fourth largest, after those in Rome (St. Peter's), Sevilla, and Milan. The spaciousness is accentuated by the relative lack of decoration. The simple, cream-colored ceiling and the clear glass in the windows light everything evenly. Wren wanted this: a simple, open church with nothing to hide. Unfortunately, only this entrance area keeps his original vision—the rest was encrusted with 19th-century Victorian ornamentation.

Ahead and on the left is the towering, black-and-white ❷ **Wellington Monument.** Wren would have been appalled,

Majestic St. Paul's Cathedral is one of London's most iconic buildings.

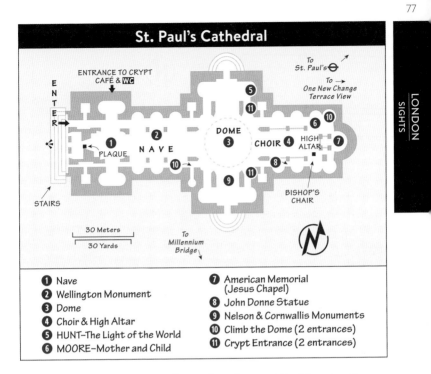

St. Paul's Cathedral

ENTRANCE TO CRYPT
CAFÉ & WC

ENTER

PLAQUE

NAVE

DOME

CHOIR

HIGH
ALTAR

STAIRS

30 Meters
30 Yards

To
Millennium
Bridge

To
St. Paul's

To →
One New Change
Terrace View

BISHOP'S
CHAIR

❶ Nave
❷ Wellington Monument
❸ Dome
❹ Choir & High Altar
❺ HUNT–The Light of the World
❻ MOORE–Mother and Child
❼ American Memorial (Jesus Chapel)
❽ John Donne Statue
❾ Nelson & Cornwallis Monuments
❿ Climb the Dome (2 entrances)
⓫ Crypt Entrance (2 entrances)

but his church has become so central to England's soul that many national heroes are buried here (in the basement crypt).

The ❸ **dome** you see from here, painted with scenes from the life of St. Paul, is only the innermost of three. From the painted interior of the first dome, look up through the opening to see the light-filled lantern of the second dome. Finally, the whole thing is covered on the outside by the third and final dome, the shell of lead-covered wood that you see

from the street. Wren's ingenious three-in-one design was psychological as well as functional—he wanted a low, shallow inner dome so worshippers wouldn't feel diminished.

The ❹ **choir** area blocks your way, but you can see the altar at the far end under a golden canopy. Do a quick clockwise spin around the church. In the north transept (to your left as you face the altar), find the big painting ❺ *The Light of the World* (1904), by the Pre-Raphaelite William

The cathedral's interior is dazzling.

Views from St. Paul's dome are worth the climb.

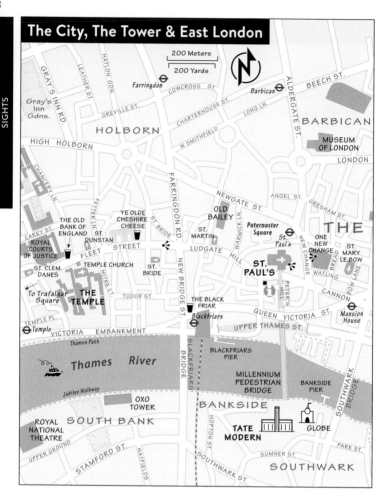

The City, The Tower & East London

200 Meters
200 Yards

Farringdon
COWCROSS ST.
Barbican
BEECH ST.
ALDERSGATE ST.

Gray's Inn Gdns.
GRAY'S INN RD.
LEATHER ST.
HATTON GDN.
GREVILLE ST.

BARBICAN

HOLBORN
CHARTERHOUSE ST.
LONG LN.

MUSEUM OF LONDON
LONDON

HIGH HOLBORN
W. SMITHFIELD

CHANCERY LN.

FARRINGDON RD.
NEWGATE ST.
ANGEL ST.
GRESHAM ST.

FETTER LN.
YE OLDE CHESHIRE CHEESE
OLD BAILEY
Paternoster Square
THE

CAREY ST.
THE OLD BANK OF ENGLAND
ST. DUNSTAN
ST. BRIDE
WARWICK LN.
ST. MARTIN
St. Paul's
ONE NEW CHANGE
ST. MARY LE BOW

ROYAL COURTS OF JUSTICE
FLEET STREET
LUDGATE HILL
NEW CHANGE
BREAD ST.
WATLING
BOW LANE

ST. CLEM. DANES
TEMPLE CHURCH
ST. BRIDE
ST. PAUL'S
PETER'S HILL

To Trafalgar Square
THE TEMPLE
MITRE CT.
TUDOR ST.
NEW BRIDGE ST.
THE BLACK FRIAR
QUEEN VICTORIA ST.
CANNON ST.
Mansion House

TEMPLE PL.
Temple
VICTORIA EMBANKMENT
Blackfriars
UPPER THAMES ST.

Thames Path

Thames River
BLACKFRIARS BRIDGE
BLACKFRIARS PIER

Jubilee Walkway
OXO TOWER
MILLENNIUM PEDESTRIAN BRIDGE
BANKSIDE PIER
SOUTHWARK BRIDGE

ROYAL NATIONAL THEATRE
SOUTH BANK
BANKSIDE
HOPTON ST.
TATE MODERN
GLOBE

UPPER GROUND
STAMFORD ST.
HATFIELDS
SOUTHWARK ST.
SUMNER ST.
PARK ST.
SOUTHWARK

Holman Hunt. Inspired by Hunt's own experience of finding Christ during a moment of spiritual crisis, the crowd-pleasing work was criticized by art highbrows for being "syrupy" and "simple"—even as it became the most famous painting in Victorian England.

Along the left side of the choir is the statue ❻ *Mother and Child* (1983), by the great modern sculptor Henry Moore. Typical of Moore's work, this Mary and Baby Jesus—inspired by the sight of British moms nursing babies in WWII bomb shelters—renders a traditional subject in an abstract, minimalist way.

The area behind the main altar, with three stained-glass windows, is the ❼ **American Memorial Chapel,** honoring the Americans who sacrificed their lives to save Britain in World War II. In brightly colored panes that arch around the big windows, spot the American eagle (center window, to the left of Christ), George Washington (right window, upper-right corner), and symbols of all 50 states (find your state seal). The Roll of Honor, a 500-page book under glass (immediately behind the altar), lists the names of

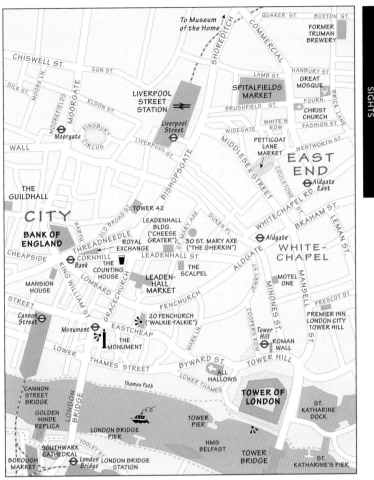

28,000 US servicemen and women based in Britain who gave their lives during the war.

Around the other side of the choir is a shrouded statue honoring **8 John Donne** (1573-1631), a passionate preacher in old St. Paul's, as well as a great poet ("never wonder for whom the bell tolls—it tolls for thee.") In the south transept are monuments to military greats **9 Horatio Nelson,** who fought Napoleon, and **Charles Cornwallis,** who was finished off by George Washington at Yorktown.

Climb the Dome: The 528-step climb is worthwhile. First you get to the Whispering Gallery (257 shallow steps, with views of the church interior). Whisper sweet nothings into the wall, and your partner (and anyone else) standing far away can hear you. For best effects, try whispering (not talking) with your mouth close to the wall, while your partner stands a few dozen yards away with his or her ear to the wall.

After another set of (steeper, narrower) stairs, you're at the Stone Gallery, with views of London. Finally, a long, tight metal staircase takes you to the very top of the cupola, the Golden Gallery, with stunning, unobstructed views of the city.

Crypt: The crypt is a world of historic bones and interesting cathedral models. Many legends are buried here—Horatio Nelson, who wore down Napoleon; the Duke of Wellington, who finished off Napoleon; and even Wren himself. Wren's actual tomb is marked by a simple black slab with no statue, though he considered this church to be his legacy. Back up in the nave, on the floor directly under the dome, is Christopher Wren's name and epitaph (written in Latin): "Reader, if you seek his monument, look around you."

▲MUSEUM OF LONDON

Scale models and costumes help you visualize everyday life in the city through history—from Neanderthals, to Romans, to Elizabethans, to Victorians, to Mods, to today. It's informative without being overwhelming, with enough whiz-bang multimedia displays to spice up otherwise humdrum artifacts.

Cost and Hours: Free, daily 10:00-18:00, last entry one hour before closing, see the day's events board for special talks and tours, café, lockers, 150 London Wall at Aldersgate Street, Tube: Barbican or St. Paul's plus a 5-minute walk, tel. 020/7001-9844, www.museumoflondon.org.uk.

▲▲▲TOWER OF LONDON

The Tower has served as a castle in wartime, a king's residence in peacetime, and, most notoriously, as the prison and execution site of rebels. You can see the crown jewels, take a witty Beefeater tour, and ponder the executioner's block that dispensed with troublesome heirs to the throne and a couple of Henry VIII's wives.

Cost and Hours: £28.90, cheaper online, family ticket available; Tue-Sat 9:00-17:30, Sun-Mon from 10:00; Nov-Feb closes one hour earlier; free Beefeater tours available, skippable audioguide-£5, Tube: Tower Hill, tel. 0333-206-000, www.hrp.org.uk.

Advance Tickets: To avoid long ticket-buying lines, and save a few pounds, buy tickets in advance for a specific day on the Tower website (print at home or collect on-site at group ticket office—see map). Alternatively, buy a voucher on your way to the Tower at the Trader's Gate gift shop, down the steps from the Tower Hill Tube stop (look for the blue awning). The voucher is good any day and can be exchanged for a ticket at the group ticket office.

Visiting the Tower: Even an army the size of the ticket line couldn't storm this castle. The ❶ **entrance gate** where you'll show your ticket was just part of two concentric rings of complete defenses. When you're all set, go 50 yards straight ahead to the ❷ **traitors' gate.** This was the boat entrance to the Tower from the Thames. Turn left to pass underneath the archway into the inner courtyard. The big,

Tower of London

A Beefeater on duty

London's Best Views

For some viewpoints, you need to pay admission, and at the bars or restaurants, you'll need to buy a drink.

London Eye: Ride the giant Ferris wheel for stunning London views. See page 86.

St. Paul's Dome: You'll earn a striking, unobstructed view by climbing hundreds of steps to the cramped balcony of the church's cupola. See page 75.

One New Change: Get fine, free views of St. Paul's Cathedral and surroundings—nearly as good as those from St. Paul's Dome—from the rooftop terrace of the One New Change shopping mall just behind and east of the church.

Tate Modern: Head to the Tate Modern's annex—the Blavatnik Building—and ride the elevator to floor 10, where you'll enjoy sweeping views of the skyline (plus the Tate's own tower in the foreground). You can also ride to floor 6 of the main building. See page 88.

20 Fenchurch (a.k.a. "The Walkie-Talkie"): Get 360-degree views of London from the mostly enclosed Sky Garden. It's free but you'll need to make reservations in advance and bring photo ID (Mon-Fri 10:00-18:00, Sat-Sun 11:00-21:00, 20 Fenchurch Street, Tube: Monument, https://skygarden.london/sky-garden).

National Portrait Gallery: A mod top-floor restaurant peers over Trafalgar Square and the Westminster neighborhood. See page 61.

Waterstones Bookstore: Its hip, low-key, top-floor café/bar has reasonable prices and sweeping views of the London Eye, Big Ben, and the Houses of Parliament (Mon-Sat 9:00-22:00, Sun 12:00-18:30, on Sun bar closes one hour before bookstore, 203 Piccadilly, www.5thview.co.uk).

The Shard: The observation decks that cap this 1,020-foot-tall skyscraper offer London's most commanding views, but at an outrageously high price (£39—book online in advance, advance ticket includes free return ticket in case of bad weather, otherwise pay 25 percent more on-site; daily 10:00-22:00, shorter hours Oct-March; Tube: London Bridge—use London Bridge exit and follow signs, www.theviewfromtheshard.com).

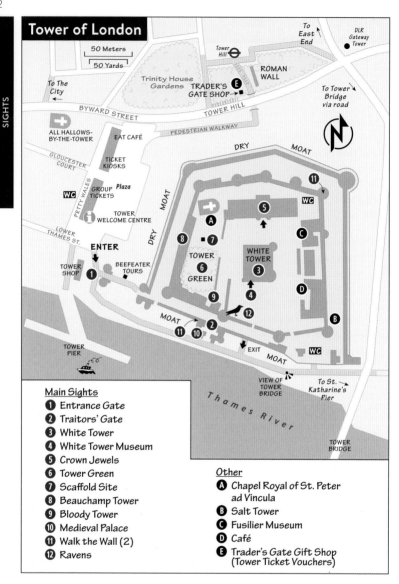

Tower of London

50 Meters
50 Yards

To East End

DLR Gateway Tower

Tower Hill

ROMAN WALL

Trinity House Gardens

TRADER'S GATE SHOP **E**

To The City

BYWARD STREET

TOWER HILL

To Tower Bridge via road

ALL HALLOWS-BY-THE-TOWER

EAT CAFÉ

PEDESTRIAN WALKWAY

GLOUCESTER COURT

TICKET KIOSKS

DRY MOAT

PETTY WALES

WC GROUP TICKETS Plaza

DRY MOAT

11

WC

TOWER WELCOME CENTRE

A

5

LOWER THAMES ST.

ENTER

8 ■ **7**

WHITE TOWER

C

TOWER SHOP **1**

BEEFEATER TOURS

TOWER GREEN **6**

3

4

D

9

MOAT

12

B

11 **10** **2**

WC

TOWER PIER

EXIT MOAT

VIEW OF TOWER BRIDGE

To St. Katharine's Pier

Thames River

TOWER BRIDGE

Main Sights

1 Entrance Gate
2 Traitors' Gate
3 White Tower
4 White Tower Museum
5 Crown Jewels
6 Tower Green
7 Scaffold Site
8 Beauchamp Tower
9 Bloody Tower
10 Medieval Palace
11 Walk the Wall (2)
12 Ravens

Other

A Chapel Royal of St. Peter ad Vincula
B Salt Tower
C Fusilier Museum
D Café
E Trader's Gate Gift Shop (Tower Ticket Vouchers)

white tower in the middle is the **3** **White Tower,** the original structure that gave this castle complex its name. William the Conqueror built it more than 950 years ago to put 15 feet of stone between himself and those he conquered. The White Tower provided a gleaming reminder of the monarchy's absolute power. You could be feasting on roast boar in the Banqueting Hall one night and chained to the walls of the prison the next.

Inside the White Tower is a **4** museum with exhibits re-creating medieval life and the Tower's bloody history of torture and executions. The first suits of armor you see belonged to Henry VIII—on a horse,

Henry VIII (1491-1547)

The notorious king who single-handedly transformed England was a true Renaissance Man—six feet tall, handsome, charismatic, well-educated, and brilliant. He spoke English, Latin, French, and Spanish. A legendary athlete, he hunted, played tennis, and jousted with knights and kings. When 17-year-old Henry, the second monarch of the House of Tudor, was crowned king in Westminster Abbey, all of England rejoiced.

Henry left affairs of state in the hands of others, and filled his days with sports, war, dice, women, and the arts. But in 1529, Henry's personal life became a political atom bomb, and it changed the course of history.

Henry wanted a divorce, partly because his wife had become too old to bear him a son, and partly because he'd fallen in love with Anne Boleyn. Henry begged the pope for an annulment, but—for political reasons—the pope refused. Henry went ahead and divorced his wife anyway, and he was excommunicated.

Henry's rejection of papal authority sparked the English Reformation. He forced monasteries to close, sold off some church land, and confiscated everything else for himself and the Crown. Meanwhile, the Catholic Church was reorganized into the (Anglican) Church of England, with Henry as its head. Though Henry himself basically adhered to Catholic doctrine, he discouraged the veneration of saints and relics, and commissioned an English translation of the Bible.

Henry famously had six wives. The issue was not his love life (which could have been satisfied by his numerous mistresses), but the politics of royal succession. To guarantee the Tudor family's dominance, he needed a male heir born by a recognized queen. Henry's first marriage, to Catherine of Aragon, had been arranged to cement an alliance with her parents, Ferdinand and Isabel of Spain. Catherine bore Henry a daughter, but no sons. Next came Anne Boleyn, who also gave birth to a daughter. After a turbulent few years with Anne and several miscarriages, a frustrated Henry had her beheaded at the Tower of London. His next wife, Jane Seymour, finally had a son (but Jane died soon after giving birth). A blind marriage with Anne of Cleves ended quickly when she proved to be both politically useless and ugly. Next, teen bride Catherine Howard ended up cheating on Henry, so she was executed. Henry finally found comfort—but no children—in his later years with his final wife, Catherine Parr.

Henry's last years were marked by paranoia, sudden rages, and despotism. He gave his perceived enemies the pink slip in his signature way—charged with treason and beheaded. Once-wealthy England was becoming depleted, thanks to Henry's expensive habits, which included making war on France, building and acquiring 50 palaces, and collecting fine tapestries and archery bows.

Henry forged a large legacy. He expanded the power of the monarchy, making himself the focus of a rising, modern nation-state. Simultaneously, he strengthened Parliament—largely because it agreed with his policies. He annexed Wales, and imposed English rule on Ireland (provoking centuries of resentment). He expanded the navy, paving the way for Britannia to soon rule the waves. And—thanks to Henry's marital woes—England would forever be a Protestant nation.

Execution ax and block

slender in his youth (c. 1515), then more heavyset by 1540 (with his bigger-is-better codpiece). On the top floor are the Tower's actual execution ax and chopping block.

Across from the White Tower is the entrance to the ❺ **crown jewels.** The Sovereign's Scepter is encrusted with the world's largest cut diamond—the 530-carat Star of Africa, beefy as a quarter-pounder. The Crown of the Queen Mother (Elizabeth II's famous mum, who died in 2002) has the 106-carat Koh-I-

Noor diamond glittering on the front (considered unlucky for male rulers, it adorns the crown of the king's wife). The Imperial State Crown is what the Queen wears for official functions such as the State Opening of Parliament. Among its 3,733 jewels are Queen Elizabeth I's former earrings (the hanging pearls, top center), a stunning 13th-century ruby look-alike in the center, and Edward the Confessor's ring (the blue sapphire on top, in the center of the Maltese cross of diamonds).

Exiting the tower, turn right and walk past the White Tower, straight ahead to the grassy field called ❻ **Tower Green.** In medieval times, this was the "town square" for those who lived in the castle. Near the middle of Tower Green is a granite-paved square, the ❼ **Scaffold Site.** It was here that enemies of the Crown would kneel before the king for the final time. On the left as you face the chapel, is the ❽ **Beauchamp Tower** (pronounced "BEECH-um"), one of several places in the complex that housed Very Important Prisoners.

Down toward the river, at the bot-

The Tower Bridge has spanned the Thames since 1894.

tom corner of the green is the **⑨ Bloody Tower,** and beyond that the **⑩ Medieval Palace.** From the palace's throne room, continue up the stairs to **⑪ walk the wall** for a fine view of the Tower Bridge. Between the White Tower and the Thames are cages housing the **⑫ ravens.** According to tradition, the Tower and the British throne are only safe as long as ravens are present here. Other sights at the Tower include the Salt Tower and the Fusilier Museum.

TOWER BRIDGE

The iconic Tower Bridge (often mistakenly called London Bridge) was built in 1894 to accommodate the growing East End. While fully modern and hydraulically powered, the drawbridge was designed with a retro Neo-Gothic look. The bridge is most interesting when the drawbridge lifts to let ships pass, as it does a thousand times a year (best viewed from the Tower side of the Thames). For the bridge-lifting schedule, check the website or call.

You can tour the bridge at the **Tower Bridge Exhibition,** with a history display and a peek at the Victorian-era engine room that lifts the span. Included in your entrance is the chance to cross the bridge—138 feet above the road along a partially see-through glass walkway. As an exhibit, it's overpriced, though the adrenaline rush and spectacular city views from the walkway may help justify the cost.

Cost and Hours: £9.80, daily 10:00-18:00 in summer, 9:30-17:30 in winter, enter at northwest tower, Tube: Tower Hill, tel. 020/7403-3761, www.towerbridge.org.uk.

South Bank
▲JUBILEE WALKWAY

This riverside path is a popular pub-crawling pedestrian promenade that stretches all along the South Bank, offering grand views of the Houses of Parliament and St. Paul's. On a sunny day, this is the place to see Londoners out strolling. The Walkway hugs the river except just east of London Bridge, where it cuts inland for a couple of blocks. It has been expanded into a 60-mile "Greenway" circling the city, including the 2012 Olympics site.

The London Eye adds whimsical fun to London's stately skyline.

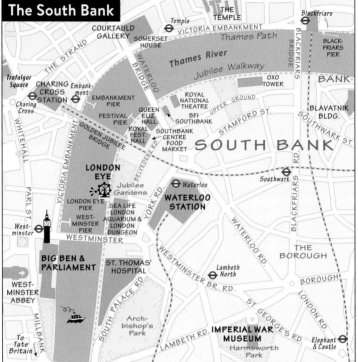

▲▲LONDON EYE

This giant Ferris wheel, towering above London opposite Big Ben, is one of the world's highest observational wheels and London's answer to the Eiffel Tower. Riding it is a memorable experience, even though London doesn't have much of a skyline, and the price is borderline outrageous. Whether you ride or not, the wheel is a sight to behold.

Twenty-eight people ride in each of its 32 air-conditioned capsules (representing the boroughs of London) for the 30-minute rotation (you go around only once). From the top of this 443-foot-high wheel—the second-highest public viewpoint in the city—even Big Ben looks small.

Cost and Hours: £30, cheaper online, family ticket and combo-ticket with Madame Tussauds and other attractions available; daily 10:00-20:30 or later, Sept-

May generally 11:00-18:00, check website for latest schedule, these are last-ascent times, Tube: Waterloo or Westminster. Thames boats come and go from London Eye Pier at the foot of the wheel.

Rick's Tip: *The* **London Eye** *is busiest between 11:00 and 17:00, especially on weekends year-round and every day in July and August.* **Book your ticket at** *www.londoneye.com,* *then print it at home, retrieve it from an onsite ticket machine (bring your payment card and confirmation code), or stand in the "Ticket Collection" line. Even if you buy in advance, you may wait to board (but it's not worth paying extra for a Fast Track ticket).*

▲▲IMPERIAL WAR MUSEUM

This impressive museum covers the wars and conflicts of the 20th and 21st centu-

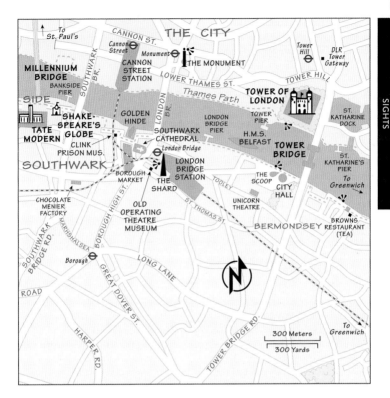

ries. You can walk chronologically through World War I, to the rise of fascism, World War II, the Cold War, the Troubles in Northern Ireland, the wars in Iraq and Afghanistan, and terrorism. Rather than glorify war, the museum explores the human side of the wartime experience and its effect on people back home. It raises thoughtful questions about one of civilization's more uncivilized, persistent

traits. Allow plenty of time; lots of artifacts, interactive experiences, and multimedia exhibits can be engrossing.

Cost and Hours: Free, £5 suggested donation, special exhibits extra, daily 10:00-18:00, last entry one hour before closing, Tube: Lambeth North or Elephant and Castle; buses #3, #12, and #159 from Westminster area; tel. 020/7416-5000, www.iwm.org.uk.

Imperial War Museum

Imperial War Museum atrium

Visiting the Museum: Start in the atrium to grasp the massive scale of warfare as you wander among and under notable battle machines. The Spitfire plane overhead flew in the Battle of Britain. From here, the displays unfold chronologically as you work your way up from floor to floor. On level 0, enter **The First World War.** The highlight of the exhibit is a reconstructed trench, with a massive tank rearing overhead, where you're bombarded with the sounds of war. Climb the stairs for exhibits on **World War II.** A video clip shows the mesmerizing Adolf Hitler, who roused a defeated Germany to rearm for war again. At the museum shop, double back to see displays on Britain's fight against the Nazis in North Africa and Operation Overlord—i.e., D-Day.

Level 2, which may be under renovation, covers the **Post-War Years,** which began (as the plaque says) "In the shadow of The Bomb" (alongside an actual casing made for the Hiroshima bomb). Level 3 generally has **temporary exhibits** shedding light on why humans fight. The most powerful exhibit is on level 4—**The Holocaust.** Photos, video clips, and a few artifacts trace the sad story. A room-size model of the Auschwitz camp testifies to the scale of the slaughter and its banal orderliness. Crowning the museum on level 5, the **Lord Ashcroft Gallery** celebrates Britain's heroes who received the Victoria and George Crosses.

▲▲TATE MODERN

This striking museum fills a former power station across the river from St. Paul's with a powerhouse collection including Dalí, Picasso, Warhol, and much more.

Cost and Hours: Free, £5 suggested donation, fee for special exhibits; daily 10:00-18:00, Fri-Sat until 22:00, last entry to special exhibits 45 minutes before closing, especially crowded on weekend days (crowds thin out Fri and Sat evenings); view restaurant on top floor, across the Millennium Bridge from St. Paul's; Tube:

Tate Modern

Southwark, London Bridge, St. Paul's, Mansion House, or Blackfriars plus a 10- to 15-minute walk; or connect by Tate Boat museum ferry from Tate Britain—see page 90; tel. 020/7887-8888, www.tate.org.uk.

Tours: Free 45-minute guided tours are offered at 12:00 and 13:00 (Natalie Bell Building) and 14:00 (Blavatnik Building); free 10-minute gallery talks sometimes offered (see info desk).

Visiting the Museum: The permanent collection is generally on levels 2, 4, and part of level 3 of the Natalie Bell Building. Paintings are arranged according to theme, not artist. Paintings by Picasso, for example, might be scattered in different rooms on different levels. To help you get started, find the "Start Display" room on level 2—highlighting a range of artworks.

Since 1960, London has rivaled New York as a center for the visual arts. You'll find British artists displayed here—look for work by David Hockney, Henry Moore, and Barbara Hepworth. American art is also prominently represented—keep an eye out for abstract expressionist works by Mark Rothko and Jackson Pollock, and the pop art of Andy Warhol and Roy Lichtenstein. After you see the Old Masters of Modernism (Matisse, Picasso, Kandinsky, and so on), push your mental envelope with works by Pollock, Miró, Bacon, Picabia, Beuys, Twombly, and beyond.

You'll find temporary exhibits throughout the museum—some free, some requiring a special admission. Additionally, the main hall features a different monumental installation by a prominent artist each year. The museum's newer twisted-pyramid, 10-story Blavatnik Building also hosts changing themed exhibitions, performance art, experimental film, and interactive sculpture incorporating light and sound.

▲MILLENNIUM BRIDGE

The pedestrian bridge links St. Paul's Cathedral and the Tate Modern across the Thames. This is London's first new bridge in a century. When it opened, the $25 million bridge wiggled when people walked on it, so it promptly closed for repairs; 20 months and $8 million later, it reopened. Nicknamed the "blade of light" for its sleek minimalist design (370 yards long, four yards wide, stainless steel with teak planks), its clever aerodynamic handrails deflect wind over the heads of pedestrians.

▲▲SHAKESPEARE'S GLOBE

This replica of the original Globe Theatre was built, half-timbered and thatched, to appear as it was in Shakespeare's time. (This is the first thatched roof constructed in London since they were outlawed after the Great Fire of 1666.) It serves as a working theater by night and offers tours by day. The original Globe opened in 1599, debuting Shakespeare's play *Julius Caesar*. The Globe originally accommodated 2,200 seated and another 1,000 standing. Today, slightly smaller and leaving space for reasonable aisles,

the theater holds 800 seated and 600 groundlings.

Its promoters brag that the theater melds "the three A's"—actors, audience, and architecture—with each contributing to the play. The working theater hosts authentic performances of Shakespeare's plays with actors in period costumes, modern interpretations of his works, and some works by other playwrights. For details on attending a play, see page 100. The complex's smaller Sam Wanamaker Playhouse—an indoor, horseshoe-shaped Jacobean theater—allows the show to go on in the winter, when it's too cold for performances in the outdoor Globe. Seating fewer than 350, the playhouse is more intimate and sometimes uses authentic candle lighting for period performances. While the Globe mainly presents Shakespeare's works, the playhouse tends to focus on the works of his contemporaries (Jonson, Marlow, Fletcher) and some new plays.

Touring the Globe: Tours depart from the box office every half-hour and last for 40 minutes (£17, £10 for kids 5-15; during outdoor theater season—April-mid-Oct—last tours depart Mon at 17:00, Tue-Sat at 12:30, Sun at 11:30; off-season last tours Mon-Sat at 12:30, Sun at 17:00; Tube: Mansion House or London Bridge plus a 10-minute walk; or a short walk across the Millennium Bridge from St. Paul's Cathedral; tel. 020/7902-1400, www.shakespearesglobe.com).

Eating: The **$$$ Swan at the Globe** café offers a sit-down restaurant (for

Millennium Bridge

Shakespeare's Globe

lunch and dinner, reservations recommended, tel. 020/7928-9444, www.swanlondon.co.uk), a drinks-and-plates bar, and a sandwich-and-coffee cart (Mon-Fri 8:00-closing, depends on performance times, Sat-Sun from 10:00).

West London

▲▲TATE BRITAIN

One of Europe's great art houses, Tate Britain specializes in British painting from the 16th century through modern times. The museum has a good representation of William Blake's religious sketches, the Pre-Raphaelites' naturalistic and detailed art, Gainsborough's aristocratic ladies, and the best collection anywhere of J. M. W. Turner's swirling works.

Cost and Hours: Free, £4 suggested donation, fee for special exhibits; daily 10:00-18:00, last entry 45 minutes before closing; free tours generally daily; on the Thames River, south of Big Ben and north of Vauxhall Bridge, Tube: Pimlico, Tate Boat museum ferry goes directly to the museum from Tate Modern—see page 88; tel. 020/7887-8888, www.tate.org.uk.

Tours: Free guided tours are generally offered daily at 11:00 (the best overview tour), with specialty tours at 12:00, 14:00, and 15:00.

Visiting the Museum: Works from the early centuries are located in the west half of the building (to your left), and 20th-century art is in the east half. Also to the east, in the adjacent Clore Gallery, are the works of J. M. W. Turner, John Constable, and William Blake. The Tate rotates its vast collection of paintings, so it's difficult to predict exactly which works will be on display. Pick up a map as you enter (£1 suggested donation) or download the museum's helpful app for a room-by-room guide.

1700-1800—Art Blossoms: With peace at home (under three King Georges), a strong overseas economy, and a growing urban center in London, England's artistic life began to bloom.

As the English grew more sophisticated, so did their portraits. Painters branched out into other subjects, capturing slices of everyday life (find William Hogarth's unflinchingly honest portraits, and Thomas Gainsborough's elegant, educated women).

1800-1850—The Industrial Revolution: Newfangled inventions were everywhere, but along with technology came factories coating towns with soot, urban poverty, regimentation, and clock-punching. Many artists rebelled against "progress" and the modern world. They escaped the dirty cities to commune with nature. Or they found a new spirituality in intense human emotions, expressed in dramatic paintings of episodes from history. In rooms dedicated to the 1800s, you may see a number of big paintings devoted to the power of nature.

1837-1901—The Victorian Era: In the world's wealthiest nation, the prosperous middle class dictated taste in art. They admired paintings that were realistic (showcasing the artist's talent and work ethic), depicting slices of everyday life. Some paintings tug at the heartstrings, with scenes of parting couples, the grief of death, or the joy of families reuniting.

Overdosed with the gushy sentimentality of their day, a band of 20-year-old artists—including Sir John Everett Millais, Dante Gabriel Rossetti, and William Holman Hunt—said "Enough!" and dedicated themselves to creating less saccharine art

Victorian-era Lady of Shalott

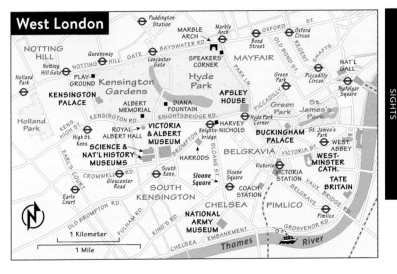

(the Pre-Raphaelites). Like the Impressionists who followed them, they donned their scarves, barged out of the stuffy studio, and set up outdoors, painting trees, streams, and people, like scientists on a field trip. Still, they often captured nature with such a close-up clarity that it's downright unnatural.

British Impressionism: Realistic British art stood apart from the modernist trends in France, but some influences drifted across the Channel (Rooms 1890 and 1900). John Singer Sargent (American-born) studied with Parisian Impressionists, learning the thick, messy brushwork and play of light at twilight. James Tissot used Degas' snapshot technique to capture a crowded scene from an odd angle. And James McNeill Whistler (born in America, trained in Paris, lived in London) composed his paintings like music—see some of his paintings' titles.

1900-1950—World Wars: As two world wars whittled down the powerful British Empire, it still remained a major cultural force. British art mirrored many of the trends and "-isms" pioneered in Paris (Room 1930). You'll see Cubism like Picasso's, abstract art like Mondrian's, and so on. But British artists also continued the British tradition of realistic paintings of people and landscapes.

If British painters were less than avant-garde, their sculptors were cutting edge. Henry Moore's statues—mostly female, mostly reclining—capture the human body in a few simple curves, with minimal changes to the rock itself. Francis Bacon has become Britain's best-known 20th-century painter, exemplifying the angst of the early post-WWII years. His deformed half-humans/half-animals express the existential human predicament of being caught in a world not of your own making, isolated and helpless to change it.

1950-2000—Modern World: No longer a world power, Britain in the Swinging '60s became a major exporter of pop culture. British art's traditional strengths—realism, portraits, landscapes, and slice-of-life scenes—were redone in the modern style. Look for works by David Hockney, Lucian Freud, Bridget Riley, and Gilbert and George.

Clore Gallery: Walking through J. M. W. Turner's life's work, you can watch Turner's style evolve from clear-eyed realism to hazy proto-Impressionism (1775-1851). You'll also see how Turner dabbled in different subjects: landscapes, seascapes, Roman ruins, snapshots of Venice, and so on. The corner room of the Clore Gallery is dedicated to John Constable (1776-1837), who painted the English landscape realistically, without idealizing it.

▲HYDE PARK AND SPEAKERS' CORNER

London's "Central Park," originally Henry VIII's hunting grounds, has more than 600 acres of lush greenery, Santander Cycles rental stations (described on page 126), the huge man-made Serpentine Lake (with rental boats and a lakeside swimming pool), the royal Kensington Palace (described next), and the ornate Neo-Gothic Albert Memorial across from the Royal Albert Hall (for more about the park, see www.royalparks.org.uk/parks/hyde-park). The western half of the park is known as Kensington Gardens. The park is huge—study a Tube map to choose the stop nearest to your destination.

On Sundays, from just after noon until early evening, **Speakers' Corner** offers soapbox oratory at its best (northeast corner of the park, Tube: Marble Arch). Characters climb their stepladders, wave their flags, pound emphatically on their sandwich boards, and share what they are convinced is their wisdom. Regulars have resident hecklers who know their lines and are always ready with a verbal jab or barb. "The grass roots of democracy" is actually a holdover from when the gallows stood here and the criminal was allowed to say just about anything he wanted to before he swung. I dare you to raise your voice and gather a crowd—it's easy to do.

The **Princess Diana Memorial Fountain** honors the "People's Princess," who once lived in nearby Kensington Palace. The low-key circular stream, great for cooling off your feet on a hot day, is in the south-central part of the park, near the Albert Memorial and Serpentine Gallery (Tube: Knightsbridge). A similarly named but different sight, the **Diana, Princess of Wales Memorial Playground,** in the park's northwest corner, is loads of fun for kids (Tube: Queensway).

KENSINGTON PALACE

For nearly 150 years (1689-1837), Kensington was the royal residence, before Buckingham Palace became the official home of the monarch. Sitting primly on its pleasant parkside grounds, the palace gives a barren yet regal glimpse into royal life—particularly that of Queen Victoria, who was born and raised here.

After Queen Victoria moved the monarchy to Buckingham Palace, lesser royals bedded down at Kensington. Princess Diana lived here both during and after her marriage to Prince Charles (1981-1997). More recently, Will and Kate moved in here. However—as many disappointed visitors discover—none of these more recent apartments are open to the public. The palace hosts a revolving series of temporary exhibits. To see what's on during your visit, check online.

Cost and Hours: £17.50; daily 10:00-18:00, Nov-Feb until 16:00, last entry one

Hyde Park

Kensington Palace

hour before closing; a long 10-minute stroll through Kensington Gardens from either High Street Kensington or Queensway Tube stations, tel. 0844-482-7788, www.hrp.org.uk.

Outside: Garden enthusiasts enjoy popping into the secluded Sunken Garden, 50 yards from the exit. Consider afternoon tea at the nearby Orangery (see page 117), built as a greenhouse for Queen Anne in 1704.

▲▲▲VICTORIA AND ALBERT MUSEUM

The world's top collection of decorative arts encompasses 2,000 years of art and design (ceramics, stained glass, fine furniture, clothing, jewelry, carpets, and more), displaying a surprisingly interesting and diverse assortment of crafts from the West, as well as from Asian and Islamic cultures. There's much to see, including Raphael's tapestry cartoons, Leonardo da Vinci's notebooks, the huge Islamic Ardabil Carpet (4,914 knots in every 10 square centimeters), a cast of Trajan's Column that depicts the emperor's conquests, and pop culture memorabilia, including the jumpsuit Mick Jagger wore for The Rolling Stones' 1972 world tour.

Cost and Hours: Free, £5 donation requested, fee for some special exhibits, daily 10:00-17:45, some galleries open Fri until 22:00, free tours daily, on Cromwell Road in South Kensington, Tube: South Kensington, from the Tube station a long tunnel leads directly to museum, tel. 020/7942-2000, www.vam.ac.uk.

Visiting the Museum: In the Grand Entrance lobby, look up into the rotunda to see the **Dale Chihuly chandelier,** epitomizing the spirit of the V&A's collection—beautiful manufactured objects that demonstrate technical skill and innovation, wedding the old with the new, and blurring the line between arts and crafts.

Now look up to the balcony (above the shop) and see the pointed arches of the **Hereford Screen,** a 35-by-35-foot, eight-ton rood screen (built for the Her-

eford Cathedral's sacred altar area). It looks medieval, but it was created with the most modern materials the Industrial Revolution could produce. George Gilbert Scott (1811-1878), who built the screen, redesigned much of London in the Neo-Gothic style, restoring old churches such as Westminster Abbey, renovating the Houses of Parliament, and building new structures like St. Pancras Station and the Albert Memorial—some 700 buildings in all.

Rick's Tip: *The Victoria and Albert Museum is huge and tricky to navigate. Spend £1 for the* **museum map** *available from the info desk.*

The V&A has (arguably) the best collection of Italian Renaissance sculpture outside Italy. One prime example is *Samson Slaying a Philistine,* by Giambologna (c. 1562), carved from a single block of marble, which shows the testy Israelite warrior rearing back, brandishing the jawbone of an ass, preparing to decapitate a man who'd insulted him.

The **Medieval and Renaissance Galleries** display 1,200 years of decorative arts, showing how the mix of pagan-Roman and medieval-Christian elements created modern Europe. In Room 8 is a glass case displaying the blue-and-gold, shoebox-sized **Becket Casket,** which contains the mortal remains (or relics) of St. Thomas Becket, who was brutally murdered. The enamel-and-metal workbox is a specialty of Limoges, France. In Room 10a, you'll run into the **Boar and Bear Hunt Tapestry.** Though most medieval art depicted the Madonna and saints, this colorful wool tapestry—woven in Belgium—provides a secular slice of life.

Two floors up, you'll see the tiny, pocket-size **notebook by Leonardo da Vinci** (Codex Forster III, 1490-1493), which dates from the years when he was living in Milan, shortly before undertaking his

Victoria and Albert Museum

Greenwich

famous *Last Supper* fresco. The book's contents are all over the map: meticulous sketches of the human head, diagrams illustrating nature's geometrical perfection, a horse's leg for a huge equestrian statue, and even drawings of the latest ballroom fashions. The adjacent computer lets you scroll through three of his notebooks and even flip his backwards handwriting to make it readable.

Back on level 0, enter Room 46b, and find **Michelangelo casts** and other replica statues. These plaster-cast versions of famous Renaissance statues allowed 19th-century art students who couldn't afford a rail pass to study the classics. In Room 42, you'll see **Islamic art,** reflecting both religious influences and a sophisticated secular culture. Many Islamic artists expressed themselves with beautiful but functional objects, such as the 630-square-foot Ardabil Carpet (1539-1540), which likely took a dozen workers years to complete. Also in the room are ceramics and glazed tile—all covered top to bottom in similarly complex patterns. The intricate interweaving, repetition, and unending lines suggest the complex, infinite nature of God (Allah).

In the hallway (technically "Room" 47b) is a glass case with a statue of **Shiva Nataraja,** one of the hundreds, if not thousands, of godlike incarnations of Hinduism's eternal being, Brahma. As long as Shiva keeps dancing, the universe will continue. In adjoining Room 41, a glass

case in the center of the room contains **possessions of Emperor Shah Jahan,** including a cameo portrait, thumb ring, and wine cup (made of white nephrite jade, 1657). Shah Jahan—or "King of the World"—ruled the largest empire of the day, covering northern India, Pakistan, and Afghanistan. At the far end of Room 41 is the huge wood-carved **Tipu's Tiger,** a life-size robotic toy, once owned by an oppressed Indian sultan. When you turned the crank, the Brit's left arm would flail, and both he and the tiger would roar through organ pipes. (The mechanism still works.)

The **Fashion Galleries** display centuries of English fashion, from ladies' underwear, hoop skirts, and rain gear to high-society evening wear, men's suits, and more. Across the hall are **Raphael's tapestry cartoons.** The V&A owns seven of these full-size designs (approximately 13 by 17 feet, done in tempera on paper, now mounted on canvas). The cartoons were sent to factories in Brussels, cut into strips (see the lines), and placed on the looms.

Upstairs, Room 57 is the heart of the **British Galleries,** which cover the era of Queen Elizabeth I. Find rare miniature portraits—a popular item of the day— including Hilliard's oft-reproduced *Young Man Among Roses* miniature, capturing the romance of a Shakespeare sonnet. Back in the Grand Entrance lobby, climb the staircase to level 2 to see **jewelry, theater artifacts, silver,** and more.

▲▲ NATURAL HISTORY MUSEUM

Across the street from the Victoria and Albert, this mammoth museum covers everything from life ("creepy crawlies," human biology, our place in evolution, and awe-inspiring dinosaurs) to earth science (meteors, volcanoes, and earthquakes).

Cost and Hours: Free, £5 donation requested, fee for special exhibits, daily 10:00-18:00, helpful £1 map, long tunnel leads directly from South Kensington Tube station to museum (follow signs), tel. 020/7942-5000, exhibit info and reservations tel. 020/7942-5011, www.nhm.ac.uk. Free visitor app available via the "Visit" section of the website.

Greenwich

This borough of London (worth ▲▲) is an easy, affordable boat trip or Docklands Light Railway (DLR) journey from downtown. Along with majestic, picnic-perfect parks are the stately trappings of Britain's proud nautical heritage and the Royal Observatory Greenwich, with a fine museum on how Greenwich Mean Time came to be, and a chance to straddle the eastern and western hemispheres at the prime meridian.

Getting There: Ride a boat to Greenwich for the scenery and commentary, and take the DLR back. Various tour boats—with commentary and open-deck seating (2/hour, 30-75 minutes)—and faster Thames Clippers (every 20-30 minutes, 20-55 minutes) depart from several piers in central London. Thames Clippers also connects Greenwich to the Docklands' Canary Wharf Pier (2-3/hour, 15 minutes).

By DLR, ride from the Bank-Monument Station to Cutty Sark Station in central Greenwich; it's one stop before the main—but less central—Greenwich Station (departs at least every 10 minutes, 20-minute ride, all in Zone 2). Or, catch bus #188 from Russell Square near the British Museum (about 45 minutes to Greenwich).

Eating: Greenwich's parks are picnic-perfect, especially around the National Maritime Museum and Royal Observatory. **$ Marks & Spencer Simply Food** sells ready-made lunches (55 Greenwich Church Street), and Greenwich Market offers an international variety of tasty food stalls (farmers market, arts and crafts, and food stands; daily 10:00-17:30; antiques Mon-Tue and Thu-Fri, www.greenwichmarketlondon.com). **$$$ The Old Brewery,** in the Discover Greenwich center, is a gastropub with classic British cuisine. **$$ The Trafalgar Tavern,** with a casual pub and pricier, elegant dining room, is a historical place for an overpriced meal. Up by the Royal Observatory, the elegant 1906 **$ Pavilion Café** offers tea, coffee, and counter-service food. At the bottom of Greenwich Park, **$$ White House Café** offers baked goodies and sandwiches.

Cutty Sark

Old Royal Naval College

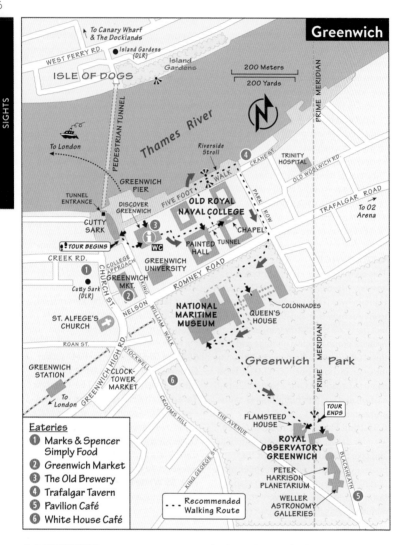

Greenwich

To Canary Wharf & The Docklands
WEST FERRY RD.
Island Gardens (DLR)
Island Gardens
ISLE OF DOGS
200 Meters
200 Yards
PEDESTRIAN TUNNEL
Thames River
Riverside Stroll
To London
GREENWICH PIER
TUNNEL ENTRANCE
FIVE FOOT WALK
CRANE ST.
PARK ROW
TRINITY HOSPITAL
OLD WOOLWICH RD.
TRAFALGAR ROAD
To O2 Arena
PRIME MERIDIAN
CUTTY SARK
DISCOVER GREENWICH
TOUR BEGINS
OLD ROYAL NAVAL COLLEGE
CHAPEL
PAINTED HALL
Tunnel
WC
CREEK RD.
COLLEGE APPROACH
GREENWICH UNIVERSITY
GREENWICH MKT.
ROMNEY ROAD
Cutty Sark (DLR)
CHURCH ST.
KING WILLIAM WALK
NELSON RD.
ST. ALFEGE'S CHURCH
ROAN ST.
STOCKWELL ST.
NATIONAL MARITIME MUSEUM
QUEEN'S HOUSE
COLONNADES
PRIME MERIDIAN
Greenwich Park
GREENWICH STATION
CLOCK-TOWER MARKET
GREENWICH HIGH RD.
CROOMS HILL
THE AVENUE
6
To London
FLAMSTEED HOUSE
TOUR ENDS
ROYAL OBSERVATORY GREENWICH
BLACKHEATH
KING GEORGE ST.
PETER HARRISON PLANETARIUM
WELLER ASTRONOMY GALLERIES

Eateries
1 Marks & Spencer Simply Food
2 Greenwich Market
3 The Old Brewery
4 Trafalgar Tavern
5 Pavilion Café
6 White House Café

- - - Recommended Walking Route

▲▲CUTTY SARK

When first launched in 1869, the Scottish-built *Cutty Sark* was the last of the great China tea clippers and the queen of the seas. She was among the fastest clippers ever built, the culmination of centuries of ship design. With 32,000 square feet of sail—and favorable winds—she could travel 300 miles in a day. But as a new century dawned, steamers began to outmatch sailing ships for speed, and

by the mid-1920s the *Cutty Sark* was the world's last operating clipper ship.

In 2012, the ship was restored and reopened with a spectacular new glass-walled display space (though one critic groused that the ship now "looks like it has run aground in a giant greenhouse"). Displays explore the *Cutty Sark*'s 140-year history and the cargo she carried—everything from tea to wool to gunpowder—as she raced between London and ports all around the world.

Cost and Hours: £15 weekdays, £17 weekends, cheaper online, kids ages 4-15—£7.50, free for kids under age 4, family tickets available, combo-ticket with Royal Observatory—£26.25, kids combo-ticket—£17.60; daily 10:00-17:00; to skip the ticket-buying line reserve timed-entry tickets online or by phone, or show up around 13:00; unnecessary £6 guidebook, reservation tel. 020/8312-6608, www.rmg.co.uk.

OLD ROYAL NAVAL COLLEGE

Despite the name, these grand structures were built (1692) as a veterans' hospital to house disabled and retired sailors who'd served their country. In 1873, the hospital was transformed into one of the world's most prestigious universities for training naval officers. Today, the buildings host university students, music students, business conventions, concerts, and film crews drawn to the awe-inspiring space.

▲PAINTED HALL

Originally intended as a dining hall for pensioners, this sumptuously painted room was deemed too glorious (and, in the winter, too cold) for that purpose. So almost as soon as it was completed, it became simply a showcase for visitors. Impressive as it is, the admission is quite steep to see gigantic paintings by an artist you've never heard of, featuring second-rate royals. But those who appreciate artistic spectacles and picking out lavish

details will find it worthwhile.

Cost and Hours: £12, daily 10:00-17:00, sometimes closed for private events, www.ornc.org. Ticket includes audioguide and a 45-minute guided tour of the Old Royal Naval College grounds, not including the Painted Hall (departs from Discover Greenwich at the top of each hour).

▲NATIONAL MARITIME MUSEUM

Great for anyone interested in the sea, this museum holds everything from a giant working paddlewheel to the uniform Admiral Horatio Nelson wore when he was killed at Trafalgar. A big glass roof tops three levels of slick, modern, kid-friendly exhibits about all things seafaring.

Cost and Hours: Free, daily 10:00-17:00, tel. 020/8858-4422, www.rmg.co.uk. The museum hosts frequent family-oriented events—ask at the desk.

▲▲ROYAL OBSERVATORY GREENWICH

Located on the prime meridian (0° longitude), this observatory is famous as the point from which all time and distances on earth are measured. A visit here gives you a taste of the sciences of astronomy, timekeeping, and seafaring—and how they all meld together—along with great views over Greenwich and the distant London skyline. In the courtyard, snap a selfie straddling the famous prime meridian line in the pavement. In the museum, there's the original 1600s-era observatory, the **Weller Astronomy Galleries,**

Royal Observatory

Kew Gardens

and the state-of-the-art, **Peter Harrison Planetarium** (£10, shows about every 45 minutes during the observatory's opening times, no morning shows on school days, check schedule online).

Cost and Hours: £16 weekdays, £18 weekends, includes audioguide, combo-ticket with *Cutty Sark*—£26.25; daily 10:00-17:00; tel. 020/8858-4422, reservations tel. 020/8312-6608, www.rmg.co.uk.

Greater London
▲▲KEW GARDENS

For a fine riverside park and a palatial greenhouse jungle to swing through, take the Tube or the boat to every botanist's favorite escape. Garden lovers could spend days exploring Kew's 300 acres. For a quick visit, spend a fragrant hour wandering through three buildings: the Palm House, a humid Victorian world of iron, glass, and tropical plants that was built in 1844; a Waterlily House that Monet would swim for; and the Princess of Wales Conservatory, a meandering modern greenhouse with many different climate zones growing countless cacti, bug-munching carnivorous plants, and more. Check out the Xstrata Treetop Walkway, a 200-yard-long scenic steel walkway that puts you high in the canopy 60 feet above the ground.

Cost and Hours: £18, June-Aug £11 after 16:00, kids 4-16—£6, kids under 4—free; Mon-Thu 10:00-19:00, Fri-Sun until 20:00, closes earlier Sept-March—check schedule online, glasshouses close at 17:30 in high season—earlier off-season, free one-hour walking tours daily at 11:00 and 13:30, tel. 020/8332-5000, www.kew.org.

Getting There: By Tube, ride to Kew Gardens station, then cross the footbridge over the tracks, which drops you in a little community of plant-and-herb shops, a two-block walk from Victoria Gate (the main garden entrance). Boats also run to Kew Gardens from Westminster Pier (see page 44).

Eating: For a sun-dappled lunch or snack, walk 10 minutes from the Palm House to the **$$ Orangery Cafeteria** (Mon-Thu 10:00-17:30, Fri-Sun until 18:30, until 15:15 in winter, closes early for events).

EXPERIENCES

Shopping

Most stores are open Monday through Saturday from roughly 9:00 or 10:00 until 17:00 or 18:00, with a late night on Wednesday or Thursday (usually until 19:00 or 20:00). Many close on Sundays. Large department stores stay open later during the week (until about 21:00 Mon-Sat) with shorter hours on Sundays. If you're looking for bargains, visit one of the city's many street markets.

Shopping Streets

The best and most convenient shopping streets are in the West End and West London (roughly between Soho and Hyde Park). You'll find midrange shops along **Oxford Street** (running east from

Tube: Marble Arch), and fancier shops along **Regent Street** (stretching south from Tube: Oxford Circus to Piccadilly Circus) and **Knightsbridge** (where you'll find Harrods and Harvey Nichols; Tube: Knightsbridge). Other streets are more specialized, such as **Jermyn Street** for old-fashioned men's clothing (just south of Piccadilly) and **Charing** Cross Road for books. **Floral Street,** connecting Leicester Square to Covent Garden, is lined with boutiques.

Department Stores

Harrods is London's most famous and touristy department store, with more than four acres of retail space covering seven floors (Mon–Sat 10:00–21:00, Sun 11:30–18:00, Brompton Road, Tube: Knightsbridge, tel. 020/7730-1234, www.harrods.com).

Harvey Nichols was once Princess Diana's favorite and later Duchess Kate's. "Harvey Nick's" remains the department store *du jour* (Mon–Sat 10:00–20:00, Sun 11:30–18:00, near Harrods, 109 Knightsbridge, Tube: Knightsbridge, tel. 020/7235-5000, www.harveynichols.com).

Fortnum & Mason, the official department store of the Queen, embodies old-fashioned, British upper-class taste, with a storybook atmosphere. An elegant tea is served in their Diamond Jubilee Tea Salon (Mon–Sat 10:00–21:00, Sun 11:30–18:00, 181 Piccadilly, Tube: Green Park, tel. 020/7734-8040, www.fortnumandmason.com).

Liberty is a still-thriving 19th-century institution known for its artful displays and castle-like interior (Mon–Sat 10:00–20:00, Sun 11:30–18:00, Great Marlborough Street, Tube: Oxford Circus, tel. 020/7734-1234, www.liberty.co.uk).

Street Markets

Antique buffs and people-watchers love London's street markets. The best markets—which combine lively stalls and a colorful neighborhood with cute and characteristic shops of their own—are Portobello Road and Camden Lock Market. Hagglers will enjoy the no-holds-barred bargaining.

IN NOTTING HILL

Portobello Road stretches for several blocks through the delightful, colorful, funky-yet-quaint Notting Hill neighborhood. Charming streets lined with pastel-painted houses and offbeat antique shops are enlivened on Fridays and Saturdays with 2,000 additional stalls (9:00–19:00), plus food, live music, and more (Tube: Notting Hill Gate, near recommended accommodations, tel. 020/7727-7684, www.portobelloroad.co.uk).

Rick's Tip: *Browse* **Portabello Road on Friday.** *Most stalls are open, with half the crowds of Saturday.*

IN CAMDEN TOWN

Camden Lock Market is a huge, trendy arts-and-crafts festival divided into three areas, each with its own vibe. The main market, set alongside the picturesque canal, features a mix of shops and stalls selling boutique crafts and artisanal foods. The market on the opposite side of Chalk Farm Road is edgier, with cheap ethnic food stalls, lots of canalside seating, and punk crafts. The Stables, a sprawling, incense-scented complex, is squeezed into tunnels under the old rail bridge just behind the main market (daily 10:00-19:00, busiest on weekends, tel. 020/3763-9999, www.camdenmarket.com).

IN THE EAST END

Spitalfields Market combines old brick buildings with sleek modern ones, all covered by a giant glass roof. Shops, stalls, and a rainbow of restaurant options are open every day (Mon-Fri 10:00-17:00, Sat from 11:00, Sun from 9:00; Tube: Liverpool Street; from the Tube stop, take Bishopsgate East exit, turn left, walk to Brushfield Street, and turn right; www.spitalfields.co.uk).

Petticoat Lane Market, a block from Spitalfields Market, sits on the otherwise dull Middlesex Street; adjoining Wentworth Street is grungier and more characteristic (Sun 9:00-14:00, sometimes later; smaller market Mon-Fri on Wentworth Street only; Middlesex Street and Wentworth Street, Tube: Liverpool Street).

The **Truman Markets,** housed in the former Truman Brewery on Brick Lane, are gritty and avant-garde. The markets are in full swing on Sundays (roughly 10:00-17:00), though you'll see some action on Saturdays (11:00-18:00). Surrounding shops and eateries are open all week (Tube: Liverpool Street or Aldgate East, www.vintage-market.co.uk).

Brick Lane is lined with Sunday market stands from about Buxton Street to Bethnal Green Road—about a 10-minute walk. Continuing another 10 minutes north, then turning right onto Columbia Road, takes you to **Columbia Road Flower Market** (Sun 8:00-15:00, www.columbiaroad.info). Halfway up Columbia Road, be sure to loop left up little Ezra Street, with characteristic eateries, boutiques, and antique vendors.

IN THE WEST END

The iron-and-glass **Covent Garden Market,** originally the garden for Westminster Abbey, hosts a mix of fun shops, eateries, and markets. Mondays are for antiques, while arts and crafts dominate the rest of the week. Produce stalls are open daily 10:30-18:00, and on Thursdays, a food market brightens up the square (Tube: Covent Garden, tel. 020/7395-1350, www.coventgardenlondonuk.com).

Jubilee Market features antiques on Mondays (5:00-17:00); a general market Tuesday through Friday (10:30-19:00); and arts and crafts on Saturdays and Sundays (10:00-18:00). It's located on the south side of Covent Garden (tel. 020/7379-4242, www.jubileemarket.co.uk).

Theater (a.k.a. "Theatre")

London's theater scene rivals Broadway's in quality and often beats it in price. Choose from 200 offerings—Shakespeare, musicals, comedies, thrillers, sex farces, cutting-edge fringe, revivals starring movie celebs, and more. London does it all well.

Rick's Tip: *Just like at home, London's theaters* **sell seats in a range of levels***—but the Brits use different terms: stalls (ground floor), dress circle (first balcony), upper circle (second balcony), balcony (sky-high third balcony), and slips (cheap seats on the fringes). Discounted tickets are called "concessions" (abbreviated as "conc" or "s").*

West End Shows

Nearly all big-name shows are hosted in the theaters of the West End, clustering around Soho between Piccadilly and Covent Garden. With a centuries-old tradition of pleasing the masses, they present London theater at its grandest.

Well-known musicals may draw the

biggest crowds, but the West End offers plenty of other crowd-pleasers, from revivals of classics to cutting-edge works by the hottest young playwrights. These productions tend to have shorter runs than famous musicals. Many productions star huge-name celebrities—London is a magnet for movie stars who want to stretch their acting chops.

The *Official London Theatre Guide,* a free booklet that's updated every two weeks, is a handy tool (find it at hotels, box offices, the City of London TI, and online at www.officiallondontheatre.co.uk). Check reviews at www.timeout.com/london.

Most performances are nightly except Sunday, usually with two or three matinees a week. The few shows that run on Sundays are mostly family fare (such as *The Lion King*).

TICKETS

Most shows have tickets available on short notice—likely at a discount. But if your time in London is limited—and you have your heart set on a particular show that's likely to sell out, you can buy peace of mind by booking tickets from home. For floor plans of the various theaters, see www.theatremonkey.com.

Advance Tickets: It's generally cheapest to buy your tickets directly from the theater, either through its website or by calling the theater box office. In most cases, a theater will reroute you to a third-party ticket vendor such as Ticketmaster (typically with a £3/ticket fee). You can have your tickets emailed to you or pick them up before show time at Will Call.

Rick's Tip: *The* **real TKTS booth** *(with its prominent sign) is a freestanding kiosk at the south edge of Leicester Square. Several dishonest outfits nearby advertise "official half-price tickets"—avoid these, where you'll pay closer to full price.*

Discount Tickets: The **TKTS Booth** at Leicester Square sells discounted tickets (25-50 percent off) for many shows (£3/ticket service charge, open Mon-Sat 10:00-19:00, Sun 11:00-16:30). You must buy in person at the kiosk, and the best deals are same-day only. The list of shows and prices is continually updated and posted outside the booth and on their website (www.tkts.co.uk). For the best choice and prices, come early in the day—the line starts forming even before the booth opens (it moves quickly).

Theater Box Office: Even if a show is "sold out," there's usually a way to get a seat. Many theaters offer various discounts or "concessions": same-day tickets, cheap returned tickets, standing-room, matinee, senior or student standby deals, and more. Start by checking the show's website, then call the box

office or simply drop by (many theaters are right in the tourist zone).

Same-day tickets (called **"day seats"**) can be an excellent deal. These generally go on sale *only in person* when the box office opens (typically at 10:00; people start lining up before then). These tickets (£20 or less) tend to be either in the nosebleed rows or with a restricted view. Another strategy is to show up at the box office shortly before show time (best on weekdays) and—before paying full price—ask about cheaper options. Last-minute return tickets are often sold at great prices as curtain time approaches.

For a helpful guide to "day seats"—including recent user reports on how early you need to show up—consult www.theatremonkey.com/dayseatfinder.htm; for tips on getting cheap and last-minute tickets, visit www.londontheatretickets.org and www.timeout.com/london/theatre.

Other Agencies: Although booking through a middleman such as your hotel or a ticket agency is quick and easy, prices are greatly inflated (legitimate resellers add up to a 25 percent booking fee). Ticket agencies and third-party websites are often just scalpers with an address. If you do buy from an agency, choose one who is a member of the Society of Ticket Agents and Retailers (look for the STAR logo—short for "secure tickets from authorized retailers").

Scalpers ("Touts"): You'll find scalpers hawking tickets outside theaters. Just like at home, those people may either be honest folk whose date just happened to cancel at the last minute...or unscrupulous thieves selling forgeries. London has many of the latter.

Beyond the West End

Tickets for lesser-known shows tend to be cheaper (figure £15-30), in part because most of the smaller theaters are government-subsidized. Read up on the latest offerings online; Timeout.com is a great place to start. Major noncommercial theaters include the National Theatre, Barbican Centre, Royal Court Theatre, Menier Chocolate Factory, and Bridge Theatre. The Royal Shakespeare Company performs at various theaters around London.

SHAKESPEARE'S GLOBE

To see Shakespeare in a replica of the theater for which he wrote his plays, attend a play at the Globe. In this round, thatched-roof, open-air theater, the plays are performed much as Shakespeare intended—under the sky, with no amplification.

The play's the thing from late April through mid-October (usually Tue-Sat 14:00 and 19:30, Sun either 13:00 and/or 18:30, tickets can be sold out months in advance). You'll pay £5 to stand and £23-47 to sit, usually on a backless bench (only a few rows and the pricier Gentlemen's Rooms have seats with backs, £2 cushions and £4 add-on backrests a good investment; dress for the weather).

The £5 "groundling" or "yard" tickets—which are open to rain—are most fun. Scurry in early to stake out a spot on the stage's edge, where the most interaction with the actors occurs. You're a crude peasant. You can lean your elbows on the stage, munch a snack (yes, you can bring in food—but bag size is limited), or walk around. I've never enjoyed Shakespeare as much as here, performed as it was meant to be in the "wooden O." If you can't get

A performance at Shakespeare's Globe

Evensong

One of my favorite experiences in Britain is to attend evensong at a great church. Evensong is an evening worship service that is typically sung rather than said (though some parts—including scripture readings, a few prayers, and a homily—are spoken). It follows the traditional Anglican service in the Book of Common Prayer, including prayers, scripture readings, canticles (sung responses), and hymns that are appropriate for the early evening—traditionally the end of the working day and before the evening meal. In major churches with resident choirs, a singing or chanting priest leads the service, and a choir—usually made up of both men's and boys' voices (to sing the lower and higher parts, respectively)—sings the responses. The choir usually sings a cappella, or is accompanied by an organ. Visitors are welcome and are given an order of service or a prayer book to help them follow along.

Impressive places for evensong include Westminster Abbey and St. Paul's. Evensong typically takes place in the small choir area, which is far more intimate than the main nave. It generally occurs daily between 17:00 and 18:00 (often two hours earlier on Sun)—check with individual churches for specifics. At smaller churches, evensong is sometimes spoken, not sung.

Note that evensong is not a performance—it's a somewhat somber worship service. If you enjoy worshipping in different churches, attending evensong can be a highlight. Most major churches also offer organ or choral concerts—look for posted schedules or ask at the information desk or gift shop.

a ticket, take a guided tour of the theater and museum by day (see page 89).

The indoor Sam Wanamaker Playhouse allows Shakespearean-era plays and early-music concerts to be performed through the winter. Many of the productions in this intimate venue are one-offs and can be pricey.

To reserve tickets for plays at the Globe or Playhouse, drop by the box office (Mon-Sat 10:00-18:00, Sun until 17:00, open one hour later on performance days, New Globe Walk entrance, box office tel. 020/7401-9919, info tel. 020/7902-1400). You can also reserve online (www.shakespearesglobe.com, £2.50 booking fee). Try calling around noon the day of the performance to see if the box office expects any returned tickets. If so, they'll advise you to show up a little more than an hour before the show, when these tickets are sold (first-come, first-served).

The theater is on the South Bank,

directly across the Thames over the Millennium Bridge from St. Paul's Cathedral (Tube: Mansion House or London Bridge).

Concerts at Churches

For easy, cheap, or free concerts in historic churches, attend a **lunch concert,** especially:

St. Bride's Church, with free half-hour lunch concerts twice a week at 13:15 (usually Tue and Fri—confirm in advance, church tel. 020/7427-0133, www.stbrides.com).

Temple Church, also in The City, with free organ recitals weekly (Wed at 13:15, www.templechurch.com).

St. James's at Piccadilly, with 50-minute concerts on Mon, Wed, and Fri at 13:10 (suggested £5 donation, info tel. 020/7734-4511, www.sjp.org.uk).

St. Martin-in-the-Fields, offering concerts on Mon, Tue, and Fri at 13:00

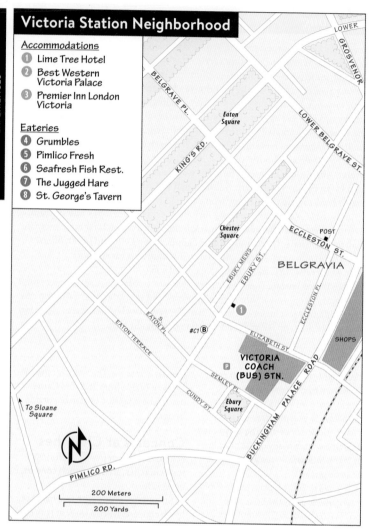

Victoria Station Neighborhood

Accommodations

1 Lime Tree Hotel
2 Best Western Victoria Palace
3 Premier Inn London Victoria

Eateries

4 Grumbles
5 Pimlico Fresh
6 Seafresh Fish Rest.
7 The Jugged Hare
8 St. George's Tavern

LOWER GROSVENOR

BELGRAVE PL.

Eaton Square

LOWER BELGRAVE ST.

KING'S RD.

Chester Square

ECCLESTON ST.

POST

EBURY MEWS

EBURY ST.

BELGRAVIA

ECCLESTON PL.

S. EATON PL.

EATON TERRACE

#C1 B

ELIZABETH ST.

SHOPS

P

VICTORIA COACH (BUS) STN.

SEMLEY PL.

BUCKINGHAM PALACE ROAD

CUNDY ST.

To Sloane Square

Ebury Square

N

PIMLICO RD.

200 Meters

200 Yards

(suggested £3.50 donation, church tel. 020/7766-1100, www.stmartin-in-the-fields.org).

St. Martin-in-the-Fields also hosts fine **evening concerts** by candlelight (£9-29, several nights a week at 19:30) and live jazz in its underground Café in the Crypt (£8-15, Wed at 20:00).

Evensong services are held at several churches, including St. Paul's Cathedral (see page 75) and Westminster Abbey (see page 47).

Free **organ recitals** are usually held on Sunday at 17:45 in Westminster Abbey (30 minutes, tel. 020/7222-5152). Many other churches have free concerts; ask for the *London Organ Concerts Guide* at the TI.

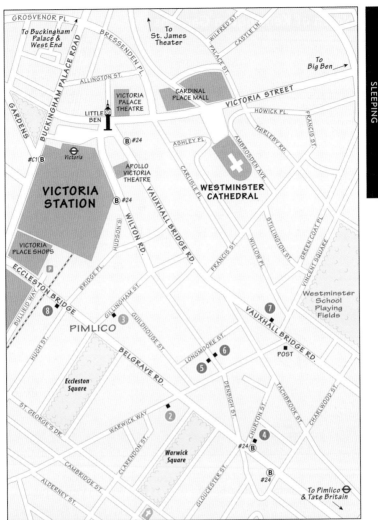

SLEEPING

London is an expensive city for lodging. Expect cheaper rooms to be relatively dumpy. Focus on choosing the right neighborhood, which is as important as selecting the right hotel. I rank accommodations from $ budget to $$$$ splurge. For the best deal, contact my family-run places directly by phone or email. Book well in advance for peak season or if your trip coincides with a major holiday or festival. For more details on reservations, short-term rentals, and more, see the "Sleeping" section in the Practicalities chapter.

Looking for Hotel Deals Online: Given London's high hotel prices, it's worth searching for a deal. For more options, browse these accommodation discount sites: www.londontown.com (an informative site with a discount booking service),

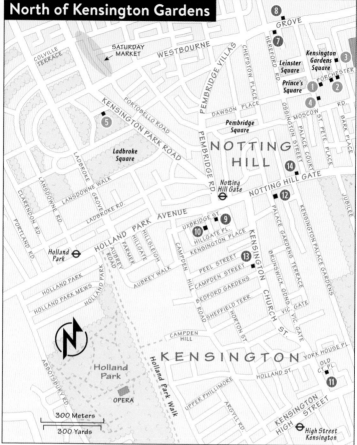

North of Kensington Gardens

www.athomeinlondon.co.uk and www. londonbb.com (both list central B&Bs), www.lastminute.com, www.visitlondon. com, and www.eurocheapo.com.

Near Victoria Station

The safe, surprisingly tidy streets behind Victoria Station teem with little, moderately-priced-for-London B&Bs.

$$$$ Lime Tree Hotel has 28 spacious, stylish, comfortable, thoughtfully decorated rooms, a helpful staff, a fun-loving breakfast room, and a delightful garden in back (135 Ebury Street, tel. 020/7730-8191, www.limetreehotel.co.uk, info@ limetreehotel.co.uk, Charlotte and Matt,

Laura manages the office).

$$ Best Western Victoria Palace offers modern, if slightly worn, business-class comfort compared with some of the other creaky old guesthouses in the neighborhood. Choose from the 43 rooms in the main building (at 60 Warwick Way), or pay about 20 percent less by booking a nearly identical room in one of the annexes, each a half-block away—an excellent value for this neighborhood if you skip breakfast (air-con, elevator in main building only, 17 Belgrave Road and 1 Warwick Way, reception at main building, tel. 020/7821-7113, www. bestwesternvictoriapalace.co.uk, info@

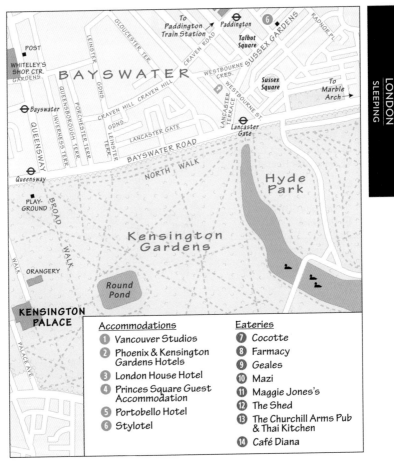

Accommodations

1. Vancouver Studios
2. Phoenix & Kensington Gardens Hotels
3. London House Hotel
4. Princes Square Guest Accommodation
5. Portobello Hotel
6. Stylotel

Eateries

7. Cocotte
8. Farmacy
9. Geales
10. Mazi
11. Maggie Jones's
12. The Shed
13. The Churchill Arms Pub & Thai Kitchen
14. Café Diana

bestwesternvictoriapalace.co.uk).

If considering chain hotels, there's also a fine **$$$ Premier Inn** in this area (82 Eccleston Square, www.premierinn.com).

North of Kensington Gardens

From the core of the tourist's London, vast Hyde Park spreads west, eventually becoming Kensington Gardens. Bayswater anchors the area; it's bordered by Notting Hill to the west and Paddington to the east. This area has quick bus and Tube access to downtown and, for London, is very cozy.

Bayswater and Notting Hill

$$$ Vancouver Studios has 45 modern, tastefully furnished rooms that come with fully equipped kitchenettes, or you can pay for a continental breakfast. It's nestled between Kensington Gardens Square and Prince's Square and has its own tranquil garden patio out back (laundry, 30 Prince's Square, tel. 020/7243-1270, www.vancouverstudios.co.uk, info@ vancouverstudios.co.uk).

$$$ Phoenix Hotel offers spacious, stately public spaces and 125 modern-feeling rooms with classy decor. While the rates can vary wildly, it's a good choice if you can get a deal (ele-

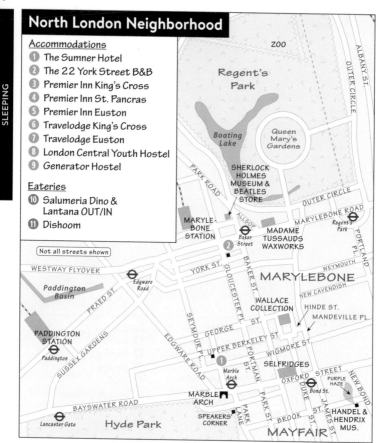

North London Neighborhood

Accommodations

1. The Sumner Hotel
2. The 22 York Street B&B
3. Premier Inn King's Cross
4. Premier Inn St. Pancras
5. Premier Inn Euston
6. Travelodge King's Cross
7. Travelodge Euston
8. London Central Youth Hostel
9. Generator Hostel

Eateries

10. Salumeria Dino & Lantana OUT/IN
11. Dishoom

Not all streets shown

vator, 1 Kensington Gardens Square, tel. 020/7229-2494, www.phoenixhotel.co.uk, reservations@phoenixhotel.co.uk).

$$$ London House Hotel has 103 spiffy, modern, cookie-cutter rooms at reasonable prices (family rooms, air-con, elevator, 81 Kensington Gardens Square, tel. 020/7243-1810, www. londonhousehotels.com, reservations@ londonhousehotels.com).

$$$ Princes Square Guest Accommodation is a crisp (if impersonal) place renting 50 businesslike rooms with pleasant, modern decor. It's well located, practical, and a very good value, especially if you can score a good rate (elevator, 23 Prince's Square, tel. 020/7229-9876,

www.princessquarehotel.co.uk, info@ princessquarehotel.co.uk).

$$ Kensington Gardens Hotel, with the same owners as the Phoenix Hotel, laces 17 rooms together in a tall, skinny building (breakfast served at Phoenix Hotel, 9 Kensington Gardens Square, tel. 020/7243-7600, www. kensingtongardenshotel.co.uk, info@ kensingtongardenshotel.co.uk).

$$$$ Portobello Hotel is on a quiet residential street in the heart of Notting Hill. Its 21 rooms are funky yet elegant—both the style and location give it an urban-fresh feeling (elevator, 22 Stanley Gardens, tel. 020/7727-2777, www.portobellohotel.com, stay@portobellohotel.com).

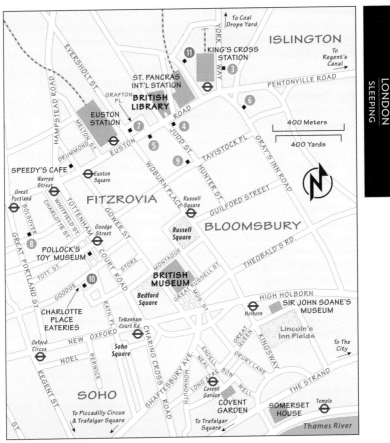

Near Paddington Station

$$ Stylotel feels like the stylish, super-modern, aluminum-clad big sister of the EasyHotel chain. While the 42 rooms can be cramped, the beds have space for luggage underneath (RS%, family rooms, air-con, elevator, 160 Sussex Gardens, tel. 020/7723-1026, www.stylotel.com, info@stylotel.com, Andreas).

North London

$$$$ The Sumner Hotel rents 19 rooms in a 19th-century Georgian townhouse sporting large contemporary rooms and a lounge with fancy modern Italian furniture. This swanky place packs in all the amenities and is conveniently located north of Hyde Park and near Oxford Street, a busy shopping destination—close to Selfridges and a Marks & Spencer (RS%, air-con, elevator, 54 Upper Berkeley Street, a block-and-a-half off Edgware Road, Tube: Marble Arch, tel. 020/7723-2244, www.thesumner.com, hotel@thesumner.com).

$$$ The 22 York Street B&B offers a casual alternative in the city center, with an inviting lounge and 10 traditional, hardwood, comfortable rooms, each named for a notable London landmark (near Marylebone/Baker Street: From Baker Street Tube station, walk 2 blocks down Baker Street and take a right to 22 York

Street—no sign, just look for #22; tel. 020/7224-2990, www.22yorkstreet.co.uk, mc@22yorkstreet.co.uk, energetically run by Liz and Michael Callis).

Other Sleeping Options
Big, Good-Value, Modern Hotels

If you can score a double for £100 (or less—often possible with promotional rates) and don't mind a modern, impersonal, American-style hotel, one of these can be a decent value in pricey London (for details on chain hotels, see page 392).

I've listed a few of the dominant chains, along with a quick rundown on their more convenient London locations. Quality can vary wildly so check online reviews. Some of these branches sit on busy streets in dreary train-station neighborhoods. While I wouldn't necessarily rule these out, ask for a quieter room, use common sense when exploring after dark, and wear a money belt.

$$ Motel One, the German chain that specializes in affordable style, has a branch at Tower Hill, a 10-minute walk north of the Tower of London (24 Minories—see map on page 78, tel. 020/7481-6420, www.motel-one.com, london-towerhill@motel-one.com).

$$ Premier Inn has more than 70 hotels in greater London. Convenient locations include a branch inside London County Hall (next to the London Eye), at Southwark/Borough Market (near Shakespeare's Globe, 34 Park Street), Southwark/Tate Modern (15 Great Suffolk Street), Kensington/Earl's Court (11 Knaresborough Place), Victoria (82 Eccleston Square), and Leicester Square (1 Leicester Place). In North London, several locations cluster between King's Cross St. Pancras and the British Museum: King's Cross, St. Pancras, and Euston. Avoid the Tower Bridge location, south of the bridge and a long walk from the Tube—but London City Tower Hill, north of the bridge on Prescot Street (see map on page 78)—works fine (www.premierinn.com).

$$ Travelodge has close to 70 locations in London, including at King's Cross (200 yards in front of King's Cross Station, Gray's Inn Road) and Euston (1 Grafton Place). Other handy locations include King's Cross Royal Scot, Marylebone, Covent Garden, Liverpool Street, Southwark, and Farringdon; www.travelodge.co.uk.

$$ Ibis, the budget branch of the AccorHotels group, has a few dozen options across the city, with a handful of locations convenient to London's center, including London Blackfriars (49 Blackfriars Road) and London City Shoreditch (5 Commercial Street). The more design-focused Ibis Styles has branches near Earl's Court (15 Hogarth Road) and Southwark, with a theater theme (43 Southwark Bridge Road; https://ibis.accorhotels.com).

$ EasyHotel, with several branches in good neighborhoods, offers generally tiny, super-efficient, no-frills rooms that feel popped out of a plastic mold, down to the prefab ship's head-type "bathroom pod." Rates can be surprisingly low (with doubles as cheap as £30 if you book early enough)—but you'll pay à la carte for expensive add-ons, such as TV use, Wi-Fi, luggage storage, fresh towels, and daily cleaning (breakfast, if available, comes from a vending machine). If you go with the base rate, it's like hosteling with privacy. But you get what you pay for (thin walls, flimsy construction, noisy fellow guests, and so on). They're only a good deal if you book far enough ahead to get a good price and skip the many extras. Locations include Victoria (34 Belgrave Road), South Kensington (14 Lexham Gardens), and Paddington (10 Norfolk Place); www.easyhotel.com.

$ Hub by Premier Inn—the budget chain's no-frills, pod-style division—offers extremely small rooms (just a little bigger than the bed) in convenient locations for low prices (from £69, www.premierinn.com/gb/en/hub.html).

Hostels

¢ London Central Youth Hostel is the flagship of London's hostels. Families and travelers of any age will feel welcome in this wonderful facility. You'll pay the same price for any bed—so try to grab one with a bathroom (families welcome to book an entire room, book long in advance; between Oxford Circus and Great Portland Street Tube stations at 104 Bolsover Street—see map on page 108, tel. 0345-371-9154, www.yha.org.uk, londoncentral@yha.org.uk).

¢ Generator Hostel is a brightly colored, hip hostel with a café and a DJ spinning the hits. It's in a renovated building tucked behind a busy street halfway between King's Cross and the British Museum (37 Tavistock Place—see map on page 108, Tube: Russell Square, tel. 020/7388-7666, http://staygenerator.com, ask.london@generatorhostels.com).

EATING

Whether it's dining well with the upper crust, sharing hearty pub fare with the blokes, or venturing to a fringe neighborhood to try the latest hotspot or street food at a market, eating out is an essential part of the London experience. The sheer variety of foods—from every corner of Britain's former empire and beyond—is astonishing. I rank restaurants from $ budget to $$$$ splurge. For more advice on eating, including ordering, tipping, and British cuisine and beverages, see the "Eating" section of the Practicalities chapter.

Central London
Soho

With its status as *the* place where budding restaurateurs stake their claim on London's culinary map, Soho is a magnet for diners. Even if Soho isn't otherwise on your radar, make a point to dine here at least once.

$$$ Andrew Edmunds Restaurant is a tiny candlelit space where you'll want to hide your guidebook and not act like a tourist. This little place—with a loyal clientele—is the closest I've found to Parisian quality in a cozy restaurant in London. The extensive wine list, modern European cooking, and creative seasonal menu are worth the splurge (daily 12:30-15:30 & 17:30-22:45, these are last-order times, come early or call ahead, request ground floor rather than basement, 46 Lexington Street, tel. 020/7437-5708, www.andrewedmunds.com).

$$$ Temper Soho pleases well-heeled carnivores. From the nondescript office-block entrance, you'll descend to a cozy, stylish cellar filled with rich smoke from meat grilling on open fires. They carve off chunks for tacos and *parathas* (Indian-style flatbreads). The portions are small and pricey (order multiple courses), but meat lovers willing to pay leave satisfied (Mon-Sat 12:00-22:30, Sun until 21:00, 25 Broadwick Street, tel. 020/3879-3834).

$$$ Bocca di Lupo, a stylish and popular option, serves half and full portions of classic regional Italian food. Dressy but with a fun energy, it's a place where you'll be glad you made a reservation. The counter seating, on cushy stools with a view into the lively open kitchen, is particularly memorable, or you can take a table in the snug, casual back end (daily 12:30-15:00 & 17:15-23:00, 12 Archer Street, tel. 020/7734-2223, www.boccadilupo.com).

$$$ Kricket Soho serves upmarket Indian fare a few steps from Piccadilly Circus. Opt for the tight, stylish, unpretentious main floor (with counter seating surrounding an open kitchen) or the dining room in the cellar. The small-plates menu is an education in Indian cuisine beyond the corner curry house, with *kulchas* (miniature naan breads with toppings), *kheer* (rice pudding), and KFC—Keralan fried chicken (Mon-Sat 12:00-14:30 & 17:15-22:30, closed Sun, 12 Denman Street, tel. 020/7734-5612).

$$$$ Nopi is one of a handful of restaurants run by London celebrity chef Yotam Ottolenghi. The cellar features communal

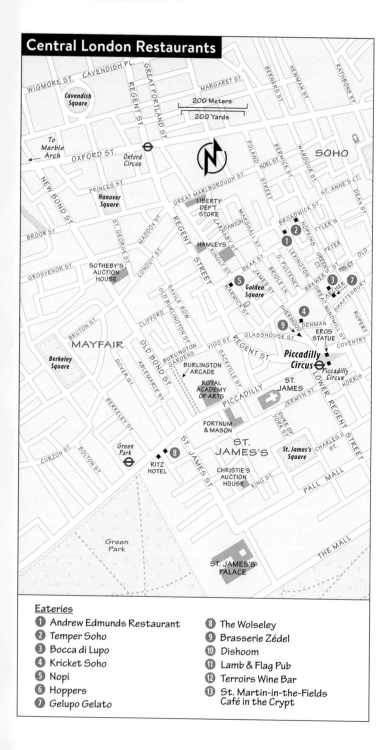

Central London Restaurants

200 Meters

200 Yards

To Marble Arch →

WIGMORE ST. CAVENDISH PL.

GREAT PORTLAND ST.

CAVENDISH

Cavendish Square

REGENT ST.

MARGARET ST.

BERNERS ST.

NEWMAN ST.

RATHBONE ST.

OXFORD ST.

Oxford Circus

SOHO

POLAND STREET

NOEL ST.

BERWICK ST.

WARDOUR ST.

ST. ANNE'S CT.

DEAN ST.

NEW BOND ST.

PRINCES ST.

Hanover Square

GREAT MARLBOROUGH ST.

LIBERTY DEP'T STORE

CARNABY ST.

BROADWICK ST.

HOPKINS

TYLER'S

PETER

ST.

BROOK ST.

ST. GEORGE'S ST.

MADDOX ST.

CONDUIT ST.

HAMLEYS

KINGLY ST.

MARSHALL ST.

BEAK ST.

JAMES ST.

LEXINGTON

G. PULTENEY

BRIDLE LN.

GREEN'S CT.

BREWER ST.

GREAT WINDMILL ST.

ARCHER

OLD

ST S CT.

SHAFTESBURY

2

1

3

7

GROSVENOR ST.

SOTHEBY'S AUCTION HOUSE

OLD BURLINGTON ST.

SAVILE ROW

5

Golden Square

WARWICK ST.

SHERWOOD

4

9

DENMAN

EROS STATUE

COVENTRY

REGENT STREET

BRUTON ST.

MAYFAIR

Berkeley Square

DOVER ST.

ALBEMARLE ST.

OLD BOND ST.

CLIFFORD ST.

BURLINGTON GARDENS

BURLINGTON ARCADE

VIGO ST.

SACKVILLE ST.

GLASSHOUSE ST.

REGENT ST.

Piccadilly Circus

Piccadilly Circus

LOWER REGENT STREET

NORRIS

ROYAL ACADEMY OF ARTS

PICCADILLY

ST. JAMES

JERMYN ST.

DUKE OF YORK ST.

RUPERT

BERKELEY ST.

FORTNUM & MASON

CURZON ST.

BOLTON ST.

Green Park

RITZ HOTEL

ST. JAMES ST.

8

ST. JAMES'S

CHRISTIE'S AUCTION HOUSE

KING ST.

St. James's Square

CHARLES II ST.

PALL MALL

Green Park

THE MALL

ST. JAMES'S PALACE

Eateries

1 Andrew Edmunds Restaurant
2 Temper Soho
3 Bocca di Lupo
4 Kricket Soho
5 Nopi
6 Hoppers
7 Gelupo Gelato
8 The Wolseley
9 Brasserie Zédel
10 Dishoom
11 Lamb & Flag Pub
12 Terroirs Wine Bar
13 St. Martin-in-the-Fields Café in the Crypt

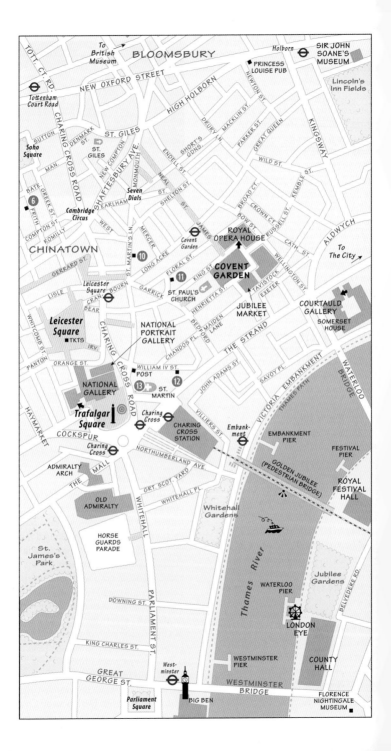

tables looking into the busy kitchen, and the cuisine is typical of Ottolenghi's masterful Eastern Mediterranean cooking, with an emphasis on seasonal produce. If you want to splurge in Soho, do it here (Mon-Sat 10:00-15:00 & 17:30-22:30, Sun until 16:00, 21 Warwick Street, tel. 020/7494-9584, www.ottolenghi.co.uk).

$$ Hoppers is an easy entry into Sri Lankan cuisine—reminiscent of Indian but with more tropical flourishes. You'll be glad the menu comes with a glossary of key terms—for example, hopper (a spongy yet firm rice-and-coconut pancake, shaped like a bowl), *kari* (Tamil for "curry"), and *roti* (flatbread). Be adventurous, and seek the waitstaff's advice (Mon-Sat 12:00-14:30 & 17:30-22:30, closed Sun, 49 Frith Street, tel. 020/3319-8110).

Gelato: Across the street from Bocca di Lupo (listed earlier) is its sister *gelateria,* **Gelupo,** with a wide array of ever-changing but always creative and delicious dessert favorites. Take away or enjoy their homey interior (daily 11:00-23:00, 7 Archer Street, tel. 020/7287-5555).

Near Piccadilly

$$$$ The Wolseley is the grand 1920s showroom of a long-defunct British car. The last Wolseley drove out with the Great Depression, but today this old-time bistro bustles with formal waiters serving traditional Austrian and French dishes in an elegant black-marble-and-chandeliers setting fit for its location next to the Ritz. Although the food can be unexceptional, prices are reasonable considering the grand presentation and setting. Reservations are a must (cheaper soup, salad, and sandwich "café menu" available in all areas of restaurant, daily 11:30-23:00, 160 Piccadilly, tel. 020/7499-6996, www.thewolseley.com). They're popular for their fancy cream tea or afternoon tea (see "Taking Tea in London" sidebar).

$$$ Brasserie Zédel is the former dining hall of the old Regent Palace Hotel, the biggest hotel in the world when built in

1915. Climbing down the stairs from street level, you're surprised by a gilded grand hall that feels like a circa 1920 cruise ship, filled with a boisterous crowd enjoying big, rich French food—old-fashioned brasserie dishes. With vested waiters, fast service, and paper tablecloths, it's great for a group of friends. After 21:30, the lights dim, the candles are lit, and it gets more romantic with live jazz (nightly inexpensive *plats du jour,* daily 11:30-24:00, 20 Sherwood Street, tel. 020/7734-4888). Across the atrium is the hotel's original Bar Américain (which feels like the 1930s) and the Crazy Coqs venue—busy with "Live at Zédel" music, theater, comedy, and literary events (see www.brasseriezedel.com for schedule).

Near Covent Garden

$$$ Dishoom is London's hotspot for upscale Indian cuisine. The dishes seem familiar, but the flavors are a revelation. People line up early (starting around 17:00) for a seat, either on the bright, rollicking, brasserie-like ground floor or in the less appealing basement. Reservations are possible only until 17:45. With its oversized reputation, long lines of tourists, and multiple locations, it's easy to think it's overrated. But the food is simply phenomenal (daily 8:00-23:00, 12 Upper St. Martin's Lane, tel. 020/7420-9320, www.dishoom.com).

$$ Lamb and Flag Pub is a survivor—a spit-and-sawdust pub serving traditional grub (like meat pies) two blocks off Covent Garden, yet seemingly a world away.

Here since 1772, this pub was a favorite of Charles Dickens and is now a hit with local workers. At lunch, it's all food. In the evening, the ground floor is for drinking and the food service is upstairs (long hours daily, 33 Rose Street, go up the narrow alley from Floral Street, tel. 020/7497-9504).

Near Trafalgar Square

$$$ **Terroirs Wine Bar** is an enticing place with a casual but classy ambience that exudes happiness. It's a few steps below street level, with a long zinc bar that has a kitchen view and two levels of tables. The fun menu is mostly Mediterranean and designed to share. The meat and cheese plates complement the fine wines available by the glass (Mon-Sat 12:00-23:00, small bites only from 15:00-17:30, closed Sun, reservations smart, two blocks from Trafalgar Square but tucked away at 5 William IV Street, tel. 020/7036-0660, www.terroirswinebar.com).

$$ **St. Martin-in-the-Fields Café in the Crypt** is just right for a tasty meal on a monk's budget—maybe even on a monk's tomb. You'll dine sitting on somebody's gravestone in an ancient crypt. Their enticing buffet line is kept stocked all day, serving breakfast, lunch, and dinner (hearty traditional desserts, free jugs of water). They also serve a restful £11 afternoon tea (daily 12:00-18:00). You'll find the café directly under St. Martin-in-the-Fields, facing Trafalgar Square—enter through the glass pavilion next to the church (generally daily 10:00-19:30, profits go to the church, Tube: Charing Cross, tel. 020/7766-1158). On Wednesday evenings you can dine to the music of a live jazz band at 20:00 (food available until 21:00, band plays until 22:00, £8-15 tickets). While here, check out the concert schedule for the busy church upstairs (or visit www.stmartin-in-the-fields.org).

West London
Victoria Station Area

$$ **Grumbles** brags it's been serving "good food and wine at non-scary prices since 1964." Offering a delicious mix of "modern eclectic French and traditional English," this unpretentious little place with cozy booths inside (on two levels) and a few nice sidewalk tables is the best spot to eat well in this otherwise workaday neighborhood. Their traditional dishes are their forte (early-bird specials, open daily 12:00-14:30 & 18:00-23:00, reservations wise, a half-block north of Belgrave Road at 35 Churton Street, tel. 020/7834-0149, www.grumblesrestaurant.co.uk).

$ **Pimlico Fresh**'s breakfasts and lunches feature fresh, organic ingredients, served up with good coffee and/or fresh-squeezed juices. This place is heaven if you need a break from your hotel's bacon-eggs-beans routine (takeout lunches, vegetarian options, Mon-Fri 7:30-18:00—breakfast served until 15:00, Sat-Sun 8:30-18:00, 86 Wilton Road, tel. 020/7932-0030).

$$$ **Seafresh Fish Restaurant** is the neighborhood place for plaice—and classic and creative fish-and-chips cuisine. You can either step up to the cheaper **takeout counter,** or eat in—enjoying a white-fish ambience. Though Mario's father started this place in 1965, it feels like the chippy of the 21st century (Mon-Sat 12:00-15:00 & 17:00-22:30, closed Sun, 80 Wilton Road, tel. 020/7828-0747).

$$ **The Jugged Hare,** a 10-minute walk from Victoria Station, fills a lavish old bank building, with vaults replaced by kegs of beer and a kitchen. They have a traditional menu and a plush, vivid pub scene good for a meal or just a drink (food served Mon-Fri 11:00-21:00, Sat-Sun until 20:00, 172 Vauxhall Bridge Road, tel. 020/7828-1543).

$$ **St. George's Tavern** is the neighborhood's best pub for a full meal. They serve dinner from the same menu in three zones: on the sidewalk to catch the sun and enjoy some people-watching (mostly travelers with wheelie bags), in the ground-floor pub, and in a classier downstairs dining

room with full table service. The scene is inviting for just a beer, too (food served daily 12:00–22:00, corner of Hugh Street and Belgrave Road, tel. 020/7630-1116).

North of Kensington Gardens
Bayswater and Notting Hill

$$ Cocotte is a "healthy rotisserie" restaurant specializing in delectable roast chicken, plus tempting sides and healthy salads (dine in or take away; daily 12:00–22:00, 95 Westbourne Grove, tel. 020/3220-0076).

$$$ Farmacy is focused on organic vegan fare...with a side of pretense. The menu includes earth bowls, meat-less burgers and tacos, and superfood smoothies. With an all-natural, woodgrain vibe, it feels like a top-end health food store (daily 9:00–16:00 & 18:00–22:00, 74 Westbourne Grove, tel. 020/7221-0705).

$$$ Geales, which opened its doors in 1939 as a fish-and-chips shop, has been serving Notting Hill ever since. Today, while the menu is more varied, the emphasis is still on fish. The interior is casual, but the food is upscale. The crispy battered cod that put them on the map is still the best around (£15 two-course express menu for lunch and until 20:00 Tue-Fri; open Tue-Sun 12:00–15:00 & 18:00–22:00, closed Mon; reservations smart, 2 Farmer Street, just south of Notting Hill Gate Tube stop, tel. 020/7727-7528, www.geales.com).

$$$$ Mazi is a highly regarded Greek restaurant serving refined renditions of classic dishes, including Greek salad, grilled octopus, and *loukoumades* (dough-nuts) in a contemporary, sophisticated setting. Since ordering several small plates can add up, the £15 two-course lunch is a good deal (daily 18:30–22:30, also Tue-Sun 12:00–15:00, 12 Hillgate Street, tel. 020/7229-3794).

Near Kensington Gardens

$$$$ Maggie Jones's has been feeding locals for over 50 years. Its countryside antique decor and candlelight make a visit a step back in time. It's a longer walk than most of my recommendations, but you'll get solid English cuisine. The por-tions are huge (especially the meat-and-fish pies, their specialty), and prices are a bargain at lunch. You're welcome to split your main course. The candlelit upstairs is the most romantic, while the basement is lively (daily 12:00–14:00 & 18:00–22:30, reservations recommended, 6 Old Court Place, east of Kensington Church Street, near High Street Kensington Tube stop, tel. 020/7937-6462, www.maggie-jones.co.uk).

$$$$ The Shed offers farm-to-table dishes in a rustic-chic setting. Owned by three brothers—a farmer, a chef, and a restaurateur—The Shed serves locally sourced modern English dishes. The por-tions are hearty, with big, meaty flavors—a change of pace from London's delicate high-end dining scene. It's tucked a block off busy Notting Hill Gate (Mon-Sat 18:00–24:00, also open for lunch Tue-Sat 12:00–15:00, closed Sun, reservations smart, 122 Palace Gardens Terrace, tel. 020/7229-4024, www.theshed-restaurant.com).

$$ The Churchill Arms Pub and Thai Kitchen is a combo establishment that's a hit in the neighborhood. It offers good beer and a thriving old-English ambi-ence in front and hearty Thai dishes in an enclosed patio in the back. You can eat the Thai food in the tropical hideaway (table service) or in the atmospheric pub section (order at the counter). Bedecked with flowers on the exterior, it's festooned with Churchill memorabilia and chamber pots. Arrive by 18:00 or after 21:00 to avoid a line (food served daily 12:00–22:00, 119 Kens-ington Church Street, tel. 020/7727-4242 for the pub or 020/7792-1246 for restau-rant, www.churchillarmskensington.co.uk).

$ Café Diana is a healthy little eatery

While visiting London, consider partaking in this most British of traditions. While some tearooms—such as the finicky Fortnum & Mason—still require a jacket and tie, most others happily welcome tourists in jeans and sneakers (and cost, on average, £35-50). Most tearooms are usually open for lunch and close about 17:00.

Popular choices are a "cream tea," which consists of tea and a scone or two, or the pricier "afternoon tea," which comes with pastries and finger foods such as small, crust-less sandwiches (for more tea options, see page 398). It's perfectly acceptable for two people to order one afternoon tea and one cream tea and share the afternoon tea's goodies. At many places, you can spring an extra £10 or so to upgrade to a boozy "champagne tea."

Many museum restaurants offer a fine inexpensive tea service: For example, the **$$ Victoria and Albert Museum** café serves a classic cream tea in an elegant setting that won't break your budget.

$$$ The Wolseley serves a good afternoon tea between their meal service (generally served 15:00-18:30 daily, see full listing on page 114).

$$$$ Fortnum & Mason department store offers tea at several different restaurants. You can "Take Tea in the Parlour" for a reasonably priced experience (including ice cream and scones; Mon-Sat 10:00-19:30, Sun 11:30-17:00). The pièce de resistance is their Diamond Jubilee Tea Salon, named in honor of the Queen's 60th year on the throne. At royal prices, consider it dinner (Mon-Sat 12:00-19:00, Sun until 18:00, dress up a bit—no shorts, "children must be behaved," 181 Piccadilly, smart to reserve at least a week in advance, tel. 020/7734-8040, www.fortnumandmason.com).

$$$$ The Orangery at Kensington Palace may be closed for restoration when you visit. If so, you can take tea next door at the Kensington Palace Pavilion (daily 12:00-16:00, a 10-minute walk through Kensington Gardens from either Queensway or High Street Kensington Tube stations—see the map on page 106; tel. 020/3166-6113, www.hrp.org.uk).

serving sandwiches, salads, and Middle Eastern food. It's decorated with photos of Princess Diana, who used to drop by for pita sandwiches (daily 8:00-23:00, cash only, 5 Wellington Terrace, on Bayswater Road, opposite Kensington Palace Garden gates, where Di once lived, tel. 020/7792-9606, Abdul).

North London

To avoid the touristy crush right around the British Museum, head a few blocks west to the Fitzrovia area. Here, tiny Charlotte Place is lined with small eateries (including my first two listings); nearby,

the much bigger Charlotte Street has several more good options (Tube: Goodge Street). See the map on page 108 for locations.

$ Salumeria Dino serves up hearty £5 sandwiches, pasta, and Italian coffee. Dino, a native of Naples, has run his little shop for more than 30 years and has managed to create a classic-feeling Italian deli (cheap takeaway cappuccinos, Mon-Sat 7:30-18:00, closed Sun, 15 Charlotte Place, tel. 020/7580-3938).

$ Lantana OUT is an Australian coffee shop that sells modern soups, sandwiches, and salads at their takeaway window (£8 daily hot dish). **Lantana IN** is an adjacent sit-down café that serves pricier meals (both Mon-Fri 8:00-18:00, Sat-Sun 9:00-17:00, 13 Charlotte Place, tel. 020/7637-3347).

Near the British Library: Farther north, in the Coal Drops Yard development just behind King's Cross Station, is a branch of the renowned Indian restaurant **$$$ Dishoom** (see description for Covent Garden branch, earlier). Not only is the food excellent, but it's a fun excuse to explore this development—a repurposing of an old industrial site on Regent's Canal.

TRANSPORTATION

Getting Around London

To travel smart in a city this size, you must get comfortable with public transportation. London's excellent taxis, buses, and subway (Tube) system can take you anywhere you need to go—a blessing for travelers' precious vacation time, not to mention their feet.

For more information about public transit (bus and Tube), the best source is the helpful *Welcome to London* brochure, which includes both a Tube map and a handy schematic map of the best bus routes (available free at TIs, museums, and hotels).

For specific directions on how to get from point A to point B on London's transit, detailed transit maps, updated prices, and general information, check www.tfl.gov.uk, or call the info line at 0343-222-1234.

Tickets and Cards

For most tourists, the Oyster card transit pass is better than individual tickets. The transit system has nine zones, but almost all tourist sights are within Zones 1 and 2, so those are the prices I've listed. For more information, visit www.tfl.gov.uk/tickets.

Individual Tickets: Paper tickets for the Tube are ridiculously expensive (£5/ride). At every Tube station, tickets are sold at easy-to-use self-service machines (hit "Adult Single" and enter your destination). Tickets are valid only on the day of purchase. Unless you're literally taking only one Tube ride your entire visit, you'll save money and time with an Oyster card.

Oyster Card: A pay-as-you-go Oyster card allows you to ride the Tube, buses, Docklands Light Railway (DLR), and Overground (suburban trains) for about half the rate of individual tickets. To use the card, simply touch it against the yellow card reader at the turnstile or entrance. It flashes green and the fare is automatically deducted. (You must also tap your card again to "touch out" as you exit the Tube, but not buses.)

Buy the card at any Tube station ticket machine, or look for nearby shops displaying the Oyster logo, where you can purchase a card or add credit without the wait. You'll pay £5 up front for the card, then load it with credit. One ride between Zones 1 and 2 during peak time costs £2.90; (£2.40 during off-peak). An automatic price cap guarantees you'll never pay more than £7.20 in one day for rides within Zones 1 and 2. If you think you'll take two or more rides in a day, £8 of credit will cover you, but it's smart to add a little more if you expect to travel outside the city center. If you're staying six or more days, consider adding a 7-Day Travelcard to your Oyster card (details below).

Oyster cards are not shareable among companions taking the same ride; all travelers need their own. If your balance gets

low, simply add credit—or "top up"—at a ticket machine, shop, or with the Transport for London (TFL) Oyster app (available on the App Store or Google Play). You can always see how much credit remains on your card with the app or by touching your card to the pad at any ticket machine. After your last ride you can have your unused balance up to £10 refunded by selecting "Pay as you go refund" on any ticket machine that gives change. For balances of more than £10, you can claim a refund online. The credit never expires—use it again on a future trip.

PASSES AND DISCOUNTS

7-Day Travelcard: Various Tube passes and deals are available but the only option of note is the 7-Day Travelcard. This is the best choice if you're staying six or more days and plan to use public transit a lot (£36.10 for Zones 1-2; £66 for Zones 1-6). For most travelers, the Zone 1-2 pass works best. Heathrow Airport is in Zone 6, but there's no need to buy the Zones 1-6 version if that's the only ride outside the city center you plan to take—instead you can pay a small supplement to cover the difference. You can add the 7-Day Travelcard to your Oyster card, or purchase the paper version at any National Rail train station.

Families: A paying adult can take up to four kids (ages 10 and under) for free on the Tube, DLR, Overground, and buses. Kids ages 11-15 get a discount. Explore other child and student discounts at www.tfl.gov.uk/tickets—or ask a Tube station employee.

River Cruises: A Travelcard gives you a 33 percent discount on most Thames cruises. The Oyster card gives you roughly a 10 percent discount on Thames Clippers (including the Tate Boat museum ferry).

By Tube

London's subway system is called the Tube or Underground (but never "subway," which, in Britain, refers to a pedestrian underpass). The Tube is one of this planet's great people-movers and usually the fastest long-distance transport in town (runs Mon-Sat about 5:00-24:00, Sun about 7:00-23:00; Central, Jubilee, Northern, Piccadilly, and Victoria lines also run Fri-Sat 24 hours). Two other commuter rail lines are tied into the network and use the same tickets: the Docklands Light Railway (called DLR) and the Overground.

Each line has a name (such as Circle, Northern, or Bakerloo) and two directions (indicated by the end-of-the-line stops). Find the line that will take you to your destination, and figure out roughly which direction (north, south, east, or west) you'll need to go to get there.

At the Tube station, with an Oyster card, touch it flat against the turnstile's yellow card reader, both when you enter and exit the station. With a paper ticket or paper Travelcard, feed it into the turnstile, reclaim it, and hang on to it—you'll need it later.

Find your train by following signs to your line and the (general) direction it's headed (such as Central Line: Eastbound). Since some tracks are shared by several lines, double-check before boarding: Make sure your destination is one of the stops listed on the sign at the platform. Also, check the electronic signboards that announce which train is next, and make sure the destination (the end-of-the-line stop) is the direction you want. Some trains, particularly on the Circle and District lines, split off for other directions, but each train has its final destination marked above its windshield and on the side of the cars.

Trains run about every 3-10 minutes. (A general rule of thumb is that it takes 30 minutes to travel six Tube stops (including walking time within stations), or roughly 5 minutes per stop. Check maps and signs for the most convenient exit.

The system can be fraught with construction delays and breakdowns. Pay

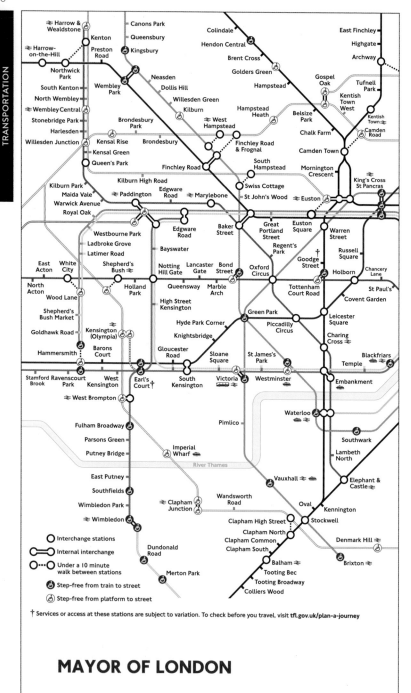

MAYOR OF LONDON

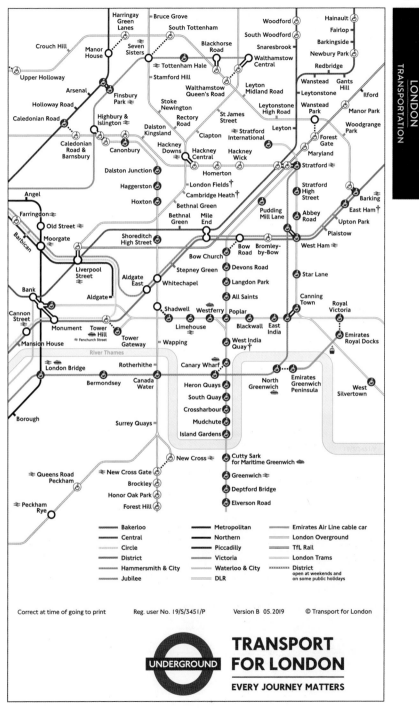

attention to signs and announcements explaining necessary detours. Rush hours (8:00-10:00 and 16:00-19:00) can be packed and sweaty. If one train is stuffed—and another is coming in three minutes—it may be worth a wait to avoid the sardine routine. For help, check out the "Plan a Journey" feature at www.tfl. gov.uk.

TUBE ETIQUETTE

When your train arrives, stand off to the side and let riders exit before you board.

When the car is jam-packed, avoid using the hinged seats near the doors of some trains—they take up valuable stand-ing space.

If you're blocking the door when the train stops, step out of the car and off to the side, let others off, then get back on.

Talk softly. Listen to how quietly Lon-doners communicate and follow their lead.

On escalators, stand on the right and pass on the left. But note that in some passageways or stairways, you might be directed to walk on the left (the direction Brits go when behind the wheel).

Discreet eating and drinking are fine; drinking alcohol and smoking are banned.

Be zipped up to thwart thieves.

Carefully check exit options before sur-facing to street level. Signs point clearly to nearby sights—you'll save lots of walking by choosing the right exit.

By Bus

If you figure out the bus system, you'll swing like Tarzan through the urban jungle of London (see sidebar for a list of handy routes). Get in the habit of hopping buses for quick little straight shots, even just to get to a Tube stop. But during bump-and-grind rush hours (8:00-10:00 and 16:00-19:00), you'll usually go faster by Tube.

You can't buy single-trip tickets for buses, and you can't use cash to pay when boarding. Instead, you must have an Oys-ter card, a paper Travelcard, or a one-day Bus & Tram Pass (£5, can buy on day of travel only—not beforehand—from ticket machine in any Tube station). If you're using your Oyster card, any bus ride in downtown London costs £1.50 (capped at £4.50/day).

When your bus approaches, it's wise to hold your arm out to let the driver know you want on. Hop on and confirm your

destination with the driver (often friendly and helpful).

As you board, touch your Oyster card to the card reader, or show your paper Travelcard or Bus & Tram Pass to the driver. Unlike on the Tube, there's no need to show or tap your card when you hop off. On the older heritage "Routemaster" buses without card readers (used on the #15 route on summer weekends), you simply take a seat, and the conductor comes around to check cards and passes.

To alert the driver that you want to get off, press one of the red buttons (on the poles between the seats) before your stop.

By Taxi

London is the best taxi town in Europe. Big, black, carefully regulated cabs are everywhere—there are about 25,000 of them.

I've never met a crabby cabbie in London. They love to talk, and they know every nook and cranny in town. I ride in a taxi each day just to get my London questions answered. Drivers must pass a rigorous test on "The Knowledge" of London geography to earn their license.

If a cab's top light is on, just wave it down. Drivers flash lights when they see you wave. They have a tight turning radius, so you can hail cabs going in either direction. If waving doesn't work, ask someone where you can find a taxi stand. Telephoning a cab will get you one in a few minutes, but costs a little more (tel. 0871-871-8710).

Rides start at £3. The regular tariff #1 covers most of the day (Mon-Fri 5:00-20:00), tariff #2 is during "unsociable hours" (Mon-Fri 20:00-22:00 and Sat-Sun 5:00-22:00), and tariff #3 is for nighttime (22:00-5:00) and holidays. Rates go up about 20 percent with each higher tariff. Extra charges are explained in writing on the cab wall. All cabs accept credit and debit cards. Tip a cabbie by rounding up (maximum 10 percent).

Connecting downtown sights is quick and easy, and will cost you about £8-12 (for example, St. Paul's to the Tower of London, or between the two Tate museums). For a short ride, three adults in a cab generally travel at close to Tube prices—and groups of four or five adults should taxi everywhere. All cabs can carry five passengers, and some take six, for the same cost as a single traveler.

Don't worry about meter cheating. Licensed British cab meters come with a sealed computer chip and clock that ensures you'll get the correct tariff. The only way a cabbie can cheat you is by taking a needlessly long route. Don't, however, take a cab in bad traffic—especially to a destination efficiently served by the Tube.

By Uber

Uber faces legal challenges in London and may not be operating when you visit. If Uber is running, it can be much cheaper than a taxi and is a handy alternative if there's a long line for a taxi or if no cabs are available. Uber drivers generally don't know the city as well as regular cabbies, and they don't have the access to some fast lanes that taxis do. Still, if you like using Uber, it can work great here.

By Car

If you have a car, stow it—you don't want to drive in London. An £11.50 **congestion charge** is levied on any private car

Handy Bus Routes

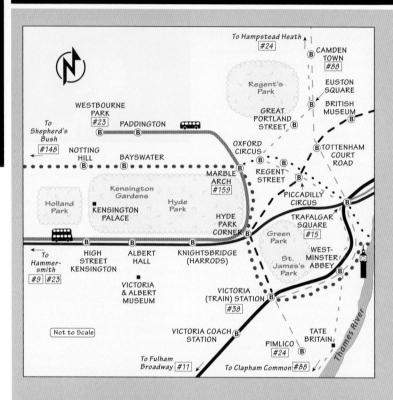

The best views are upstairs on a double-decker. Here are some of the most useful routes:

Route #9: High Street Kensington to Knightsbridge (Harrods) to Hyde Park Corner to Trafalgar Square to Aldwych (Somerset House).

Route #11: Victoria Station to Westminster Abbey to Trafalgar Square to St. Paul's and Liverpool Street Station and the East End.

Route #15: Trafalgar Square to St. Paul's to Tower of London (occasionally with heritage "Routemaster" old-style double-decker buses).

Route #159: Marble Arch to Oxford Circus to Piccadilly Circus to Trafalgar Square to Westminster and the Imperial War Museum. In addition, bus #139 also makes the corridor run between Marble Arch, Oxford Circus, Piccadilly Circus, and Trafalgar Square.

Route #23: Paddington Station to Marble Arch, Hyde Park Corner, Knightsbridge, Albert Hall, High Street Kensington, and on to Hammersmith.

Route #24: Pimlico to Victoria Station to Westminster Abbey to Trafalgar

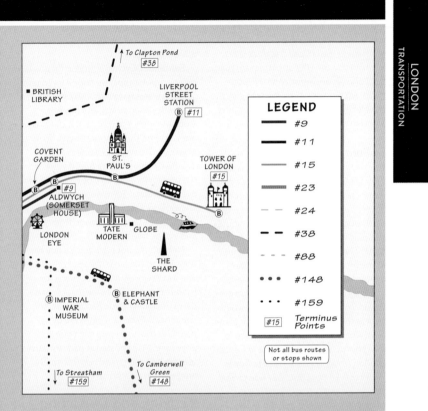

Square to Euston Square, then all the way north to Camden Town (Camden Lock Market) and Hampstead Heath.

Route #38: Victoria Station to Hyde Park Corner to Piccadilly Circus to British Museum.

Route #88: Tate Britain to Westminster Abbey to Trafalgar Square to Piccadilly Circus to Oxford Circus to Great Portland Street Station (Regent's Park), then north to Camden Town.

Route #148: Westminster Abbey to Victoria Station to Notting Hill and Bayswater (by way of the east end of Hyde Park and Marble Arch).

entering the city center during peak hours (Mon-Fri 7:00-18:00, no charge Sat-Sun and holidays). You can pay the fee either online or by phone (www.cclondon.com, from within the UK call 0343/222-2222, from outside the UK call 011-44-20/7649-9122, phones answered Mon-Fri 8:00-22:00, Sat 9:00-15:00, be ready to give the vehicle registration number and country of registration).

By Boat

The sleek, 220-seat catamarans used by **Thames Clippers** are designed for commuters rather than sightseers. Think of the boats as express buses on the river—they zip through London every 20-30 minutes, stopping at most of the major docks en route. They're fast: roughly 20-30 minutes from Embankment to Tower, 10 more minutes to Docklands/Canary Wharf, and 15 more minutes to Greenwich. However, the only outside access is on a crowded deck at the exhaust—choked back of the boat, where you're jostling for space to take photos. Any one-way ride in Central London (roughly London Eye to Tower Pier) costs £8.60; a one-way ride to East London (Canary Wharf and Greenwich) is £10, and a River Roamer all-day ticket costs £19.80 (discounts online and with Travelcard and Oyster card, www. thamesclippers.com).

The **Tate Boat** ferry service, which directly connects the Tate Britain (Millbank Pier) and the Tate Modern (Bankside Pier), is made for art lovers (£9 one-way, covered by River Roamer day ticket; buy ticket at kiosks or self-service machines before boarding or use Oyster card; for frequency and times, see www. tate.org.uk/visit/tate-boat).

By Bike

London operates a citywide bike-rental program similar to ones in other major European cities, and new bike lanes are still cropping up around town. Still, London isn't (yet) ideal for biking. Its network of designated bike lanes is far from complete, and the city's many one-way streets (not to mention the need to bike on the "wrong" side) can make biking here a bit more challenging.

Santander Cycles, intended for quick point-to-point trips, are fairly easy to rent. These cruisers have big, cushy seats, a bag rack with elastic straps, and three gears. Approximately 750 bike-rental stations are scattered throughout the city. To rent a bike, you'll pay an access fee (£2/day). The first 30 minutes are free; if you keep the bike for longer, you'll be charged £2 for every additional 30-minute period. Maps showing docking stations are available at major Tube stations, at www.tfl.gov.uk, and via the free app.

Helmets are not provided, so ride carefully. Stay to the far-left side of the road and watch closely at intersections for *left*-turning cars. Be aware that in most parks (including Hyde Park/Kensington Gardens) only certain paths are designated for bike use—you can't ride just anywhere. Maps posted at park entrances identify bike paths, and non-bike paths are generally clearly marked.

Arriving and Departing
By Plane

London has six airports; I've focused my coverage on the two most widely used—Heathrow and Gatwick—with a few tips for using the others (Stansted, Luton, London City, and Southend).

HEATHROW AIRPORT

For Heathrow's airport, flight, and transfer information, call the switchboard at 0844-335-1801, or visit the helpful website www. heathrow.com (code: LHR).

Heathrow's terminals are numbered T-2 through T-5. Each terminal is served by different airlines and alliances; for example, T-5 is exclusively for British Air and Iberia Air flights, while T-2 serves mostly Star Alliance flights, such as United and Lufthansa.

London's Airports

Luton●
✈ Luton
✈ Stansted

#757 & A1

N

Not to Scale

ST. PANCRAS
PADDINGTON
LIVERPOOL STREET
Southend
✈
Reading
Windsor
#71 & 77
Southend●
Tube
D.L.R. ✈
Rail Air Link
VICTORIA
To Bath
Heathrow
VICTORIA COACH STN.
London City
Thames
London
Guildford
EUROSTAR

- - - - - Rail
━━━━━ Eurostar Rail
━━━━━ Tube & D.L.R.
- - - - Bus

✈ Gatwick

Ashford
To Paris, Amsterdam & Brussels

ALL BUSES ARE NATIONAL EXPRESS
UNLESS NOTED

↓To Brighton

English Channel

You can walk between T-2 and T-3. From this central hub (called "Heathrow Central"), T-4 and T-5 split off in opposite directions (and are not walkable). The easiest way to travel between the T-2/T-3 cluster and either T-4 or T-5 is by Heathrow Express train (free to transfer between terminals, but tickets are required—hold onto your ticket even once you've passed through the turnstile—train departs every 15-20 minutes). You can also take a shuttle bus (free, serves all terminals), or the Tube (requires a ticket, serves all terminals).

If you're flying out of Heathrow, it's critical to confirm which terminal your flight will use (look at your ticket/boarding pass, check online, or call your airline in advance)—if it's T-4 or T-5, allow extra time. Taxi drivers generally know which terminal you'll need based on the airline, but bus drivers may not.

Services: Each terminal has an airport information desk (open long hours daily),

car-rental agencies, exchange bureaus, ATMs, a pharmacy, a VAT refund desk (tel. 0845-872-7627), and pay baggage storage (long hours daily, www.left-baggage.co.uk). Heathrow offers both free Wi-Fi and pay internet access points (in each terminal, check map for locations). You'll find a post office on the first floor of T-3 (departures area). Each terminal also has cheap eateries.

Heathrow's small **"TI"** (tourist info shop), even though it's a for-profit business, is worth a visit if you're nearby and want to pick up free information, including the *London Planner* visitors guide (long hours daily, 5-minute walk from T-3 in Tube station, follow signs to Underground; bypass queue for transit info to reach window for London questions).

Getting Between Heathrow and Downtown London: Options for traveling the 14 miles between Heathrow Airport and downtown London include Tube (about £6/person), bus (£8-10/person),

express train with connecting Tube or taxi (£22-25, price does not include connecting Tube fare), or most expensive—taxi or car service. The one that works best for you will depend on your arrival terminal, your destination in central London, and your budget.

By Tube (Subway): The Tube takes you from any Heathrow terminal to downtown London in 50-60 minutes on the Piccadilly Line (6/hour, buy ticket at Tube station self-service machine). If you plan to use the Tube in London, it makes sense to buy a pay-as-you-go Oyster card (possibly adding a 7-Day Travelcard) at the airport's Tube station ticket machines. If you add a Travelcard that covers only Zones 1-2, you'll need to pay a small supplement for the initial trip from Heathrow (Zone 6) to downtown.

If you're taking the Tube from downtown London *to* the airport, note that Piccadilly Line trains don't stop at every terminal. Trains either stop at T-4, then T-2/T-3 (also called Heathrow Central), in that order; or T-2/T-3, then T-5. When leaving central London on the Tube, allow extra time if going to T-4 or T-5, and check the reader board in the station to make sure that the train goes to the right terminal before you board.

By Bus: Most buses depart from the outdoor common area called the Central Bus Station, a five-minute walk from the T-2/T-3 complex. To connect between T-4 or T-5 and the Central Bus Station, ride the free Heathrow Express train or the shuttle buses.

National Express has regular service from Heathrow's Central Bus Station to Victoria Coach Station in downtown London, near several of my recommended hotels. While slow, the bus is affordable and convenient for those staying near Victoria Station (£8-10, 1-2/hour, less frequent from Victoria Station to Heathrow, 45-75 minutes depending on time of day, tel. 0871-781-8181, www.nationalexpress.com). A less-frequent National Express bus goes from T-5 directly to Victoria Coach Station.

By Train: The **Heathrow Express** runs between Heathrow Airport and London's Paddington Station. At Paddington, you're in the thick of the Tube system, with easy access to any of my recommended neighborhoods.

The Heathrow Express is fast but pricey (£22-25 one-way, price depends on time of day, £37 round-trip, cheaper if purchased online in advance, covered by BritRail pass; 4/hour, Mon-Sat 5:00-24:00, Sun from 6:00, 15 minutes to downtown from Heathrow Central Station serving

T-2/T-3, 21 minutes from T-5; for T-4 take free transfer to Heathrow Central, tel. 0345-600-1515, www.heathrowexpress.co.uk).

A cheaper alternative to the Heathrow Express—the new **Crossrail Elizabeth line**—may not yet be operational by the time you visit, but when it opens, it will be faster (and more expensive) than the Tube; see www.tfl.gov.uk for updates.

By Car Service: Just Airports offers a private car service between five London airports and the city center (see website for price quote, tel. 020/8900-1666, www.justairports.com).

By Taxi or Uber: Taxis from the airport cost £45-75 to west and central London (one hour). For four people traveling together, this can be a reasonable option. Hotels can often line up a cab back to the airport for about £50. If running, Uber also offers London airport pickup and drop-off.

Gatwick Airport

Gatwick Airport is halfway between London and the south coast (code: LGW, tel. 0844-892-0322, www.gatwickairport.com). Gatwick has two terminals, North and South, which are easily connected by a free monorail (two-minute trip, runs 24 hours). Note that boarding passes say "Gatwick N" or "Gatwick S" to indicate your terminal. Gatwick Express trains (described next) stop only at Gatwick South. Schedules in each terminal show only arrivals and departures from that terminal.

Getting Between Gatwick and Downtown London: Gatwick Express trains are the best way into London from this airport. They shuttle conveniently between Gatwick South and London's **Victoria Station,** with many of my recommended hotels close by (£20 one-way, £35 round-trip, at least 10 percent cheaper if purchased online, Oyster cards accepted but no discount offered, 4/hour, 30 minutes, runs 5:00-24:00 daily, a few

trains as early as 3:30, tel. 0845-850-1530, www.gatwickexpress.com). If you buy your tickets at the station before boarding, ask about possible group deals. (If you see others in the ticket line, you could suggest buying your tickets together.) When going *to* the airport, at Victoria Station note that Gatwick Express has its own ticket windows right by the platform (tracks 13 and 14). You'll also find easy-to-use ticket machines nearby.

A train also runs between Gatwick South and **St. Pancras International Station** (£12.10, 3-5/hour, 45-60 minutes, www.thetrainline.com)—useful for travelers taking the Eurostar train (to Paris, Amsterdam, or Brussels) or staying in the St. Pancras/King's Cross neighborhood.

While even slower, the **bus** is a cheap and handy option to the Victoria Station neighborhood. National Express runs a bus from Gatwick directly to Victoria Station (£10, at least hourly, 1.5 hours, tel. 0871-781-8181, www.nationalexpress.com); EasyBus has one that stops near the Earl's Court Tube stop (£4-10 depending on how far ahead you book, 2-3/hour, www.easybus.com).

London's Other Airports

Stansted Airport: From Stansted (code: STN, tel. 0844-335-1803, www.stanstedairport.com), **buses** connect the airport and London's Victoria Station neighborhood: National Express (£9-12, every 15 minutes, 2 hours, runs 24 hours a day, picks up and stops throughout London, ends at Victoria Coach Station or Liverpool Street Station, tel. 0871-781-8181, www.nationalexpress.com) and Airport Bus Express (£9, 2/hour, 1.5-2 hours). Or you can take the faster, pricier Stansted Express **train** (£19, cheaper if booked online, connects to London's Tube system at Tottenham Hale or Liverpool Street, 2-4/hour, 45 minutes, 4:30-23:00, www.stanstedexpress.com). Stansted is expensive by **cab;** figure £100-120 one-way from central London.

London's Major Train Stations

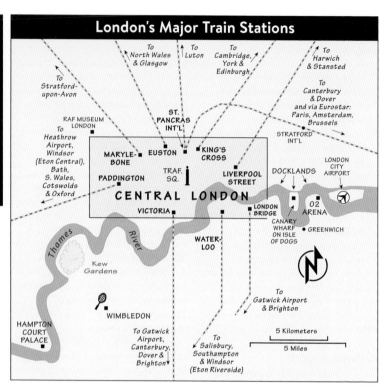

To North Wales & Glasgow

To Luton

To Cambridge, York & Edinburgh

To Harwich & Stansted

To Stratford-upon-Avon

To Canterbury & Dover and via Eurostar: Paris, Amsterdam, Brussels

RAF MUSEUM LONDON

To Heathrow Airport, Windsor (Eton Central), Bath, S. Wales, Cotswolds & Oxford

ST. PANCRAS INT'L

STRATFORD INT'L

MARYLE-BONE

EUSTON

KING'S CROSS

LONDON CITY AIRPORT

PADDINGTON

TRAF. SQ.

LIVERPOOL STREET

DOCKLANDS

CENTRAL LONDON

VICTORIA

LONDON BRIDGE

O2 ARENA

CANARY WHARF ON ISLE OF DOGS

GREENWICH

WATER-LOO

Thames River

Kew Gardens

To Gatwick Airport & Brighton

HAMPTON COURT PALACE

WIMBLEDON

To Gatwick Airport, Canterbury, Dover & Brighton

To Salisbury, Southampton & Windsor (Eton Riverside)

5 Kilometers

5 Miles

Luton Airport: For Luton (code: LTN, tel. 01582/405-100, www.london-luton.co.uk), the fastest way to get into London is by **train** to St. Pancras International Station (£14-17 one-way, 1-5/hour, 35-45 minutes—check schedule to avoid slower trains, tel. 0345-712-5678, www.eastmidlandstrains.co.uk); catch the 10-minute shuttle bus (every 10 minutes) from outside the terminal to the Luton Airport Parkway Station. You can purchase a shuttle bus and train combo-ticket from kiosks or ticket machines inside the airport. When buying your train ticket *to* Luton, make sure you select "Luton Airport" as your destination rather than "Parkway Station" to ensure the shuttle fare is included.

The **National Express bus** A1 runs from Luton to Victoria Coach Station (£7-11 one-way, 2/hour, 1-1.5 hours, runs 24 hours, tel. 0871-781-8181, www.

nationalexpress.com). The **Green Line express bus** #757 runs to Buckingham Palace Road, just south of Victoria Sta-

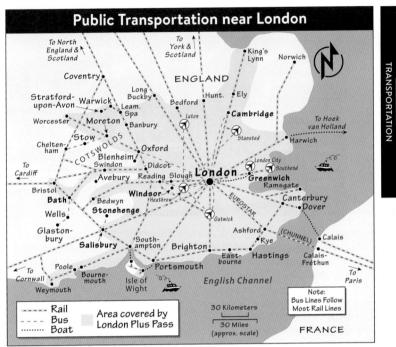

Public Transportation near London

To North England & Scotland
To York & Scotland
King's Lynn
Norwich

Coventry
ENGLAND

Stratford-upon-Avon
Warwick
Leam.
Spa
Long Buckby
Bedford
Hunt.
Ely
Cambridge

Worcester
Moreton
Banbury
Luton
Stansted
To Hoek van Holland

Cheltenham
Stow
COTSWOLDS
Oxford
Harwich

To Cardiff
Blenheim
Swindon
Didcot
Avebury
Reading
Slough
London
London City
Southend
Greenwich
Ramsgate

Bristol
Windsor
Heathrow
EUROSTAR
Canterbury
Dover

Bath
Bedwyn
Stonehenge
Wells
Gatwick

Glaston-bury
Salisbury
South-ampton
Brighton
Ashford
Rye
(CHUNNEL)
Calais

Poole
Bourne-mouth
Portsmouth
East-bourne
Hastings
Calais-Fréthun
To Paris

To Cornwall
Weymouth
Isle of Wight
English Channel

- - - - - Rail
- - - - Bus
.... Boat

Area covered by London Plus Pass

30 Kilometers
30 Miles (approx. scale)

Note: Bus Lines Follow Most Rail Lines

FRANCE

---

tion, and stops en route near the Baker Street Tube station—best if you're staying near Paddington Station or in North London (£10 one-way, 2-4/hour, 1-1.5 hours, runs 24 hours, tel. 0344-800-4411, www.greenline.co.uk).

London City and Southend Airports: To get into the city center from London City Airport (code: LCY, tel. 020/7646-0088, www.londoncityairport.com), take the Docklands Light Railway (DLR) to the Bank Tube station, which is one stop east of St. Paul's on the Central Line (less than £6 one-way, covered by Travelcard, a bit cheaper with an Oyster card, 20 minutes, www.tfl.gov.uk/dlr). Some EasyJet flights land farther out, at Southend Airport (code: SEN, tel. 01702/538-500, www.southendairport.com). Trains connect this airport to London's Liverpool Street Station (£16.20 one-way, 3-8/hour, 55 minutes, www.abelliogreateranglia.co.uk).

By Train

London has nine main stations:

Euston: Serves northwest England, North Wales, and Scotland.

St. Pancras International: Serves north and south England, plus the Eurostar to Paris, Amsterdam, or Brussels.

King's Cross: Serves northeast England and Scotland, including York and Edinburgh.

Liverpool Street: Serves east England, including Essex and Harwich.

London Bridge: Serves south England, including Brighton.

Waterloo: Serves south England, including Salisbury and Southampton.

Victoria: Serves Gatwick Airport, Canterbury, Dover, and Brighton.

Paddington: Serves south and southwest England, including Heathrow Airport, Windsor, Bath, Oxford, South Wales, and the Cotswolds.

Marylebone: Serves southwest and central England, including

Stratford-upon-Avon.

Any train station has schedule information, can make reservations, and can sell tickets for any destination. Most stations offer a baggage-storage service (look for *left luggage* signs); because of long security lines, it can take a while to check or pick up your bag (www.left-baggage.co.uk). For more details on the services available at each station, see www.nationalrail.co.uk/stations. UK train and bus info is available at www.traveline.org.uk. For information on tickets and rail passes, see the Practicalities chapter.

TRAIN CONNECTIONS FROM LONDON

From Paddington Station to: Windsor (Windsor & Eton Central Station, 2/hour, 35 minutes, easy change at Slough), **Bath** (2/hour, 1.5 hours), **Oxford** (4/hour direct, 1 hour, more with transfer), **Moreton-in-Marsh** (hourly, 1.5 hours), **Penzance** (every 2 hours, 5 hours, more with change in Plymouth), **Cardiff** (2/hour, 2 hours).

From **King's Cross Station**: **York** (3/hour, 2 hours), **Durham** (hourly, 3 hours), **Edinburgh** (2/hour, 4.5 hours).

From **Euston Station**: **Liverpool** (hourly, 3 hours, transfer at Liverpool South Parkway), **Keswick/Lake District** (train to Penrith—hourly, 3.5 hours, then bus at Keswick).

From Marylebone Station: Stratford-upon-Avon (2/day direct, 2.5 hours; also 1-2/hour, 2 hours, transfer in Leamington Spa, Dorridge, or Birmingham Moor).

By Bus

Buses are slower but considerably cheaper than trains. Most depart from **Victoria Coach Station,** which is one long block south of Victoria Station, Tube: Victoria). Inside the station, you'll find basic eateries, kiosks, and a helpful information desk.

Ideally you'll buy your tickets online (for tips on buying tickets and taking buses, see page 404). But if you must buy one at the station, arrive an hour before the bus departs, or drop by the day before. Ticketing machines are scattered around the station (separate machines for National Express/Eurolines and Megabus; you can buy either for today or for tomorrow); there's also a ticket counter near gate 21. For UK train and bus info, check www.traveline.info.

National Express buses go to: **Bath** (hourly, 3 hours), **Oxford** (2/hour, 2 hours), **Stratford-upon-Avon** (3/day, 3.5 hours), **Liverpool** (8/day direct, 5.5 hours, overnight available), **York** (3/day direct, 6 hours), **Durham** (3/day direct, 7 hours, train is better), **Edinburgh, Scotland** (2/day direct, 10 hours, go by train instead).

NEAR LONDON

Windsor and Stonehenge are two great day-trip possibilities near London. Windsor Castle, the primary residence of Her Majesty the Queen, is regally lived-in yet open to the public (23 miles west of London). Stonehenge, the world's most famous rock group, sits lonesome and adored in a mysterious field 90 miles southwest of the city.

Rick's Tip: *Take advantage of* **British Rail's "off-peak day return" ticket.** *This round-trip fare costs virtually the same as one-way, provided you depart London outside rush hour (usually after 9:30 on weekdays and anytime Sat-Sun). Ask for the "day return" ticket (round-trip within a single day) rather than the more expensive standard "return."*

Windsor Castle

Windsor Castle, rated ▲▲, the official home of England's royal family for 900 years, claims to be the largest and oldest occupied castle in the world. (The current Queen considers Windsor her primary residence, and she generally hangs her crown here on weekends.) Thankfully, touring it is simple. You'll see sprawling grounds, lavish staterooms, a crowd-pleasing dollhouse, and an exquisite Perpendicular Gothic chapel.

Day Plan
Follow my self-guided tour or the included audioguide through the grounds and castle. You could also take the free guided walk of the grounds. A typical castle visit lasts at least two hours.

Orientation
Tourist Information: The TI is in the Windsor Royal Shopping Centre's Old Booking Hall, immediately adjacent to Windsor & Eton Central Station (Thu-Mon 10:00-16:00, closed Tue-Wed, tel. 01753/743-900, www.windsor.gov.uk).

Cost: £22.50, includes entry to castle grounds and all exhibits inside.

Hours: Grounds and most interiors open daily 10:00-17:15, Nov-Feb until 16:15, except St. George's Chapel, which is closed Sun (but open to worshippers; wait at the exit gate to be escorted in).

Information: Tel. 0303/123-7304, www.rct.uk.

Crowd Control: In summer, it's smart to buy tickets in advance at www.rct.uk (collect them at the prepaid ticket window), or in person at the Buckingham Palace ticket office in London. All visitors must go through a security checkpoint, which can slow entry.

Possible Closures: On rare occasions when the Queen is entertaining guests,

Windsor Castle

Changing of the Guard at Windsor

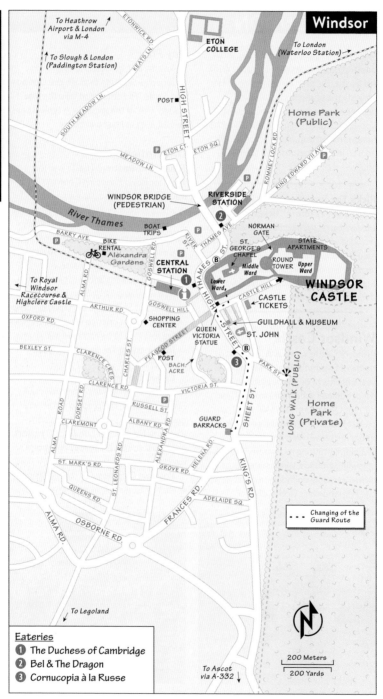

Windsor

To Heathrow
Airport & London
via M-4

↑ To Slough & London
(Paddington Station)

ETONWICK RD.

KEATS LN.

ETON COLLEGE

HIGH STREET

To London
(Waterloo Station)

POST

Home Park
(Public)

SOUTH MEADOW LN.

ROMNEY LOCK RD.

KING EDWARD VII AVE.

MEADOW LN.

ETON CT.

ETON SQ.

WINDSOR BRIDGE
(PEDESTRIAN)

RIVERSIDE
STATION

THAMES AVE.

NORMAN GATE

River Thames

BARRY AVE.

BOAT TRIPS

RIVER ST.

GOSWELL RD.

ST. GEORGE'S CHAPEL

STATE APARTMENTS

BIKE RENTAL

Alexandra Gardens

CENTRAL STATION

THAMES ST.

HIGH STREET

Middle Ward

ROUND TOWER

Upper Ward

WINDSOR CASTLE

To Royal
Windsor
Racecourse &
Highclere Castle

ALMA RD.

Lower Ward

CASTLE HILL

CASTLE TICKETS

ARTHUR RD.

GOSWELL HILL

OXFORD RD.

SHOPPING CENTER

GUILDHALL & MUSEUM

BEXLEY ST.

CLARENCE CRES.

CHARLES ST.

PEASCOD STREET

QUEEN VICTORIA STATUE

ST. JOHN

POST

BACH-ACRE

PARK ST.

CLARENCE RD.

VICTORIA ST.

Home Park
(Private)

DORSET RD.

RUSSELL ST.

LONG WALK (PUBLIC)

ROAD

ALBANY RD.

ALEXANDRA RD.

CLAREMONT

ALMA

ST. LEONARDS RD.

GROVE RD.

HELENA RD.

GUARD BARRACKS

SHEET ST.

KING'S RD.

ST. MARK'S RD.

QUEENS RD.

FRANCES RD.

ADELAIDE SQ.

ALMA RD.

OSBORNE RD.

- - - Changing of the
Guard Route

To Legoland

N

To Ascot
via A-332 ↓

200 Meters

200 Yards

Eateries

1. The Duchess of Cambridge
2. Bel & The Dragon
3. Cornucopia à la Russe

the State Apartments close. Check the website (especially in mid-June) to make sure everything is open when you want to go.

Tours: An included **audioguide** covers both the grounds and interiors. Consider the free 30-minute **guided walk** around the grounds (about 5/day, schedule posted on path up to the main gate).

Changing of the Guard: The Changing of the Guard usually takes place Tuesday, Thursday, and Saturday at 11:00 (confirm schedule on website). The fresh guards, led by a marching band, leave their barracks on Sheet Street and march up High Street, hanging a right at Victoria, then a left into the castle's Lower Ward, arriving at about 11:00. After about a half-hour, the tired guards march back the way the new ones came. To view the ceremony from inside the castle, arrive as early as possible (no later than 10:30 on quiet days) to have time to buy tickets, clear security, and stake out a spot with a clear view. If you arrive late, just wait for them to march by on High Street or on the lower half of Castle Hill.

Evensong: An evensong takes place in the chapel nightly at 17:15 (free for worshippers, line up at exit gate to be admitted).

Eating: The Undercroft Café, on the ground floor below St. George's Hall, serves sandwiches, wraps, salads, teas sweets, and ice cream under medieval arches. Around the castle, look for restaurants on High and Thames streets, and down pedestrian Peascod Street (PESS-cot). Consider the Duchess of Cambridge for pub grub right across from the castle walls (3 Thames Street), the charming Bel & The Dragon (on Thames Street, near the bridge), or the cozy Cornucopia a la Russe (closed Sun, 6 High Street).

Getting There

By Train: Windsor has two train stations—London's Paddington Station connects with Windsor & Eton Central (2-3/

hour, 35 minutes, easy change at Slough—typically just across the platform, www.gwr.com). London's Waterloo Station connects with Windsor & Eton Riverside (2/hour, no changes but slower—55 minutes, www.nationalrail.co.uk). Either trip costs about £11 one-way (a few pounds more for same-day return).

Whichever train station you arrive at, you're only a five-minute walk to the castle. From Windsor & Eton Central, walk through the Windsor Royal Shopping Centre (which houses the TI), and up the hill to the castle. From Windsor & Eton Riverside, you'll see the castle as you exit—just follow the wall as you walk up the street and around to the ticket office.

By Bus: Green Line buses #702 and #703 run from London's Victoria Colonnades to the Parish Church stop on Windsor's High Street (1-2/hour, 1.5 hours to Windsor, prices typically £6-10 each way, tel. 0871-200-2233, www.firstgroup.com).

By Car: Windsor is well-signposted from the M-4 motorway. Follow signs from the motorway for pay-and-display parking in the center.

⊙ Visiting the Castle

The Grounds: Emerging from security, head up the hill (WCs to your right, audioguides up the path on the left), enjoying the first of many fine castle views you'll see today. The tower-topped conical hill on your left represents the historical core of the castle. William the Conqueror built this motte (artificial mound) and bailey (fortified stockade around it) in 1080—his first castle in England. Among the later monarchs who spiffed up Windsor were Edward III (flush with French war booty, he made it a palace fit for a 14th-century king), Charles II (determined to restore the monarchy properly in the 1660s), and George IV (Britain's "Bling King," who financed many such vanity projects in the 1820s).

The castle has three "baileys" (castle yards), which today make up Windsor's

Upper Ward (where the Queen lives), Middle Ward (with St. George's Chapel), and Lower Ward (residences for castle workers). The Upper Ward's **Quadrangle** is surrounded by the State Apartments and the Queen's private apartments. The **Round Tower** sits atop the original motte. The red, yellow, and blue royal standard flies here when the Queen is in residence.

Queen Mary's Dolls' House: This palace in miniature (1:12 scale, from 1924) is "the most famous dollhouse in the world." It was a gift for the adult Queen Mary (the current Queen's grandmother), who greatly enjoyed miniatures. It's basically one big, dimly lit room with the large dollhouse in the middle, executed with an astonishing level of detail. Each fork, knife, and spoon on the expertly set banquet table is perfect and made of real silver—and the tiny pipes of its plumbing system actually have running water.

State Apartments: Dripping with chandeliers, finely furnished, and strewn with history and the art of a long line of kings and queens, they're the best I've seen in Britain. This is where Henry VIII

Round Tower

and Charles I once lived, and where the current Queen wows visiting dignitaries.

On your way in, you may pass through the **China Museum,** featuring items from the Queen's many exquisite settings for royal shindigs.

You'll climb the Grand Staircase up to the peach-colored **Grand Vestibule,** decorated with exotic items seized by British troops during their missions to colonize various corners of the world. Immediately to the left of the door into the next room, look for the bullet that killed Lord Nelson at Trafalgar. The magnificent wood-ceilinged **Waterloo Chamber** is wallpapered with portraits of figures from the pan-European alliance that defeated Napoleon.

Many rooms are decorated with some of the finest works from the royal collection, including by Rubens, Van Dyck, and Holbein. **St. George's Hall** is decorated with emblems representing the knights of the prestigious Order of the Garter, established by Edward III in 1834. This hall is the site of elaborate royal banquets—imagine one long table stretching from one end of the hall to the other and seating 160 VIPs. The **Garter Throne Room** is where new members of the Order of the Garter are invested (ceremonially granted their titles).

St. George's Chapel: This church is an exquisite example of the Perpendicular Gothic style (dating from about 1500). More recently, it's where Prince Harry and Meghan Markle tied the knot in 2018. Pick up a free map and circle the interior to find the highlights, including the burial spots of the current Queen's parents, **King George VI and "Queen Mum" Elizabeth,** and **King Henry VIII** and Jane Seymour, Henry's favorite wife (perhaps because she was the only one who died before he could behead her). The body of King Charles I, who was beheaded by Oliver Cromwell's forces, was also discovered here...with its head sewn back on.

On your way out, pause at the door of the sumptuous 13th-century **Albert Memorial Chapel** (#28), redecorated in

1861 after the death of Queen Victoria's husband, Prince Albert, and dedicated to his memory.

Lower Ward: This area is a living town where some 160 people who work for the Queen reside.

Stonehenge

As old as the pyramids, and far older than the Acropolis and the Colosseum, this iconic stone circle amazed medieval Europeans, who figured it was built by a race of giants. And it still impresses visitors today. As one of Europe's most famous sights, Stonehenge, worth ▲▲▲, does a valiant job of retaining an air of mystery and majesty (partly because cordons, which keep hordes of tourists from trampling all over it, foster the illusion that it stands alone in a field). Most of its almost one million annual visitors agree that it's well worth the trip.

Day Plan

Tour the visitors center, then head to Stonehenge by shuttle bus or on foot. Allow at least two hours to see everything.

Orientation

The visitors center, located 1.5 miles west of the circle, is a minimalist steel structure with a subtly curved roofline, evoking the landscape of Salisbury Plain.

Cost: £19.50, purchase timed-entry ticket in advance online, ticket includes shuttle-bus ride to stone circle, covered by English Heritage membership (see page 390).

Hours: Daily 9:30-19:00, June-Aug 9:00-20:00, mid-Oct-March 9:30-17:00. Note that the last ticket is sold two hours before closing. Expect shorter hours and possible closures June 20-22 due to huge, raucous solstice crowds.

Information: Tel. 0370-333-1181, www.english-heritage.org.uk/stonehenge.

Advance Tickets Recommended: In busy times, avoid the long ticket-buying line by purchasing tickets at least 24 hours in advance at www.english-heritage.org.uk/stonehenge. You'll select a 30-minute entry window.

Tours: Worthwhile audioguides are available behind the ticket counter (included with Heritage Pass, otherwise

Stonehenge is the most famous of Britain's stone circles.

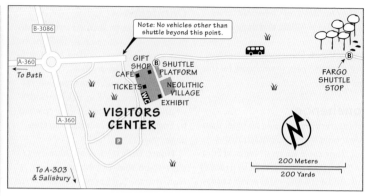

Note: No vehicles other than shuttle beyond this point.

B-3086
A-360
To Bath
GIFT SHOP
CAFE
TICKETS
SHUTTLE PLATFORM
NEOLITHIC VILLAGE
WC
EXHIBIT
VISITORS CENTER
A-360
P
To A-303 & Salisbury
FARGO SHUTTLE STOP
200 Meters
200 Yards

£3). Or use the visitors center's free Wi-Fi to download the free "Stonehenge Audio Tour" app.

Visiting the Inner Stones: Special one-hour access to the stones' inner circle is available early in the morning or after closing to the general public. Only 30 people are allowed at a time, so reserve well in advance (£45, for details see the English Heritage website).

Services: The visitors center has WCs and a large gift shop. Services at the circle itself are limited to emergency WCs. Even in summer, carry a jacket.

Eating: A large **$ café** within the visitors center serves hot drinks, soup, sandwiches, and salads.

Rick's Tip: *For a less crowded, more mystical experience, **visit Stonehenge early or late.** Things are pretty quiet before about 10:30 (head out to the stones first, then circle back to the exhibits); at the end of the day, aim to arrive just before the "last ticket" time (two hours before closing).*

Getting There

By Bus Tour: Several companies offer big-bus day trips to Stonehenge from London. These generally cost about £50-100 (including Stonehenge admission), last 8-12 hours, and pack a 45-seat bus. Well-known companies are **Evan Evans** (www.evanevanstours.co.uk) and **Golden Tours** (www.goldentours.com). **International Friends** runs pricier but smaller 16-person tours that include Windsor and Bath (www.internationalfriends.co.uk).

By Guided Tour on Public Transport: The "Stonehenge and Salisbury Excursion" from **London Walks** travels by train and bus on Tuesdays from mid-May through early October (£93, cash only, www.walks.com).

On Your Own on Public Transport: Catch a train (2/hour, 1.5 hours) from London's Waterloo station to Salisbury (www.southwesternrailway.com or www.nationalrail.co.uk). From Salisbury, you can get to Stonehenge by taxi (£40-60) or take the **Stonehenge Tour bus** (£15, £30 includes Stonehenge as well as Old Sarum—whether you want it or not; daily June-Aug 10:00-17:00, 2/hour; may not run on solstice—June 21, shorter hours and hourly departures off-season; 30 minutes, timetable at www.thestonehengetour.info).

By Car: Stonehenge is well-signed just off the A-303, about 15 minutes north of Salisbury, an hour southeast of Bath, an hour east of Glastonbury, and an hour south of Avebury.

◗ Self-Guided Tour

Start by touring the visitors center, then take a shuttle (or walk) to the stone circle.
• *As you enter the complex, on the right is the...*

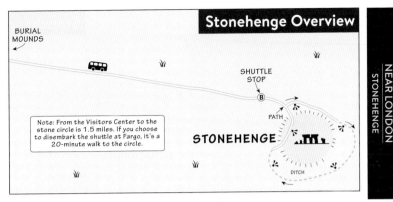

Rick's Tip: *If you want to see a* **large Bronze Age burial mound,** *get off the shuttle bus at the Fargo Plantation. From there, you can walk the rest of the way to the stone circle in about 20 minutes. Some visitors prefer this more authentic approach.*

PERMANENT EXHIBIT

This excellent, state-of-the-art exhibit uses an artful combination of multimedia displays and actual artifacts to provide context for the stones.

Prehistoric bones, tools, and pottery shards tell the story of the people who built Stonehenge, how they lived, and why they might have built the stone circle. Step outside and explore a village of reconstructed **Neolithic huts** modeled after the traces of a village discovered just northeast of Stonehenge.

• *Shuttle buses to the stone circle depart every 5-10 minutes from just behind the gift shop. Or, you can walk 1.5 miles through the fields to the site.*

STONE CIRCLE

As you approach the massive structure, walk right up to the knee-high cordon and let your fellow 21st-century tourists melt away. It's just you and the druids...

England has hundreds of stone circles,

Stonehenge's builders may have used sledges like this one.

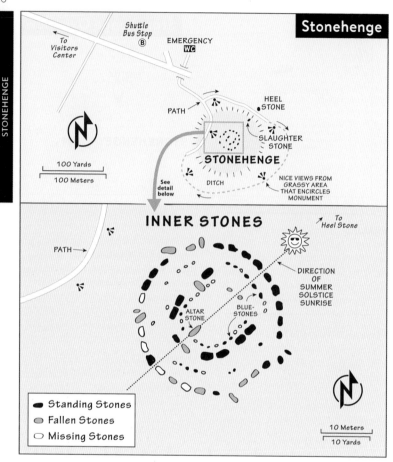

but Stonehenge—which literally means "hanging stones"—is unique. It's the only one that has horizontal cross-pieces (called lintels) spanning the vertical monoliths, and the only one with stones that have been made smooth and uniform. What you see here is a bit more than half the original structure—the rest was quarried centuries ago for other buildings.

Now do a slow **clockwise spin** around the monument. As you walk, mentally flesh out the missing pieces and re-erect the rubble.

It's now believed that Stonehenge, which was built in phases between 3000 and 1500 BC, was originally used as a cremation cemetery. This was a hugely significant location to prehistoric peoples. There are several hundred burial mounds within a three-mile radius of Stonehenge—some likely belonging to kings or chieftains. Some of the human remains are of people from far away, and others show signs of injuries—evidence that Stonehenge may have been used as a place of medicine or healing.

Whatever its original purpose, Stonehenge still functions as a celestial calendar. As the sun rises on the summer solstice (June 21), the **"heel stone"**— the one set apart from the rest, near the road—lines up with the sun and the altar

at the center of the stone circle. A study of more than 300 similar circles in Britain found that each was designed to calculate the movement of the sun, moon, and stars, and to predict eclipses in order to help early societies know when to plant, harvest, and party. Even in modern times, as the summer solstice sun sets in just the right slot at Stonehenge, pagans boogie.

Stonehenge's builders used two different types of stone. The tall, stout monoliths and lintels are sandstone blocks called **sarsen stones.** Most of the monoliths weigh about 25 tons (the largest is 45 tons), and the lintels are about 7 tons apiece. These sarsen stones were brought from "only" 20 miles away. The shorter stones in the middle—called **bluestones**—came from the south

coast of Wales...240 miles away. Imagine the logistical puzzle of floating six-ton stones across Wales' Severn Estuary and up the River Avon, then rolling them on logs about 20 miles to this position...an impressive feat.

Why didn't the builders of Stonehenge use what seem like perfectly adequate stones nearby? This, like many other questions about Stonehenge, remains shrouded in mystery. Imagine congregations gathering here 5,000 years ago, raising thought levels, creating a powerful life force. Maybe a particular kind of stone was essential for maximum energy transmission. Maybe the stones were levitated here. Maybe psychics really do create powerful vibes. Maybe not. It's as unbelievable as electricity used to be.

Bath

Bath is within easy striking distance of London—just a 1.5-hour train ride away. Two hundred years ago, this city of 90,000 was the trendsetting Tinseltown of Britain. If ever a city enjoyed looking in the mirror, Bath's the one. Built of the creamy warm-tone limestone called "Bath stone," it beams in its cover-girl complexion. It's a triumph of the Neoclassical style of the Georgian era (1714-1830), and—even with its mobs of tourists and high prices—is a joy to visit.

Long before the Romans arrived in the first century, Bath was known for its healing hot springs. In 1687, Queen Mary, fighting infertility, bathed here. Within 10 months, she gave birth to a son...and Bath boomed as a spa resort, which was rebuilt in the 18th century as a "new Rome" in the Neoclassical style. It became a city of balls, gaming, and concerts—the place to see and be seen.

Today, tourism has stoked its economy, as has the fast morning train to London. Renewed access to Bath's soothing hot springs at the Thermae Bath Spa also attracts visitors in need of a cure or a soak.

BATH IN 2 DAYS

Day 1: Take the City Sightseeing bus tour (the City Tour—rather than the Skyline Tour—offers the better city overview). Visit the abbey. Take the city walking tour at 14:00. Have afternoon tea and cakes in the Pump Room (or a cheaper tearoom). Stroll to Pulteney Bridge (visiting the Guildhall Market en route) and enjoy the gardens.

On any evening: Take a walking tour—the fun Bizarre Bath comedy walk (best choice), a ghost walk, or the free city walking tour. Visit the Roman Baths (open until 22:00 in July-Aug) or soak in the Thermae Bath Spa (both are also open during the day). Linger over dinner, enjoy a pub, or see a play in the classy theater. Just strolling in the evening is a pleasure, given Bath's elegant architecture.

Rick's Tip: *Consider* **starting your trip in Bath** (*using it as your jet-lag recovery pillow*)*, and then* **visit London at the end of your trip.** *You can get from Heathrow Airport to Bath by train, bus, a bus/train combination, or a taxi service (offered by Celtic Horizons, page 150; for train and bus info, see page 167).*

Day 2: Tour the Roman Baths (buy a ticket online in advance to save time in line). Then visit any of these sights, clustered in the neighborhood that features the architectural splendor of the Royal Crescent and the Circus: the No. 1 Royal Crescent Georgian house, Fashion Museum, or the Museum of Bath at Work. Consider a late afternoon stroll on my Canalside Walk to Bathampton.

With Extra Time: If you have another

day, explore nearby sights—such as Stonehenge, Wells, or Glastonbury by car, bus, or minibus tour.

ORIENTATION

Think of Bath as three sightseeing neighborhoods. In the center of town is the main cluster of sights: the Roman Baths, Pump Room, and Bath Abbey. A few blocks northeast is another group of sights around Pulteney Bridge. And, a 10-minute walk to the northwest, are the Georgian-era sights: the Circus, Royal Crescent, and several museums. Bath is hilly. In general, you'll gain elevation as you head north.

Tourist Information

The TI is next to The Huntsman Inn pub and a block south of the abbey (Mon-Sat 9:30-17:30, Sun 10:00-16:00, Bridgwater House, 2 Terrace Walk, tel. 01225/614-420, www.visitbath.co.uk). It houses the Bath Box Office, where you can check for events going on all around town (see listing below, under "Helpful Hints").

Helpful Hints

Festivals: In late May, the 10-day **Bath Festival** celebrates art, music, and literature (bathfestivals.org.uk/the-bath-festival/), overlapped by the eclectic **Bath Fringe Festival** (theater, walks, talks, bus trips; www.bathfringe.co.uk). The **Jane Austen Festival** unfolds genteelly in late September (www.janeausten.co.uk/festival). And for three weeks in December, the squares around the abbey are filled with a **Christmas market.**

Event Tickets and Listings: The **Bath Box Office** sells tickets for festivals and most events (except those at the Theatre Royal), and can tell you exactly what's on tonight (inside the TI, tel. 01225/463-362, www.bathfestivals.org.uk). The city's weekly paper, the Bath Chronicle, publishes a "What's On" events listing each Thursday (www.thisisbath.com).

Laundry: Try **Spruce Goose Launderette** between the Circus and the Royal Crescent (bring coins, self-service, daily 8:00-20:00, last load at 19:00), or **Speedy Wash,** which picks up your laundry on weekdays before 9:30 for same-day service (no pickup Sat, closed Sun, tel. 01225/427-616).

Tours

▲▲▲FREE CITY WALKING TOURS

Free two-hour tours are led by the **Mayor of Bath's Honorary Guides,** volunteers who share their love of Bath with its many visitors (as the city's mayor first did when he took a group on a guided walk back in the 1930s). These chatty, historical, and gossip-filled walks give you the lay of the land while you learn about the evolution of the city, its architecture, and its amazing Georgian social scene. How else would you learn that the old "chair ho" call for your sedan chair evolved into today's "cheerio" farewell? Tours leave from outside the Pump Room in the Abbey Churchyard (free, no tips, year-round Sun-Fri at 10:30 and 14:00, Sat at 10:30 only; additional evening walks May-Aug Tue and Thu at 18:00; www.bathguides.org.uk).

▲▲CITY BUS TOURS

City Sightseeing's hop-on, hop-off bus tours zip through Bath. Jump on a bus at one of 17 signposted pickup points, pay the driver, climb upstairs, and hear recorded commentary about Bath. City Sightseeing has two 45-minute routes: the City Tour of Bath's center and the Skyline Tour outside town. On a sunny day, this is a multitasking tourist's dream come true: You can munch a sandwich, work on a tan, snap great photos, and learn a lot—all at once. Try to get one with a live guide—select tours only—confirm with driver (£16.50, ticket valid for 24 hours and both tour routes; City Tour generally 4/hour daily in summer 9:30-17:30, in winter 10:00-17:00, no buses Dec-Feb;

BATH AT A GLANCE

▲▲▲**Free City Walking Tours** Top-notch tours helping you make the most of your visit, led by the Mayor of Bath's Honorary Guides. **Hours:** Sun-Fri at 10:30 and 14:00, Sat at 10:30 only; additional evening walks offered May-Aug Tue and Thu at 18:00. See page 145.

▲▲▲**Roman Baths** Ancient baths that gave the city its name, tourable with good audioguide. **Hours:** Daily 9:00-18:00, July-Aug until 22:00, Nov-Feb 9:30-18:00. See page 150.

▲▲**Bath Abbey** 500-year-old Perpendicular Gothic church, graced with beautiful fan vaulting and stained glass. **Hours:** Mon-Sat 9:30-17:30, Sun 13:00-14:30 & 16:30-17:30. See page 154.

▲▲**The Circus and Royal Crescent** Stately Georgian (Neoclassical) buildings from Bath's 18th-century glory days. See page 156.

▲▲**No. 1 Royal Crescent** Your best look at the interior of one of Bath's high-rent Georgian beauties. **Hours:** Daily 10:00-17:00. See page 157.

▲▲**Canalside Walk to Bathampton** This easy, hour-long stroll along an Industrial Age canal is a delightful escape from the busy town. See page 159.

▲**Pump Room** Swanky Georgian hall, ideal for a spot of tea or a taste of unforgettably "healthy" spa water. **Hours:** Daily 9:30-16:00 for breakfast, lunch, and afternoon tea (open 18:00-21:00 for dinner July-Aug). See page 153.

▲**Pulteney Bridge and Parade Gardens** Shop-strewn bridge and relaxing riverside gardens. **Hours:** Bridge—always open; gardens—daily 10:00-18:00, Oct-April open 24 hours. See page 155.

▲**Fashion Museum** 400 years of clothing under one roof. **Hours:** Daily 10:30-18:00, Nov-Feb until 17:00. See page 157.

▲**Museum of Bath at Work** Gadget-ridden circa-1900 engineer's shop, foundry, factory, and office. **Hours:** Daily 10:30-17:00, Nov and Jan-March weekends only, closed Dec. See page 158.

▲**Thermae Bath Spa** Relaxation center that put the bath back in Bath. **Hours:** Daily 9:00-21:30. See page 159.

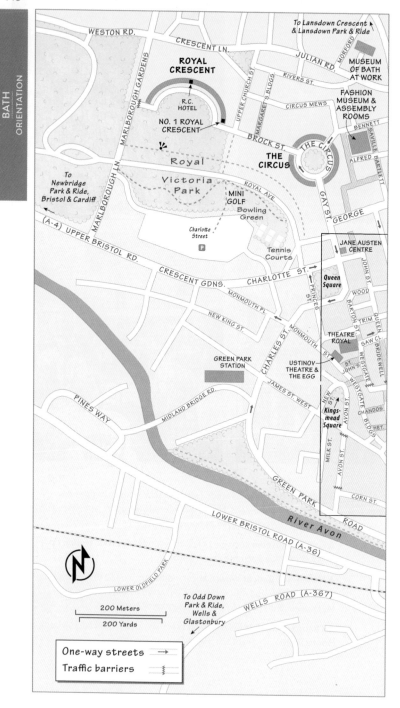

WESTON RD.

CRESCENT LN.

To Lansdown Crescent
& Lansdown Park & Ride

MORFORD

JULIAN RD.

MUSEUM
OF BATH
AT WORK

**ROYAL
CRESCENT**

UPPER CHURCH ST.

RIVERS ST.

MARGARET'S BLDGS.

CIRCUS MEWS

FASHION
MUSEUM &
ASSEMBLY
ROOMS

MARLBOROUGH GARDENS

R.C.
HOTEL

NO. 1 ROYAL
CRESCENT

BROCK ST.

BENNETT

SAVILLE

BARTLETT

THE CIRCUS

**THE
CIRCUS**

ALFRED

Royal

MARLBOROUGH LN.

Victoria
Park

ROYAL AVE.

MINI
GOLF

GAY ST.

GEORGE

To
Newbridge
Park & Ride,
Bristol & Cardiff

Bowling
Green

Charlotte
Street

Ⓟ

Tennis
Courts

JANE AUSTEN
CENTRE

(A-4) UPPER BRISTOL RD.

CRESCENT GDNS.

CHARLOTTE ST.

PRINCES ST.

*Queen
Square*

JOHN ST.

WOOD

BARTON ST.

MONMOUTH PL.

NEW KING ST.

CHARLES ST.

MONMOUTH

MONMOUTH ST.

TRIM

QUEEN

THEATRE
ROYAL

SAW CL.

WESTGATE

BRIDEWELL

GREEN PARK
STATION

JAMES ST. WEST

USTINOV
THEATRE &
THE EGG

JOHN'S ST.

WESTGATE BLDGS.

CHANDOS

PINES WAY

MIDLAND BRIDGE RD.

*Kings-
mead
Square*

NEW

AVON ST.

HET.

MILK ST.

AVON ST.

GREEN PARK

CORN ST.

ROAD

LOWER BRISTOL ROAD (A-36)

River Avon

N

LOWER OLDFIELD PARK

200 Meters

200 Yards

To Odd Down
Park & Ride,
Wells &
Glastonbury

WELLS ROAD (A-367)

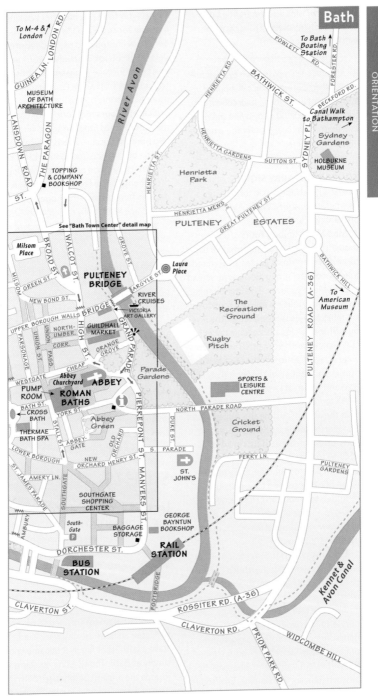

Skyline Tour runs less frequently but year-round; tel. 01225/330-444, www.bathbuscompany.com).

Rick's Tip: *Local taxis, driven by good talkers, go where big buses can't. A group of up to four can rent a cab for an hour (about £40; try to negotiate) and enjoy a fine, informative, and—with the right cabbie—entertaining private joyride.*

TOURS TO NEARBY SIGHTS

Bath is a good launchpad for visiting nearby Glastonbury, Wells, Avebury, Stonehenge, and more.

Mad Max Minibus Tours offers thoughtfully organized, informative tours run with entertaining guides and limited to 16 people per group. Book as far ahead as possible in summer. The Stonehenge, Avebury, and Villages full-day tour covers 110 miles and visits Stonehenge, the Avebury Stone Circles, photogenic Lacock (LAY-cock), and the southernmost Cotswold village, Castle Combe (£42 plus £20 Stonehenge entry, tours depart daily at 8:30 and return at 17:30).

All tours depart from downtown Bath near the abbey (outside the Abbey Hotel on 1 North Parade, arrive 15 minutes early, book at least 48 hours in advance; RS%—£10 rebate with online purchase of two separate tour itineraries, request when booking second tour, discount refunded to credit card; mobile 07990-505-970, phone answered daily 8:00-18:00, www.madmaxtours.co.uk, maddy@madmaxtours.co.uk).

Lion Tours runs full-day tours of Cotswold villages and "King Arthur's Realm" (£45 each), and gets you to Stonehenge with half- or full-day tours (Stonehenge and Lacock tour-£49; Stonehenge, Salisbury, and Cotswold villages-£61; Stonehenge inner circle access-£130; these prices include Stonehenge admission; RS%—£10/adult discount when you book any two full-day tours online, £5 discount for half-day tours—email after booking first tour for code; mobile 07769-668-668, www.liontours.co.uk, see website for details). If you ask in advance, you can bring your luggage along and use this tour to get to the Cotswolds (£5/person, minimum two people).

Scarper Tours runs four-hour narrated minibus tours to Stonehenge, giving you two hours at the site. This is basically a shuttle bus service from Bath with tickets (£25 transportation only, £40 including Stonehenge entry fee and reservation, departs from outside the Abbey Hotel on Terrace Walk, daily mid-March-Oct at 9:30 and 14:00, Nov-mid-March at 13:00, www.scarpertours.com, sally@scarpertours.com).

Celtic Horizons is a car service offering tours from Bath to destinations such as Stonehenge, Avebury, and Wells. They also provide a convenient transfer service (to or from London; Heathrow, Bristol, and other airports; the Cotswolds, and so on), with or without a tour itinerary en route. Allow about £35/hour for a group (comfortable minivans seat up to 8 people) and £150 for Heathrow-Bath transfers (1-3 people). Make arrangements and get pricing by email at info@celtichorizons.com (tel. 01373/800-500, US tel. 855-407-3200, www.celtichorizons.com).

SIGHTS

In the Town Center
▲▲▲ROMAN BATHS

For thousands of years, humans have marveled at the hot water that bubbles out of the earth on this spot. In ancient Roman times, high society enjoyed soaking in the mineral springs, and they built a large bathhouse around it. From Londinium, Romans traveled so often to Aquae Sulis, as the city was called, to "take a bath" that finally it became known simply as Bath. Today, a fine museum surrounds the ancient bathhouse. With the help of a great audioguide, you'll wander

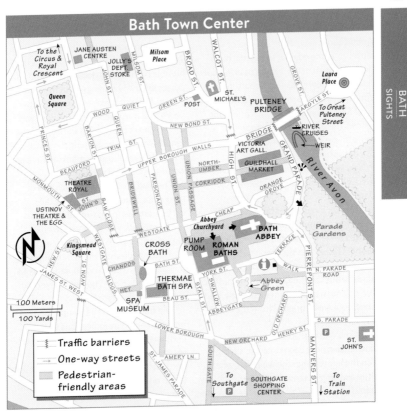

Bath Town Center

past Roman artifacts, a temple pediment with an evocative bearded face, a bronze head of the goddess Sulis Minerva, excavated ancient foundations, and the actual mouth of the health-giving spring. At the end, you'll have a chance to walk around the big, steaming pool itself, where Romans once lounged, splished, splashed, and thanked the gods for the gift of therapeutic hot water.

Cost and Hours: £22, £20 off-peak days—see website, includes audioguide; daily 9:00-18:00, July-Aug until 22:00, Nov-Feb 9:30-18:00, last entry one hour before closing; tel. 01225/477-784, www. romanbaths.co.uk.

Combo-Ticket: If you plan to see both the Roman Baths and the Fashion Museum, you can save a little with the £25 Museums Saver combo-ticket, which also covers the temporary exhibit at the Victoria Art Gallery. If you buy the combo-ticket online, you'll save more—and avoid ticket lines at both sights. Family Saver tickets fare also available.

Rick's Tip: To avoid long ticket lines, use the "fast track" lane by buying a ticket online in advance, or by purchasing a combo-ticket at the Fashion Museum or Victoria Art Gallery. Visit early or late; peak time is between 13:00 and 15:00

Tours: Take advantage of the excellent, included **audioguide**. In addition to the basic commentary, look for posted numbers to key into your audioguide for specialty topics—including a kid-friendly tour and musings from American expat writer

Bill Bryson. For those with a big appetite for Roman history, in-depth 30-minute **guided tours** leave from the end of the museum at the edge of the actual bath (included with ticket, on the hour, a poolside clock shows the next departure time). You can revisit the museum after the tour.

◯ Self-Guided Tour: This brief tour follows the baths' one-way route; for more in-depth commentary, make ample use of the audioguide.

• *Begin by walking around the upper terrace, overlooking the swimming-pool-like Great Bath.*

Terrace: Lined with **statues** of VIRs (Very Important Romans), the terrace evokes ancient times but was built in the 1890s. The terrace sits atop the remarkably well-preserved lower story, which was actually built by the Romans: The bases of the columns, the pavement, and the lead-lined pool are all original from the first century AD.

At the end of the terrace, before going downstairs, peer down into the **spring** (on the left through the window), where little air bubbles remind you that each day 240,000 gallons of water emerge from the earth—magically, it must have seemed to Romans—at a constant 115°F.

• *Now you'll head downstairs to the...*

Museum: Start with its helpful **models.** The first model (of plexiglass) shows the humble baths that stood here around AD 70. It's just two buildings, with the spring in between, but it makes clear the complex's dual purpose: The bathhouse was for soaking in the healing waters, and the temple was for worshipping the goddess Sulis Minerva who gave mankind such a wondrous thermal spring.

The next model shows the baths at their peak, around AD 325. The tallest building (with a barrel-arch roof) is the Great Bath you see today, with its big swimming pool. The smaller arched roofs alongside were other bathhouse buildings—dressing rooms, saunas, cold plunges, and so on. The red-tile-roofed section was the temple.

The fragments of the **temple pediment**—carved by indigenous Celtic craftsmen but with Roman themes—represent a remarkable cultural synthesis. Sit and watch for a while as a slide projection fills in historians' best guesses as to what once occupied the missing bits.

The next exhibits examine every day

The ancient Roman baths are surrounded by an excellent museum.

Roman life—living, dying, and worshipping here in Aquae Sulis. You'll see vases, coins, and a stone head of a big-haired woman with her trendy first-century 'fro.

Next up are a couple of rooms dedicated to **Roman worship.** You'll see some of the small but extremely heavy stone altars that pilgrims hauled here as an offering to the goddess.

• *Next you'll walk through the ruins of the...*

Temple Courtyard: Imagine being a Roman arriving here to worship at the temple, which would have stood at the far end of the room. (That's made easy by the monitors, which recreate the scene from where you're standing.) In the temple itself, you'd come face-to-face with a gilded-bronze **statue** of the goddess Sulis Minerva (the surviving head is on display). The goddess was a powerful multicultural hybrid of the Celtic goddess Sulis (who presided over the Aquae Sulis, or "waters of Sulis" in prehistoric times) and Minerva (a Roman life-giving mother-goddess), with hints of the Greek warrior-goddess Athena.

• *Now head down a hall (with more exhibits), until you emerge outside in the...*

Great Bath: Take a slow lap (by foot) around the perimeter, imagining the frolicking Romans who once immersed themselves in this five-foot-deep pool. (These days, the water has turned greenish because of algae—don't touch it.) Originally, this pool was housed in a spacious hall with a three-story-tall arched ceiling, and sunlight filtered in through vast windows.

• *Now explore more of the...*

Bath Complex: The **East Baths** is a series of rooms showing how Romans typically bathed (with naked bodies artfully and modestly projected). You'd undress in the first room, warm up in the next room, get a massage in another, then start the cool-down process in another room. The large **central hall** was a sauna, heated from below.

Nearby is a giant red brick chunk of **roof span,** from when this was a cavernous covered swimming hall. At the corner, you'll see a length of original **lead pipe** (on the right, remarkably preserved since ancient times) and step over a small **canal** where hot water still trickles into the main pool.

When you're ready to cool down, follow the route away from the big pool and into the **West Baths** with its big round *frigidarium,* or "cold plunge" pool sparkling with coins. Across the hall (up a few steps) you have a close-up look at the source of this entire complex—the **sacred spring.**

• *After returning your audioguide, pop over to the fountain for a free taste of the spa water, which purportedly has health benefits (see minerals listed on the wall). Then pass the WC, head up the stairs, go through the gift shop, and exit via (or stop for tea in) the Pump Room.*

▲PUMP ROOM

The Pump Room, an elegant Georgian hall just above the Roman Baths, offers visitors their best chance to raise a pinky in Neoclassical grandeur. Above the clock, a statue of Beau Nash—who promoted Bath as an aristocratic playground in the 1700s—sniffles down at you. Come for tea or a light meal, or to try a famous (but forgettable) "Bath bun" with your spa water (the same water that's in the fountain at the end of the baths tour; also free in the Pump Room if you present your ticket). The spa water is served by an appropri-

Sulis Minerva

ately attired waiter, who will tell you the water is pumped up from nearly 100 yards deep and marinated in 43 wonderful minerals. Or for just the price of a coffee, drop in anytime—except during lunch—to enjoy live music (string trio or piano; times vary) and the atmosphere. Even if you don't eat here, you're welcome to enter the foyer for a view of the baths and dining room.

▲▲BATH ABBEY

The town of Bath wasn't much in the Middle Ages, but an important church has stood on this spot since Anglo-Saxon times. King Edgar I was crowned here in 973, when the church was much bigger (before the bishop packed up and moved to Wells). Dominating the town center, today's abbey—the last great church built in medieval England—is 500 years old and a fine example of the Late Perpendicular Gothic style, with breezy fan vaulting and enough stained glass to earn it the nickname "Lantern of the West."

Cost and Hours: £4 suggested donation, Mon-Sat 9:30-17:30, Sun 13:00-14:30 & 16:30-17:30, handy flier narrates a self-

Bath Abbey

guided tour, ask about events—including concerts, services, and evensong, schedule also posted on the door and online, tel. 01225/422-462, www.bathabbey.org.

Evensong: Choral evensong generally takes place twice a week (Thu at 17:30 and Sun at 15:30, 45 minutes); spoken evening prayers on other days are also a beautiful 20 minutes of worship (17:30).

Tower Climb: You can reach the top of the tower only with a worthwhile 50-minute guided tour. You'll hike up 212 steps for views across the rooftops of Bath and a peek down into the Roman Baths (£8, generally at the top of each hour when abbey is open, more often during busy times; Mon-Sat 10:00-16:00, no tours Sun, tour times usually posted outside abbey entrance, buy tickets in abbey gift shop).

Visiting the Abbey: This impressive church encapsulates Bath's long history in stone. It stands near the mineral springs where, even in pagan times, people came to worship. When Christianity arrived, a monastery was built here (8th century), then a larger church (11th century). The present church was begun in 1499. No sooner was the church finished than it was stripped of its furnishings by King Henry VIII (1539), who dissolved the monastery and sold off its valuable lead roof and glass windows.

For the next phase of the abbey's story, step inside and admire the **nave** and one of the abbey's most splendid features—the fan vaulting. Next to a tomb, a stained-glass **window** depicts coats of arms of donors who financed the church's windows. Cross to the opposite side of the nave toward the right transept. Just before entering the transept, find a gravestone on the wall for "Ricardi Nash"—better known as Beau Nash, Bath's 18th-century master of festivities.

At the far end of the church (above the altar), the large **window** shows 52 scenes from Christ's life—good for weekly sermons for a year. The window to the left of the altar shows **King Edgar** being

Pulteney Bridge

crowned. Edgar (in red) sits on a throne clutching the orb and scepter while the Archbishop of Canterbury (in purple) places the crown on his head. Edgar was one of the first monarchs of what we now call England. His coronation in AD 973 established the protocols used by all future English monarchs up to the present—and it all started here in Bath.

Along the River

These pleasant, low-key sights are located along the River Avon behind Bath Abbey. Taken together, they create an enjoyable scene of shops, cafés, galleries, and people-watching.

PARADE GARDENS

Opposite the abbey, the Parade Gardens is a riverside park with manicured lawns, knockout flowerbeds, a café, and good views of the Pulteney Bridge. A great way to enjoy a sunny day is to pack a picnic lunch and pay to enter the gardens (£2, fee includes deck chairs, daily 10:00-18:00, Oct-April free and open 24 hours, ask about summer concerts some Sun at 15:00, entrance a block south of Pulteney Bridge).

GUILDHALL MARKET

The little old-school shopping mall just north of the Parade Gardens is a frumpy time warp in this affluent town. The Humbug shop sells traditional candy by the weight. Stephane has been the cheese-monger here since 1975. The leather goods shop offers Bath belts made to order. The old-fashioned barber offers old-fashioned shaves. And the Market Café has customers who've enjoyed it since the 1950s (opens at 9:00 for breakfast).

▲VICTORIA ART GALLERY

This small gallery, between the Guildhall Market and Pulteney Bridge, was opened in 1897 to celebrate the 60th anniversary of Queen Victoria's reign. The ground floor houses temporary exhibits, while the upstairs is filled with paintings from the late 15th century to the present, along with a small collection of decorative arts, including 187 porcelain and pottery dog figures.

Cost and Hours: Free, £2 suggested donation, temporary exhibits-£5, covered by combo-ticket with Roman Baths and Fashion Museum, daily 10:30-17:00, tel. 01225/477-233, www.victoriagal.org.uk.

▲PULTENEY BRIDGE

Bath is inclined to compare its shop-lined Pulteney Bridge with Florence's Ponte Vecchio. That's pushing it. The bridge was commissioned by Frances Pulteney and designed in 1770 by Scottish architect Robert Adam in the same Georgian, or "Palladian," style that John Wood the Younger was applying to the row of townhouses known as Bath's Royal Crescent. The best view of the bridge is from its downstream side. The most Palladian feature is the center of the bridge with the outline of a Greek temple seemingly stamped into the stone.

Across the bridge at Pulteney Weir, tour boat companies run **cruises**—see "Experiences," later.

Northwest of the Town Center

Several worthwhile public spaces and museums can be found an uphill 10-minute walk to the northwest of the town center. If Bath is an architectural cancan, these are its knickers. The entire area is a palatial housing development built during Bath's Golden Age of the 1700s. It's the masterpiece of the visionary father-and-son architects John Wood the Elder and John Wood the Younger.

▲▲THE CIRCUS

True to its name, this is a circular housing complex. It was Wood the Elder's great expansion, consisting of 30 symmetrical townhouses arranged in a perfect circle. The best views are from the middle of the Circus among the grand plane trees, on the capped old well.

The circle of houses is broken into three segments, so that anyone approaching from the street has a great view of the crescent-shaped facades. Each residence has five stories. You'd enter at street level into the workaday public rooms. The entrances were made large enough that aristocrats could be carried right through the door in their sedan chairs, and women could enter without disturbing their sky-high hairdos. The next floor up (with bigger windows) generally had ballrooms and dining rooms for hosting parties. The floor

above that held bedrooms. The top floor (the tiny dormer windows in the roof) housed servant bedrooms, and the basement (below street level) held the kitchen and workrooms. Wood united it all with a symmetrical facade, but the arrangement of the actual rooms behind the facade was left to the owner's discretion. If you circled around, you'd see that the backs are a jumble, infamous for their "hanging loos" (bathrooms added years later).

Note the frieze—a continuous band of sculpted reliefs—located just above the ground floor. There are 525 different panels, each one unique, depicting everything from dogs to eagles to roses, scrolls, guitars, anchors, leaves, and roosters.

▲▲ROYAL CRESCENT

This long, graceful arc of buildings evokes the wealth and gentility of Bath's glory days. The Royal Crescent was the majestic showpiece of John Wood the Younger. He took the Georgian style his father had pioneered and supersized it. The Crescent is a semicircular row of 30 townhouses 500 feet long and 50 feet tall. It's lined with 114 Ionic columns that span the middle two stories. A ground floor of large blocks and a balustrade across the roofline unites

Bath's curved Royal Crescent is England's greatest example of Georgian architecture.

it all. In typical Georgian style, the only deviation from the symmetry is in the very center of the crescent, which has two pairs of columns and a taller arched window. The building's warm golden color is typical of the city, made of limestone from the surrounding hills.

The refined and stylish **Royal Crescent Hotel** sits virtually unmarked in the center of the Crescent (with the giant magnolia growing up its wall). You're welcome to (politely) drop in to explore its fine ground-floor public spaces and back garden, where a gracious and traditional tea is served.

▲▲NO. 1 ROYAL CRESCENT

This former residence at the east end of the Crescent is now a museum, taking visitors behind the classy Georgian facade for a glimpse into the everyday life of wealthy residents during the mid-1700s. At the time, Britain was on the leading edge of global exploration and scientific discovery, and the period artifacts show the wide-ranging interests of the educated rich.

Cost and Hours: £10.60, half price after 16:00, daily 10:00-17:00, tel. 01225/428-126, http://no1royalcrescent.org.uk.

Visiting the Museum: Start on the ground floor with the **Parlour,** the main room of the house used for breakfast in the mornings, business affairs in the afternoon, and various other everyday activities throughout the evening. The **Gentleman's Retreat**—an educated fellow's man-cave—has various proto-scientific objects, like a globe, telescope, and clock. You could turn the crank of one gadget to generate a spark—a shocking marvel to show party guests before the age of electricity.

In the **Dining Room,** refined 18th-century gentlemen ate with elegant dinnerware, drank, smoked, talked business, and relieved themselves behind the folding screen. Before going upstairs, pause at the **Cabinet of Curiosities**—it's fine to open the drawers. This is a collection of odd and precious objects that a host would show his guests: fossils, tribal masks, and exotic weapons.

Heading upstairs, you enter more intimate rooms. The **Withdrawing Room** (later called simply a "drawing" room) is where the ladies would withdraw from the rude company of men to play the harpsichord and take tea on the sofa. In the **Lady's Bedroom,** you can picture her ladyship waking from her canopied bed, attended by her maid (who arrived through the hidden door), dressing at her table, and donning her big-hair wig. See the typical trinkets of a Georgian socialite, like a framed love letter and a wig scratcher. Up another flight is the **Gentleman's Bedroom,** with his wig, engravings of old cityscapes, and a great view out the window of the Royal Crescent. The visit ends (down the servants' back stairs) in the basement with the **Servants Hall and Kitchen.** Remember, the servants lived way up in the attic, worked in the basement, and served the family on the middle floors—lots of upstairs and downstairs.

ASSEMBLY ROOMS

Back when Bath was the liveliest city in Britain, festive partygoers would "assemble" here almost nightly to dance, drink, gamble, and mingle. The building was designed by John Wood the Younger as part of his real estate development. You can tour the four rooms, which, though mostly empty, still retain echoes of 18th-century gaiety.

Cost and Hours: Free, same hours as the Fashion Museum (in the Assembly Rooms basement; see next).

▲FASHION MUSEUM

Housed underneath Bath's Assembly Rooms, this museum displays four centuries of fashion on one floor. The fact-filled audioguide can stretch a visit to an informative and enjoyable hour. Like fashion itself, the exhibits change all the time, but there's always a section on historical trends. You'll see how fashion evolved— ·

just like architecture and other arts—from Georgian to Regency, Victorian, the Swinging '60s, and so on. A major feature is the "Dress of the Year" display: Since 1963 a fashion expert has anointed a new look to add to this collection.

Cost and Hours: £9.50, includes audioguide; £25 combo-ticket includes Roman Baths and Victoria Art Gallery temporary exhibits, cheaper online, family ticket available; daily 10:30-18:00, Nov-Feb until 17:00, last entry one hour before closing; free 30-minute guided tour in summer at 12:00 and 16:00, in winter at 12:00 and 13:00; self-service café, Bennett Street, tel. 01225/477-789, www.fashionmuseum.co.uk.

▲MUSEUM OF BATH AT WORK

This modest but informative museum north of the Assembly Rooms explains the industrial history of Bath. The core of the museum is the well-preserved, circa-1900 fizzy-drink business of one Mr. Bowler. It includes a Dickensian office, engineer's shop, brass foundry, essence room lined with bottled flavorings, and factory floor. It's just a pile of defunct gadgets—until the included audioguide resurrects Mr. Bowler's creative genius.

Cost and Hours: £8, includes audioguide, daily 10:30-17:00, Nov and Jan-March weekends only, closed Dec, last entry one hour before closing, Julian Road, 2 steep blocks up Russell Street from Assembly Rooms, tel. 01225/318-348, www.bath-at-work.org.uk.

JANE AUSTEN CENTRE

Although it has no actual historic artifacts, this exhibition does a good job of illuminating the world of Bath's most famous writer. Jane Austen spent five tumultuous, sometimes troubled years in Bath (circa 1800, during which time her father died), where she bristled at the vapid social scene. Visitors are briefed on Austen's life and family history through a short film and docent talk, and then head downstairs where they are free to try on Regency-era costumes and sniff era-appropriate scents, taste Regency biscuits, play parlor games such as spillikins, and pen a note with a quill.

Cost and Hours: £12, family ticket available; the friendly doorman (Martin)

Museum of Bath at Work

Jane Austen Centre

welcomes you daily 9:45-17:30, July-Aug until 18:00; Nov-March Sun-Fri 11:00-16:30, Sat from 10:00; docent talks on the hour and at :20 and :40 past the hour, last entry one hour before closing; just northeast of Queen's Square at 40 Gay Street, tel. 01225/443-000, www.janeausten. co.uk. Austen fans appreciate an included pamphlet that locates a dozen "Jane Austen points" around town.

Tea: Upstairs, the **Regency Tea Rooms** (free entrance) hits the spot for Austen-ites with costumed waitstaff and themed teas (£8-12), including the all-out "Tea with Mr. Darcy" for £19.50 (same hours as museum, last order taken one hour before closing).

EXPERIENCES

Activities
▲ THERMAE BATH SPA

After simmering unused for a quarter-century, Bath's natural thermal springs once again offer R&R for the masses. The state-of-the-art spa is housed in a complex of three buildings that combine historic structures with new glass-and-steel architecture. This is the only natural thermal spa in the UK and your one chance to actually bathe in Bath.

Cost: The cheapest spa pass is £36 for two hours (£40 on weekends), which includes towel, robe, and slippers and gains you access to the Royal Bath's large, ground-floor "Minerva Bath"; four steam

Thermae Bath Spa

rooms and a waterfall shower; and the view-filled, open-air, rooftop thermal pool. Longer stays are £10 for each additional hour. The much-hyped £49 Twilight Package includes three hours and a meal (one plate, drink, robe, towel, and slippers). Bring your own swimsuit.

Thermae has all the "pamper thyself" extras (not included): massages, scrubs, and facials. Book treatments in advance by phone.

Hours: Daily 9:00-21:30, last entry at 19:00, pools close at 21:00. No kids under 16.

Information: It's 100 yards from the Roman Baths, on Beau Street (tel. 01225/331-234, www.thermaebathspa. com).

The Cross Bath: Operated by Thermae Bath Spa, this renovated circular Georgian structure across the street from the main spa provides a simpler and less-expensive bathing option. It has a hot-water fountain that taps directly into the spring, making its water hotter than the spa's (£20/1.5 hours, daily 10:00-19:30, last entry at 18:00, check in at Thermae Bath Spa's main entrance across the street—you'll be escorted to the Cross Bath, changing rooms, no access to Royal Bath, no kids under 12). If you're not comfortable playing footsie with strangers, it can feel cramped.

▲▲ CANALSIDE WALK TO BATHAMPTON

An idyllic towpath leads three miles from Bath along the Kennet and Avon Canal to the sleepy village of Bathampton. For an unforgettable hour that gets you totally out of the city, don't miss this memorable little walk.

From Pulteney Bridge walk straight down Great Pulteney Street to the Holburne Museum with its fine modern café facing Sydney Gardens. Continue straight a hundred yards through the gardens, over the train tracks to the Kennet and Avon Canal. At the canal, turn left and walk the towpath for about an hour to Bathampton. Consider the classic **George pub** there for a nice meal and a beer (reservations smart, tel. 01225/425-079, www.chefandbrewer.com).

From The George you can hike back to Bath, or walk (on the left) along the road for five more minutes to the River Avon. There you'll find the bigger **Bathampton Mill pub,** with garden tables overlooking the Avon (tel. 01225/469-758, www.thebathamptonmill.co.uk) and the pier for the *Pulteney Princess* river cruise that glides back to Bath (see below). From here it's a £10 taxi back to Bath.

RIVER CRUISE TO BATHAMPTON

The *Pulteney Princess* cruises to the neighboring village of Bathampton about hourly from Pulteney Weir. The cruise is a sleepy float with sporadic commentary, but it's certainly relaxing, and the boat has picnic-friendly sundecks. The Bathampton Mill pub awaits at the dock in Bathampton (£5 one-way, up to 12/day in good weather, one hour to Bathampton and back, WCs on board, mobile 07791-910-650, www.pulteneyprincess.co.uk).

Shopping

Shops in Bath close at about 17:30, and many are open on Sunday (11:00-16:00). The Southgate area across from the train station hosts myriad chain stores. Guildhall Market is fun for old-school shopping (see page 155). There's great browsing between the abbey and the Assembly Rooms/Fashion Museum. East of Queen

Square, sprawling along Milsom Street is Jolly's (the UK's oldest department store), now home to upmarket boutiques. Explore the antique shops around Bartlett Street, below the Fashion Museum. The Bartlett Street Antique Centre is a collection of a dozen or so shops under one roof (Mon-Sat 10:00-16:30).

Nightlife

▲▲BIZARRE BATH STREET THEATER

For an entertaining walking-tour comedy act "with absolutely no history or culture," follow Toby or Noel on their creative and lively Bizarre Bath walk. This 1.5-hour "tour," which combines stand-up comedy with cleverly executed magic tricks, plays off unsuspecting passersby as well as tour members.

Cost and Hours: £10, RS%—£8 with this book, April-Oct nightly at 20:00, smaller groups Mon-Thu, promises to insult all nationalities and sensitivities, just racy enough but still good family fun, leaves from the Huntsman Inn, North Parade Passage, next to the TI, www.bizarrebath.co.uk.

▲THEATRE ROYAL PERFORMANCE

The restored 18th-century, 800-seat Theatre Royal, one of England's loveliest, offers a busy schedule of London West End-type plays, including many "pre-London" dress-rehearsal runs. The Theatre Royal also oversees performances at two other theaters around the corner from the main box office: Ustinov Studio (edgier,

Take a fun walking tour in Bath.

Theatre Royal

more obscure titles, many of which are premier runs in the UK) and "the egg" (for children, young people, and families).

Cost and Hours: £23-48; shows generally start at 19:30 or 20:00, matinees at 14:30, box office open Mon-Sat 10:00-20:00, Sun from 12:00 if there's a show; book in person, online, or by phone; on Saw Close, tel. 01225/448-844, www. theatreroyal.org.uk.

EVENING WALKS

Take your choice: comedy (Bizarre Bath, described earlier), history, or ghost tour. Free city walking tours are offered on some evenings in high season (described on page 145). Ghost Walks are a popular way to pass the after-dark hours (£8, cash only, 1.5 hours, year-round Thu-Sat at 20:00, leave from The Garrick's Head pub—to the left and behind Theatre Royal as you face it, tel. 01225/350-512, www.ghostwalksofbath.co.uk).

SLEEPING

Bath is a busy tourist town: Reserve in advance. B&Bs favor those lingering longer; it's worth asking for a weekday, three-nights-in-a-row, or off-season deal. If you're driving to Bath, stowing your car near the center will cost you: Take advantage of the Park & Ride lots outside of town or ask your hotelier for the best option.

Near the Royal Crescent

These listings are all a 5- to 10-minute walk from the town center, and an easy 15-minute walk from the train station.

$$$ Marlborough House, exuberantly run by hands-on owner Peter, mixes modern style with antique furnishings and features a welcoming breakfast room with an open kitchen. Each of the six rooms comes with a sip of sherry (RS%, family room, air-con, minifridges, free parking, 1 Marlborough Lane, tel. 01225/318-175, www.marlborough-house.net, mars@manque.dircon.co.uk).

$$ Brocks Guest House rents six rooms in a Georgian townhouse built by John Wood in 1765. Located between the prestigious Royal Crescent and the courtly Circus, it's been redone in a way that would make the great architect proud. Each room has its own Bath-related theme (little top-floor library, 32 Brock Street, tel. 01225/338-374, www.brocksguesthouse.co.uk, brocks@brocksguesthouse.co.uk, Marta and Rafal).

$$ Brooks Guesthouse is the biggest and most polished of the bunch, albeit the least personal, with 22 modern rooms and classy public spaces, including an exceptionally pleasant breakfast room (limited pay parking, 1 Crescent Gardens, Upper Bristol Road, tel. 01225/425-543, www.brooksguesthouse.com, info@brooksguesthouse.com). They also rent two apartments.

$$ 2 Crescent Gardens, owner Giacomo's former family home, has six attractive rooms—some with views—and a bright, open breakfast room and homey living room (family room, limited free parking, closed Jan, 2 Crescent Gardens, tel. 01225/331-186, www.2crescentgardens.co.uk, 2crescentgardens@gmail.com, managed by Monika).

East of the River

These listings are a 5- to 10-minute walk from the city center. From the train station, it's best to take a taxi, as there are no good bus connections.

$$$ The Kennard is a short walk from the Pulteney Bridge. Each of the 12 rooms is colorfully and elaborately decorated (free street parking permits, peaceful little Georgian garden out back, 11 Henrietta Street, tel. 01225/310-472, www.kennard.co.uk, reception@kennard.co.uk, Priya and Ajay).

$$$ Henrietta House, with large rooms, hardwood floors, and daily home-made biscuits and jam, is cloak-and-cravat cozy. Even the name reflects English aristocracy, honoring the daughter of the mansion's former owners, Lord and Lady Pulteney. Now it's smartly run by Peter and another Henrietta (family-size suites, limited free parking, 33 Henrietta Street, tel. 01225/632-632, www.henriettahouse.co.uk, reception@henriettahouse.co.uk).

$$ At Apple Tree Guesthouse, near a shady canal, hostess Ling rents five comfortable rooms sprinkled with Asian decor (family rooms, 2-night minimum Fri-Sat nights, free parking, 7 Pulteney Gardens, tel. 01225/337-642, www.appletreebath.com, enquiries@appletreebath.com).

In the Town Center

Since Bath is so pleasant and manageable by foot, a downtown location isn't essential, but these options are close to the baths and abbey.

$$$ Three Abbey Green Guest House offers 10 spacious rooms off a quiet, traffic-free courtyard just 50 yards from the abbey and the Roman Baths. There's a different breakfast special every day (family rooms, 2-night minimum on weekends, limited free parking, 2 ground-floor rooms work well for those with limited mobility, tel. 01225/428-558, https://threeabbeygreen.com, stay@threeabbeygreen.com, Sue, daughter Nicola, and son-in-law Alan). They also rent an apartment (2-night minimum).

$$ Harington's Hotel rents 13 fresh, modern rooms on a quiet street. This stylish place feels like a boutique hotel, but with a friendlier, laid-back vibe (pay parking, 8 Queen Street, tel. 01225/461-728, www.haringtonshotel.co.uk, post@haringtonshotel.co.uk, manager Julian). Owners Melissa and Peter rent nine apartments nearby (2-night minimum on weekends).

$$ Laura's Townhouse Apartments rents three flats on Abbey Green and others scattered around the city. The apartment called Abbey View comes with a washer/dryer and has views of the abbey from its nicely equipped kitchen.

Laura provides a simple breakfast, but it's fun and cheap to stock the fridge. When Laura meets you to give you the keys, you become a local (2-night minimum, rooms can sleep four with Murphy and sofa beds, tel. 01225/464-238, www.laurastownhouseapartments.co.uk, bookings@laurastownhouseapartments.co.uk).

$$ The Henry Guest House is a simple, vertical place, renting seven clean rooms. It's friendly, well-run, and just two blocks from the train station (family room, 2-night minimum on weekends, 6 Henry Street, tel. 01225/424-052, www.thehenry.com, stay@thehenry.com, Christina).

Bargain Accommodations

$ Z Hotel Bath (the Brits say "zed") rents spare, modern rooms just big enough for the bed—your suitcase slides in a nook below. Though tight on space, hotel frills include organic linen and a daily wine-and-cheese buffet—and best of all, it's right in the center, just across from the Theatre Royal (breakfast extra, cheaper "inside" rooms lack windows, air-con, elevator, 7 Saw Close, tel. 01225/613-160, www.thezhotels.com, bath@thezhotels.com).

¢ The YMCA, centrally located on a leafy square, is safe, secure, quiet, and efficiently run with a youthful, dorm vibe (private en suite rooms and family rooms available, includes continental breakfast, laundry facilities, down a tiny alley off Broad Street on Broad Street Place, tel. 01225/325-900, www.bathymca.co.uk, stay@bathymca.co.uk).

EATING

Bath is bursting with eateries. There's something for every appetite and budget—just stroll around the center of town. The restaurants I recommend are mostly small and popular—reserve a table for dinner—especially on Friday and Saturday.

Upscale English

$$$$ The Circus Restaurant is a relaxing eatery serving well-executed seasonal dishes with European flair. Choose between the modern interior—with seating on the main floor or in the less-charming cellar—and a few tables on the peaceful street connecting the Circus and the Royal Crescent (Mon-Sat 12:00-late, closed Sun, 34 Brock Street, tel. 01225/466-020, www.thecircusrestaurant. co.uk).

$$$ Eight Restaurant looks simple—like a tidy living room with six tables crowded into it. But each dish is a beautifully presented work of edible art, the price is right, and the service is perfectly attentive. The eight seasonal Italian/French/English dishes (at around £14 each) are small, and while you can make it a light meal, a couple could enjoy trying three or four dishes family-style (daily 17:30-21:30, 3 North Parade Passage, tel. 01225/724-111, https://eightinbath.co.uk).

$$$$ Clayton's Kitchen is where Michelin-star chef Rob Clayton aims to offer affordable British cuisine without pretense. The food is artfully prepared and presented (daily from 12:00 and 18:00, a few outside tables, 15 George Street, tel. 01225/585-100, www.claytonskitchen. com).

$$$ The Chequers is so nice I raised it out of the pub category. It's pubby gourmet, serving a small menu of creative, beautifully presented British dishes to enjoy in their handsome bar on the ground floor or refined upstairs restaurant (with open kitchen). Reasonable fixed-price meals are available from 17:30-18:30 except Sunday (daily, just above the Royal Crescent at 50 Rivers Street, tel. 01225/360-017, www.thechequersbath. com).

Rick's Tip: Most pricey little bistros offer big savings with their two- and three-course lunches and "pretheatre" specials. Look for early-bird specials: If you order within the time window, you're in for a less-expensive meal.

Pub Grub

$$$ The Garrick's Head, an elegantly simple gastropub around the corner from the Theatre Royal, serves traditional English dishes with a few Mediterranean options. There's a restaurant with table service on one side, a more casual bar on the other, and some tables outside great for people-watching—all with the same menu and prices (lunch and pretheater specials until 19:00, daily 12:00-23:00, 8 St. John's Place, tel. 01225/318-368).

$$ Crystal Palace, a casual and inviting standby a block from the abbey, faces the delightful little Abbey Green. With a focus on food rather than drink, they serve "pub grub with a Continental flair" in three different spaces: a bar, a full-service restaurant, and an airy back patio (daily 11:00-23:00, 10 Abbey Green, tel. 01225/482-666). Their lunch menu, a simpler and cheaper option, is served until 17:00.

$$ The Raven attracts a boisterous local crowd. It emphasizes beer—with an impressive selection of real ales—but serves some delicious savory pies for nourishment. The ground floor has a thick pub vibe while upstairs feels more like a restaurant (Mon-Fri 12:00-15:00 & 17:00-21:00, Sat-Sun 12:30-20:30, open longer for drinks; no kids under 10, 6 Queen Street, tel. 01225/425-045).

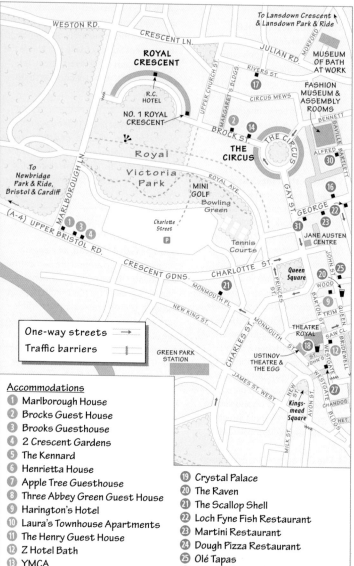

Accommodations

1. Marlborough House
2. Brocks Guest House
3. Brooks Guesthouse
4. 2 Crescent Gardens
5. The Kennard
6. Henrietta House
7. Apple Tree Guesthouse
8. Three Abbey Green Guest House
9. Harington's Hotel
10. Laura's Townhouse Apartments
11. The Henry Guest House
12. Z Hotel Bath
13. YMCA

Eateries

14. The Circus Restaurant
15. Eight Restaurant & Acorn Vegetarian Kitchen
16. Clayton's Kitchen
17. The Chequers
18. The Garrick's Head
19. Crystal Palace
20. The Raven
21. The Scallop Shell
22. Loch Fyne Fish Restaurant
23. Martini Restaurant
24. Dough Pizza Restaurant
25. Olé Tapas
26. Eastern Eye
27. Thai Balcony Restaurant
28. Yak Yeti Yak
29. Market Café & Guildhall Market
30. Boston Tea Party
31. Chandos Deli
32. The Cornish Bakehouse
33. Supermarket (3)

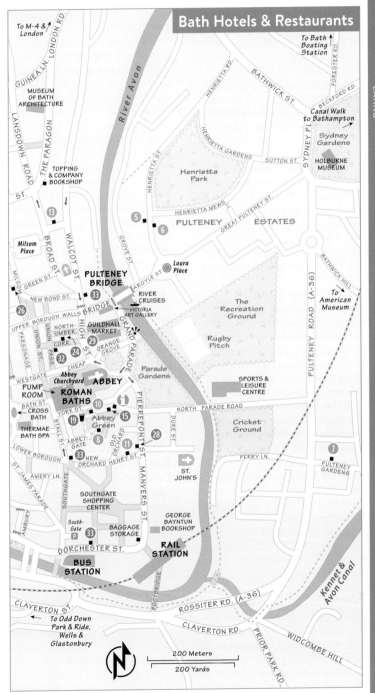

Bath Hotels & Restaurants

To M-4 &
London

GUINEA LN. LONDON RD.

MUSEUM
OF BATH
ARCHITECTURE

To Bath
Boating
Station

FORESTER RD.

BECKFORD RD.

Canal Walk
to Bathampton

BATHWICK ST.

HENRIETTA RD.

LANSDOWN ROAD

THE PARAGON

ST.

TOPPING
& COMPANY
BOOKSHOP

HENRIETTA ST.

River Avon

HENRIETTA GARDENS

SUTTON ST.

SYDNEY PL.

Sydney
Gardens

HOLBURNE
MUSEUM

Henrietta
Park

BROAD ST.

Milsom
Place

WALCOT ST.

MILSOM

GREEN ST.

NEW BOND ST.

13

PULTENEY
BRIDGE

5

6

HENRIETTA MEWS

PULTENEY   ESTATES

GREAT PULTENEY ST.

GROVE ST.

Laura
Place

33

ARGYLE ST.

RIVER
CRUISES

BATHWICK HILL

To
American
Museum

PULTENEY ROAD (A-36)

26

UPPER BOROUGH WALLS

BRIDGE

VICTORIA
ART GALLERY

HIGH ST.

GUILDHALL
MARKET

29

ORANGE
GROVE

The
Recreation
Ground

PARSONAGE

UNION ST.

NORTH-
UMBER-

32

24

CORR.

CHEAP

GRAND PARADE

Parade
Gardens

Rugby
Pitch

WESTGATE

Abbey
Churchyard

ABBEY

SPORTS &
LEISURE
CENTRE

PUMP
ROOM

ROMAN
BATHS

10

i

BATH ST.

CROSS
BATH

YORK ST.

19

Abbey
Green

15

PIERREPONT ST.

NORTH PARADE ROAD

THERMAE
BATH SPA

ABBEY-
GATE

8

OLD
ORCHARD

DUKE ST.

28

Cricket
Ground

LOWER BOROUGH

33

NEW
ORCHARD HENRY ST.

11

MANVERS ST.

ST. JAMES PARADE

AMERY LN.

AMBURY

SOUTHGATE

SOUTHGATE
SHOPPING
CENTER

St.
JOHN'S

FERRY LN.

7

PULTENEY
GARDENS

South-
Gate
P

33

BAGGAGE
STORAGE

GEORGE
BAYNTUN
BOOKSHOP

RAIL
STATION

DORCHESTER ST.

BUS
STATION

FOOTBRIDGE

Kennet &
Avon Canal

CLAVERTON ST.

To Odd Down
Park & Ride,
Wells &
Glastonbury

ROSSITER RD. (A-36)

CLAVERTON RD.

PRIOR PARK RD.

WIDCOMBE HILL

N

200 Meters

200 Yards

Fish

$$ The Scallop Shell is my top choice for fish in Bath. Hard-working Garry and his family offer grilled seafood along with fish-and-chips. Their £10 lunch special is served daily until 15:00. The ground floor is energized by the open kitchen while upstairs is quieter with a breezy terrace (Mon-Sat 12:00-21:30, Sun until 16:00, 22 Monmouth Place, tel. 01225/420-928).

$$$ Loch Fyne Fish Restaurant is an inviting outpost of this chain, serving fresh fish at reasonable prices. The big dining hall occupies what was once a lavish bank building and comes with a fun and family-friendly energy (two-course special until 18:00, daily 12:00-22:00, 24 Milsom Street, tel. 01225/750-120).

Italian and Spanish

$$$ Martini Restaurant, a hopping, purely Italian place with jovial waiters, serves family-style Italian food and pizza with class (daily 12:00-14:30 & 18:00-22:30, daily fish specials, extensive wine list, 9 George Street, tel. 01225/460-818; Nunzio, Franco, and chef Luigi).

$$ Dough Pizza Restaurant serves the best pizza in town in a fun and casual atmosphere with an open oven adding to the energy (daily 12:00-22:00, 14 The Corridor, tel. 01255/443-686).

$$ Olé Tapas bounces to a flamenco beat, turning out tasty tapas from their minuscule kitchen. If you're hungry for a trip to Spain, arrive early or make a reservation, as it's both tiny and popular (Sun-Thu 12:00-22:00, Fri-Sat until 23:00, up the stairs at 1 John Street, tel. 01225/424-274, www.oletapas.co.uk).

Vegetarian and Asian

$$$$ Acorn Vegetarian Kitchen is pricey but highly rated (with an impressive tasting menu) and ideal for the well-heeled vegetarian. Its tight interior is elegant with a quiet and understated vibe (completely vegan menu, daily 12:00-15:00 & 17:30-21:30, 2 North Parade Passage, tel. 01225/446-059).

$$$ Eastern Eye serves large portions of Indian and Bangladeshi dishes in an impressive, triple-domed Georgian hall (Mon-Fri 12:00-14:30 & 18:30-23:30, Sat-Sun 12:00-23:30, RS%—free glass of wine or beer for those dining with this book, 8A Quiet Street, tel. 01225/422-323).

$$ Thai Balcony Restaurant has an open, spacious interior so plush, it'll have you wondering, "Where's the Thai wedding?" While residents debate which of Bath's handful of Thai restaurants serves the best food or value, there's no doubt that Thai Balcony's fun and elegant atmosphere makes for a memorable and enjoyable dinner (daily 12:00-14:30 & 18:00-22:00, Saw Close, tel. 01225/444-450).

$$ Yak Yeti Yak is a basic and earnest Nepalese restaurant with both Western and sit-on-the-floor seating. Sera and his wife, Sarah, along with their cheerful, hardworking Nepali team, cook up great traditional food (including plenty of vegetarian plates). It's a simple and honest place with prices that would delight a Sherpa (daily 12:00-14:00 & 18:00-22:00, downstairs at 12 Pierrepont Street, tel. 01225/442-299).

Simple Lunch and Breakfast Options

$ Market Café, in the Guildhall Market, is where you can munch cheaply on a homemade meat pie or sip tea while surrounded by stacks of used books and old-time locals (traditional English meals including fried breakfasts all day, cash only, Mon-Sat 8:00-17:00, closed Sun, tel. 01225/461-593 a block north of the abbey, on High Street).

$ Boston Tea Party is what Starbucks aspires to be—the neighborhood coffeehouse and hangout. Its extensive breakfasts, bakery items, light lunches, and salads are fresh and healthy. They're popular with vegetarians and famously ethical in their business practices (daily 7:00-18:00, across from the Assembly Rooms at 8 Alfred Street, tel. 01225/476-465).

$ Chandos Deli has good coffee, breakfast pastries, and tasty £4 sandwiches made on artisan breads—plus meats, cheese, baguettes, and wine for assembling a gourmet picnic. Upscale yet casual, this place satisfies dedicated foodies who don't want to pay too much (Mon-Fri 8:00-17:30, Sat from 9:00, Sun from 10:00, 12 George Street, tel. 01225/314-418).

$ The Cornish Bakehouse has freshly baked takeaway pasties (Mon-Sat 7:30-18:00, Sun 9:00-17:30, off High Street at 11A The Corridor, tel. 01225/426-635). Munch your goodies at the nearby Parade Gardens or Abbey Churchyard.

Supermarkets: Waitrose has a café upstairs and racks of inexpensive picnic-type meals to go on the ground level. There are some stools inside and a few tables on the street out front (Mon-Fri 7:30-21:00, Sat until 20:00, Sun 11:00-17:00, just west of Pulteney Bridge and across from post office on High Street). **Marks & Spencer,** near the bottom end of town, has a grocery at the back of its department store and the M&S Café on the top floor (Mon-Sat 8:30-19:00, Sun 11:00-17:00, 16 Stall Street). **Sainsbury's Local,** across the street from the bus station, has the longest hours (daily 7:00-23:00, 2 Dorchester Street).

TRANSPORTATION

Arriving and Departing
By Train

Bath's train station, called Bath Spa, has a staffed ticket desk and ticket machines (tel. 0345-748-4959). The best route into the town center is the 10-minute walk up Southgate Street. Exiting the train station, turn left on Dorchester, then right onto pedestrian-only Southgate, Bath's main modern shopping street. Continue uphill as Southgate changes names to Stall

Street, glance right at a photogenic arch, then keep going another block to a row of columns on the right. Stepping through the columns, you enter Abbey Churchyard—Bath's historic center.

You can store bags at **@Internet & Luggage,** a half-block in front of the train station (£2.50/bag per day, daily 8:00-22:00, 13 Manvers Street, tel. 01225/312-685).

Train Connections to: Salisbury (hourly direct, 1 hour), **Moreton-in-Marsh** (hourly, 2.5 hours, 1 transfer, more with additional transfers), **York** (hourly with transfer in Bristol, 4.5 hours, more with additional transfers), **Oxford** (hourly, 1.5 hours, transfer in Didcot).

To/From London: You can catch a **train** to London's Paddington Station (2/hour, 1.5 hours, best deals for travel after 9:30 and when purchased in advance, www.gwr.com).

To/From Heathrow Airport: It's fastest and most pleasant to take the **train via London;** it takes about three hours total (airport to London Paddington-4/hour, Paddington to Bath-2/hour). With a rail pass, it's also the cheapest option, as the whole trip is covered. Without a rail pass, it's the most expensive way to go (£60 total for off-peak travel, cheaper bought in advance, up to £60 more for full-fare peak-time ticket; 2/hour, 2.25 hours depending on airport terminal, easy change between First Great Western train and Heathrow Express at London's Paddington Station.

Doing a **train-and-bus combination** via the town of Reading can make sense for travelers without a rail pass, as it's more frequent, can take less time than the direct bus—allow 2.5 hours total—and can be much cheaper than the train via London (RailAir Link shuttle bus from Heathrow to Reading: 2-3/hour, 45 minutes; train from Reading to Bath: 2/hour, 1 hour; £31-41 for off-peak, nonrefundable travel booked in advance—but up to double for peak-time trains; tel. 0118-957-

9425, buy bus ticket from www.railair.com, train ticket from www.gwr.com). Another option is the **minibus** operated by recommended tour company Celtic Horizons (see page 150).

Rick's Tip: Take the train or bus to Bath from London, and rent a car when you leave Bath.

By Bus

The National Express **bus station** is just west of the train station (bus info tel. 0871-781-8181, www.nationalexpress. com). For all public bus services in southwestern England, see www.travelinesw. com.

Bus Connections to: Salisbury (hourly, 3 hours), **Stratford-upon-Avon** (1/day, 4 hours, transfer in Bristol), and **Oxford** (1/day direct, 2 hours, more with transfer).

To/From London: You can save money—but not time—by taking the National Express **bus** to Victoria Coach Station (direct buses nearly hourly, 3.5 hours, avoid those with layover in Bristol, one-way—£7-12, cheapest to purchase online several days in advance).

To/From Heathrow Airport: The **National Express bus** is direct and often much cheaper for those without a rail pass, but it's less frequent and can take nearly twice as long as the train (nearly hourly, 3.5 hours, £24-40 one-way depending on time of day, tel. 0871-781-8181, www.nationalexpress.com).

By Plane

Bristol Airport, located about 20 miles west of Bath, is closer to Bath than Heathrow and has good connections by bus (Bristol Air Decker bus #A4, £14, 2/hour, 1.25 hours, www.airdecker.com). Otherwise, you can take a taxi (£40) or call Celtic Horizons (see page 150).

By Car

Parking: Park for free at one of the big **Park & Ride lots** just outside of Bath at Newbridge, Lansdown, or Odd Down, and ride a shuttle bus 10 minutes into town (£3.40 round-trip, £6/group round-trip; tel. 0345-602-0121, www.firstgroup. com/bath-park-and-ride). In town, try the **Southgate shopping center** lot on the corner of Southgate and Dorchester streets, a five-minute walk from the abbey (£5/up to 3 hours, £14/24 hours, open 24/7). For more info on parking (including Park & Ride service), see the "Maps and Guides" section of http://visitbath.co.uk.

Renting a Car: If you'll be exploring more of England by car, rent it as you leave Bath. **Enterprise** provides a pickup service for customers to and from their hotels (extra fee for one-way rentals, at Lower Bristol Road outside Bath, tel. 01225/443-311, www.enterprise.com). Others include **Thrifty** (pickup service and one-way rentals available, in the Burnett Business Park in Keynsham—between Bath and Bristol, tel. 01179/867-997, www.thrifty. co.uk), **Hertz** (one-way rentals possible, at Windsor Bridge, tel. 0843-309-3004, www.hertz.co.uk), and **National/Europcar** (one-way rentals available, about £15 by taxi from the train station, at Brassmill Lane—go west on Upper Bristol Road, tel. 0871-384-9985, www.europcar.co.uk). Most offices close Saturday afternoon and all day Sunday, which complicates weekend pickups.

NEAR BATH

The countryside surrounding Bath holds two particularly fine cathedral towns. Glastonbury is the ancient resting place of King Arthur, and home (maybe) to the Holy Grail. Nearby, medieval Wells gathers around its grand cathedral. Drivers can tour the towns easily in a same-day loop trip from Bath; visit Wells last to attend the afternoon evensong service (Sept-June only).

Glastonbury and Wells are each about 20-25 miles from Bath and 140 miles from London. The nearest train station is in Bath, served by regular trains from London's Paddington Station (2/hour, 1.5 hours).

Day Trip from Bath: Wells and Glastonbury are both easily accessible by bus from Bath. Bus #173 goes direct from Bath to **Wells** (nearly hourly, less frequent on Sun, 75 minutes), where you can continue on to **Glastonbury** by catching bus #376 (2/hour, 20 minutes, drops off directly in front of abbey entrance on Magdalene Street). To return to Bath, you'll likely go back through Wells (as direct bus service from Glastonbury to Bath is very limited). First Bus Company's £11 day pass is a good deal if you plan on connecting Glastonbury and Wells from your Bath home base.

Glastonbury

Marked by its hill, or "tor," and located on England's most powerful line of prehistoric sites, the town of Glastonbury gurgles with history and mystery. The extensive Glastonbury Abbey, laid waste by Henry VIII, is among England's oldest religious centers. It's the legendary resting place of the fifth-century King Arthur and his Queen Guinevere. Lore has it that the

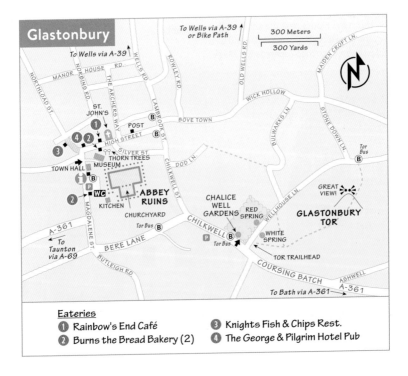

Eateries
1. Rainbow's End Café
2. Burns the Bread Bakery (2)
3. Knights Fish & Chips Rest.
4. The George & Pilgrim Hotel Pub

Holy Grail, the cup used by Christ at the Last Supper, was buried here, inducing a healing spring to flow (now known as the Chalice Well, located near Glastonbury Tor).

Today, Glastonbury and its tor are a center for "searchers"—just right for those looking for a place to recharge their crystals. Glastonbury is also synonymous with its summer music-and-arts festival, a long-hair-and-mud Woodstock re-creation.

Day Plan

Tour the abbey when you arrive in town, then ride the shuttle out to the base of the tor. Enjoy the views as you climb to the top of the tor, then stroll back to town (on the way, drop by the Chalice Well Gardens). You can picnic at the abbey or on the tor—pick something up from the shops on High Street.

Orientation

Tourist Information: The TI, located in St. Dunstan's House near the abbey, sells several booklets about area walks and bike rides, and a £1.50 map (open daily, 1 Mag-dalene Street, tel. 01458/832-954, www. glastonburytic.co.uk). The TI also **rents bikes** (£20/day, £50 deposit).

Market Day: Tuesday is market day for crafts, knickknacks, and local produce on the main street. There's also a country market Tuesday mornings in the Town Hall.

---

*Rick's Tip: Nearly every summer around the summer solstice in June, music fans and London's beautiful people make the trek to the **Glastonbury Festival** to see some of the world's hottest bands (www.glastonburyfestivals.co.uk). Expect increased traffic and crowds.*

Getting There

The nearest train station is in Bath. Local buses are run by First Bus Company (sparse on Sundays, tel. 0845-602-0156, www.firstgroup.com). The bus leaves you right in the town center, in sight of the abbey. Parking is immediately adjacent to the abbey.

Glastonbury

Sights

▲▲GLASTONBURY ABBEY

The massive and evocative ruins of the first Christian sanctuary in the British Isles stand mysteriously alive in a lush 36-acre park. Because it comes with a small museum, a dramatic history, and enthusiastic guides dressed in period costumes, this is one of the most engaging to visit of England's many ruined abbeys.

The space that these ruins occupy has been sacred ground for centuries. Druids used it as a pagan holy site. In the 12th century—because of its legendary connection to King Arthur and the Holy Grail—Glastonbury was the leading Christian pilgrimage site in all of Britain. The popular abbey grew powerful and very wealthy, employing a thousand people to serve the needs of the pilgrims. Then, in 1539, King Henry VIII ordered the abbey's destruction (as head of the new Church of England, he wanted to remove any reminders of the power of the Catholic Church).

Cost and Hours: £8.25, daily 9:00-18:00, June-Aug until 20:00, Nov-Feb until 16:00.

The ruined Glastonbury Abbey

Information: Tel. 01458/832-267, www.glastonburyabbey.com.

Tours: Costumed guides offer 30-minute tours (generally daily March-Oct on the hour from 10:00).

❸ **Self-Guided Tour:** Start by touring the informative **museum** at the entrance building. A model shows the abbey in its pre-Henry VIII splendor, and exhibits tell the story of a place "grandly constructed to entice the dullest minds to prayer."

Next, head out to explore the green park, dotted with bits of the **ruined abbey.** Before poking around the ruins, circle to the left behind the entrance building to find the two **thorn trees.** According to legend, when Joseph of Arimathea came here, he climbed nearby Weary-all Hill and stuck his staff into the soil. A thorn tree sprouted, and its descendant still stands there today; the trees here in the abbey are its offspring. If the story seems far-fetched to you, don't tell the Queen—a blossom from the abbey's trees sits proudly on her breakfast table every Christmas morning.

Ahead and to the left of the trees, inside what was the north wall, look for two **trap doors** in the ground. Lift up the doors to see surviving fragments of the abbey's original tiled floor.

Now hike through the remains of the ruined complex to the far end of the abbey. From here, you can envision the longest church nave in England. In this area, you'll find the tombstone (formerly in the floor of the church's choir) marking the spot where the supposed relics of **Arthur and Guinevere** were interred.

Continue around the far side of the abbey ruins, and head for the only surviving intact building on the grounds—the abbot's conical **kitchen,** with a simple exhibit about life in the abbey.

CHALICE WELL GARDENS

When Joseph of Arimathea brought the Holy Grail to Glastonbury, it supposedly ended up in the bottom of a well, which is now the centerpiece of the peaceful and inviting Chalice Well Gardens. Have a drink or take some of the precious water home—they sell empty bottles to fill.

Cost and Hours: £4.50, daily 10:00-18:00, Nov-March until 16:30, on Chilkwell Street/A-361, tel. 01458/831-154, www.chalicewell.org.uk.

▲GLASTONBURY TOR

Seen by many as a Mother Goddess symbol, the Glastonbury Tor—a natural plug of sandstone on clay—has an undeniable geological charisma. A fine Somerset view rewards those who hike to its 520-foot summit.

Climbing the Tor: From the base of the tor, a trail leads up to the top (about 15-20 uphill minutes, if you keep a brisk pace). While you can hike up the tor from either end, the less-steep approach starts next to the Chalice Well.

As you climb, survey the surrounding land—a former swamp. The ribbon-like man-made drainage canals that glisten as they slice through the farmland are the work of engineers—Huguenot refugees who turned the marsh into arable land. The tor-top tower is the remnant of a chapel dedicated to St. Michael, the warrior angel employed to combat pagan gods.

Getting There: The base of the tor is a 20-minute walk from the town center. You can also take the **Tor Bus** shuttle (£3.30 round-trip, 2/hour, departs from St. Dunstan's parking lot next to the abbey, daily, doesn't run Oct-March) or a **taxi** to the tor trailhead (about £7 one-way).

Eating

$ Burns the Bread makes hearty pasties (savory meat pies) as well as fresh pies, sandwiches, delicious cookies, and pastries (daily, at 14 High Street and in parking lot next to the abbey). **$ Knights Fish and Chips Restaurant** is the town's top chippy (daily, closed Sun off-season, 5 Northload Street). **$$ The George & Pilgrim Hotel**'s wonderfully Old World pub serves up a traditional menu (daily, 1 High Street). They also rent **$$** rooms.

Wells

This well-preserved little town (pop. just under 12,000) has one of the country's most interesting cathedrals and a wonderful afternoon evensong service (Sept-June only). You can still spot a number of wells, water, and springs that helped give the town its name. Markets fill the town square on Wednesday (farmers market) and Saturday (general goods).

Day Plan

Little Wells is easy to handle in a half-day. You're here to see the cathedral (try to take in the evensong service). Save time

Glastonbury Tor

Wells

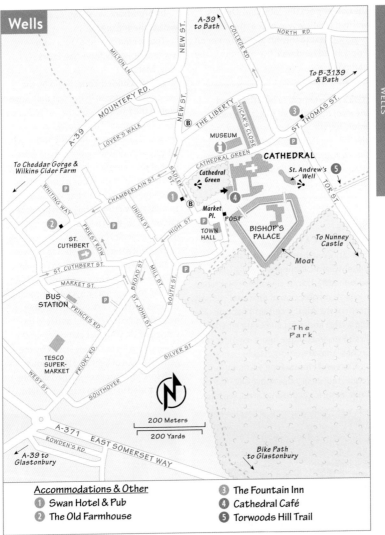

Accommodations & Other
1 Swan Hotel & Pub
2 The Old Farmhouse
3 The Fountain Inn
4 Cathedral Café
5 Torwoods Hill Trail

to explore the quaint town, especially the medieval, picturesque street called the Vicars' Close.

Orientation

Tourist Information: The TI is in the Wells & Mendip Museum, across the green from the cathedral (Mon-Sat 10:00-17:00, Nov-March until 16:00, closed Sun year-round, 8 Cathedral Green, tel. 01749/671-770, www.wellssomerset.com).

Walking Tour: If you're here on a Wednesday, consider a town walking tour (£7, departs 11:00 in peak season, 1.5 hours, leaves from The Crown on Market Place, www.wellswalkingtours.co.uk).

Getting There

If you're coming by **bus,** get off in the city center at the Sadler Street stop, around the corner from the cathedral. **Drivers** will find it simplest to park at the Princes Road lot next to the bus station (enter on Priory Road) and walk five minutes to the cathedral.

Rick's Tip: *It's hard to beat the* **grand views** *of the cathedral from the green in front...but the reflecting pool tucked inside the Bishop's Palace grounds tries hard. For a fine cathedral-and-town view, hike 10 minutes up Torwoods Hill (trail starts on Tor Street behind Bishop's Palace).*

Sights

▲▲WELLS CATHEDRAL

The city's highlight is England's first completely Gothic cathedral (dating from about 1200). Locals claim this church has the largest collection of medieval statuary north of the Alps. It certainly has one of the widest and most elaborate facades I've seen, and unique figure-eight "scissor arches" that are unforgettable.

Cost and Hours: Free, £6 donation requested; daily 7:00-19:00, Oct-March until 18:00; for evensong times, see later.

Information: Tel. 01749/674-483, www. wellscathedral.org.uk.

Tours: Free one-hour tours run 4-5 times per day Mon-Sat; fewer Nov-March.

❍ **Self-Guided Tour:** Begin on the large, inviting **green** in front of the cathedral. In the Middle Ages, the cathedral was enclosed within "The Liberty," an area free from civil jurisdiction until the 1800s. The Liberty included the green on the west side of the cathedral, which, from the 13th to the 17th centuries, was a burial place for common folk, including 17th-century plague victims. The green became a cricket pitch, then a field for grazing animals and picnicking people.

Today, it's the perfect spot to marvel at an impressive cathedral and its magnificent **facade.** The west front displays almost 300 original 13th-century carvings of kings and the Last Judgment. Now head through the cloister and into the cathedral. At your first glance down the nave, you're immediately struck by the general sense of light and the unique "scissors" or hourglass-shaped **double arch** (added in 1338 to transfer weight

Wells Cathedral

The nave culminates at the ingenious scissor arch.

away from where the foundations were sinking). Until Henry VIII and the Reformation, the interior was opulently painted in golds, reds, and greens. Later it was whitewashed. Then, in the 1840s, the church experienced the Victorian "great scrape," as locals peeled moldy whitewash off and revealed the bare stone we see today. The floral ceiling painting is based on the original medieval design.

Rick's Tip: *Lined with perfectly pickled 14th-century houses,* **Vicar's Close** *is the oldest continuously occupied complete street in Europe (since 1348). It's just a block north of the cathedral—go under the big arch and look left.*

Small, ornate, 15th-century pavilion-like chapels flank the altar, carved in lacy Gothic for church VIPs. On the right, the **pulpit** features a post-Reformation, circa-1540 English script—rather than the standard Latin (see where the stonemason ran out of space when carving the inscription—we've all been there).

In the apse you'll find the **Lady Chapel.** Examine the medieval stained-glass windows. Do they look jumbled? In the 17th century, Puritan troops trashed the precious original glass. Much was repaired, but many of the broken panes were like a puzzle that was never solved. That's why today many of the windows are simply kaleidoscopes of colored glass.

As you walk, notice that many of the black **tombstones** set in the floor have decorative recesses that aren't filled with brass. After the Reformation in the 1530s, the church was short on cash, so they sold the brass lettering to raise money for roof repairs.

Once you reach the south transept, you'll find several items of interest. The **old Saxon font** survives from the previous church (AD 705) and has been the site of Wells baptisms for more than a thousand years. (Its carved arches were added by Normans in the 12th century, and the cover is from the 17th century.) Nearby, notice the **carvings** in the capitals of the freestanding pillars, with whimsical depictions of medieval life. On the first pillar, notice the man with a toothache and another man with a thorn in his foot.

Also in the south transept, you'll find the entrance to the cathedral **Reading Room** and **Chained Library** (free). Housing a few old manuscripts, it offers a peek into a real 16th-century library.

▲▲CATHEDRAL EVENSONG SERVICE

The cathedral choir takes full advantage of heavenly acoustics with a nightly 45-minute evensong service. You'll sit right in the old "quire" as you listen to a great pipe organ and the world-famous Wells Cathedral choir.

Cost and Hours: Free, Mon-Sat at 17:15, Sun at 15:00, usually not offered July-Aug—confirm times in advance, tel. 01749/674-483, www.wellscathedral.org.uk.

Rick's Tip: *If you attend evensong and* **miss the last bus back to Bath,** *here's what to do: Catch the bus to Bristol instead (hourly, one-hour trip), then take a 15-minute train ride to Bath.*

Sleeping and Eating

The comfortable **$$$ Swan Hotel** faces the cathedral; you can get a pub lunch in their garden with views over the green and cathedral (Sadler Street, www.swanhotelwells.co.uk). For a B&B, try **$$ The Old Farmhouse** (62 Chamberlain Street).

For good pub grub, head to **$$ The Fountain Inn** (no dinner on Sun and no lunch on Mon, St. Thomas Street). The **$ café** in the cathedral welcome center offers a handy—if not heavenly—lunch.

The
Cotswolds

The Cotswold Hills, a 25-by-90-mile chunk of Gloucestershire, are dotted with enchanting villages. Enjoy a harmonious blend of man and nature—the most pristine of English countrysides decorated with time-passed villages, rich wool churches, tell-me-a-story stone fences, and "kissing gates" you wouldn't want to experience alone.

The beauty of the Cotswolds is the result of an economic disaster. Wool was a huge industry in medieval England, and Cotswold sheep grew the best wool. But with the rise of cotton and the Industrial Revolution, the woolen industry collapsed and the Cotswold towns fell into a depressed time warp. Now appreciated by 21st-century Romantics, the Cotswolds are enjoying new prosperity.

Two of the region's coziest towns and best home bases are Chipping Campden and Stow-on-the-Wold. Those without a car should also consider Moreton-in-Marsh, which has the best public transportation connections. Exploring the thatch-happiest of Cotswold villages and countryside is an absolute delight by car and, with a well-organized plan—and patience—is enjoyable even without one.

THE COTSWOLDS IN 2 DAYS

Decide first if you want to rent a car, rely on public transportation (budgeting for an inevitable taxi ride), or reserve a day with a tour company or private driver. Whatever you choose, you can see Chipping Campden (and nearby sights) on one day, and Stow-on-the-Wold (and nearby sights) on the other.

Technically, you could do it all in a day. Distances are short, so you could visit Chipping Campden and Stow, each in a half-day (they're 10 miles apart, and respectively 8 and 4 miles from Moreton-in-Marsh). But rushing the Cotswolds isn't experiencing them. Their charm has a softening effect on many uptight itineraries.

With More Time: Several worthwhile sights are nearby, which you could visit on your way into or out of the Cotswolds. To the south lies Oxford, a historic university town, plus Blenheim, England's top countryside palace. Allow a day if you visit both. To the north are Stratford-upon-Avon and Warwick Castle. Shakespeare fans could easily spend a day in Stratford, and castle lovers storm Warwick in a half-day's time.

With a Car: On **day 1,** spend the morning in Chipping Campden, then head south for a loop drive, joyriding through Snowshill (lavender farm nearby), Stanway (Stanway House open Tue and Thu afternoon), and Stanton. If you're a garden lover, head north and sniff out Hidcote Manor Garden. On **day 2,** focus on Stow-on-the-Wold in the morning, then drive to the Slaughters, Bourton-on-the-Water, and Northleach (avoiding Bourton mid-day, when big bus tours overwhelm the town). If you're up for a hike instead of a drive, walk from Stow to the Slaughters to Bourton (about 3 hours at a relaxed pace), then catch the bus back to Stow. **On any evening,** you could have dinner at a pub; take a seat at the bar if you want to talk with locals. An after-dinner stroll is especially appealing in summer, when you're treated to long hours of daylight.

Using Public Transportation: This plan is best for any day except Sunday—when virtually no buses run—and assumes you're home-basing in Moreton-in-Marsh.

On **day 1,** take the morning bus to Chipping Campden (likely departing around 9:30) to explore that town. Hike up Dover's Hill and back (about one-hour round-trip), or take the bus to Mickleton and walk (uphill, 45 minutes) to Hidcote Manor Garden. Eat lunch in Chipping Campden, then squeeze in either Broad Campden or Broadway before returning directly from Broadway (bus #1 only) or Chipping Campden (bus #1 or #2) to Moreton.

On **day 2,** take a morning bus to Stow. After poking around the town, hike from Stow through the Slaughters to Bourton-on-the-Water (about 3 hours at a relaxed pace), then return by bus or taxi to Moreton for dinner.

Getting Around the Cotswolds

By Car: Joyriding here truly is a joy. Distances are wonderfully short, and easily navigable with GPS. Here are driving distances from Moreton: **Stow-on-the-Wold** (4 miles), **Chipping Campden** (8 miles), **Broadway** (10 miles), **Stratford-upon-Avon** (17 miles), **Warwick** (23 miles), **Blenheim Palace** (20 miles).

Car hiking is great. In this chapter, I cover the postcard-perfect (but discov-ered) villages. With a car and a good map (either GPS or the local Ordnance Survey), you can easily ramble about and find your own gems. The problem with having a car is that you are less likely to walk. Consider taking a taxi or bus somewhere, so that you can walk back to your car and enjoy the scenery.

Rick's Tip: *If you want to sample a bit of* **Shakespeare,** *note that* **Stratford is only a 30-minute drive** *from Stow, Chipping Campden, and Moreton-in-Marsh. On the afternoon of your last day in the Cotswolds, you could drive to Stratford, set up in a hotel, and see a play that evening.*

By Bus: The Cotswolds are so well-preserved, in part, because public transportation to and within this area has long been miserable. Fortunately, trains link the region to larger towns, and a few key buses connect the more interesting villages. Centrally located Moreton-in-Marsh is the region's transit hub—with the only train station and several bus lines.

To explore the towns, use the bus routes that hop through the Cotswolds about every 1.5 hours, lacing together main stops and ending at train stations. In each case, the entire trip takes about an hour. Individual fares are around £4. If you plan on taking more than two rides in a day, consider the Cotswolds Discoverer pass, which offers unlimited travel on most buses including those listed below (£10/day, www.escapetothecotswolds.org.

THE COTSWOLDS AT A GLANCE

Chipping Campden and Nearby

▲▲**Chipping Campden** Picturesque market town with finest High Street in England, accented by a 17th-century Market Hall, wool-tycoon manors, and a characteristic Gothic church. See page 186.

▲▲**Stanway House** Grand, aristocratic home of the Earl of Wemyss, with the tallest fountain in Britain and a 14th-century tithe barn. **Hours:** June-Aug Tue and Thu only 14:00-17:00, closed Sept-May. See page 194.

▲**Stanton** Classic Cotswold village with flower-filled exteriors and 15th-century church. See page 195.

▲**Hidcote Manor Garden** Fragrant garden organized into color-themed "outdoor rooms" that set a trend in 20th-century garden design. **Hours:** Daily 10:00-18:00; Oct until 17:00; Nov-mid-Dec Sat-Sun 11:00-16:00, closed Mon-Fri; closed mid-Dec-Feb. See page 197.

▲**Broad Campden, Blockley, and Bourton-on-the-Hill** Trio of villages with sweeping views and quaint homes, far from the madding crowds. See page 198.

Stow-on-the-Wold and Nearby

▲▲**Stow-on-the-Wold** Convenient Cotswold home base with charming shops and pubs clustered around town square, plus popular day hikes. See page 198.

▲**Lower and Upper Slaughter** Inaptly named historic villages—home to a working waterwheel, peaceful churches, and a folksy museum. See page 206.

▲**Bourton-on-the-Water** The "Venice of the Cotswolds," touristy yet undeniably striking, with petite canals and impressive Cotswold Motoring Museum. See page 206.

▲**Cotswold Farm Park** Kid-friendly park with endangered breeds of native British animals, farm demonstrations, and tractor rides. **Hours:** Daily 10:30-17:00, Nov-Dec until 16:00, closed Jan-Feb. See page 207.

▲**Bibury** Extremely touristy village of antique weavers' cottages, best for outdoor activities like fishing and picnicking. See page 208.

▲**Cirencester** Ancient 2,000-year-old city noteworthy for its crafts center and museum, showcasing artifacts from Roman and Saxon times. See page 209.

Moreton-in-Marsh

▲**Moreton-in-Marsh** Relatively flat and functional home base with the best transportation links in the Cotswolds and a bustling Tuesday market. See page 210.

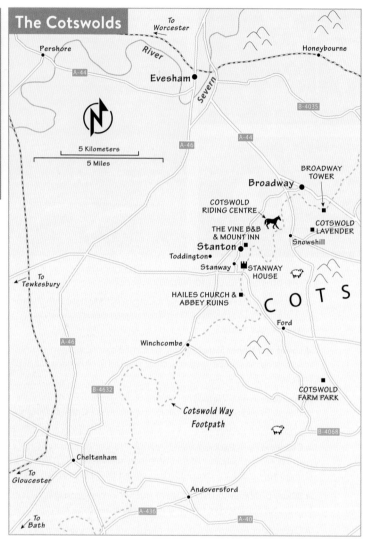

The Cotswolds

uk/discoverer).

The TI hands out easy-to-read bus schedules for the key lines described here (or check www.traveline.info, or call the Traveline info line, tel. 0871-200-2233). Put together a one-way or return trip by public transportation, making for a fine Cotswold day. If you're traveling one-way between two train stations, remember that the Cotswold villages—gener-ally pretty clueless when it comes to the needs of travelers without a car—have no official baggage-check services. You'll need to improvise; ask sweetly at the nearest TI or business.

Note that no single bus connects the three major towns described in this chapter (Chipping Campden, Stow, and More-ton); to get between Chipping Campden and Stow, you'll need to change buses in

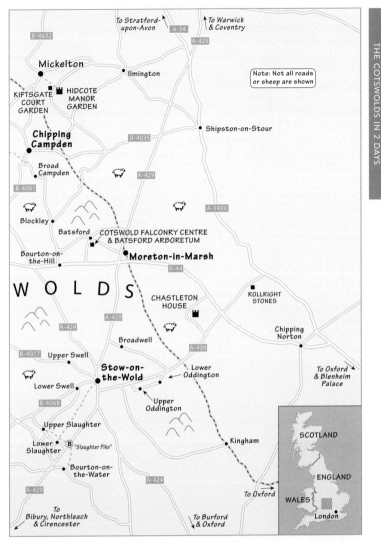

To Stratford-upon-Avon
To Warwick & Coventry
A-34
A-429
B-4632

Note: Not all roads or sheep are shown

Mickelton
Ilmington

KIFTSGATE COURT GARDEN
HIDCOTE MANOR GARDEN

Chipping Campden

Shipston-on-Stour
B-4035

Broad Campden
A-429

B-4081

Blockley

Batsford
COTSWOLD FALCONRY CENTRE & BATSFORD ARBORETUM

Bourton-on-the-Hill
Moreton-in-Marsh
A-44

A-3400

CHASTLETON HOUSE
ROLLRIGHT STONES

W O L D S

A-424
A-429

Broadwell
A-436

Chipping Norton

B-4077 Upper Swell
Stow-on-the-Wold
Lower Oddington

Lower Swell
B-4068
Upper Oddington

To Oxford & Blenheim Palace

Upper Slaughter

Lower Slaughter
B "Slaughter Pike"

Kingham

Bourton-on-the-Water

A-424

A-429
To Bibury, Northleach & Cirencester

To Burford & Oxford

To Oxford

SCOTLAND

ENGLAND

WALES

London

Moreton. Since buses can be unreliable and connections aren't timed, it may be better to call a driver or taxi to go between Chipping Campden and Stow.

The following bus lines are operated by Johnsons Excelbus (tel. 01564/797-070, www.johnsonscoaches.co.uk): Buses **#1** and **#2** run from Moreton-in-Marsh to Blockley (#1 also stops in Broadway) on their way to Chipping Campden, and

pass through Mickleton before ending at Stratford-upon-Avon.

The following buses are operated by Pulham & Sons Coaches (tel. 01451/820-369, www.pulhamscoaches.com): Bus **#801** goes nearly hourly in both directions from Moreton-in-Marsh to Stow-on-the-Wold to Bourton-on-the-Water (connecting towns in about 15 minutes); most continue on to Northleach and Cheltenham (limited service on Sun in summer). Bus **#802** runs between Stow-on-the-Wold and Bourton-on-the-Water (4-5/day, 1 hour, none on Sun). Bus **#855** goes from Moreton-in-Marsh and Stow to Northleach to Bibury to Cirencester.

Leave yourself a sizeable cushion if using buses to make another connection (such as a train to London). Remember that bus service is essentially nonexistent on Sundays.

By Bike: Despite narrow roads, high hedgerows (blocking some views), and even higher hills, bikers enjoy the Cotswolds free from the constraints of bus schedules. For each area, TIs have fine route planners that indicate which peaceful, paved lanes are particularly scenic for biking. In summer, it's smart to book your rental bike a couple of days ahead.

TY Cycles in Chipping Norton can deliver bikes to your hotel if it's within 15 miles of their shop (includes Stow, Chipping Campden, and Moreton-in-Marsh; hybrid bike—£25/first day, £15/additional day; ebike—£50/first day, £30/additional day; rates include pickup, delivery, helmet, lock, and map; Mon-Fri 8:30-17:00, Sat until 16:00, closed Sun, tel. 01608/238-150, www.tycycles.co.uk, enquiries@tycycles.

co.uk, Tom and Rob Yeatman,). If you make it to **Bourton-on-the-Water,** you can rent bicycles through **Hartwells** on High Street (see page 207). In **Broadway,** ebikes are rentable at **Broadway Tower** (see page 194).

If you're interested in a biking vacation, **Cotswold Country Cycles** offers self-led bike tours of the Cotswolds and surrounding areas (tours last 3-7 days and include accommodations and luggage transfer, see www.cotswoldcountrycycles.com).

By Foot: Walking guidebooks and leaflets abound, giving you a world of choices for each of my recommended stops. If you're doing any hiking whatsoever, get the excellent Ordnance Survey Explorer OL #45 map, which shows every road, trail, and ridgeline (£9 at local TIs). Nearly every hotel and B&B offers hiking advice and has a box or shelf of local walking guides and maps, including Ordnance Survey #45. Don't hesitate to ask for a loaner. For a quick **circular hike** from a particular village, peruse the books and brochures offered by that village's TI, or search online for maps and route descriptions; one good website is www.nationaltrail.co.uk—select "Cotswold Way," then "Be Inspired," then "Circu-

lar Walks." Villages are generally no more than three miles apart, and most have pubs that would love to feed and water you.

Each of the home-base villages I recommend has several options. Stow-on-the-Wold, immersed in pleasant but not-too-hilly terrain, is within easy walking distance of several interesting spots and is probably the best starting point. Chipping Campden sits along a ridge, which means that hikes from there are extremely scenic, but also more strenuous. Moreton—true to its name—sits on a marsh, offering flatter and less picturesque hikes.

Consider the following two hikes, both convenient to the home-base towns and with start and/or end points on bus lines (allowing you to hitch a ride back to where you started—or on to the next town—rather than backtracking by foot): **Stow, the Slaughters, and Bourton-on-the-Water** (see page 203) and **Chipping Campden, Broad Campden, Blockley, and Bourton-on-the-Hill** (see page 192).

Another option is to leave the planning to a company such as Cotswold Walking Holidays, which can help you design a walking vacation, provide route instructions and maps, transfer your bags, and even arrange lodging. They also offer six-night walking tours that come with a local guide (www.cotswoldwalks.com).

By Taxi or Private Driver: Two or three town-to-town taxi trips can make more sense than renting a car—the distances are short, and one-way walks are lovely. If you call a cab, confirm that the meter will start only when you are actually picked up. Consider hiring a private driver at the hourly "touring rate" (generally around £35), rather than the meter rate. Whether you book a taxi or a private driver, expect to pay about £25 between Chipping Campden and Stow and about £20 between Chipping Campden and Moreton.

Note that the drivers listed here are not typical city taxi services (with many drivers on call), but are mostly individuals—it's smart to call ahead if you're arriving in high season, since they can be booked in advance on weekends.

In **Moreton,** try Stuart and Stephen at **ETC,** "Everything Taken Care of" (tel. 01608/650-343, www.cotswoldtravel.co.uk); see also the taxi phone numbers posted outside the Moreton train station office. In Stow, try **Tony Knight** (mobile 07887-714-047, anthonyknight205@btinternet.com).

In **Chipping Campden,** call James at **Cotswold Private Hire** (mobile 07980-857-833) or **Les Proctor,** who offers village tours and station pick-ups (mobile 07580-993-492, Les also co-runs the recommended Cornerways B&B, listed later).

Tim Harrison at **Tour the Cotswolds** specializes in tours of the Cotswolds and its gardens, but will also do tours outside the area (mobile 07779-030-820, www.tourthecotswolds.co.uk). Peter Shelley at **Cotswolds by Car** offers custom tours in a comfy Range Rover (mobile 07968-330-485, www.cotswoldsbycar.com).

By Minibus Tour: Go Cotswolds offers a fast blitz of the most famous stops. It's an efficient way to see some of the Cotswold's most picturesque places (with seven stops in a 16-seat bus). Energetic Tom or Colin will pick you up from Stratford-upon-Avon, Chipping Campden, or Moreton-in-Marsh for a jam-packed day including about an hour each in Chipping Campden, Stow-on-the-Wold, and Bourton-on-the-Water (£40/person, Wed-Sun 9:45-17:00, tel. 07786-920-166, www.gocotswolds.co.uk, info@gocotswolds.co.uk).

Secret Cottage Cotswold Tours doesn't give you the famous stops; it's an intimate look at offbeat villages in a seven-seat minibus. You get short, guided visits to a selection of lesser-known villages, and tours include a cream tea served in a private cottage. Meet Becky at Moreton-in-Marsh's train station at 10:00 and you'll return to the station by 16:20 (£95/person, must reserve ahead online, tel. 01608/674-700, www. cotswoldtourismtours.co.uk).

CHIPPING CAMPDEN

Just touristy enough to be convenient, the north Cotswold town of Chipping Campden (CAM-den) is a ▲▲ sight. This market town, once the home of the richest Cotswold wool merchants, has some incredibly beautiful thatched roofs. Both the great British historian G. M. Trevelyan and I call Chipping Campden's High Street the finest in England.

Orientation

Drivers can find a spot anywhere along High Street and park for free with no time limit. There's also a pay-and-display lot on High Street, across from the TI (2-hour maximum). If those are full, there is free parking on the street called Back Ends. On weekends, you can also park for free at the school (see map).

Tourist Information: Chipping Campden's TI is tucked away in the old police station on High Street. Buy the cheap town guide with map, or the local *Footpath Guide* (daily 9:30-17:00; off-season Mon-Thu until 13:00, Fri-Sun until 16:00; tel. 01386/841-206, www. chippingcampdenonline.org).

Tours: The local members of the **Cotswold Voluntary Wardens** are happy to show you around town for a small donation to the Cotswold Conservation Fund (suggested donation-£4/person, 1.5-hour walks run May-Sept Tue at 14:00 and Thu at 10:00, meet at Market Hall; mobile 07761-565-661, Vin Kelly).

❷ Chipping Campden Walk

This self-guided stroll through "Campden" (as locals call their town) takes you from the Market Hall west to the old silk mill, and then back east the length of High Street to the church. It takes about an hour.

Market Hall: Begin at Campden's most famous monument—the Market Hall. It stands in front of the TI, marking the town center. The Market Hall was built in 1627 by the 17th-century Lord of the Manor, Sir Baptist Hicks. (Look for the Hicks family coat of arms on the east end of the building's facade.) Back then, it was an elegant shopping hall for the townsfolk who'd come here to buy their produce.

The timbers inside are true to the original. Study the classic Cotswold stone roof, still held together with wooden pegs nailed in from underneath. (Tiles were

Quaint and cute Cotswolds

Chipping Campden Market Hall

Chipping Campden

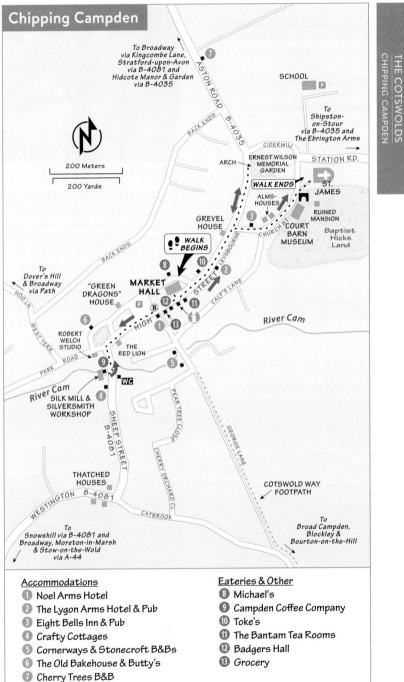

To Broadway
via Kingcombe Lane,
Stratford-upon-Avon
via B-4081 and
Hidcote Manor & Garden
via B-4035

SCHOOL

To
Shipston-
on-Stour
via B-4035 and
The Ebrington Arms

STATION RD.

ASTON ROAD

B-4035

BACK ENDS

CIDERMILL

ARCH

ERNEST WILSON
MEMORIAL
GARDEN

WALK ENDS

ST.
JAMES

ALMS-
HOUSES

RUINED
MANSION

GREVEL
HOUSE

Baptist
Hicks
Land

COURT
BARN
MUSEUM

CHURCH ST.

LEYSBOURNE

**WALK
BEGINS**

To
Dover's Hill
& Broadway
via Path

BACK ENDS

**MARKET
HALL**

"GREEN
DRAGONS"
HOUSE

River Cam

HIGH

STREET

CALF'S LANE

ROBERT
WELCH
STUDIO

THE
RED LION

HOO LN

WEST TERR.

PARK ROAD

River Cam

SILK MILL &
SILVERSMITH
WORKSHOP

WC

PEAR TREE CLOSE

SHEEP STREET

B-4081

GEORGE LANE

CHERRY ORCHARD CL.

THATCHED
HOUSES

WESTINGTON B-4081

COTSWOLD WAY
FOOTPATH

CATBROOK

To
Snowshill via B-4081 and
Broadway, Moreton-in-Marsh
& Stow-on-the-Wold
via A-44

To
Broad Campden,
Blockley &
Bourton-on-the-Hill

200 Meters

200 Yards

Accommodations

1. Noel Arms Hotel
2. The Lygon Arms Hotel & Pub
3. Eight Bells Inn & Pub
4. Crafty Cottages
5. Cornerways & Stonecroft B&Bs
6. The Old Bakehouse & Butty's
7. Cherry Trees B&B

Eateries & Other

8. Michael's
9. Campden Coffee Company
10. Toke's
11. The Bantam Tea Rooms
12. Badgers Hall
13. Grocery

cut and sold with peg holes, and stacked like waterproof scales.) Buildings all over the region still use these stone shingles. Today, the hall, which is rarely used, stands as a testimony to the importance of trade to medieval Campden.

Adjacent to the Market Hall is the sober WWI monument—a reminder of the huge price paid by nearly every little town. Walk around it, noticing how 1918 brought the greatest losses.

Between the Market Hall and the WWI monument you'll find a limestone disc embedded in the ground marking the ceremonial start of the Cotswold Way (you'll find its partner in front of the abbey in Bath—100 miles away—marking the southern end).

The TI is across the street, in the old police courthouse. If it's open, you're welcome to climb the stairs and peek into the **Magistrate's Court** (free, same hours as TI, ask at TI to go up). Under the open-beamed courtroom is a humble little exhibit on the town's history.

• *Walk west, passing the Town Hall (with the cute little bell tower) and the parking lot that was originally the sheep market, until you reach the Red Lion Inn. Across High Street (and a bit to the right), look for the house with a sundial and sign over the door reading...*

"Green Dragons": The house's decorative, black cast-iron fixtures (originally in the stables) once held hay and functioned much like salad bowls for horses. Fine-cut stones define the door, but "rubble stones" make up the rest of the wall. The pink stones are the same limestone but have been heated, and likely were scavenged from a house that burned down.

• *At the Red Lion, leave High Street and walk a block down Sheep Street. At the little creek just past the public WC, a 30-yard-long lane on the right leads to an old Industrial-Age silk mill (and the Hart silversmith shop).*

Silk Mill: The tiny River Cam powered a mill here since about 1790. Today it houses the handicraft workers guild and

On High Street

some interesting history. In 1902, Charles Robert Ashbee (1863-1942) revitalized this sleepy hamlet of 2,500 by bringing a troupe of London artisans and their families (160 people in all) to town. Ashbee was a leader in the romantic Arts and Crafts movement—craftspeople repulsed by the Industrial Revolution who idealized the handmade crafts and preindustrial ways. Ashbee's idealistic craftsmen's guild lasted only until 1908, when it ran into financial difficulties and the individual artisans were left to run their own businesses.

Today, the only shop surviving from the originals is that of **silversmith David Hart.** His grandfather came to town with Ashbee, and the workshop (upstairs in the mill building) is an amazing time warp—little has changed since 1902 (Mon-Fri 9:00-17:00, Sat until 12:00, closed Sun, tel. 01386/841-100).

• *While you could continue 200 yards farther to see some fine thatched houses, this walk instead returns to High Street. On the corner is the studio shop of **Robert Welch,** a local industrial designer who worked in the spirit of the Arts and Crafts movement. His son and daughter carry on his legacy in the fine shop with sleek tableware, glassware, and bath fittings (with a little museum case in the back). Now turn right, and walk through town.*

High Street: Chipping Campden's High Street has changed little architecturally since 1840. (The town's street plan

Cotswold Appreciation 101

In the Cotswolds, a town's main street (called High Street) needed to be wide to accommodate the sheep and cattle being marched to market. Some of the most picturesque cottages were once humble row houses of weavers' cottages, usually located along a stream for their waterwheels (good examples in Bibury and Lower Slaughter). Walls and roofs are made of the local limestone. The limestone roof tiles hang by pegs. To make the weight more bearable, smaller and lighter tiles are higher up. An extremely strict building code keeps towns looking what many locals call "overly quaint."

While you'll still see lots of sheep, the commercial wool industry is essentially dead. It costs more to shear a sheep than the 50 pence the wool will fetch. In the old days, sheep lived long lives, producing lots of wool. When they were finally slaughtered, the meat was tough and eaten as "mutton." Today, you don't find mutton much because the sheep are raised primarily for their meat, and slaughtered younger. When it comes to Cotswold sheep these days, it's lamb (not mutton) for dinner (not sweaters).

Towns are small, and everyone seems to know everyone. In contrast to the village ambience are the giant manors and mansions that have private gated driveways you'll drive past. Many of these now belong to A-list celebrities, who have country homes here. If you live in the Cotswolds, you can call Madonna, Elizabeth Hurley, and Kate Moss your neighbors.

This is walking country. The English love their walks and vigorously defend their age-old right to free passage. Once a year the Ramblers, Britain's largest walking club, organizes a "Mass Trespass," when each of the country's 50,000 miles of public footpaths is walked. By assuring that each path is used at least once a year, they stop landlords from putting up fences. Any paths found blocked are unceremoniously unblocked.

and property lines survive from the 12th century.) As you now walk the length of England's finest historic High Street, study the skyline, see the dates on the buildings, and count the sundials. Notice the harmony of the long rows of buildings. While the street comprises different styles through the centuries, everything you see was made of the same Cotswold stone—the only stone allowed today.

To remain level, High Street arcs with the contour of the hillside. Because it's so wide, you know this was a market town. In past centuries, livestock and packhorses laden with piles of freshly shorn fleece would fill the streets. Campden was a sales and distribution center for the wool industry, and merchants from as far away as Italy would come here for the prized raw wool.

High Street has no house numbers: Locals know the houses by their names. In the distance, you'll see the town church (where this walk ends). Notice that the power lines are buried underground, making the scene delightfully uncluttered.

As you stroll High Street, you'll find the finest houses on the uphill side. Decorative features (like the Ionic capitals near the TI) are added for nonstructural touches of class. Most High Street buildings are half-timbered, but with cosmetic stone facades. You may see some exposed half-timbered walls. Study the crudely beautiful framing, made of hand-hewn oak (you can see the adze marks) and held together by wooden pegs.

Peeking down alleys, you'll notice how the lots are narrow but very deep (33 x 330 feet). Called "burgage plots," this platting goes back to 1170. In medieval times, rooms were lined up long and skinny like train cars: Each building had a small storefront, followed by a workshop, living quarters, staff quarters, stables, and a garden at the very back. Now the private alleys that still define many of these old lots lead to comfy gardens. While some of today's buildings are wider, virtually all the widths are exact multiples of that basic first unit.

• *Hike the length of High Street toward the church. After a couple hundred yards, just before Church Street, there's a fine mansion on the left.*

Grevel House: In 1367, William Grevel built what's considered Campden's first stone house. Sheep tycoons had big homes. Imagine back then, when this fine building was surrounded by humble wattle-and-daub huts. It had newfangled chimneys, rather than a crude hole in the roof. (No more rain inside!) Originally a "hall house" with just one big, tall room, it got its upper floor in the 16th century. The finely carved central bay window is a good early example of the Perpendicular Gothic style. The gargoyles scared away bad spirits—and served as rain spouts. The boot scrapers outside the door were fixtures in that muddy age—especially in market towns, where the streets were filled with animal dung.

• *Continue up High Street for about 100 yards. Go past Church Street (which we'll walk up later). On the right, at a big tree behind a low stone wall, you'll find a small Gothic arch leading into a garden.*

Ernest Wilson Memorial Garden: Once the church's vegetable patch, this small and secluded garden is a botanist's delight today. Pop inside if it's open. The garden is filled with well-labeled plants that the Victorian botanist Ernest Wilson brought back to England from his extensive travels in Asia. There's a complete history of the garden on the board to the left of the entry.

• *Backtrack to Church Street. Turn left, walk past the recommended Eight Bells pub, and hook left with the street. Along your right-hand side stretches...*

Baptist Hicks Land: Sprawling adja-

Grevel House

Baptist Hicks Land

Tomb of Sir Baptist Hicks and his wife

cent to the town church, the area known as Baptist Hicks Land held Hicks' huge estate and manor house. This influential Lord of the Manor was from "a family of substance," who were merchants of silk and fine clothing as well as moneylenders. Beyond the ornate gate (which you'll see ahead, near the church), only a few outbuildings and the charred corner of his **mansion** survive. The mansion was burned by royalists in 1645 during the Civil War—notice how Cotswold stone turns red when burned. Hicks housed the poor, making a show of his generosity, adding a long row of almshouses (with his family coat of arms) for neighbors to see as they walked to church. These almshouses (lining Church Street on the left) house pensioners today, as they have since the 17th century. Across the street is a ditch built as a "cart wash"—it was filled with water to soak old cart wheels so they'd swell up and stop rattling.

On the right, filling the old **Court Barn,** is a small, fussy museum about crafts and designs from the Arts and Crafts movement, with works by Ashbee and his craftsmen (£5, Tue-Sun 10:00-17:00, Oct-March until 16:00, closed Mon, tel. 01386/841-951, www.courtbarn.org.uk).

• *Next to the Hicks gate, a scenic lane leads to the front door of the church. It's lined with 11 linden trees: Planted in about 1760, there used to be one for each of the apostles. But recently one of the trees died.*

St. James Church: One of the finest churches in the Cotswolds, St. James Church graces one of its leading towns. Both the town and the church were built by wool wealth. Go inside. The church is Perpendicular Gothic, with lots of light and strong verticality. Notice the fine vestments and altar hangings (intricate c. 1460 embroidery) behind protective blue curtains (near the back of the church). Tombstones pave the floor in the chancel (often under protective red carpeting)—memorializing great wool merchants through the ages.

At the altar is a brass relief of William Grevel, the first owner of the Grevel House (described earlier), and his wife. But it is Sir Baptist Hicks who dominates the church. His huge canopied tomb is the ornate final resting place for Hicks and his wife, Elizabeth. Study their faces, framed by fancy lace ruffs (trendy in the 1620s). Adjacent—as if in a closet—is a statue of their daughter, Lady Juliana, and her husband, Lutheran Yokels. Juliana commissioned the statue in 1642, when her husband died, but had it closed up until *she* died in 1680. Then, the doors were opened, revealing these two people holding hands and living happily ever after—at least in marble. The hinges were likely used only once.

Just outside as you leave the church, look immediately around the corner to the right of the door. A small tombstone reads "Thank you Lord for Simon, a dearly loved cat who greeted everyone who entered this church. RIP 1986."

Experiences
Walks and Hikes

Since this is a particularly hilly area, long-distance hikes are challenging. The easiest and most rewarding stroll is to the thatch-happy hobbit village of **Broad Campden** (about a mile, mostly level). From there, you can walk or take the bus (#2) back to Chipping Campden.

Or, if you have more energy, continue from Broad Campden up over the ridge and into picturesque **Blockley**—and, if your stamina holds out, all the way to **Bourton-on-the-Hill** (Blockley is connected by buses #1 and #2 to Chipping Campden and Moreton).

Alternatively, you can hike up to **Dover's Hill,** just north of the village. Ask locally about this easy, circular one-hour walk that takes you on the first mile of the 100-mile-long Cotswold Way (which goes from here to Bath).

For more about hiking, see "Getting Around the Cotswolds—By Foot," earlier.

Sleeping

In Chipping Campden—as in any town in the Cotswolds—B&Bs offer a better value than hotels. Most of my listings are centrally located on the main street (or just off of it). Try to book well in advance, as rooms are snapped up early in the spring and summer by happy hikers heading for the nearby Cotswold Way.

$$$ Noel Arms Hotel, the characteristic old hotel on the main square, has welcomed guests for 600 years. Its lobby was remodeled in a medieval-meets-modern style, and its 27 rooms are well furnished with antiques (some ground-floor doubles, attached restaurant/bar and café, free parking, High Street, tel. 01386/840-317, www.noelarmshotel.com, reception@noelarmshotel.com).

$$$ The Lygon Arms Hotel (pronounced "lig-un"), attached to the popular pub of the same name, has small public areas and 10 cheery, open-beamed rooms (family rooms available, free parking, High Street, go through archway and look for hotel reception on the left, tel. 01386/840-318, www.lygonarms.co.uk, sandra@lygonarms.co.uk, Sandra Davenport).

$$$ Eight Bells Inn rents six old-school rooms with modern en suite baths above a recommended pub (Church Street, tel. 01386/840-371, wwww.eightbellsinn.co.uk, info@eightbellsinn.co.uk).

$$$ Crafty Cottages, run by helpful lifelong Cotswolds residents Sally and Paul, supply home-away-from-home modern amenities in three cottages—two one-bedroom and one two-bedroom—right next to the silk mill (3-night minimum, Sheep Street, tel. 01386/849-079, www.craftycottages.com, enquiries@craftycottages.com).

$$ Cornerways B&B is a fresh, bright, and comfy home a block off High Street. It's run by the delightful Carole Proctor, who can "look out the window and see the church where we were married." The two huge, light, airy loft rooms are great for families with children over 10 (2-night minimum, cash only, off-street parking, George Lane—walk through the arch beside Noel Arms Hotel, tel. 01386/841-307, www.cornerways.info, carole@cornerways.info). For a fee, Les can pick you up from the train station or take you on village tours.

$$ Stonecroft B&B, next to Cornerways, has three polished, well-maintained rooms (one with low, slanted ceilings—unfriendly to tall people). The lovely garden with a patio and small stream is a tranquil place for meals or an early-evening drink (family rooms but no kids under 12, George Lane, tel. 01386/840-486, www.stonecroft-chippingcampden.co.uk, info@stonecroft-chippingcampden.co.uk, Roger and Lesley Yates).

$$ The Old Bakehouse, run by energetic young mom Zoe, rents two small-but-pleasant rooms in a 600-year-old home with exposed beams and cottage charm (cash only, Lower High Street, near intersection with Sheep Street, tel.

01386/840-979, mobile 07717-330-838, www.theoldbakehouse.org.uk, zoegabb@ yahoo.co.uk).

$$ Cherry Trees B&B, set well off the road, is bubbly Angie's spacious, modern home, with three king rooms, one with balcony (2-night minimum, cash only, 10-minute walk from Market Hall or take bus to Aston Road, tel. 01386/840-873, www.cherrytreescampden.com, sclrksn7@tiscali.co.uk).

Eating

This town—filled with wealthy residents and tourists—comes with several good choices.

$$$ Eight Bells pub is a charming 14th-century inn. It's the best deal going for top-end pub dining in town, with English dishes both classic and modern. They serve a daily special, summer salads, and always have a good vegetarian dish. The restaurant, classy pub, and terrace out back (lunch only) all have the same menu. Reservations are smart (daily 12:00-14:00 & 18:30-21:00, Church Street, tel. 01386/840-371, www.eightbellsinn. co.uk).

$$$ Michael's, a fun Mediterranean restaurant on High Street, serves hearty portions and breaks plates at closing every Saturday night. Michael, who runs his place with a contagious love of life, is from Cyprus: The forte here is Greek, with plenty of *mezes*—small dishes. "The Meze" special gives you the works with a hearty selection of small plates (Tue-Sun 18:45-22:00, closed Mon, tel. 01386/840-826).

$ Butty's is a practical little eatery offering salads, tasty sandwiches, and wraps made to order (Mon-Fri 7:00-14:00, Sat 8:00-13:00, closed Sun, Lower High Street, tel. 01386/840-401).

$ Campden Coffee Company is a cozy little café with local goodies including salads, sandwiches, and homemade sweets (Sat-Mon 10:00-16:00, Tue-Fri from 9:00, on the ground floor of the Silk Mill, tel.

01386/849-251).

$ Toke's has a tempting selection of cheeses, meats, and wine for a make-your-own ploughman's lunch (Mon-Fri 9:00-18:00, Sat 10:00-17:00, Sun 10:00-16:00, just past the Market Hall, tel. 01386/849-345).

Afternoon Tea: The Bantam Tea Rooms (daily 9:30-17:00) and **Badgers Hall** (Thu-Sat 10:00-16:00), each a scone's throw from the Market Hall, are sweet and pastel places popular for their cakes, bakery goods, lunches, and afternoon tea.

Picnic and Groceries: The **Co-op grocery** (daily 7:00-22:00, next to TI on High Street) is handy for a picnic, with a good selection of sandwiches and takeaway items.

NEAR CHIPPING CAMPDEN

Because the countryside around Chipping Campden is particularly hilly, it's also especially scenic. This is a very rewarding area to poke around and discover little thatched villages. Due west of Chipping Campden lies the famous and touristy town of Broadway. Just south of that, you'll find my nominations for the cutest Cotswold villages. Like marshmallows in hot chocolate, Stanway, Stanton, and Snowshill nestle side by side, awaiting your arrival. (Note the Stanway House's limited hours when planning your visit.) Hidcote Manor Garden is just northeast of Chipping Campden, while Broad Campden, Blockley, and Bourton-on-the-Hill lie roughly between Chipping Campden and Stow (or Moreton)—handy if you're connecting those towns.

Broadway

This postcard-pretty town, a couple of miles west of Chipping Campden, is filled with inviting shops and fancy teahouses. With a "broad way" indeed running through its middle, it's one of the big-

The countryside around Chipping Campden is dotted with charming villages.

ger towns in the area. This means you'll likely pass through at some point if you're driving—but, since all the big bus tours seem to stop here, I usually give Broadway a miss. However, with a new road that allows traffic to skirt the town, Broadway has gotten cuter than ever. If driving, check out the top end of High Street (which is a dead end, residential, and a classic/modern Cotswolds neighborhood). Broadway has limited bus connections with Chipping Campden.

To rent an **ebike,** follow *Tower Barn* signs from the Broadway Tower ticket office to a slick café and shop with fine Cotswolds goods bike rentals. From here, it's an easy pedal over country lanes to the nearby lavender fields (£9/hour, £35/day, daily 10:00-16:00, tel. 01386/852-390, https://broadwaytower.co.uk). There's also a nuclear bunker open on weekends (£4.50, closed Nov-March).

Broadway Tower ornaments a hill above Broadway. Just outside of town, on the road to Chipping Campden, signs direct you to the tower, which looks like a turreted castle fortification stranded in the countryside without a castle in sight.

This 55-foot-tall observation tower is a "folly"—a uniquely English term for a quirky, outlandish novelty erected as a giant lawn ornament by some aristocrat with more money than taste. If you're also weighted down with too many pounds, you can relieve yourself of £5 to climb to its top for a view over the pastures. But the view from the tower's parklike perch is free, and almost as impressive (daily 10:00-17:00). A short hike beyond the tower just before sunset can be unforgettable.

Stanway

More of a humble crossroads community than a true village, sleepy Stanway is worth a visit mostly for its manor house, which offers an intriguing insight into the English aristocracy today. If you're in the area when it's open, it's well worth visiting.

▲▲STANWAY HOUSE

The Earl of Wemyss (pronounced "Weemz"), whose family tree charts relatives back to 1202, opens his melancholy home and grounds to visitors two days a week in the summer. Walking through his house offers a unique glimpse into the lifestyles of England's eccentric and fading nobility.

Cost and Hours: £9 ticket covers house and fountain, includes a wonderful and intimate audioguide narrated by the lordship himself; June-Aug Tue and Thu only 14:00-17:00, closed Sept-May, tel. 01386/584-469, www.stanwayfountain.co.uk.

Getting There: By car, leave the B-4077 at a statue of (the Christian) George slaying the dragon (of pagan superstition); you'll round the corner and see the manor's fine 17th-century Jacobean gatehouse. Park in the lot across the street. There's no public transportation to Stanway.

Visiting the Manor: The 14th-century **Tithe Barn** (near where you enter the grounds) predates the manor. It was originally where monks—in the days before money—would accept one-tenth of whatever the peasants produced. Peek inside: This is a great hall for village hoedowns. While the Tithe Barn is no longer used to greet motley peasants and collect

Stanway House

their feudal "rents," the lord still gets rent from his vast landholdings, and hosts village fêtes in his barn.

You're free to wander around the **manor** pretty much as you like, but keep in mind that a family does live here. His lordship is often roaming about as well. The place feels like a time warp. Ask a staff member to demonstrate the spinning rent-collection table. In the great hall, marvel at the one-piece oak shuffleboard table and the 1780 Chippendale exercise chair (a half-hour of bouncing on this was considered good for the liver).

The manor dogs have their own cutely painted "family tree," but the Earl admits that his last dog, C. J., was "all character and no breeding." Poke into the office. You can psychoanalyze the lord by the books that fill his library, the DVDs stacked in front of his bed (with the mink bedspread), and whatever's next to his toilet.

The place has a story to tell. And so do the docents stationed in each room—modern-day peasants who, even without family trees, probably have relatives going back just as far in this village. Learn what you can about this side of England.

Wandering through the expansive backyard you'll see the earl's pet project: restoring "the tallest **fountain** in Britain"—300 feet tall, gravity-powered, and running for 30 minutes twice a day (at 14:45 and 16:00).

Signs lead to a working **watermill,** which produces flour from wheat grown on the estate (about 100 yards from the house, requires separate £4 ticket to enter).

Stanton

Pristine Cotswold charm cheers you as you head up the main street of the village of Stanton (worth ▲), served by a scant few buses. Go on a photo safari for flower-bedecked doorways and windows.

Stanton's **Church of St. Michael** (with the pointy spire) betrays a pagan past. It's safe to assume any church dedicated to St. Michael (the archangel who fought the devil) sits upon a sacred pagan site. Stanton is actually at the intersection of two ley lines (a line connecting prehistoric or ancient sights). You'll see St. Michael's well-worn figure (and, above that, a sundial) over the door as you enter. Inside, above the capitals in the nave, find the pagan symbols for the sun and the moon. While the church probably dates back to the ninth century, today's building is mostly from the 15th century, with 13th-century transepts. On the north transept (far side from entry), medieval frescoes show faintly through the 17th-century whitewash. (Once upon a time, these frescoes were considered too "papist.") Imagine the church interior colorfully decorated throughout. Original medieval glass is behind the altar. The list of rectors (at the very back of the church, under the organ loft) goes back to 1269. Finger the grooves in the back pews, worn away by sheepdog leashes. (A man's sheepdog accompanied him everywhere.)

Horse Riding: Jill Carenza's **Cotswolds Riding Centre,** set just outside Stanton village, is in the most scenic corner of the region. The facility's horses can take anyone from rank beginners to more experienced riders on a scenic "hack" through the village and into the high country (per-hour prices: £34/person on a group hack, £44/person semiprivate hack, £54 private one-person hack; lessons, longer/ expert rides, and pub tours available; tel. 01386/584-250, www.cotswoldsriding. co.uk, info@cotswoldsriding.co.uk). From Stanton, head toward Broadway and watch for the riding center on your right after about a third of a mile.

Sleeping: $$ The Vine B&B has four rooms in a lovingly worn family home near the center of town, next to the cricket pitch (most rooms share a WC but have a private shower, one room en suite, family room available, some stairs; for contact info, see listing for riding center, earlier).

Eating: High on a hill at the far end of Stanton's main drag, nearest to Broadway, the aptly named **$$$ Mount Inn** serves upscale meals on its big, inviting terrace with grand views (daily 12:00-15:00 & 18:00-23:00, may be closed Mon-Tue off-season, Old Snowshill Road, tel. 01386/584-316).

Snowshill

Another nearly edible little bundle of cuteness, the village of Snowshill (SNAH-zul) has a photogenic triangular square with a characteristic pub at its base.

SNOWSHILL MANOR

Dark and mysterious, this old manor house is stuffed with the lifetime collection of Charles Paget Wade (its management made me promise not to promote it as an eccentric collector's pile of curiosities). It's one big, musty celebration of craftsmanship, from finely carved spinning wheels to frightening samurai armor to tiny elaborate figurines carved by prisoners from the bones of meat served at

Pagan symbol in the Church of St. Michael

Snowshill Manor

Cotswold lavender

A "garden room" at Hidcote Manor

dinner. Taking seriously his family motto, "Let Nothing Perish," Wade dedicated his life and fortune to preserving things finely crafted.

Cost and Hours: £12.20; manor house open daily 11:00-17:30, closed Nov-March; gardens and ticket window open at 11:00, last entry one hour before closing, restaurant, tel. 01386/852-410, www.nationaltrust.org.uk/snowshillmanor.

Getting There: There's no direct access from the square; instead, the entrance and parking lot are about a half-mile up the road toward Broadway. Park there and follow the long walkway through the garden to get to the house. A golf-cart-type shuttle to the house is available for those who need assistance.

Getting In: This popular sight strictly limits the number of entering visitors by doling out entry times. No reservations are possible; to get a slot, you must report to the ticket desk. It can be up to an hour's wait—even more on busy days, especially weekends (when they can sell out for the day as early as 14:00). Tickets go on sale and the gardens open at 11:00. A good strategy is to arrive close to the opening time, and if there's a wait, enjoy the gardens (it's a 10-minute walk to the manor).

COTSWOLD LAVENDER

In 2000, farmer Charlie Byrd realized that tourists love lavender. He planted his farm with 250,000 plants, and now visitors come to wander among his 53

acres, which burst with gorgeous lavender blossoms from mid-June through late August. His fragrant fantasy peaks late each July. Lavender—so famous in France's Provence—is not indigenous to this region, but it fits the climate and soil just fine. A free flier in the shop explains the variations of blooming flowers. Farmer Byrd produces lavender oil (an herbal product valued since ancient times for its healing, calming, and fragrant qualities) and sells it in a delightful shop, along with many other lavender-themed items. In the café, enjoy a pot of lavender-flavored tea with a lavender scone.

Cost and Hours: Free to enter shop and café, £4 to walk through the fields and the distillery; generally open June-Aug daily 10:00-17:00, closed Sept-May, schedule changes annually depending on when the lavender blooms—call ahead or check their website; tel. 01386/854-821, www.cotswoldlavender.co.uk.

Getting There: It's a half-mile out of Snowshill on the road toward Chipping Campden (easy parking). Entering Snowshill from the road to the manor (described earlier), take the left fork, then turn left again at the end of the village.

Hidcote Manor Garden

Less "on the way" between towns than the other sights in this section, the grounds around this manor house are well worth a detour (and ▲) if you like gardens. Hidcote is where garden designers pioneered the notion of creating a series of outdoor "rooms," each with a unique theme (such as maple room, red room, and so on) and separated by a yew-tree hedge. The garden's design, inspired by the Arts and Crafts movement, is most formal near the house and becomes more pastoral as it approaches the countryside. Follow your nose through a clever series of small gardens that lead delightfully from one to the next. Among the best in England, Hidcote Gardens are at their fragrant peak from May through August.

Cost and Hours: £13.50; daily 10:00-18:00, Oct until 17:00; Nov-mid-Dec Sat-Sun 11:00-16:00, closed Mon-Fri; closed mid-Dec-Feb; last entry one hour before closing, café, restaurant, tel. 01386/438-333, www.nationaltrust.org.uk/hidcote.

Getting There: If you're driving, it's four miles northeast of Chipping Campden—roughly toward Ilmington. The gardens are accessible by bus, then a 45-minute country walk uphill. Buses #1 and #2 take you to Mickleton (one stop past Chipping Campden), where a footpath begins next to the churchyard. Continuing more or less straight, the path leads through sheep pastures and ends at Hidcote's driveway.

Broad Campden, Blockley, and Bourton-on-the-Hill

This trio of pleasant villages (worth ▲) lines up along an off-the-beaten-path road between Chipping Campden and Moreton or Stow. **Broad Campden,** just on the outskirts of Chipping Campden, has some of the cutest thatched-roof houses I've seen. **Blockley,** nestled higher in the picturesque hills, is a popular setting for films. The same road continues on to **Bourton-on-the-Hill** (pictured), with fine views looking down into a valley. Blockley is connected to Chipping Campden by bus #1 and #2, or you can walk (easy to Broad Campden, more challenging to the other two—see page 192).

STOW-ON-THE-WOLD

Located 10 miles south of Chipping Campden, Stow-on-the-Wold—with a name that means "meeting place on the uplands"—is the highest town in the Cotswolds. Despite its crowds, it retains its charm, and it merits ▲▲. Most of the tourists are day-trippers, so nights—even

Stow-on-the-Wold

in the peak of summer—are peaceful. Stow has no real sights other than the town itself, some good pubs, antiques stores, and cute shops draped seductively around a big town square. Visit the church, with its evocative old door guarded by ancient yew trees and the tombs of wool tycoons. A visit to Stow is not complete until you've locked your partner in the stocks on the village green.

Orientation

Drivers can park anywhere on Market Square free for two hours, and overnight between 18:00 and 9:00 (combining overnight plus daily 2-hour allowances means you can park free 16:00-11:00—they note your license, so you can't just move to another spot after your time is up; £50 tickets for offenders). You can also park for free on some streets farther from the center (such as Park Street and Well Lane) for an unlimited amount of time. A convenient pay-and-display lot is at the bottom of town (toward the Oddingtons), and there's free long-stay parking adjacent to the lot at Tesco Supermarket—an easy five-minute walk north of town (follow the signs).

Tourist Information: A small visitor information center—little more than a rack of brochures staffed by volunteers—is run out of the library in St. Edwards Hall on the main square (hours generally Mon-Sat 10:00-14:00, sometimes as late as 19:00, closed Sun; Oct-April Sat 10:00-14:00 only, tel. 01451/870-998). The TI in Moreton-in-Marsh is more serious (see page 210).

Sunday Morning Town Walk: Volunteers give charming guided town walks once a week to raise a little money for community projects. It's fun to mix with English visitors as a local tells the town's story (£5, April-Sept Sun at 10:30, just show up at the stocks on Market Square).

◐ Stow-on-the-Wold Walk

This six-stop self-guided walk covers about 500 yards and takes about 45 minutes. We'll start in the small park on the main square.

The Stocks on Market Square: Imagine this village during the 17th century when people were publicly ridiculed in stocks like this as a punishment. (Lock up your travel partner for a fun photo op.) Stow was born in pre-Roman times; it's where three trade routes crossed at a high point in the region (altitude: 800 feet). This square was the site of an Iron Age fort, and then a Roman garrison town. Starting in 1107, Stow was the site of an international fair, and people came from as far away as Italy to shop for wool fleeces on this vast, grassy expanse. Picture it in the Middle Ages (minus all the parked cars, and before the buildings in the center were added): a public commons and grazing ground, paths worn through the grass, and no well. Until the late 1800s, Stow had no running water; women fetched water from the "Roman Well" a quarter-mile down the hill.

With as many as 20,000 sheep sold in a single day, this square was a thriving scene. And Stow was filled with inns and pubs to keep everyone housed, fed, and watered.

Most of the buildings you see date from the 17th and 18th centuries. A thin skin of topsoil covers the Cotswold limestone, from which these buildings were made. The local limestone is easy to cut, hardens after contact with the air, and darkens with age. Many buildings were made of stone quarried right on site—with the mini quarries becoming their cellars.

That's why the **Stow Lodge** (next to the church) lies a little lower than the church. It sits on the spot where locals quarried stones for the church. That building, originally the rectory, is now a hotel. The church (where we'll end this little walk) is made of Cotswold stone, and marks the summit of the hill upon

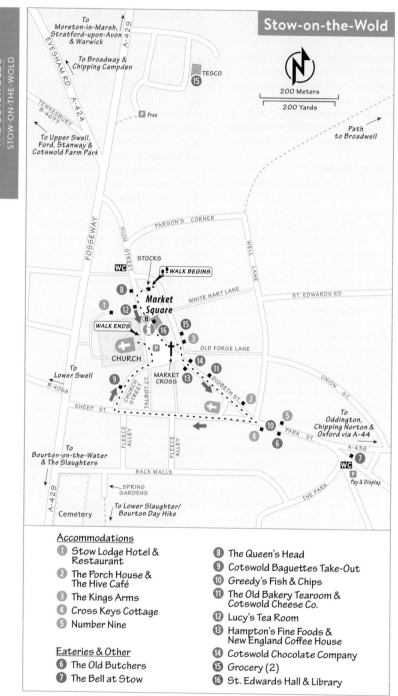

Stow-on-the-Wold

Accommodations

1. Stow Lodge Hotel & Restaurant
2. The Porch House & The Hive Café
3. The Kings Arms
4. Cross Keys Cottage
5. Number Nine

Eateries & Other

6. The Old Butchers
7. The Bell at Stow
8. The Queen's Head
9. Cotswold Baguettes Take-Out
10. Greedy's Fish & Chips
11. The Old Bakery Tearoom & Cotswold Cheese Co.
12. Lucy's Tea Room
13. Hampton's Fine Foods & New England Coffee House
14. Cotswold Chocolate Company
15. Grocery (2)
16. St. Edwards Hall & Library

which the town was built.

The **Stag Inn,** ahead on the left, was a typical coaching inn from a time before trains and cars, when land transport was literally horsepower. As horses could manage about 25 miles without a rest, coaches stopped at coaching inns to swap teams of horses. Taking advantage of such a relay of horses, travelers could go from London to Liverpool in 10 days.

As you walk, notice how locals stop to chat with each other to catch up on local news: This is a tight-knit little community.

• *Walk around the right of the building in the middle of the square and enter the library.*

St. Edwards Hall: The stately building in the square with the wooden steeple is St. Edwards Hall. Back in the 1870s, a bank couldn't locate the owner of an account containing a small fortune, so it donated the funds to the town to build this civic center. It serves as a City Hall, library, TI, and meeting place. When it's open, you can wander around upstairs to see the largest collection of Civil War portrait paintings in England—well described and an education in local 17th-century history.

The library offers a candid peek at town life: community bulletin board, volunteers, history in a glass case, and historic town photos.

• *Beyond the library, at the far end of the square find the free-standing stone cross.*

The Market Cross: For 500 years, the Market Cross stood in the market reminding all Christian merchants to "trade fairly under the sight of God." Notice the stubs of the iron fence in the stone base—a reminder of how countless wrought-iron fences were cut down and given to the government to be melted down during World War II. One of the plaques on the cross honors the Lord of the Manor, who donated money back to his tenants, allowing the town to finally finance running water in 1878. Panels at the top of the cross feature St. Edward, the Crucifixion, the wool trade, and a memorial to the Battle of Stow.

This is the site of the 1646 Battle of Stow. During the English Civil War, which pitted Parliamentarians against Royalists, Stow-on-the-Wold remained staunchly loyal to the king. The final battle of

St. Edward's Hall

Market Cross

England's first Civil War was fought on this square as about 3,000 troops loyal to the king made their last stand. About 200 Royalist troops were killed (and survivors were locked up in the church). Ultimately, this cleared the way for the beheading of King Charles I and the rise of Oliver Cromwell.

Scan the square for **The Kings Arms,** with its great gables and spindly chimney. This square was where travelers parked their horses before spending the night at the inn. In the 1600s, this inn was considered the premium "posting house" between London and Birmingham. Because of its allegiance to the king, the town has an abundance of pubs with royal names (King's This and Queen's That).

Today, The Kings Arms cooks up pub grub and rents rooms upstairs. It's the opposite of a "free house"—it's part of a big chain owned by a national brewery and therefore does not offer any of the local beers on tap.

• Walk down Digbeth Street.

Digbeth Street: This street is lined with workaday shops, cute gift shops, many good little eateries, and beautiful Cotswold stone. It starts with a handy ATM. Then, from top to bottom you'll find: Hampton's Fine Foods (local gifty edibles), Cotswold Chocolate Company (pop in to watch Tony working in the back kitchen and his wife, Heidi, decorating his concoctions), the New England Coffee House (which feels like a village Starbucks with cozy lounge rooms upstairs), a "saddlery" for the many local horse enthusiasts, Lambournes (a traditional butcher), Cotswold Cheese Company (with old milk churns flanking the door), and the recommended Old Bakery Tearoom (good for a cream tea or lunch).

Digbeth ends at a little triangular park in front of the former Methodist Church and across from the Porch House Hotel, with timbers that date from 947 (it claims—along with about 20 others—to be the oldest in England).

Just beyond the small grassy triangle was the place where locals gathered for bloody cockfights and bearbaiting (watching packs of hungry dogs tear at bears).

Today this is where—twice a year, in May and October—the Stow Horse Fair attracts thousands of nomadic Roma and Travellers from far and wide. (It's a challenging time for the town, and many shops and pubs actually close up for the fair.)

• Hook right and hike up the wide street.

Sheep Street: As you head up Sheep Street, you'll pass a boutique-filled former brewery yard (on the left). Notice the old brewery's fancy street-front office, with its striking Welsh flint facade. This was the bad side of town (with the "smelly trades"). Across the street from the brewery was the slaughterhouse. And Sheep Street was originally not a street, but a staging place for medieval sheep markets. The sheep would be gathered here, then paraded into the market on the main square.

You'll notice narrow lanes on either side of the street. There are two explanations: one I like to believe (paths just wide enough for a single file of sheep to walk down, making it easier for merchants to count them) and another that's more likely true (practical walks between the long, narrow, medieval strips of land allotments). You'll see several of these so-called "fleece alleys" as you walk up the street.

• Walk a couple blocks until you're one block from the traffic light and the highway, then make a right onto cute little Church Street, which leads to the church.

St. Edwards Church: Before entering the church, circle it. On the back side, a wooden door is flanked by two ancient yew trees. While many see the door and think of the Christian scripture, "Behold, I stand at the door and knock," J. R. R. Tolkien fans see something quite different. Tolkien hiked the Cotswolds, and had a passion for sketching evocative trees such

sons defending the realm. It's sliced from an ancient fluted column (which locals believe is from Ephesus, Turkey).

During the English Civil War in the mid-1600s, the church was ransacked, and hundreds of soldiers were imprisoned here. The tombstone on the floor in front of the altar remembers the Royalist Captain Francis Keyt. His long hair, lace, and sash indicate he was a "cavalier," and true-blue to the king (Cromwellians were called "round heads"—named for their short hair). Study the crude provincial art—childlike skulls and (in the upper corners) symbols of his service to the king (armor, weapons).

Finally, don't miss the kneelers tucked in the pews. These are made by a committed band of women known as "the Kneeler Group." And with Reverend Martin Short for the pastor, the services could be pretty lively.

The door claimed by Tolkien fans as the portal to Middle Earth

as this. *Lord of the Rings* enthusiasts are convinced this must be the inspiration for the Doors of Durin, leading into Moria.

Notice the two "bale tombs" (10 steps to the right of the door). Wool merchant gravestones were topped with a carved image of a tightly bound bale of wool.

Enter the church (usually open 9:00-17:00, except during services). While a wooden Saxon church stood here in the 10th century, today's structure is mostly from the 15th century. Its history is played up in leaflets and plaques just inside the door. The floor is paved with the tombs of big shots, who made their money from wool and are still boastful in death. (Find the tombs crowned with the bales of wool.) Most of the windows are traditional Victorian (19th century) designs, but the two sets high up in the clerestory are from the dreamier Pre-Raphaelite school.

On the right wall, as you approach the altar, a monument remembers the many boys from this small town who were lost in World War I (50 out of a population of 2,000). There were far fewer in World War II. The biscuit-shaped plaque remembers an admiral from Stow who lost four

Hiking

Stow is made to order for day hikes. The most popular is the downhill stroll to **Lower Slaughter** (3 miles), then on to **Bourton-on-the-Water** (about 1.5 miles more). It's a two-hour walk if you keep up a brisk pace and don't stop, but dawdlers should allow three to four hours. At the end, from Bourton-on-the-Water, a bus can bring you back to Stow. While those with keen eyes can follow this walk by spotting trail signs, it can't hurt to download or bring a map (ask to borrow one at your B&B). Note that these three towns are described in more detail starting on page 206.

To reach the trail from Stow, walk to the top of Sheep Street. At the busy A-429 highway, turn left. Head south of town on a footpath alongside the busy highway, past the gas station for a couple hundred yards. Leave the highway on a well-marked trail (on the right) at Quarwood Cottage. You'll see a gravel lane with a green sign noting *Public Footpath/Gloucestershire Way/Monarch's Way*.

Follow this trail for a delightful hour across farms, through romantic gates, across a fancy driveway, and past Gainsborough-painting vistas. You'll enjoy an intimate backyard look at local farm life. Although it seems like you could lose the trail, tiny easy-to-miss signs (yellow *Public Footpath* arrows—sometimes also marked *Gloucestershire Way* or *The Monarch's Way*—usually embedded in fence posts) keep you on target—watch for these very carefully to avoid getting lost. Finally, passing a cricket pitch, you reach Lower Slaughter, with its fine church and a mill creek leading up to its mill. (The people at the mill can call a taxi for a quick return to Stow.)

From Lower Slaughter, you can continue 30 minutes on Monarch's Way (follow green signs) into touristy Bourton-on-the-Water. Enjoy some time in Bourton itself and—when ready—catch the bus from in front of the Edinburgh Woolen Mill back to Stow (bus #801 departs roughly hourly, none on Sun, 10-minute ride; bus #802 also connects to Stow).

Sleeping

$$$ Stow Lodge Hotel fills the historic church rectory with lots of old English charm. Facing the town square, with its own sprawling and peaceful garden, this lavish old place offers 21 large, thoughtfully appointed rooms with soft beds, stately public spaces, and a cushy-chair lounge (closed Jan, free parking, The Square, tel. 01451/830-485, www.stowlodge.co.uk, info@stowlodge.co.uk, helpful Hartley family).

$$ The Porch House rents 13 updated rooms with stone-wall and wood-beam accents (Digbeth Street, tel. 01451/870-048, www.porch-house.co.uk, info@porch-house.co.uk).

$$ The Kings Arms, with 10 rooms above a pub, manages to keep its historic Cotswold character while still feeling fresh and modern in all the right ways (steep stairs, three slightly shabby "cottages" out back, free parking, Market Square, tel. 01451/830-364, www.kingsarmsstow.co.uk, info@kingsarmsstow.co.uk, Chris).

$$ Cross Keys Cottage offers four smallish but smartly updated rooms—

The old mill at Lower Slaughter

some bright and floral, others classy white—with modern bathrooms. Kindly Margaret and Roger Welton take care of their guests in this 17th-century beamed cottage (RS%, call ahead to confirm arrival time, Park Street, tel. 01451/831-128, www.crosskeyscottage.co.uk, rogxmag@hotmail.com).

$ Number Nine has three large, bright, refurbished, and tastefully decorated rooms. This 200-year-old home comes with watch-your-head beamed ceilings and beautiful old wooden doors (9 Park Street, tel. 01451/870-333, mobile 07779-006-539, www.number-nine.info, enquiries@number-nine.info, James and Carol Brown).

Eating

These places are all within a five-minute walk of each other, either on the main square or downhill on Queen and Park streets.

Restaurants and Pubs

$$$ The Old Butchers, named for its location rather than its menu, specializes in fish. Serving oysters, scallops, and fish along with steak and burgers, they offer both indoor and outdoor tables and a good wine list (daily 12:00-14:30 & 18:30-21:30, 7 Park Street, tel. 01451/831-700) .

$$ Stow Lodge is *the* choice of the town's proper ladies. There are two parts: The formal but friendly bar serves fine pub grub (daily 12:00-14:00 & 19:00-20:30); the restaurant serves a popular £30 three-course dinner (nightly, veggie options, good wines, just off main square, tel. 01451/830-485, Val). On a sunny day, the pub serves lunch in the well-manicured garden, where you'll feel quite aristocratic.

$$$ The Bell at Stow, at the end of Park Street (on the edge of town), has a youthful pub energy for a drink or for a full meal. They serve up classic English dishes with seasonal, locally sourced ingredients (daily 12:00-21:00, reservations recommended, tel. 01451/870-916, www.thebellatstow.com).

$$ The Queen's Head faces Market Square, near Stow Lodge. With a classic pub vibe, it's a great place to bring your dog and watch the eccentrics while you eat pub grub and drink the local Cotswold brew, Donnington Ale. They have a meat pie of the day and good fish-and-chips (beer garden out back, Mon-Sat 12:00-14:30 & 18:30-21:00, Sun 12:30-16:00, tel. 01451/830-563).

Cheaper Options

$ Cotswold Baguettes Take-Out has a line out the door for tasty takeout jacket potatoes, pasties, made-to-order sandwiches, and soup (Mon-Fri 9:00-16:00, Sat until 13:00, closed Sun, Church Street, tel. 01451/831-362).

$ Greedy's Fish and Chips, on Park Street, is the go-to place for takeout. There's no seating, but they have benches out front (Mon-Sat 12:00-14:00 & 16:30-20:30, closed Sun, tel. 01451/870-821).

$ The Old Bakery Tearoom is a local favorite hidden away in a tiny mall at the bottom of Digbeth Street with traditional cakes and light lunches (Mon-Wed & Fri-Sat 10:30-16:00, closed Thu and Sun, Digbeth Street, Alan and Jackie). Come here for soup, salad, sandwiches, and tea and scones (£6 cream tea is splittable).

$ The Hive is a quality modern café, where Jane and Sally offer breakfast, lunch, and tea with a warm welcome (Thu-Mon 9:00-17:00, closed Tue-Wed, Digbeth Street, tel. 01451/831-087).

$ Lucy's Tea Room is a nice option if you fancy a light lunch or cream tea on Market Square (daily 9:00-16:00, next to Stow Lodge).

Groceries: The **Co-op,** a small grocery store, faces the main square next to the Kings Arms (daily 7:00-22:00) and a big **Tesco** supermarket is 400 yards north of town.

NEAR STOW-ON-THE-WOLD

These sights are all south of Stow: Some are within walking distance (the Slaughters and Bourton-on-the-Water), and one is 20 miles away (Cirencester). The Slaughters and Bourton are tied together by the countryside walk described on page 203.

Lower and Upper Slaughter

"Slaughter" has nothing to do with lamb chops. It likely derives from an Old English word, perhaps meaning sloe tree (the one used to make sloe gin). These villages are worth ▲ and a quick stop.

Lower Slaughter is a classic village, with ducks, a charming little church, a picturesque water mill, and usually an artist busy at her easel somewhere. The Old Mill Museum is a folksy ensemble with a tiny museum, shop, and café complete with a delightful terrace overlooking the millpond, enthusiastically run by Gerald and his daughter Laura, who just can't resist giving generous tastes of their homemade ice cream (£1 for museum, daily 10:00-18:00, Nov-Feb until dusk, tel. 01451/822-127, www.oldmill-lowerslaughter.com). Just behind the Old Mill, two kissing gates lead to the path that goes to nearby Upper Slaughter, a 15-minute walk or 2-minute drive away (leaving the Old Mill, take two lefts, then follow sign for *Wardens Way*). And if you follow the mill creek downstream, a bridle path leads to Bourton-on-the-Water (described next).

In **Upper Slaughter,** walk through the yew trees (sacred in pagan days) down a lane through the raised graveyard (a buildup of centuries of graves) to the peaceful church. In the far back of the fine cemetery, the statue of a wistful woman looks over the tomb of an 18th-century rector (sculpted by his son). Notice the town is missing a war memorial—that's because every soldier who left Upper Slaughter for World War I and World War II survived the wars. As a so-called "Doubly Thankful Village" (one of only 13 in England and Wales), the town instead honors those who served in war with a simple wood plaque in the Town Hall.

Getting There: Though the stop is not listed on schedules, you should be able to reach these towns on bus #801 (from Moreton or Stow) by requesting the "Slaughter Pike" stop (along the main road, near the villages). Confirm with the driver before getting on. If driving, the small roads from Upper Slaughter to Ford and Kineton (and the Cotswold Farm Park, described later) are some of England's most scenic. Roll your window down and joyride slowly.

Bourton-on-the-Water

I can't figure out whether they call this "the Venice of the Cotswolds" because of

The church at Upper Slaughter

Bourton-on-the-Water

Motoring Museum

its quaint canals or its miserable crowds. Either way, this town—four miles south of Stow and a mile from Lower Slaughter—is very pretty and worth ▲. But it can be mobbed with tour groups during the day: Sidewalks become jammed with disoriented tourists wearing nametags.

If you can avoid the crowds, it's worth a drive-through and maybe a short stop. It's pleasantly empty in the early evening and after dark.

The **Cotswold Motoring Museum** is lovingly presented. This good, jumbled museum shows off a lifetime's accumulation of vintage cars, old lacquered signs, threadbare toys, prewar memorabilia, and sundry British pop culture knick-knacks. If you appreciate old cars, this is nirvana. Wander the car-and-driver displays, which range from the automobile's early days to slick 1970s models, including period music to set the mood. Talk to an elderly Brit who's touring the place for some personal memories (£6.25, daily 10:00-18:00, closed mid-Dec–mid-Feb, in the mill facing the town center, tel. 01451/821-255, www.cotswoldmotoringmuseum.co.uk).

Getting There: It's conveniently connected to Stow and Moreton by bus #801. Bus #802 also connects to Stow.

Parking: Finding a spot here can be tough. Even during the busy business day, rather than park in the pay-and-display parking lot a five-minute walk from the center, you can drive right into town and wait for a spot on High Street just past the village green. (Where the road swings left, turn a hard right [watch for signs for museums and TI] to go along the babbling brook and down High Street; there's a long row of free 1.5 hour spots starting just past the brook in front of the Edinburgh Woolen Mills Shop, on the right). After 18:00 you can park free just along the brook.

Tourist Information: The TI is tucked across the stream a short block off the main drag, on Victoria Street, behind The Victoria Hall (Mon-Sat 9:30-17:00, Sun 10:00-14:00 except closed Sun Oct-April, tel. 01451/820-211).

Bike Rental: Hartwells on High Street rents bikes by half-day or day and includes a helmet, map, and lock (£11/3 hours; £16/day, Mon-Sat 9:00-18:00, Sun from 10:00, tel. 01451/820-405, www.hartwells.supanet.com).

Cotswold Farm Park

This park, worth ▲ and a delight for young and old alike, is the private venture of the Henson family, who are passionate about preserving rare and endangered breeds of native British animals. While it feels like a kids' zone (with all the family-friendly facilities you can imagine), it's a fascinating chance for anyone to get up close and (very) personal with piles of mostly cute animals, including the sheep that made this region famous—the big and woolly Cotswold Lion. The "listening posts" deliver audio information on each rare breed.

Check the events board for seasonal demonstrations of farm life—such as milking, bottle-feeding, shearing, sheep shows (meet the seven local breeds), and more.

Cost and Hours: £10.50, kids-£9, daily 10:30-17:00, Nov-Dec until 16:00, closed Jan-Feb, good guidebook (£5), restaurant and café, tel. 01451/850-307, www.cotswoldfarmpark.co.uk.

Getting There: It's well-signposted

Cotswold Farm Park

about halfway between Stow and Stanway (15 minutes from either). A visit here makes sense if you're traveling from Stow to Chipping Campden.

Northleach

While other towns may be cuter with more tourist-oriented sights, Northleach (nine miles south of Stow-on-the-Wold) is the best of the "untouched and untouristed" Cotswold villages. Officials made sure the main road didn't pass through town back in the 1980s, and today there's no TI and no place to park a big bus. It's invisible to mass tourism...and I like it.

The town's impressive main square (Market Place) and church attest to its position as a major wool center in the Middle Ages. Along with the **Cotswolds Discovery Centre** (on the big road at the edge of town; free, daily 9:30-16:30, on the A-429—Fosse Way—at the edge of Northleach, tel. 01451/862-000), the town mostly consists of a main street leading to a fine old square facing a glorious church, and some quality restaurants nearby. The **$$ Sherborne Arms** pub (long hours daily) is a classic, family- and pet-friendly local, with a big fireplace, pool table,

traditional ales and pub grub, outdoor seating, and a sloppy vibe. **$$$$ The Wheatsheaf Inn** is the foodie's favorite for fine dining, with a pleasantly traditional dining room and a gorgeous sprawling garden (long hours daily, on the main street into town one block before Market Place, tel. 01451/860-244, www. cotswoldswheatsheaf.com).

Drivers can park in the square called The Green or the adjoining Market Place. Bus #801 (with good Stow and Moreton connections) stops on the square, where there's an outdated map posted by the WC. For better information, find the nicely done Northleach map/guide (free at the church, post office, or Black Cat Community Café). Information is also online (www.northleach.gov.uk). Your best bet for a friendly and knowledgeable local might be the volunteer greeters at the church.

Bibury

Six miles northeast of Cirencester, this ▲ village—long a favorite with British fond of strolling and fishing—is now so touristy I'd only visit after hours. Bibury (BYE-bree) caters to tour buses, and lately has become a stop on the Instagram circuit and can be overwhelmed by selfie-stick tourists. After about 17:00, the light is warm and the masses are gone. The town offers some relaxing sights, including a row of very old weavers' cottages, a trout farm, a stream teeming with fat fish and proud ducks, and a church surrounded by rosebushes. A protected wetlands area on the far side of the stream hosts newts and water voles.

From the small parking lot, check out the posted map and information. Then walk the loop: up the main street (enjoying achingly beautiful homes with gardens and signs in Chinese that say keep out), then turn right along the old weavers' Arlington Row and back along the made-for-tour-groups paved path on the far side of the marsh, peeking into the rushes for wildlife.

For a closer look at the fish, cross the little bridge to the 15-acre **Trout Farm,** where you can feed them—or catch your own (£4.50 to walk the grounds, fish food-£0.60; daily 8:00-18:00, shorter hours off-season; catch-your-own only on weekends March-Oct 10:00-17:00, no fishing in winter, call or email to confirm fishing schedule, tel. 01285/740-215, www.biburytroutfarm.co.uk).

Getting There: Take bus #801 from Moreton-in-Marsh or Stow, then change to #855 in Northleach or Bourton-on-the-Water (3/day, 1 hour total).

Cirencester

Almost 2,000 years ago, Cirencester (SIGH-ren-ses-ter) was the ancient Roman city of Corinium. Worth ▲, it's the largest town of the Cotswold district, and while it's less cute and feels more bustling than surrounding towns, it has a pleasant and pedestrianized historic center. It's 20 miles from Stow down the A-429, which was called Fosse Way in Roman times. The **TI,** in the shop at the Corinium Museum, answers questions and sells a town map and a town walking-tour brochure (same hours as museum, tel. 01285/654-180).

Stop by the impressive **Corinium Museum** to find out why they say, "If you scratch Gloucestershire, you'll find Rome." The museum chronologically displays well-explained artifacts from the town's rich history, with a focus on Roman times—when Corinium was the second-biggest city in the British Isles (after Londinium). You'll see column capitals and fine mosaics before moving on to the Anglo-Saxon and Middle Ages exhibits (£6, Mon-Sat 10:00-17:00, Sun from 14:00, shorter hours off-season, Park Street, tel. 01285/655-611, www.coriniummuseum.org).

Cirencester's **church,** built in about 1490, is the largest of the Cotswold "wool" churches. The cutesy **New Brewery Arts** crafts center entertains visitors with traditional weaving and potting, workshops, an interesting gallery, and a good coffee shop (www.newbreweryarts.org.uk). Mon-

Bibury

Cirencester

day and Friday are general-**market** days, Friday features an antique market, and a crafts market is held every Saturday.

Getting There: By bus, take #801 from Moreton-in-Marsh or Stow, then change to #855 in Northleach or Bourton-on-the-Water for Cirencester (3/day, 1.5 hours total). Drivers follow *Town Centre* signs and find parking right on the market square; if it's full, retreat to the Waterloo pay-and-display lot (a 5-minute walk away).

MORETON-IN-MARSH

This workaday town—worth ▲—is like Stow or Chipping Campden without the touristy sugar. Rather than gift and antique shops, you'll find streets lined with real shops: ironmongers selling cottage nameplates and carpet shops strewn with the remarkable patterns that decorate B&B floors. A traditional market of 100-plus stalls fills High Street each Tuesday, as it has for the last 400 years (9:00-15:00, handicrafts, farm produce, clothing, books, and people-watching; best if you go early). The Cotswolds has an economy aside from tourism, and you'll feel it here.

Orientation

Moreton has a tiny, sleepy train station two blocks from High Street and lots of bus connections. Drivers can park anywhere on High Street any time, as long as you want, for free (though there is a 2-hour parking limit for the small lot in the middle of the street). On Tuesdays, when the market makes parking tricky, try the Budgens supermarket, where you can park for two hours.

Tourist Information: Moreton has the best TI in the region. Peruse the racks of fliers, confirm rail and bus schedules, and consider the £0.50 *Town Trail* self-guided walking tour leaflet (Mon-Fri 8:45-17:00, Sat 10:00-13:00, closed Sat Nov-Easter and Sun year-round, good public WC, tel.

Moreton-in-Marsh

01608/650-881).

Laundry: The handy launderette is a block in front of the train station on New Road (daily 7:00-19:00, last self-service wash at 17:00, drop-off service options available—call ahead to arrange, tel. 01608/650-888).

Hikes and Walks from Moreton-in-Marsh: As its name implies, Moreton-in-Marsh sits on a flat, boggy landscape, making it a bit less appealing for hikes; I'd bus to Chipping Campden or to Stow for a better hike (this is easy, since Moreton is a transit hub).

Sleeping

$$$$ Manor House Hotel is Moreton's big old hotel, dating from 1545 but sporting such modern amenities as toilets and electricity. Its 35 classy-for-the-Cotswolds rooms and its garden invite relaxation (elevator, log fire in winter, attached restaurants, free parking, on far end of High Street away from train station, tel. 01608/650-501, www.cotswold-inns-hotels.co.uk, info@manorhousehotel.info).

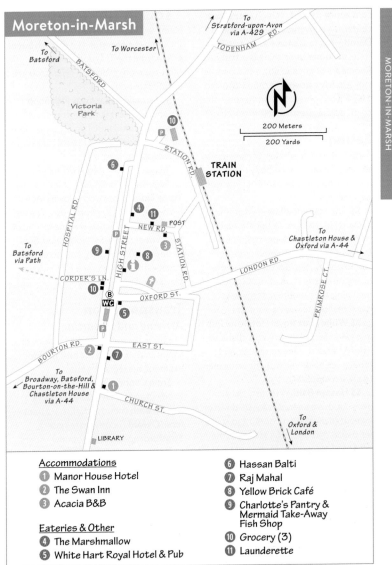

Moreton-in-Marsh

Accommodations
① Manor House Hotel
② The Swan Inn
③ Acacia B&B

Eateries & Other
④ The Marshmallow
⑤ White Hart Royal Hotel & Pub
⑥ Hassan Balti
⑦ Raj Mahal
⑧ Yellow Brick Café
⑨ Charlotte's Pantry & Mermaid Take-Away Fish Shop
⑩ Grocery (3)
⑪ Launderette

$$ The Swan Inn is wonderfully perched on the main drag, with 10 en-suite rooms. Though the halls look a bit worn and you enter through a bar/restaurant that can be noisy on weekends, the renovated rooms themselves are classy and the bathrooms modern (free parking, restaurant gives guests 10 percent discount, High Street, tel. 01608/650-711, www.swanmoreton.co.uk, info@swanmoreton.co.uk, Sara and Terry Todd). Terry can pick up guests from the train station and may be able to drive guests to destinations within 20 miles if no public transport is available.

$ Acacia B&B, on the short road

connecting the train station to the town center, is a convenient budget option. Dorothy has four small rooms: one is en suite, the other three share one bathroom. Rooms are bright and tidy, and most overlook a lovely garden (tel. 01608/650-130, 2 New Road, www.acaciainthecotswolds. co.uk, acacia.guesthouse@tiscali.co.uk).

Eating

A stroll up and down High Street lets you survey your options. Nobody travels to Moreton for its restaurants but you won't go hungry.

$$ The Marshmallow is a dainty little place, relatively upscale but affordable, with a menu that includes traditional English dishes and afternoon tea (Sun-Tue 10:00-17:00, Wed-Sat until 20:00, reservations smart, shady back garden for dining, tel. 01608/651-536, www. marshmallow-tea-restaurant.co.uk).

$$ White Hart Royal Hotel and Pub is a solid bet for pub grub with a characteristic bar, finer restaurant seating, and a terrace out back—all with the same menu (daily, tel. 01608/650-731).

$$ Hassan Balti, with tasty Bangladeshi food, is a fine value for sit-down or takeout (daily 12:00-14:00 & 17:30-23:30, tel. 01608/650-798). **Raj Mahal,** at the other end of town (on High Street, just past the White Hart), is also good.

$$ Yellow Brick Café, run by Tom and Nicola, has a delightful outdoor patio, cozy indoor seating, cheap and cheery menu, and a tempting display of homemade cakes (daily 9:00-17:00, just off High Street at 3 Old Market Way, tel. 01608/651-881).

$ Charlotte's Pantry serves fresh soups, salads, sandwiches, and pastries for lunch in a cheerful spot on High Street across from the TI (good cream tea, Mon-Sat 9:00-17:00, Sun from 10:00, tel. 01608/650-000).

$ Mermaid Take-Away Fish Shop is popular for its takeout fish and tasty selection of traditional savory pies (Mon-Sat 11:30-14:00 & 17:00-22:00, closed Sun, tel. 01608/651-391).

Picnic: There's a small **Co-op** grocery on High Street (daily 7:00-20:00), and a **Tesco Express** two doors down (Mon-Fri 6:00-23:00, Sat-Sun from 7:00). The big **Budgens** supermarket is at the far end of High Street (Mon-Sat 7:00-22:00, Sun 10:00-16:00). You can picnic across the street in pleasant Victoria Park (with a playground).

Transportation
Arriving and Departing

Moreton, the only Cotswold town with a train station, is also the best base for exploring the region by bus.

Train Connections to: London's Paddington Station (every 1-2 hours, 2 hours), **Bath** (hourly, 3 hours, 1-2 transfers), **Oxford** (hourly, 40 minutes), **Stratford-upon-Avon** (hourly, 3 hours, 2 transfers, slow and expensive, better by bus). Train info: Tel. 0345-748-4950, www. nationalrail.co.uk.

Bus Connections to: Stratford-upon-Avon (#1 and #2 go via Chipping Campden: Mon-Sat 5/day, none on Sun, 1.5 hours, Johnsons Excelbus, tel. 01564/797-070, www.johnsonscoaches. co.uk).

BEST OF THE REST

Central England hosts a number of worthwhile sights. **Oxford** is one of England's great university towns. Historic **Blenheim Palace** is nearby; this marvelous Baroque building, with a sumptuous interior, also has beautiful gardens.

Stratford-upon-Avon is a must for Shakespeare fans; stay for a play. Near Stratford is **Warwick Castle,** a fine stop for families and knights and maidens of any age.

Oxford

Oxford, founded in the seventh century and home to the oldest university in the English-speaking world, originated as a simple trade crossroads. Ever since the first homework was assigned in 1167, its stellar graduates have influenced Western civilization. Its alumni include 27 British prime ministers, more than 60 Nobel Prize winners, well-known writers and actors, and even 11 saints.

For tourists, Oxford offers a pleasant town center plus historic colleges with literary connections. And just a half-hour outside town is magnificent Blenheim Palace.

Day Plan

Oxford is a convenient stop for people visiting the Cotswolds, Blenheim Palace, Stratford-upon-Avon, and Bath. In a single busy day, you could see the essential Oxford: my self-guided walk, Christ Church College, and the Ashmolean Museum.

Rick's Tip: *For a* **do-it-yourself tour,** *find the* **information panels** *around town that explain nearby sights. On the opposite side of each panel, a map will help you navigate the maze of streets.*

Orientation

While a typical American university has one self-contained campus, Oxford has colleges and buildings scattered throughout town.

The spires of All Souls College, Oxford

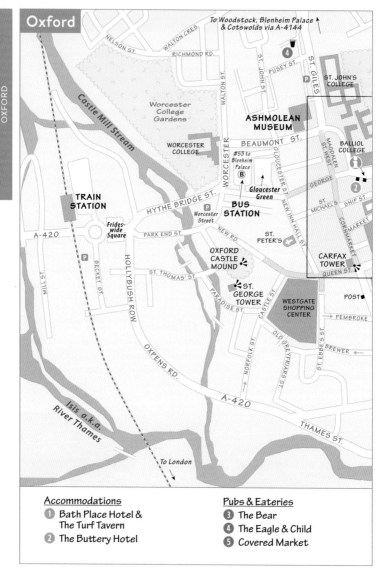

Oxford

To Woodstock, Blenheim Palace & Cotswolds via A-4144

ASHMOLEAN MUSEUM

ST. JOHN'S COLLEGE

BALLIOL COLLEGE

Worcester College Gardens

WORCESTER COLLEGE

BEAUMONT ST.

#53 to Blenheim Palace

Gloucester Green

TRAIN STATION

Frideswide Square

HYTHE BRIDGE ST.

BUS STATION

Worcester Street

PARK END ST.

NEW RD.

ST. PETER'S

A-420

OXFORD CASTLE MOUND

ST. THOMAS' ST.

ST. GEORGE TOWER

WESTGATE SHOPPING CENTER

CARFAX TOWER

QUEEN ST.

POST

PEMBROKE

BREWER

Isis a.k.a. River Thames

A-420

THAMES ST.

To London

Accommodations
1 Bath Place Hotel & The Turf Tavern
2 The Buttery Hotel

Pubs & Eateries
3 The Bear
4 The Eagle & Child
5 Covered Market

But the sightseer's Oxford is walkable and compact, and many streets are pedestrian-only.

Tourist Information: The TI offers walking tours and sells a detailed town map and *A Quick Guide to Oxford*. They also offer baggage storage for a fee. If you're headed to Blenheim Palace,

buy your tickets here at a discount (15 Broad Street, tel. 01865/686-441, www. experienceoxfordshire.org).

Local Guide: William Underhill is a good Oxford-educated private guide (£55/hour, mobile 07802-328-956, williamunderhill@gmail.com).

Tours: Walking Tours of Oxford

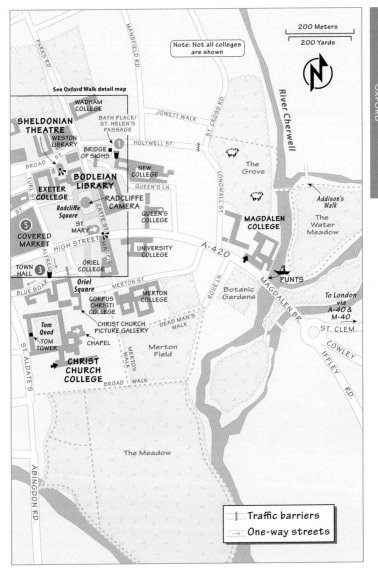

Note: Not all colleges are shown

200 Meters
200 Yards

Traffic barriers
One-way streets

offers themed group tours and private tours (tel. 07833/176-196, www. walkingtoursofoxford.com). **Oxford Walking Tours** are more casual and depart hourly from the Trinity College gates (daily 11:00-16:00, 1.5 hours, mobile 07790-734-387, www.oxfordwalkingtours. com).

Getting There

Oxford is linked by train with London (Paddington Station, 2/hour direct, 1 hour), Bath (2/hour, 1.5 hours), and Moreton-in-Marsh (hourly, 40 minutes). Competing bus companies run frequently from London to Oxford's Gloucester Green bus station (about 2 hours, www.oxfordtube.

com or www.oxfordbus.co.uk).

From the **train** station, the city center is a 10-minute walk (exit straight ahead and follow the signs). A taxi costs around £6. The **bus** station is a five-minute walk from the heart of Oxford and the TI. **Drivers** day-tripping into Oxford should use one of the outlying park-and-ride lots, which are about a 10-minute shuttle-bus ride from the town center. There are some pay parking lots closer to the center.

Rick's Tip: *For great views of Oxford's many spires and colleges, climb the 127 narrow, twisting stairs of the bell tower of the University Church of St. Mary the Virgin (£5, High Street) or the 99 steps of Carfax Tower (£3, intersection of High and Cornmarket streets).*

⊙ Oxford Walk

This stroll takes you through the heart of Oxford's colleges and university buildings. Budget about 2.5 hours, which includes going inside some of the sights.
• *Start at the intersection of Broad and Cornmarket streets.*

❶ **Oxford's Birth:** Gazing down pedestrian-only Cornmarket with its modern shops, you see the historic town of Oxford. Looking east down Broad Street, you see the realm of the university. It's these two elements—"town and gown"—that combined to make the Oxford of today. Take a few steps down Cornmarket to see Oxford's oldest building—the tall, stone Saxon Tower, from around AD 1000. The town began as a fortified trading post with a "corn market." Then, in 1167, a university was founded—one of Europe's first—bringing a new and sometimes troublesome element: students.
• *Walk east along Broad Street about 100 yards. Stop at a small patch of bricks embedded in the middle of the road.*

❷ **Broad Street:** The **brick patch,** in the shape of a cross, marks the spot where three local bishops, known as the "Oxford Martyrs," were burned at the stake for heresy in 1555-56. Their crime: Protestantism.

Ahead on the left is **Balliol College,** one of 38 colleges that make up Oxford University. Most colleges allow visitors (for a small admission fee) to stroll the grounds and pop into a few select buildings. Balliol features atmospheric medieval-style buildings, a chapel with stained glass and carved-wood pews, and an impressive dining hall.
• *Continue east, seeing...*

❸ **More Along Broad Street:** At #17 (on the right) is an **Oxfam** shop. This tiny building is where the charitable organization Oxfam was founded in 1942 (by a Balliol grad) to feed starving victims of World War II.

A few steps farther (on the left) is the entrance to **Trinity College,** and on the right is **Exeter College,** where J. R. R. Tolkien lived while an undergrad.

At #48 (on the left), step into **Blackwell's Bookshop.** This store may not look impressive initially, but beneath your feet in underground tunnels are an additional three miles of bookshelves.
• *Directly across the street is the...*

❹ **Museum of the History of Science:** One of Europe's oldest museums, this place is worth ▲ (free, Tue-Sun 12:00-17:00, closed Mon). It's an easily manageable display of scientific bric-a-brac (including Einstein's blackboard) that the scholars of Oxford used to change our world. Upstairs you'll find early globes, sundials, telescopes, and calculating machines. Downstairs you'll see early radios, equipment used in developing penicillin, and Lewis Carroll's photo-developing kit.
• *We now dive into the university, starting next door with the...*

❺ **Sheldonian Theatre:** This ▲ venue for concerts and lectures is best known as the grand space for graduations and other important campus ceremonies (£3.50, generally daily 10:00-16:00). It was

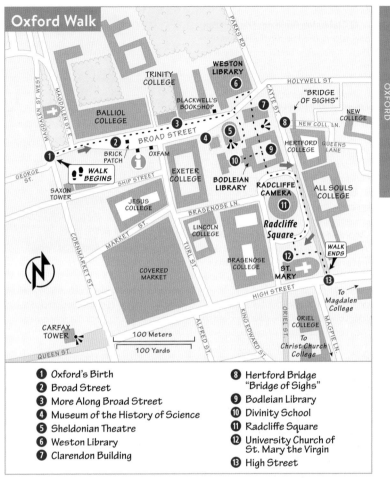

Oxford Walk

❶ Oxford's Birth
❷ Broad Street
❸ More Along Broad Street
❹ Museum of the History of Science
❺ Sheldonian Theatre
❻ Weston Library
❼ Clarendon Building
❽ Hertford Bridge "Bridge of Sighs"
❾ Bodleian Library
❿ Divinity School
⓫ Radcliffe Square
⓬ University Church of St. Mary the Virgin
⓭ High Street

the first major building designed by Sir Christopher Wren—an Oxford graduate and astronomy professor who went on to become England's best-known architect. Wren's domed ceiling was an engineering marvel, spanning a 70-by-80-foot hole. You can climb 114 steps, walking among big oak trusses, to a glass-covered cupola with great views.

• Cross Broad Street to the...

❻ **Weston Library:** This building was constructed in the 1930s to house the overflow of university books when the venerable Bodleian Library began running

out of space. Today, the ▲ Weston welcomes visitors to enjoy its "Treasures"— an ever-changing selection of precious books, manuscripts, and letters (free, suggested £5 donation, Mon-Sat 10:00-17:00, Sun from 11:00). You may see a Shakespeare First Folio, a copy of the Magna Carta, handwritten scores by Handel, or even a sixth-century scrap of birch bark with a recipe in Sanskrit to remove wrinkles and gray hair.

• From the Weston Library, cross Broad Street to enter the historic core of the university. Walk through the stately four-columned *facade into the...*

❼ Clarendon Building: This building originally housed the Oxford University Press. Among the books printed here was the Lincoln Bible—used to inaugurate Presidents Lincoln and Obama. Exit the Clarendon out the other side.

• *Pause and look left for a glimpse of*

❽ Hertford Bridge, *known as the "Bridge of Sighs," after the one in Venice. Keep going straight ahead, into the next building. You emerge in a courtyard called the Schools Quadrangle. You're in the center of the...*

❾ Bodleian Library: As the university's main library (and one of the oldest in Europe), this is arguably the heart of Oxford's academic life, and worth ▲▲. With some 11 million books—some dating to medieval times—and more than 100 miles of shelving in its underground stacks, "the Bod" is one of the world's largest and most famous libraries. The doors branching off the courtyard led to the various university departments—the music school *(Schola Musica),* astronomy *(Schola Astronomae),* and so on—where classes were taught in Europe's universal language, Latin. The courtyard's main tower is called the Tower of the Five Orders, because of the five types of columns: Tuscan, Doric, Ionic, Corinthian, and Composite. The statue of King James I (ruler when the Bodleian was built) shows him handing out books.

• *The ticket office for the Divinity School is directly beneath that tower. You can also book a guided tour for Duke Humfrey's Library (which includes a tour of the Divinity School).*

❿ Divinity School: The ▲▲ Divinity School was the university's first purpose-built classroom, constructed in 1427 for teaching theology (£2, Mon-Sat 9:00-17:00, Sun from 11:00). The room, brilliantly lit by tall clear windows, is worth a look for its impressive fan-vaulted ceiling.

Duke Humfrey's Library, upstairs and only accessible on a guided tour, dates from 1488. Ancient-looking books are

Bodleian Library

stacked neatly under a beautifully painted wooden ceiling (£9 one-hour tour, £6 30-minute tour; check the schedule and buy your ticket at the kiosk, www.tickets. ox.ac.uk).

• *Exit the Schools Quadrangle through the passageway between "Schola Musicae" and "Naturalis Philosophiae." You emerge in...*

⓫ Radcliffe Square: The round, columned structure is Radcliffe Camera. Originally housing medical books, the building is a reading "room" (or "camera"). Only students and staff with special credentials can enter. Circle around the left side for a peek into **All Souls College.** It's named for the dead of the Hundred Years' War that England fought with France in the 14th and 15th centuries. The college is notorious for having the toughest entrance exam; famous alums include Lawrence of Arabia and Christopher Wren.

• *Just past Radcliffe Camera is the most important church in town.*

⓬ University Church of St. Mary the Virgin: A thousand years ago, this church stood at the center of the small, walled town. As the university formed, this church was its only building: where scholars prayed, lectured, kept their books, administered affairs, and received graduation degrees. The church interior reflects the delicate balance Oxford keeps between various religious ideologies: Protestants, Catholics, and secularists (free, £5 tower climb with great views; Mon-Sat 9:30-17:00, Sun from 11:30; garden café, crypt).

• *Circle around behind the church to...*

⓭ High Street: The central axis of Oxford, High Street has more colleges to the left (east) and the city center to the right (west, beyond the church tower a couple of blocks away). Traditionally, there's been tension between the privileged university population and the hardscrabble citizens of Oxford. In fact, it was a town-and-gown riot in 1209 that drove a group of professors and students out of Oxford to quieter Cambridge to found a rival university.

• *Your walk is over.*

Colleges and Sights
▲CHRIST CHURCH COLLEGE
Of Oxford's colleges, Christ Church is the largest and most prestigious. It was founded by Henry VIII's chancellor, Cardinal Thomas Wolsey, in 1524 on the site of an abbey dissolved by the king. The buildings survived the tumult of the Reformation because the abbey and its cathedral served as part of the king's new Church of England. While all colleges boast of their esteemed alumni, none has a list as esteemed as Christ Church College: 13 of

the 27 Oxford-educated prime ministers were Christ Church alums. William Penn (founder of Pennsylvania), John Wesley (influential Methodist leader), John Locke (English Enlightenment thinker), and Charles Dodgson (a.k.a. Lewis Carroll) also studied here.

Your entry ticket comes with an essential self-guided tour booklet with map. "Custodians" wearing bowler hats are posted around the college to answer questions. You'll be sent along a one-way route with these main stops: dining hall (familiar to Harry Potter fans), quadrangle, cathedral, and picture gallery.

Rick's Tip: The entrance to each college is easy to spot—just look for a doorway with crests and a flagpole on the top. Each entry has an office with a porter (live-in caretaker). Inquire there to find out which buildings are open to visitors, and if any plays, music, evensong services, or lectures are scheduled.

Cost and Hours: £10—buy timed-entry ticket online in advance to bypass line, family ticket available; Mon-Sat 10:00-17:00, Sun from 14:00, last entry 45 minutes before closing; tel. 01865/276-492, www.chch.ox.ac.uk. Note that the dining hall is closed to outsiders when students are eating here. Call ahead or check the website and plan your visit accordingly.

Evensong: Most evenings in Christ Church Cathedral, an excellent choir service is open to anyone (free, Tue-Sun

Christ Church College

Christ Church dining hall

at 18:00, enter at Tom Tower, arrive 15-20 minutes early).

MAGDALEN COLLEGE

Sitting on the upper edge of town, this college (pronounced "maudlin")—where C. S. Lewis taught for 25 years—gets my vote for the prettiest in Oxford. Magdalen has the largest grounds of any of the Oxford colleges (big enough to include its own deer park, with actual deer browsing the grounds) and a peaceful café overlooking the sleepy river and lively punting scene.

Cost and Hours: £7, July-Sept daily 10:00-19:00, rest of the year open 13:00-18:00 or dusk—whichever is earlier, £10 guided tours sometimes offered in summer—ask at visitor desk, High Street next to Magdalen Bridge, tel. 01865/276-000.

Evensong: Evensong services in the exquisite chapel take place Tue-Sun at 18:00 (except July-Sept).

EXETER COLLEGE

A smaller college, 700-year-old Exeter is centrally located, free to visit, and worth a peek. The highlight is its jewel-like Neo-Gothic chapel—oh-so Victorian from the 1860s and inspired by Paris' Sainte-Chapelle. It features William Morris' *Adoration of the Magi* tapestry and a bust of J. R. R. Tolkien, who studied here.

Cost and Hours: Free, usually open daily 14:00-17:00, Turl Street, tel. 01865/279-600.

▲▲ ASHMOLEAN MUSEUM OF ART AND ARCHAEOLOGY

In 1683, celebrated antiquary Elias Ashmole insisted his collection of curiosities deserved its own building. Half of his trove originated with an even-more-eccentric royal gardener, John Tradescant, who loved to seek out interesting items while traveling in search of plants. You won't see any particularly famous items, but you'll find intriguing and offbeat bits and pieces (such as Lawrence of Arabia's ceremonial dress, prehistoric Cycladic figurines from

Greece, gorgeous Turkish and Middle Eastern tiles, and a Stradivarius violin).

Cost and Hours: Free, suggested £5 donation, daily 10:00-17:00, basic café, rooftop restaurant open until 22:00 Thu-Sat, Beaumont Street, tel. 01865/278-000, www.ashmolean.org.

PUNTING

Long, flat boats can be rented for punting (pushing with a long pole) along the River Cherwell. Chauffeurs are available, while the do-it-yourself crowd tends to get a little wet. Punting looks easier than it is; the guided ride includes a short lesson so you can actually learn how to do it right.

Cost and Hours: £22-24/hour per boat rental, £30 deposit if paying cash, leave ID with credit card; chauffeured punts-£30-32 per boat for 30 minutes and up to 4 people, higher prices for Sat-Sun; book ahead for weekends, rowboats and paddle boats available for the less adventurous, daily 9:30-dusk, closed Dec-Jan, Magdalen Bridge Boathouse, tel. 01865/202-643, www.oxfordpunting.co.uk.

Sleeping and Eating

$$$ Bath Place Hotel is a bit worn but full of charm (off Holywell Street at 4 Bath Place, www.bathplace.co.uk). **$$ The Buttery Hotel** rents good-value rooms (11 Broad Street, www.thebutteryhotel.co.uk).

$$$ The Bear, close to the Christ Church Picture Gallery, is one of Oxford's

The Bear pub

most charming pubs (corner of Alfred and Blue Boar streets). The big and boisterous **$$$ Turf Tavern** is popular for its solid grub and outdoor beer garden (4 Bath Place). **$$ The Eagle and Child** was the gathering place for such writers as J. R. R. Tolkien and C. S. Lewis (49 St. Giles Street). **$ Covered Market**—a farmers market maze of shops and stands—has a fine selection for lunch or a picnic (between Market and High streets, near Carfax Tower).

Blenheim Palace

Just 30 minutes' drive from Oxford (and convenient to combine with a drive through the Cotswolds), Blenheim Palace is one of England's best—worth ▲▲▲. The 2,000-acre yard, designed by Lancelot "Capability" Brown, is as majestic to some as the palace itself.

Rick's Tip: *Americans who pronounce the place "blen-HEIM" are the butt of jokes. It's "BLEN-em."*

John Churchill, first Duke of Marlborough, achieved a stunning victory over Louis XIV's armies at the Battle of Blenheim in 1704. A thankful Queen Anne rewarded Churchill by building him this nice home, perhaps the finest Baroque building in England. Eleven dukes of Marlborough later, the palace is as impressive as ever. In 1874, a later John Churchill's American daughter-in-law, Jennie Jerome, gave birth at Blenheim to another historic baby in that line...and named him Winston.

Day Plan

To include Blenheim Palace with a stop in Oxford, head to Blenheim first (by bus); on your return, visit Oxford.

Getting There

Blenheim Palace sits at the edge of the cute cobbled town of Woodstock.

From Oxford by Bus: Take bus #S3 (2/hour, 40 minutes, www.stagecoachbus.com) from the bus station at Gloucester Green or the train station. It stops twice near Blenheim Palace: The "Blenheim Palace Gates" stop is about a half-mile walk to the palace itself; the "Woodstock/Marlborough Arms" stop is in the village of Woodstock and offers the most spectacular view of the palace and lake.

From the Cotswolds by Train: Your easiest train connection is from Moreton-in-Marsh to Hanborough—just 1.5 miles from the palace (£10, hourly, 30 minutes). From Hanborough station, take bus #233 (£3, buy on bus, 2/hour, 10 minutes, Mon-Sat only). Taxis don't wait at the station, but you can book one in advance (try A2B Taxis, tel. 07767/685-257; or Cabs 4U, tel. 07919/675-150).

By Car: Head for Woodstock; the palace is well-signposted once in town. Buy your ticket at the gate, then park near the palace.

Orientation

Cost: £27, includes audioguide; park and gardens only-£17; 30% discount when you buy on site and show your train or bus ticket; discount palace tickets are available at TIs in surrounding towns—including Oxford and Moreton-in-Marsh—or on the #S3 bus from Oxford; family ticket available.

Hours: Daily 10:30-17:30, Nov-mid-Dec generally closed Mon-Tue, park open but palace closed mid-Dec-mid-Feb. Doors to the palace close at 16:45, and the park closes at 18:00.

Information: Tel. 0199/381-0530, www.blenheimpalace.com.

Tours: Audioguides are available for the state rooms (included in admission). Guided tours are available for the duke's private apartment (£5, 2/hour, about 40 minutes, tickets are limited), the servants' quarters (£5, about 40 minutes), and the gardens (included in admission).

Eating: The **$$ Water Terrace Café** at

Blenheim Palace

the garden exit is delightful for basic lunch and teatime treats. Just outside the palace gates, **$ Hampers Deli** is a good place to pick up provisions for a picnic (31 Oxford Street).

Visiting the Palace

State Rooms: The state rooms are the fancy halls the dukes use to impress visiting dignitaries. These most sumptuous rooms in the palace are ornamented with fine porcelain, gilded ceilings, portraits of past dukes, photos of the present duke's family, and "chaperone" sofas designed to give courting couples just enough privacy...but not *too* much.

Enjoy the series of 10 Brussels tapestries that commemorate military victories of the First Duke of Marlborough, including the Battle of Blenheim. After winning that pivotal conflict, he scrawled a quick note on the back of a tavern bill notifying the queen of his victory (you'll see a replica).

Finish with the remarkable "long library"—with its tiers of books and stuccoed ceilings.

Winston Churchill Exhibition: This is a fascinating display of letters, paintings, and other artifacts of the great statesman who was born here. Along with lots of intimate artifacts from his life, you'll see the bed in which Sir Winston was born in 1874.

Private Apartment: For a more extensive visit, book a spot to tour the duke's private digs (see "Tours," earlier). You'll see the chummy billiards room, luxurious china, the servants quarters with 47 bells—one for each room to call the servants, private rooms, 18th-century Flemish tapestries, family photos, and so on.

Churchills' Destiny: In the "stables block" is an exhibit that traces the military leadership of two great men who shared the name Churchill: John, who defeated Louis XIV at the Battle of Blenheim in the 18th century, and in whose honor this palace was built; and Winston, who was born in this palace, and who won the Battle of Britain and helped defeat Hitler in the 20th century. It's remarkable that arguably two of the most important military victories in the nation's history were overseen by distant cousins.

Gardens: The palace's expansive gardens stretch nearly as far as the eye can see in every direction. From the main courtyard, you'll emerge into the Water

Terraces; from there, you can loop around to the left, behind the palace, to see (but not enter) the Italian Garden. Or, head down to the lake to walk along the waterfront trail; going left takes you to the rose gardens and arboretum, while turning right brings you to the Grand Bridge.

Stratford-Upon-Avon

To see or not to see? Stratford, Shakespeare's hometown, is a must for every big bus tour in England, and one of the most popular side-trips from London. Sure, it's touristy, and nonliterary types might find it's much ado about nothing. But the play's the thing to bring the Bard to life—and here you can see the Royal Shakespeare Company (the world's best Shakespeare ensemble) performing in their state-of-the-art theater complex.

Just north of the Cotswolds, Stratford makes a convenient stop for Shakespeare fans—either before, after, or even during a Cotswold stay.

Day Plan

If you're just passing through Stratford, it's worth a half-day—stroll the charming core, visit your choice of Shakespeare sights (Shakespeare's Birthplace is best and easiest), and watch the swans along the river. But if you can squeeze it in, it's worth it to stick around to see a play; in this case, you'll need to spend the night or drive in from the Cotswolds (just 30 minutes away).

Rick's Tip: *If coming by train or bus, be sure to request a ticket for "Stratford-up-on-Avon," not just "Stratford" (to avoid a mix-up with Stratford Langthorne, near London). And don't get off at the Stratford Parkway train station—you want Stratford-upon-Avon.*

Orientation

Stratford, with around 30,000 people, has a compact old town, with the TI and theater along the riverbank, and Shakespeare's Birthplace a few blocks inland; you can easily walk to everything except Mary Arden's Farm.

Tourist Information: The TI is in a small brick building on Bridgefoot,

Stratford-upon-Avon is notable for its half-timbered architecture.

Stratford-upon-Avon

To Mary Arden's Farm

BIRMINGHAM RD.

SHAKESPEARE ST.

ARDEN ST.

MANSELL ST.

WINDSOR ST.

11

SHAKESPEARE'S BIRTHPLACE

4

MEER ST.

TRAIN STATION

STATION RD.

To Worcester via A-46

ALCESTER RD.

GREENHILL ST.

9

5

Market Place

AMERICAN FOUNTAIN

ALBANY RD.

GROVE RD.

ELY ST.

200 Meters
200 Yards

ROTHER ST.

SCHOLARS LN.

1

SHAKESPEARE'S SCHOOLROOM & GUILDHALL

CHURCH ST.

CHESTNUT WALK

To Anne Hathaway's Cottage

BROAD WALK

BROAD ST.

BULL ST.

OLD TOWN

HALL'S CROFT

NARROW LN.

COLLEGE ST.

SANCTUS ST.

COLLEGE LN.

Accommodations
1 Adelphi & Salamander Guest Houses
2 Mercure Shakespeare Hotel

Eateries
3 The Fourteas 1940s Tea Room
4 Bensons Restaurant & Tea Rooms
5 The Old Thatch Tavern
6 Barnaby's Fish & Chips
7 Lambs & The Opposition
8 The Vintner Restaurant

Other
9 Mailboxes Etc (Bag Storage)
10 Swan Fountain (Town Walks)
11 Jester Statue (Bard Walks)
12 City Bus Tours

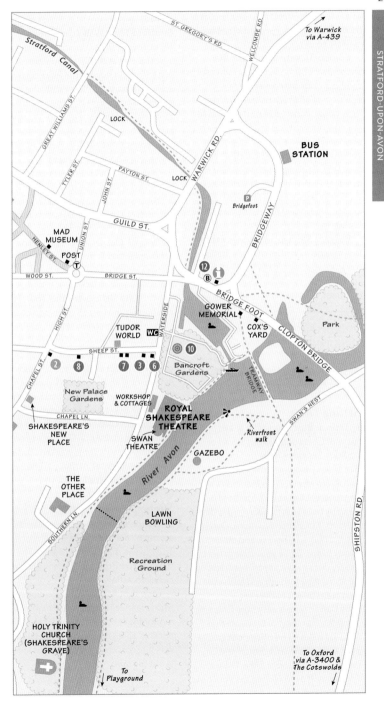

where the main street hits the river (daily, tel. 01789/264-293, www.shakespeare-country.co.uk).

Combo-Tickets: The TI and the Shakespeare Birthplace Trust sights sell combo-tickets that cover the five Trust sights (the **Full Story ticket,** a.k.a. the "five-house ticket"; £22.50 if purchased at a covered sight, £21 at TI). However, only the TI offers a special "any-three" option covering your pick of three of the five (£18). Booking online saves you 10 percent. The TI also sells discount tickets for Warwick Castle (£18 versus £29 on-site). Individual tickets are also sold at the sights.

Baggage Storage: Mailboxes Etc., a five-minute walk from the train station, can store your luggage (£2.50/bag, Mon-Fri hours vary, closed Sat-Sun, 12a Greenhill Street, tel. 01789/294-968).

Rick's Tip: *Expect crowds on the weekend nearest Shakespeare's birthday on April 23 (also the day he died); if overnighting, book your room and a play well in advance.*

Getting There

By Train or Bus: Stratford is linked by **bus** with Cotswolds towns (bus #1 or #2, Mon-Sat 5/day, none on Sun, 50 minutes to Chipping Campden, 1.5 hours from Moreton-in-Marsh, www.johnsonscoaches.co.uk). Stratford is linked by **train** with London (3/day direct, 2.5 hours, Marylebone Station), Oxford (every 2 hours, 1.5 hours), and other nearby towns. Once you arrive at the train station, exit straight ahead, bear right up the stairs, then turn left and follow the main drag straight to the river.

By Car: Driving is easy from Chipping Campden (12 miles) or Stow-on-the-Wold (22 miles). The Bridgefoot garage is big, easy, cheap, and central; the City Sightseeing bus stop and the TI are a block away. If overnighting, ask your hotelier about parking.

Tours

Stratford Town Walks can introduce you to the town and its famous playwright. Just show up at the Swan fountain (on the waterfront) in front of the Royal Shakespeare Theatre (£6, ticket stub offers discounts to some sights, shops, and restaurants; daily, mobile 07855-760-377, www.stratfordtownwalk.co.uk). They also run an evening ghost walk (£7, Sat at 19:30, 1.5 hours, must book in advance).

On a **Bard Walks** tour, trained, costumed actors describe the city with Shakespearean flair, incorporating some of the Bard's most famous speeches and sonnets (£10, cash only, 1.5 hours, generally April-Oct Thu-Sun 14:00, book in advance, leaves from Jester statue on Henley Street, mobile 07932-336-593, www.bardwalk.co.uk).

With **City Sightseeing Bus Tours,** you can hop on and hop off open-top buses at stops within the compact town, and head out to Anne Hathaway's Cottage and Mary Arden's Farm. The full 11-stop circuit takes about an hour and comes with entertaining and informative commentary (£15, ticket valid 24 hours, discount with town walk ticket stub, buy tickets on bus or at the TI; buses leave from the TI every 20 minutes, mid-April-Oct 9:30-17:00, no buses off-season, some weekend buses have live guides; tel. 01789/412-680, www.citysightseeing-stratford.com).

Shakespearean Sights

Stratford's five biggest Shakespeare sights are run by the Shakespeare Birthplace Trust (www.shakespeare.org.uk). The sights are well-run, all different, and genuinely interesting.

Each sight has helpful, eager docents who love to tell a story; you'll have a far more informative visit if you listen to the docents' spiels or chat them up. They provide fun, gossipy insight into what life was like at the time.

IN STRATFORD
▲▲SHAKESPEARE'S BIRTHPLACE

While the birthplace itself is a bit underwhelming, it's rewarding to stand in the bedroom where Shakespeare was born, and helpful docents make this a good introduction to the Bard. A modern exhibit and live mini performances emphasize how his work continues to inspire.

Cost and Hours: £17.50, daily 9:00-17:00, Nov-March 10:00-16:00, in town center on Henley Street, tel. 01789/204-016, www.shakespeare.org.uk.

Visiting Shakespeare's Birthplace: An introductory **exhibit** shows Shakespeare's enduring influence, with a video mash-up ranging from *The Simpsons* to the Hip-Hop Shakespeare Company. Check out the timeline of Shakespeare's plays, information about his upbringing and family life, and career in London. A few historical artifacts, including an original 1623 First Folio of Shakespeare's work, are also on display.

I find the **half-timbered Elizabethan building,** where young William grew up, a bit disappointing, as if millions of visitors have rubbed it clean of anything authentic. It was restored in the 1800s, and the furnishings are true to 1575, when William was 11. This is also the house where Shakespeare and his bride, Anne Hathaway, began their married life together. Upstairs are the rooms where young Will, his siblings, and his parents slept (along with their servants).

Look for the window etched with the names of important visitors, from Sir Walter Scott to actor Henry Irving. After Shakespeare's father died and William inherited the building, the thrifty playwright converted it into a pub to make a little money.

Exit into the fine **garden** where Shakespearean **actors** often perform brief scenes (they may even take requests). Pull up a bench and listen, imagining the playwright as a young boy stretching his imagination in this very place.

SHAKESPEARE'S NEW PLACE

While nothing remains of the house the Bard inhabited when he made it big (it was demolished in the 18th century), its manicured grounds are a tranquil spot to soak up some history. Today, modern sculptures and traditional gardens adorn the grounds of the mansion Shakespeare called home for nearly 20 years. Next

Shakespeare's Birthplace

William Shakespeare (1564-1616)

To many, William Shakespeare is the greatest author, in any language, period. He expanded and helped define modern English—the unrefined tongue of everyday people—and granted it a beauty and legitimacy that put it on par with Latin.

Using borrowed plots, outrageous puns, and poetic language, Shakespeare wrote comedies (c. 1590—*Taming of the Shrew, As You Like It*), tragedies (c. 1600—*Hamlet, Othello, Macbeth, King Lear*), and fanciful combinations (c. 1610—*The Tempest*), exploring the full range of human emotions.

Think of his stock of great characters and great lines: Hamlet ("To be or not to be, that is the question"), Othello and his jealousy ("It is the green-eyed monster"), ambitious Mark Antony ("Friends, Romans, countrymen, lend me your ears"), rowdy Falstaff ("The better part of valor is discretion"), and the star-crossed lovers Romeo and Juliet ("But soft, what light through yonder window breaks").

With plots that entertained both the highest and the lowest minds, Shakespeare taught the play-going public about human nature. Even today, his characters strike a familiar chord.

His friend and fellow poet, Ben Jonson, wrote in the preface to the First Folio, "He was not of an age, but for all time!"

door, Nash's House (which belonged to Shakespeare's granddaughter and her husband) hosts a model of Shakespeare's house, domestic artifacts, period clothing, and a balcony view of the knot garden.

Cost and Hours: £12.50, daily 10:00-17:00, Nov-March until 16:00, 22 Chapel Street, tel. 01789/338-536.

HALL'S CROFT

This former home of Shakespeare's eldest daughter, Susanna, gives a good idea of how the wealthy lived in the 17th century, with finer furnishings compared to the other Shakespeare properties. Since Susanna married a doctor, exhibits focus on Elizabethan-era medicine, leaving visitors grateful to live in modern times.

Cost and Hours: £8.50, daily 10:00-

17:00, Nov-March 11:00-16:00, on-site tearoom, between Church Street and the river on Old Town Street, tel. 01789/338-533.

JUST OUTSIDE STRATFORD

To reach either of these sights, it's best to drive or take the hop-on, hop-off bus tour unless you're staying at one of the Grove Road B&Bs, which are an easy 20-minute walk from Anne Hathaway's Cottage.

▲▲MARY ARDEN'S FARM

Along with Shakespeare's Birthplace, this is my favorite of the Shakespearean sights. Three miles from Stratford in Wilmcote, it's famous as the girlhood home of William's mom. Built around two historic farmhouses, it's an open-air folk museum depicting 16th-century farm life...which happens to have ties to Shakespeare.

Cost and Hours: £15, daily 10:00-17:00, closed Nov-mid-March, on-site café and picnic tables, tel. 01789/338-535.

Visiting Mary Arden's Farm: The museum hosts many special **events**—check the board by the entry. There are always plenty of active, hands-on activities to engage kids. Save some time for a walk: There are 23 acres of bucolic trails, orchards, and meadows to explore.

Pick up a map (and handful of organic animal feed) at the entrance and wander the grounds and buildings. Throughout the complex, you'll see interpreters in Tudor costumes performing daily 16th-century chores, such as milking the sheep and cutting wood to do repairs on the house. Look out for heritage breeds of farmyard animals including goats, woolly pigs, and friendly donkeys.

The first building, **Palmer's farm** (mistaken for Mary Arden's home for hundreds of years, and correctly identified in 2000), holds a kitchen where food is prepared over an open fire; at 13:00 each day the "servants" (employees) sit down in the adjacent dining room for a traditional dinner.

Mary Arden actually lived in the neighboring **farmhouse,** covered in brick facade and less impressive. The house is filled with kid-oriented activities, including period dress-up clothes, board games from Shakespeare's day, and a Tudor alphabet so kids can write their names in fancy lettering.

Of the many events here, the most enjoyable is the daily **bird of prey display** (call ahead for times). Chat with the falconers about their methods for earning the birds' trust: the birds are motivated by food. You may be given a bit of meat to feed the bird yourself.

▲**ANNE HATHAWAY'S COTTAGE**
Located 1.5 miles out of Stratford, this home is a 12-room farmhouse where the Bard's wife grew up. William courted Anne here—she was 26, he was only 18—and his tactics proved successful. (Maybe a little too much, as she was several months pregnant at their wedding.) Their 34-year marriage produced two more children, and lasted until his death in 1616 at age 52. The Hathaway family lived here from the 1500s until 1911, and much of the family's 92-acre farm remains part of the sight.

Cost and Hours: £12.50, daily 9:00-17:00, Nov-March 10:00-16:00, tearoom, tel. 01789/338-532.

Visiting Anne Hathaway's Cottage: The thatched-roof **cottage** looks cute enough to eat, and it's fun to imagine the writer of some of the world's greatest romances wooing his favorite girl right here during his formative years.

Maybe even more interesting than the cottage are the **gardens,** which have several parts (including a prizewinning "traditional cottage garden"). Follow the signs to the "Woodland Walk" (look for the music-note willow sculpture on your way), along with a fun sculpture garden littered with modern interpretations of Shakespearean characters. From April through June, the gardens are at their best, with birds chirping, bulbs in bloom, and a large sweet-pea display. You'll also find a music trail, a butterfly trail, and various exhibits.

THE ROYAL SHAKESPEARE COMPANY
The Royal Shakespeare Company (RSC), undoubtedly the best Shakespeare company on earth, performs year-round in Stratford and in London. The RSC makes it easy to take in a play, thanks to their very user-friendly website, painless ticket-booking system, and chock-a-block schedule that fills the summer with mostly big-name Shakespeare plays. The smaller attached Swan Theatre hosts plays on a more intimate scale.

▲▲▲**SEEING A PLAY**
Performances take place most days (Mon-Sat generally at 19:15 at the Royal Shakespeare Theatre or 19:30 at the Swan,

The Royal Shakespeare Theatre

matinees around 13:15 at the RST or 13:30 at the Swan, sporadic Sun shows). Shows generally last three hours or more, with one intermission. There's no strict dress code—nice jeans and short-sleeve shirts are fine—but shorts are discouraged.

Getting Tickets: Tickets range from £5 (standing) to £75, with most around £45 (discounts for families). Saturday-evening shows—the most popular—are the most expensive. Tickets go on sale months in advance. You can book tickets as you like it: online (www.rsc.org. uk), by phone (tel. 01789/331-111, Mon-Sat 10:00-18:00, Sun until 17:00) or in person at the box office (Mon-Sat 10:00-20:00, until 18:00 on nonperformance days, Sun until 17:00).

▲▲VISITING THE ROYAL SHAKESPEARE THEATRE

The RSC's flagship theater is one of Stratford's most fascinating sights. If you're seeing a play here, come early to poke around the building and check out interesting tidbits of theater history. You need to take a guided tour (explained below) to see the backstage areas, but you're welcome to wander the theater's public areas

any time the building is open.

Cost and Hours: Free entry, £8.50 for *The Play's the Thing* exhibit; Mon-Sat 10:00-23:00, Sun until 17:00.

Information: Tel. 01789/331-111, www. rsc.org.uk.

Guided Tours: Well-informed RSC volunteers lead entertaining, one-hour tours (£9; behind-the-scenes tour and front-of-the-house tours are at Royal Shakespeare Theatre; tour schedule varies by day; call, check online, or go to box office to confirm schedule; best to book ahead).

Tour Combo-Ticket: The £15 Explorer Pass includes a theater tour of your choice, the tower climb, and *The Play's the Thing* exhibit (book at box office or online).

Background: The original Victorian-style theater was built in 1879 to honor the Bard, but it burned down in 1926. The big Art Deco-style building you see today was erected in 1932 and outfitted with a stodgy Edwardian "picture frame"-style stage. The 2011 renovation added an updated thrust-style stage. They've left the shell of the 1930s theater, but with the seats stacked at an extreme vertical pitch.

There's not a bad seat in the house—no matter what, you're no more than 50 feet from the stage.

Visiting the Theater: From the main lobby and box office/gift shop area, there's plenty to see. First head left. In the circular **atrium** between the brick wall of the modern theater and fragments of the previous theater, notice the ratty old floorboards—pried up from the 1932 stage and laid down here. Upstairs on level 2, find the **Paccar Room,** with exhibits assembled from the RSC's substantial collection of historic costumes, props, manuscripts, and other theater memorabilia. Continue upstairs to level 3 to the Rooftop Restaurant (described later). High on the partition that runs through the restaurant, facing the brick theater wall, notice the four **chairs** affixed to the wall. These are original seats from the earlier theater, situated where the back row used to be (90 feet from the stage)—illustrating how much more audience-friendly the new design is.

Tower View: For a God's-eye view of all of Shakespeare's houses, ride the elevator to the top of the RSC's tower (£3, £1 with tour ticket, buy ticket at box office or book online; tower open daily 10:00-17:00; Oct-March Sun-Fri 10:00-16:30, Sat until 12:15; closed 12:00-14:00 year-round during matinees). The main attraction here is the 360-degree view over the theater building, the Avon, and the lanes of Stratford.

Rick's Tip: *For a cheap lunch out, get fish-and-chips from* **Barnaby's** *across from the riverfront park and have a picnic.*

Eating: The theater has a casual **$ café** with a terrace overlooking the river (sandwiches, daily 10:00-21:00), as well as the fancier **$$ Rooftop Restaurant**—though I'd dine elsewhere (Mon-Sat 11:30 until late, Sun 10:30-18:15, dinner reservations smart, tel. 01789/403-449, www.rsc.org.uk/rooftop).

Sleeping and Eating

If staying overnight, consider the homey **$$ Adelphi Guest House** (RS%, 39 Grove Road, www.adelphi-guesthouse.com), the cheaper **$ Salamander Guest House** (40 Grove Road, www.salamanderguesthouse.co.uk), or the central, business-class **$$ Mercure Shakespeare Hotel** (Chapel Street, www.mercure.com).

For lunch, try the retro-designed **$$ FourTeas 1940s Tea Room** (24 Sheep Street) or friendly **$$ Bensons Restaurant and Tea Rooms** (40 Henley Street). **$$ The Old Thatch Tavern** is the town's best pub (also open for dinner, on Greenhill Street overlooking the market square).

For dinner, these pricey, trendy eateries on Sheep Street have good-value pre-theater menus before 19:00: the half-timbered **Lambs** (12 Sheep Street), the less formal **The Opposition** next door (closed Sun), and the popular **The Vintner** up the street (4 Sheep Street).

Warwick Castle

Just north of Stratford, you'll find England's single most spectacular castle: Warwick (rated ▲▲). This medieval masterpiece, which has been turned into a virtual theme park, is extremely touristy—but it's also historic and fun, and may well be Britain's most kid-friendly experience.

The town of Warwick, huddled protectively against the castle walls, is a half-timbered delight—enjoyable for lunch or dinner, or even for an overnight.

Day Plan

Warwick Castle deserves at least three hours, but it can be an all-day outing for families. You can tour the sumptuous staterooms, climb the towers and ramparts for the views, stroll through themed exhibits populated by aristocratic wax figures, explore the sprawling grounds and gardens, and—best of all—interact with costumed docents who explain the place and perform fantastic demonstrations of medieval weapons and other skills.

Warwick Castle is a great family destination.

Orientation

Warwick is small and manageable. The castle and old town center sit side by side, with the train station about a mile to the north. From the castle's main gate, a lane leads into the old town center a block away, where you'll find the TI and plenty of eateries.

Cost: Steep £29 entry fee; entrance includes gardens and most castle attractions except for the gory (skippable) Castle Dungeon.

Hours: Daily July-Sept 10:00-17:00, Oct-June generally until 16:00 or 17:00.

Information: Recorded info tel. 0871/265-2000, www.warwick-castle.com.

Events: When you buy your castle ticket, be sure to pick up the daily events flier. Plan your day around these events, which can include jousting, archery, sword fights, jester acts, and falconry shows.

Getting There

By Train: Warwick has two train stations; you want the one called simply "Warwick" (Warwick Parkway Station is farther from the castle). To reach the castle or the town center, take a taxi (about £5) or walk (15 minutes, one mile).

By Car: Warwick is easy for drivers—the main Stratford-Coventry road cuts right through Warwick. Coming from Stratford (8 miles to the south), you'll hit two castle parking lots first (£6, buy token from machines at the castle entrance). You'll find plenty of other lots throughout Warwick.

Rick's Tip: *Warwick's TI sells same-day Fast Track ticket vouchers to Warwick Castle for a reduced rate, about a £5 savings over buying them on-site (TI open daily in season but closed Sun Jan-Easter, The Court House, Jury Street, www.visitwarwick.co.uk).*

Visiting the Castle

Buy your ticket and head through the turnstile into the moat area, where you'll get your first view of the dramatic castle—it's a 14th- and 15th-century fortified shell, holding an 18th- and 19th-century royal residence. From the moat, two entrance gateways lead to the castle's **inner court-**

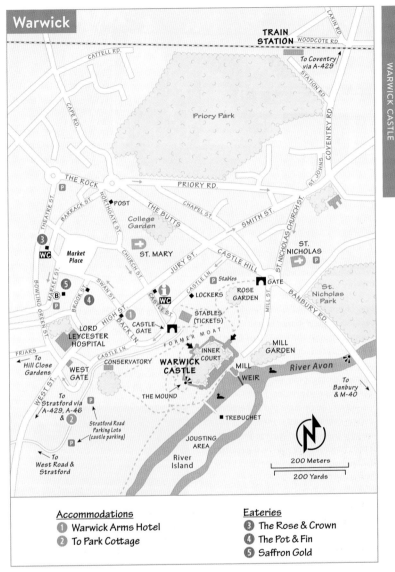

Warwick

TRAIN STATION — WOODCOTE RD.

LAKIN RD.

To Coventry via A-429

CATTELL RD.

STATION RD.

CAPE RD.

Priory Park

ST. JOHNS.

COVENTRY RD.

THE ROCK

P

POST

PRIORY RD.

BARRACK ST.

NORTHGATE ST.

THEATRE ST.

CHAPEL ST.

THE BUTTS

SMITH ST.

ST. NICHOLAS CHURCH ST.

College Garden

ST. NICHOLAS

3

WC

Market Place

ST. MARY

CHURCH ST.

JURY ST.

CASTLE HILL

P

MILL ST.

St. Nicholas Park

BOWLING GREEN ST.

MARKET ST.

BROOK ST.

SWAN ST.

HIGH ST.

BACK LN.

5

B

4

1

Stables

P

LOCKERS

CASTLE LN.

ROSE GARDEN

GATE

BANBURY RD.

CASTLE ST.

WC

STABLES (TICKETS)

CASTLE GATE

FORMER MOAT

MILL GARDEN

LORD LEYCESTER HOSPITAL

FRIARS

To Hill Close Gardens

CASTLE LN.

CONSERVATORY

WARWICK CASTLE

INNER COURT

MILL

River Avon

WEST GATE

WEST ST.

THE MOUND

MILL WEIR

To Banbury & M-40

To Stratford via A-429, A-46 & 2

P

Stratford Road Parking Lots (castle parking)

P

TREBUCHET

N

To West Road & Stratford

JOUSTING AREA

River Island

200 Meters

200 Yards

Accommodations
1 Warwick Arms Hotel
2 To Park Cottage

Eateries
3 The Rose & Crown
4 The Pot & Fin
5 Saffron Gold

yard. The bulge of land at the far right end, called **The Mound,** is where the original Norman castle of 1068 stood. Under this "motte," the wooden stockade (the "bailey") defined the courtyard in the way the castle walls do today.

GREAT HALL AND STATE ROOMS

The main attractions are in the largest buildings along the side of the courtyard: the Great Hall, five lavish staterooms, and the chapel. Progressing through these rooms, you'll see how the castle complex evolved over the centuries, from the militarized Middle Ages to civilized Victorian

A Warwick state room

times, from a formidable defensive fortress to a genteel manor home.

Enter through the cavernous **Great Hall,** decorated with suits of equestrian armor. Adjoining the Great Hall is the state dining room, with portraits of English kings and princes. Then follow the one-way route through the **staterooms,** keeping ever more esteemed company as you go—the rooms closest to the center of the complex were the most exclusive, reserved only for those especially close to the Earl of Warwick.

You'll pass through a series of three drawing rooms: first, one decorated in a deep burgundy; then the cedar drawing room, with intricately carved wood paneling, a Waterford crystal chandelier, and a Carrara marble fireplace; and the green drawing room, with a beautiful painted coffered ceiling and wax figures of Henry VIII and his six wives. The sumptuous Queen Anne Room was decorated in preparation for a planned 1704 visit by the monarch. Finally comes the blue boudoir, an oversized closet decorated in blue silk wallpaper. The portrait of King Henry VIII over the fireplace faces a clock once owned by Marie-Antoinette.

RAMPARTS AND TOWERS
You can climb up onto the ramparts and tower—a one-way, no-return route that leads you up and down the tallest tower (on very tight spiral stairs), leaving you at

A young knight

Bring a picnic lunch and enjoy the lush grounds at Warwick Castle.

a fun perch from which to fire your imaginary longbow. The halls and stairs can be very crowded with young kids, and—as the signs warn—it takes 530 steep steps (both up and down) to follow the whole route; claustrophobes may want to skip it.

The **Princess Tower** offers children (ages 3-8) the chance to dress up as princesses and princes for a photo op. While it's included in the castle ticket, those interested must first sign up for a 15-minute time slot at the information tent in the middle of the courtyard, near the staterooms.

CASTLE GROUNDS

Surrounding everything is a lush, peacock-patrolled, picnic-perfect park, complete with a Victorian rose garden. The castle grounds are often enlivened by a knight in shining armor on a horse or a merry band of musical jesters. The grassy moat area is typically filled with costumed characters and demonstrations, including archery and falconry. Near the entrance to

the complex is the **Pageant Playground,** with medieval-themed slides and climbing areas for kids, and the **Horrible Histories Maze,** which includes six "history zones" that cover the Vikings to World War I.

Sleeping and Eating

If you want to overnight in Warwick, try the charming **$$ Warwick Arms Hotel** (17 High Street, www.warwickarmshotel. com) or half-timbered **$$ Park Cottage** (113 West Street/A-429, www. parkcottagewarwick.co.uk).

Consider bringing a picnic to enjoy on the gorgeous grounds (otherwise you'll be left with the overpriced food stands). It's worth the 100-yard walk from the castle turnstiles to Warwick town's Market Place, with several lunch options on or near the square: **$$$ The Rose and Crown** (pub classics, daily), **$ The Pot & Fin** (excellent fish-and-chips, closed Sun-Mon), or **$$ Saffron Gold** (tasty Indian food, daily).

The Lake District

The Lake District is nature's lush green playground. Here, William Wordsworth's poems still shiver in trees and ripple on ponds. Nature rules this pristine land, and humanity keeps a wide-eyed but low profile. It's a place to relax, recharge, and maybe even write a poem.

Located in the northwestern county of Cumbria, the Lake District is about 30 miles long and 30 miles wide. Explore it by foot, bike, bus, or car.

There's a walking-stick charm about the way nature and the culture mix here. Cruising a lake, hiking along a windblown ridge, or climbing over a rock fence to look into the eyes of a ragamuffin sheep, even tenderfeet get a chance to feel very outdoorsy.

Dress in layers, and expect rain mixed with "bright spells." Drizzly days can be followed by delightful evenings. Pubs offer atmospheric shelter at every turn.

Plan to spend the majority of your time in the unspoiled North Lake District. Make your home base in the town of Keswick, near the lake called Derwentwater. The North Lake District works great by car or by bus (with easy train access via Penrith), delights nature lovers, and has good accommodations to boot. Side-trip to the South Lake District only if you're interested in its Wordsworth and Beatrix Potter sights.

THE LAKE DISTRICT IN 2 DAYS

Nearly all the activities on Day 1 can be enjoyed without a car.

Day 1: Spend the morning (3-4 hours) combining a Derwentwater lake cruise with a hike: Take the boat partway around the lake, get off at one of the stops to do either the Catbells high-ridge hike or the easier lakeside walk, then hop back on the boat at a later stop to finish the cruise.

For the afternoon, choose among hiking to Castlerigg Stone Circle (1 mile from Keswick), taking the Walla Crag hike (allow 2 hours), or visiting the Pencil Museum. Drivers could take the Latrigg Peak hike (trailhead is just outside Keswick).

On any evening: Enjoy a pub dinner and stroll through Keswick. Take a hike or evening cruise (or rent a rowboat), play pitch-and-putt golf, or see a play. Hike to the ancient stone circle—if you haven't yet—to toast the sunset.

Day 2: Drivers have these options:

Take the **scenic loop drive** from Keswick through the Newlands Valley, Buttermere, Honister Pass, and Borrowdale. Allow two hours for the drive; by adding stops for the Buttermere hike (an easy 4 miles) and the slate-mine tour at Honister Pass (check last tour time), you'll have a full, fun day.

Drive to Glenridding for a **cruise and seven-mile hike** along Ullswater (allow a day). For a shorter Ullswater experience, hike up to the Aira Force waterfall (1 hour) or up to and around Lanty's Tarn (2 hours).

You could day-trip into the **South Lake District** for the Wordsworth and Beatrix Potter sights. Visiting the sights also works well en route if you're driving between Keswick and points south.

Those **without a car** can use Keswick as a springboard: Cruise the lake and take a hike in the Catbells area or hop on a minibus tour. Or take advantage of two public bus routes: The Honister Rambler (#77/#77A) makes the gorgeous circle from Keswick around Derwentwater, over Honister Pass, through Buttermere, and down the Whinlatter Valley. The Borrowdale Rambler (#78) goes topless in the summer, affording a wonderful sightseeing experience in and of itself, heading from Keswick to Lodore Hotel, Grange Bridge, Rosthwaite, and Seatoller at the base of Honister Pass (see page 266 for bus details).

KESWICK AND THE NORTH LAKE DISTRICT

Keswick (KEZ-ick, population 5,000) is far more enjoyable than other touristy Lake District towns. An important mining center for slate, copper, and lead through the Middle Ages, Keswick became a resort in the 19th century. Its fine Victorian buildings recall the days when city slickers first learned about communing with nature, inspired by the Romantic poets (Wordsworth, Coleridge) who wandered the trails here. Today, the compact town is lined with tearooms, pubs, gift shops, and hiking-gear shops. The shore of the lake called Derwentwater is a pleasant 10-minute walk from the town center.

The Lake District is arguably the most scenic district in all of England.

THE LAKE DISTRICT AT A GLANCE

North Lake District

▲▲▲**Scenic Circle Drive South of Keswick** Hour-long drive through the best of the Lake District's scenery, with plenty of fun stops. See page 253.

▲▲**Castlerigg Stone Circle** Evocative and extremely old (even by British standards) ring of Neolithic stones. See page 250.

▲▲**Catbells High Ridge Hike** Two-hour hike along dramatic ridge southwest of Keswick. See page 251.

▲▲**Buttermere Hike** Four-mile, low-impact lakeside loop in a gorgeous setting. See page 252.

▲▲**Theatre by the Lake** Top-notch theater a pleasant stroll from Keswick's main square. See page 255.

▲**Derwentwater** Lake immediately south of Keswick, with good boat service and trails. See page 245.

▲**Honister Slate Mine Tour** Guided 1.5-hour hike through a 19th-century mine at the top of Honister Pass. **Hours:** Daily in season at 10:30, 12:30, and 15:30; also at 14:00 in summer. See page 254.

▲ **Pitch-and-Putt Golf** Cheap, easygoing nine-hole course in Keswick's Hope Park. **Hours:** Daily from 10:00, shorter hours off-season. See page 250.

Ullswater Lake Area

▲▲ **Ullswater Hike and Boat Ride** Long lake best enjoyed via steamer boat and seven-mile walk. See page 258.

▲▲ **Lanty's Tarn and Keldas Hill** Moderately challenging 2.5-mile loop hike from Glenridding with sweeping views of Ullswater. See page 258.

▲ **Aira Force Waterfall** Easy uphill hike to picturesque waterfall. See page 259.

South Lake District

▲▲ **Dove Cottage at Wordsworth Grasmere** The poet's humble home, with a museum that tells the story of his remarkable life. **Hours:** Daily 9:30-17:30, Nov-Feb 10:00-16:30 except closed Jan. See page 260.

▲ **Rydal Mount and Gardens** Wordsworth's later, more upscale home. **Hours:** Daily 9:30-17:30; Nov-Dec and Feb 10:00-16:30 and closed Mon-Tue; closed Jan. See page 262.

▲ **Hill Top Farm** Beatrix Potter's painstakingly preserved cottage. **Hours:** June-Aug daily 10:00-17:30; mid-Feb-May and Sept-Oct until 16:30 and closed Fri; house closed Nov-Dec but gardens and shop open Sat-Sun, closed Jan-mid-Feb. See page 263.

▲ **Beatrix Potter Gallery** Collection of artwork by and background on the creator of Peter Rabbit. **Hours:** Daily 10:30-16:00, closed Nov-mid-Feb. See page 264.

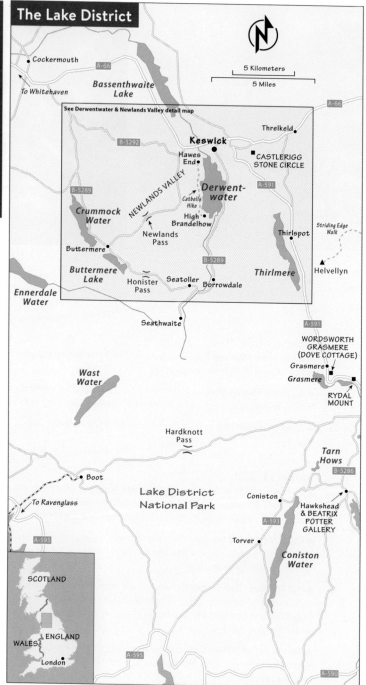

The Lake District

5 Kilometers

5 Miles

Cockermouth

A-66

To Whitehaven

Bassenthwaite Lake

A-66

Threlkeld

See Derwentwater & Newlands Valley detail map

B-5292

Keswick

Hawes End

CASTLERIGG STONE CIRCLE

A-591

Derwentwater

Catbells Hike

NEWLANDS VALLEY

High Brandelhow

Striding Edge Walk

Thirlspot

Crummock Water

Newlands Pass

Buttermere

Newlands Pass

B-5289

Thirlmere

Helvellyn

Buttermere Lake

Honister Pass

Seatoller

Borrowdale

B-5289

Ennerdale Water

Seathwaite

A-591

WORDSWORTH GRASMERE (DOVE COTTAGE)

Grasmere

Grasmere

RYDAL MOUNT

Wast Water

Hardknott Pass

Tarn Hows

B-5286

Boot

Lake District National Park

Coniston

Hawkshead & BEATRIX POTTER GALLERY

To Ravenglass

A-593

A-595

Torver

Coniston Water

SCOTLAND

ENGLAND

WALES

London

A-595

A-590

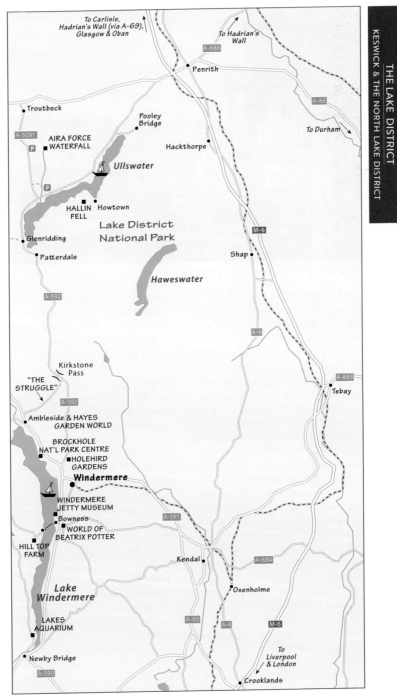

Stone and slate buildings predominate in Keswick.

Orientation

Keswick is an ideal home base, with plenty of good B&Bs, an easy bus connection to the nearest train station at Penrith, and a prime location near the best lake in the area, Derwentwater. In Keswick, everything is within a 10-minute walk of everything else: the pedestrian town square, the TI, recommended B&Bs, grocery stores, the wonderful municipal pitch-and-putt golf course, the main bus stop, a lakeside boat dock, and a central parking lot.

Keswick town is a delight for wandering. Its centerpiece, Moot Hall (meaning "meeting hall"), was a 16th-century copper warehouse upstairs with a market arcade below. The town square is lively every day throughout the summer, especially on market days—Thursdays and Saturdays.

Tourist Information

The National Park Visitors Centre/TI is in Moot Hall, right on the town square (daily 9:30-17:30, Nov-Easter until 16:30, tel. 0845-901-0845, www.keswick.org; you'll also find helpful planning info at www. lakedistrict.gov.uk, tel. 01539/724-555).

Staffers are pros at advising you about hiking routes. They can also help you figure out public transportation to outlying sights. For information about the TI's guided walks, see "Tours," below.

Helpful Hints

Laundry: The town's launderette is on Bank Street, just up the side street from the post office (full- and self-service; Mon-Fri 8:00-19:00, Sat-Sun 9:00-18:00, tel. 017687/75448).

Groceries and More: Booths, a huge, modern supermarket (facing the Keswick bus stop), has a fine cafeteria, handy food to-go, a great book and map section, and a public WC (daily 7:00-22:00, shorter Sun hours, Tithebarn Street, tel. 017684/73518).

Tours

WALKING TOURS

The **Keswick TI** offer guided walks several times weekly, some free and others £5-10, led by "Voluntary Rangers" in summer (depart from Keswick TI; check the Events and Guided Walks page at www. lakedistrict.gov.uk for schedule, descriptions, and advance booking).

Rick's Tip: *Be sure to try Kendal mint cakes, a longtime favorite among hikers. You'll find them in area supermarkets and gift stores.*

PRIVATE GUIDES

Show Me Cumbria Private Tours, run by Andy, offers personalized tours all around the Lake District (£140/half-day for 3-6 people, tel. 017688/64825, mobile 07809-026-357, www.showmecumbria.co.uk, andy@showmecumbria.co.uk).

Discover Lakeland, led by friendly and experienced Blue Badge guide Anna Grey, gives tours all over Cumbria and beyond (£160/half-day, £260/full day, mobile 07557-915-855, www.discoverlakeland.uk, anna@discoverlakeland.co.uk).

Keswick Rambles Guided Walks, led by Pete and Lynn Armstrong, offers private guided hikes of varying difficulty, including the popular Catbells trail (typically £90/day or £20-25/person if more than 4, Easter-Oct, must book in advance, tel. 017687/71302, mobile 07342-637-813, keswickrambles.blogspot.co.uk, armstrongps1@gmx.com).

BUS TOURS

Mountain Goat Tours is the region's dominant tour company and runs half- and full-day minibus excursions nearly every morning and afternoon from Keswick to all the scenic highlights. Customizable private tours are also available (£22-40/half-day, £48/full day, tours run April-Oct, maximum of 16 persons, book in advance, tel. 015394/45161, www.mountain-goat.com, tours@mountain-goat.com).

Sights

▲DERWENTWATER

One of Cumbria's most photographed and popular lakes, Derwentwater has four islands, good boat service, and plenty of trails. While you can walk around the lake, you're better off mixing a hike and boat ride, or simply enjoying a boat cruise around the lake.

Boating on Derwentwater: The Keswick Launch Company runs two **cruises** an hour, alternating clockwise and "anticlockwise" (boats depart on the half-hour, daily 10:00-16:30, July-Aug until 17:30, in winter 6/day generally weekends and holidays only, at end of Lake Road, tel. 017687/72263,

Derwentwater is just a 10-minute walk from the ideal home-base town of Keswick.

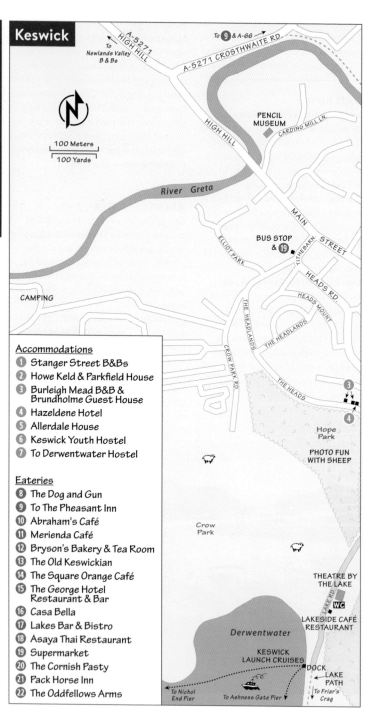

Keswick

PENCIL MUSEUM

CAMPING

BUS STOP & ⑲

Accommodations
① Stanger Street B&Bs
② Howe Keld & Parkfield House
③ Burleigh Mead B&B & Brundholme Guest House
④ Hazeldene Hotel
⑤ Allerdale House
⑥ Keswick Youth Hostel
⑦ To Derwentwater Hostel

Eateries
⑧ The Dog and Gun
⑨ To The Pheasant Inn
⑩ Abraham's Café
⑪ Merienda Café
⑫ Bryson's Bakery & Tea Room
⑬ The Old Keswickian
⑭ The Square Orange Café
⑮ The George Hotel Restaurant & Bar
⑯ Casa Bella
⑰ Lakes Bar & Bistro
⑱ Asaya Thai Restaurant
⑲ Supermarket
⑳ The Cornish Pasty
㉑ Pack Horse Inn
㉒ The Oddfellows Arms

To ⑨ & A-66

A-5271 HIGH HILL
To Newlands Valley B & Bs
A-5271 CROSTHWAITE RD.

HIGH HILL

CARDING MILL LN.

River Greta

MAIN STREET

ELLIOT PARK

TITHEBARN

HEADS RD.

HEADS MOUNT

THE HEADLANDS

THE HEADLANDS

THE HEADS

CROW PARK RD.

Hope Park

PHOTO FUN WITH SHEEP

Crow Park

THEATRE BY THE LAKE

LAKE RD. WC

LAKESIDE CAFÉ RESTAURANT

Derwentwater

KESWICK LAUNCH CRUISES

DOCK
LAKE PATH

To Nichol End Pier

To Ashness Gate Pier

To Friar's Crag

100 Meters
100 Yards

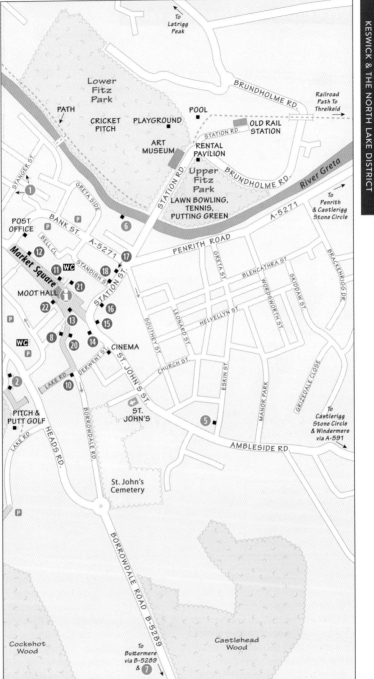

Derwentwater & Newlands Valley

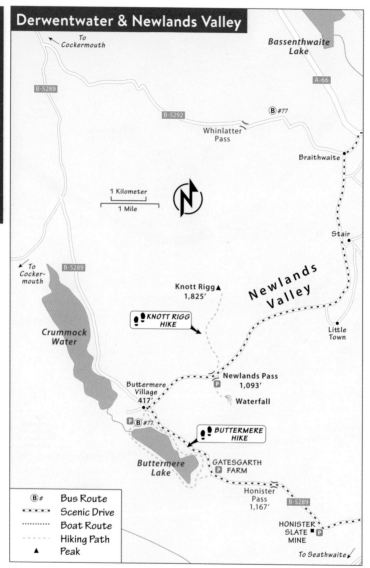

www.keswick-launch.co.uk). Boats make seven stops on each 50-minute round-trip (may skip some stops or not run at all if the water level is very high—such as after a heavy rain). The boat trip costs about £2 per segment or £11 per round-trip circuit (£1 less if you book through TI) with free stopovers; you can get on and off all you want, but tickets are collected on the boat's last leg to Keswick, marking the end of your ride. If you want to hop on the scenic #77/#77A bus and also cruise Derwentwater, the Derwentwater Bus & Boat all-day pass covers both (see "Getting Around the Lake District" at the end of this chapter). To be picked up at a certain stop, stand at the

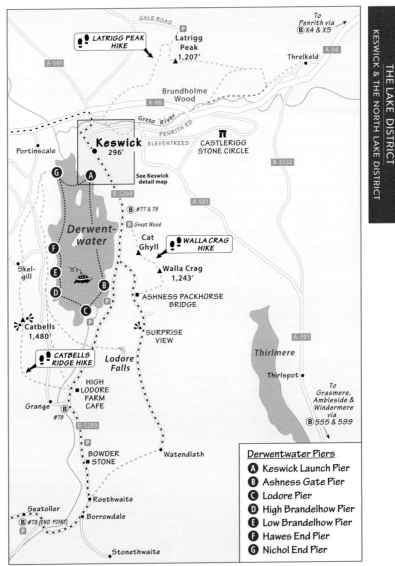

GALE ROAD

To Penrith via B X4 & X5

LATRIGG PEAK HIKE

Latrigg Peak 1,207'

Threlkeld

A-591

A-66

Brundholme Wood

A-66

Greta River

PENRITH RD.

Keswick 296'

Portinscale

ELEVENTREES

CASTLERIGG STONE CIRCLE

See Keswick detail map

B-5532

G

A

B-5289

A-591

B #77 & 78

P Great Wood

Derwent-water

Cat Ghyll

WALLA CRAG HIKE

F

Skel-gill

E

Walla Crag 1,243'

B

D

ASHNESS PACKHORSE BRIDGE

C

P

Catbells 1,480'

SURPRISE VIEW

A-591

Thirlmere

CATBELLS RIDGE HIKE

Lodore Falls

Thirlspot

HIGH LODORE FARM CAFE

To Grasmere, Ambleside & Windermere via B 555 & 599

Grange

B

#78

B-5289

P

BOWDER STONE

Watendlath

Seatoller

B #78 (END POINT)

P

Rosthwaite

Borrowdale

Stonethwaite

Derwentwater Piers
- **A** Keswick Launch Pier
- **B** Ashness Gate Pier
- **C** Lodore Pier
- **D** High Brandelhow Pier
- **E** Low Brandelhow Pier
- **F** Hawes End Pier
- **G** Nichol End Pier

end of the pier and wave, or the boat may not stop. See the "Derwentwater & Newlands Valley" map in this chapter for an overview of all the boat stops.

Keswick Launch also rents **rowboats** for up to three people (£10/30 minutes, £15/hour, open Easter-Oct, larger rowboats and motorboats available).

Derwentwater Lakeside Walk: A fine, marked trail runs all along Derwentwater (9 miles, 4 hours, floods after heavy rains), but much of it (especially the Keswick-to-Hawes End stretch) is not that interesting. The best hour-long section is the 1.5-mile path between the docks at High Brandelhow and Hawes End, where you'll stroll a level trail through peaceful trees. This walk works well with the lake boat described above.

For a very easy, paved stroll, walk 10 minutes from the Keswick dock clockwise to the Friar's Crag viewpoint. The Lakeside Café Restaurant overlooking the Keswick landing can be handy (daily 9:00-20:30).

DERWENT PENCIL MUSEUM

Graphite was first discovered centuries ago in Keswick. A hunk of the stuff proved great for marking sheep in the 15th century. In 1832, the first crude Keswick pencil factory opened, and the rest is history (which is what you'll learn about here). While the factory that made the famous Derwent pencils is closed, a small modern building tells the story in a kid-friendly exhibit filling one small room.

Cost and Hours: £5, daily 9:30-17:00, last entry one hour before closing, humble café, 3-minute walk from town center, signposted off Main Street, tel. 017687/73626, www.pencilmuseum.co.uk.

GOLF AND HOPE PARK

A nine-hole ▲ pitch-and-putt golf course near the lush gardens in Hope Park separates the town from the lake and offers a classy, cheap, and convenient chance to golf near the birthplace of the sport (daily from 10:00, last round starts around 18:00, possibly later in summer, shorter hours off-season, café, tel. 017687/73445, www.hopeleisure.com).

Even if you're not a golfer, Hope Park is a fine place to walk among grazing sheep, with great photo ops.

SWIMMING

While the leisure center lacks a serious adult pool, it does have an indoor pool kids love, with a huge waterslide and wave machine (swim times vary by day and by season—call or check website, no towels or suits for rent, lockers available, 10-minute walk from town center, follow Station Road past Fitz Park and veer left, tel. 017687/72760, www.better.org.uk).

Near Keswick

▲▲CASTLERIGG STONE CIRCLE

For some reason, 70 percent of England's stone circles are here in Cumbria. Castlerigg is one of the best and oldest in Britain, and an easy stop for drivers. The circle—90 feet across and 5,000 years old—has 38 stones mysteriously laid out on a line between the two tallest peaks on the horizon. They may have served as a celestial calendar for ritual celebrations. Imagine the ambience here, as ancient people filled this clearing in spring to celebrate fertility, in late summer to commemorate the harvest, and in the winter to celebrate the winter solstice and the coming renewal of light. Festival dates may have been dictated by how the sun rose and set in relation to the stones. The more that modern academics study this circle, the more meaning they find in the

Hope Park golf course

Castlerigg Stone Circle

placement of the stones. For maximum "goose pimples" (as they say here), show up at sunset.

Cost and Hours: Free, always open, located 1.5 miles east of Keswick on Eleventrees Road; about 30 minutes from town on foot; by car, follow brown signs—it's 3 minutes off the A-66, limited but easy parking, www.english-heritage.org.uk.

Experiences
Hikes and Drives

Don't hike without a good, detailed map (wide selection at Keswick TI and outdoor gear stores, or borrow one from your B&B). Helpful fliers at TIs and B&Bs describe the most popular routes. For an up-to-date weather report, check LakeDistrictWeatherLine.co.uk or call the local weather line: 0844-846-2444. Wear suitable clothing and footwear (you can rent boots in town), and plan for rain.

▲▲CATBELLS HIGH RIDGE HIKE

For a great "king of the mountain" feeling, 360-degree views, and a close-up look at the weather blowing over the ridge, take a two-hour hike above Derwentwater from Hawes End up along the ridge to Catbells

(1,480 feet) and down to High Brandelhow. This is probably the most dramatic family walk in the area (wear sturdy shoes and bring a raincoat).

Because the mountaintop is basically treeless, you're treated to dramatic panoramas the entire way up. From High Brandelhow, you can catch the boat back to Keswick or take the easy path along the Derwentwater shore to your Hawes End starting point. (Extending the hike farther around the lake to Lodore takes you to a waterfall, rock climbers, a fine café, and another boat dock for a convenient return to Keswick—for more about Lodore, see page 254). Note: When the water level is very high, boats can't stop at Hawes End—ask at the TI or boat dock before setting out.

Getting There: To reach the trailhead from Keswick, catch the "anticlockwise" boat (see "Boating on Derwentwater," earlier) and ride for 10 minutes to the second stop, Hawes End. Note the schedule for your return boat ride. If driving, there's free but limited parking at Hawes End, and the road can be hard to find—get clear directions in town before heading out. (Hardcore hikers can walk to the foot

Catbells High Ridge

of Catbells from Keswick via Portinscale, which takes about 40 minutes—ask your B&B or the TI for directions.)

The Route: The path is not signposted, but it's easy to follow, and you'll see plenty of other walkers. From Hawes End, walk away from the lake through a kissing gate to the turn just before the car park. Then turn left and go up, up, up. After about 20 minutes, you'll hit the first of two short scrambles (where the trail vanishes into a cluster of steep rocks), which leads to a bluff. From the first little summit (great for a picnic break), and then along the ridge, you'll enjoy sweeping views of the lake on one side and of Newlands Valley on the other. The bald peak in the distance is Catbells. Broken stones crunch under each step, wind buffets your ears, clouds prowl overhead, and the sheep baa comically. To anyone looking up from the distant farmhouse B&Bs, you are but a stick figure on the ridge. Just below the summit, the trail disintegrates into another short, steep scramble. Your reward is just beyond: a magnificent hilltop perch.

After the Catbells summit, descend along the ridge to a saddle ahead. The ridge continues much higher, and while it may look like your only option, at its base a small, unmarked lane with comfortable steps leads left. Take this path down to the lake. To get to High Brandelhow Pier, take the first left fork you come across down through a forest to the lake. When you reach Abbot's Bay, go left through a swinging gate, following a lakeside trail around a gravelly bluff, to the idyllic High Brandelhow Pier, a peaceful place to wait for your boat back to Keswick. (You can pay your fare when you board.)

Rick's Tip: *Tiny biting* **midges** *might bug you in this region from late May through September, particularly at dawn and dusk. Be prepared with* **insect repellant** *to fend them off.*

LATRIGG PEAK

For the easiest mountain-climbing sensation around, take the short drive to the Latrigg Peak parking lot just north of Keswick, and hike 15 minutes to the top of the 1,200-foot-high hill, where you'll be rewarded with a commanding view of the town, lake, and valley, all the way to Bassenthwaite, the next lake over. At the traffic circle just outside Keswick, take the A-591 Carlisle exit, then an immediate right (direction: Ormathwaite/Underscar). Take the next right, a hard right, at the *Skiddaw* sign, where a long, steep, one-lane road leads to the Latrigg parking lot at the end of the lane. With more time, you can walk all the way from your Keswick B&B to Latrigg and back (it's a popular evening walk for locals).

WALLA CRAG

From your Keswick B&B, a fine two-hour walk to Walla Crag offers great fell (mountain) and ridge walking without the necessity of a bus or car. Start by strolling along the lake to the Great Wood parking lot (or drive to this lot), and head up Cat Ghyl (where "fell runners"—trail-running enthusiasts—practice) to Walla Crag. You'll be treated to great panoramic views over Derwentwater and surrounding peaks—especially beautiful when the heather blossoms in the summer. You can do a shorter version of this walk from the parking lot at Ashness Packhorse Bridge.

▲▲BUTTERMERE HIKE

The ideal little lake with a lovely circular four-mile stroll offers nonstop, no-sweat Lake District beauty. If you're not a hiker but wish you were, take this walk. If you're short on time, at least stop here and get your shoes dirty.

Buttermere is connected with Borrowdale and Derwentwater by a dramatic road that runs over rugged Honister Pass. Bus #77/#77A make a 1.75-hour round-trip loop between Keswick and Buttermere that includes a trip over this pass. The two-pub hamlet of Buttermere has

Buttermere hike

two pay-and-display parking lots and free parking along the roadside by the church. There's also a pay parking lot at the Honister Pass end of the lake (at Gatesgarth Farm). The Syke Farm Tea Room in Buttermere is popular for its enticing farm-made ice cream (daily 11:30-17:00, light lunches, box lunches for hikers).

While you can circumnavigate the entire lake, the side opposite the road is nicest. You can walk from one end to the other—Buttermere to Gatesgarth Farm—in about an hour (using a pay and display lot at either end and/or bus #77). In Buttermere the trail starts at The Fish Hotel.

▲▲▲SCENIC CIRCLE DRIVE SOUTH OF KESWICK

This hour-long drive, which includes Newlands Valley, Buttermere, Honister Pass, and Borrowdale, offers the North Lake District's best scenery. (To do a similar route without a car from Keswick, take loop bus #77/#77A and use it as a do-it-yourself, hop-on, hop-off tour.) Distances are short, roads are narrow and have turnouts, and views are rewarding. Get a good map and ask your B&B host for advice. (For an overview of the route, see the "Derwentwater & Newlands Valley" map in this chapter.)

Keswick to Newlands Pass: From Keswick, leave town on Crosthwaite Road, then, at the roundabout, head west on Cockermouth Road (A-66, following *Cockermouth* and *Workington* signs). Don't take the first Newlands Valley exit (to Grange), but do take the second one (through Braithwaite), and follow signs up the majestic Newlands Valley (also signed for *Buttermere*).

If the **Newlands Valley** had a lake, it would be packed with tourists. But it doesn't—and it isn't. The valley is dotted with 500-year-old family-owned farms. Shearing day is reason to rush home from school. Sons get school out of the way ASAP and follow their dads into the family business. Neighbor girls marry those sons and move in with them. Grandparents retire to the cottage next door. With the price of wool depressed, most of the wives supplement the family income by running B&Bs (virtually every farm in the valley rents rooms). The road (six miles to the pass) has one lane, with turnouts for passing. From the Newlands Pass summit, notice the glacial-shaped wilds, once forested, now not.

At **Newlands Pass** (unmarked, but you'll see a waterfall on the left and a parking pullout), an easy 300-yard hike leads to a little waterfall. On the other side of the road, a one-mile hike climbs up to **Knott Rigg,** which offers lots of TPCB (thrills per calorie burned). If you don't have time for even a short hike, at least get out of the car, hike a couple of minutes to your own private bluff, and get a feel for the setting.

Newlands Pass to Honister Pass and Slate Mine: From the pass, descend to Buttermere (scenic lake, tiny hamlet with pubs and an ice-cream store—see "Buttermere Hike," earlier), turn left, drive the length of the lake, and climb over rugged Honister Pass—strewn with glacial debris, remnants from the old slate mines, and curious shaggy sheep. The U-shaped valleys you'll see are textbook examples of those carved out by glaciers. Look high on the hillsides for small "hanging valleys"—they were cut off by the huge flow of the much larger glacier that swept down the main valley floor.

The **Honister Slate Mine,** England's last still-functioning slate mine (and worth ▲), stands at the summit of Honister Pass. The youth hostel next to it was built to house miners in the 1920s. The mine offers worthwhile tours into a shaft to learn about the region's slate industry. Even if you don't have time to take the tour, stop here for the slate-filled shop (£17.50, 1.5-hour tour; departs daily at 10:30, 12:30, and 15:30; additional tour at 14:00 in summer; Dec-Jan 12:30 tour only; reserve online or call ahead to confirm times and to book a spot, helmets and lamps provided, wear good walking shoes and bring warm clothing even in summer, café and nice WCs, tel. 017687/77230, www.honister.com, Roland).

From Honister Slate Mine to Lodore: From the mine, you'll drop into the sweet and homey **Borrowdale Valley,** with a few lonely hamlets. Circling past Borrowdale, you'll turn north onto the B-5289 (a.k.a. the Borrowdale Valley Road), which takes you past the following popular attractions:

The house-size **Bowder Stone,** thought to have cleaved from the top of a nearby cliff, sits about 15 minutes off the main road (signposted); a ladder lets you climb to the top. For a great lunch or snack, including tea and homemade quiche and cakes, drop in to the much-loved **$ High Lodore Farm Café** (daily

You'll find scenic vistas everywhere you venture in the Lake District.

9:00-18:00, closed Nov-Easter, short drive uphill from the main road and over a tiny bridge, tel. 017687/77221).

Nearby is the village of **Grange,** which must be the cutest hamlet in the area. It's built of locally quarried Lakeland Green slate, and mostly by one builder, which adds to the tidy feel. Grange has a couple of inviting cafés and two tiny churches—one vibrant and welcoming; the other is home to the free "Borrowdale Story" history exhibit.

Farther along, **Lodore Falls** is a short walk from the road, behind the Lodore Hotel (a nice place to stop for tea and beautiful views). **Shepherds Crag,** a cliff overlooking Lodore, was made famous by pioneering rock climbers as far back as the 1890s. (Their descendants hang from little ridges on its face today.)

From Lodore, with a Detour, to Keswick: A very hard right off the B-5289 at the Ashness Gate Pier (signposted *Ashness Bridge, Watendlath*) and a steep half-mile climb on a narrow lane takes you to the postcard-pretty **Ashness Packhorse Bridge,** a quintessential Lake District scene (parking lot just above on right). A half-mile farther up, park the car and hop out (parking lot on left, no sign). You'll be startled by the "surprise view" of Derwentwater—great for a lakes photo op. Continuing from here, the road gets extremely narrow en route to the hamlet of **Watendlath,** which has a tiny lake and lazy farm animals.

Return to the B-5289 and head back to Keswick. If you have yet to see it, cap your drive with a short detour from Keswick to the Castlerigg Stone Circle.

Nightlife
▲▲THEATRE BY THE LAKE
Keswickians brag that they enjoy "London theater quality at Keswick prices." Their theater offers events year-round on two stages and a wonderful rotation of six plays from late May through October (plays vary throughout the week,

with music concerts on Sun in summer). Attending a play here is a fine opportunity to enjoy a classy night out.

Cost and Hours: £10-36, discounts for those under 26; shows generally at 19:30; café, restaurant (pretheater dinners start at 17:30 and must be booked 24 hours ahead by calling 017687/81102), located off Lake Road with parking in adjacent lot. It's smart to buy tickets in advance—book at box office (daily 9:30-19:30 on performance days, other days until 18:00), by phone (tel. 017687/74411), at TI, or at www.theatrebythelake.com.

PUB EVENTS
To socialize with locals, head to a pub for one of their special evenings. **Quiz nights** are popular at many local pubs, and tourists are more than welcome. Drop in, say you want to join a team, and you're in (the Pack Horse Inn, on Packhorse Court, hosts quiz nights most Wed at 21:30).

The Oddfellows Arms has free **live music** (often classic rock) in summer (April-Oct Thu-Sun from 21:30, 19 Main Street). The Square Orange occasionally has live music on Wednesday evenings (20 St. John's Street) and the Pack Horse Inn on weekends.

Sleeping
Reserve your room in advance in high season. Many Keswick listings charge extra for a one-night stay and most won't book one-night stays on weekends. Some add a surcharge for credit cards. Most don't welcome young children. None have elevators and all have lots of stairs—ask about a ground-floor unit if steps are a problem.

On Stanger Street
This street, quiet but just a block from Keswick's town center, is lined with B&Bs situated in Victorian slate townhouses. Each of these places is small and family-run. They all offer comfortably sized rooms, free parking, and a friendly welcome.

$$ Ellergill Guest House has four spic-and-span rooms with an airy, contemporary feel—several with views (2-night minimum, no children under age 10, 22 Stanger Street, tel. 017687/73347, www.ellergill.co.uk, stay@ellergill.co.uk, Clare and Robin Pinkney).

$$ Badgers Wood B&B, at the top of the street, has six modern, bright, unfrilly view rooms, each named after a different tree (2-night minimum, no children under age 12, special diets accommodated, 30 Stanger Street, tel. 017687/72621, www.badgers-wood.co.uk, enquiries@badgers-wood.co.uk, chatty Scotsman Andrew and his charming wife, Anne).

$$ Abacourt House, with a daisy-fresh breakfast room, has five pleasant doubles (2-night minimum on weekends, no children, sack lunches available, 26 Stanger Street, tel. 017687/72967, www.abacourt.co.uk, abacourt.keswick@btinternet.com, John and Heather).

$ Dunsford Guest House rents four updated rooms at bargain prices. Stained glass and wooden pews give the bright breakfast room a country-chapel vibe (RS%, cash only, 16 Stanger Street, tel. 017687/75059, www.dunsfordguesthouse.co.uk, info@dunsfordguesthouse.co.uk, Deb and Keith).

On the Heads

The classy area known as The Heads has B&Bs with bigger and grander Victorian architecture and great views.

$$$ Howe Keld has the polished feel of a boutique hotel, but offers all the friendliness of a B&B. Its 12 contemporary-posh rooms are spacious and tastefully decked out in native woods and slate. It's warm, welcoming, and family-run, with an à la carte breakfast cooked to order by chef Jerome (cash and 2-night minimum preferred, sack lunches available, tel. 017687/72417, www.howekeld.co.uk, laura@howekeld.co.uk, run with care by Laura and Jerome Bujard).

$$ Parkfield House, thoughtfully run and decorated by John and Susan Berry, is a big Victorian house with a homey lounge. Its six rooms, some with fine views, are bright and classy (RS%, 2-night minimum, no children under age 16, free parking, tel. 017687/72328, www.parkfieldkeswick.co.uk, parkfieldkeswick@hotmail.co.uk).

$$ Burleigh Mead B&B is a slate mansion from 1892. Gill (pronounced "Jill," short for Gillian) rents seven lovely rooms and offers a friendly welcome, as well as a lounge and peaceful front-yard sitting area that's perfect for enjoying the view (cash only, discount for longer stays, no children under age 8, tel. 017687/75935, www.burleighmead.co.uk, info@burleighmead.co.uk).

$$ Hazeldene Hotel, on the corner of The Heads, rents 10 spacious rooms, many with commanding views. There's even a "boot room" that doubles as a guest rec room with a ping-pong table. It's run with care by delightful Helen and Howard (ground-floor unit available, free parking, tel. 017687/72106, www.hazeldene-hotel.co.uk, info@hazeldene-hotel.co.uk).

$$ Brundholme Guest House has four bright and comfy rooms, most with sweeping views at no extra charge—especially from the front side—and a friendly and welcoming atmosphere (mini fridge, free parking, tel. 017687/73305, mobile 07739-435-401, www.brundholme.co.uk, bazaly@hotmail.co.uk, Barry and Allison Thompson).

On Eskin Street

Just southeast of the town center, the area around Eskin Street is still within easy walking distance and has stress-free parking.

$$ Allerdale House, a classy, nicely decorated stone mansion with five rooms, is well run by Mat and Leigh Richards (RS%, free parking, 1 Eskin Street, tel. 017687/73891, www.allerdale-house.co.uk, reception@allerdale-house.co.uk).

Hostels

¢ **Keswick Youth Hostel,** with a big lounge and a great riverside balcony, fills a converted mill. Travelers of all ages feel at home here, but book ahead—family rooms book up July through September (breakfast extra, café, bar, office open 7:00-23:00, center of town just off Station Road before river, tel. 017687/72484, www.yha.org.uk, keswick@yha.org.uk).

¢ **Derwentwater Hostel,** in a 220-year-old mansion on the shore of Derwentwater, is two miles south of Keswick (breakfast extra, family rooms; follow the B-5289 from Keswick—entrance is 2 miles along the Borrowdale Valley Road about 150 yards after Ashness exit—look for cottage and bus stop at bottom of the drive; tel. 017687/77246, www.derwentwater.org, contact@derwentwater.org).

Eating in Keswick

$$ The Dog and Gun serves good pub food (their rump of lamb is a hit) with great pub ambience. Upon arrival, muscle up to the bar to order your beer or meal. Then snag a table as soon as one opens up (food served daily 12:00-21:00, famous goulash, dog treats, 2 Lake Road, tel. 017687/73463).

$$ The Pheasant Inn is a walk outside town, but locals trek here regularly for the food. The menu offers Lake District pub standards (fish pie, Cumberland sausage, guinea fowl) as well as more inventive choices. There's a small restaurant section, but I much prefer eating in the bar (food served daily 12:00-14:00 & 18:00-21:00, bar open until 23:00, Crosthwaite Road, tel. 017687/72219). From the town square, walk past the Pencil Museum, hang a right onto Crosthwaite Road, and walk 10 minutes. For a more scenic route, cross the river into Fitz Park, go left along the riverside path until it ends at the gate to Crosthwaite Road, turn right, and walk five minutes.

$ Abraham's Café, popular with townspeople, is a fine value for lunch. It's tucked away on the upper floor of the giant George Fisher outdoor store (Mon-Sat 10:00-17:00, Sun 10:30-16:30, on the corner of Borrowdale and Lake streets, tel. 017687/71811).

$$ Merienda Café, with a friendly staff and a contemporary space, can be a welcome break from pub grub, serving up an inviting menu of international, North African, and vegetarian dishes (daily 9:00-21:00, 10 Main Street, tel. 017687/72024).

$$ Bryson's Bakery and Tea Room has an enticing ground-floor bakery, with sandwiches and light lunches. The upstairs is a popular tearoom. Order lunch to-go from the bakery, or for a few pence more, eat in, either sitting on stools or at a sidewalk table (daily 9:00-17:00, 42 Main Street, tel. 017687/72257).

$ The Old Keswickian, a fish-and-chips shop, is a fixture on the main square, with an old-fashioned takeaway bar on the ground floor and 70 seats upstairs in a proper dining room (£10 plates and meat pies, daily 11:00-19:30, takeaway until 20:00, on Market Square, tel. 017687/73861).

$$ The Square Orange Café—small and very orange—is a quirky place that just makes you want to smile. It's popular—and they take no reservations, so grab one of their eight little tables when you can and then order at the bar. The eclectic menu features Spanish tapas, Neapolitan pizzas, fun cocktails, and fine European beers (daily 12:00-15:00 & 17:00-21:00, 20 St. John's Street, tel. 017687/73888).

$$ The George Hotel Restaurant and Bar, with a good solid pub and a large hotel dining room adjacent, is a warm and cozy Old World place. They offer the same extensive and very English menu in both the restaurant and bar (order at the pub's bar or wait to be served in the restaurant, tel. 017687/72076, St. John's Street, reservations in dining room only).

Eateries on Station Street: The street leading from the town square to the leisure center has several restaurants, including **$$ Casa Bella,** a popular and well-priced Italian place that's good for families—reserve ahead (daily 12:00-15:30 & 17:00-21:00, 24 Station Street, tel. 017687/75575, www.casabellakeswick.co.uk). **$$ Lakes Bar and Bistro** is popular for its burgers, meat pies, and good fixed-price meal deals (daily 10:00-23:00, 25 Station Street, tel. 017687/74080). **$ Asaya Thai Restaurant,** a hard-working, bright-and-mellow place, is a solid, inexpensive bet (daily 17:00-22:00, 21 Station Street, tel. 017687/75111).

Picnic Food: $ The Cornish Pasty offers an enticing variety of fresh meat pies to-go (daily 9:00-17:00 or until the pasties are all gone, across from The Dog and Gun on Borrowdale Road, tel. 017687/72205). Or stop by the huge **Booths** grocery store (see "Helpful Hints," earlier).

ULLSWATER LAKE AREA

Long, narrow Ullswater, which some consider the loveliest lake in the area, offers miles of diverse and grand Lake District scenery. The main town on Ullswater is the stony village of **Glenridding,** which is little more than a few pubs and shops along the bank of a spritely stream. Visit the **TI** there for advice on the area (daily 9:30-17:30, Nov-March weekends only until 15:30, located in the village's pay parking lot, tel. 017684/82414, www.visiteden.co.uk).

▲▲ULLSWATER HIKE AND BOAT RIDE

While you can drive it or cruise the lake, I'd ride the boat from the south tip halfway up (to Howtown—which is nothing more than a dock) and hike back. Or walk first, then enjoy an easy boat ride back.

An old-fashioned **"steamer" boat** (actually diesel-powered) leaves Glenridding regularly for Howtown (departs daily generally 9:45-16:55, 6-9/day April-Oct, fewer off-season, 40 minutes; £7.30 one-

Ullswater steamer boat

way, £12 round-trip, £17 round-the-lake ticket lets you hop on and off, covered by Ullswater Bus & Boat day pass, family rates, drivers can use safe pay-and-display parking lot, by public transit take bus #508 from Penrith, café at dock, tel. 017684/82229, www.ullswater-steamers.co.uk).

From Howtown, spend three to four hours hiking and dawdling along the well-marked path by the lake south to Patterdale, and then along the road back to Glenridding. This is a serious seven-mile walk with good views, varied terrain, and a few bridges and farms along the way. For a shorter hike from the Howtown pier, consider a three-mile loop around Hallin Fell. A rainy-day plan is to ride the covered boat up and down the lake to Howtown and Pooley Bridge at the northern tip of the lake (2 hours). Boats don't run in bad weather—call ahead if it looks iffy.

▲▲LANTY'S TARN AND KELDAS HILL

If you like the idea of an Ullswater-area hike but aren't up for the long huff from Howtown, consider this shorter loop that leaves right from the TI's pay parking lot in Glenridding (about 2.5 miles, allow 2 hours; buy the leaflet at the TI that describes this walk).

From the parking lot, head to the main road, turn right to cross the Glenridding Beck river, then immediately turn right again and follow the river up into the hills. After passing a row of cottages, turn left,

Hike the Keldas Hill for a great view.

cross the wooden bridge, and proceed up the hill through the swing gate. Just before the next swing gate (set in a stone wall—do not go through this gate), turn left (following *Grisedale* signs) and head to yet another gate. From here you can see the small lake called Lanty's Tarn.

While you'll eventually go through this gate and walk along the lake to finish the loop, first you can detour to the top of the adjacent hill, called Keldas, for sweeping views over the near side of Ullswater (to reach the summit, climb over the step gate and follow the faint path up the hill). Returning to—and passing through—the swing gate, you'll walk along Lanty's Tarn on your left, then begin your slow, steep, and scenic descent into the Grisedale Valley. Reaching the valley floor (and passing a noisy dog breeder's farm), cross the stone bridge, then turn left and follow the road all the way back to the lakefront, where a left turn returns you to Glenridding.

▲AIRA FORCE WATERFALL

On the north bank of Ullswater, there's a delightful little park with parking, a ranger trailer, and easy trails leading a half-mile uphill to a powerful 60-foot-tall waterfall. At the falls a little loop trail takes you over two romantic stone arched bridges. Wordsworth was inspired to write three poems here...and after taking this little walk, you'll know why. Park at the pay-and-display lot just where the A-5091

from Troutbeck hits the lake and the A-592. To get to the falls with a much shorter walk (10 minutes), drivers can find the Park Brow pay & display lot above the lake on A-5091 (direction Troutbeck).

▲KIRKSTONE PASS

Heading south from Ullswater to Windermere, you drive over the 1500-foot Kirkstone Pass. The stark Ullswater Valley is famous for its old, dry stone walls, built without mortar. To this day, these fine walls still define the valley's family farms. If you look carefully, you can see "sheep creeps"—small holes in the walls to allow sheep to be moved conveniently from one field to the next.

At the summit, stop to enjoy the view and check out the Kirkstone Pass Inn, a 500-year-old coaching stop. The steep road just across from the inn is called "The Struggle" for the work it took for those long-ago coaches to climb it.

▲HOLEHIRD GARDENS

South of Kirkstone Pass on the Ullswater-Windermere road, Holehird is a haven for gardeners. Run by Lakeland Horticultural Society volunteers for 50 years, it's one of the most enjoyable gardens in England. Of particular interest are several National Plant Collections, a scheme to systematically collect and preserve particular plant families cultivated in the UK. The Holehird examples are well worth seeking out.

Cost and Hours: Free, donations welcome, open dawn to dusk, car park, WC, on the A-592 one mile north of Windermere, tel. 105394/46008, www. holehirdgardens.org.uk.

SOUTH LAKE DISTRICT

The South Lake District has a cheesiness that's similar to other popular English resort destinations. But the area around Windermere is worth a drive-through if you're a fan of Wordsworth or Beatrix Potter.

If you're without a car, buses #599 and #555 are a fine and stress-free way to lace together the sights. Consider leaving your car at Grasmere and enjoying the breezy and extremely scenic bus #599, hopping off and on as you like (see "Getting Around the Lake District," later, for details).

By Boat: Windermere Lake Cruises run from Bowness to Ambleside and other points on the lake all year (several itineraries offered, some are seasonal; tel. 015394/43360, www.windermerelakecruises.co.uk).

Sights
Wordsworth Sights

William Wordsworth was one of the first writers to reject fast-paced city life. During England's Industrial Age, hearts were muzzled and brains ruled. Science was in, machines were taming nature, and factory hours were taming humans. In reaction to these brainy ideals, a rare few—dubbed Romantics—began to embrace untamed nature and undomesticated emotions.

Back then, nobody climbed a mountain just because it was there—but Wordsworth did. He'd "wander lonely as a cloud" through the countryside, finding inspiration in "plain living and high thinking." He soon attracted a circle of likeminded creative friends.

Today, the Romantic appreciation of the natural world thrives as visitors continue to inundate the region.

▲▲DOVE COTTAGE AT WORDSWORTH GRASMERE

Following a year-long renovation, Dove Cottage has a new name (Wordsworth Grasmere) and new galleries to celebrate the 250th anniversary of Wordsworth's birth. For literary types, this visit is the top sight of the Lake District. Take a short tour of William Wordsworth's humble cottage; get inspired in its excellent museum, which displays original writings, sketches, personal items, and fine paintings; and wander the garden/orchard.

The poet whose appreciation of nature and a back-to-basics lifestyle put this area on the map spent his most productive years (1799-1808) in this well-preserved stone cottage on the edge of Grasmere. This is where Wordsworth got

Dove Cottage

Wordsworth at Dove Cottage

Lake District homeboy William Wordsworth (1770-1850) was born in Cockermouth and schooled in Hawkshead. In adulthood, he married a local girl, settled down in Grasmere and Ambleside, and was buried in Grasmere's St. Oswald's churchyard.

But the 30-year-old man who moved into Dove Cottage in 1799 was not the carefree lad who'd once roamed the district's lakes and fields. At Cambridge University, he'd been a C student, graduating with no job skills and no interest in a nine-to-five career. Instead, he hiked through Europe, where he had an epiphany of the "sublime" atop Switzerland's Alps. Wordsworth lived a year in France during its revolution, and fell in love with a Frenchwoman, with whom he had a daughter. But lack of money forced him to return to England, and the outbreak of war with France kept them apart.

Pining away in London, William hung out in the pubs and coffeehouses with fellow radicals, where he met poet Samuel Taylor Coleridge. They inspired each other to write and jointly published a groundbreaking book of poetry.

In 1799, his head buzzing with words and ideas, William and his sister (and soul mate), Dorothy, moved into the whitewashed, slate-tiled former inn now known as Dove Cottage. He came into a small inheritance, dedicated himself to poetry full time, and married a former kindergarten classmate, Mary.

The time at Dove Cottage was Wordsworth's "Golden Decade," when he penned his masterpieces. But after almost nine years here, Wordsworth's family and social status had outgrown the humble cottage. They moved first to a house in Grasmere before settling down in Rydal Hall. Wordsworth was changing. After the Dove years, he would write less, settle into a regular government job, quarrel with Coleridge, drift to the right politically, and endure criticism from old friends who branded him a sellout. Still, his poetry—most of it written at Dove—became increasingly famous, and he died honored as England's Poet Laureate.

married, had kids, and wrote much of his best poetry. The place comes with some amazing artifacts, including the poet's passport and suitcase (he packed light) and his own furniture. Even during his lifetime, Wordsworth was famous, and Dove Cottage was turned into a museum in 1891—it's now protected by the Wordsworth Trust.

Cost and Hours: £9, daily 9:30-17:30, Nov-Feb 10:00-16:30 except closed Jan and for events in Dec and Feb (call ahead), café, bus #555 from Keswick, bus #555 or #599 from Windermere, tel. 015394/35544, www.wordsworth.org.

uk. Pay parking in the Dove Cottage lot off the main road (A-591), 50 yards from the site.

Visiting the Cottage and Museum: The cottage tour and adjoining museum, with lots of actual manuscripts handwritten by Wordsworth and his illustrious friends, are both excellent. In dry weather, the garden where the poet was much inspired is lovely. (Visit this after leaving the cottage tour and pick up the description at the back door. The garden is closed when wet.) Allow 1.5 hours for this visit.

Wordsworth's Poetry

At Dove Cottage, Wordsworth was immersed in the beauty of nature. The following stanzas are selected from two well-known poems from this fertile time.

Ode: Intimations of Immortality

There was a time when meadow, grove, and stream,
The earth, and every common sight, to me did seem
Apparelled in celestial light,
The glory and the freshness of a dream.
It is not now as it hath been of yore;—
Turn wheresoe'er I may,
By night or day,
The things which I have seen I now can see no more.

I Wandered Lonely as a Cloud (Daffodils)

I wandered lonely as a cloud
That floats on high o'er vales and hills,
When all at once I saw a crowd,
A host, of golden daffodils;
Beside the lake, beneath the trees,
Fluttering and dancing in the breeze...

. . . .

For oft, when on my couch I lie
In vacant or in pensive mood,
They flash upon that inward eye
Which is the bliss of solitude,
And then my heart with pleasure fills,
And dances with the daffodils.

▲ **RYDAL MOUNT AND GARDENS**

Located just down the road from Dove Cottage, this sight is worthwhile for Wordsworth fans. The poet's final, higher-class home, with a lovely garden and view, lacks the humble charm of Dove Cottage, but still evokes the creative spirit of the literary giant who lived here for 37 years. Wander through the garden William himself designed, which has changed little since then. Surrounded by his nature, you can imagine the poet enjoying it all with you. "O happy garden! Whose seclusion deep hath been so friendly to industrious hours; and to soft slumbers, that did gently steep our spirits, carrying with them dreams of flowers, and wild notes warbled among leafy bowers."

Cost and Hours: £7.50; daily 9:30-17:30, Nov-Dec and Feb 11:00-16:30 and closed Mon-Tue, closed Jan; occasionally

Rydal Mount

closed for private functions—check website; tearoom, 1.5 miles north of Ambleside, well-signed, free and easy parking, bus #555 from Keswick, tel. 015394/33002, www.rydalmount.co.uk.

Beatrix Potter Sights

Author and illustrator Beatrix Potter, of Peter Rabbit fame, lived and worked in the Lake District for years. Of the many attractions in the area that claim a connection to her, there are two serious sights: Hill Top, her farm, and the Beatrix Potter Gallery, filled with her sketches and paintings. The sights are two miles apart: Beatrix Potter Gallery is in Hawkshead, an extremely cute but extremely touristy town that's a 20-minute drive south of Ambleside; Hill Top Farm is south of Hawkshead, in Near Sawrey village.

On busy summer days, the wait to get into Hill Top Farm can last several hours. If you like quaint towns engulfed in Potter tourism (Hawkshead), this extra waiting time can be a blessing. Otherwise, you'll wish you were in the woods somewhere with Wordsworth. If you have questions, visit the Hawkshead TI inside the Ooh-La-La gift shop (tel. 015394/36946).

▲HILL TOP FARM

A hit with Beatrix Potter fans (and skippable for others), this dark and intimate cottage, swallowed up in the inspirational and rough nature around it, provides an enjoyable if quick experience. The six-room farm was left just as it was when Potter died in 1943. At her request, the house is set as if she had just stepped out—flowers on the tables, fire on, low lights. While there's no printed information here, guides in each room are eager to explain things. Fans of the classic *Tale of Samuel Whiskers* will recognize the home's rooms, furniture, and views—the book and its illustrations were inspired by an invasion of rats when Potter bought this place. If exasperated by long lines, remember you can enjoy the garden and see the house from outside for free at any time.

Cost and Hours: Farmhouse-£12, gardens-free; June-Aug daily 10:00-17:30; mid-Feb-May and Sept-Oct until 16:30 and closed Fri; house closed Nov-Dec but gardens and shop open Sat-Sun; closed Jan-mid-Feb; tel. 015394/36269, www.nationaltrust.org.uk/hill-top.

Getting In: Admission is by timed tickets, which cannot be booked in advance

Hill Top Farm

Beatrix Potter (1866-1943)

As a girl growing up in London, Beatrix Potter vacationed in the Lake District, where she became inspired to write her popular children's books. Unable to get a publisher, she self-published the first two editions of *The Tale of Peter Rabbit* in 1901 and 1902. When she finally landed a publisher, sales of her books were phenomenal. With the money she made, she bought Hill Top Farm, a 17th-century cottage, and fixed it up, living there sporadically from 1905 until she married in 1913. Potter was more than a children's book writer; she was a fine artist, an avid gardener, and a successful farmer. She married a lawyer and put her knack for business to use, amassing a 4,000-acre estate. An early conservationist, she used the garden-cradled cottage as a place to study nature. She willed it—along with the rest of her vast estate—to the National Trust, which she enthusiastically supported.

(only eight people are let in every five minutes). To beat the lines, get to the ticket office 15 minutes before it opens. Otherwise, call the farm for the current wait times (if no one answers, leave a message for the administrator; if the office is attended, someone will call you back). Big bus or student groups (common in late July and Aug) can book up several hours of entries at any moment if you're unlucky.

Getting There: Mountain Goat Tours runs a shuttle bus (Mountain Goat #525) from across the Hawkshead TI to the farm every 20-40 minutes (tel. 015394/45161). Drivers can take the B-5286 and B-5285 from Ambleside or the B-5285 from Coniston—be prepared for extremely narrow roads with no shoulders that are often lined

Hill Top Farm, Beatrix Potter's home

with stone walls. You'll find the museum parking lot and ticket office about 150 yards down the road from the farm.

▲BEATRIX POTTER GALLERY

Located in the cute town of Hawkshead, this gallery fills the one-time law office of Potter's husband with the wonderful and intimate drawings and watercolors she made to illustrate her books. Each year the museum highlights a new theme and brings out a different set of Potter's paintings, drawings, and other items. Unlike Hill Top, the gallery has plenty of explanation about her life and work, including touchscreen displays and information panels. Anyone will find this museum rather charming and her art surprisingly interesting.

Cost and Hours: £6.80, daily 10:30-16:00, closed Nov-mid-Feb, Main Street, drivers use the nearby Hawkshead pay-and-display lot and walk 200 yards to the town center, tel. 015394/36355, www.nationaltrust.org.uk/beatrix-potter-gallery.

HAWKSHEAD GRAMMAR SCHOOL MUSEUM

This interesting museum, just across from the pay-and-display parking lot, was founded in 1585 and is where William

Boats on display at the Windermere Jetty Museum

Wordsworth studied from 1779 to 1787. It shows off old school benches and desks whittled with penknife graffiti.

Cost and Hours: £2.50 includes guided tour on the hour; Mon-Sat 10:00-13:00 & 14:00-17:00, closed Sun and Nov-March; tel. 015394/36735, www.hawksheadgrammar.org.uk.

WINDERMERE JETTY MUSEUM

On the east shore of Windermere, this museum of "boats, steam, and stories" offers a fun opportunity to learn about the boating history of the lake over the past 200 years. Brush up on your maritime vocabulary with the display of mooring warps, splicing fids, fenders, and more. Then view the museum's collection of 40 boats (about half are exhibited at any one time). Kids will enjoy the model boat pond.

Cost and Hours: £9, £19 includes trip on the steam launch *Osprey*, daily 10:00-17:30; Nov-Feb 10:30-16:00; last entry one hour before closing, free parking, view café, tel. 01539/637-940, www.windermerejetty.org.

Getting There: The museum is just off the A-592, near Bowness Pier. Bus #599 from Ambleside (daily mid-July-Aug) stops at Bowness Pier (8-minute walk), where Windermere Lake Cruises also stop (www.windermere-lakecruises.co.uk).

TRANSPORTATION

Getting Around the Lake District

By Car

Nothing is very far from Keswick and Derwentwater. Pick up a good map (any hotel can loan you one), get off the big roads, and leave the car, at least occasionally, for some walking. In summer, the Keswick-Ambleside-Windermere-Bowness corridor (A-591) suffers from congestion. Back lanes are far less trampled and lead you through forgotten villages, where sheep outnumber people.

To **rent a car** here, try Enterprise in Penrith. They'll transport you between Keswick and their office when you're picking up and dropping off the car (Mon-Fri 8:00-18:00, Sat 9:00-12:00, closed Sun, requires driver's license and second ID, reserve a day in advance, located at the David Hayton Peugeot dealer, Haweswater Road, tel. 01768/893-840). Larger outfits are more likely to have a branch in Carlisle, which is a bit to the north but well served by train (on the same Glasgow-Birmingham line as Penrith) and only a few minutes farther from the Keswick area.

Without a Car

Those based in Keswick without a car manage fine. Because of the region's efforts to cut down on car traffic, the bus service can be quite efficient for hiking and sightseeing.

BY BUS

Keswick has no real bus station; buses stop in front of the Booths supermarket where well-designed maps and posted schedules make your bus options very clear. Check the schedule carefully to make sure you can catch the last bus home. For bus schedules, look for the Lakes by Bus booklet (available at TIs or on any bus) or visit StagecoachBus.com and set your location for Keswick.

Bus Passes/Bus & Boat Passes: On board, you can purchase an Explorer pass that lets you ride any Stagecoach bus throughout the area (£11.50/1 day, £26/3 days), or you can get one-day passes for certain routes; tickets can also be purchased via the Stagecoach Bus app. Bus & Boat all-day passes combine bus rides with boat cruises on Derwentwater (£14, covers #77/#77A bus and Derwentwater cruise).

Bus routes: Buses #X4 and #X5 connect Penrith train station to Keswick (April-Oct hourly, every 2 hours on Sun, 45 minutes).

Bus #77/#77A, the Honister Rambler, makes the circle trip from Keswick around Derwentwater, over Honister Pass, through Buttermere, and down the Whinlatter Valley (5-7/day clockwise, 4/day "anticlockwise," daily Easter-Oct, 1.75-hour loop). Bus #78, the Borrowdale

Rambler, goes from Keswick to Lodore Hotel, Grange Bridge, Rosthwaite, and Seatoller at the base of Honister Pass (hourly, daily Easter-Oct, 2/hour July-Sept, 30 minutes each way). Both routes are covered by the £8.50 Keswick and Honister Dayrider all-day pass.

Bus #508, the Kirkstone Rambler, runs between Penrith and Patterdale Hotel (near the bottom of Ullswater), stopping in Pooley Bridge (5/day, more frequent June-Aug with open-top buses, 50 minutes). Bus #508 also connects Glenridding and Windermere (1 hour).

Bus #505, the Coniston Rambler, connects Windermere with Hawkshead (about hourly, daily Easter-Oct, 35 minutes).

Bus #555 connects Keswick with the south and Windermere (hourly, 2/hour July-Sept, 1 hour to Windermere).

Bus #599, the open-top Lakeland Experience, runs along the main Windermere corridor, connecting the big tourist attractions in the south: Grasmere and Dove Cottage, Rydal Mount, Ambleside, Brockhole (National Park Visitors Centre), Windermere, and lake cruises from Bowness Pier (3/hour June-Sept, 2/hour May and Oct, 50 minutes each way, £8.50 Central Lakes Dayrider all-day pass).

BY BIKE

Keswick works well as a springboard for several fine days out on a bike; consider a three-hour loop trip up Newlands Valley. Ask about routes at the TI or your bike rental shop. Try **Whinlatter Bikes** (best prices, daily 10:00-17:00, free touring maps, 82 Main Street, tel. 017687/73940, www.whinlatterbikes.com); **E-Venture** (happy to store bags while you rent for no cost, daily 9:00-17:00, Elliot Park—facing the Keswick bus stop, tel. 017687/71363, www.e-venturebikes.co.uk); or **Keswick Bikes** (daily 9:00-17:30, 133 Main Street, tel. 017687/73355, www.keswickbikes.co.uk).

BY BOAT

A circular boat service glides you around Derwentwater, with several hiker-aiding stops along the way (for details, see "Boating on Derwentwater," page 245).

Arriving and Departing

The nearest train station to Keswick is in Penrith (no lockers). For train and bus info, check at a TI, visit Traveline.info, or call 0345-748-4950 (for train). Most routes run less frequently on Sundays.

From Penrith by Bus to: Keswick (hourly, every 2 hours on Sun in Nov-April, 45 minutes, pay driver, Stagecoach bus #X4 or #X5), **Ullswater** and **Glenridding** (5/day, more frequent June-Aug with open-top buses, 50 minutes, bus #508). The Penrith bus stop is just outside the train station (bus schedules posted inside and outside station).

From Penrith by Train to: Liverpool (2/hour, 2.5 hours, change in Wigan or Preston), **Durham** (hourly, 3 hours, 1-2 transfers), **York** (roughly 2/hour, 4 hours, 1-2 transfers), **London**'s Euston Station (hourly, 3.5 hours), **Edinburgh** (8/day direct, more with transfer, 1.5 hours).

York

Historic York is loaded with world-class sights. Marvel at the York Minster, England's finest Gothic church. Ramble The Shambles, York's wonderfully preserved medieval quarter. Enjoy a walking tour led by an old Yorker. Hop a train at one of the world's greatest railway museums, travel to the 1800s in the York Castle Museum, head back 1,000 years to Viking times at the Jorvik Viking Centre, or dig into the city's buried past at the Yorkshire Museum.

In AD 71 York was a Roman provincial capital—the northernmost city in the empire. In the fifth century, as Rome was toppling, it became the capital of the Anglo-Saxon kingdom of Northumbria. The city's first church was built in 627, and the town became an early Christian center of learning. The Vikings later took the town, and from the 9th through the 11th century, it was a Danish trading center called Jorvik. The invading and conquering Normans destroyed and then rebuilt the city, fortifying it with a castle and the walls you see today.

Medieval York, with 9,000 inhabitants, grew rich on the wool trade and became England's second city. In the Industrial Age, York was the railway hub of northern England. Today, it feels like a big, traffic-free amusement park for adults. With its strollable cobbles and half-timbered buildings, grand cathedral and excellent museums, thriving restaurant scene and welcoming locals, York delights.

YORK IN 2 DAYS

Day 1: Take the free city walking tour on your first day. It's offered in the morning and afternoon (and in the summer, also in the evening).

After lunch, tour the Yorkshire Museum (or save it for tomorrow morning, before the self-guided walk). Visit the York Minster, and attend the evensong service (Tue-Sat and occasional Mon at 17:15, Sun at 16:00).

On any evening: Splurge on dinner at one of the city's bistros (cheaper if you go for an early-bird dinner). Enjoy the ghost walk of your choice (or the free city walking tour in summer). Stroll or bike along the riverside path, or settle in at a pub.

Day 2: Take my self-guided York Walk, which starts from the Yorkshire Museum's garden. Explore The Shambles.

In the afternoon, tour any of these fine museums: York Castle Museum, National Railway Museum, Merchant Adventurers' Hall, or the Fairfax House.

YORK AT A GLANCE

▲▲▲**York Minster** York's pride and joy, and one of England's finest churches, with stunning stained-glass windows, textbook Decorated Gothic design, and glorious evensong services. **Hours:** Mon-Sat 9:00-16:30, Sun 12:30-15:00; evensong services Tue-Sat and some Mon at 17:15, Sun at 16:00. See page 279.

▲▲▲**Walking Tours** Variety of guided town walks and evening ghost walks covering York's history. See page 272.

▲▲**York Castle Museum** Far-ranging collection displaying everyday objects from Victorian times to the present. **Hours:** Daily 9:30-17:00. See page 287.

▲▲**National Railway Museum** Train buff's nirvana, tracing the history of all manner of rail-bound transport. **Hours:** Daily 10:00-18:00. See page 289.

▲**Yorkshire Museum** Archaeology and natural history museum with York's best Viking exhibit, plus Roman, Saxon, Norman, and Gothic artifacts. **Hours:** Daily 10:00-17:00. See page 285.

▲**Merchant Adventurers' Hall** Vast medieval guildhall with displays recounting life and commerce in the Middle Ages. **Hours:** Sun-Fri 10:00-16:30, Sat until 13:30. See page 286.

▲**Jorvik Viking Centre** Entertaining and informative Disney-style exhibit/ride exploring Viking lifestyles and artifacts. **Hours:** Daily 10:00-17:00, Nov-March until 16:00. See page 287.

▲**Fairfax House** Glimpse into an 18th-century Georgian family house, with enjoyably chatty docents. **Hours:** Tue-Sat 10:00-17:00, Sun 11:00-16:00, Mon by tour only at 11:00 and 14:00, closed Jan-mid-Feb. See page 287.

▲**The Shambles** Atmospheric old butchers' quarter, with colorful, tipsy medieval buildings. See page 279.

If you want to visit the popular Jorvik Viking Centre, you'll minimize your time in line if you go early, late, or pay a bit extra for a timed-entry ticket.

Have afternoon tea at the elegant Bettys Café Tea Rooms.

ORIENTATION

There are roughly 200,000 people in York and its surrounding area; about one in ten is a student. But despite the city's size, the sightseer's York is small. Virtually everything is within a few minutes' walk: sights, train station, TI, and B&Bs. The longest walk a visitor could take (from a B&B across the old town to the York Castle Museum) is about a half-hour.

Bootham Bar, a gate in the medieval town wall, is the hub of your York visit. (In York, a "bar" is a gate and a "gate" is a street. Blame the Vikings.) At Bootham Bar and on Exhibition Square, you'll find the starting points for most walking tours and bus tours, handy access to the medieval town wall, a public WC, and Bootham Street (which leads to my recommended B&Bs). To find your way around York, use the Minster's towers as a navigational landmark, or follow the strategically placed signposts, which point out all places of interest to tourists.

Tourist Information

York's TI is a block in front of the Minster (Mon-Sat 9:00-17:00, Sun 10:00-16:00, 1 Museum Street, tel. 01904/550-099, www. visityork.org). They sell a quality £1 map.

Rick's Tip: *The TI sells a £45 one-day* **York Pass** *that covers all the sights, but you'd have to be a very busy sightseer to make it worth the cost (multiday options available, www.yorkpass.com).*

Helpful Hints

Festivals: The **Viking Festival** features *lur* horn-blowing, warrior drills,

and re-created battles in mid-February (www.jorvikvikingfestival.co.uk). The **Early Music Festival** (medieval minstrels, Renaissance dance, and so on) zings its strings in early July (www.ncem.co.uk/yemf.shtml). The **Great Yorkshire Fringe Festival** happens the last two weeks of July (www.greatyorkshirefringe.com). York fills up on horse-race weekends (once a month May-Oct, check schedules at www.yorkracecourse.co.uk). The **York Food and Drink Festival** takes a bite out of late September (www.yorkfoodfestival. com). And the **St. Nicholas Fair** Christmas market jingles its bells from mid-November through Christmas. For a complete list of festivals, see www.visityork. org/whats-on/festivals.

Baggage Storage: Yorbag Left Luggage has a tiny office at 20 High Petergate (daily 9:00-19:00, just inside Bootham Bar, 10-minute walk to train station, mobile 07561-852-654).

Laundry: Some B&Bs will do laundry for a reasonable charge. Otherwise the nearest place is **Haxby Road Launderette,** a long 15-minute walk north of the town center (or take a bus—ask your B&B for directions, 124 Haxby Road, call ahead for prices and hours—tel. 01904/623-379).

Tours
Walking Tours

A walking tour in York is worth ▲▲▲.

FREE TWO-HOUR WALKS WITH VOLUNTEER GUIDES

Charming locals give energetic, entertaining walks that often go long because the guides love to teach and tell stories. You're welcome to cut out early—but let them know, or they'll worry that they've lost you (daily at 10:15 and 13:15, June-Aug also at 18:15; depart from Exhibition Square in front of the art gallery, tel. 01904/550-098, www.avgyork.co.uk).

YORK TOUR

York Tour offers two more intellectually demanding walks with a history focus

(£18, daily at 14:00, 90 minutes; £15, daily at 18:00, 1 hour; meet at Exhibition Square, must book online, mobile 07963-791-937, www.yorktour.com). **Alfred Hickling,** who runs York Tour, has a passion for York's history and also gives private tours (£90/half-day, mobile 07963-791-937www.yorktour.com).

Rick's Tip: Hop-on, hop-off buses *circle York, taking tourists past secondary sights on the mundane perimeter of town. To hit the best sights,* **take a walking tour.**

Ghost Walks

Each evening, the old center of York crawls with creepy ghost walks. (York claims to be the most haunted city in Europe.) These walks are generally 1.5 hours long, cost £5-7, and go rain or shine. Reservations are usually not necessary. You simply show up at the advertised time and place, your black-clad guide appears, and you follow him or her to the first stop. Your guide gives a sample of the entertainment you have in store, humorously collects the "toll," and you're off.

Companies come and go, but I find there are three general styles of walks: street theater, historic, and storytelling (discount for children under 14).

The **Terror Trail Walk** has entertaining guides and are thought-provoking and historic (£5, daily at 18:45, meet in front of

Ye Old Shambles Tavern on The Shambles, www.yorkterrortrail.co.uk).

The **Bloody Tour of York,** led by Mad Alice (an infamous figure in York lore), is an engaging walk offering a fine blend of history, violence, and mayhem (£7, Thu-Sat at 18:00, also at 20:00 in April-Oct, no tours Sun-Wed, Dec-Jan by reservation only, meet outside St. Williams College behind the Minster on College Street, www.thebloodytourofyork.co.uk).

The **Original Ghost Walk,** said to be the first of its kind (dating to the 1970s), has more classic spooky storytelling than comedy (£5, daily at 20:00, meet outside The Kings Arms at Ouse Bridge, www.theoriginalghostwalkofyork.co.uk).

YORK WALK

Get a taste of Roman and medieval York on this easy, self-guided stroll that begins in the gardens just in front of the Yorkshire Museum, covers a stretch of the medieval city walls, and then cuts through the middle of the old town.

❷ Self-Guided Walk

Start at the ruins of St. Mary's Abbey in the Museum Gardens (see the "York" map).

❶ St. Mary's Abbey

This abbey dates to the age of William the Conqueror—whose harsh policies (called the "Harrowing of the North")

Walking tours are both educational and entertaining.

St. Mary's Abbey

York

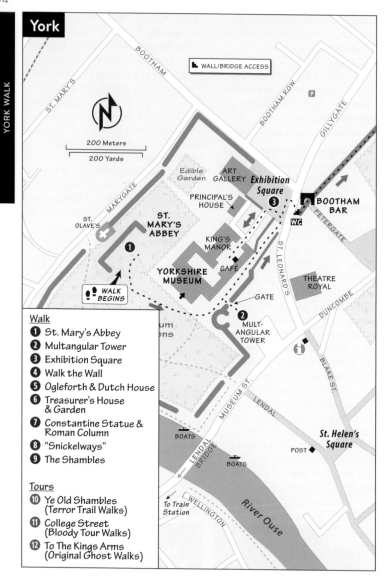

WALL/BRIDGE ACCESS

200 Meters
200 Yards

BOOTHAM

ST. MARY'S

BOOTHAM ROW

GILLYGATE

MARYGATE

Edible Garden

ART GALLERY

Exhibition Square

3

BOOTHAM BAR

PRINCIPAL'S HOUSE

ST. OLAVE'S

ST. MARY'S ABBEY

KING'S MANOR

WC

PETERGATE

1

YORKSHIRE MUSEUM

CAFÉ

ST. LEONARD'S

THEATRE ROYAL

WALK BEGINS

GATE

DUNCOMBE

...um ...ens

2 MULT-ANGULAR TOWER

BLAKE ST.

Walk
1 St. Mary's Abbey
2 Multangular Tower
3 Exhibition Square
4 Walk the Wall
5 Ogleforth & Dutch House
6 Treasurer's House & Garden
7 Constantine Statue & Roman Column
8 "Snickelways"
9 The Shambles

MUSEUM ST.

LENDAL

St. Helen's Square

POST

Tours
10 Ye Old Shambles (Terror Trail Walks)
11 College Street (Bloody Tour Walks)
12 To The Kings Arms (Original Ghost Walks)

BOATS

LENDAL BRIDGE

BOATS

To Train Station

WELLINGTON

River Ouse

consisted of massacres and destruction, including the burning of York's main church. His son Rufus, who tried to improve relations in the 11th century, established a great church here. The church became an abbey that thrived from the 13th century until the Dissolution of the Monasteries in the 16th

century. The Dissolution, which accompanied the Protestant Reformation and break with Rome, was a power play by Henry VIII. The king wanted much more than just a divorce: He wanted the land and riches of the monasteries.

As you gaze at this ruin, imagine magnificent abbeys like this scat-

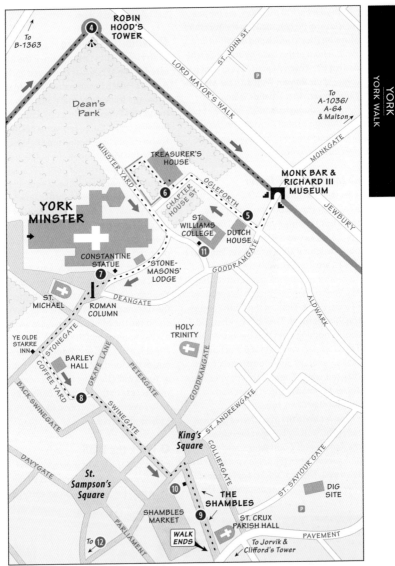

tered throughout the realm. Henry VIII destroyed most of them, taking the lead from their roofs and leaving the stones to scavenging townsfolk. Scant as they are today, these ruins still evoke a time of immense monastic power. The one surviving wall was the west half of a very long, skinny nave. The tall arch marked the start of the transept. Stand on the nearby plaque that reads *Crossing beneath central tower,* and look up at the air that now fills the space where a huge tower once stood. (Fine carved stonework from the ruined abbey is on display in a basement room of the adjacent Yorkshire Museum.)

• *With your back to the abbey, see the fine Neoclassical building housing the* **Yorkshire Museum** *(worth a visit and described later). Walk in front of this building and circle left down a tree-covered lane. On your right is a corner of the* **Roman Wall** *with the* **Multangular Tower***. After 30 yards, a lane on the right leads through a garden, past yew trees and through a small gated arch in the wall. Step through the wall and look right for a peek into the ruined tower.*

❷ Multangular Tower

This 12-sided tower (c. AD 300) was likely a catapult station built to protect the town from enemy river traffic. The red ribbon of bricks was a Roman trademark—both structural and decorative. The lower stones are Roman, while the upper (and bigger) stones are medieval. After Rome fell, York suffered through two centuries of a Dark Age. Then, in the ninth century, the Vikings ruled. They built with wood, so almost nothing from that period remains. The Normans came in 1066 and built in stone, generally atop Roman structures (like this wall). The wall that defined the ancient Roman garrison town worked for the Norman town, too.

• *Now, return to the tree-covered lane and turn right, walking between the museum and the Roman wall. Continuing straight, the lane goes between the abbot's palace and the town wall. This is a "snickelway"—a small, characteristic York lane or footpath. The snickelway pops out on...*

❸ Exhibition Square

With Henry VIII's Dissolution of the Monasteries, the abbey was destroyed and the Abbot's Palace became the **King's Manor** (from the snickelway, make a U-turn to the left and through the gate). Enter the building under the coat of arms of Charles I, who stayed here during the English Civil War in the 1640s. Today, the building is part of the University of York. Because the northerners were slow to embrace the king's reforms, Henry VIII came here to personally enforce the Dissolution. He stayed 17 days in this mansion and brought along 1,000 troops to make his determination clear.

Exhibition Square is the departure point for various walking and bus tours. You can see the towers of the Minster in the distance. Travelers in the Middle Ages could see the Minster from miles away as they approached the city. Across the street is a pay WC and **Bootham Bar**—one of the fourth-century Roman gates in York's wall (this one faced Scotland)—with access to the best part of the city walls (free, walls open 8:00-dusk).

• *Climb up the bar.*

❹ Walk the Wall

Hike along the top of the wall behind the Minster to the first corner. (While there may be a padlock on an entry gate,

Multangular Tower

Bootham Bar

it's generally open. Just push.) York's 13th-century walls are three miles long. This stretch follows the original Roman wall. Norman kings built up the walls to assert control over northern England. Notice the pivots in the crenellations (square notches at the top of a medieval wall), which once held wooden hatches to provide cover for archers. The wall was extensively renovated in the 19th century. (Victorians added little touches, such as Romantic arrow slits.)

At the corner with the benches— **Robin Hood's Tower**—you can lean out to see the moat. This was originally the Roman ditch that surrounded the fortified garrison town. Continue walking for a fine view of the Minster, with its truncated main tower and the pointy rooftop of its chapter house.

Continue on to the next gate, **Monk Bar.** This fine medieval gatehouse is the home of the little **Richard III Museum.**

• *Descend the wall at Monk Bar, and step outside the city's protective wall. Pass the portcullis (last lowered in 1953 for the Queen's coronation). Take 10 paces and gaze up at the tower. Imagine 10 archers behind*

the arrow slits. Keep an eye on the 17th-century guards, with their stones raised and primed to protect the town.

Return through the city wall. After a short block, turn right on Ogleforth.

York's Old Town

Walking down ❺ **Ogleforth,** ogle (on your left) a charming little brick house from the 17th century called the **Dutch House.** It was designed by an apprentice architect showing off for his master, and was the first entirely brick house in town—a sign of opulence. Next, also of brick, is a former brewery, with a 19th-century industrial feel.

Ogleforth jogs left and becomes **Chapter House Street,** which leads on to the Minster. On your way you'll pass the ❻ **Treasurer's House** on the right, where a short detour to a tranquil garden awaits. While admission is charged to visit the stately house (daily 11:00-16:30), it's free to visit its garden and café. Pass through the ornate iron gate into the hallway and take a sharp left into the garden. Pause to enjoy this pint-sized walled oasis before exiting onto Minster Yard with the pointed

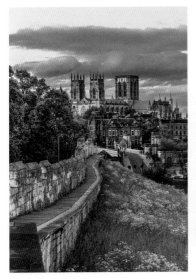

City walls

Monk Bar

A York's Old Town

B Constantine statue

C Snickelways

D The Shambles

tower of the octagonal Chapter House looming in front of you.

Then, circle left around the back side of the Minster, past the stonemasons' lodge (where craftsmen are chiseling local limestone for the church, as has been done here since the 13th century), to the statue of Roman Emperor Constantine and an ancient Roman column.

Step up to lounging ❼ **Constantine.** Five emperors visited York when it was the Roman city of Eboracum. Constantine was here when his father died. The troops declared him the Roman emperor in AD 306 at this site, and six years later, he went to Rome to claim his throne. In AD 312, Constantine legalized Christianity, and in AD 314, York got its first bishop.

The **ancient column,** across the street from Constantine, is a reminder that the Minster sits upon the site of the Roman headquarters, or *principia*. The city placed this column here in 1971, just before celebrating the 1,900th anniversary of the founding of Eboracum—a.k.a. York.

• *If you want to visit the* **York Minster** *now, find the entrance on its west side, ahead and around the corner. Otherwise, head into the town center. From opposite the Minster's south transept door (near Constantine), take a narrow pedestrian walkway—which becomes Stonegate—into the tangled commercial center of medieval York. Walk down Stonegate, lined with inviting cafés, pubs, and restaurants. Just before the Ye Old Starre Inne banner hanging over the street, turn left down the snickelway called Coffee Yard (marked by a red devil). Enjoy strolling another of York's...*

❽ *"Snickelways"*

This is a made-up York word combining "snicket" (a passageway between walls or fences), "ginnel" (a narrow passageway between buildings), and "alleyway" (any narrow passage)—snickelway. York—with its population packed densely inside its protective walls—has about 50 of these public passages. In general, when exploring the city, you should duck into these—both for the adventure and to take a shortcut. While some of York's history has been bulldozed by modernity, bits of it hide and survive in the snickelways.

Coffee Yard leads past Barley Hall, popping out at the corner of Grape Lane and Swinegate. Medieval towns named streets for the business done there. Swinegate, a lane of pig farmers, leads to the market. Grape Lane is a polite version of that street's original crude name, Gropec*nt Lane. If you were here a thousand years ago, you'd find it lined by brothels. Throughout England, streets for prostitutes were called by this graphic name. If you see a street named Grape Lane, that's usually its heritage.

Skip Grape Lane and turn right down Swinegate to a market (which you can see in the distance). The **Shambles Market,** popular for cheap produce and clothing, was created in the 1960s with the demolition of a bunch of colorful medieval lanes. (The food trucks at the far end are good for a fast, cheap, and memorable little lunch.)
• *In the center of the market, tiny "Little Shambles" lane (on the left) dead-ends into the most famous lane in York.*

❾ *The Shambles*

This colorful old street (rated ▲) was once the "street of the butchers." The name was derived from "shammell"—a butcher's bench upon which he'd cut and display his meat. In the 16th century, this lane was dripping with red meat. You can still see the hooks—once used to hang rabbit, pheasant, beef, lamb, and pigs' heads—under the eaves. Fresh slabs were displayed on the fat sills, while people lived above the shops. All the garbage and sewage flushed down the street to a mucky pond at the end—a favorite hangout for the town's cats and dogs. Tourist shops now fill these fine, half-timbered Tudor buildings. While fires gutted most old English town centers, York's old town survives intact.

Turn right and slalom down The Shambles. Just past the tiny sandwich shop at #37, pop in to the snickelway and look for very old **woodwork.** Study the 16th-century carpentry: mortise-and-tenon joints with wooden plugs rather than nails, and the wattle-and-daub construction (timber frames filled in with rubble and plastered over).

Next door (back on The Shambles) is the **shrine of St. Margaret Clitherow,** a 16th-century Catholic crushed by Protestants under her own door (as was the humiliating custom when a city wanted to teach someone a lesson). She was killed for refusing to testify about hiding priests in her home. Step into the tiny shrine for a peaceful moment to ponder Margaret, who, in 1970, was sainted for her faith.

The Shambles reminds many of Diagon Alley in Harry Potter films. While this lane inspired the set design, no filming was ever done here.

At the bottom of The Shambles is the cute, tiny **St. Crux Parish Hall,** which charities use to raise funds by selling light meals. Take time to chat with the volunteers.

With blood and guts from The Shambles' 20 butchers all draining down the lane, it's no wonder The Golden Fleece, just below, is considered the most haunted pub in town.
• *Your town walk is finished. From here, you're just a few minutes from plenty of fun: street entertainment and lots of cheap eating options on King's Square, good restaurants on Fossgate, the York Castle Museum (a few blocks farther downhill).*

SIGHTS

Inside York's Walls
▲▲▲YORK MINSTER
The pride of York, this largest Gothic church north of the Alps (540 feet long, 200 feet tall) brilliantly shows that the High Middle Ages were far from dark. The word "minster" means an important

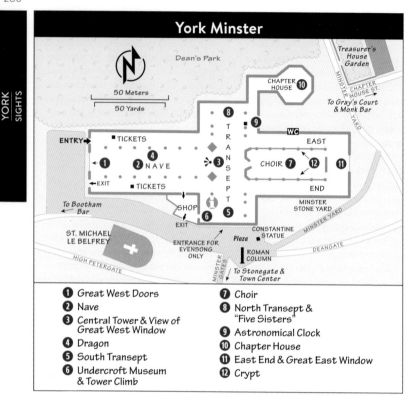

York Minster

Dean's Park

50 Meters

50 Yards

CHAPTER HOUSE **10**

Treasurer's House Garden

CHAPTER HOUSE ST.

To Gray's Court & Monk Bar

ENTRY

■ TICKETS

8

9

WC

EAST

T R A N S E P T

1 **2** N A V E **4** **3**

CHOIR **7** **12** **11**

←EXIT

■ TICKETS

END

To Bootham ← Bar

SHOP

MINSTER STONE YARD

EXIT

6 **5**

ST. MICHAEL LE BELFREY

ENTRANCE FOR EVENSONG ONLY

Plaza

CONSTANTINE ■ STATUE

MINSTER YARD

DEANGATE

HIGH PETERGATE

MINSTER GATES

ROMAN COLUMN

To Stonegate & Town Center

1 Great West Doors
2 Nave
3 Central Tower & View of Great West Window
4 Dragon
5 South Transept
6 Undercroft Museum & Tower Climb

7 Choir
8 North Transept & "Five Sisters"
9 Astronomical Clock
10 Chapter House
11 East End & Great East Window
12 Crypt

church chartered with a mission to evangelize. As it's the seat of a bishop, York Minster is also a cathedral. While Henry VIII destroyed England's great abbeys, this was not part of a monastery (and Henry needed an ecclesiastical center for his Anglican Church in the north), so it was left standing. It seats 2,000 comfortably; on Christmas and Easter, at least 4,000 worshippers pack the place. Today, more than 250 employees and 500 volunteers work to preserve its heritage and welcome more than a million visitors each year.

Cost: £12, includes guided tour, Undercroft Museum, and crypt; free for kids under age 16. You can skip the ticket line if you buy your ticket online in advance.

Hours: The cathedral is open for sightseeing Mon-Sat 9:00-16:30, Sun 12:30-15:00. It opens for worship daily at 7:30. Sights within the Minster have shorter

hours (see below). The Minster may close for special events (check calendar on website).

Information: Tel. 01904/557-217 or 0844-393-0011, www.yorkminster.org.

Visitor Information: You'll get a free map with your ticket. For more information, pick up the inexpensive *York Minster Short Guide.* Helpful Minster guides stationed throughout are happy to answer your questions (but not on Sundays).

Tower Climb: It costs £5 for 30 minutes of exercise (275 steps) and forgettable views. The tower opens at 9:30 (13:15 on Sun), with ascents every 45 minutes (no children under 8, not good for acrophobes, closes in extreme weather). Get your timed-entry ticket upon arrival, as only 50 visitors are allowed up at once.

Undercroft Museum: This museum focuses on the history of the site and its origins as a Roman fortress (Mon-Sat 10:00-16:30, Sun 13:00-15:15).

Tours: Free, guided hour-long tours depart from the ticket desk every hour on the hour (Mon-Sat 10:00-15:00, can be more frequent during busy times, none on Sun, they go even with just one or two people). You can join a tour in progress.

Evensong: To experience the cathedral in musical and spiritual action, attend an evensong (Tue-Sat at 17:15, Sun at 16:00, Mon spoken service at 17:15, enter at south door). Visiting choirs perform when the Minster's choir is on summer break (mid-July-Aug). Arrive 15 minutes early and wait just outside the choir in the center of the church. You'll be ushered in and can sit in one of the big wooden stalls. As evensong is a worship service, attendees enter the church free of charge. For more on evensong, see page 103.

Church Bells: If you're a fan of church bells, you'll experience ding-dong ecstasy Sunday morning at about 10:00 and during the Tuesday practice session between 19:00 and 22:00. These performances are especially impressive, as the church holds a full carillon of 35 bells (it's

York Minster, south transept

the only English cathedral to have such a range). Stand in front of the church's west portal and imagine the gang pulling on a dozen ropes (halfway up the right tower—you can actually see the ropes through a little window) while a talented carillonneur plays 22 more bells with a keyboard and foot pedals.

➔ SELF-GUIDED TOUR

Enter the great church through the west portal (under the twin towers). Upon entering, decide whether you're climbing the tower. If so, get a ticket (with an assigned time). Also consider visiting the Undercroft Museum (described later) if you want to get a comprehensive history and overview of the Minster before touring the church.

• *Entering the church, turn 180 degrees and look back at the...*

❶ **Great West Doors:** These are used only on special occasions. Flanking the doors is a list of archbishops (and other church officials) that goes unbroken back to the 600s. The statue of Peter with the key and Bible (between the doors) is a reminder that the church is dedicated to St. Peter, and the key to heaven is found through the word of God. While the Minster sits on the remains of a Romanesque church (c. 1100), today's church was begun in 1220 and took 250 years to complete. Up above, look for the female, headless "semaphore saints" (from 2004), using semaphore flag code to spell out a message with golden discs: "Christ is here".

• *Grab a chair and enjoy the view down the...*

❷ **Nave:** Your first impression might be of its spaciousness and brightness. One of the widest Gothic naves in Europe, it was built between 1280 and 1360—the middle period of the Gothic style, called "Decorated Gothic." Rather than risk a stone roof, builders spanned the space with wood. Colorful shields on the arcades are the coats of arms of nobles who helped tall and formidable Edward I, known as "Longshanks," fight

England's Anglican Church

The Anglican Church (a.k.a. the Church of England) came into existence in 1534, when Henry VIII declared that he, and not Pope Clement VII, was the head of England's Catholics. The pope had refused to allow Henry to divorce his wife to marry his mistress Anne Boleyn (which Henry did anyway, resulting in the birth of Elizabeth I). Still, Henry regarded himself as a faithful Catholic—just not a *Roman* Catholic—and made relatively few changes in how and what Anglicans worshipped.

It's interesting to think of the Dissolution of the Monasteries in 1534 as "the first Brexit." It was spearheaded by a much-married, arrogant, overweight, egomaniacal Henry VIII—matched today by the Conservative Party's Boris Johnson. Henry (like Boris) wanted "to be free" from European meddling (the pope then, the EU today). The local sentiment (then as now) was no more money to Europe (tithes to the pope then, taxes to Brussels today) and no more intrusions into English life from the Continent.

Henry's son, Edward VI, later instituted many of the changes that Reformation Protestants were bringing about in continental Europe: an emphasis on preaching, people in the pews actually reading the Bible, clergy being allowed to marry, and a more "Protestant" liturgy in English from the revised Book of Common Prayer (1549). The next monarch, Edward's sister Mary I, returned England to the Roman Catholic Church (1553), earning the nickname "Bloody Mary" for her brutal suppression of Protestant elements. When Elizabeth I succeeded Mary (1558), she soon broke from Rome again. Today, many regard the Anglican Church as a compromise between the Catholic and Protestant traditions.

the Scots in the 13th century.

The coats of arms in the clerestory (upper-level) glass represent the nobles who helped Edward I's son, Edward II, in the same fight. There's more medieval glass in this building than in the rest of England combined. This precious glass survived World War II—hidden in stately homes throughout Yorkshire.

Walk to the very center of the church, under the ❸ **central tower.** Look up. An exhibit in the undercroft explains how gifts and skill saved this 197-foot tower from collapse. Use the neck-saving mirror to marvel at it.

Look back at the west end to marvel at the **Great West Window,** especially the stone tracery. While its nickname is the "Heart of Yorkshire," it represents the sacred heart of Christ, meant to remind

people of his love for the world.

Find the ❹ **dragon** on the right of the nave (two-thirds of the way up the wall, affixed to the top of a pillar). While no one is sure of its purpose, it pivots and has a hole through its neck—so it was likely a mechanism designed to raise a lid of a saint's coffin. Carved out of Scandinavian oak, it's considered part of the earlier church built during Viking times.

• *Facing the altar, turn right and head into the...*

❺ **South Transept:** Look up. The new "bosses" (carved medallions decorating the point where the ribs meet on the ceiling) are a reminder that the roof of this wing of the church was destroyed by fire in 1984, caused when lightning hit an electricity box. Some believe the lightning was

Choir screen with carvings of English monarchs

God's angry response to a new bishop, David Jenkins, who questioned the literal truth of Jesus' miracles. (Jenkins had been interviewed at a nearby TV studio the night before, leading locals to joke that the lightning occurred "12 hours too late, and 17 miles off-target.")

Two other sights can be accessed through the south transept: the ❻ **Undercroft Museum** (explained later) and the **tower climb** (explained earlier). But for now, stick with this tour; we'll circle back to the south transept at the end, before exiting the church.

• *Head back into the middle of the nave and face the front of the church. You're looking at the...*

❼ **Choir:** Examine the choir screen—the ornate wall of carvings separating the nave from the choir. It's lined with all English kings from William I (the Conqueror) to Henry VI (during whose reign it was carved, in 1461). Numbers indicate the years each reigned. It is literally covered in gold leaf, but the gold is very thin...a nugget the size of a sugar cube can be pounded into a foil-like sheet the size of a driveway.

Step into the choir, where a service is held daily. All the carving was redone after an 1829 fire, but its tradition of glorious evensong services (sung by choristers from the Minster School) goes all the way back to the eighth century.

• *To the left as you face the choir is the...*

❽ **North Transept:** In this transept, the grisaille windows—dubbed the **"Five Sisters"**—are dedicated to British servicewomen who died in war. They were made in 1260, before colored glass was produced in England.

The 18th-century ❾ **astronomical clock** is worth a look (the sign helps you make sense of it). It's dedicated to the heroic Allied aircrews from bases here in northern England who died in World War II. The Book of Remembrance below the clock contains 18,000 names.

• *A corridor leads to the Gothic, octagonal...*

❿ **Chapter House:** This was the traditional meeting place of the governing body (or chapter) of the Minster. On the pillar in the middle of the doorway, the Virgin holds Baby Jesus while standing on the devilish serpent. The Chapter House, without an interior support, is remarkable (almost frightening) for its breadth. A model of the wooden construction (in the hallway just outside the door) illustrates the impressive 1285 engineering: with a wooden frame from which the ceiling actually hangs.

The fanciful carvings decorating the canopies above the stalls date from 1280 (80 percent are originals) and are some of the Minster's finest. Stroll slowly around the entire room and imagine that the tiny sculpted heads are a 14th-century parade—a fun glimpse of medieval society.

The Chapter House was the site of an important moment in England's parliamentary history. In the late 1200s, the Scots under William Wallace and Robert the Bruce were threatening London. Fighting the Scots in 1295, Edward I (the "Longshanks" we met earlier) convened his parliament (a war cabinet) here, rather than down south in London. The government met here through the 20-year reign of Edward II, before moving to London during Edward III's rule in the 14th century.
• *Return to the main part of the church, turn left, and continue all the way down the nave (behind the choir) to the...*

Chapter House

⓫ East End and Great East Window: This part of the church is square, lacking a semicircular apse, typical of England's Perpendicular Gothic style (15th century). Monuments (almost no graves) were once strewn throughout the church, but in the Victorian Age, they were gathered into the east end, where you see them today.

The Great East Window, the size of a tennis court, is one of the great treasures of medieval art in Europe. It's completely original, looking today as it did when finished in 1408. Imagine being a worshipper here the day it was unveiled—mesmerized by this sweeping story told in more than 300 panels of painted glass climaxing with the Apocalypse...vivid scenes from the book of Revelation. A hundred years before Michelangelo frescoed the story of the beginning and end of time at the Sistine Chapel in Rome, this was done by one man: John Thornton of Coventry.

Because of the Great East Window's immense size, the east end has an extra layer of supportive stonework, parts of it wide enough to walk along. For special occasions, the church choir has sung from the walkway halfway up the window.
• *Looking under the central altar and choir (or going down a flight of steps) you can see the...*

⓬ Crypt: Here you can view the boundary of the much smaller, but still huge, Norman church from 1100 that stood on this spot (look for the red dots, marking where the Norman church ended, and note how thick the wall was). You can also see some of the old columns and additional remains from the Roman fortress that once stood here, the tomb of St. William of York (a Roman sarcophagus that was reused), and the modern concrete save-the-church foundations (much of this church history is covered in the Undercroft Museum).
• *You'll exit the church through the gift shop in the south transept. If you've yet to climb the* **tower,** *the entrance is in the south tran-*

sept before the exit. Also before leaving, look for the entrance to the...

Undercroft Museum: Well-described exhibits follow the history of the site from its origins as a Roman fortress to the founding of an Anglo-Saxon/Viking church, the shift to a Norman place of worship, and finally the construction of the Gothic structure that stands today. Videos re-create how the fortress and Norman structure would have been laid out, and various artifacts provide an insight into each period. Highlights include:

- The remains of the Roman fort's basilica (its hall of justice), including patches of Roman frescoes from what was the basilica's anteroom.
- The Horn of Ulf, the finest Viking treasure in York. This intricately carved elephant's tusk was presented to the Minster in 1030 by Ulf, a Viking nobleman, as a symbol that he was dedicating his land to God and the Church.
- The personal effects of Archbishop Walter de Gray who, in the 13th century, started the current church.
- The York Gospels manuscript, a thousand-year-old text containing the four gospels. Made by Anglo-Saxon monks at Canterbury, it's the only book in the Minster's collection that dates prior to the Norman Conquest.

• This finishes your visit. Before leaving, take a moment to just be in this amazing building. Then, go in peace.

Nearby: As you leave through the south transept, notice the people-friendly plaza created here and how effectively it ties the church in with the city that stretches before you. To your left are the Roman column from the ancient headquarters, which stood where the Minster stands today (and from where Rome administered the northern reaches of Britannia 1,800 years ago); a statue of Emperor Constantine; and the York Minster Stone Yard, where masons chisel stone—as they have for centuries—to keep the religious pride and joy of York standing strong and looking good.

▲YORKSHIRE MUSEUM

Located in a lush, picnic-perfect park next to the stately ruins of St. Mary's Abbey (described in my "York Walk," earlier), the Yorkshire Museum is the city's serious "archaeology of York" museum. You can't dig a hole in York without hitting some remnant of the city's long past, and most of what's found ends up here. While the hordes line up at Jorvik Viking Centre, this museum has no crowds and provides a broader historical context, with more real artifacts. The three main collections— Roman, medieval, and natural history— are well described, bright, and good for kids.

Cost and Hours: £8, kids under 16 free with paying adult, daily 10:00-17:00, within Museum Gardens, tel. 01904/687-687, www.yorkshiremuseum.org.uk.

Visiting the Museum: At the entrance, you're greeted by an original, early fourth-century Roman statue of the god Mars. If he could talk, he'd say, "Hear me, mortals. There are three sections here: Roman (on this floor), medieval (downstairs), and natural history (a kid-friendly, fossil-based archaeology wing opposite the Roman stuff).

The **Roman** collection starts with a large map of the Roman Empire, set on the floor. Then, you'll see slice-of-life exhibits about Roman baths, a huge floor mosaic, and skulls accompanied by artists' renderings of how the people originally looked. (One man was apparently killed by a sword blow to the head—making it graphically clear that the struggle between Romans and barbarians was violent.) These artifacts are particularly interesting when you consider that you're standing in one of the farthest reaches of the Roman Empire.

The **medieval** collection is in the basement. During the Middle Ages, York was England's second city. One large room is dominated by ruins of the St. Mary's

Abbey complex; one wall of the abbey still stands just out front—be sure to see it before leaving. In the center of the rooms is the Vale of York Hoard, displaying a silver cup and the accompanying treasures it held—more than 600 silver coins as well as silver bars and jewelry. A father-and-son team discovered the hoard (thought to have been buried by Vikings in 927) while out for a day of metal detecting in 2007. You'll also see old weapons, glazed vessels, and a well-preserved 13th-century leather box.

The museum's prized pieces, a helmet and a pendant, are housed in this section. The eighth-century Anglo-Saxon helmet (known as the York Helmet or the Coppergate Helmet) shows a bit of barbarian refinement. Examine the delicate carving on its brass trim. The exquisitely etched 15th-century pendant—called the Middleham Jewel—is considered the finest piece of Gothic jewelry in Britain. The noble lady who wore this on a necklace believed that it helped her worship and protected her from illness. The back of the pendant, which rested near her heart, shows the Nativity. The front shows the Holy Trinity crowned by a sapphire (which people believed put their prayers at the top of God's to-do list).

In addition to the Anglo-Saxon pieces, the Viking collection is one of the best in England. Looking over the artifacts, you'll find that the Vikings (who conquered most of the Anglo-Saxon lands) wore some pretty decent shoes and actually combed their hair. The Cawood Sword, nearly 1,000 years old, is one of the finest surviving swords from that era.

Rick's Tip: *Lively* **King's Square***, with inviting benches, is great for people-watching. Once the site for the town's gallows, today it's prime real estate for buskers and street performers. Just beyond is York's most characteristic street, The Shambles.*

▲MERCHANT ADVENTURERS' HALL

The word "adventurers" refers to investors of the day, and this was a kind of merchants' corporate headquarters/early stock exchange. Claiming to be the finest surviving medieval guildhall in Britain (built from 1357 to 1361), the vast half-timbered building with marvelous exposed beams contains interesting displays about life and commerce in the Middle Ages when the economy revolved around guilds. Sitting by itself in its own little picnic-friendly park, the classic old building is worth a stop even just to see it from the outside.

Cost and Hours: £7, includes audioguide, Sun-Fri 10:00-16:30, Sat until 13:30, inviting café, south of The Shambles between Fossgate and Piccadilly, tel. 01904/654-818, www.merchantshallyork.org.

Yorkshire Museum

Eighth-century helmet

Jorvik Viking Centre

17:00, Nov-March until 16:00, these are last-entry times, tel. 01904/615-505, www. jorvikvikingcentre.co.uk.

Rick's Tip: *The popular* **Jorvik Viking Centre** *can have* **long lines.** *At the busiest times (roughly 11:00-15:00), you may have to wait an hour or more, especially on school breaks or in midsummer. For £2 extra, you can book a slot in advance, either over the phone or on their website. Or, try visiting early or late in the day.*

▲JORVIK VIKING CENTRE

Take the "Pirates of the Caribbean," sail them northeast and back in time 1,000 years, sprinkle in some real artifacts, and you get Jorvik (YOR-vik). In the late 1970s, more than 40,000 artifacts were dug out of the peat bog right here in downtown York—the UK's largest archaeological dig of Viking-era artifacts. When the archaeologists were finished, developers were allowed to build the big Fenwick Department store next door, and the dig site was converted into this attraction, opened in 1984.

Jorvik blends museum exhibits with a 16-minute ride on theme-park-esque "time capsules" that glide through the re-created Viking street of Coppergate as it looked circa the year 975. Animatronic characters and modern-day interpreters bring the scenes to life. Innovative when it first opened, the commercial success of Jorvik inspired copycat rides/museums all over England. Some love Jorvik, while others call it gimmicky and overpriced. If you think of it as Disneyland with a splash of history, Jorvik's fun. To me, Jorvik is a commercial venture designed for kids, with too much emphasis on its gift shop. But it's also undeniably entertaining, and—if you take the time to peruse its exhibits and substantial museum with a rich trove of Viking artifacts—it can be quite informative.

Cost and Hours: £13, daily 10:00-

▲FAIRFAX HOUSE

This well-furnished home, one of the first Georgian townhouses in England, is perfectly Neoclassical inside. Its seven rooms on two floors are each staffed by pleasant docents eager to talk with you. They'll explain how the circa-1760 home was built as the dowry for an aristocrat's daughter. The house is compact and bursting with stunning period furniture (the personal collection of a local chocolate magnate), gorgeously restored woodwork, and lavish stucco ceilings that offer clues as to each room's purpose. Stuccoed philosophers look down on the library, while the goddess of friendship presides over the drawing room. Altogether, this house provides fine insights into aristocratic life in 18th-century England.

Cost and Hours: £7.50, Tue-Sat 10:00-17:00, Sun 11:00-16:00, Mon by one-hour guided tour only at 11:00 and 14:00, closed Jan-mid-Feb, near Jorvik Viking Centre at 29 Castlegate, tel. 01904/655-543, www. fairfaxhouse.co.uk.

▲▲YORK CASTLE MUSEUM

This fascinating social-history museum is a Victorian home show, and one of the closest things to a time-tunnel experience England has to offer. The one-way plan ensures that you'll see everything, including remakes of rooms from the 17th to 20th century, a re-creation of a Victorian street, a heartfelt WWI exhibit, and eerie prison cells.

Reconstructed Victorian-era street and shops at the York Castle Museum

Cost and Hours: £10, kids under 16 free with adult, daily 9:30-17:00, roaming guides happily answer your questions (no audioguide), cafeteria at entrance, tel. 01904/687-687, www.yorkcastlemuseum. org.uk. It's at the bottom of the hop-on, hop-off bus route. The museum can call you a taxi (worthwhile if you're hurrying to the National Railway Museum, across town).

Visiting the Museum: The exhibits are divided between two wings: the North Building (the former women's prison, to the left as you enter) and the South Building (former debtors' prison, to the right).

Follow the one-way route, starting in the **North Building.** You'll first visit the Period Rooms, illuminating Yorkshire lifestyles during different time periods (1600s-1950s) and among various walks of life. Toy Stories is an enchanting review of toys through the ages. Next is the Shaping the Body exhibit, detailing diet and fashion trends over the past 400 years. Check out the codpieces, bustles, and corsets that used to "enhance" the human

form, and ponder some of the odd diet fads that make today's craziest diets seem normal. For foodies and chefs, the exhibit showcasing fireplaces and kitchens from the 1600s to the 1980s is especially tasty.

Next, stroll down the museum's re-created Kirkgate, a street from the Victorian era (1890s), when Britain was at the peak of its power. It features old-time shops and storefronts, including a pharmacist, sweet shop, school, and grocer for the working class, along with roaming guides in period dress. Around the back is a slum area depicting how the poor lived in those times.

Circle back to the entry and cross over to the **South Building.** In the WWI exhibit you can follow the lives of five York citizens as they experience the horrors and triumphs of the war years. One room plunges you into the gruesome world of trench warfare, where the average life expectancy was six weeks (and if you fell asleep during sentry duty, you'd be shot). A display about the home front notes that York suffered from Zeppelin attacks in which six died. At the end you're encouraged to share your thoughts in a room lined with chalkboards.

Exit outside and cross the castle yard. A detour to the left leads to a flour mill (open sporadically). Otherwise, your tour continues through the door on the right, where you'll find another reconstructed historical street, this one capturing the spirit of the swinging 1960s—"a time when

Period room—a slice of Yorkshire life

the cultural changes were massive but the cars and skirts were mini." Slathered with DayGlo colors, this street scene examines fashion, music, and television (including clips of beloved kids' shows and period news reports).

Finally, head into the York Castle Prison, which recounts the experiences of people who were thrown into the clink here. Videos, eerily projected onto the walls of individual cells, show actors telling tragic stories about the cells' one-time inhabitants.

Across the River

▲▲NATIONAL RAILWAY MUSEUM

If you like model railways, this is train-car heaven. The thunderous museum—displaying 200 illustrious years of British railroad history—is one of the biggest and best railroad museums anywhere.

Cost and Hours: Free but £5 suggested donation, daily 10:00-18:00, lockers-£3, café, restaurant, tel. 0333-016-1010, www. railwaymuseum.org.uk.

Getting There: It's about a 15-minute walk from the Minster (southwest of town, behind the train station). From the TI walk down Museum Street and

cross the Lendal Bridge, then take a right and follow the signs. To skip the walk, a cute little "road train" shuttles you more quickly between the Minster and the Railway Museum (£3 one-way, runs daily Easter-Oct, leaves museum every 30 minutes 11:00-16:00 at :00 and :30 past each hour; leaves town—from Duncombe Place, 100 yards in front of the Minster—at :15 and :45 past each hour).

Visiting the Museum: Pick up the floor plan to locate the various exhibits, which sprawl through several gigantic buildings on both sides of the street. Throughout the complex are info stands with staff eager to talk trains.

The museum's most impressive room is the **Great Hall** (head right from the entrance area and take the stairs to the underground passage). Fanning out from this grand roundhouse is an array of historic cars and engines, starting with the very first "stagecoaches on rails," with a crude steam engine from 1830. You'll trace the evolution of steam-powered transportation, from a replica of the Rocket (one of the first successful steam locomotives) to the era of the aerodynamic Mallard (famous as the first train to travel at a

National Railway Museum

startling two miles per minute—a marvel back in 1938) and the striking Art Deco-style Duchess of Hamilton. The collection spans to the present day, with a replica of the Eurostar (Chunnel) train and the Shinkansen Japanese bullet train.

In the **North Shed** you find **The Works**—an actual workshop where engineers scurry about, fixing old trains. Live train switchboards show real-time rail traffic on the East Coast Main Line. Next to the diagrammed screens, you can look out to see the actual trains moving up and down the line. **The Warehouse** is loaded with more than 10,000 items relating to train travel (including dinnerware, signage, and actual trains). Exhibits feature dining cars, post cars, sleeping cars, and info on the Flying Scotsman (the first London-Edinburgh express rail service, now running all over Britain in private tours).

Crossing back to the entrance side, continue to the **Station Hall,** with a collection of older trains, including Queen Victoria's lavish royal car and a WWII royal carriage reinforced with armor. Behind the hall are the South Yard and the Depot, with actual trains in storage. Train fans can hop on a steam train for a 10-minute ride (£4, daily 11:30-16:00, every 30 minutes).

EXPERIENCES

Shopping

With its medieval lanes lined with classy as well as tacky little shops, York is a hit with shoppers.

Antique Malls: Two places within a few blocks of each other are filled with stalls and cases owned by antique dealers from the countryside (all open daily). The malls, a warren of rooms on three floors with cafés buried deep inside, sell the dealers' bygones on commission. Serious shoppers do better heading for the country, but if you brake for garage sales you'll love these: The **Antiques Centre York** (41 Stonegate, www.theantiquescentreyork. co.uk), and the **Red House Antiques Centre** (a block from the Minster at Duncombe Place, www.redhouseyork.co.uk).

Nightlife

York's atmospheric **pubs** make for convivial eating and drinking. Many serve inexpensive lunches and/or early dinners, and then focus on beer in the evening.

The Maltings, just over Lendal Bridge, has classic pub ambience. Their fine local and international beers and light-and-mellow vibe are conducive to drinking

and talking (cross the bridge and look down and left to Tanners Moat, tel. 01904/655-387).

The Blue Bell is one of my favorites for old-school York vibes. This tiny, traditional establishment with a time-warp Edwardian interior is the smallest pub in York (no music, east end of town at 53 Fossgate, tel. 01904/654-904).

The House of the Trembling Madness is another fine watering hole with a cozy atmosphere; it sits above a "bottle shop" that sells a stunning variety of beers by the bottle to go (48 Stonegate).

Evil Eye Lounge, a hit with York's young crowd, is a creaky, funky, hip space famous for its strong cocktails and edgy ambience. You can order downstairs at the bar (with a small terrace out back) or head upstairs (42 Stonegate, tel. 01904/640-002).

The Golden Fleece—a sloppy, dingy place with tilty floors that make you feel drunk even if you aren't—claims to be the oldest and most haunted coaching inn in York (music nightly at 21:00, 16 Pavement, across the street from southern end of The Shambles, tel. 01904/625-171).

Entertainment
THEATRE ROYAL
This spiffed-up theater sporting an 18th-century facade offers a full variety of dramas, comedies, and works by Shakespeare (tickets £15-35, shows usually Tue-Sat at 19:30, tickets easy to get, on St. Leonard's Place near Bootham Bar,

booking tel. 01904/623-568, www. yorktheatreroyal.co.uk). Those under 18 and students of any age can get tickets for £10-15.

Riverside Walk or Bike Ride
The New Walk is a mile-long, tree-lined riverside lane created in the 1730s as a promenade for York's dandy class to stroll, see, and be seen—and is a fine place for today's visitors to walk or bike (Cycle Heaven rents bikes at the train station).

This hour-long walk is a delightful way to enjoy a dose of countryside away from York. It's paved, illuminated in the evening, and a popular jogging route any time of day.

Start from the riverside under Skeldergate Bridge (near the York Castle Museum) and walk south away from town about a mile to the striking, modern **Millennium Bridge.** Cross the bridge and take a right to head back toward York, passing **Rowntree Park** (you can enter the park through its fine old gate, stroll along the duck-filled pond near the Rowntree Park Café, and return to the riverside lane). Continue into York.

SLEEPING

July through October are the busiest (and usually most expensive) months. B&Bs often charge more for weekends and sometimes turn away one-night bookings, particularly for peak-season Saturdays. (York is worth two nights anyway.)

Rick's Tip: Book a room well in advance *during* **festival times** *and on weekends any time of year. For info on festivals, go to www. visityork.org.*

B&Bs and Guesthouses
These places are all small and family-run. They come with plenty of steep stairs (and no elevators) but no traffic noise.

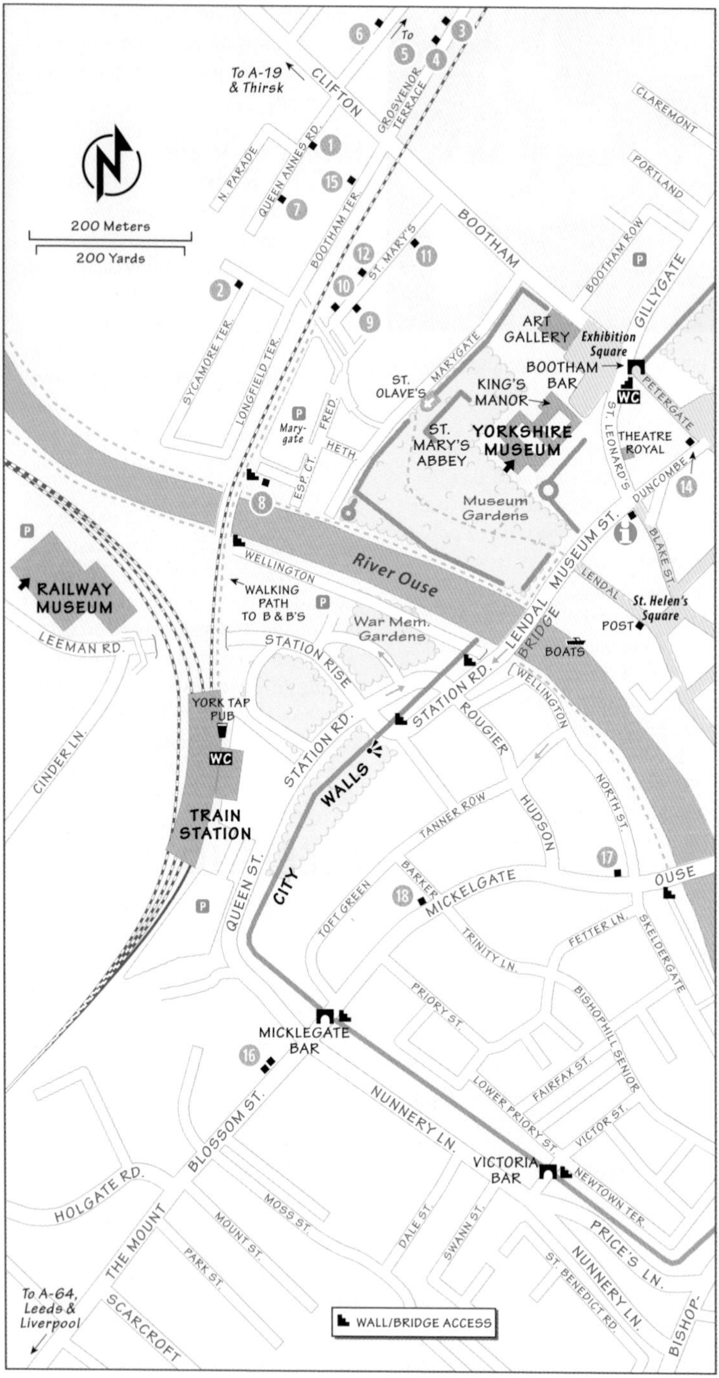

To A-19
& Thirsk

CLIFTON

GROSVENOR TERRACE

CLAREMONT

PORTLAND

200 Meters

200 Yards

N. PARADE

QUEEN ANNE'S RD.

BOOTHAM TER.

ST. MARY'S

BOOTHAM

BOOTHAM ROW

GILLYGATE

SYCAMORE TER.

LONGFIELD TER.

MARYGATE

ART
GALLERY

Exhibition
Square

BOOTHAM
BAR

PETERGATE

WC

Marygate

FRED.

HETH.

ESP. CT.

ST.
OLAVE'S

KING'S
MANOR

ST.
MARY'S
ABBEY

YORKSHIRE
MUSEUM

ST. LEONARD'S

THEATRE
ROYAL

DUNCOMBE

Museum
Gardens

BLAKE ST.

LENDAL

MUSEUM ST.

St. Helen's
Square

POST

RAILWAY
MUSEUM

LEEMAN RD.

WELLINGTON

River Ouse

WALKING
PATH
TO B & B'S

LENDAL
BRIDGE

BOATS

CINDER LN.

YORK TAP
PUB

WC

TRAIN
STATION

STATION RISE

War Mem.
Gardens

STATION RD.

STATION RD.

ROUGIER

WELLINGTON

CITY

WALLS

QUEEN ST.

TANNER ROW

TOFT GREEN

BARKER

HUDSON

NORTH ST.

OUSE

SKELDERGATE

MICKLEGATE

FETTER LN.

TRINITY LN.

PRIORY ST.

BISHOPHILL SENIOR

MICKLEGATE
BAR

BLOSSOM ST.

NUNNERY LN.

LOWER PRIORY ST.

FAIRFAX ST.

VICTOR ST.

VICTORIA
BAR

NEWTOWN TER.

HOLGATE RD.

THE MOUNT

MOSS ST.

MOUNT ST.

PARK ST.

DALE ST.

SWANN ST.

PRICE'S LN.

NUNNERY LN.

ST. BENEDICT RD.

BISHOP

To A-64,
Leeds &
Liverpool

SCARCROFT

WALL/BRIDGE ACCESS

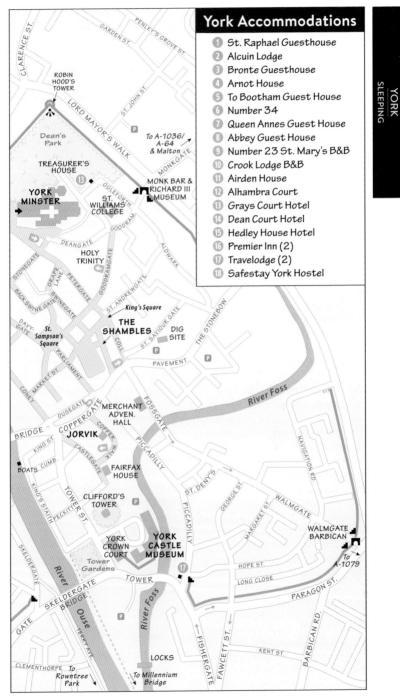

York Accommodations

1. St. Raphael Guesthouse
2. Alcuin Lodge
3. Bronte Guesthouse
4. Arnot House
5. To Bootham Guest House
6. Number 34
7. Queen Annes Guest House
8. Abbey Guest House
9. Number 23 St. Mary's B&B
10. Crook Lodge B&B
11. Airden House
12. Alhambra Court
13. Grays Court Hotel
14. Dean Court Hotel
15. Hedley House Hotel
16. Premier Inn (2)
17. Travelodge (2)
18. Safestay York Hostel

Rooms can be tight; if maneuverability is important, say so when booking. For a good selection, contact them well in advance. Most can provide permits for street parking.

The handiest B&B neighborhood is the quiet residential area just outside the old town wall's Bootham Bar, along the road called Bootham. All of these are within a 10-minute walk of the Minster and TI, and a 5- to 15-minute walk from the station.

Getting There: From the train station it's an easy five-minute **walk** to the B&B neighborhood: Head to the north end of the station along track 2 (past the York Tap pub and racks of bicycles) and into the short-stay parking lot. You'll continue essentially straight along the tracks, never taking any stairs, over the river and along a footpath, and ultimately to a short stairway (on the right) that leads to the base of St. Mary's Street.

If **driving** into town**,** head for the cathedral and follow the medieval wall to Bootham Bar. The street called Bootham leads away from Bootham Bar.

On or near Bootham Terrace

$$ St. Raphael Guesthouse, run by Fran and Jamie, has seven comfy rooms. Each is themed after a York street and lovingly accented with a fresh rose and home-baked banana bread. For more space, ask for their small apartment with a private entrance and courtyard (RS%, family rooms, 44 Queen Annes Road, tel. 01904/645-028, www.straphaelguesthouse.co.uk, info@straphaelguesthouse.co.uk).

$$ Alcuin Lodge, run by welcoming Darren and Mark, is a cozy place, with five rooms that feel personal yet up to date (1 room with private WC in the hallway just outside; 15 Sycamore Place, tel. 01904/629-837, www.alcuinlodge.com, darren@alcuinlodge.com).

$$ Bronte Guesthouse is a modern B&B with five airy, bright rooms and a lovely back garden (family room available,

22 Grosvenor Terrace, tel. 01904/621-066, www.bronte-guesthouse.com, enquiries@bronte-guesthouse.com).

$$ Arnot House, run by a hardworking daughter-and-mother team, is old-fashioned, homey, and lushly decorated with Victorian memorabilia (2-night minimum preferred, no children, huge DVD library, 17 Grosvenor Terrace, tel. 01904/641-966, www.arnothouseyork.co.uk, kim.robbins@virgin.net).

$$ Bootham Guest House features creamy walls and contemporary furniture. Of the eight rooms, six are en suite, while two share a bath (RS%, 56 Bootham Crescent, tel. 01904/672-123, www.boothamguesthouse.co.uk, boothamguesthouse1@hotmail.com, Andrew).

$ Number 34, run by Jason, has five simple, light rooms at fair prices. It has a clean, uncluttered feeling, with modern decor (RS%, ground-floor room, 5-person apartment next door, 34 Bootham Crescent, tel. 01904/645-818, www.number34york.co.uk, enquiries@number34york.co.uk).

$ Queen Annes Guest House has nine basic rooms in two adjacent houses. While it doesn't have the plushest beds or richest decor, it's respectable, affordable, and clean (RS%, family room, lounge, 24 and 26 Queen Annes Road, tel. 01904/629-389, www.queen-annes-guesthouse.co.uk, info@queen-annes-guesthouse.co.uk).

On the River

$$ Abbey Guest House is a peaceful refuge overlooking the River Ouse, with five cheerful, contemporary-style rooms and a cute little garden. A tasty homemade breakfast is served, and the river-view rooms will ramp up your romance with York (RS%, pay laundry service, 13 Earlsborough Terrace, tel. 01904/627-782, www.abbeyguesthouseyork.co.uk, info@abbeyguesthouseyork.co.uk).

On St. Mary's Street

$$ Number 23 St. Mary's B&B, run by Simon, has nine extravagantly decorated and spaciously comfortable rooms, plus a classy lounge and all the doily touches (discount for longer stays, family room, honesty box for drinks and snacks, lots of stairs, 23 St. Mary's, tel. 01904/622-738, www.23stmarys.co.uk, stmarys23@hotmail.com).

$$ Crook Lodge B&B, with six tight but elegantly charming rooms, serves breakfast in an old Victorian kitchen. The 21st-century style somehow fits this old house (one ground-floor room, free parking, quiet, 26 St. Mary's, tel. 01904/655-614, www.crooklodgeguesthouseyork.co.uk, crooklodge@hotmail.com).

$$ Airden House rents nine nice, mostly traditional rooms, though the two basement-level rooms are more mod—one has a space age-looking hot tub (RS%, lounge, free parking, 1 St. Mary's, tel. 01904/638-915, www.airdenhouse.co.uk, info@airdenhouse.co.uk, Emma and Heather).

$$ Alhambra Court is a family-run hotel with 24 charmingly appointed rooms. Relax outside in the quiet courtyard or inside in the two splendidly decorated lounges (elevator, pay laundry service, free parking, 31 St. Mary's, tel. 01904/628-474, www.alhambracourt.co.uk, stay@alhambracourt.co.uk)

Hotels

$$$$ Grays Court Hotel is a historic mansion—the home of dukes and archbishops since 1091—that now rents 12 rooms to travelers. While its public spaces and gardens are lavish, its rooms are elegant yet modest. If it's too pricey for lodging, consider coming here for its fine-dining **$$$$ Bow Room Restaurant** serving modern English cuisine (Chapter House Street, tel. 01904/612-613, www.grayscourtyork.com).

$$$ Dean Court Hotel, a Best Western facing the Minster, is a big stately hotel with classy lounges and 37 comfortable rooms. It has a great location and friendly vibe for a business-class establishment. A few rooms have views for no extra charge (elevator, restaurant, Duncombe Place, tel. 01904/625-082, www.deancourt-york.co.uk, sales@deancourt-york.co.uk).

$$$ Hedley House Hotel, well run by a wonderful family, has 30 clean and spacious rooms. The outdoor hot tub/sauna is a fine way to end your day (ask for a deal with stay of three or more nights, family rooms, good two-course evening meals, in-house massage and beauty services, free parking, 3 Bootham Terrace, tel. 01904/637-404, www.hedleyhouse.com, greg@hedleyhouse.com). They also have three luxury studio apartments.

Budget Chain Hotels: If looking for something a little less spendy than the hotels listed earlier, consider several chains, with central locations in town. These include **Premier Inn** (two branches side-by-side) and **Travelodge** (one location near the York Castle Museum at 90 Piccadilly; second location on Micklegate).

Hostel

¢ Safestay York is a boutique hostel on a rowdy street (especially on Fridays and Saturdays). Located in a big old Georgian house, they rent 158 beds in 4- to 12-bed rooms, with great views, private prefab "pod" bathrooms, and reading lights. They also offer fancier, hotel-quality doubles (family room, breakfast extra, 4 floors, no elevator, air-con, Wi-Fi in public areas only, laundry, TV lounge, game room, bar, no curfew, 5-minute walk from train station at 88 Micklegate, tel. 01904/627-720, www.safestay.com/ss-york-micklegate.html, reception-yk@safestay.com).

EATING

York is a great food city, with a wide range of ethnic options and foodie bistros. Thanks to the local high-tech industry, the university, and tourism, there's a demand that sustains lots of creative and fun eateries. Most bistros have good vegetarian options and offer economical lunch specials and early dinners (generally order by 18:30). After 19:00 or so, main courses cost £16-26. If you're set on a particular place for dinner, reservations are smart.

City Center
Fine Dining
$$$$ Skosh serves a smart local clientele gourmet tapas—modern, creative, and shareable small dishes that are a fusion of English and international cuisine. Its bright dining room is loud and fun, with an open kitchen adding energy to the mix. It's top quality with no pretense (£10 plates—three or four per person makes a meal, Wed-Sat 12:00-14:00 & 17:30-22:00, closed Sun-Tue, 98 Micklegate, tel. 01904/634-849).

Cheap Eats Around King's Square
King's Square is about as central as can be, and from here you can see several fine quick-and-cheap lunch options. After buying your takeout, sit on the square and enjoy the street entertainers. Or, for a peaceful place, find the Holy Trinity Church yard on Goodramgate (half a block to the right of York Roast Company).

$ York Roast Company is a local fixture, serving their Yorkshire pudding wrap (a kind of old English burrito) and hearty pork sandwiches. If Henry VIII wanted fast food, he'd have eaten here (daily 10:00-23:00, order at counter then eat upstairs or take away for the same price, 74 Low Petergate, tel. 01904/629-197, second location at 4 Stonegate).

$ Drakes Fish & Chips across the street from York Roast Company, is a local favorite chippy. For £3 extra you can sit and eat in their simple backroom dining area (daily 11:00-22:30, 97 Low Petergate, tel. 01904/624-788).

$ The Cornish Bakery, facing King's Square, cooks up pasties to eat in or take away (30 Colliergate, tel. 01904/671-177).

$ Shambles Market and Food Court has many food stalls and street-food vendors—like a corral of food trucks—offering fun, nutritious, and ethnic light meals. The Moros stand is particularly popular for its North African plates. This lively scene is wedged between The Shambles and Parliament Street (daily 7:00-17:00, until 16:00 in winter).

$ St. Crux Parish Hall is used by a medley of charities that sell tea, homemade cakes, and light meals (Tue-Sat 10:00-16:00, closed Sun-Mon, at bottom of The Shambles at its intersection with Pavement, tel. 01904/621-756).

$ Harlequin Café, a charming place, is appreciated for its good coffee, homemade cakes, and light meals. It's up a creaky staircase overlooking King's Square. On weekend nights it morphs into a gin bar (Mon-Sat 10:00-16:00, Sun 11:00-15:00, 2 King's Square, tel. 01904/630-631).

Groceries: A **Marks & Spencer Food Hall** is a block away from Shambles Market on Parliament Street (Mon-Sat 8:00-18:30, Sun 10:30-17:00).

Near Stonegate
$$ Ask Italian Restaurant is part of a cheap and cheery chain, but the food's fine, the price is right, and you'll slurp your pasta in the majestic Neoclassical hall of York's Grand Assembly Rooms, lined with Corinthian marble columns (daily 11:00-22:00, weekends until 23:00; Blake Street, tel. 01904/637-254).

Near Bootham Bar and Recommended B&Bs
$$$$ Roots Restaurant feels formal and romantic, with a classy dining room and small gourmet dishes designed to be

enjoyed family-style. I'd opt for the £55 tasting menu (lots of fine wine by the glass, lunch from noon, dinner 17:30-21:00, closed Tue, 68 Marygate, no phone, reserve at info@rootsyork.co.uk or www.rootsyork.com).

$$ Café Concerto, a casual and cozy bistro with wholesome food and a charming musical theme, has a loyal following. The fun menu features updated English favorites with some international and vegetarian options (daily 9:30-17:00, facing the Minster at 21 High Petergate, tel. 01904/610-478, www.cafeconcerto.biz).

$$$ Café No. 8 is a romantic and modern little bistro. Grab one of the tables in front or in the sunroom, or enjoy a shaded little garden out back. Chef Chris Pragnell uses what's fresh in the market to shape his elegant, creative modern British menu. An early dinner special is offered Tuesday through Thursday until 18:30 (Mon 12:00-16:00, Tue-Fri 12:00-22:00, Sat 9:00-22:00, Sun until 16:00, 8 Gillygate, tel. 01904/653-074, www.cafeno8.co.uk).

$$ Mamma Mia Italian Restaurant is a popular choice for its pizza, pasta, and a full menu of Italian *secondi*. The eating area features a tempting gelato bar, and in nice weather the back patio is *molto bello* (Tue-Sun 11:30-14:00 & 17:30-23:00, closed Mon, 20 Gillygate, tel. 01904/622-020).

$$ Hole-in-the-Wall Pub is the place if you're looking for a ye olde pub with good grub and a £10 dinner. They have an extensive menu with light bites, burgers, fish-and-chips, meat pies, and veggie dishes—and it's a fine spot for a traditional Yorkshire pudding (daily 11:30-22:00, on High Petergate just inside Bootham Bar, tel. 01904/634-468).

$$$ The Star Inn the City has quality modern Yorkshire cuisine and a dressy dining hall. Lunch is served on its enticing riverside terrace, but in the evening that's for drinks only (daily 12:00-22:00, next to the river in Lendal Engine House, Museum Street, tel. 01904/619-208, www.starinnthecity.co.uk).

$$ The Minster Inn, an Edwardian alehouse serving stone-baked pizzas, tapas, and a good selection of cask ales and wines, is a friendly neighborhood hangout with an open courtyard that's fun in the summer (daily 12:00-23:00, 24 Marygate, tel. 01904/849-240).

Groceries: Sainsbury is handy for picnic provisions or a simple cheap dinner (daily 6:00-24:00, 50 yards outside Bootham Bar, on Bootham).

East End of Town

This neighborhood is across town from my recommended B&Bs, but still central (and a short walk from the York Castle Museum). Reservations are smart for all.

$$ The Hop York Pizzeria Beerhall is a favorite for its simple approach and winning combo: pizza and beer. The pub pulls real ales in the front, serves wood-fired pies in an inviting space in the back, and offers live music (daily 12:00-23:00, food served until 21:00—Sun until 20:00, music Wed-Sun at 21:00; 11 Fossgate, tel. 01904/541-466).

$$ Mumbai Lounge Indian Restaurant is a local choice for Indian food (daily 12:00-14:00 & 17:30-23:30, 47 Fossgate, tel. 01904/654-155, www.mumbailoungeyork.co.uk).

$$ Loch Fyne Seafood and Grill is a fine fish value with an inviting and affordable menu served in a classic and spacious old hall. Their three-course, £13 lunch special is served until 18:00 (daily 12:00-22:30, Foss Bridge House, Walmgate, tel. 01904/650-910).

$$ Khao San Road Thai Bistro hits the spot if you need a Thai fix (daily from 17:00, 52 Walmgate, tel. 01904/635-599).

$$ The Barbakan Polish Restaurant is run by a Krakow family offering an inviting little Polish dining room with a passion for homemade cakes (Mon-Sat 9:00-13:00 & 18:00-22:00, Sun 10:00-21:00, 58 Walmgate, tel. 01904/672-474, www.deli-barbakan.co.uk).

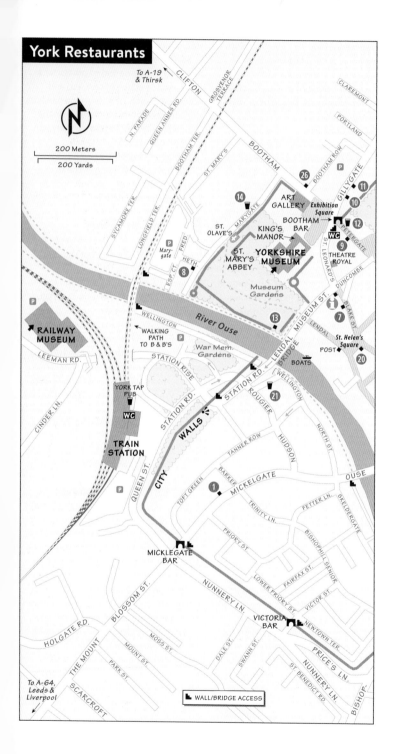

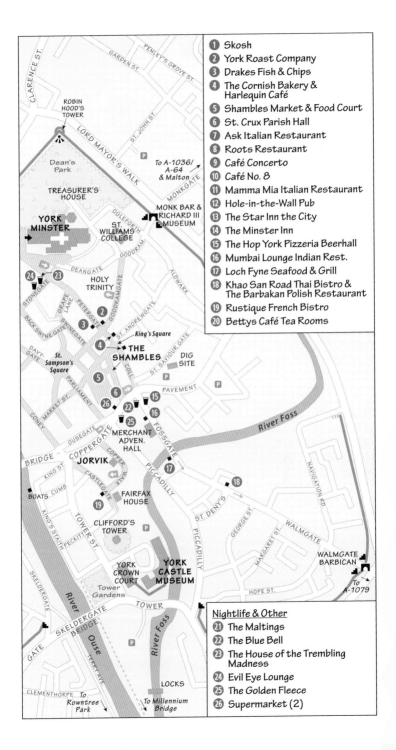

1. Skosh
2. York Roast Company
3. Drakes Fish & Chips
4. The Cornish Bakery & Harlequin Café
5. Shambles Market & Food Court
6. St. Crux Parish Hall
7. Ask Italian Restaurant
8. Roots Restaurant
9. Café Concerto
10. Café No. 8
11. Mamma Mia Italian Restaurant
12. Hole-in-the-Wall Pub
13. The Star Inn the City
14. The Minster Inn
15. The Hop York Pizzeria Beerhall
16. Mumbai Lounge Indian Rest.
17. Loch Fyne Seafood & Grill
18. Khao San Road Thai Bistro & The Barbakan Polish Restaurant
19. Rustique French Bistro
20. Bettys Café Tea Rooms

Nightlife & Other

21. The Maltings
22. The Blue Bell
23. The House of the Trembling Madness
24. Evil Eye Lounge
25. The Golden Fleece
26. Supermarket (2)

$$$ Rustique French Bistro has one big room of tight tables and good prices (£20 three-course meal), and is straight French—right down to the welcome (daily 12:00–22:00, across from Fairfax House at 28 Castlegate, tel. 01904/612-744, www. rustiqueyork.co.uk).

Tearoom

$$ Bettys Café Tea Rooms is a destination restaurant for many. Choose between a Yorkshire Cream Tea (tea and scones with clotted Yorkshire cream and strawberry jam) or a full traditional English afternoon tea (tea, delicate sandwiches, scones, and sweets). With the afternoon tea, your table is so full of doily niceties that the food is served on a little three-tray tower. While you'll pay a little extra here, the ambience and people-watching are hard to beat. They'll offer to seat you sooner in the bigger and less atmospheric basement, but I'd be patient and wait for a place upstairs—ideally by the window. It's permissible for travel partners on a budget to enjoy the experience for about half the price by one ordering a "full tea"—£20, with enough little sandwiches and sweets for two to share—and the other a simple cup of tea (daily 9:00–21:00, tel.

01904/659-142, www.bettys.co.uk, St. Helen's Square). During World War II, Bettys was a drinking hangout for Allied airmen based nearby. Downstairs near the WC is a mirror signed by bomber pilots—read the story.

TRANSPORTATION

Arriving and Departing
By Train

The train station is a 10-minute walk from downtown (see directions below). Day-trippers can pay to store baggage at the small hut next to the Europcar office just off Queen Street—as you exit the station, turn right and walk along a bridge to the first intersection, then turn right (daily 8:00–20:00). Baggage storage is also available near Bootham Bar—see "Helpful Hints," earlier.

My recommended B&Bs are a 5- to 15-minute walk from the station. For walking directions to the B&Bs, see page 294.

Or, a **taxi** can zip you from the train station to your B&B for £7-9. Queue up at the taxi stand, or call 01904/623-332; cabbies don't start the meter until you get in.

To **walk downtown** from the station,

exit straight, crossing the street through the bus stops, and turn left down Station Road, keeping the wall on your right. At the first intersection, turn right through the gap in the wall and then left across the river, and follow the crowd toward the Gothic towers of the Minster. After the bridge, a block before the Minster, you'll see the TI on your right.

Train Connections to: Durham (4/hour, 50 minutes), **London**'s King's Cross Station (3/hour, 2 hours), **Bath** (hourly with change in Bristol, 4.5 hours, more with additional transfers), **Oxford** (hourly direct, 3.5 hours, more with transfers), **Birmingham** (2/hour, 2.5 hours), **Keswick/Lake District** (train to Penrith: roughly 2/hour, 4 hours, 1-2 transfers; then bus, allow about 5 hours total), **Edinburgh** (2/hour, 2.5 hours). Train info: Tel. 0345-748-4950, www.nationalrail.co.uk.

Connections with London's Airports: Heathrow (allow 4 hours minimum; from airport take Heathrow Express train to London's Paddington Station, transfer by Tube to King's Cross, then take train to York); **Gatwick** (allow 4 hours minimum; from Gatwick South, catch Thameslink train to London's St. Pancras International Station; from there, walk to neighboring King's Cross Station, and catch train to York).

By Car

Driving and parking in York is maddening. Those day-tripping here should follow signs to one of several park-and-ride lots ringing the perimeter. Parking is free (though they don't generally allow over-night parking), and cheap shuttle buses go every 10 minutes into the center.

If you're sleeping here, park your car where your B&B advises and walk. As you near York (and your B&B), you'll hit the A-1237 ring road. Follow this to the A-19/Thirsk roundabout (next to river on northwest side of town). From the roundabout, follow signs for *York,* traveling through Clifton into Bootham. All recommended B&Bs are four or five blocks before you hit the medieval city gate.

If you're approaching York from the south, take the M-1 until it becomes the A-1M, exit at junction 45 onto the A-64, and follow it for 10 miles until you reach York's ring road (A-1237), which allows you to avoid driving through the city center.

Rick's Tip: *If you're nearing the end of your trip,* **drop off your rental car upon arrival in York.** *The money saved by turning it in early just about pays for the train ticket that whisks you effortlessly to London.*

Car Rental: In York, you'll find these agencies: **Avis** (3 Layerthorpe, tel. 0844-544-6117); **Hertz** (at train station, tel. 0843-653-503); **Budget** (near the National Railway Museum behind the train station at 75 Leeman Road, tel. 01904/644-919); and **Europcar** (off Queen Street near train station, tel. 0371-384-3458). Beware: Car-rental agencies close early on Saturday afternoons and all day Sunday. This is OK when dropping off, but picking up at these times is possible only by prior arrangement (and for an extra fee).

BEST OF THE REST

Once a grimy manufacturing city, **Liverpool** now sparkles with a revived waterfront and a buzzing cultural scene that pays homage to the city's musical past (Beatles, anyone?).

Marvel at England's greatest Norman church—**Durham's** cathedral—and enjoy an evensong service there. At the excellent Beamish Museum nearby, travel back in time to the 19th and 20th centuries. If you're looking for more ancient history, go for a Roman ramble at **Hadrian's Wall,** a reminder that Britain was an important Roman colony 2,000 years ago.

Liverpool

Liverpool provides the best look at urban England outside of London. Beatles fans flock to Liverpool to learn about the Fab Four's early days, but the city has much more to offer, including quality, free museums, a dramatic skyline mingling old red-brick maritime buildings and glassy new skyscrapers, and—most of all—the charm of the Liverpudlians. Anyone who still thinks of Liverpool as a depressed industrial center is behind the times.

Day Plan

For the quickest visit, focus your time around the Albert Dock area, home to The Beatles Story, Merseyside Maritime Museum, Museum of Liverpool, and the British Music Experience. If time allows, consider a Beatles bus tour (departs from the Albert Dock). A full day buys you time either to delve into the rest of the city, to binge on more Beatles sights (the Magical Beatles Museum or the boyhood homes of John and Paul), or a bit of both.

Orientation

For visitors, most points of interest are concentrated in the generally pedestrian-friendly downtown area. Beatles sights, however, are spread far and wide—it's most efficient to connect them with a tour.

Tourist Information: Liverpool's TIs are just tiny desks freeloading in the Central Library (near the train station) and at the Magical Beatles Museum on Mathew Street (tel. 0151/707-0729, www.visitliverpool.com).

Tours: If you want to see as many Beatles-related sights as possible in a short time, these tours are the way to go. Your choices include the **Magical Mystery Big Bus Tour** (£20, 5-8/day, fewer on Sun and in off-season, 2 hours, buses depart from the Albert Dock near the Beatles Story, tel. 0151/703-9100, www.cavernclub.org); the **Phil Hughes Minibus Beatles and Liverpool Tours** (£150 for private group tour with 1-5 people; £30/person in peak season if he can assemble a group of 5-8 people; 5 hours, 8-seat minibus, tel. 0151/228-4565, www.tourliverpool.co.uk); or **Jackie Spencer Private Tours** (up to 5 people in her chauffeur-driven minivan-£240, 3 hours, mobile 0799-076-1478, www.jackiespencerbeatleguide.com).

Getting There: Liverpool is linked by train with the Lake District (via Penrith, 2/hour with change in Wigan or Lancaster, 2.5 hours), York (hourly, 2 hours), Edinburgh (2/hour, 4 hours, most change in Preston, Wigan, or York), and London's Euston Station (3/hour, 2.5 hours). From the main Lime Street Station to the Albert Dock is about a 20-minute walk or a quick trip by subway or taxi.

Drivers approaching Liverpool first follow signs to *City Centre* and *Waterfront,* then brown signs to *Albert Dock,* where you'll find a huge pay parking lot.

Sights

▲THE BEATLES STORY

The Beatles seem like they're becoming a bigger and bigger attraction in Liverpool these days. This exhibit—while overpriced

BEST OF THE REST
LIVERPOOL

Albert Dock

and a bit small—is well done. There are many artifacts (from George Harrison's first boyhood guitar to John Lennon's orange-tinted "Imagine" glasses), as well as large dioramas celebrating landmarks in Beatles lore (a reconstruction of the Cavern Club, a life-size re-creation of the *Sgt. Pepper* album cover, and a walk-through yellow submarine). The story's a fascinating one, and even an avid fan will pick up some new information.

Cost and Hours: £17, includes audioguide; daily 9:00-19:00, Nov-March 10:00-18:00; tel. 0151/709-1969, www.beatlesstory.com.

▲**MERSEYSIDE MARITIME MUSEUM AND INTERNATIONAL SLAVERY MUSEUM**

These museums tell the story of Liverpool, once the second city of the British Empire. The **International Slavery Museum** has a harrowing exhibit about enslavement and the Middle Passage (as the voyage to the Americas was called). The **Maritime Museum** celebrates Liverpool's shipbuilding heritage and covers emigration to America. There are also extensive exhibits on the *Titanic* and another maritime disaster—the 1915 sinking of the *Lusitania,* which was torpedoed by a German U-boat.

Cost and Hours: Free, donations accepted, daily 10:00-17:00, café, tel. 0151/478-4499, www.liverpoolmuseums.org.uk.

▲▲**MUSEUM OF LIVERPOOL**

This museum does a good job of fulfilling its goal to "capture Liverpool's vibrant character and demonstrate the city's unique contribution to the world." The *People's Republic* exhibit examines what it means to be a Liverpudlian (a.k.a. "Scouser") and covers everything from

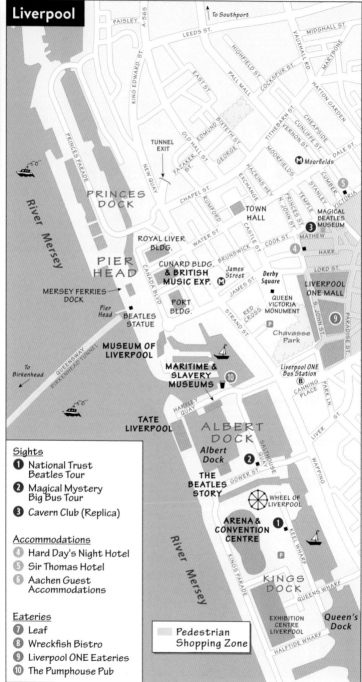

Liverpool

To Southport

PAISLEY · A-565 · LEEDS ST. · MIDGHALL ST. · MARYBONE

KING EDWARD ST. · HIGHFIELD ST. · VAUXHALL RD. · HATTON GARDEN

EAST ST. · PALL MALL · COCKSPUR ST. · CHEAPSIDE · HATTON GARDEN

PRINCES PARADE · NEW QUAY · OLD HALL ST. · GEORGE · BIXTETH ST. · EDMUND ST. · TITHEBARN ST. · CUNLIFFE ST. · VERNON ST. · DALE ST.

TUNNEL EXIT

FAZAKERLEY ST.

M Moorfields

PRINCES DOCK

CHAPEL ST. · RUMFORD · EXCHANGE · HACKINS HEY · N. JOHN ST. · PRINCES ST. · TEMPLE · STANLEY · CUMBER · VICTORIA · **5**

River Mersey

CANADA BLVD.

PIER HEAD

ROYAL LIVER BLDG.

TOWN HALL

M MAGICAL BEATLES MUSEUM

3 MATHEW

WATER ST. · CASTLE ST. · COOK ST.

BRUNSWICK ST.

4 HARR.

MERSEY FERRIES DOCK

CUNARD BLDG. & BRITISH MUSIC EXP. **M**

James Street

Derby Square

LORD ST.

LIVERPOOL ONE MALL

Pier Head

BEATLES STATUE

PORT BLDG.

JAMES ST. · RED CROSS

QUEEN VICTORIA MONUMENT

S. JOHN ST. · PARADISE ST.

9

To Birkenhead

QUEENSWAY BIRKENHEAD TUNNEL

MUSEUM OF LIVERPOOL

STRAND ST.

P Chavasse Park

MARITIME & SLAVERY MUSEUMS **10**

Liverpool ONE Bus Station

B CANNING PLACE

PARK LN.

HARTLEY QUAY

TATE LIVERPOOL

LIVER ST.

ALBERT DOCK

Albert Dock **2**

SALTHOUSE QUAY

WAPING

THE BEATLES STORY

GOWER ST.

WHEEL OF LIVERPOOL

ARENA & CONVENTION CENTRE **1**

KEEL WHARF

P

River Mersey

KINGS PARADE

KINGS DOCK

QUEENS WHARF

EXHIBITION CENTRE LIVERPOOL

Queen's Dock

HALFTIDE WHARF

Sights
1 National Trust Beatles Tour
2 Magical Mystery Big Bus Tour
3 Cavern Club (Replica)

Accommodations
4 Hard Day's Night Hotel
5 Sir Thomas Hotel
6 Aachen Guest Accommodations

Eateries
7 Leaf
8 Wreckfish Bistro
9 Liverpool ONE Eateries
10 The Pumphouse Pub

Pedestrian Shopping Zone

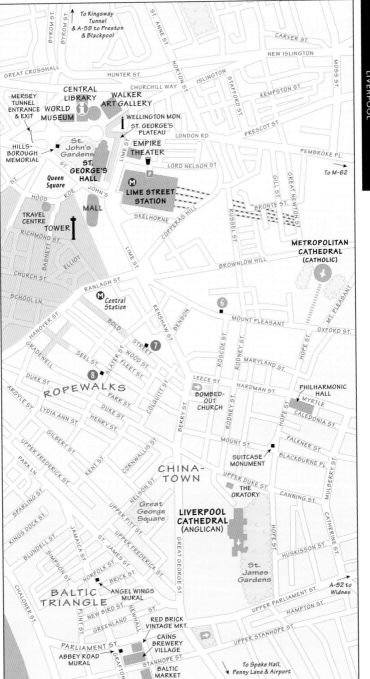

housing and health issues to military and religious topics. Music is the other big focus here, with plenty of fun interactive stops that include quizzes, a karaoke booth, and listening stations. The museum is full of fascinating facts that bring a whole new depth to your Liverpool experience.

Cost and Hours: Free, donations encouraged, daily 10:00-17:00, guidebook-£1, café, Mann Island, Pier Head, tel. 0151/478-4545, www.liverpoolmuseums.org.uk.

▲▲BRITISH MUSIC EXPERIENCE

This museum, located in the Cunard Building at Pier Head, goes beyond Liverpool's Beatlemania, immersing visitors in the history of British music of all genres from 1945 until today. The multimedia exhibits include costumes, instruments, recordings, and memorabilia from artists and bands such as David Bowie, Queen, Amy Winehouse, Coldplay, and Adele, plus the chance to play professional-grade instruments in a sound studio. You could easily spend hours here, but plan for at least 90 minutes.

Cost and Hours: £14, daily 10:00-18:00, last entry 1.5 hours before closing, multimedia guide-£2; tel. 0344-335-0655, www.britishmusicexperience.com.

▲WALKER ART GALLERY

Though it has few recognizable works, Liverpool's main art gallery offers an enjoyable walk through an easy-to-digest collection of European (mostly British) paintings, sculpture, and decorative arts. There's no audioguide, but many of the works are well explained by posted descriptions. You'll see a famous Nicholas Hilliard portrait of Queen Elizabeth I (nicknamed "The Pelican," for her brooch) and a well-known royal portrait of Henry VIII by Hans Holbein. The collection also features a Rembrandt self-portrait, canvases by Gainsborough and Hogarth, plus a delightful array of Pre-Raphaelite works.

Cost and Hours: Free, donations accepted, daily 10:00-17:00, William Brown Street, tel. 0151/478-4199, www.liverpoolmuseums.org.uk.

MATHEW STREET

The narrow, bar-lined Mathew Street, right in the heart of downtown, is ground zero for Beatles fans. The Beatles frequently performed in their early days together at the original Cavern Club, deep in a cellar along this street. While that's long gone, a mock-up of the historic nightspot (built with many of the original bricks) lives on a few doors down. Still billed as "the **Cavern Club**," this noisy bar is worth a visit to see the reconstructed cellar that's often filled by Beatles cover bands (open daily 10:00-24:00; live music daily from noon until late evening, free admission most of the time, small entry fee Thu-Sun evenings; tel. 0151/236-9091, www.cavernclub.org).

Across the street and run by the same owners, the **Cavern Pub** lacks its sibling's troglodyte aura, but makes up for it with walls lined with old photos and memorabilia from The Beatles and other bands who've performed here. Like the Cavern Club, the pub features frequent performances by Beatles cover bands and other acts (no cover, daily 11:00-24:00, tel. 0151/236-4041).

▲▲MAGICAL BEATLES MUSEUM

Claiming to be "the world's most authentic Beatles museum," this fascinating-to-Beatles-fans collection is spread chronologically over three floors with thoughtful descriptions. Neil Aspinall, a roadie-hoarder, collected this memorabilia during the early years as if he knew The Beatles would make history. Filled with a trove of artifacts (letters, clothing, photos, and so on), each floor covers an era: before they were famous, the touring years, and the studio/psychedelic years. Beatle-geek staffers are standing by to tell stories and answer questions. It's strong on pre-Ringo days, because Neil was "a kind of stepfather" to Pete Best (the original drummer)...it's complicated.

Cost and Hours: £15, RS%—Roag Best (the owner and half-brother of Pete) promises 20 percent off with this book; daily 10:00-18:00, last entry one hour before closing, 50 yards from the Cavern Club at 23 Mathew Street, tel. 0151/236-1337, www.magicalbeatlesmuseum.com.

▲**LENNON AND MCCARTNEY HOMES**
John's and Paul's boyhood homes are now owned by the National Trust and have both been restored to how they looked during the lads' 1950s childhoods. While some Beatles bus tours stop here for photo ops, only the National Trust minibus tour gets you inside the homes. For die-hard Beatles fans who want to get a glimpse into the time and place that created these musical masterminds, the National Trust tour is worth ▲▲▲.

Cost: £25, £31 includes a guidebook.

Reservations: Advance booking is strongly advised, especially in summer and on weekends or holidays (tel. 0344-249-1895, www.nationaltrust.org.uk/beatles).

Visitor Information: Limited to 15 or so Beatlemaniacs each, tours run daily from the Albert Dock at 10:00, 11:00, and 14:10 (tours do not run Mon-Tue in mid-Feb–mid-March and Nov; no tours at all Dec–mid-Feb). They depart from the Jurys Inn (south across the bridge from The Beatles Story). The entire visit takes about 2.5 hours.

Visiting the Homes: A minibus takes you to the homes of John and Paul, with about 45 minutes inside each (no photos allowed inside either home). Each home has a caretaker who acts as your guide. These folks give an entertaining, insightful-to-fans talk that lasts about 30 minutes. You then have 10-15 minutes to wander through the house on your own.

Mendips (John Lennon's Home): Even though he sang about being a working-class hero, John grew up in the suburbs of Liverpool, surrounded by doctors,

lawyers, and—beyond the back fence—Strawberry Field.

This was the home of John's Aunt Mimi, who raised him in this house from the time he was five years old and once told him, "A guitar's all right, John, but you'll never earn a living by it."

On the surface, it's just a 1930s house carefully restored to how it would have been in the past. But if you're a John Lennon fan, it's fun to picture him as a young boy drawing and imagining at his dining room table. His bedroom, with an Elvis poster and his favorite boyhood books, offers tantalizing hints at his later musical genius. Sing a song to yourself in the enclosed porch—John and Paul did this when they wanted an echo-chamber effect.

20 Forthlin Road (Paul McCartney's Home): In comparison to Aunt Mimi's house, the home where Paul grew up is simpler, much less "posh," and even a little ratty around the edges. More than a hundred Beatles songs were written in this house (including "I Saw Her Standing There") during days Paul and John spent skipping school. The photos from Paul's brother, Michael, taken in this house, help make the scene of what's mostly a barren interior much more interesting. Ask your guide how Paul would sneak into the house late at night without waking up his dad.

Rick's Tip: *Your best budget options for sleeping in this thriving city are the boring, predictable, and central chain hotels.*

Sleeping

If you're interested in overnighting, consider the Beatle-themed **$$ Hard Day's Night Hotel** (North John Street, www.harddaysnighthotel.com); the centrally located **$$ Sir Thomas Hotel** (24 Sir Thomas Street, www.thesirthomas.co.uk); or the straightforward **$ Aachen Guest Accommodations** (89 Mount Pleasant, www.aachenhotel.co.uk).

Eating

The Ropewalks area, a 20-minute walk east of the Albert Dock, has several good eateries, including **$$ Leaf,** serving fresh bakery items, salads, vegetarian plates, soups, sandwiches, fun cocktails, and lots of tea (65 Bold Street) and **$$$ Wreckfish Bistro,** a dynamic and friendly place serving modern British cuisine (reservations smart, corner of Slater and Seel streets). Closer to the Albert Dock is the **Liverpool ONE** shopping center, with a row of popular chain eateries, all with outdoor seating, or **$ The Pumphouse Pub,** at the north edge of Albert Dock—a touristy place for pub grub with a noisy interior and great harborside tables outside.

Durham

Without its cathedral, Durham would hardly be noticed. But this magnificently situated structure is hard to miss (even if you're zooming by on the train). Seemingly happy to go nowhere, Durham sits along the tight curve of its river, snug below its castle and famous church. Durham is home to England's third-oldest university, with a student vibe jostling against its lingering working-class mining-town feel.

Day Plan

For the best quick visit to Durham, arrive by midafternoon, in time to tour the cathedral and enjoy the evensong service (Tue-Sat at 17:15, Sun at 15:30). If you're sleeping in Durham, you can visit the Beamish Museum the next morning before continuing on to your next destination.

Orientation

As it has for a thousand years, tidy little Durham (pop. 65,000) clusters everything safely under its castle, within the protective hairpin bend of the River Wear. Because of the town's hilly topography, going just about anywhere involves a lot of up and down...and back up again. The main spine through the middle of town (Framwellgate Bridge, Silver Street, and Market Place) is level to moderately steep, but walking in any direction from that area involves some serious uphill climbing.

Tourist Information: Durham does not have a physical TI, but the town does maintain a call center and a useful website (tel. 03000-262-626, www.thisisdurham.com). During the summer, volunteer Durham Pointers staff a tourist information cart in Market Place (late May-early Oct, mobile 0758-233-2621, www.durhampointers.co.uk).

Tours: Each Saturday at 14:00 in peak season, **Blue Badge guides** offer 1.5-hour city walking tours (£4, meet at Durham World Heritage Site Visitor Centre, 7 Owengate, contact TI call center to confirm schedule).

Getting There

Frequent trains run from York (4/hour, 50 minutes) and Edinburgh (hourly, 2 hours); from London, there's a direct train hourly (3 hours). From the station, the fastest and easiest way to reach the cathedral is to hop on the Cathedral Bus #40, which runs between the train station, Market Place, and the Palace Green (£1 all-day ticket, none on Sun).

Durham, near the A-1/M-1 motorway, is an easy stop for drivers.

The 400-space Prince Bishops Shopping Centre parking lot is at the roundabout at the base of the old town, a short block from Market Place.

Sights
IN DURHAM
▲▲▲DURHAM'S CATHEDRAL

Built to house the much-venerated bones of St. Cuthbert, Durham's cathedral offers the best look at Norman architecture in England. ("Norman" is British for "Romanesque.") In addition to touring the cathedral, try to fit in an evensong service.

Cost and Hours: Free but £3 donation suggested; fee to climb the tower and

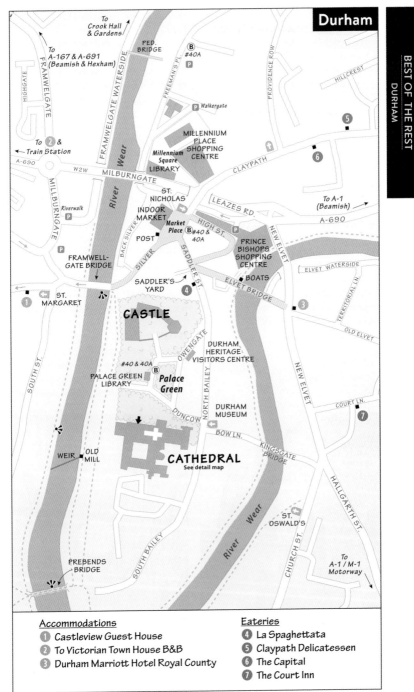

Durham

Accommodations
1. Castleview Guest House
2. To Victorian Town House B&B
3. Durham Marriott Hotel Royal County

Eateries
4. La Spaghettata
5. Claypath Delicatessen
6. The Capital
7. The Court Inn

to enter *Open Treasure* exhibit; Mon-Sat 9:00-18:00, Sun 12:30-17:00, daily until 20:00 mid-July-Aug, opens daily at 7:15 for worship and prayer; tel. 0191/386-4266, www.durhamcathedral.co.uk.

Evensong and Organ Recitals: To really experience the cathedral, attend an evensong service. Arrive early and ask to be seated in the choir (Tue-Sat at 17:15, Sun at 15:30, 1 hour, sometimes sung on Mon). Noted organists play most Wednesday evenings from July to early September (£10, 19:30).

Tours: Regular tours run Monday through Saturday (£5; tours at 10:30, 11:00, and 14:00; fewer in winter, call or check website to confirm schedule; £10 combo-ticket for guided tour and the *Open Treasure* exhibit).

Open Treasure Exhibit: This collection of the church's rare artifacts is housed in the former monks' quarters (£7.50, Mon-Sat 10:00-17:00, Sun from 12:30).

○ SELF-GUIDED TOUR

Begin your visit at the cathedral **door.** Check out the big, bronze, lion-faced knocker (a replica of the 12th-century original) used by criminals seeking sanctuary.

Inside, a handy ❶ **information desk** at the back (right) end of the nave sells tickets for guided tours. Notice the ❷ **modern window** with the novel depiction of the Last Supper (above and to the left of the entry door).

Spanning the nave, the ❸ **black marble strip** on the floor was as close to the altar as women were allowed in the days when this was a Benedictine church (until 1540). Take a seat and admire the fine proportions, rounded arches, and zig-zag-carved decorations of England's best Norman nave. It is particularly harmonious because it was built in a mere 40 years (1093-1133) by well-traveled French masons and architects who knew the latest innovations from Europe. Its stone and ribbed roof, pointed arches, and flying buttresses were revolutionary in England.

At the back of the nave, enter the ❹ **Galilee Chapel** (late Norman, from 1175). The paintings of St. Cuthbert and St. Oswald (seventh-century king of Northumbria) on the side walls of the niche are rare examples of Romanesque

Durham Cathedral

Cathedral nave

Durham's Cathedral

To #40A Bus Stop & Castle

Palace Green

To Town Center

DUN COW LANE

ENTRY

COLUMNS

NAVE

TRANSEPT

CHOIR

THE CLOISTER

UNDERCROFT

SHOP

WC

CAFÉ

SOUTH BAILEY

50 Meters

50 Yards

1 Information Desk
2 Modern Window
3 Black Marble Strip
4 Galilee Chapel & Tomb of the Venerable Bede
5 Chapel of the Nine Altars
6 LAWSON - Pietà
7 Illumination Window
8 Tomb of St. Cuthbert
9 Tower Entry
10 Miners' Memorial
11 Cloister Entry
12 Stairs to Open Treasure Exhibit

(Norman) paintings. On the right side of the chapel, the upraised tomb topped with a black slab contains the remains of the **Venerable Bede,** an eighth-century Christian scholar who wrote the first history of England.

Back in the main church, stroll down the nave to the center, under the highest **bell tower** in Europe (218 feet). Monks worshipped many times a day, and the choir in the center of the church provided a cozy place to gather. Mass has been said daily here in the heart of the cathedral for 900 years. The fancy wooden benches are from the 17th century. Behind the altar is the delicately carved Neville Screen from 1380 (made of Normandy stone in London, shipped to Newcastle by sea, then

brought here by wagon). Until the Reformation, the niches contained statues of 107 saints.

Step down behind the high altar into the east end of the church, which contains the 13th-century ❺ **Chapel of the Nine Altars.** Built later than the rest of the church, this is Gothic—taller, lighter, and relatively more extravagant than the Norman nave—but look up to see if you can spot an error in the symmetry. On the right, see the powerful modern ❻ **pietà** made of driftwood, with brass accents by local sculptor Fenwick Lawson.

Walk through the chapel to the north end where you will find an ❼ **illumination window,** a memorial to a Durham University student who tragically died from a cardiac-related condition. The window casts vibrant colors onto the ❾ **tomb of St. Cuthbert,** an inspirational leader of the early Christian Church in north England. This cathedral was built over Cuthbert's tomb.

In the **south transept** (to your left) is the ❾ **tower entry** as well as an astronomical clock and the Chapel of the Durham Light Infantry, a regiment of the British Army. The old flags and banners hanging above were actually carried into battle.

Find your way toward the cloister (opposite the entry door). Along the wall by the cloister door, notice the ❿ **memorial honoring coal miners.** The last pit of the Durham coalfields closed in the 1980s, but the mining legacy here is still strong.

It's worth making a circuit of the Gothic ⓫ **cloister** for a fine view back up to the church towers. From there, you can climb some stairs to enter the ⓬ *Open Treasure* **exhibit,** which holds artifacts from the cathedral treasury and monks' library, including a copy of the *Magna Carta* from 1216 and relics from St. Cuthbert's tomb.

DURHAM CASTLE

The castle still stands—as it has for a thousand years—on its motte (man-made mound) and now houses Durham University. Look into the old courtyard from the castle gate. It traces the very first and smallest bailey (protected area). As future bishops expanded the castle, they left their coats of arms as a way of "signing" the wing they built. Because the Norman kings appointed prince bishops here to rule this part of their realm, Durham was the seat of power for much of northern England. The bishops had their own army and even minted their own coins. The castle is accessible with a 45-minute guided tour, which includes the courtyard, kitchens, great hall, and chapel.

Cost and Hours: £5, open most days when school is in session—but schedule varies so call ahead, buy tickets at Durham World Heritage Site Visitor Centre (near the cathedral) or Palace Green Library (on the green near the castle), tel. 0191/334-2932, www.dur.ac.uk/durham.castle.

Near Durham
BEAMISH MUSEUM

This huge, 300-acre open-air museum, located 12 miles from Durham, re-creates life in northeast England from the Victorian era to the 1950s. It is England's best museum of its type. You'll want at least three hours to explore its five sections: Pit Village (a coal-mining settlement with an actual mine); The Town (a 1913 street lined with actual shops); Pockerley Old Hall (the manor house of a "gentleman farmer"); Home Farm (a preserved farm and farmhouse); and the newest section, 1950s Town (mid-century street still under development). Attendants at each stop happily explain everything. In fact, the place is only really interesting if you talk to the attendants—who make it worth ▲▲▲.

A vintage building at the Beamish Museum

Cost and Hours: £19.50, children 5-16-£11.50, under 5-free; open daily 10:00-17:00; off-season until 16:00, weekends only Dec-mid-Feb, last entry one hour before closing; check events schedule on chalkboard as you enter, tel. 0191/370-4000, www.beamish.org.uk.

Getting There: By car, the museum is five minutes off the A-1/M-1 motorway (one exit north of Durham at Chester-le-Street/Junction 63, well-signposted; 25-minute drive northwest of Durham).

Getting to Beamish from Durham by bus is an uncomplicated affair. Catch bus #21, #X21, or #50 from the Durham bus station (3-4/hour, 25 minutes) and transfer at Chester-le-Street to bus #8, #78A, #28, or #28A, which takes you right to the museum entrance (2/hour Mon-Sat, hourly Sun, 15 minutes, leaves from South Burns Stand L at the central bus kiosk, tel. 0191/420-5050, www.simplygo.com). Show your bus ticket for a 25 percent museum discount.

Eating: Several eateries are scattered around Beamish, including a pub and tearooms (in The Town), a fish-and-chips stand (in the Pit Village), and various cafeterias and snack stands. Or bring a picnic.

Visiting the Museum: From the entrance building, bear left along the road, then watch for the turnoff on the right to the Pit Village & Colliery. This is a company town built around a coal mine, with a schoolhouse, a Methodist chapel, and a row of miners' homes with long, skinny pea-patch gardens out front. Poke into some of the homes to see their modest interiors.

Next, cross to the adjacent colliery (coal mine), where you can take a fascinating—if claustrophobic—20-minute tour into the drift mine (check in at the "lamp cabin"—tours depart when enough people gather, generally every 5-10 minutes). Nearby (across the tram tracks) is the fascinating **mine elevator,** where you can see the actual steam-powered winding engine used to operate it.

A path leads through the woods to Georgian-era **Pockerley,** which has two parts. First you'll see the **Waggonway,** a big barn filled with steam engines, including the re-created, first-ever passenger train from 1825. (Occasionally this train takes modern-day visitors for a spin on 1825 tracks—a hit with railway buffs.)

Then, walk back and climb the hill to **Pockerley Old Hall,** the manor house of a gentleman farmer and his family. The house dates from the 1820s, and while not extremely wealthy, the farmer who lived here owned large tracts of land and could afford to hire help to farm it for him. This rustic home is no palace, but it was comfortable for the period. The small garden terrace out front provides beautiful views across the pastures.

From the manor house, hop on a vintage tram or bus or walk 10 minutes to the **1950s Town,** a new zone where the mid-century buildings include a replica of a local welfare hall and community center. From here, another short tram ride or five-minute walk takes you back to the Edwardian-era in **The Town** (c. 1913). In the Masonic Hall at the beginning of the town, ogle the grand high-ceilinged meeting room. Farther on, check out the fun, old metal signs inside the garage. The heavenly-smelling candy store sells old-timey sweets and has an actual workshop in back with trays of free samples. The newsagent sells stationery, cards, and old toys, while in the grocery, you can see old packaging and the scales used for weighing out products.

Finally, walk or ride a tram or bus to the **Home Farm** (skippable if you're running short on time). Here you'll get to experience a petting zoo and see a "horse gin" (a.k.a. "gin gan")—where a horse walking in a circle turned a crank on a gear to amplify its "horsepower," helping to replace human hand labor.

Sleeping

$$$ Castleview Guest House rents five airy, restful rooms (4 Crossgate, www.

castle-view.co.uk); **$$ Victorian Town House B&B** offers three spacious, boutique-like rooms (cash only, 2 Victoria Terrace, www.durhambedandbreakfast. com); and **$$ Durham Marriott Hotel Royal County** has 150 posh, four-star but slightly scruffy rooms (Old Elvet, www. marriott.co.uk).

Eating

$$ La Spaghettata has some of the best Italian food in town (66 Saddler Street); **$ Claypath Delicatessen** offers tasty sandwiches, salads, and sampler platters (closed Sun-Mon, 57 Claypath); **$$ The Capital** has well-executed Indian food (69 Claypath); and **$$ The Court Inn** offers an eclectic menu of pub grub (Court Lane).

Hadrian's Wall

In about AD 122, during the reign of Emperor Hadrian, the Romans constructed this great stone wall, stretching 73 miles coast to coast. Not just a wall, it was a military complex with forts, ditches, settlements, and roads. At every mile of the wall, a castle guarded a gate, and two turrets stood between each castle. Once a towering 20-foot-tall fortification, these days the wall is only about three feet wide and three to six feet high. (The conveniently precut stones were carried away by peasants during the post-Rome Dark Ages for other structures.) In most places, what's left of the wall has been covered over by centuries of sod, making it effectively disappear into the landscape.

But for those intrigued by Roman history, Hadrian's Wall provides a fine excuse to take your imagination for a stroll. These are the most impressive Roman ruins in Britain.

Day Plan

While a dozen Roman sights cling along the wall's route, focus on the easily digestible six-mile stretch right in the middle, where you'll find the best museums and some of the most enjoyable-to-hike stretches of the wall. Three top sights are worth visiting: From east to west, Housesteads Roman Fort shows you where the Romans lived; Vindolanda's museum shows you how they lived; and the Roman Army Museum explains the empire-wide military organization that brought them here.

Orientation

Hadrian's Wall is anchored by the big cities of Newcastle to the east and Carlisle to the west; many key sights are located between the midsize towns of Bardon Mill and Haltwhistle, along the busy A-69 highway. To get right up close to the wall, you'll need to head a couple of miles north to the adjacent villages of Once Brewed and Twice Brewed (along the B-6318 road).

Tourist Information: The **Walltown Visitor Centre** lies along the Hadrian's Wall bus #AD122 route (closed Nov-Easter, just off the B-6318 next to the Roman Army Museum, follow signs to *Walltown Quarry*, tel. 01434/344-396, www. northumberlandnationalpark.org.uk).

Also consider **The Sill National Landscape Discovery Centre,** about a half-mile from the Steel Rigg trailhead (daily, served by bus #AD122, on the B-6318 near Bardon Mill, tel. 01434/341-200, www. thesill.org.uk).

A helpful TI is in **Haltwhistle,** a block from the train station inside the library (closed Sun, tel. 01434/321-863, www. visitnorthumberland.com).

For an overview, visit the helpful website at HadriansWallCountry.co.uk.

Getting Around Hadrian's Wall

Driving is the most convenient way to see Hadrian's Wall. If you're coming by train, consider renting a car for the day at either Newcastle or Carlisle; otherwise, you'll need to rely on trains and a bus to connect the sights, hire taxis, or book a private guide with a car. Nondrivers who want to see everything—or even hike part of the

Hadrian's Wall is the finest Roman relic in Britain.

wall—will need to stay one or two nights along the bus route.

By Car: Zip to this "best of Hadrian's Wall" zone on the speedy A-69; when you get close, head a few miles north and follow the B-6318, which parallels the wall. Official Hadrian's Wall parking lots have pay-and-display machines.

By Bus: To reach the Roman sights without a car, take the made-for-tourists Hadrian's Wall bus #AD122 (runs only in peak season). Essential resources for navigating the wall by public transit include the *Hadrian's Wall Country Map,* the bus #AD122 schedule, and a local train timetable for Northern Line #4—all available at local visitors centers and train stations (also see www.hadrianswallcountry.co.uk). The bus connects the Roman sights with train stations in Haltwhistle and Hexham (from £2/ride, £12.50 unlimited Day Rover ticket, buy tickets on board, 8/day in each direction Easter-Sept, no service Oct-Easter). If you're coming from Carlisle or Newcastle, you'll need to take the train to Haltwhistle or Hexham and pick up the bus there (tel. 01434/322-002, www.gonortheast.co.uk/ad122).

By Train: Northern Line's train route #4 runs parallel to and a few miles south of the wall. While the train doesn't take you near the actual Roman sights, you can reach them by catching bus #AD122 (described above) at Hexham or Haltwhistle (train runs hourly; www.northernrail.org).

By Taxi: These Haltwhistle-based taxi companies can help you connect the dots: Sprouls (mobile 07712-321-064) or Diamond (mobile 07597-641-222). It costs about £14 one-way from Haltwhistle to Housesteads Roman Fort.

By Private Tour: Peter Carney, a former history teacher who waxes eloquently on all things Roman, offers tours with his car and also leads guided walks around Hadrian's Wall. He can pick you up from your B&B or the train station (£200/day for up to 4 people, £150/half-day, mobile 07585-139-016, www.hadrianswall-walk.com).

Sights
▲▲HIKING THE WALL

For a good, craggy, three-mile, one-way, up-and-down walk along the wall, hike between Steel Rigg and Housesteads Roman Fort. For a shorter hike, begin at

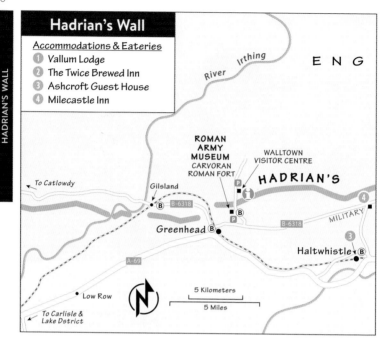

Hadrian's Wall

Accommodations & Eateries

1. Vallum Lodge
2. The Twice Brewed Inn
3. Ashcroft Guest House
4. Milecastle Inn

E N G

River Irthing

ROMAN
ARMY
MUSEUM
CARVORAN
ROMAN FORT

WALLTOWN
VISITOR CENTRE

H A D R I A N ' S

To Catlowdy

Gilsland

B-6318

MILITARY

B-6318

Greenhead

Haltwhistle

A-69

Low Row

5 Kilometers

5 Miles

To Carlisle &
Lake District

Steel Rigg (where there's a pay parking lot) and walk a mile to Sycamore Gap, then back again (described next; the Sill and Walltown visitors centers hand out a free description of this walk). These hikes are moderately strenuous and are best for those in good shape. You'll need sturdy shoes and a windbreaker to comfortably overcome the often-blustery environment. As you would while driving in Britain, stay on the left side of the path when you meet other hikers.

To reach the trailhead for the short hike from **Steel Rigg to Sycamore Gap,** take the little road off the B-6318 near the Twice Brewed Inn and park in the pay-and-display parking lot on the right at the crest of the hill. Walk through the gate to the shoulder-high stretch of wall, go to the left, and follow the wall running steeply down the valley below you. Walk down the steep slope into the valley, then back up the other side. Following the wall, you'll do a similar up-and-down routine three more times.

In the second gap is one of the best-preserved milecastles (called Castle Nick). Soon after, you'll reach the third gap, called Sycamore Gap for the large

A hiker walking along Hadrian's Wall

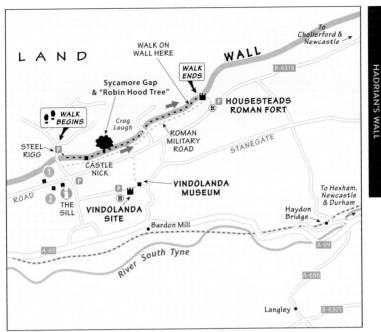

symmetrical tree in the middle. You can either hike back the way you came or walk down a short stretch toward the main road to find a less strenuous path that leads back to the base of the Steel Rigg hill, where you can huff back up to your car.

If you continue on to Housesteads, you'll pass a traditional Northumbrian sheep farm, windswept lakes, and more ups and downs.

▲▲HOUSESTEADS ROMAN FORT

With its respectable museum, powerful scenery, and the best-preserved segment of the wall, this is your best single stop at Hadrian's Wall. It requires a steep hike up from the parking lot, but once there it's just you, the bleating sheep, and memories of ancient Rome.

Cost and Hours: £8 for site and museum, discount with bus ticket; if the main entrance line is long, you can pay admission fee at the museum; daily 10:00-18:00, Oct until 17:00, Nov-March until 16:00; last entry 45 minutes before closing, pay parking, bus #AD122 stops here; info tel. 0870-333-1181, www.english-heritage. org.uk/housesteads.

Visiting the Museum and Fort: Hike about a half-mile uphill to the fort, and duck into the **museum** (on the left) before touring the site. Look for the giant Victory statue, which once adorned the fort's East Gate; her foot is stepping on a globe, serving as an intimidating reminder to outsiders of the Romans' success in battle.

Then head out to the sprawling ruins of the **fort.** All Roman forts were the same rectangular shape and design, containing a commander's headquarters, barracks, and latrines (Housesteads has the best-preserved Roman toilets found anywhere—look for them at the lower-right corner). This fort also had a hospital, granary, and a bakery where the soldiers would bake bread and cook meals. The fort was built right up to the wall, which runs along its upper end. Even if you're not

The remains of Housesteads Roman Fort, part of Hadrian's Wall

a hiker, take some time to walk the wall here. This is the one place along the wall where you're actually allowed to get up and walk on top of it for a photo op.

▲▲VINDOLANDA

This larger Roman fort (which actually predates the wall by 40 years) and museum are just south of the wall. Although Housesteads has better ruins and the wall, Vindolanda has the more impressive museum, packed with artifacts that reveal intimate details of Roman life.

Cost and Hours: £8.25, £12.20 combo-ticket includes Roman Army Museum, discount with bus ticket; daily 10:00-18:00, mid-Feb-March and Oct-Nov until 17:00, winter hours variable, last entry one hour before closing, call first during bad weather, free parking with entry, bus #AD122 stops here, café; tel. 01434/344-277, www.vindolanda.com.

Tours: Free guided tours are offered in high season (July-Aug Sat-Sun 10:30, 11:00, 13:00, and 14:00; Mon-Fri 11:00 and 13:00; April-June and Sept Sat-Sun 11:00 and 13:00 only, call to confirm).

Archaeological Dig: The Vindolanda site is an active dig—from Easter through September, you'll see the excavation work in progress (usually Mon-Fri, weather permitting).

Visiting the Site and Museum: Head out to the **site,** walking through 500 yards of grassy parkland decorated by the foundation stones of the Roman fort and a full-size replica chunk of the wall. Over the course of 400 years, at least nine forts were built on this spot. The Romans, by lazily sealing the foundations from each successive fort, left modern-day archaeologists with a 20-foot-deep treasure trove of remarkably well-preserved artifacts.

At the far side of the site, pass through the pleasant riverside garden area on the way to the museum. The well-presented **museum** pairs actual artifacts with insightful explanations—such as a collection of Roman shoes with a description about what each one tells us about its wearer. The weapons (including arrowheads and spearheads) and fragments of armor are a reminder that Vindolanda was an important outpost on Rome's northern boundary.

But the museum's main attraction is its collection of writing tablets. These letters bring Romans to life in a way that ruins alone can't. The most famous piece (described but not displayed here) is the first known example of a woman writing to a woman (an invitation to a birthday party). A large interactive screen lets you choose and read tablets selected by Robin Birley, a British archaeologist and former leader of the excavations.

Finally, you'll pass through an exhibit about the history of the excavations.

▲▲ROMAN ARMY MUSEUM

This museum, a few miles farther west at Greenhead (near the site of the Carvoran Roman fort), has cutting-edge, interactive exhibits illustrating the structure of the Roman Army that built and monitored this wall, with a focus on the everyday lifestyles of the Roman soldiers stationed here. Bombastic displays, life-size figures, and several different films—but few actual artifacts—make this entertaining museum a good complement to the archaeological emphasis of Vindolanda. If you plan to visit all three Roman sights, this is an ideal place to start, as it sets the stage for what you're about to see.

Cost and Hours: £7, £12.20 combo-ticket includes Vindolanda, discount with bus ticket; daily 10:00-18:00, mid-Feb-March and Oct until 17:00, Nov-Dec Sat-Sun only until 16:00, closed Jan-mid-Feb; free parking with entry, bus #AD122 stops here, tel. 01697/747-485, www.vindolanda.com.

Sleeping

$$ Vallum Lodge is a cushy, comfortable, nicely renovated base half-mile from the wall (Military Road, www.vallum-lodge.co.uk); **$$ The Twice Brewed Inn,** also a half-mile from the wall, rents 19 basic, workable rooms (Military Road, www.twicebrewedinn.co.uk); and the **$$ Ashcroft Guest House** in Haltwhistle has seven big, luxurious rooms, huge terraced gardens, and views (Lanty's Lonnen, www.ashcroftguesthouse.co.uk).

Eating

West of Once/Twice Brewed, the **$$ Milecastle Inn** cooks up all sorts of exotic game and offers the best dinner around (reserve in summer, North Road, www.milecastle-inn.co.uk). The recommended Twice Brewed Inn's friendly **$$ brewpub** serves real ales and large portions of good pub grub.

Edinburgh

Edinburgh is the historical, cultural, and political capital of Scotland. For nearly a thousand years, Scotland's kings, parliaments, writers, thinkers, and bankers have called Edinburgh home. Today, it remains Scotland's most sophisticated city.

Edinburgh (ED'n-burah—only tourists pronounce it like "Pittsburgh") is two cities in one. The Old Town stretches along the Royal Mile, from the grand castle on top to the palace on the bottom. Along this colorful labyrinth of cobbled streets and narrow lanes, medieval skyscrapers stand shoulder to shoulder, hiding peaceful courtyards.

A few hundred yards north of the Old Town lies the New Town. It's a magnificent planned neighborhood (from the 1700s). Here, you'll enjoy upscale shops, broad boulevards, straight streets, and Georgian mansions decked out in Greek-style columns and statues.

Just to the west of the New Town, the West End is a prestigious and quieter neighborhood boasting more Georgian architecture, cobbled lanes, fine dining options, and a variety of concert and theater venues.

Since 1999, when Scotland regained a measure of self-rule, Edinburgh reassumed its place as home of the Scottish Parliament. The city hums with life. Students and professionals pack the pubs and art galleries. It's especially lively in August, when the Edinburgh Festival takes over the city. Historic, monumental, fun, and well organized, Edinburgh is a tourist's delight.

EDINBURGH IN 2 DAYS

While the major sights can be seen in a day, I'd give Edinburgh two days and three nights.

Day 1: Tour the castle, then take my self-guided Royal Mile walk, stopping in at St. Giles' Cathedral and whichever shops and museums interest you. At the bottom of the Mile, consider visiting the Scottish Parliament, the Palace of Holyroodhouse, or both. If the weather's good and the trail is open, you could hike along the Salisbury Crags.

On any evening: Options include various "haunted Edinburgh" walks, the literary pub crawl, or live music in pubs.

Day 2: Visit the National Museum of Scotland. After lunch, stroll through the

Scottish National Gallery. Then, follow my self-guided walk through the New Town, visiting the Scottish National Portrait Gallery and the Georgian House—or squeeze in a quick tour of the good ship *Britannia* (check last entry time before you head out).

ORIENTATION

With 500,000 people (835,000 in the metro area), Edinburgh is Scotland's second-biggest city (after Glasgow). But the tourist's Edinburgh is compact: Old Town, New Town, West End, and the B&B area south of the city center.

Edinburgh's **Old Town** stretches across a ridgeline slung between two bluffs. From west to east, this "Royal Mile" runs from the Castle Rock—which is visible from anywhere—to the base of the 822-foot extinct volcano called Arthur's Seat. For visitors, this east-west axis is the center of the action. Just south of the Royal Mile is the National Museum of Scotland; farther to the south is a handy B&B neighborhood that lines up along **Mayfield Gardens.** North of the Royal

Old Town

Mile ridge is the **New Town,** a neighborhood of grid-planned streets and elegant Georgian buildings, and the **West End,** near Charlotte Square—a posh, quiet neighborhood that's still close to the sightseeing action.

In the center of it all—in a drained lake bed between the Old and New Towns—sit the Princes Street Gardens park and Waverley Bridge, where you'll find the Waverley train station, Waverley Mall, bus info office (starting point for most city bus tours), Scottish National Gallery, and a covered dance-and-music pavilion.

Tourist Information

The TI, branded "iCentre," is on the Royal Mile across from St. Giles' Cathedral (Mon-Sat 9:00-17:00, Sun from 10:00, June daily until 18:00, July-Aug daily until 19:00, 249 High Street, tel. 0131/473-3868, www.visitscotland.com). The staff is scattered at various tables with laptops on and ready to help.

For more information than what's included in the TI's free map, buy the excellent *Collins Discovering Edinburgh* map (which comes with opinionated commentary and locates almost every major sight). If you're interested in evening music, ask for the comprehensive entertainment listing, *The List.*

Rick's Tip: *If visiting during the* **Edinburgh Festival** *in August, book ahead for your must-see events, hotels, and dinners. Expect huge crowds and sky-high hotel prices.*

Helpful Hints

Baggage Storage: At the train station, a luggage storage office is near platform 2 (£7.50/3 hours, daily 7:00-23:00). Cheaper lockers are at the bus station on St. Andrew Square, just two blocks north of the train station (£8/12 hours, daily 4:30-24:00). Apps like Stasher can also help you find convenient baggage storage locations around big cities like Edinburgh.

EDINBURGH AT A GLANCE

▲▲▲**Royal Mile** Historic road—good for walking—stretching from the castle down to the palace, lined with museums, pubs, and shops. See page 329.

▲▲▲**Edinburgh Castle** Iconic hilltop fort and royal residence complete with crown jewels, Romanesque chapel, memorial, and fine military museum. **Hours:** Daily 9:30-18:00, Oct-March until 17:00. See page 342.

▲▲▲**National Museum of Scotland** Intriguing, well-displayed artifacts from prehistoric times to the 20th century. **Hours:** Daily 10:00-17:00. See page 353.

▲▲**Gladstone's Land** Seventeenth-century Royal Mile merchant's residence. **Hours:** Daily 11:00-16:30. See page 348.

▲▲**St. Giles' Cathedral** Preaching grounds of Scottish Reformer John Knox, with spectacular organ, Neo-Gothic chapel, and distinctive crown spire. **Hours:** Mon-Fri 9:00-19:00, Sat until 17:00; Nov-March Mon-Sat 9:00-17:00; Sun 13:00-17:00 year-round. See page 349.

▲▲**Scottish Parliament Building** Striking headquarters for parliament, which returned to Scotland in 1999. **Hours:** Mon-Sat 10:00-17:00, longer hours Tue-Thu when parliament is in session (Sept-June), closed Sun year-round. See page 351.

▲▲**Palace of Holyroodhouse** The Queen's splendid official residence in Scotland, with lavish rooms, 12th-century abbey, and gallery with rotating exhibits. **Hours:** Daily 9:30-18:00, Nov-March until 16:30, closed during royal visits. See page 352.

▲▲**Scottish National Gallery** Choice sampling of European masters and Scotland's finest. **Hours:** Fri-Wed 10:00-17:00, Aug until 18:00; Thu 10:00-19:00 year-round. See page 356.

▲▲**Scottish National Portrait Gallery** Beautifully displayed Who's Who of Scottish history. **Hours:** Daily 10:00-17:00. See page 357.

▲▲**Georgian House** Intimate peek at upper-crust life in the late 1700s. **Hours:** Daily 10:00-17:00, March and Nov 11:00-16:00, closed Dec-Feb. See page 359.

▲▲**Royal Yacht** *Britannia* The Queen's former floating palace, with a history of distinguished passengers, a 15-minute trip out of town. **Hours:** Daily 9:30-16:30, Oct until 16:00, Nov-March 10:00-15:30. See page 360.

▲**Scotch Whisky Experience** Gimmicky but fun and educational introduction to Scotland's most famous beverage. **Hours:** Generally daily 10:00-18:30. See page 348.

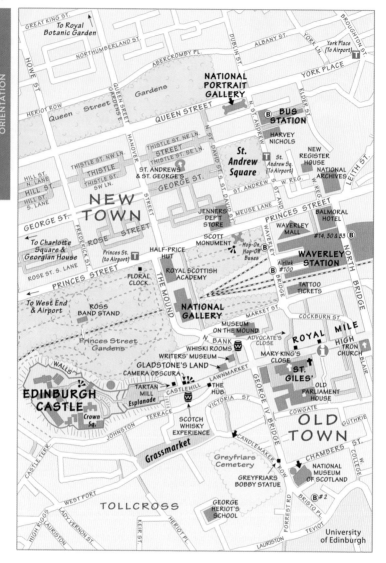

Laundry: The **Ace Cleaning Centre** launderette is located near my recommended B&Bs south of town. You can pay for full-service laundry (drop off in the morning for same-day service) or stay and do it yourself. For a small extra fee, they'll collect your laundry from your B&B and drop it off the next day (Mon-Fri 8:00-19:30, Sat 9:00-17:00, Sun 10:00-16:00, along bus route to city center at 13 South Clerk Street, opposite Queens Hall, tel. 0131/667-0549). In the West End, **Johnsons the Cleaners** will do your laundry (no hotel or B&B drop-off, Mon-Fri 9:30-18:00, Sat until 17:00, closed Sun, 5 Drumsheugh Place, tel. 0131/225-8077).

Bike Rental and Tours: The laid-back crew at **Cycle Scotland** happily recommends good bike routes with your rental

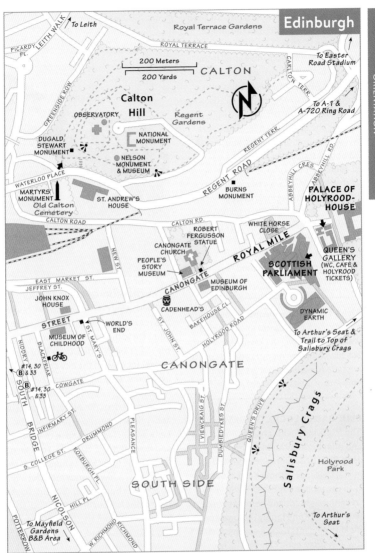

(prices starting at £20/3 hours or £30/day, electric bikes available for extra fee, daily 10:00–18:00, may be closed in winter, just off Royal Mile at 29 Blackfriars Street, tel. 0131/556-5560, mobile 0779-688-6899, www.cyclescotland.co.uk, Peter). They also run guided three-hour bike tours daily (£45/person, extra fee for e-bike, book ahead).

Tours
ROYAL MILE WALKING TOURS
Walking tours are an Edinburgh specialty; you'll see groups trailing entertaining guides all over town. Below I've listed good all-purpose walks; for **literary pub crawls** and **ghost tours,** see "Night Walks" on page 365.

Edinburgh Tour Guides offers a good historical walk (without all the ghosts and goblins). Their Royal Mile tour is a gentle three-hour downhill stroll from the top of the Mile to the palace (£25; daily at 9:30 and 19:00—evening tour is only two hours; meet outside Gladstone's Land, near the top of the Royal Mile, must reserve ahead, mobile 0785-888-0072, www.edinburghtourguides.com, info@edinburghtourguides.com).

Mercat Tours offers a 1.5-hour "Secrets of the Royal Mile" walk that's more entertaining than intellectual (£14; £30 includes optional, 45-minute guided Edinburgh Castle visit; daily at 10:00 and 13:00, leaves from Mercat Cross on the Royal Mile, tel. 0131/225-5445, www.mercattours.com). They also offer other themed tours (check their website).

Rick's Tip: **Sunday means fewer crowds,** *making this a good day to take* **a guided walking tour** *along the Royal Mile or a city bus tour. Although many Royal Mile sights are closed on Sunday (except in August), other major sights and shops are open.*

BLUE BADGE LOCAL GUIDES

The following guides charge similar prices and offer half-day and full-day tours: **Jean Blair** (a delightful teacher and guide, £230/day without car, £450/day with car, mobile 0798-957-0287, www.travelthroughscotland.com, scotguide7@gmail.com); **Ken Hanley** (who wears his kilt as if pants don't exist, £130/half-day, £250/day, extra charge if he uses his car—seats up to six, tel. 0131/666-1944, mobile 0771-034-2044, www.small-world-tours.co.uk, kennethhanley@me.com); and **Maggie McLeod** (another top-notch guide, £175/half-day walking tour, £660 day trips with car to farther-flung destinations, mobile 0775-151-6776, www.scotlandandmore.com, margaret.mcleod@live.co.uk).

HOP-ON, HOP-OFF BUS TOURS

The following one-hour hop-on, hop-off bus tour routes, all run by the same company, circle the town center, stopping at the major sights. **Edinburgh Tour** (green buses) focuses on the city center, with live guides. **City Sightseeing** (red buses, focuses on Old Town) has recorded commentary, as does the **Majestic Tour** (blue-and-yellow buses, goes to the port of Leith and includes a stop at the *Britannia* and Royal Botanic Garden). You can pay for just one tour (£16/24 hours), but most people pay a few pounds more for a ticket covering all buses (£24/48 hours; buses run April-Oct roughly 9:00-19:00, shorter hours off-season; about every 10 minutes, buy tickets on board, tel. 0131/220-0770, www.edinburghtour.com).

The Royal Edinburgh Ticket costs £57 and covers 48 hours of unlimited travel on all three hop-on, hop-off buses, as well as admission at Edinburgh Castle, the Palace of Holyroodhouse, and *Britannia* (www.royaledinburghticket.co.uk). This is a good deal if you plan to use the buses and see all three sights. You'll also save time by skipping ticket lines at the included sights.

EDINBURGH WALKS

I've outlined two walks in Edinburgh: along the Royal Mile, and through the New Town.

❍The Royal Mile

The Royal Mile is one of Europe's most interesting historic walks—it's worth ▲▲▲. The following self-guided stroll is also available as a free 🎧 downloadable Rick Steves audio tour.

This 1.5-hour walk covers the Royal Mile's landmarks, but skips the many museums and indoor sights along the way (these are described under "Sights," later). Doing this walk in the morning or evening allows you to focus on the past without having to dodge crowds. You can return later to stroll during the much livelier business hours when shops, museums, and the cathedral are all open.

Another option is to review the sight descriptions beforehand, plan your walk around their open hours, and pop into those that interest you as you pass them.

Overview

Start at Edinburgh Castle at the top and amble down to the Palace of Holyroodhouse. The street itself changes names—Castlehill, Lawnmarket, High Street, and Canongate—but it's a straight, downhill shot totaling just over one mile. And nearly every step is packed with shops, cafés, and lanes leading to tiny squares.

As you walk, you'll be tracing the growth of the city—its birth atop Castle Hill, its Old Town heyday in the 1600s, its expansion in the 1700s into the Georgian New Town (leaving the old quarter an overcrowded, disease-ridden Victorian slum), and on to the 21st century at the modern Scottish parliament building (2004).

Despite the drizzle, be sure to look up—spires, carvings, and towering Gothic "skyscrapers" give this city its unique urban identity.

As you stroll this mostly traffic-free tourist strip, you'll navigate a can-can of low-grade souvenir shops, eateries, and tour groups following their guides' umbrellas. Along the way, you'll be entertained by buskers, perused by pickpockets, hit up by beggars, and tempted by

The Royal Mile

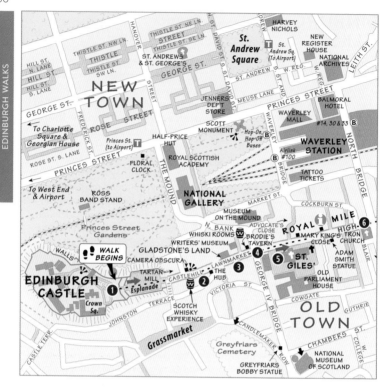

street merchants. Oh, and as it's quite haunted, you may feel the presence of a few ghosts.

• *We'll start at the castle esplanade, the big parking lot at the entrance to...*

❶ Edinburgh Castle

Edinburgh was born on the bluff—a big rock—where the castle now stands. Since before recorded history, people have lived on this strategic, easily defended perch.

The **castle** is an imposing symbol of Scottish independence (for a self-guided tour of Edinburgh Castle, see page 342.) Its esplanade—built as a military parade ground (1816)—is now the site of the annual Military Tattoo. This spectacular massing of regimental bands fills the square nightly for most of August.

Facing north from the esplanade, you'll see the body of water called the Firth of Forth, and Fife beyond that. (The

Firth of Forth is the estuary where the River Forth flows into the North Sea.) Still facing north, find the lacy spire of the Scott Monument and two Neoclassical buildings housing art galleries. Beyond them, the stately buildings of Edinburgh's New Town rise. Panning to the right, find the Nelson Monument and some faux

Edinburgh Castle's Esplanade

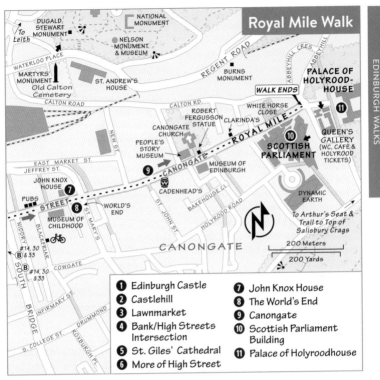

Royal Mile Walk

Map labels:
- DUGALD STEWART MONUMENT
- To Leith
- NATIONAL MONUMENT
- NELSON MONUMENT & MUSEUM
- WATERLOO PLACE
- REGENT ROAD
- MARTYRS' MONUMENT
- Old Calton Cemetery
- ST. ANDREW'S HOUSE
- BURNS MONUMENT
- ABBEYHILL CRES.
- ABBEYHILL
- PALACE OF HOLYROOD-HOUSE
- WALK ENDS
- CALTON ROAD
- CALTON RD.
- WHITE HORSE CLOSE
- ROBERT FERGUSSON STATUE
- CLARINDA'S
- ROYAL MILE
- NEW ST.
- CANONGATE CHURCH
- PEOPLE'S STORY MUSEUM
- EAST MARKET ST.
- JEFFREY ST.
- CANONGATE
- MUSEUM OF EDINBURGH
- SCOTTISH PARLIAMENT
- QUEEN'S GALLERY (WC, CAFE & HOLYROOD TICKETS)
- JOHN KNOX HOUSE
- PUBS
- STREET
- WORLD'S END
- CADENHEAD'S
- BAKEHOUSE CL.
- ST. JOHN ST.
- HOLYROOD ROAD
- DYNAMIC EARTH
- MUSEUM OF CHILDHOOD
- ST. MARY'S
- BLACKFRIAR
- #14, 30 & 33
- COWGATE
- SOUTH BRIDGE
- NIDDRY
- #14, 30 & 33
- INFIRMARY ST.
- DRUMMOND
- S. COLLEGE ST.
- ROXBURGH PL.
- CANONGATE
- To Arthur's Seat & Trail to Top of Salisbury Crags
- 200 Meters
- 200 Yards
- N

Legend:
1. Edinburgh Castle
2. Castlehill
3. Lawnmarket
4. Bank/High Streets Intersection
5. St. Giles' Cathedral
6. More of High Street
7. John Knox House
8. The World's End
9. Canongate
10. Scottish Parliament Building
11. Palace of Holyroodhouse

Greek ruins atop Calton Hill.

• *Start walking down the bustling Royal Mile. The first block is a street called...*

❷ Castlehill

The big, squat, tank-like building immediately on your left was once the Old Town's reservoir. While it once held 1.5 million gallons of water, today it's filled with the touristy **Tartan Weaving Mill** (open daily 9:00-17:30), a massive complex of four floors selling every kind of Scottish cliché. At the bottom level (a long way down) is a floor of big looms and weavers sometimes at work.

The black-and-white tower ahead on the left has entertained visitors since the 1850s with its **camera obscura,** a darkened room where a mirror and a series of lenses capture live images of the city surroundings outside. (Giggle at the funny mirrors as you walk fatly by.) Across the

street, filling the old Castlehill Primary School, is a gimmicky-if-intoxicating whisky-sampling exhibit called the **Scotch Whisky Experience** (a.k.a. "Malt Disney," described later).

• *Just ahead, in front of the church with the tall, lacy spire, is the old market square known as...*

❸ Lawnmarket

During the Royal Mile's heyday, in the 1600s, this intersection was bigger and served as a market for fabric (especially "lawn," a linen-like cloth).

Towering above Lawnmarket, with the highest spire in the city, is the former Tolbooth Church. This impressive Neo-Gothic structure (1844) is now home to **the Hub,** Edinburgh's festival-ticket and information center. This is a handy stop for its WC, café, and free Wi-Fi, and for information on Edinburgh's many festivals: The world-famous Edinburgh Festival fills the month of August with cultural action, while other August festivals feature classical music, traditional and fringe theater (especially comedy), art, books, and more.

In the 1600s, this—along with the next stretch, called High Street—was the city's main street. At that time, Edinburgh was bursting with breweries, printing presses, and banks. Tens of thousands of citizens were squeezed into the narrow confines of the Old Town.

Here on this ridge, they built tenements (multiple-unit residences) similar to the more recent ones you see today. These tenements, rising 10 stories and more, were some of the tallest domestic buildings in Europe.

• Continue a half-block down the Mile.

Gladstone's Land (at #477b, on the left), a surviving original tenement, was acquired by a wealthy merchant in 1617. Stand in front of the building and look up at this centuries-old skyscraper. This design was standard for its time: a shop or shops on the ground floor, with columns and an arcade, and residences on the floors above. Because window glass was expensive, the lower halves of window openings were made of cheaper wood, which swung out like shutters for ventilation—and were convenient for tossing out garbage. Now a museum, Gladstone's Land is worth visiting for its intimate look at life here 400 years ago (see "Sights," later).

Branching off the spine of the Royal Mile are a number of narrow alleyways that go by various local names. A "wynd" (rhymes with "kind") is a narrow, winding lane. A "pend" is an arched gateway. "Gate" is from an Old Norse word for street. And a "close" is a tiny alley between two buildings (originally with a door that "closed" at night). A "close" usually leads to a "court," or courtyard.

Opposite Gladstone's Land (at #322), a close leads to **Riddle's Court.** Wander through here and imagine Edinburgh in the 17th and 18th centuries, when tourists came here to marvel at its skyscrapers. Some 40,000 people were jammed into the few blocks between here and the World's End pub (which we'll reach soon). Visualize the labyrinthine maze of the old city, with people scurrying through these back alleyways, buying and selling, and popping into taverns.

No city in Europe was as densely populated—or perhaps as filthy. The dirt streets were soiled with sewage from bedpans emptied out windows. By the 1700s, the Old Town was rife with poverty and disease. The smoky home fires rising from tenements and the infamous smell (or "reek" in Scottish) that wafted across the city gave it a nickname that sticks today: "Auld Reekie."

• Return to the Royal Mile and continue down it a few steps to take in some sights at the…

❹ Bank/High Streets Intersection

Several sights cluster here, where Lawnmarket changes its name to High Street and intersects with Bank Street and George IV Bridge.

Begin with **Deacon Brodie's Tavern.** Read the "Doctor Jekyll and Mr. Hyde" story of this pub's notorious namesake on the wall facing Bank Street. Then, to see his spooky split personality, check out both sides of the hanging signpost. Brodie—a pillar of the community by day but a burglar by night—epitomizes the divided personality of 1700s Edinburgh. It was a rich, productive city—home to great philosophers and scientists, who actively contributed to the Enlightenment. Meanwhile, the Old Town was riddled with crime and squalor. (In the next century, in the late 1800s, novelist Robert Louis Stevenson would capture the dichotomy of Edinburgh's rich-poor society in his *Strange Case of Dr. Jekyll and Mr. Hyde.*)

In the late 1700s, Edinburgh's upper class moved out of the Old Town into a

Scottish Enlightenment of the mid-1700s.

Follow David Hume's gaze to the opposite corner, where a **brass H** in the pavement marks the site of the last public execution in Edinburgh in 1864. Deacon Brodie himself would have been hung about here (in 1788, on gallows whose design he had helped to improve—smart guy).

• *From the brass H, continue down the Royal Mile, pausing just before the church square at a stone wellhead with the pyramid cap.*

All along the Royal Mile, **wellheads** like this (from 1835) provided townsfolk with water in the days before buildings had plumbing. These neighborhood wells were served by the reservoir up at the castle.

• *Ahead of you (past the Victorian statue of some duke), embedded in the cobblestones near the street, is a big heart.*

The **Heart of Midlothian** marks the spot of the city's 15th-century municipal building and jail. In times past, in a nearby open space, criminals were hanged, traitors were decapitated, and witches were burned.

• *Make your way to the entrance of the church.*

❺ *St. Giles' Cathedral*

This is the flagship of the Church of Scotland (Scotland's largest denomination)—called the "Mother Church of Presbyterianism." The interior serves as a kind of Scottish Westminster Abbey, filled with monuments, statues, plaques, and

planned community called the New Town (a quarter-mile north of here). Eventually, most tenements were torn down and replaced with newer Victorian buildings. You'll see some at this intersection.

Look left down Bank Street to the green-domed **Bank of Scotland.** This was the headquarters of the bank, which had practiced modern capitalist financing since 1695.

If you detour left down Bank Street toward the bank, you'll find the recommended **Whiski Rooms Shop.** If you head in the opposite direction, down George IV Bridge, you'll reach the excellent **National Museum of Scotland,** photogenic Victoria Street, which leads to the pub-lined Grassmarket square, and several recommended eateries. Victoria Street (to the left) is so dreamy, many Potterheads figure it must be the inspiration for J. K. Rowling's Diagon Alley.

Across the street (downhill) from Deacon Brodie's Tavern is a seated green statue of hometown boy **David Hume** (1711-1776)—one of the most influential thinkers not only of Scotland, but in all of Western philosophy. The atheistic Hume was one of the towering figures of the

St. Giles' Cathedral

stained-glass windows dedicated to great Scots and moments in history.

The reformer John Knox (1514-1572) was the preacher here. His fiery sermons helped turn once-Catholic Edinburgh into a bastion of Protestantism. During the Scottish Reformation, St. Giles was transformed from a Catholic cathedral to a Presbyterian church. The spacious interior is well worth a visit (see "Sights," later).

• Facing the church entrance, curl around its right side, into a parking lot.

Sights Around St. Giles

The grand building across the parking lot from St. Giles is the **Old Parliament House.** From the early 1600s until 1707, this building evolved to become the seat of a true parliament of elected officials. That came to an end in 1707, when Scotland signed an Act of Union, joining what's known today as the United Kingdom and giving up their right to self-rule. (More on that later in the walk.)

The great reformer **John Knox** is buried—with appropriate austerity—under parking lot spot #23. The statue among the cars shows King Charles II riding to a toga party back in 1685.

• Continue through the parking lot, around the back end of the church.

Every Scottish burgh (town licensed by the king to trade) had three standard features: a "tolbooth" (basically a Town Hall, with a courthouse, meeting room, and jail); a "tron" (official weighing scale); and a "mercat" (or market) cross. The **mercat cross** standing just behind St. Giles' Cathedral has a slender column decorated with a unicorn holding a flag with the cross of St. Andrew. Royal proclamations have been read at this mercat cross since the 14th century. In 1952, a town crier heralded the news that Britain had a new queen—three days after the actual event (traditionally the time it took for a horse to speed here from London). Today, Mercat Cross is the meeting point for many of Edinburgh's walking tours.

• Circle around to the street side of the church.

The statue to **Adam Smith** honors the Edinburgh author of the pioneering *Wealth of Nations* (1776), in which he laid out the economics of free-market capitalism. Smith theorized that an "invisible hand" wisely guides the unregulated free market.

• Head on down the Royal Mile.

❻ More of High Street

Continuing down this stretch of the Royal Mile, which is traffic-free most of the day (notice the bollards that raise and lower for permitted traffic), you'll see the Fringe Festival office (at #180), street musicians, and another wellhead (with horse "sippies," dating from 1675).

Notice those **three red boxes.** In the 20th century, people used these to make telephonic calls to each other. (Imagine that!)

At the next intersection, on the left, is **Cockburn Street** (pronounced "COE-burn"), with a reputation for its eclectic independent shops and string of trendy bars and eateries.

• When you reach the Tron Church (with a fine 17th-century interior, currently housing historic exhibits and shops), you're at the intersection of **North and South Bridge** streets. These major streets lead left to Waverley Station and right to the Mayfield Gardens B&Bs. Several handy bus lines run along here.

This is the halfway point of this walk. Stand on the corner diagonally across from the church. Look up to the top of the Royal Mile at the Hub and its 240-foot spire. In front of that, take in the spire of St. Giles' Cathedral—inspired by the Scottish crown and the thistle, Scotland's national flower.

With its faux turret and made-up 16th-century charm, the **Radisson Blu Hotel** just across the street is entirely new construction (1990), but built to fit in. The city is protecting its historic look.

In the next block downhill are three **characteristic pubs** (The Mitre, Royal Mile, and Whiski), side by side, that offer free folk music many evenings.

• *Go down High Street another block, passing near the Museum of Childhood (on the right, at #42).*

Directly across the street, just below another wellhead, is the...

❼ *John Knox House*

Remember that Knox was a towering figure in Edinburgh's history, converting Scotland to a Calvinist style of Protestantism. His religious bent was "Presbyterianism," in which parishes are governed by elected officials rather than appointed bishops. This more democratic brand of Christianity also spurred Scotland toward political democracy. Full disclosure: It's not certain that Knox ever actually lived here. Attached to the Knox House is the Scottish Storytelling Centre, where locals with the gift of gab perform regularly; check the posted schedule.

• *A few steps farther down High Street, at the intersection with St. Mary's and Jeffrey streets, you'll reach...*

❽ *The World's End*

For centuries, a wall stood here, marking the end of the burgh of Edinburgh. For residents within the protective walls of the city, this must have felt like the "world's end," indeed. You can even pop in for a pint at the recommended The World's End pub, to your right. At the intersection, find the brass bricks in the street that trace the gate (demolished in 1764).

Look left down Jeffrey Street past the train tracks for a good view of the **Calton Cemetery** up on Calton Hill. The obelisk, called Martyrs' Monument, remembers a group of 18th-century patriots exiled by London to Australia for their reform politics. The round building to the left is the grave of philosopher David Hume. Today, the main reason to go up Calton Hill is for the fine views.

• *Continue down the Royal Mile—leaving old Edinburgh—as High Street changes names to...*

❾ *Canongate*

A couple hundred yards farther along (on the right at #172) you reach **Cadenhead's,** a serious whisky shop (see page 363)

• *About 30 yards beyond that, you'll pass*

Calton Hill

Canongate Kirk

White Horse Close

two worthwhile and free museums, the **People's Story Museum** *(on the left, in the old tollhouse at #163) and the* **Museum of Edinburgh** *(on the right, at #142), with the entry to the characteristic Bakehouse Close next door. But our next stop is the church just across from the Museum of Edinburgh.*

The 1688 **Canongate Kirk** (Church)—located not far from the royal residence of Holyroodhouse—is where Queen Elizabeth II and her family worship whenever they're in town. (So don't sit in the front pew, marked with her crown.) The gilded emblem at the top of the roof, high above the door, has the antlers of a stag from the royal estate of Balmoral.

The church is open only when volunteers have signed up to welcome visitors. Chat them up and borrow the description of the place. Then step inside the lofty blue and red interior, renovated with royal money; the church is filled with light and the flags of various Scottish regiments. In the narthex, peruse the photos of royal family events here, and find the list of priests and ministers of this parish—it goes back to 1143 (with a clear break with the Reformation in 1561).

• After leaving the church, walk about 300 yards farther along (past the recommended **Clarinda's Tea Room**). *In the distance you can see the Palace of Holyroodhouse (the end of this walk) and soon, on the right, you'll come to the modern Scottish parliament building.*

Just opposite the parliament building is **White Horse Close** (on the left, in the white arcade that juts into the sidewalk). Step into this 17th-century courtyard. It was from here that the Edinburgh stagecoach left for London. Eight days later, the horse-drawn carriage would pull into its destination: Scotland Yard. Note that bus #35 leaves in two directions from here—downhill for the Royal Yacht *Britannia*, and uphill along the Royal Mile (as far as South Bridge) and on to the National Museum of Scotland.

• Now walk up around the corner to the flag-poles (flying the flags of Europe, Britain, and Scotland) in front of the...

❿ *Scottish Parliament Building*

Finally, after centuries of history, we reach the 21st century. And finally, after three centuries of London rule, Scotland has a parliament building...in Scotland. When Scotland united with England in 1707, its parliament was dissolved. But in 1999, the Scottish parliament was reestablished, and in 2004, it moved into this striking new home. Notice how the eco-friendly building, by the Catalan architect Enric Miralles, mixes wild angles, lots of light, bold windows, oak, and native stone into a startling complex.

Since it celebrates Scottish democracy, the architecture is not a statement of authority. There are no statues of old heroes. There's not even a grand entry.

Given its neighborhood, the media often calls the Scottish Parliament "Holyrood" for short (similar to calling the US Congress "Capitol Hill"). For details on touring the building and seeing parliament in action, see page 351.

• Across the street is the **Queen's Gallery**, where her majesty shares part of her amazing personal art collection in excellent revolving exhibits—each with a theme (see page 353). Finally, walk to the end of the road (Abbey Strand), and step up to the impressive wrought-iron gate of the Queen's palace. Look up at the stag with its holy cross, or "holy rood," on its forehead, and peer into the palace grounds. (The ticket office and palace entryway, a fine café, and a handy WC are just through the arch on the right.)

⓫ Palace of Holyroodhouse

Since the 16th century, this palace has marked the end of the Royal Mile. Because Scotland's royalty preferred living at Holyroodhouse to the blustery castle on the rock, the palace grew over time. If the Queen's not visiting, the palace welcomes visitors (get tickets in the Queen's Gallery; see page 352 for details).

• Your walk—from the castle to the palace, with so much Scottish history packed in between—is complete. But if your appetite is whetted, don't worry, there's much more to see. Enjoy the rest of Edinburgh.

❷ New Town Walk: Georgian Edinburgh

With the city's finest Georgian architecture (from its 18th-century boom period), the New Town has a completely different character than the Old Town. This self-guided walk—worth ▲▲—gives you a quick orientation in about one hour.

• Begin on Waverley Bridge, spanning the gully between the Old and New towns; to get there from the curved Cockburn Street near the Tron Church (or cut down any of the "close" lanes opposite St. Giles Cathedral). Stand on the bridge overlooking the train tracks, facing the castle.

❶ **View from Waverley Bridge:** From this vantage point, you can enjoy fine views of medieval Edinburgh, with its 10-story-plus "skyscrapers." It's easy to imagine how miserably crowded this area was, prompting the expansion of the city during the Georgian period. Pick out

View from Waverley Bridge

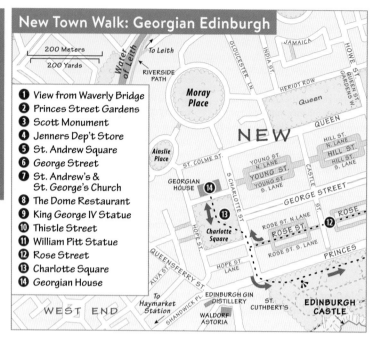

New Town Walk: Georgian Edinburgh

200 Meters
200 Yards

To Leith
RIVERSIDE PATH

Water of Leith

JAMAICA

GLOUCESTER LN.

INDIA ST.

HOWE ST.

QUEEN ST. GARDENS W.

HERIOT ROW

Moray Place

Queen

1 View from Waverly Bridge
2 Princes Street Gardens
3 Scott Monument
4 Jenners Dep't Store
5 St. Andrew Square
6 George Street
7 St. Andrew's & St. George's Church
8 The Dome Restaurant
9 King George IV Statue
10 Thistle Street
11 William Pitt Statue
12 Rose Street
13 Charlotte Square
14 Georgian House

NEW

QUEEN

HILL ST.
N. LANE

HILL ST.

HILL ST.
S. LANE

Ainslie Place

ST. COLME ST.

YOUNG ST.
N. LANE

YOUNG ST.

YOUNG ST.
S. LANE

CASTLE ST.

GEORGE STREET

GEORGIAN HOUSE 14

S. CHARLOTTE ST.

Charlotte Square 13

ROSE ST. N. LANE

ROSE ST.

ROSE ST. S. LANE

ROSE

12

HOPE ST.

PRINCES

QUEENSFERRY ST.

HOPE ST. LANE

ALVA ST.

To Haymarket Station

SHANDWICK PL.

EDINBURGH GIN DISTILLERY

WALDORF ASTORIA

ST. CUTHBERT'S

EDINBURGH CASTLE

WEST END

landmarks along the Royal Mile, most notably the open-work "thistle steeple" of St. Giles.

A big lake called the **Nor' Loch** once was to the north (nor') of the Old Town; now it's a valley between Edinburgh's two towns. The lake was drained around 1800 as part of the expansion. Before that, the lake was the town's water reservoir...and its sewer. Much has been written about the town's infamous stink. The town's nickname, "Auld Reekie," referred to both the smoke of its industry and the stench of its squalor.

The long-gone loch was also a handy place for drowning witches. With their thumbs tied to their ankles, they'd be lashed to dunking stools. Those who survived the ordeal were considered "aided by the devil" and burned as witches. If they died, they were innocent and given a good Christian burial. Edinburgh was Europe's witch-burning mecca—any perceived "sign," including a small birthmark, could condemn you. Scotland burned

more witches per capita than any other country—17,000 souls between 1479 and 1722.

Visually trace the train tracks as they disappear into a tunnel below the **Scottish National Gallery** (with the best collection anywhere of Scottish paintings; see "Sights," later).

Turning 180 degrees (and facing the ramps down into the train station), notice the huge, turreted building with the clock tower. (The clock is famously four minutes fast to help locals not miss their trains.) **The Balmoral** was one of the city's two grand hotels during its glory days (its opposite bookend, the **Waldorf Astoria Edinburgh,** sits at the far end of the former lakebed—near the end of this walk). Today The Balmoral is known mostly as the place where J. K. Rowling completed the final Harry Potter book.

• Now walk across the bridge toward the New Town. Before the corner, enter the gated gardens on the left, and head toward the big, pointy monument. You're at the edge of...

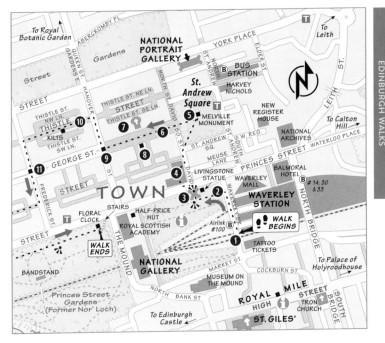

② **Princes Street Gardens:** This grassy park, filling the former lakebed, offers a wonderful escape from the bustle of the city. Once the private domain of the wealthy, it was opened to the public around 1870—not as a democratic gesture, but in hopes of increasing sales at the Princes Street department stores (Jenners is across the street).

• *Take a seat on the bench as encouraged by the Livingstone (Dr. Livingstone, I presume?) statue. (The Victorian explorer is well equipped with a guidebook but is hardly packing light—his lion skin doesn't even fit in his rucksack carry-on.)*

Look up at the towering...

③ **Scott Monument:** Built in the early 1840s, this elaborate Neo-Gothic monument honors the great author Sir Walter Scott, one of Edinburgh's many illustrious sons. When Scott died in 1832, it was said that "Scotland had never owed so much to one man." Scott almost singlehandedly created the image of the Scotland we know. Just as the country

Scott Monument

Jenners Department Store

St. Andrew Square

was in danger of being assimilated into England, Scott celebrated traditional songs, legends, myths, architecture, and kilts, thereby reviving the Highland culture and cementing a national identity. And, as the father of the Romantic historical novel, he contributed to Western literature in general. Nicknamed "the Gothic Rocket," this 200-foot-tall monument shelters a marble statue of Scott and his favorite pet, Maida, a deerhound who was one of 30 canines this dog lover owned during his lifetime. Climbing the tight, stony spiral staircase of 220 steps earns you a peek at a tiny museum midway and a fine city view at the top (£8, open daily 10:00-17:00, Oct-March until 16:00; 30-minute tours depart on the half-hour, last tour 30 minutes before closing; tel. 0131/529-4068).

• *Exit the park and head across busy Princes Street to the venerable...*

❹ Jenners Department Store: As you wait for the light to change, notice how statues of women support the building—just as real women support the business.

Step inside and head upstairs into the grand, skylit atrium. The central space—filled with a towering tree at Christmas—is classic Industrial Age architecture. The Queen's coat of arms high above the clock indicates she shops here. But Jenners, like most department stores, is struggling in the age of online shopping.

• *Walk through the atrium, turn right, and exit onto South St. David Street. Turn left and follow this street uphill one block up to...*

❺ St. Andrew Square: This green space is dedicated to the patron saint of Scotland. In the early 19th century, there were no shops around here—just fine residences; this was a private garden for the fancy people living here. Now open to the public, the square is a popular lunch hangout for workers.

One block beyond the top of the park on Queen Street is the excellent **Scottish National Portrait Gallery,** which introduces you to all of the biggest names in Scottish history (described later, under "Sights").

• *Follow the Melville Monument's gaze straight ahead out of the park. Cross the street and stand at the top of...*

❻ George Street: This is the main drag of Edinburgh's grid-planned New Town. Laid out in 1776, when King George III was busy putting down a revolution in a troublesome overseas colony, the New Town was a model of urban planning in its day. The architectural style is "Georgian"—British for "Neoclassical."

If you look at a map, you'll see the politics in the street plan: St. Andrew Square (patron saint of Scotland) and Charlotte Square (George III's queen) bookend the New Town, with its three main streets named for the royal family of the time (George, Queen, and Princes). Thistle

Charlotte Square

Scottish National Gallery

and Rose streets—which we'll see near the end of this walk—are named for the national flowers of Scotland and England.
• *Halfway down the first block of George Street, on the right, is...*

❼ St. Andrew's and St. George's Church: Designed as part of the New Town plan in the 1780s, the church is a product of the Scottish Enlightenment. It has an elliptical plan (the first in Britain) so that all can focus on the pulpit. If it's open, step inside. The church conveys the idea that God is space, light, reason, and ordered beauty.

❽ The Dome: Directly across the street from the church is another temple, this one devoted to money. This former bank building (now housing a recommended restaurant) has a pediment filled with figures demonstrating various ways to make money, which they do with all the nobility of classical gods. Consider scurrying across the street and ducking inside to view the stunning domed atrium.

❾ Statue of King George IV: Continue down George Street to the intersection with a statue commemorating the visit by George IV.
• *Turn right on Hanover Street; after just one (short) block, cross over and go left down...*

❿ Thistle Street: This street seems sleepy, but holds characteristic boutiques and good restaurants. Halfway down the street on the left is a rare kilt-making artisan in action: Howie Nicholsby's shop,

21st Century Kilts, updates traditional Scottish menswear (though it's usually open by appointment only).
• *You'll soon reach Frederick Street. Turn left and head toward the...*

⓫ Statue of William Pitt the Younger: Pitt was a prime minister under King George III during the French Revolution and the Napoleonic Wars. His father gave his name to the American city of Pittsburgh.
• *For an interesting contrast, we'll continue down another side street. Pass the statue of Pitt (heading toward Edinburgh Castle), and turn right onto...*

⓬ Rose Street: This stretch of Rose Street feels more commercialized, jammed with chain stores. The far end is packed with pubs and restaurants. As you walk, keep an eye out for the cobbled Tudor rose embedded in the brick sidewalk. When you cross the aptly named Castle Street, linger over the grand views to Edinburgh Castle. It's almost as if they planned it this way... just for the views.
• *Popping out at the far end of Rose Street, across the street and to your right is...*

⓭ Charlotte Square: The building of the New Town started cheap with St. Andrew Square, but finished well with this stately space, designed by Scottish Robert Adam in 1791. Adam's design, which raised the standard of New Town architecture to "international class," created Edinburgh's finest Georgian square. To this day, the fine garden filling the square is private, reserved for residents only.

• *Along the right side of Charlotte Square, at #7, you can visit the* ⓮ **Georgian House,** *which gives you a great peek behind all of these harmonious Neoclassical facades (see "Sights," later).*

Return Through Princes Street Gardens: From Charlotte Square, drop down to busy Princes Street (noticing the red building to the right—the grand Waldorf Astoria Hotel and twin sister of The Balmoral at the start of our walk). But rather than walking along the busy bus-and-tram-lined shopping drag, head into **Princes Street Gardens** (cross Princes Street and enter the gate on the left). With the castle looming overhead, you'll pass a playground, a fanciful Victorian fountain, more monuments to great Scots, war memorials, and a bandstand. Finally, you'll reach a staircase up to the Scottish National Gallery (though access from this entrance may be limited); and the oldest **floral clock** in the world—perhaps telling you it's time for a spot of tea.

• *Our walk is over. From here, you can tour the gallery; head up Bank Street just behind it to reach the Royal Mile; hop on a bus along Princes Street to your next stop (or B&B); or continue through another stretch of the Princes Street Gardens to the Scott Monument and our starting point.*

SIGHTS

▲▲▲EDINBURGH CASTLE

The fortified birthplace of the city 1,300 years ago, this imposing symbol of Edinburgh sits proudly on a rock high above the town. The home of Scotland's kings and queens for centuries, the castle has witnessed royal births, medieval pageantry, and bloody sieges. Today it's a complex of various buildings, the oldest dating from the 12th century, linked by cobbled roads that survive from its more recent use as a military garrison. The

castle—with expansive views, plenty of history, and the stunning crown jewels of Scotland—is a fascinating and multifaceted sight that deserves several hours of your time.

Cost and Hours: £20, daily 9:30-18:00, Oct-March until 17:00, last entry one hour before closing, tel. 0131/225-9846, www.edinburghcastle.scot.

Avoiding Lines: The castle is usually less crowded after 15:00. To avoid ticket lines (worst in Aug), buy your ticket in advance online. You can print your ticket at home or pick it up at the black kiosk—with several nearby computer stations—just below the esplanade (facing the Tartan Weaving Mill) before joining the castle crowds. You can also pick up tickets at the machines just inside the castle entrance or at the visitor information desk a few steps uphill on the right.

Getting There: Simply walk up the Royal Mile (if arriving by bus from the B&B area south of the city, get off at South Bridge and huff up the Mile for about 15 minutes). Taxis get you closer, dropping you a block below the esplanade at the Hub/Tolbooth Church.

Tours: Thirty-minute introductory guided tours are free with admission (2-4/hour, depart from Argyle Battery, see clock for next departure; fewer off-season). The informative audioguide provides four hours of descriptions, including the National War Museum Scotland (£3.50, pick up inside Portcullis Gate).

Eating: The $ Redcoat Café—just past the Argyle Battery—is a big, bright, efficient cafeteria with great views.

➲ SELF-GUIDED TOUR

❶ **Entry Gate:** Flanking the entryway are statues of the fierce warriors who battled English invaders, William Wallace (on the right) and Robert the Bruce (left). Between them is the Scottish motto, *Nemo me impune lacessit*—roughly, "No one messes with me and gets away with it."

Once inside, start winding your way uphill toward the main sights—the crown

ipice looks impregnable. But on the night of March 14, 1314, 30 armed men silently scaled this rock face. They were loyal to Robert the Bruce and determined to recapture the castle, which had fallen into English hands. They caught the English by surprise, took the castle, and—three months later—Bruce defeated the English at the Battle of Bannockburn.

• *A little farther along, to the right of the Redcoat Café, is the...*

❸ **One O'Clock Gun:** Crowds gather for the 13:00 gun blast (which comes with a little military ceremony), a tradition that gives ships in the bay something to set their navigational devices by. (Locals joke that the frugal Scots don't fire it at high noon, as that would cost 11 extra rounds a day.) For more information, there's a small exhibit just down the stairs.

• *Continue uphill, winding to the left and passing through **Foog's Gate**. At the very top of the hill, climb up the stairs on your left to reach...*

❹ **St. Margaret's Chapel:** This tiny stone chapel is Edinburgh's oldest building (around 1120) and sits atop its highest point (440 feet). It represents the birth of the city.

In 1057, Malcolm III murdered King Macbeth (of Shakespeare fame) and assumed the Scottish throne. Later, he married Princess Margaret, and the family settled atop this hill. Their marriage united Malcolm's Highland Scots with Margaret's

jewels and the Royal Palace—located near the summit. Since the castle was protected on three sides by sheer cliffs, the main defense had to be here at the entrance. During the castle's heyday in the 1500s, a 100-foot tower loomed overhead, facing the city.

• *Passing through the **portcullis gate**, you reach the...*

❷ **Argyle (Six-Gun) Battery, with View:** These front-loading, cast-iron cannons are from the Napoleonic era, around 1800, when the castle was still a force to be reckoned with.

From here, look north across the valley to the grid of the New Town. The valley (directly below) sits where the Nor' Loch once was; this lake was drained and filled in when the New Town was built in the late 1700s, its swamps replaced with gardens. Later the land provided sites for the Greek-temple-esque Scottish National Gallery (above the train line tunnels), Waverley Station, and the tall, lacy Sir Walter Scott Memorial.

Now look down. The sheer north prec-

St. Margaret's Chapel

Edinburgh Castle

50 Meters
50 Yards

Cliffs

WESTERN
DEFENCES

WALLS

HOSPITAL

HAIG
STATUE

REDCOAT
CAFÉ

(RAMP)

10 NATIONAL
WAR MUSEUM
SCOTLAND

GOVERNOR'S
HOUSE

WALLS

NEW
BARRACKS

Gardens

Cliffs

Tour
1 Entry Gate
2 Argyle Battery
3 One O'Clock Gun
4 St. Margaret's Chapel,
Mons Meg & Dog Cemetery
5 Crown Square
6 Scottish Crown Jewels
(Honours of Scotland)
7 Royal Apartments
8 Great Hall
9 Scottish National War
Memorial
10 National War Museum
Scotland

Lowland Anglo-Saxons—the cultural mix that would define Edinburgh.

Step inside the tiny, unadorned church—a testament to Margaret's reputed piety. The elegant-yet-simple stone structure is Romanesque. The nave is wonderfully simple, with classic Norman zigzags decorating the round arch that separates the tiny nave from the sacristy. You'll see a facsimile of St. Margaret's 11th-century gospel book. The small (19th-century Victorian) stained-glass windows feature St. Margaret herself, St. Columba, St. Ninian (who brought Christianity to Scotland in AD 397), St. Andrew (Scotland's patron saint), and William

Wallace (the defender of Scotland).

Margaret died at the castle in 1093, and her son King David I built this chapel in her honor (she was sainted in 1250). David expanded the castle and also founded Holyrood Abbey, across town. These two structures were soon linked by a Royal Mile of buildings, and Edinburgh was born.

Mons Meg, in front of the church, is a huge and once-upon-a-time frightening 15th-century siege cannon that fired 330-pound stones nearly two miles. Look at the huge granite cannon balls and imagine.

Nearby, belly up to the banister and look down to find the **Dog Cemetery,** a

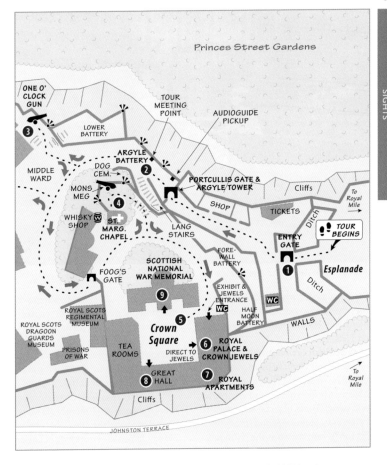

tiny patch of grass with a sweet little line of doggie tombstones, marking the graves of soldiers' faithful canines-in-arms.

• Continue on, curving downhill into...

❺ **Crown Square:** This courtyard is the center of today's Royal Castle complex. You're surrounded by the crown jewels, the Royal Palace (with its Great Hall), and the Scottish National War Memorial.

• We'll tour the buildings around Crown Square. First up: the crown jewels. There are two entrances—both usually with a line. The one on Crown Square, only open in peak season, deposits you straight into the room with the crown jewels but usually comes with a longer line. The other entry, around the left side (near the WCs), takes you—at a shuffle—to the jewels the long way, through the interesting, Disney-esque "Honours of

Crown Square

Diorama in the Honours of Scotland *exhibit*

Scotland" exhibit, which tells the story of the crown jewels and how they survived the harrowing centuries, but lacks any actual artifacts.

❻ Scottish Crown Jewels: For centuries, Scotland's monarchs were crowned in elaborate rituals involving three wondrous objects: a jewel-studded crown, scepter, and sword. These objects—along with the ceremonial Stone of Scone (pronounced "skoon")—are known as the "Honours of Scotland." Scotland's crown jewels may not be as impressive as England's, but locals treasure them as a symbol of Scottish nationalism. They're also older than England's; while Oliver Cromwell destroyed England's jewels, the Scots managed to hide theirs.

History of the Jewels: The Honours of Scotland exhibit that leads up to the Crown Room traces the evolution of the jewels, the ceremony, and the often-turbulent journey of this precious regalia. Here's the short version:

In 1306, Robert the Bruce was crowned with a "circlet of gold" in a ceremony at Scone—a town 40 miles north of Edinburgh, which Scotland's earliest kings had claimed as their capital. Around 1500,

King James IV added two new items to the coronation ceremony—a scepter (a gift from the pope) and a huge sword (a gift from another pope). In 1540, James V had the original crown augmented by an Edinburgh goldsmith, giving it the imperial-crown shape it has today.

These Honours were used to crown every monarch: nine-month-old Mary, Queen of Scots (she cried); her one-year-old son James VI (future king of England); and Charles I and II. But the days of divine-right rulers were numbered.

In 1649, the parliament had Charles I (king of both England and Scotland) beheaded. Soon Cromwell's rabid English antiroyalists were marching on Edinburgh.

When the monarchy was restored, the regalia were used to crown Scotland's last king, Charles II (1660). Then, in 1707, the Treaty of Union with England ended Scotland's independence. The Honours came out for a ceremony to bless the treaty.

As it represents the monarchy, the crown is present whenever a new session of parliament opens. (And if Scotland ever secedes, you can be sure that crown will be in the front row.)

The Honours: Finally, you enter the

Crown Room to see the regalia itself. The four-foot steel **sword** was made in Italy under orders of Pope Julius II (the man who also commissioned Michelangelo's Sistine Chapel and St. Peter's Basilica). The **scepter** is made of silver, covered with gold, and topped with a rock crystal and a pearl. The gem- and pearl-encrusted **crown** has an imperial arch topped with a cross. Legend says the band of gold in the center is the original crown that once adorned the head of Robert the Bruce.

The **Stone of Scone** (a.k.a. the "Stone of Destiny") sits plain and strong next to the jewels. It's a rough-hewn gray slab of sandstone, about 26 by 17 by 10 inches. As far back as the ninth century, Scotland's kings were crowned atop this stone, when it stood at the medieval capital of Scone. But in 1296, the invading army of Edward I of England carried the stone off to Westminster Abbey. For the next seven centuries, English (and subsequently British) kings and queens were crowned sitting on a coronation chair with the Stone of Scone tucked in a compartment underneath.

In 1996, in recognition of increased Scottish autonomy, Queen Elizabeth II agreed to let the stone go home, on one condition: that it be returned to Westminster Abbey for all British coronations. Assuming Scotland remains in the United Kingdom, one day, the next monarch of the UK—Prince Charles is first in line—

will sit atop this stone, re-enacting a coronation ritual that dates back a thousand years.

• *Exit the crown jewel display, heading down the stairs. But just before exiting into the courtyard, turn left through a door that leads into the...*

❼ **Royal Apartments:** Scottish royalty lived in the Royal Palace only when safety or protocol required it (they preferred the Palace of Holyroodhouse at the bottom of the Royal Mile). Here you can see several historic but unimpressive rooms. The first one, labeled **Queen Mary's Chamber,** is where Mary, Queen of Scots (1542-1587) gave birth to James VI of Scotland, who later became King James I of England. Nearby **Laich Hall** (Lower Hall) was the dining room of the royal family.

• *Head back outside, across the square, to find the entry on the left to the...*

❽ **Great Hall:** Built by James IV to host the castle's official banquets and meetings, the Great Hall is still used for such purposes today. Most of the interior—its fireplace, carved walls, pikes, and armor—is Victorian. But the well-constructed wood ceiling is original. This hammer-beam roof (constructed like the hull of a ship) is self-supporting.

• *Across the Crown Square courtyard is the...*

❾ **Scottish National War Memorial:** This commemorates the 149,000 Scottish soldiers lost in World War I, the 58,000 who died in World War II, and the nearly 800 (and counting) lost in British battles

Laich Hall

Great Hall

since. To appreciate how important this place is, consider that Scottish soldiers died at twice the rate per capita of other British soldiers in World War I.

• *There are several other exhibits (including "Prisons of War," covering the lives of POWs held in the castle in 1781), memorials, and regimental museums in the castle. If you have seen enough, the Lang Stairs near St. Margaret's Chapel are a shortcut leading down to the Argyle Battery and the exit.*

But there is one more important stop— the National War Museum. Backtrack down the hill toward the Redcoat Café (and the One O'Clock Gun). Just before the café head downhill to the left to the museum courtyard.

🔟 **National War Museum Scotland:** This thoughtful museum covers four centuries of Scottish military history. There's a compelling mix of videos, uniforms, weapons, medals, mementos, and eloquent excerpts from soldiers' letters. Your castle audioguide includes coverage of this museum, and the introductory video in the theater is worth watching.

Here you'll learn the story of how the fierce and courageous Scottish warrior changed from being a symbol of resistance against Britain to being a champion of that same empire.

Leaving the castle complex, you're surrounded by cannons that no longer fire, dramatic views of this grand city, and the clatter of tourists (rather than soldiers) on cobbles. Consider for a moment all the bloody history and valiant struggles, along with British power and Scottish pride, that have shaped the city over which you are perched.

Sights on and near the Royal Mile

▲**THE SCOTCH WHISKY EXPERIENCE** This attraction seems designed to distill money out of your pocket. The 50-minute experience consists of a "Malt Disney" whisky-barrel ride through the production process followed by an explanation

and movie about Scotland's five main whisky regions. Though gimmicky, it does succeed in providing an entertaining yet informative orientation to the creation of Scottish firewater. Your ticket also includes sampling a wee dram and the chance to stand amid the world's largest Scotch whisky collection (almost 3,500 bottles). At the end, you'll find yourself in the bar, with a fascinating wall of unusually shaped whisky bottles. Serious connoisseurs should stick with the more substantial shops in town, but this place can be worthwhile for beginners.

Cost and Hours: £16 "silver tour" includes one sample, £28 "gold tour" includes five samples—one from each main region, generally daily 10:00-18:30, last "silver tour" at 17:00, tel. 0131/220-0441, www.scotchwhiskyexperience.co.uk.

▲▲**GLADSTONE'S LAND** This is a typical 16th- to 17th-century merchant's "land," or tenement building. These multistory structures—in which merchants ran their shops on the ground

Gladstone's Land

Stained-glass window in St. Giles' Cathedral

floor and lived upstairs—were typical of the time (the word "tenement" didn't have the slum connotation then that it has today). At six stories, this one was still just half the height of the tallest "skyscrapers."

Gladstone's Land comes complete with an almost-lived-in, furnished interior and 400-year-old Renaissance painted ceiling. You'll explore five rooms, each with a docent posted to answer your questions.

Cost and Hours: £7, daily 11:00-16:30, tel. 0131/226-5856, www.nts.org.uk/visit/gladstones-land.

▲▲ST. GILES' CATHEDRAL

This is Scotland's most important church. Its ornate spire—the Scottish crown steeple from 1495—is a proud part of Edinburgh's skyline. The fascinating interior contains nearly 200 memorials honoring distinguished Scots through the ages.

Cost and Hours: Free, but consider the suggested £5 donation as a fair admission cost; Mon-Fri 9:00-19:00, Sat until 17:00; Nov-March Mon-Sat 9:00-17:00; Sun 13:00-17:00 year-round; info sheet-£1, guidebook-£6, tel. 0131/226-0677, www.stgilescathedral.org.uk.

Concerts: St. Giles' busy concert schedule includes free organ recitals and visiting choirs (frequent events at 13:30 and concerts Sun at 18:00; also sometimes Wed, Thu, or Fri at 20:00; see schedule or ask for *Music at St. Giles* pamphlet at welcome desk or gift shop).

❷ Self-Guided Tour: Today's facade is 19th-century Neo-Gothic, but most of what you'll see inside is from the 14th and 15th centuries. Engage the cathedral guides in conversation; you'll be glad you did.

Just inside the entrance, turn around to see the modern stained-glass **Robert Burns window,** which celebrates Scotland's favorite poet. The top is a rosy red sunburst of creativity, reminding Scots of Burns' famous line, "My love is like a red, red rose"—part of a song near and dear to every Scottish heart.

To the right of the Burns window is a fine **Pre-Raphaelite window.** Like most in the church, it's a memorial to an important patron (in this case, John Marshall). From here stretches a great swath of war memorials.

As you walk along the north wall, find **John Knox's statue** (standing like a six-

Scotland's Literary Greats

Edinburgh was home to Scotland's three greatest literary figures, pictured above: Robert Burns (left), Robert Louis Stevenson (center), and Sir Walter Scott (right).

Robert Burns (1759-1796), known as "Rabbie" in Scotland and quite possibly the most famous and beloved Scot of all time, moved to Edinburgh after achieving overnight celebrity with his first volume of poetry. Even though he wrote in the rough Scots dialect and dared to attack social rank, he was a favorite of Edinburgh's high society.

Robert Louis Stevenson (1850-1894) also stirred the Scottish soul with his pen. Traveling through Scotland, Europe, and around the world, he distilled his adventures into Romantic classics, including *Kidnapped* and *Treasure Island* (as well as *The Strange Case of Dr. Jekyll and Mr. Hyde*).

Sir Walter Scott (1771-1832) wrote the *Waverley* novels, including *Ivanhoe* and *Rob Roy*. He's considered the father of the Romantic historical novel. His writing generated a worldwide interest in Scotland, and reawakened his fellow countrymen's pride in their heritage.

The best way to learn about these literary greats is to take Edinburgh's Literary Pub Tour (see page 365).

While these three writers dominate your Edinburgh sightseeing, consider also the other great writers with Edinburgh connections: J. K. Rowling (who captures the "Gothic" spirit of Edinburgh with her Harry Potter series); Ian Rankin (with his "tartan noir" novels); J. M. Barrie (who created Peter Pan); Sir Arthur Conan Doyle (who is best known for inventing Sherlock Holmes); and James Boswell (revered for his biography of Samuel Johnson).

foot-tall bronze chess piece). Knox, the great religious reformer and founder of austere Scottish Presbyterianism, first preached here in 1559. His insistence that every person should be able to personally read the word of God—notice that he's pointing to a book—gave Scot-land an educational system 300 years ahead of the rest of Europe.

Knox preached Calvinism. Consider that the Dutch and the Scots both embraced this creed of hard work, frugality, and strict ethics. This helps explain why the Scots are so different

Scottish Parliament exterior

Scottish Parliament interior

from the English (and why the Dutch and the Scots—both famous for their thriftiness and industriousness—are so much alike).

The oldest parts of the cathedral—the **four massive central pillars**—are Norman and date from the 12th century.

Cross over to the **organ** (1992, Austrian-built, one of Europe's finest) and take in its sheer might.

Immediately to the right of the organ is a tiny chapel for silence and prayer. The dramatic **stained-glass window** above shows the commotion that surrounded Knox when he preached. The bearded, fiery-eyed Knox had a huge impact on this community.

Head toward the east (back) end of the church, and turn right to see the Neo-Gothic **Thistle Chapel** (the volunteer guide is a wealth of information). The interior is filled with intricate wood carving. Built in two years (1910-1911), entirely with Scottish materials and labor, it is the private chapel of the Order of the Thistle, the only Scottish chivalric order.

Downstairs you'll find handy public WCs and an inviting **$ café**—a good place for paupers to munch prayerfully—quick, quaint, and supporting the church (simple, light lunches, coffee and cakes; Mon-Sat 9:00-17:00, Sun from 11:00, in basement on back side of church, tel. 0131/225-5147).

▲▲SCOTTISH PARLIAMENT BUILDING

Scotland's parliament originated in 1293 and was dissolved when Scotland united with England in 1707. But after the Scottish electorate and the British parliament gave their consent, in 1997 it was decided that there should again be "a Scottish parliament guided by justice, wisdom, integrity, and compassion." Formally reconvened by Queen Elizabeth in 1999 (note that, while she's "II" in England, she's only the first "QE" for the people of Scotland), the Scottish parliament now enjoys self-rule in many areas (except for matters of defense, foreign policy, immigration, and taxation). The current government, run by the Scottish Nationalist Party (SNP), is pushing for even more independence.

The innovative building, opened in 2004, brought together all the functions of the fledgling parliament in one complex. It's a people-oriented structure conceived by Catalan architect Enric Miralles. Signs are written in both English and Gaelic (the Scots' Celtic tongue).

For a peek at the building and a lesson in how the Scottish parliament works, drop in, pass through security, and find the visitors' desk. You're welcome in the public parts of the building, including a small ground-floor exhibit on the parliament's history and function and, up the stairs, a viewing gallery overlooking the impressive Debating Chambers.

Palace of Holyroodhouse

Cost and Hours: Free; Mon-Sat 10:00-17:00, Tue-Thu 9:00-18:00 when parliament is in session (Sept-June), closed Sun year-round. For a complete list of recess dates or to book tickets for debates, check their website or call their visitor services line, tel. 0131/348-5200, www.parliament.scot.

Tours: Proud locals offer worthwhile free hour-long tours covering history, architecture, parliamentary processes, and other topics. Tours generally run throughout the day Mon and Fri-Sat in session (Sept-June) and Mon-Sat in recess (July-Aug). While you can try dropping in, these tours can book up—it's best to book ahead online or over the phone.

Seeing Parliament in Session: The public can witness the Scottish parliament's hugely popular debates (usually Tue-Thu 14:00-18:00, but hours can vary). Book ahead online no more than seven days in advance, over the phone, or at the info desk. You're not required to stay the whole session.

▲▲PALACE OF HOLYROODHOUSE

Built on the site of the abbey/monastery founded in 1128 by King David I, this palace was the true home, birthplace, and coronation spot of Scotland's Stuart kings in their heyday (James IV; Mary, Queen of Scots; and Charles I). It's particularly memorable as the site of some dramatic moments from the short reign of Mary, Queen of Scots—including the murder of her personal secretary, David Rizzio, by agents of her jealous husband. Today, it's one of Queen Elizabeth II's official residences. She usually manages her Scottish affairs here during Holyrood Week, from late June to early July (and generally stays at Balmoral Castle, in Scotland, in August). Holyrood is open to the public outside of the Queen's visits. The one-way audioguide route leads you through the fine apartments and tells some of the notable stories that played out here.

Cost: £15, includes quality one-hour audioguide; £20 combo-ticket includes the Queen's Gallery; £24.50 combo-ticket adds guided tour of palace gardens (April-Oct only); tickets sold in Queen's Gallery to the right of the castle entrance (see next listing).

Ruined abbey

Queen's Gallery

Hours: Daily 9:30-18:00, Nov-March until 16:30, last entry 1.5 hours before closing, tel. 0131/556-5100, www.rct.uk. It's still a working palace, so it's closed when the Queen or other VIPs are in residence.

Eating: The **$$$ café** on the palace grounds, to the right of the palace entrance, has an inviting afternoon tea.

Visiting the Palace: The building, rich in history and decor, is filled with elegantly furnished Victorian rooms and a few darker, older rooms with glass cases of historic bits and Scottish pieces that locals find fascinating. Bring the palace to life with the audioguide. The tour route leads you into the grassy inner courtyard, then up to the royal apartments: dining rooms, *Downton Abbey*-style drawing rooms, and royal bedchambers, including the private chambers of Mary, Queen of Scots, where conspirators stormed in and stabbed her secretary 56 times.

After exiting the palace, you're free to stroll through the evocative **ruined abbey** (destroyed by the English during the time of Mary, Queen of Scots, in the 16th century) and the **palace gardens** (closed Nov-March except some weekends).

Nearby: Hikers, note that the wonderful trail up Arthur's Seat starts just across the street from the gardens (see "Urban Hikes," later). From the palace, face parliament, turn left, and head straight.

▲QUEEN'S GALLERY, PALACE OF HOLYROODHOUSE

Over more than five centuries, the royal family has collected a wealth of art treasures. While the Queen keeps most of the royal collection in her many private palaces, she shares an impressive sampling of it in this small museum, with themed exhibits changing about every six months.

Cost and Hours: £8 includes excellent audioguide, £20 combo-ticket includes Palace of Holyroodhouse, daily 9:30-18:00, Nov-March until 16:30, last entry one hour before closing, www.rct.uk. Buses #35 and #36 stop outside, saving you a walk to or from Princes Street/North Bridge.

South of the Royal Mile

▲▲▲NATIONAL MUSEUM OF SCOTLAND

This huge museum has amassed more historic artifacts than every other place I've seen in Scotland combined. It's all wonderfully displayed, with fine descriptions offering a best-anywhere hike through the history of Scotland.

Cost and Hours: Free, daily 10:00-17:00; two long blocks south of St. Giles' Cathedral and the Royal Mile, on Chambers Street off George IV Bridge, tel. 0131/123-6789, www.nms.ac.uk.

Tours: Free one-hour general tours are offered daily at 11:00 and 13:00; themed tours at 15:00 (confirm tour schedule at

National Museum of Scotland

Replica tomb of Mary, Queen of Scots

info desk or on TV screens). The National Museum of Scotland Highlights app provides thin coverage of select items but is free and downloadable using their free Wi-Fi. Scattered interactive kiosks help navigate the stories behind important artifacts and figures.

Services: Bag check is on the ground floor (£1.50).

Eating: A **$$ brasserie** is on the ground floor near the information desks, and a **$ café** with coffee, tea, cakes, and snacks is on the level 3 balcony overlooking the Grand Gallery. On the museum's fifth floor, the dressy and upscale **$$$$ Tower restaurant** serves good food with a castle view (lunch/early-bird special, afternoon tea, three-course dinner specials; daily 10:00-22:00—use Tower entry if eating after museum closes, reservations recommended, tel. 0131/225-3003, www.tower-restaurant.com). A number of good eating options are within a couple of blocks of the museum (see "Eating," later).

Overview: The museum can be confusing to navigate, so pick up the map when you enter for a color-coded guide to each wing. The place gives you several museums in one, with each gallery rising vertically up several floors: the Natural World galleries (T. Rex skeletons and other animals), the Science and Technology galleries, and more.

We'll focus on the Scotland galleries, which sweep you through Scottish his-

tory covering Roman and Viking times, Edinburgh's witch-burning craze and clan massacres, the struggle for Scottish independence, the Industrial Revolution, and right up to Scotland in the 21st century.

🕨 **Self-Guided Tour:** Get oriented on level 1, in the impressive glass-roofed Grand Gallery right above the entrance hall. Just outside the Grand Gallery is the **millennium clock,** a 30-foot high clock with figures that move to a Bach concerto on the hour from 11:00 to 16:00. The clock has four parts (crypt, nave, belfry, and spire) and represents the turmoil of the 20th century, with a pietà at the top.

• *To reach the **Scottish history wing,** exit the Grand Gallery at the far right end, under the clock and past the statue of Scottish inventor James Watt.*

Continue into Hawthornden Court (level 1, past the little snack bar), where our tour begins. (It's possible to detour downstairs from here to level -1 for Scotland's prehistoric origins—geologic formation, Celts, Romans, Vikings.) Enter the door marked...

Kingdom of the Scots (c. 900s-late 1600s): From its very start, Scotland was determined to be free. You're greeted with proud quotes from what's been called the Scottish Declaration of Independence—the Declaration of Arbroath, a defiant letter written to the pope in 1320. As early as the ninth century, Scotland's patron saint, Andrew (see the small statue in the next room), had—according to legend—

miraculously intervened to help the Picts and Scots of Scotland remain free by defeating the Angles of England. Andrew's X-shaped cross still decorates the Scottish flag today.

Enter the first room on your right, with imposing swords and other objects related to Scotland's most famous patriots—William Wallace and Robert the Bruce. Bruce's descendants, the Stuarts, went on to rule Scotland for the next 300 years. Eventually, James VI of Scotland (see his baby cradle) came to rule England as well (as King James I of England).

In the next room, a big guillotine recalls the harsh justice meted out to criminals, witches, and "Covenanters" (17th-century political activists who opposed interference of the Stuart kings in affairs of the Presbyterian Church of Scotland). Look for the creepy mask of Covenanter Alexander Peden, who preached illegally in this disguise. Nearby, also check out the tomb (a copy) of Mary, Queen of Scots, the 16th-century Stuart monarch who opposed the Presbyterian Church of Scotland. Educated and raised in Renaissance France, Mary brought refinement to the Scottish throne. After she was imprisoned and then executed by Elizabeth I of England in 1587, her supporters rallied each other by invoking her memory. Pendants and coins with her portrait stoked the irrepressible Scottish spirit (see display case next to tomb).

Browse the rest of level 1 to see everyday objects from that age: carved panels, cookware, and sculptures.

• *Backtrack to Hawthornden Court and head up to level 3.*

Scotland Transformed (1700s): You'll see artifacts related to Bonnie Prince Charlie and the Jacobite rebellions as well as items related to the Treaty of Union document, signed in 1707 by the Scottish parliament. This act voluntarily united Scotland with England under the single parliament of the United Kingdom. For some Scots, this move was an inevitable step in connecting to the wider world, but for others it symbolized the end of Scotland's existence.

Union with England brought stability and investment to Scotland. In this same era, the advances of the Industrial Revolution were making a big impact on Scottish life. Mechanized textile looms (on display) replaced hand craftsmanship. The huge Newcomen steam-engine water pump helped the mining industry to develop sites with tricky drainage. Nearby is a model of a coal mine (or "colliery"); coal-rich Scotland exploited this natural resource to fuel its textile factories.

• *Leave this hall the way you came in, and journey up to level 5.*

Industry and Empire (1800s): Turn right and do a counterclockwise spin around this floor to survey Scottish life in the 19th century. Industry had transformed the country. Highland farmers left their land to find work in Lowland factories and foundries. Modern inventions—the phonograph, the steam-powered train, the kitchen range—revolutionized everyday life. In Glasgow near the turn

Newcomen steam-engine water pump

Scottish National Gallery

of the century, architect Charles Rennie Mackintosh helped to define Scottish Art Nouveau. Scotland was at the forefront of literature (Robert Burns, Sir Walter Scott, Robert Louis Stevenson), science (Lord Kelvin, James Watt), world exploration (John Kirk in Africa, Sir Alexander Mackenzie in Canada), and whisky production.

• *Climb the stairs to level 6.*

Scotland: A Changing Nation

(1900s-present): Turn left and do a clockwise spin through this floor to bring the story to the present day. The two world wars decimated the population of this already wee nation. In addition, hundreds of thousands emigrated, especially to Canada (where one in eight Canadians has Scottish origins). Other exhibits include shipbuilding and the fishing industry; Scots in the world of entertainment (from folk singer Donovan to actor-comedian Billy Connolly); a look at the recent trend of devolution from the United Kingdom; and a sports Hall of Fame (from tennis star Andy Murray to auto racers Jackie Stewart and Jim Clark).

• *Finish your visit on level 7, the rooftop.*

Garden Terrace: The well-described roof garden features grasses and heathers from every corner of Scotland and spectacular views of the city.

Museums in the New Town

These sights are linked by my "New Town Walk" on page 337.

▲▲SCOTTISH NATIONAL GALLERY

This delightful, small museum has Scotland's best collection of paintings—both European and Scottish. In a short visit, you can admire well-described works by Old Masters (Raphael, Rembrandt, Rubens), Impressionists (Monet, Degas, Gauguin), and a few underrated Scottish painters. Although there are no iconic masterpieces, it's a surprisingly enjoyable collection that's truly world class. The museum is undergoing renovation until 2021, but it's still worthwhile.

Cost and Hours: Free; Fri-Wed 10:00-17:00, Aug until 18:00; Thu 10:00-19:00 year-round; café downstairs, The Mound (between Princes and Market streets), tel. 0131/624-6200, www.nationalgalleries.org.

Expect Changes: The museum is undergoing major renovation to increase the space of its Scottish collection and build a grand main entrance from Princes Street Gardens. As a result, some exhibits may be closed, and pieces may be relocated, on loan, or in storage.

Visiting the Museum: The collection is arranged chronologically, mostly on one floor with the more modern paintings (19th and early 20th century) upstairs.

The main floor includes exquisite medieval altarpieces and works by the great masters (Botticelli, Raphael, Rubens, Rembrandt), as well as English artists (Gainsborough, Constable). Highlights of the more modern paintings (mostly upstairs) cover Celtic Revival, Pre-Raphaelites, Impressionists, and Post-Impressionists.

For the heart of the Scottish collection (on the main floor) look for the section labeled "Scottish, 1650-1850." But works by these homegrown artists are scattered throughout the museum:

Allan Ramsay, the son of the well-known poet of the same name, painted portraits of curly-wigged men of the Enlightenment era (the philosopher David Hume, King George III) as well as likenesses of his two wives. Ramsay's portrait of the duke of Argyll—founder of the Royal Bank of Scotland—appears on the front of notes printed by this bank.

Sir Henry Raeburn chronicled the next generation: Sir Walter Scott, the proud kilt-wearing Alastair MacDonell, and the ice-skating Reverend Robert Walker, minister of the Canongate Church.

Sir David Wilkie's forte was small-scale scenes of everyday life. *The Letter of Introduction* (1813) captures Wilkie's own experience of trying to impress skeptical art patrons in London; even the dog is sniffing the Scotsman out. *Distraining for Rent* (1815) shows the plight of a poor farmer about to lose his farm—a common occurrence during 19th-century industrialization.

William Dyce's *Francesca da Rimini* (1837) depicts star-crossed lovers—a young wife and her husband's kid brother—who can't help but indulge their passion. The husband later finds out and kills her; at the far left, you see his ominous hand.

William McTaggart's impressionistic landscape scenes from the late 1800s provide a glimpse of the unique light, powerful clouds, and natural wonder of the Highlands.

▲▲SCOTTISH NATIONAL PORTRAIT GALLERY

Put a face on Scotland's history by enjoying these portraits of famous Scots from the earliest times until today. From its Neo-Gothic facade to a grand entry hall highlighting Scottish history; to galleries showcasing the great Scots of each age, this impressive museum will fascinate anyone interested in Scottish culture. The gallery also hosts temporary exhibits highlighting the work of more contemporary Scots. Because of its purely Scottish focus, many travelers prefer this to the (pan-European) main branch of the National Gallery.

Cost and Hours: Free, daily 10:00-17:00, good cafeteria serving healthy meals, 1 Queen Street, tel. 0131/624-6490, www.nationalgalleries.org.

Visiting the Gallery: The meat of the collection is on the **top floor,** where Scottish history is illustrated by portraits and vividly described by information plaques next to each painting. With the 20th and 21st centuries, the chronological story spills down a level into Room 12 on the first floor. The rest of the gallery is devoted to special exhibits.

• *Start on the top floor, diving right into the thick of the struggle between Scotland and England over who should rule this land.*

Reformation to Revolution (Room 1): The collection starts with a portrait of **Mary, Queen of Scots** (1542-1587), her cross and rosary prominent. This

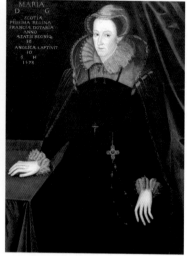

Mary, Queen of Scots

controversial ruler set off two centuries of strife. Mary was born with both Stuart blood (the ruling family of Scotland) and the Tudor blood of England's monarchs (Queen Elizabeth I was her cousin). Catholic and French-educated, Mary felt alienated from her own increasingly Protestant homeland. Her tense conversations with the reformer John Knox must have been epic. Then came a series of scandals: She married unpopular Lord Darnley, then (possibly) cheated on him, causing Darnley to (possibly) murder her lover, causing Mary to (possibly) murder Darnley, then (possibly) run off with another man, and (possibly) plot against Queen Elizabeth.

Amid all that drama, Mary was forced by her own people to relinquish her throne to her infant son, **James VI.** Find his portraits as a child and as a grown-up. James grew up to rule Scotland, and when Queen Elizabeth (the "virgin queen") died without an heir, he also became king of England (James I). But after a bitter civil war, James' son, **Charles I,** was arrested and executed in 1649: See the large *Execution of Charles I* painting, his blood-dripping head displayed to

the crowd (in a section dedicated to his beheading and that tumultuous political time). His son, Charles II, restored the Stuarts to power. He was then succeeded by his Catholic brother James VII of Scotland (II of England), who was sent into exile in France. There the Stuarts stewed, planning a return to power, waiting for someone to lead them in what would come to be known as the Jacobite rebellions.

The Jacobite Cause (a few rooms later, in Room 4): One of the biggest paintings in the room is *The Baptism of Prince Charles Edward Stuart.* Born in 1720, this Stuart heir to the thrones of Great Britain and Ireland is better known to history as "Bonnie Prince Charlie." (See his bonnie features in various portraits nearby, as a child, young man, and grown man.) Charismatic Charles convinced France to invade Scotland and put him back on the throne there. In 1745, he entered Edinburgh in triumph. But he was defeated at the tide-turning Battle of Culloden (1746). The Stuart cause died forever, and Bonnie Prince Charlie went into exile, eventually dying drunk and wasted in Rome, far from the land he nearly ruled.

The Age of Improvement (Room 7): The faces portrayed here belonged to a new society whose hard work and public spirit achieved progress with a Scottish accent. Social equality and the Industrial Revolution "transformed" Scotland—you'll see portraits of the great poet Robert Burns, the son of a farmer, and the man who perfected the steam engine, James Watt.

• *Check out the remaining galleries, then head back down to the first floor for a good look at the...*

Central Atrium (first floor): Great Scots! The atrium is decorated in a parade of late-19th-century Romantic Historicism. The **frieze** (below the bannister, working counterclockwise) is a visual encyclopedia, from an ax-wielding Stone Age man and a druid, to the early leg-

Central atrium of Scottish National Portrait Gallery

endary monarchs (Macbeth), to warriors William Wallace and Robert the Bruce, to many kings (James I, II, III, and so on), to great thinkers, inventors, and artists (Allan Ramsay, Flora MacDonald, David Hume, Adam Smith, James Boswell, James Watt), the three greatest Scottish writers (Robert Burns, Sir Walter Scott, Robert Louis Stevenson), and culminating with the historian Thomas Carlyle, who was the driving spirit (powered by the fortune of a local newspaper baron) behind creating this portrait gallery.

Around the first-floor mezzanine are large-scale **murals** depicting great events in Scottish history, including the landing of St. Margaret at Queensferry in 1068, the Battle of Stirling Bridge in 1297, the Battle of Bannockburn in 1314, and the marriage procession of James IV and Margaret Tudor through the streets of Edinburgh in 1503.

• *Also on this floor you'll find the...*

Modern Portrait Gallery: This space is dedicated to rotating art and photographs highlighting Scots who are making an impact in the world today, such as Annie Lennox, Alan Cumming, and physicist Peter Higgs (theorizer of the Higgs boson, the so-called God particle).

▲▲GEORGIAN HOUSE

This refurbished Neoclassical house, set on Charlotte Square, is a trip back to 1796. It recounts the era when a newly gentrified and well-educated Edinburgh was nicknamed the "Athens of the North." Begin on the second floor, where you'll watch a fascinating 16-minute video dramatizing the upstairs/downstairs lifestyles of the aristocrats and servants who lived here. Try on some Georgian outfits, then head downstairs to tour period rooms and even peek into the fully stocked medicine cabinet. Info sheets are available in each room, along with volunteer guides who share stories and trivia, such as why Georgian bigwigs had to sit behind a screen while enjoying a fire. A walk down George Street after your visit here can be fun for the imagination.

Cost and Hours: £8, daily 10:00-17:00, March and Nov 11:00-16:00, closed Dec-Feb, last entry 45 minutes before closing; 7 Charlotte Square, tel. 0131/225-2160, www. nts.org.uk.

Near Edinburgh

▲▲ROYAL YACHT *BRITANNIA*

This much-revered vessel, which transported Britain's royal family for more than 40 years on 900 voyages before being retired in 1997, is permanently moored in Edinburgh's port of Leith. Today it's open to the curious public, who have access to its many decks—from engine rooms to drawing rooms—and offers a fascinating time-warp look into the late-20th-century lifestyles of the rich and royal. It's worth the 20-minute bus or taxi ride from the center; figure on spending about 2.5 hours total on the outing.

Cost and Hours: £16.50, includes 1.5-hour audioguide, daily 9:30-16:30, Oct until 16:00, Nov-March 10:00-15:30, these are last-entry times, tearoom; at the Ocean Terminal Shopping Mall, on Ocean Drive in Leith; tel. 0131/555-5566, www.royalyachtbritannia.co.uk.

Getting There: From central Edinburgh, catch Lothian bus #11 or #22 from Princes Street (just above Waverley Station), or #35 from the bottom of the Royal Mile (alongside the parliament building) to Ocean Terminal (last stop). The Majestic Tour hop-on, hop-off bus stops here as well. If you're getting off the bus, go through the shopping center and take the escalator to level 2 (top floor).

Drivers can park free in the blue parking garage—park on level E (same floor as visitors center).

Visiting the Ship: First, explore the **museum,** filled with engrossing royal-family-afloat history. Then, armed with your audioguide, you're welcome aboard.

This was the last in a line of royal yachts that stretches back to 1660. With all its royal functions, the ship required a crew of more than 200. Begin in the captain's bridge, which feels like it's been preserved from the day it was launched in 1953. Then head down a deck to see the officers' quarters, then the garage, where a Rolls Royce was hoisted aboard to use in places where the local transportation wasn't up

to royal standards. The Veranda Deck at the back of the ship was the favorite place for outdoor entertainment. Ronald Reagan, Boris Yeltsin, Bill Clinton, and Nelson Mandela all sipped champagne here. The Sun Lounge, just off the back Veranda Deck, was the Queen's favorite, with Burmese teak and the same phone system she was used to in Buckingham Palace. When she wasn't entertaining, the Queen liked it quiet. The crew wore sneakers, communicated in hand signals, and (at least near the Queen's quarters) had to be finished with all their work by 8:00 in the morning.

Take a peek into the adjoining his-and-hers bedrooms of the Queen and the Duke of Edinburgh (check out the spartan twin beds), and the honeymoon suite where Prince Charles and Lady Di began their wedded bliss.

Heading down another deck, walk through the officers' lounge (and learn about the rowdy games they played) and

Royal Yacht Britannia

past the galleys (including custom cabinetry for the fine china and silver) on your way to the biggest room on the yacht, the state dining room. Now decorated with gifts given by the ship's many noteworthy guests, this space enabled the Queen to entertain a good-size crowd. The drawing room, while rather simple (the Queen specifically requested "country house comfort"), was perfect for casual relaxing among royals. Note the contrast to the decidedly less plush crew's quarters, mail room, sick bay, laundry, and engine room.

EXPERIENCES

Urban Hikes

▲▲HOLYROOD PARK: ARTHUR'S SEAT AND THE SALISBURY CRAGS

Rising up from the heart of Edinburgh, Holyrood Park is a lush green mountain squeezed between the parliament/Holyroodhouse (at the bottom of the Royal Mile) and my recommended B&B neighborhood. For an exhilarating hike, connect these two zones with a 30-minute walk along the Salisbury Crags—reddish cliffs with sweeping views over the city—but be aware that the crags occasionally close due to falling rocks. Or, for a more serious climb, make the ascent to the summit of Arthur's Seat, the 822-foot-tall remains of an extinct volcano. You can run up like they did in *Chariots of Fire,* or just stroll. At the summit, you'll be rewarded

with commanding views of the town and surroundings.

You can do this hike either from the bottom of the Royal Mile, or from the B&B neighborhood. A small road behind the bluff is accessible to taxis, so cheaters can ride halfway to the top. (Note that there are no facilities at the summit.)

From the Royal Mile: Begin in the parking lot below the Palace of Holyroodhouse. Facing the cliff, you'll see two trailheads. For the easier hike along the base of the **Salisbury Crags,** take the steps to the trail to the right. At the far end, you can descend into the B&B area or continue steeply up the switchback trail to the Arthur's Seat summit. If you know you'll want to ascend **Arthur's Seat** from the start, take the wider path on the left from the Holyroodhouse parking lot (easier grade, through the abbey ruins and "Hunter's Bog").

From the B&B Neighborhood: If you're sleeping in this area, enjoy an early-morning or late-evening hike starting from the other side (in June, the sun comes up early, and it stays light until nearly midnight). As Mayfield Gardens becomes Newington Road (heading north), turn right on Salisbury Road, and cross Dalkeith Road to take Holyrood Park Road. Bear left at the first roundabout, then turn right at the second roundabout (onto Queen's Drive). Soon you'll see the trailhead, and make your choice:

Mountain skyline of Holyrood Park

Hiking along the Salisbury Crags

Bear right up the steeper "Piper's Walk" to **Arthur's Seat** (about a 20-minute hike from here, up a steep switchback trail), or bear left for an easier ascent up the "Radial Road" to the **Salisbury Crags,** which you can follow—with great views over town—all the way up and over to Holyroodhouse Palace.

▲CALTON HILL

For an easy walk for fine views over all of Edinburgh and beyond, head up to Calton Hill—the monument-studded bluff that rises from the eastern end of the New Town. From the Waverley Station area, simply head east on Princes Street (which becomes Waterloo Place).

About five minutes after passing North Bridge, watch on the right for the gated entrance to the **Old Calton Cemetery**— worth a quick walk-through for its stirring monuments to great Scots. The can't-miss-it round monument honors the philosopher David Hume; just next to that is a memorial topped by Abraham Lincoln, honoring Scottish-American troops who were killed in combat. The obelisk honors political martyrs.

The views from the cemetery are good, but for even better ones, head back out to the main road and continue a few more minutes on Waterloo Place. Across the street, steps lead up into **Calton Hill.** Explore the park, purchased by the city in 1724 and one of the first public parks in Britain. Informational plaques identify the key landmarks. At the summit of the hill is the giant, unfinished replica of the Parthenon, honoring those lost in the Napoleonic Wars. Donations to finish it never materialized, leaving it with the nickname "Edinburgh's Disgrace." Nearby, the old observatory holds an old telescope, and the back of the hillside boasts sweeping views over the Firth of Forth and Edinburgh's sprawl. Back toward the Old Town, the tallest tower (shaped like a 19th-century admiral's telescope) celebrates Admiral Horatio Nelson—the same honoree of the giant pillar on London's Trafalgar Square. There's an interesting, free exhibit about Nelson at the base of the tower. While you can pay to climb it for the view, it doesn't gain you much. The best views are around the smaller, circular Dugald Stewart Monument, with postcard panoramas overlooking the spires of the Old Town and the New Town.

Calton Hill

Whisky and Gin Tasting
Whisky Tasting

One of the most accessible places to learn about whisky is at the **Scotch Whisky Experience** on the Royal Mile, an expensive but informative overview to whisky, including a tasting (see "Sights," earlier). Serious whisky aficionados can try an early-evening tasting at **Cadenhead's Whisky Shop** on the Royal Mile (£25, Mon-Fri at 17:45, not designed for beginners, shop open Mon-Sat 10:30-17:30, closed Sun, 172 Canongate, tel. 0131/556-5864, www.cadenhead.scot).

Whiski Rooms Shop, just off the Royal Mile, lets you order a shareable flight in the bar (with info about each whisky, options starting around £25). Or you can opt for a guided tasting (£30 introductory tasting; about one hour, reserve ahead; shop open daily 10:00-18:00, bar until 24:00, both open later in Aug, 4 North Bank Street, tel. 0131/225-1532, www.whiskirooms.co.uk).

Gin Distillery Tours

The residents of Edinburgh drink more gin per person than any other city in the United Kingdom. The city is largely responsible for the recent renaissance of this drink, so it's only appropriate that you visit a gin distillery while in town. Two distilleries right in the heart of Edinburgh offer hour-long tours with colorful guides who discuss the history of gin, show you the stills involved in the production process, and ply you with libations. Both tours are popular and fill up; book ahead on their websites.

Pickering's is between the Royal Mile and the B&Bs south of the city center. The bar and funky distillery have a cool, young, artsy vibe. The mellow bar also serves cheap pub grub (£10 includes welcome gin and tonic, tour, and 3 samples; 5/day Thu-Sun, meet at the Royal Dick Bar in the central courtyard at 1 Summerhall, tel. 0131/290-2901, www.pickeringsgin.com).

Edinburgh Gin is a showroom (not a distillery) in the West End, near the Waldorf Astoria Hotel. Besides the basic tour, there's a connoisseur tour with more tastings and a gin-making tour (basic tour £10, 3/day daily, reserve ahead, 1A Rutland Place, enter off Shandwick Place next to the Ghillie Dhu bar, tel. 0131/656-2810, www.edinburghgin.com). If you can't get on to one of their tours, visit their Heads & Tales bar to taste their gins (Tue-Sun 17:00-24:00, closed Mon).

Edinburgh's Festivals

Every summer, Edinburgh's annual festivals turn the city into a carnival of the arts. The season begins in June with the international film festival (www.edfilmfest.org.uk); then the jazz and blues festival in July (www.edinburghjazzfestival.com).

In August a riot of overlapping festivals known collectively as the **Edinburgh Festival** rages simultaneously—international, fringe, book, and art, as well as the Military Tattoo. There are enough music, dance, drama, and multicultural events to make even the most jaded traveler giddy with excitement. Every day is jammed with formal and spontaneous fun. Many city sights run on extended hours. It's a glorious time to be in Edinburgh...*if* you have (and can afford) a room.

If you'll be in town in August, book your room and tickets for major events (especially the Tattoo) as far ahead as you can lock in dates. Plan carefully to

EDINBURGH EXPERIENCES

ensure you'll have time for festival activities as well as sightseeing. Check online to confirm dates; the best overall website is www.edinburghfestivalcity.com. Several publications—including the festival's official schedule, the *Edinburgh Festivals Guide Daily*, *The List*, *Fringe Program*, and *Daily Diary*—list and evaluate festival events. The *Scotsman* newspaper reviews every show.

The official, more formal **Edinburgh International Festival** is the original. Major events sell out well in advance (ticket office at the Hub, in the former Tolbooth Church near the top of the Royal Mile, tel. 0131/473-2000, www.hubtickets.co.uk or www.eif.co.uk).

The less formal **Fringe Festival,** featuring edgy comedy and theater, is huge—with 2,000 shows—and has eclipsed the original festival in popularity (ticket/info office just below St. Giles' Cathedral on the Royal Mile, 180 High Street, bookings tel. 0131/226-0000, www.edfringe.com). Tickets may be available at the door, and half-price tickets for some events are sold on the day of the show at the Half-Price Hut, located at The Mound, near the Scottish National Gallery.

The **Military Tattoo** is a massing of bands, drums, and bagpipes, with groups from all over the former British Empire and beyond. Displaying military finesse with a stirring lone-piper finale, this grand spectacle fills the castle esplanade (nightly during most of Aug except Sun, performances Mon-Fri at 21:00, Sat at 19:15 and 22:30, £25-90, booking starts in Dec, Fri-Sat shows sell out first, all seats generally sold out by early summer, some scattered same-day tickets may be available; office open Mon-Fri 10:00-16:30, closed Sat-Sun, during Tattoo open until show time and closed Sun; 1 Cockburn Street, behind Waverley Station, tel. 0131/225-1188, www.edintattoo.co.uk).

Shopping

Shops are usually open around 10:00-18:00 (later on Thu, shorter hours or closed on Sun). Tourist shops are open longer hours.

Shopping Streets and Neighborhoods

Near the Royal Mile: The Royal Mile is intensely touristy, mostly lined with interchangeable shops selling made-in-China souvenirs. The area near Grassmarket, an easy stroll from the top of the Royal Mile, offers more originality. **Victoria Street,** which climbs steeply downhill from the Royal Mile (near the Hub/Tolbooth Church) to Grassmarket, has a fine concentration of local chain shops, including I.J. Mellis Cheesemonger and Walker Slater for designer tweed, plus Calzeat (scarves, throws, and other textiles), a Harry Potter store, and more clothing and accessory shops. On **Grassmarket,** the Hawico shop sells top quality cashmere milled in southern Scotland. Exiting Grassmarket opposite Victoria Street, **Candlemaker Row** is more artisan, with boutiques selling hats (from dapper men's caps to outrageous fascinators), jewelry, art, design items, and even fossils. The street winds a couple of blocks up toward the National Museum.

If it's **whisky** you want, try the shops I recommend for tasting (described earlier, under "Experiences"); they're on or near the Royal Mile.

Victoria Street, lined with shops

In the New Town: For mass-market shopping, you'll find plenty of big chain stores along **Princes Street.** In addition to Marks & Spencer, H&M, Zara, Primark, and a glitzy Apple Store, you'll also see the granddaddy of Scottish department stores, Jenners (Mon-Wed 9:30-18:00, Thu-Sat until 17:00, Sun 11:00-18:00). Parallel to Princes Street, **George Street** has higher-end chain stores (including many from London, such as L.K. Bennett, Molton Brown, and Karen Millen). Just off St. Andrew Square is a branch of the high-end London department store Harvey Nichols.

For more local, artisan shopping, check out **Thistle Street,** lined with some fun eateries and a good collection of shops. You'll see some fun boutiques selling jewelry, shoes, and clothing.

Night Walks
▲▲LITERARY PUB TOUR

This two-hour walk is interesting and a worthwhile way to spend an evening—even if you can't stand "Auld Lang Syne." Think of it as a walking theatrical performance, where you follow the witty dialogue of two actors as they debate the great literature of Scotland. (You may ask yourself if this is high art or the creative re-creation of fun-loving louts fueled by a passion for whisky.) You'll cover a lot of ground, wandering from Grassmarket over the Old Town and New Town, with stops in three to four pubs, as your guides share their takes on Scotland's literary greats. The tour meets at the Beehive Inn on Grassmarket (£16, just show up or book online and save £2, drinks extra; May-Sept nightly at 19:30, April and Oct Thu-Sun, Jan-March Fri and Sun, Nov-Dec Fri only; 18 Grassmarket, tel. 0800-169-7410, www. edinburghliterarypubtour.co.uk).

▲GHOST WALKS

A variety of companies lead spooky walks around town, providing an entertaining and affordable night out (offered nightly, most around 19:00 and 21:00, easy socializing for solo travelers). These two options are the most established.

Auld Reekie Tours offers a scary array of walks daily and nightly. Auld Reekie intertwines the grim and gory aspects of Scotland's history with the paranormal, witch covens, and pagan temples. They take groups into the "haunted vaults" under the old bridges "where it was so dark, so crowded, and so squalid that the people there knew each other not by how they looked, but by how they sounded, felt, and smelt." The guides are passionate, and the stories are genuinely spooky. Even if you don't believe in ghosts, you'll be entertained (£12-16, 1-1.5 hours, all tours leave from the modern Bank of Scotland building on the Royal Mile, opposite Deacon Brodie's Tavern, tel. 0131/557-4700, www.auldreekietours. com).

The theatrical **Cadies & Witchery Tours,** the most established outfit, offers two different 1.25-hour walks led by costumed actors: "Ghosts and Gore" (April-Aug only, in daylight and following a flatter route) and "Murder and Mystery" (year-round, after dark, hillier, more surprises and corny scares). The balance of historical context and slapstick humor makes these a fun pick for families (£10, includes book of stories, leaves from top of Royal Mile, outside the Witchery Restaurant, near castle esplanade, reservations required, tel. 0131/225-6745, www. witcherytours.com).

Theater

Even outside festival time, Edinburgh is a fine place for lively and affordable theater and live music. Pick up *The List* for a complete rundown of what's on (free at TI; online at www.list.co.uk).

Live Music in Pubs

While traditional music venues have been eclipsed by beer-focused student bars, Edinburgh still has a few good pubs that deliver a ▲▲ traditional folk-music experience. These days, many places that advertise "live music" offer only a solo singer/guitarist rather than a folk group. The monthly *Gig Guide* (free at TI, accommodations, and various pubs, www.gigguide.co.uk) lists several places each night that have live music, divided by genre (pop, rock, world, and folk). For locations, see the "Edinburgh Hotels & Restaurants" map, later.

South of the Royal Mile: Tight, stuffy **Sandy Bell's** is a pub with live folk music nightly from 21:30 (near the National Museum of Scotland at 25 Forrest Road, tel. 0131/225-2751). There's no food, drinks are cheap, tables are small, and the vibe is local. They also have a few sessions earlier in the day (Sat at 14:00, Sun at 16:00, Mon at 17:30 is for beginners).

Captain's Bar is a crowded-but-cozy, music-focused pub with live sessions of folk and traditional music nightly around 21:00—see website for lineup (4 South College Street, https://captainsedinburgh.webs.com).

The Royal Oak is another characteristic, snug place for a dose of folk and blues that feels like a friend's living room (just off South Bridge opposite Chambers Road at 1 Infirmary Street, tel. 0131/557-2976).

Grassmarket Neighborhood: This area below the castle bustles with live music and rowdy people spilling out of the pubs and into what was (once upon a time) a busy market square. Thanks to the music and crowds, you'll know where to go...and where not to.

The Fiddlers Arms has a charming Grassmarket pub energy with live folk, pop, or rock, depending on the night (Thu-Sat from 21:00, at the far end of the square). Check out **Biddy Mulligans** or **White Hart Inn** (both on Grassmarket and both usually with a single Irish folk singer nightly). **Finnegans Wake,** on Victoria Street (which leads down to Grassmarket), is more of a down-and-dirty, classic rock bar with dancing. **The Bow Bar,** a couple doors away on Victoria

Street, has no music but offers a hard-to-resist classic pub scene.

On the Royal Mile: Three characteristic pubs within a few steps of each other on High Street (opposite the Radisson Blu Hotel) offer a fun setting, classic pub architecture and ambience, and live music (generally just a single loud folk guitarist) for the cost of a beer: **Whiski Bar** (mostly trad and folk; nightly at 22:00), **Royal Mile** (classic pop; nightly at 22:00), and **Mitre Bar** (acoustic pop/rock with some trad; Fri-Sat at 22:00).

In the New Town: All the beer drinkers seem to head for the pedestrianized, west end of Rose Street, famous for having the most pubs per square inch anywhere in Scotland—and plenty of live music.

SLEEPING

I've recommended accommodations in three areas: the city center, the West End, and a quieter neighborhood south of town.

To stay in the city center, you'll select from large hotels and mostly impersonal guesthouses. The West End (just a few blocks from the New Town, spanning from Haymarket to Charlotte Square) offers a few comfortable and more intimate hotels and guesthouses. These places provide a calm retreat in a central location.

For the classic B&B experience (friendly hosts and great cooked breakfasts), look south of town near Mayfield Gardens. From here, it's a long walk to the city center (about 30 minutes) or a quick bus or taxi/Uber ride. While the B&Bs here are not cheap (generally $$), they're less expensive than staying at a downtown hotel.

Note that during the Festival, prices skyrocket and most places do not accept bookings for one- or even two-night stays. If coming in August, book far in advance.

I rank accommodations from $ budget to $$$$ splurge. For the best deal, contact smaller places directly by phone or email.

When you book direct, the owner avoids a commission and may be able to offer a discount.

Hotels in the City Center

These places are mostly characterless, but they're close to the sightseeing action and Edinburgh's excellent restaurant and pub scene. Prices are very high in peak season and drop substantially in off-season (a good time to shop around). In each case, I'd skip the institutional breakfast and eat out. You'll generally pay about £10 a day to park near these hotels.

$$$$ The Inn Place, part of a small chain, fills the former headquarters of The *Scotsman* newspaper—a few steep steps below the Royal Mile—with 48 classy, minimalist rooms ("bunk rooms" for 6-8 people, best deals on weekdays, breakfast extra, elevator serves some rooms, 20 Cockburn Street, tel. 0131/526-3780, www. theinnplaceedinburgh.co.uk, reception@ theinnplaceedinburgh.co.uk).

$$$$ Grassmarket Hotel's 42 rooms are quirky and fun, from the Dandy comic-book wallpaper to the giant wall map of Edinburgh equipped with planning-your-visit magnets. The hotel is in a great location right on Grassmarket overlooking the Covenanters Memorial and above Biddy Mulligans Bar (family rooms, two-night minimum on some weekends, elevator serves half the rooms, 94 Grassmarket, tel. 0131/220-2299, www.grassmarkethotel. co.uk).

$$$ The Place Hotel, sister of the Inn Place listed earlier, has a fine New Town location 10 minutes north of the train station. It occupies three grand Georgian townhouses, with no elevator and long flights of stairs leading up to the 47 contemporary, no-frills rooms. Their outdoor terrace with retractable roof and heaters is a popular place to unwind (save money with a smaller city double, 34 York Place, tel. 0131/556-7575, www.yorkplace-edinburgh.co.uk, frontdesk@yorkplace-edinburgh.co.uk).

$$ Ten Hill Place Hotel is a seven-minute walk from the Royal Mile, down a quiet courtyard. It's run in conjunction with the 500-year-old Royal College of Surgeons and profits go toward funding student education. Its 129 rooms are classy, and some have views of the Salisbury Crags (family rooms, breakfast extra, elevator, 10 Hill Place, tel. 0131/662-2080, www.tenhillplace.com, reservations@ tenhillplace.com).

$$ Motel One Edinburgh Princes is a good deal for its location, with 140 rooms, some with nice views of Waverley Station and the Old Town. The rooms are cookie cutter, but the sprawling ballroom-like lounge offers great views (family rooms, reception on first floor, breakfast extra, elevator, 10 Princes Street, enter around the corner on West Register Street, www. motel-one.com, edinburgh-princes@ motel-one.com).

Hostel

¢ SafeStay Edinburgh, just off the Royal Mile, rents 272 bunks in pleasing purple-accented rooms. Dorm rooms have 4 to 12 beds, and there are also a few private singles and twin rooms (all rooms have private bathrooms). Bar 50 in the basement has an inviting lounge. Half of the rooms function as a university dorm during the school year, becoming available just in time for the tourists (breakfast extra, kitchen, laundry, free daily walking tour, 50 Blackfriars Street, tel. 0131/524-1989, www.safestay.com, reservations-edi@safestay.com).

The West End

The area just west of the New Town and Charlotte Square is a quiet, classy, residential area of stately Georgian buildings. Hotels here can be pricey and ostentatious, catering mostly to business travelers. Though these places aren't as intimate as my recommended B&Bs south of town, the West End is convenient to most sightseeing. It's an easy 10- to 15-minute

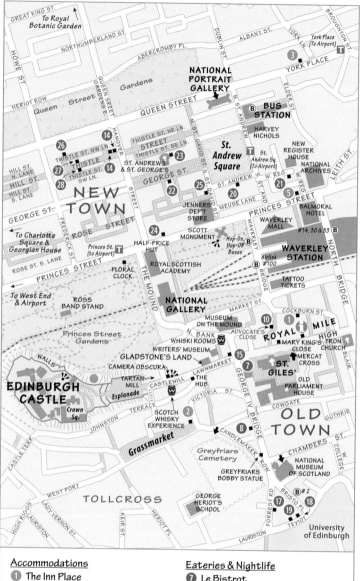

Accommodations

1 The Inn Place
2 Grassmarket Hotel
3 The Place Hotel
4 Ten Hill Place Hotel
5 Motel One Edinburgh Princes
6 SafeStay Edinburgh Hostel

Eateries & Nightlife

7 Le Bistrot
8 The Outsider
9 Hewats on the Mile,
   Mitre Bar, Whiski Pub &
   Royal Mile Pub
10 Devil's Advocate
11 Wedgwood Restaurant
12 Edinburgh Larder

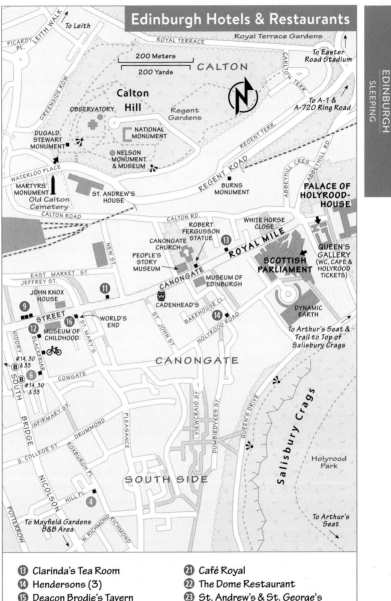

Edinburgh Hotels & Restaurants

⑬ Clarinda's Tea Room
⑭ Hendersons (3)
⑮ Deacon Brodie's Tavern
⑯ The World's End Pub
⑰ Union of Genius & Mums Diner
⑱ Ting Thai Caravan
⑲ Ting Saboteur
⑳ Dishoom

㉑ Café Royal
㉒ The Dome Restaurant
㉓ St. Andrew's & St. George's Church Undercroft Café
㉔ Marks & Spencer Food Hall
㉕ Sainsbury's
㉖ Le Café St. Honoré
㉗ The Bon Vivant
㉘ Fishers in the City

walk to bustling Princes Street.

To get here from the train station, take the Airlink #100 from Waverley Bridge to Shandwick Place, or take the train to Haymarket Station (depending on your hotel—confirm in advance). Coming from Princes Street, take the tram to the West End stop. For locations of these places, see the "West End Hotels & Restaurants" map, later.

$$$$ B+B Edinburgh is a boutique hotel with 27 comfortable rooms (some with city views). It's situated on quiet Rothesay Terrace, where you'll feel like a diplomat retreating to your private suite (RS%, family rooms, elevator, 3 Rothesay Terrace, tel. 0131/225-5084, www.bb-edinburgh.com, info@bb-edinburgh.com).

$$$ Angels Share Hotel is an elegant and inviting place with a proud Scottish heritage. Each of its tidy, stylish 31 rooms is named after a contemporary Scottish figure (his or her portrait hangs above your bed). The attached bar is glitzy, with live music on weekends. The hotel is just off Shandwick Place, the artery of the West End (RS%, breakfast extra, 11 Hope Street, tel. 0131/247-7007, www.angelssharehotel.com, reception@angelssharehotel.com).

$$$ St. Valery Guest House is on a quiet street in a perfect line of Georgian buildings close to the Haymarket train station. Its 12 simple but well-maintained rooms (a couple with peaceful garden views) have frilly old-fashioned decor with nice modern touches. It's near the Haymarket tram stop and bus routes #26, #31, and Airlink #100 (family rooms, includes breakfast, no elevator, 36 Coates Gardens, tel. 0131/337-1893, www.stvalery.co.uk, info@stvalery.co.uk, Agnes and Solveiga).

$$ 22 Chester Street offers a mix of Georgian charm and Ikea comfort, renting five smartly appointed rooms near St. Mary's Cathedral. The lounge is an elegant and cozy place to unwind. Two rooms have private bathrooms down the hall,

and a couple rooms are below street level but get plenty of light (RS%, family rooms, no breakfast but lounge has stocked fridge and microwave, street parking only, 22 Chester Street, mobile 0795-755-8658, https://22chesterstreetedinburgh.co.uk, marypremiercru@gmail.com, owner Mary and manager Lukasz).

$$ Thistle Hotel is your no-frills budget option (albeit still expensive) in this otherwise fancy neighborhood. The 16 rooms are basic but functional, and many bathrooms are remodeled (and others need to be). Two rooms have castle views (RS%, family rooms, breakfast extra, no elevator, 59 Manor Place, tel. 0131/225-6144, www.edinburghthistlehotel.com, enquiries@edinburghthistlehotel.com, Gregory).

B&Bs South of the City Center

At these not-quite-interchangeable places, character is provided by the personality quirks of the hosts and sometimes the decor. In general, cash is preferred and can lead to discounted rates. Book direct—you will pay a much higher rate through a booking website.

Near the B&Bs, you'll find plenty of fine eateries and some good, classic pubs. The nearest launderette is Ace Cleaning Centre (see page 326).

Taxi or Uber fare between the city center and these B&Bs is about £7. If taking the bus from the B&Bs into the city, hop off at the South Bridge stop for the Royal Mile. All have private parking. To reach them from the center, hop on bus #3, #7, #8, #29, #31, #37, or #49. Note: Some of these buses depart from the second bus stop, a bit farther along North Bridge.

$$$ At 23 Mayfield Guest House, Ross and Kathleen rent seven splurge-worthy, thoughtfully appointed rooms complete with high-tech bathrooms (rain showers and motion-sensor light-up mirrors). Little extras—such as locally sourced gourmet breakfasts, an inviting guest lounge,

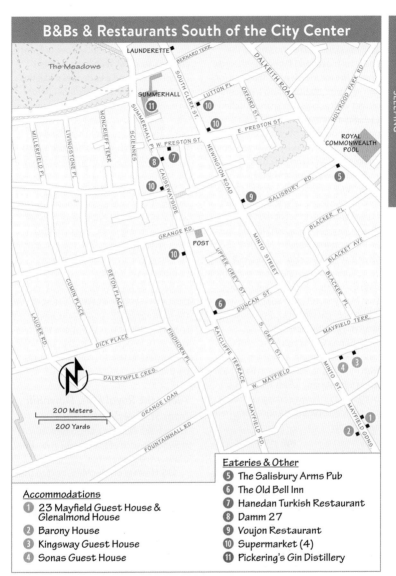

B&Bs & Restaurants South of the City Center

Accommodations
1. 23 Mayfield Guest House & Glenalmond House
2. Barony House
3. Kingsway Guest House
4. Sonas Guest House

Eateries & Other
5. The Salisbury Arms Pub
6. The Old Bell Inn
7. Hanedan Turkish Restaurant
8. Damm 27
9. Voujon Restaurant
10. Supermarket (4)
11. Pickering's Gin Distillery

an "honesty bar," and classic black-and-white movie screenings—make you feel like royalty (RS% with cash, family room, 2-night minimum preferred in summer, 23 Mayfield Gardens, tel. 0131/667-5806, www.23mayfield.co.uk, info@23mayfield.co.uk). They also rent an apartment.

$$$ Glenalmond House, run by Jimmy and Fiona Mackie, has nine smart rooms, two with garden patios (RS% with cash, discounts for longer stays, family room, no kids under 5, 25 Mayfield Gardens, tel. 0131/668-2392, www.glenalmondhouse.com, enquiries@glenalmondhouse.com).

$$ Barony House, the best value of all these places, is run with infectious enthusiasm by Aussies Paul and Susan. Their seven elegant doubles are lovingly decorated by Susan, who's made the beautiful friezes and fabric headboards. Two of the rooms are next door, in a former servants' quarters, now a peaceful retreat with access to a shared kitchen (3-night minimum preferred in summer, no kids under 9, 20 Mayfield Gardens, tel. 0131/662-9938, www.baronyhouse.co.uk, booknow@baronyhouse.co.uk).

$$ Kingsway Guest House, with seven bright and stylish rooms, is owned by conscientious, delightful Gary and Lizzie, who have thought of all the little touches, such as a DVD library and in-room internet radios, and offer good advice on neighborhood eats (RS% with cash, family rooms, one room with private bath down the hall, off-street parking, 5 East Mayfield, tel. 0131/667-5029, www.edinburgh-guesthouse.com, booking@kingswayguesthouse.com).

$$ Sonas Guest House is nothing fancy—just a simple, easygoing place with nine rooms, six of which have bathtubs (family room, 3 East Mayfield, tel. 0131/667-2781, www.sonasguesthouse.com, info@sonasguesthouse.com, Irene and Dennis).

EATING

Reservations are essential in August and on weekends, and a good idea anytime. With the ease and economy of Uber and the bus system, don't be too tied to your hotel or B&B neighborhood for dinner.

The Old Town

I prefer spots within a few minutes' walk of the tourist zone—just far enough to offer better value and a more local atmosphere.

Just off the Royal Mile on George IV Bridge

$$$ Le Bistrot is the tour guides' favorite—a delightful café hiding just steps off of the Royal Mile in the same building as the French consulate (as if put here by the consulate to promote a love of French culture). Its glowy ambience, authentic French menu, and great prices make this a welcoming spot to have dinner before an evening stroll down the Royal Mile—when all the crowds have gone to the pubs. Try their soup or fish of the day (£16 fixed-price lunch, daily 9:00-22:00, 59 George IV Bridge, tel. 0131/225-4021, www.lebistrot.co.uk).

$$$ The Outsider has a thriving energy. It's a proudly independent bistro with a social (noisy) vibe filling its sleek, sprawling dining room. The menu features good-value, fresh, modern Scottish cuisine with daily specials "until sold out" scribbled on it. You feel like a winner eating here. Ask for a window table at the back for views of the castle floating above the rooftops (daily 12:00-23:00, lunch specials until 17:00, reservations smart, 15 George IV Bridge, tel. 0131/226-3131, www.theoutsiderrestaurant.com, Eddie and partners).

Along the Royal Mile, Downhill from St. Giles' Cathedral

Though the eateries along this most-crowded stretch of the city are invariably touristy, the scene is fun.

$$$ Hewats on the Mile, next to the recommended Whiski Bar, is an intimate refuge wedged among the shops on the Royal Mile. You'll step down into an atmospheric cavern with tartan accents and enjoy fine dining at reasonable prices for such a premium location. Its colorful Scottish-Mediterranean dishes are flavorful, and ingredients are local (Mon-Sat 17:00-22:00, Sun 18:00-21:00, reservations required, 123b High Street, tel. 0131/557-5732, www.hewatsedinburgh.com).

$$$ Devil's Advocate is a popular gastropub that hides down the narrow lane called Advocates Close, directly across the Royal Mile from St. Giles. With an old cellar setting—exposed stone and heavy beams—done up in modern style, it feels like a mix of old and new Edinburgh. Creative whisky cocktails kick off a menu that dares to be adventurous, but with a respect for Scottish tradition (daily 12:00-22:00, 9 Advocates Close, tel. 0131/225-4465).

$$$$ Wedgwood Restaurant is romantic, contemporary, chic, and as gourmet as possible with no pretense. The cuisine: creative, modern Scottish with an international twist. The pigeon-and-haggis starter is scrumptious, or consider their "Wee Tour of Scotland" tasting *menu* for £55. I like the ground level with the Royal Mile view and the busy kitchen ambience better than their basement seating (fine wine by the glass, daily 12:00-15:00 & 18:00-22:00, reservations smart, 267 Canongate on Royal Mile, tel. 0131/558-8737, www.wedgwoodtherestaurant.co.uk).

QUICK, EASY, AND CHEAP BREAKFAST AND LUNCH OPTIONS

$ Edinburgh Larder promises "a taste of the country" in the center of the city. They focus on high-quality, homestyle breakfast and lunches made from seasonal, local ingredients. The café, with table service, is a convivial space with rustic tables filled by local families. Their "Little Larder" sister outlet, next door, offers more of the same (Mon-Fri 8:00-16:00, Sat-Sun from 9:00, 15 Blackfriars Street, tel. 0131/556-6922).

$ Clarinda's Tea Room, near the bottom of the Royal Mile, is a charming time warp—a fine and tasty place to relax after touring the Mile or the Palace of Holyroodhouse. Stop in for a quiche, salad, or soup lunch. It's also great for sandwiches and tea and cake any time (Mon-Sat 9:00-16:30, Sun from 10:00, 69 Canongate, tel. 0131/557-1888).

$$ Hendersons is a bright and casual local chain with good vegetarian dishes to go or eat in (daily 9:00-17:00, 67 Holyrood Road—three minutes off Royal

Mile near Scottish Parliament end, tel. 0131/557-1606).

HISTORIC PUBS FOR GRUB ALONG THE MILE

To grab some forgettable pub grub in historic surroundings, consider one of these landmark pubs described on my self-guided walk. All offer basic pub meals for £10-20 (cheaper lunch deals) and serve food daily from about 12:00 to 21:00. Deacon Brodie's is the most touristy and famous. The others have better ambience and feature music at night (see "Live Music in Pubs" on page 365).

$$ Deacon Brodie's Tavern, at a dead-center location on the Royal Mile, has a sloppy pub on the ground floor with a sloppy restaurant upstairs (435 Lawnmarket).

$$ The Mitre Bar has a classic interior, and their menu includes good meat pies (131 High Street). The neighboring **$$$ Whiski Pub** and **$$ Royal Mile Pub** are also good options.

$$ The World's End Pub, farther down the Mile at Canongate, is a colorful old place dishing up hearty meals from a creative menu in a fun, dark, and noisy space (4 High Street).

Near the National Museum

These restaurants (all within about 100 yards of each other) are happily removed from the Royal Mile melee and skew to a youthful clientele with few tourists. After passing the Greyfriars Bobby statue and the National Museum, fork left onto Forrest Road.

$ Union of Genius is a creative soup kitchen with a strong identity. They cook up a selection of delicious soups with fun foodie twists each morning at their main location in Leith, then deliver them to this shop by bicycle (for environmental reasons). These are supplemented with good salads and fresh-baked breads. The "flight" comes with three small cups of soup and three types of bread. Line up at the counter, then either take your soup to go or sit in the cramped interior, with a couple of tables and counter seating (Mon-Fri 10:00-16:00, Sat from 12:00, closed Sun, 8 Forrest Road, tel. 0131/226-4436).

$$ Mums Diner, a kitschy Scottish diner, serves up comfort food just like mum used to make. The extensive menu offers huge portions of heavy, greasy Scottish/British standards—bangers (sausages), meat pies, burgers, and artery-clogging breakfasts (served until 12:00)—and vegetarian options. There's often a line out the door on weekends (Mon-Sat 9:00-22:00, Sun from 10:00, 4 Forrest Road, tel. 0131/260-9806).

$$ Ting Thai Caravan is a loud, industrial-mod eatery serving adventurous Thai street food (soups, noodles, and curries). It's a young, stark, and simple place with thumping music, communal tables, and great food (cash only, daily 11:30-22:00, Fri-Sat until 23:00, 8 Teviot Place, tel. 0131/225-9801).

$$ Ting Saboteur, just a few doors down from Ting Thai Caravan, serves Vietnamese and Southeast Asian cuisine in a slightly more casual (but equally hip), techie-chic space. The enticing menu of bao buns and creative bowls encourages a sense of adventure—consider ordering family-style (no reservations, daily 11:30-22:00, Fri-Sat until 23:00, 19 Teviot Place, tel. 0131/623-0384).

The New Town

In the Georgian part of town, you'll find a bustling world of office workers, students, and pensioners doing their thing. These eateries are all within a 10-minute walk of Waverley Station.

Favorites on or near St. Andrew Square

$$ Dishoom is a sprawling, high-energy, Bombay Café phenom. The menu makes Indian food joyfully accessible (and affordable). You'll enjoy upscale South Asian cuisine in a bustling, dark, 1920s dining room on the second floor overlooking St. Andrew Square (I'd avoid the basement). It's a popular spot but no reservations are taken, so plan ahead (daily 12:00-23:00, 3A St. Andrew Square, tel. 0131/202-6406).

$$ Café Royal is a movie producer's dream pub—the perfect *fin de siècle* setting for a coffee, beer, or light meal. (In fact, parts of *Chariots of Fire* were filmed here.) Drop in, if only to admire the 1880 tiles featuring famous inventors. The menu is both traditional and modern with vegetarian dishes and lots of oysters (daily 12:00-22:00, 19 West Register Street, tel. 0131/556-1884, no reservations). The attached small, dressier **restaurant,** specializing in oysters, fish, and game—while stuffier and more expensive—is also good.

$$$$ The Dome Restaurant, filling what was a fancy bank, serves modern international cuisine around a classy bar and under the elegant 19th-century skylight dome. With soft jazz and chic, white-tablecloth ambience, it feels a world apart. Come here not for the food, but for the opulent atmosphere (lunch deals, early-bird special until 18:30, daily 12:00-23:00, reserve for dinner, open for a drink any time under the dome, 14 George Street, tel. 0131/624-8624, www.thedomeedinburgh.com).

$ St. Andrew's and St. George's Church Undercroft Café, in the basement of a fine old church, is the cheapest place in town for soup, sandwiches, quiche, or scones for lunch. Your tiny bill helps support the Church of Scotland (Mon-Fri 10:00-14:00, closed Sat-Sun, just off St. Andrew Square at 13 George Street, tel. 0131/225-3847). It's run by sweet volunteers who love to chat.

Supermarkets: Marks & Spencer Food Hall is just a block from the Scott Monument and the picnic-perfect Princes Street Gardens (Mon-Sat 8:00-19:00, Thu until 20:00, Sun 11:00-18:00, Princes Street 54—separate stairway next to main M&S

entrance leads directly to food hall, tel. 0131/225-2301). **Sainsbury's** supermarket, a block off Princes Street, also offers grab-and-go items (daily 7:00-22:00, on corner of Rose Street on St. Andrew Square, across the street from Jenners).

Hip Eateries on and near Thistle Street

$$$ Le Café St. Honoré, tucked away like a secret bit of old Paris, is a charming place with friendly service and walls lined with wine bottles. It serves French-Scottish cuisine in tight, Old World, cut-glass elegance to a dressy crowd (three-course lunch and dinner specials, daily 12:00-14:00 & 17:30-22:00, reservations smart—I'd ask to sit upstairs rather than in the basement, 34 Northwest Thistle Street Lane, tel. 0131/226-2211, www.cafesthonore.com).

$$$ The Bon Vivant is woody, youthful, and candlelit, with a rotating menu of French/Scottish dishes, lots of champagne by the glass, and a companion wine shop next door. They have fun tapas plates and heartier dishes, served either in the bar up front or in the restaurant in back (daily 12:00-22:00, 55 Thistle Street, tel. 0131/225-3275, www.bonvivantedinburgh.co.uk).

$$$ Fishers in the City, a good place to dine on seafood, has an inviting menu and a fine value lunch and early-bird dinner menu (served daily until 18:00). The energy is lively, the clientele is smart, and the room is bright and airy with a simple elegance (daily 12:00-22:00, lots of nice wines by the glass, reservations smart, 58 Thistle Street, tel. 0131/225-5109, www.fishersrestaurants.co.uk).

$$ Hendersons Vegetarian has fed hearty cuisine and salads to a generation of New Town vegetarians. Even carnivores love this place for its delectable salads, desserts, and smoothies. Their main restaurant, facing Hanover Street, is self-service by day but has table service after 17:00 (Mon-Sat 8:30-22:00, Sun 10:30-16:00, between Queen and George streets at 94 Hanover Street, tel. 0131/225-2131). Just around the corner on Thistle Street, **Hendersons Vegan** has a strictly vegan menu and feels a bit more casual (daily 12:00-21:30, tel. 0131/225-2605).

The West End

In this posh neighborhood of high-end eateries, the following places have character, tasty food, and fair prices.

$$$ La P'tite Folie Restaurant occupies a beautiful, half-timbered Tudor house that once housed a Polish Catholic church. Its sophisticated, local clientele goes for flavorful specialties like steak and duck—all with a French flair (good-value two-course lunch, food served Mon-Thu 12:00-15:00 & 18:00-22:00, Fri-Sat until 23:00, closed Sun, reservations smart, 9 Randolph Place, tel. 0131/225-8678, www.laptitefolie.co.uk). Under the same roof, **$$ Le Di-Vin Wine Bar** is in the nave of the church, with an extensive wine list and nice cheese-and-meat boards (Mon-Sat 12:00-late, closed Sun, tel. 0131/538-1815).

$$$ La Piazza stands out among several Italian restaurants in this neighborhood. It's a welcoming place with solid pasta dishes, pizzas, and an Italian villa vibe. Pleasant terrace tables are out back (generally Mon-Sat 12:00-23:00, Sun 16:30-22:00, reservations strongly recommended, 97 Shandwick Place, tel. 0131/221-1150, www.lapiazzaedinburgh.com).

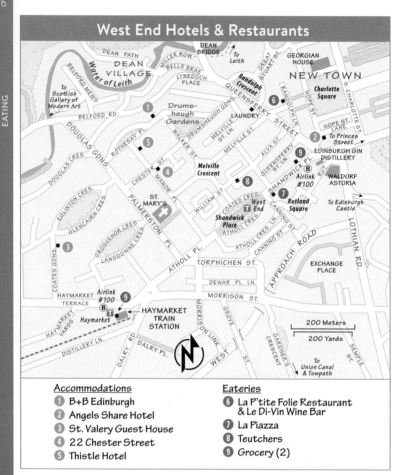

West End Hotels & Restaurants

Accommodations
1. B+B Edinburgh
2. Angels Share Hotel
3. St. Valery Guest House
4. 22 Chester Street
5. Thistle Hotel

Eateries
6. La P'tite Folie Restaurant & Le Di-Vin Wine Bar
7. La Piazza
8. Teuchers
9. Grocery (2)

$$ Teuchers is a friendly joint on cute William Street, with a fun vibe and nice tables in a rustic space. The food is a cut above typical pub grub, and the downstairs restaurant serves Scottish specialties with local ingredients (daily 10:00-late, 26 William Street, tel. 0131/225-2973).

Supermarket: There's a handy **Sainsbury's** near my recommended West End accommodations (daily 6:00-23:00, 32 Shandwick Place). A **Marks & Spencer** is at the Haymarket train station (Mon-Fri 6:00-22:00, Sat 7:00-21:00, Sun from 9:00).

South of the City Center

These places are within a 10-minute walk of my recommended B&Bs. For locations, see the map on page 369. I wouldn't eat here unless you're staying nearby.

Pub Grub

$$ The Salisbury Arms is a gastropub serving upscale, traditional classics with flair. While they have a bar area and a garden terrace, I'd dine in their elegant restaurant section. The menu ranges from burgers and salads to more sophisticated dishes (book ahead for restaurant, no reservations taken for pub, food served daily 12:00-22:00, 58 Dalkeith Road, tel. 0131/667-4518, www. thesalisburyarmsedinburgh.co.uk).

$$ The Old Bell Inn, with an old-time sports-bar ambience—fishing, golf, horses, lots of TVs—serves an extensive menu of pub meals with daily specials. This is a classic "snug pub"—all dark woods and brass beer taps, littered with evocative knickknacks (bar tables can be reserved, food served daily until 21:15, 233 Causewayside, tel. 0131/668-1573, www. oldbelledinburgh.co.uk).

Eateries Around Newington Road

$$ Hanedan serves fresh Turkish food at tiny tables in a cozy dining room. The lamb, fish, and vegetable dishes are all authentic and bursting with flavor, making this a welcome alternative to pub fare (Tue-Sun 12:00-15:00 & 17:30-late, closed Mon, 42 West Preston Street, tel. 0131/667-4242).

$$ Damm 27, tucked around the corner from Newington, is rustic-chic but unpretentious, with an appealing cocktail-and-wine list and attentive service. The menu features small plates, gourmet burgers, mussel pots, and good vegetarian and vegan options (daily 10:00-late, 27 Causewayside, tel. 0131/667-6693).

$$ Voujon Restaurant serves a fusion menu of Bengali and Indian cuisines. Vegetarians appreciate the expansive yet inexpensive offerings (daily 17:00-23:00, 107 Newington Road, tel. 0131/667-5046).

Groceries: On the main streets near the restaurants you'll find **Sainsbury's Local** and **Co-op** (on South Clerk Road), and **Tesco Express** and another **Sainsbury's Local** one block over on Causewayside (all open late—until at least 22:00).

TRANSPORTATION

Getting Around Edinburgh

By Bus: Many of Edinburgh's sights are within walking distance of one another, but buses come in handy—especially if you're staying at a B&B south of the city center (for specifics, see the "Sleeping" section earlier). Double-decker buses come with fine views upstairs. It's easy once you get the hang of it: Buses come by frequently and have free, fast Wi-Fi on board. The only hassle is that you must pay with exact change (£1.70/ride). As you board, tell your driver where you're going (or just say "single ticket") and drop your change into the box. The £4 all-day pass pays for itself in three rides and frees you from worrying about change. You can also use a payment app on your smartphone, such as ApplePay or Google Pay, to pay for your bus fare when you board. (For a day pass, tap the sensor each time you ride. If you ride three or more times, you'll be charged £4 at the end of the day.)

You can pick up a route map at the TI, in the train station, or at the transit office at the Old Town end of Waverley Bridge (tel. 0131/555-6363, www.lothianbuses.com).

By Tram: Edinburgh's single tram line (also £1.70/ride, buy at ticket machine before boarding, credit card or exact change) is designed more for locals than tourists. It's most useful for reaching the airport (£6 one-way) or getting from my recommended West End hotels to Princes Street and St. Andrew Square, near the Waverley train station.

By Taxi or Uber: The 1,300 taxis cruising Edinburgh's streets are easy to flag down (a ride between downtown and the B&B neighborhood costs about £7; rates go up after 18:00 and on weekends). They can turn on a dime, so hail them in either direction. Uber also works very well here and is substantially cheaper than taxis (with quick pickups and most rides in town averaging £5-6).

Waverley Station

Arriving and Departing
By Train
Most long-distance trains arrive at **Waverley Station** in the city center. Taxis line up outside, on Princes Street or Waverley Bridge. To catch a city bus, exit the train station via Princes Street and ride up several escalators (Waverley Mall is on your left). City buses stop around the corner to your right, along North Bridge, and are handy if you're staying in my recommended B&B neighborhood south of town. Those staying at one of my recommended West End accommodations might consider taking the train directly to **Haymarket Station** (rather than Waverley).

TRAIN CONNECTIONS FROM EDINBURGH
From Edinburgh to: Glasgow (7/hour, 50 minutes), **Inverness** (6/day direct, 3.5 hours, more with transfer), **York** (3/hour, 2.5 hours), **London** (2/hour, 4.5 hours), **Durham** (2/hour direct, 2 hours, less frequent in winter), **Newcastle** (3/hour, 1.5 hours), **Keswick/Lake District** (8/day to Penrith—more via Carlisle, 1.5 hours, then 40-minute bus ride to Keswick), **Birmingham** (hourly, 5 hours, more with transfer). Train info: Tel. 0345-748-4950, www.nationalrail.co.uk.

By Bus
Scottish Citylink, Megabus, and National Express buses use the bus station (with luggage lockers) in the New Town, two blocks north of the train station on St. Andrew Square. For bus info, stop by the station or call Scottish Citylink (tel. 0871-266-3333, www.citylink.co.uk). Additional long-distance routes may be operated by National Express (www.nationalexpress.com) or Megabus (www.megabus.com).

Rick's Tip: *If you plan to* **rent a car, pick it up on your way out of Edinburgh**—*you won't need it in town.*

By Car
No matter where you're coming from, avoid needless driving in the city by taking advantage of Edinburgh's bypass road, A-720. To conveniently reach my recommended B&Bs, circle the city on

the A-720 (direction: Edinburgh South), until the last roundabout, named *Sheriffhall*. Exit the roundabout at the sign for *A-7 (City Centre Attractions)*. About four miles and two roundabouts later, exit onto Lady Road. Turn right on A-701, which becomes Mayfield Gardens.

Car Rental: These places have offices both in the town center and at the airport: **Avis** (24 East London Street, tel. 0344-544-6059, airport tel. 0344-544-6004), **Europcar** (Waverley Station, near platform 2, tel. 0371-384-3453, airport tel. 0371-384-3406), **Hertz** (10 Picardy Place, tel. 0843-309-3026, airport tel. 0843-309-3025), and **Budget** (24 East London Street, tel. 0344-544-9064, airport tel. 0344-544-4605). Some downtown offices close or have reduced hours on Sunday, but the airport locations tend to be open daily. If you plan to rent a car, pick it up on your way out of Edinburgh—you won't need it in town.

By Plane

Edinburgh Airport is located eight miles northwest of the center (code: EDI, tel. 0844-481-8989, www.edinburghairport. com).

A **taxi** or **Uber** between the airport and city center costs about £30 (25 minutes to downtown, West End, or Mayfield Gardens).

The airport is also well connected to central Edinburgh by tram and bus. Just follow signs outside; the tram tracks are straight ahead, and the bus stop is to the right, along the main road in front of the terminal. **Trams** make several stops in town, including along Princes Street and at St. Andrew Square (£6, £8.50 round-trip, buy ticket from machine, runs every 5-10 minutes from early morning until 23:30, 35 minutes, www.edinburghtrams.com).

The Lothian **Airlink bus #100** drops you at Waverley Bridge (£4.50, £7.50 round-trip, runs every 10 minutes, 30 minutes, tel. 0131/555-6363, www. lothianbuses.com).

Britain: Past & Present

Origins
(2000 BC-AD 500)

When Julius Caesar landed on the misty and mysterious isle of Britain in 55 BC, England entered the history books. He was met by primitive Celtic tribes whose druid priests made human sacrifices and worshipped trees. (Those Celts were themselves immigrants, who had earlier conquered the even more mysterious people who built Stonehenge.) The Romans eventually settled in England (AD 43) and set about building towns and roads and establishing their capital at Londinium (today's London).

But the Celtic natives—consisting of Gaels, Picts, and Scots—were not easily subdued. Around AD 60, Boadicea, a queen of the Isle's indigenous people, defied the Romans and burned Londinium before the revolt was squelched. Some decades later, the Romans built Hadrian's Wall near the Scottish border as protection against their troublesome northern neighbors.

Dark Ages
(500-1000)

As Rome fell, so fell Roman Britain—a victim of invaders and internal troubles. Barbarian tribes from Germany, Denmark, and northern Holland, called Angles, Saxons, and Jutes, swept through the southern part of the island, establishing Angle-land. These were the days of the real King Arthur, possibly a Christianized Roman general who fought valiantly—but in vain—against invading barbarians.

In 793, England was hit with the first of two centuries of savage invasions by barbarians from Norway, called the Vikings or Norsemen. King Alfred the Great (849-899) liberated London from Danish Vikings, reunited England, reestablished Christianity, and fostered learning. Nevertheless, for most of this 500-year period, the island was plunged into a Dark Age.

Wars with France, Wars of the Roses
(1000-1500)

In 1066, William the Conqueror and his Norman troops crossed the English Chan-

Royal Families: Past and Present

802-1066:	Saxon and Danish kings
1066-1154:	William the Conqueror and Norman kings
1154-1399:	Plantagenet (kings with French roots)
1399-1461:	Lancaster
1462-1485:	York
1485-1603:	Tudor (Henry VIII, Elizabeth I)
1603-1649:	Stuart (civil war and beheading of Charles I)
1649-1653:	Commonwealth, no royal head of state
1653-1659:	Protectorate, with Cromwell as Lord Protector
1660-1714:	Restoration of Stuart dynasty
1714-1901:	Hanover (four Georges, William IV, Victoria)
1901-1910:	Saxe-Coburg (Edward VII)
1910-now:	Windsor (George V to Elizabeth II)

nel from France. William crowned him-self king in Westminster Abbey (where all subsequent coronations would take place). He began building the Tower of London, as well as Windsor Castle, which would become the residence of many monarchs to come.

Over the succeeding centuries, French-speaking kings would rule England, and English-speaking kings invaded France as the two budding nations defined their modern borders. Richard the Lionheart (1157-1199) ruled as a French-speaking king who spent most of his energy on distant Crusades. In 1215, King John (Richard's brother), under pres-sure from England's barons, was forced to sign the Magna Carta, establishing the principle that even kings must follow the rule of law.

London asserted itself as England's trade center. London Bridge—the famous stone version, topped with houses—was built (1209), and Old St. Paul's Cathedral was finished (1314).

Then followed two centuries of wars, chiefly the Hundred Years' War with France (1337-1443). In 1348, the Black Death (bubonic plague) killed half of Lon-don's population.

In the 1400s, noble families duked it out for the crown. The York and Lancaster families fought the Wars of the Roses, so-called because of the white and red flowers the combatants chose as their symbols.

The Tudor Renaissance
(1500s)

England was finally united by the "third-party" Tudor family. Henry VIII, a Tudor, was England's Renaissance king. He went through six wives in 40 years, divorcing, imprisoning, or executing them when they no longer suited his needs.

When the Pope refused to grant Henry a divorce so he could marry his mistress Anne Boleyn, Henry "divorced" England from the Catholic Church. He estab-lished the Protestant Church of England (the Anglican Church), thus setting in motion a century of bitter Protestant/ Catholic squabbles. Henry's first daughter, "Bloody" Mary, was a staunch Catholic who presided over the burning of hun-dreds of prominent Protestants.

Mary was followed by her half-sis-ter—Queen Elizabeth I—the daughter of Henry and Anne Boleyn. She reigned for 45 years, making England a great trading and naval power (defeating the Spanish Armada) and treading diplomatically over the Protestant/Catholic divide. Elizabeth presided over a cultural renaissance known (not surprisingly) as the "Elizabethan Age." Playwright William Shakespeare moved from Stratford-upon-Avon to London, beginning a remarkable career as the earth's greatest playwright. Sir Francis Drake circumnavigated the globe. Sir Walter Raleigh explored the Americas, and Sir Francis Bacon pioneered the scientific method.

But Elizabeth—the "Virgin Queen"— never married or produced an heir. So the English Parliament invited Scotland's King James (Elizabeth's first cousin twice removed) to inherit the English throne.

Kings vs. Parliament
(1600s)

The enduring quarrel between England's kings and Parliament's nobles finally erupted into the Civil War (1642). The war pitted (roughly speaking) the Protestant Puritan Parliament against the Catholic aristocracy. Parliament forces under Oliver Cromwell defeated—and beheaded—King Charles I. After Crom-

well died, Parliament invited Charles' son to take the throne—the "restoration of the monarchy."

This turbulent era was followed by back-to-back disasters—the Great Plague of 1665 (which killed 100,000) and the Great Fire of 1666 (which incinerated London). London was completely rebuilt in stone, centered around New St. Paul's Cathedral, which was built by Christopher Wren.

In the war between kings and Parliament, Parliament finally got the last word, when it deposed Catholic James II and imported the Dutch monarchs William and Mary in 1688, guaranteeing a Protestant succession.

Colonial Expansion
(1700s)

Britain grew as a naval superpower, colonizing and trading with all parts of the globe. Eventually, Britannia ruled the waves, exploiting the wealth of India, Africa, and Australia. (And America...at least until those ungrateful Yanks revolted in 1776 in the "American War.") Throughout the century, the country was ruled by the German Hanover family, including

Nelson's Column in London

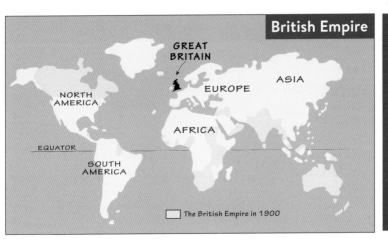

British Empire

The British Empire in 1900

four kings named George.

The "Georgian Era" was one of great wealth. London's population was now a half-million, and one in seven Brits lived in London. The nation's first daily newspapers hit the streets. The cultural scene was refined: painters (like William Hogarth, Joshua Reynolds, and Thomas Gainsborough), theater (with actors like David Garrick), music (Handel's *Messiah*), and literature (Samuel Johnson's dictionary). Scientist James Watt's steam engines laid the groundwork for a coming Industrial Revolution.

In 1789, the French Revolution erupted, sparking decades of war between France and Britain. Britain finally prevailed in the early 1800s, when Admiral Horatio Nelson defeated Napoleon's fleet at the Battle of Trafalgar and the Duke of Wellington stomped Napoleon at Waterloo. By war's end, Britain had emerged as Europe's top power.

Victorian Britain
(1800s)

Britain reigned supreme, steaming into the Industrial Age with her mills, factories, coal mines, gas lights, and trains.

In 1837, eighteen-year-old Victoria became queen. She ruled for 64 years, presiding over an era of unprecedented wealth, peace, and middle-class ("Victorian") values. Britain was at its zenith of power, with a colonial empire that covered one-fifth of the world.

Meanwhile, there was another side to Britain's era of superiority and industrial might. A generation of Romantic poets (William Wordsworth, John Keats, Percy Shelley, and Lord Byron) longed for the innocence of nature. Jane Austen and the Brontë sisters wrote romantic tales about the landed gentry. Painters like J. M. W. Turner and John Constable immersed themselves in nature to paint moody landscapes.

The gritty modern world was emerging. Popular novelist Charles Dickens brought literature to the masses, educating them about Britain's harsh social and economic realities. Rudyard Kipling critiqued the colonial system. Charles Darwin questioned the very nature of humanity when he articulated the principles of natural selection and evolution. Jack the Ripper, a serial killer of prostitutes, terrorized east London and was never caught.

World Wars and Recovery
(20TH CENTURY)

Two world wars and economic struggles whittled Britain down from a world empire to an island chain struggling to

Get It Right

Americans tend to use "England," "Britain," and the "United Kingdom" (or "UK") interchangeably, but they're not quite the same.

England is the country occupying the center and southeast part of the island.

Britain is the name of the island.

Great Britain is the political union of the island's three countries: England, Scotland, and Wales.

The **United Kingdom** (UK) adds a fourth country, Northern Ireland.

The **British Isles** (not a political entity) also includes the independent Republic of Ireland.

The **British Commonwealth** is a loose association of possessions and former colonies (including Canada, Australia, and India) that profess at least symbolic loyalty to the Crown.

You can call the modern nation either the United Kingdom ("the UK"), "Great Britain," or simply "Britain."

compete in a global economy.

In World War I, Britain joined France and other allies to battle Germany in trench warfare. A million British men died. In the 1920s, London was home to a flourishing literary scene, including T. S. Eliot (American-turned-British), Virginia Woolf, and E. M. Forster. In 1936, the country was rocked and scandalized when King Edward VIII abdicated to marry a divorced American commoner, Wallis Simpson.

In World War II, the Nazi Blitz reduced much of London to rubble, sending residents into Tube stations for shelter and the government into a fortified bunker (now the Churchill War Rooms). Britain was rallied through its darkest hour by two leaders: Prime Minister Winston Churchill, a remarkable orator, and King George VI. Amid the chaos of war, the colonial empire began to dwindle to almost nothing, and Britain emerged from the war as a shell of its former superpower self.

Culturally, Britain remained world-class. Oxford professor J. R. R. Tolkien wrote *The Lord of the Rings* and his friend C. S. Lewis wrote *The Chronicles of Narnia*.

In the 1960s, "Swinging London" became a center for rock music, film, theater, youth culture, and Austin Powers-style joie de vivre. America was conquered by a "British Invasion" of rock bands.

The 1970s brought massive unemployment, labor strikes, and recession. A conservative reaction followed in the 1980s and 90s, led by Prime Minister and Eurosceptic Margaret Thatcher—the "Iron Lady." As proponents of traditional Victorian values—community, family, hard work, thrift, and trickle-down economics—the Conservatives took a Reaganesque approach to Britain's serious social and economic problems. They cut government subsidies to old-fashioned heavy industries (closing many factories, earning working-class ire), as they tried to nudge Britain toward a more modern economy.

In 1981, the world was captivated by the spectacle of Prince Charles marrying Lady Diana in St. Paul's Cathedral. Their children, Princes William and Harry, grew up in the media spotlight, and when Diana died in a car crash (1997), the nation—and the world—mourned.

The 1990s saw Britain finally emerging

from decades of economic stagnation and social turmoil. An energized nation prepared for the new millennium.

Britain Today

In the new millennium, Britain was ruled by left-of-center Prime Minister Tony Blair, until his popularity plummeted when he supported the US invasion of Iraq. On "7/7" in 2005, London was rocked by a terrorist attack—a harbinger of others to come.

Britain suffered mightily in the global recession of 2008. Voters turned to the Conservative Prime Minister David Cameron, who introduced austerity measures, but Britain was slow to recover.

The biggest challenge facing Britain at the moment is, of course, Brexit—dealing with the consequences of the 2016 referendum in which Britain voted to leave the European Union. Brexit is inextricably tangled up with other issues that have long divided the nation, including the changing economy, immigration, terrorism, the country's place on the world stage, and the role of royalty. After the vote, the British pound dropped by 10 percent, and David Cameron resigned. His Conservative successor, Theresa May (a "Remain" supporter), was left with the thankless task of trying to carry out the will of the voters against a hostile EU and a reluctant establishment. May gave the EU two year's notice that Britain was leaving. In July 2019, May resigned.

May's successor, Boris Johnson, also tried negotiating a deal with both a bickering Parliament and with the EU. But the UK officially left the European Union on January 31, 2020, and the countdown clock started ticking on an 11-month transition period toward new arrangements for trade, customs, travel, and regulation. By the time you read this, there will likely be new wrinkles and complications.

Practicalities

TOURIST INFORMATION

Before your trip, start with the Visit Britain website, which contains a wealth of knowledge on destinations, activities, accommodations, and transport in Great Britain (www.visitbritain.com). Transportation, sightseeing, and theater tickets can also be purchased (www.visitbritainshop.com/usa).

In Britain, a good first stop is generally the tourist information office (abbreviated TI in this book and locally as TIC, for "tourist information centre"). In London, the City of London Information Centre, near St. Paul's Cathedral, is helpful (see page 40).

Swing by to pick up a city map and get information on public transit, walking tours, special events, and nightlife. Some TIs have information on the entire country or at least the region, so try to pick up maps and printed information for destinations you'll be visiting later in your trip.

HELP!

Travel Advisories: For updated health and safety conditions, including any restrictions for your destination, consult the US State Department's international travel website (travel.state.gov).

Emergency and Medical Help: For any emergency service—ambulance, police, or fire—call 112 from a mobile phone or landline. If you get sick, do as the locals do and go to a pharmacy and see a "chemist" (pharmacist) for advice. Or ask at your hotel for help—they'll know of the nearest medical and emergency services.

Theft or Loss: To replace a passport, you'll need to go in person to an embassy (see next). If your credit and debit cards disappear, cancel and replace them (see "Damage Control for Lost Cards" on page 389). File a police report, either on the spot or within a day or two; you'll need it to submit an insurance claim for lost or stolen rail passes or electronics, and it can help with replacing your passport or credit and debit cards. For more information, see RickSteves.com/help.

US Consulate and Embassy: Tel. 020/7499-9000 (all services), no walk-in passport services; for emergency two-day passport service, schedule an appointment or fill out the online Emergency Passport Contact Form, 24 Grosvenor Square, London, Tube: Bond Street, uk.usembassy.gov.

High Commission of Canada in London: Tel. 020/7004-6000, passport services available Mon-Fri 9:30-12:30, Canada House, Trafalgar Square, London, Tube: Charing Cross, www.unitedkingdom.gc.ca.

TRAVEL TIPS

Time Zones: Britain is five/eight hours ahead of the East/West Coasts of the US—and one hour earlier than most of continental Europe. The exceptions are the beginning and end of Daylight Saving Time: Europe "springs forward" the last Sunday in March (two weeks after most of North America), and "falls back" the last Sunday in October (one week before North America). For a handy time converter, use the world clock app on your phone or download one (see www.timeanddate.com/worldclock).

Business Hours: Most stores are open Monday through Saturday (roughly 9:00 or 10:00 to 17:00 or 18:00). In cities, some stores stay open later on Wednesday or Thursday (until 19:00 or 20:00). Some big-city department stores are open later throughout the week (Mon-Sat until about 21:00). Sundays have the same pros and cons as they do for travelers in the US: Sightseeing attractions are generally open, many street markets are lively with shoppers, banks and many shops are closed, public transportation options are fewer (for example, no bus service to or from smaller towns), and there's no rush hour.

Watt's Up? Britain's electrical system is 220 volts, instead of North America's 110 volts. Most electronics (laptops, phones, cameras) and hair dryers convert automatically, so you won't need a converter, but you will need an adapter plug with three square prongs, sold inexpensively at travel stores in the US.

Discounts: Discounts (called "concessions" or "concs" in Britain) for sights are generally not listed in this book. However, seniors (age 65 and over), youths under 18, and students and teachers with proper identification cards (obtain from www.isic.org) can get discounts at many sights—always ask.

MONEY

Here's my basic strategy for using money in Europe:

- Upon arrival, head for a cash machine (ATM) at the airport and withdraw some local currency, using a debit card with low international transaction fees.
- In general, pay for bigger expenses with a credit card and use cash for smaller purchases. Use a debit card only for cash withdrawals.
- Keep your cash safe in a money belt.

What to Bring

I pack the following and keep it all safe in my money belt.

Debit Card: Use at ATMs to withdraw cash.

Credit Card: Handy for bigger transactions (at hotels, shops, restaurants, car-rental agencies, and so on), payment machines, and online purchases.

Backup Card: Some travelers carry a third card (debit or credit; ideally from a different bank), in case one gets lost, demagnetized, eaten by a temperamental machine, or simply doesn't work.

Stash of Cash: I carry US $100-200 as a cash backup, which comes in handy in an emergency (such as if your ATM card gets eaten by the machine).

What NOT to Bring: Resist the urge to buy pounds before your trip or you'll pay the price in bad stateside exchange rates. I've yet to see a European airport that didn't have plenty of ATMs.

Rick's Tip: *Looking to upgrade your European travel skills? You'll find plenty of practical info at RickSteves.com/travel-tips.*

Before You Go

Know your PIN. Make sure you know the numeric, four-digit PIN for all of your cards, both debit and credit. Request it if you don't have one, as it may be required for some purchases in Europe.

Report your travel dates. Let your bank know that you'll be using your debit and credit cards in Europe, and when and where you're headed.

Adjust your ATM withdrawal limit. Find out how much you can take out daily and ask for a higher daily withdrawal limit if you want to get more cash at once. Note that European ATMs will withdraw funds only from checking accounts; you're unlikely to have access to your savings account.

Ask about fees. For any purchase or withdrawal made with a card, you may be charged a currency conversion fee (1-3 percent) and/or a Visa or MasterCard international transaction fee (less than 1 percent).

Exchange Rate

1 British pound (£1) = about $1.30

To convert prices from pounds to dollars, add about 30 percent: £20=about $26, £50=about $65. Like the dollar, the British pound (£, also called a "quid") is broken into 100 cents, called pence (p). (Check www.oanda.com for the latest exchange rates.)

In Europe

Using Cash Machines: European cash machines work just like they do at home—except they spit out local currency instead of dollars, calculated at the day's standard bank-to-bank rate.

In most places, ATMs are easy to locate—in Britain ask for a "cashpoint." When possible, withdraw cash from a bank-run ATM located just outside that bank. If your debit card doesn't work, try a lower amount—your request may have exceeded your withdrawal limit or the ATM's limit.

Avoid "independent" ATMs, such as Travelex, Euronet, Moneybox, Your Cash, Cardpoint, and Cashzone. These have high fees, can be less secure than a bank ATM, and may try to trick users with "dynamic currency conversion" (see later).

Exchanging Cash: Avoid exchanging money in Europe; it's a big rip-off. In a pinch you can always find exchange desks at major train stations or airports—convenient but with crummy rates. Banks generally do not exchange money unless you have an account with them.

Using Credit Cards: Despite some differences between European and US cards, there's little to worry about: US credit cards generally work fine in Europe. I've been inconvenienced a few times by unattended payment machines (transit-ticket kiosks, parking, self-service gas stations, tollbooths) where US cards may not work. Always carry cash as a back-up.

Dynamic Currency Conversion: If merchants offer to convert your purchase price into dollars (called dynamic currency conversion, or DCC), refuse this "service." You'll pay extra for the expensive convenience of seeing your charge in dollars. If an ATM offers to "lock in" or "guarantee" your conversion rate, choose "proceed without conversion." Other prompts might state, "You can be charged in dollars: Press YES for dollars, NO for pounds." Always choose the local currency.

Security Tips: Pickpockets target tourists. Keep your cash, credit cards, and passport secure in your money belt, and carry only a day's spending money in your front pocket or wallet.

Damage Control for Lost Cards: If you lose your credit or debit card, report the loss immediately to the respective global customer-assistance centers. With a mobile phone, call these 24-hour US numbers: Visa (tel. +1 303/967-1096), MasterCard (tel. +1 636/722-7111), and American Express (tel. +1 336/393-1111). From a landline, you can call these US numbers collect by going through a local operator. European toll-free numbers can be found at the websites for Visa and MasterCard. You can generally receive a temporary card within two or three business days in Europe (see RickSteves.com/help for more).

Tipping

Tipping in Britain isn't as automatic and generous as it is in the US. For special service, tips are appreciated, but not expected. As in the US, the proper amount depends on your resources, tipping philosophy, and the circumstances, but some general guidelines apply.

Restaurants: It's not necessary to tip if a service charge is included in the bill (common in London—usually 12.5 percent). Otherwise, it's appropriate to tip about 10-12 percent for good service.

Taxis: For a typical ride, round up your fare a bit (maximum 10 percent; for instance, if the fare is £7.40, pay £8).

Getting a VAT Refund

Wrapped into the purchase price of your British souvenirs is a value-added tax (VAT) of about 20 percent. You're entitled to get most of that tax back if you purchase more than £30 worth of goods at a store that participates in the VAT-refund scheme (although individual stores can require that you spend more—Harrods, for example, won't process a refund unless you spend £50).

Get the paperwork. Have the merchant completely fill out the necessary refund document (either an official VAT customs form, or the shop or refund company's own version of it). You'll have to present your passport. Get the paperwork done before you leave the shop to ensure you'll have everything you need (including your original sales receipt).

Get your stamp at the border or airport. Process your VAT document at your last stop in the European Union (such as at the airport) with the customs agent who deals with VAT refunds. Some customs desks are positioned before airport security; confirm the location before going through security.

Collect your refund. You can claim your VAT refund from refund companies, such as Global Blue or Planet, with offices at major airports, ports, or border crossings. These services (which extract a 4 percent fee) can refund your money in cash immediately or credit your card.

Customs for American Shoppers

You can take home $800 worth of items per person duty-free, once every 31 days. Many processed and packaged foods are allowed, including vacuum-packed cheeses, dried herbs, jams, baked goods, candy, chocolate, oil, vinegar, mustard, and honey. Fresh fruits and vegetables and most meats are not allowed, with exceptions for some canned items. As for alcohol, you can bring in one liter duty-free.

To bring alcohol (or liquid-packed foods) in your carry-on bag on your flight home, buy it at a duty-free shop at the airport. You'll increase your odds of getting it onto a connecting flight if it's packaged in a "STEB"—a secure, tamper-evident bag.

For details on allowable goods, customs rules, and duty rates, visit www.help.cbp.gov.

SIGHTSEEING

Sightseeing can be hard work. Use these tips to make your visits to England's finest sights meaningful, fun, efficient, and painless.

Plan Ahead

Set up an itinerary that allows you to fit in all your must-see sights.

Confirm open hours, and don't put off visiting a must-see sight—you never know when a place will close unexpectedly for a holiday, strike, or royal audience. Many museums are closed or have reduced hours at least a few days a year. A list of holidays is on page 413; check for possible closures during your trip.

Reservations and Advance Tickets

Given how precious your vacation time is, I recommend getting reservations for any must-see sight that offers them. Many popular sights sell advance tickets that guarantee admission at a certain time of day or allow you to skip entry lines. Either way, it's worth giving up some spontaneity to book in advance. For popular sights, you may need to book weeks or even months in advance. As soon as you're ready to commit to a certain date, book it.

Sightseeing Passes

Many sights in England are managed by either English Heritage or the National

Trust. Each organization has a combo-deal that can save some money for busy sightseers.

Membership in **English Heritage** includes free entry to more than 400 sights in England and discounted or free admission to about 100 more sights in Scotland and Wales. For most travelers, the **Overseas Visitor Pass** is a better choice than the pricier one-year membership (Visitor Pass: £35/9 days, £42/16 days, discounts for couples and families; membership: £56 for one person, £99 for two, discounts for families, seniors, and students, children under 19 free, www.english-heritage.org.uk/membership; tel. 0370-333-1181).

Membership in the **National Trust** is best suited for garden-and-estate enthusiasts, ideally those traveling by car. It covers more than 350 historic houses, manors, and gardens throughout Great Britain. From the US, it's easy to join online through the Royal Oak Foundation, the National Trust's American affiliate (one-year membership: $80 for one person, $125 for two, family and student memberships, www.royal-oak.org). For more on National Trust properties, see www.nationaltrust.org.uk.

At Sights

Here's what you can typically expect:

Entering: You may not be allowed to enter if you arrive too close to closing time. And guards start ushering people

out well before the actual closing time, so don't save the best for last.

Many sights have a security check. Allow extra time for these lines. Some sights require you to check daypacks and coats. (If you'd rather not check your daypack, try carrying it tucked under your arm like a purse as you enter.)

At ticket desks, you may see references to "Gift Aid"—a tax-deduction scheme that benefits museums—but this only concerns UK taxpayers.

Photography: If the museum's photo policy isn't clearly posted, ask a guard. Generally, taking photos without a flash or tripod is allowed. Some sights ban selfie sticks; others ban photos altogether.

Audioguides and Apps: Many sights rent audioguides with excellent recorded descriptions (about £5). Museums and sights often offer free apps that you can download to your mobile device (check their websites).

Expect Changes: Artwork can be on tour, on loan, out sick, or shifted at the whim of the curator. Pick up a floor plan as you enter, and ask museum staff if you can't find a particular item.

SLEEPING

Extensive and opinionated listings of good-value rooms are a major feature of this book's Sleeping sections. Rather than list accommodations scattered throughout a town, I choose places in my favorite neighborhoods that are convenient to your sightseeing.

Rates and Deals

I've categorized my recommended accommodations based on price, indicated with a dollar-sign rating (see sidebar). The price ranges suggest an estimated cost for a one-night stay in high season in a standard double room with a private toilet and shower, and assume you're booking directly with the hotel (not through a booking site, which extracts a commission). In London, breakfast is often not included in quoted hotel rates; you can opt out of the pricey hotel breakfast and get it on your own for less.

In Britain, small bed-and-breakfast places (B&Bs) generally provide the best value, though I also include some bigger hotels. Britain has a rating system for hotels and B&Bs, but I find they often have little to do with value.

Booking Direct: Once your dates are set, compare prices at several hotels. You can do this by checking Hotels.com or Booking.com, and hotel websites. Then book directly with the hotel itself. Contact small family-run hotels directly by phone or email. When you go direct, the owner avoids the commission paid to booking sites, thereby leaving enough wiggle room to offer you a discount, a nicer room, or a free breakfast (if it's not already included).

Sleep Code

Hotels in this book are categorized according to the average price of a standard double room with breakfast in high season.

$$$$	**Splurge:** Most rooms over £160
$$$	**Pricier:** £120-160
$$	**Moderate:** £80-120
$	**Budget:** £40-80
¢	**Backpacker:** Under £40
RS%	**Rick Steves discount**

Unless otherwise noted, credit cards are accepted and free Wi-Fi is available. Comparison-shop by checking prices at several hotels (on each hotel's own website, on a booking site, or by email). For the best deal, *book directly with the hotel.* Ask for a discount if paying in cash; if the listing includes **RS%**, request a Rick Steves discount.

If you prefer to book online or are considering a hotel chain, it's to your advantage to use the hotel's website. When establishing prices, confirm if the charge is per person or per room (if a price is too good to be true, it's probably per person).

Getting a Discount: Some hotels extend a discount to those who pay cash or stay longer than three nights. And some accommodations offer a special discount for Rick Steves readers, indicated in this guidebook by the abbreviation **RS%.** Discounts vary: Ask for details when you reserve.

Staying in B&Bs and small hotels can save money over sleeping in big hotels. Chain hotels can be even cheaper, but they don't include breakfast. When comparing prices between chain hotels and B&Bs, remember you're getting two breakfasts (about a £25 value) for each double room at a B&B.

Types of Accommodations
Hotels

Outside of pricey big cities, you can expect to find good doubles for £80-120 (about $105-155), including cooked breakfasts and tax.

A "twin" room has two single beds; a "double" has one double bed. If you'll take either, let the hotel know, or you might be needlessly turned away. Some hotels can add an extra bed (for a small charge) to turn a double into a triple; some offer larger rooms for four or more people (I call these "family rooms" in the listings). If there's space for an extra cot, they'll cram it in for you. In general, a triple room is cheaper than the cost of a double and a single. Three or four people can economize by requesting one big room.

An "en suite" room has a bathroom (toilet and shower/tub) attached to the room; a room with a "private bathroom" can mean that the bathroom is all yours, but it's across the hall. If money's tight, ask about a room with a shared bathroom.

Modern Hotel Chains: Chain hotels—

common in bigger cities all over Great Britain—can be a great value. They come with private showers/WCs, elevators, good security, and often an attached restaurant. Branches are often located near the train station, on major highways, or outside the city center.

This option is especially worth considering for families, as kids often stay for free. While most of these hotels have 24-hour reception and elevators, breakfast and Wi-Fi generally cost extra, and the service lacks a personal touch. When comparing your options, keep in mind that for about the same price, you can get a basic room at a B&B that has less predictable comfort but more funkiness and friendliness in a more enjoyable neighborhood.

The biggest chains are **Premier Inn** (www.premierinn.com) and **Travelodge** (www.travelodge.co.uk). Both have attractive deals for prepaid or advance bookings. Other chains operating in Britain include the Irish **Jurys Inn** (www.jurysinns.com) and the French-owned **Ibis** (www.ibishotel.com). Couples can consider **Holiday Inn Express,** which generally allows only two people per room (make sure Express is part of the name or you'll be paying more for a regular Holiday Inn, www.hiexpress.co.uk).

Arrival and Check-In: Hotels and B&Bs are sometimes located on the higher floors of a multipurpose building with a secured door. In that case, look for your hotel's name on the buttons by the

Using Online Services to Your Advantage

From booking services to user reviews, online businesses play a greater role in travelers' planning than ever before. Take advantage of their pluses—and be wise to their downsides.

Booking Sites

Booking websites Booking.com and Hotels.com offer one-stop shopping for hotels. To be listed, a hotel must pay a sizable commission. When you use an online booking service, you're adding a middleman. To support small, family-run hotels whose world is more difficult than ever, book direct.

Short-Term Rental Sites

Rental juggernaut Airbnb and other short-term rental sites allow travelers to rent rooms and apartments directly from locals. Airbnb fans appreciate feeling part of a real neighborhood as "temporary Europeans."

Critics view Airbnb as creating unfair competition for established guesthouse owners. As a lover of Europe, I share the worry of those who see residents nudged aside by tourists. But as an advocate for travelers, I appreciate the value and cultural intimacy Airbnb provides.

User Reviews

User-generated review sites and apps such as Yelp and TripAdvisor can give you a consensus of opinions about everything from hotels and restaurants to sights and nightlife. But a user-generated review is based on the limited experience of one person, while a guidebook is the work of a trained researcher who visits many restaurants and hotels year after year.

Both types of information have their place, and in many ways, they're complementary. If something is well reviewed in a guidebook and it also gets good online reviews, it's likely a winner.

main entrance. When you ring the bell, you'll be buzzed in.

Hotel elevators are common, though some older buildings still lack them. You may have to climb a flight of stairs to reach the elevator (if so, you can ask the front desk for help carrying your bags up). Elevators are typically very small—you may need to send your bags up without you.

The EU requires that hotels collect your name, nationality, and ID number. When you check in, the receptionist will normally ask for your passport and may keep it for anywhere from a couple of minutes to a couple of hours. If you're not

comfortable leaving your passport at the desk for a long time, ask when you can pick it up. Or, if you packed a color photocopy of your passport, you can generally leave that rather than the original.

B&Bs and Small Hotels

B&Bs and small hotels are generally family-run places with fewer amenities but more character than a conventional hotel. They range from large inns with 15-20 rooms to small homes renting out a spare bedroom. Compared to hotels, B&Bs and guesthouses give you double the cultural intimacy for half the price.

Making Hotel Reservations

Requesting a Reservation: For family-run hotels, it's generally best to book your room directly via email or phone. For business-class and chain hotels, or if you'd rather book online, reserve directly through the hotel's official website (not a booking website).

Here's what the hotelier wants to know:
- Type(s) of rooms you want and size of your party
- Number of nights you'll stay
- Your arrival and departure dates, written European-style as day/month/year (18/06/22 or 18 June 2022)
- Special requests (en suite bathroom, cheapest room, twin beds vs. double bed, quiet room)
- Applicable discounts (such as a Rick Steves reader discount, cash discount, or promotional rate)

Confirming a Reservation: Most places will request a credit-card number to hold your room. If you're using an online reservation form, make sure it's secure by looking for *https* or a lock icon at the top of your browser. If the website isn't secure, it's best to share that confidential info via a phone call.

Canceling a Reservation: If you must cancel, do so with as much notice as possible, especially for smaller family-run places. Cancellation policies can be strict; read the fine print before you book. Many discount deals require prepayment, with no cancellation refunds.

Reconfirming a Reservation: Always call or email to reconfirm your room reservation a few days in advance. For B&Bs or very small hotels, I call again on my day of arrival to tell my host what time to expect me (especially important if arriving late—after 17:00).

Phoning: For tips on how to call hotels overseas, see page 400.

B&B proprietors are selective about the guests they invite in for the night. Many do not welcome children. If you'll be staying for more than one night, you are a "desirable." In popular weekend-getaway spots, you're unlikely to find a place to take you for Saturday night only. If my listings are full, ask for guidance. Mentioning this book can help. Owners usually work together and can call up an ally to land you a bed. Many B&B owners are also pet owners. If you're allergic, ask about resident pets when you reserve.

Rules and Etiquette: B&Bs and small hotels come with their own etiquette and quirks. Keep in mind that owners are at the whim of their guests—if you're getting up early, so are they; if you check in late, they'll wait up for you. Most B&Bs have set check-in times (usually in the late afternoon). If arriving outside that time, they will want to know when to expect you (call or email ahead). Most will let you check in earlier if the room is available (or they'll at least let you drop off your bag).

Most B&Bs and guesthouses serve a hearty cooked breakfast of eggs and much more (for details on breakfast, see the "Eating" section, later). Because the owner is often also the cook, breakfast hours are usually abbreviated. Typically the breakfast window lasts for 1-1.5 hours (make sure you know when it is before you turn in for the night). Some B&Bs ask you to fill in your breakfast order the night before. It's an unwritten rule that guests shouldn't show up at the very end of the breakfast period and expect a full cooked breakfast. If you do arrive late (or need to leave before breakfast is served), most establishments are happy to let you help yourself to cereal, fruit, juice, and coffee.

B&Bs and small hotels often come with thin walls and doors, and sometimes creaky floorboards, which can make for a noisy night. If you're a light sleeper, bring earplugs.

In the Room: Your bedroom probably won't include a phone, but nearly every B&B has free Wi-Fi.

You're likely to encounter unusual bathroom fixtures. The "pump toilet" has a flushing handle or button that doesn't kick in unless you push it just right: too hard or too soft, and it won't go. (Be decisive but not ruthless.) Most B&B baths have an instant water heater. This looks like an electronic box under the showerhead with dials and buttons: One control adjusts the heat, while another turns the flow off and on (let the water run for a bit to moderate the temperature before

you hop in). If the hot water doesn't work, you may need to flip a red switch (often located just outside the bathroom).

Paying: Many B&Bs take credit cards, but may add the card service fee to your bill (about 3 percent). If you do need to pay cash for your room, plan ahead to have enough on hand when you check out.

Short-Term Rentals

A short-term rental—whether an apartment (or "flat"), house, or room in a local's home—is an increasingly popular alternative, especially if you plan to settle in one location for several nights. For stays longer than a few days, you can usually find a rental that's comparable to—and cheaper than—a hotel room with similar amenities. Websites such as Airbnb, FlipKey, Booking.com, and the HomeAway family of sites (HomeAway, VRBO, and VacationRentals), let you browse a wide range of properties. Alternatively, rental agencies such as InterhomeUSA.com or RentaVilla.com, which list more carefully selected accommodations that might cost more, can provide more personalized service.

Hostels

Britain has hundreds of hostels of all shapes and sizes. Choose your hostel selectively. Hostels can be historic castles or depressing tenements, serene and comfy or overrun by noisy school groups.

A hostel provides cheap beds in dorms where you sleep alongside strangers for about £20-30 per night. Travelers of any age are welcome if they don't mind dorm-style accommodations and meeting other travelers. Most hostels offer kitchen facilities, guest computers, Wi-Fi, and a self-service laundry.

Independent hostels tend to be easygoing, colorful, and informal (no membership required; www.hostelworld.com). You may pay slightly less by booking direct with the hostel. **Official hostels** are part of Hostelling International (HI) and share an online booking site (www.hihostels.com). HI hostels typically require that you be a member or else pay a bit more per night. In Britain, these official hostels are run by the Youth Hostel Association (YHA, www.yha.org.uk).

EATING

These days, the stereotype of "bad food in Britain" is woefully dated. Britain has caught up with the foodie revolution—in fact, they're right there, leading the vanguard—and I find it's easy to eat very well here. London, in particular, is one of Europe's best food destinations.

Tipping: At pubs and places where you order at the counter, you don't have to tip. At restaurants and fancy pubs with wait-staff, it's not necessary to tip if a service charge is already included in the bill (common in London—usually 12.5 percent). Otherwise, it's appropriate to tip about 10-12 percent; you can add a bit more for finer dining or extra good service. Tip only what you think the service warrants (if it isn't already added to your bill), and be careful not to tip double.

Breakfast (Fry-Up)

The traditional fry-up or full English breakfast—generally included in the cost of your room—is famous as a hearty way to start the day. Also known as a "heart attack on a plate," your standard fry-up is a heated plate with eggs, Canadian-style bacon and/or sausage, a grilled tomato, sautéed mushrooms, baked beans, and sometimes potatoes, kippers (herring), or fried bread (sizzled in a greasy skillet). Toast comes in a rack (to cool quickly and crisply) with butter and marmalade. At a B&B or hotel, it may start with juice and cereal or porridge. Many progressive B&B owners offer creative variations on the traditional breakfast.

As much as the full breakfast fry-up is a traditional way to start the morning, these days most places serve a healthier continental breakfast as well—with a buffet of yogurt, cereal, fruit, and pastries.

Lunch and Dinner on a Budget

Even in pricey cities, plenty of inexpensive choices are available.

I've found that portions are huge, and **sharing plates** is generally just fine. Ordering two drinks, a soup or side salad, and splitting a £10 meat pie can make a good, filling meal. If you're on a limited budget, share a main course in a more expensive place for a nicer eating experience.

Pub grub is the most atmospheric budget option. You'll usually get hearty lunches and dinners priced reasonably at £8-15 under ancient timbers (see "Pubs," later).

Classier restaurants have some affordable deals. Lunch is usually cheaper than dinner; a top-end, £30-for-dinner-type restaurant often serves the same quality two-course lunch deals for about half the price.

Many restaurants have **early-bird** or **pre-theater specials** of two or three courses, often for a significant savings. They are usually available only before 18:30 or 19:00 (and sometimes on weekdays only).

Global cuisine adds spice to Britain's food scene. Eating Indian, Bangladeshi, Chinese, or Thai is cheap (even cheaper if you do takeout).

Fish-and-chips are a heavy, greasy, but tasty British classic. Every town has at least one "chippy" selling takeaway fish-and-chips in a cardboard box or (more traditionally) wrapped in paper for about £5-7.

Picnicking saves time and money. Fine park benches and polite pigeons abound in most towns and city neighborhoods.

Pubs

Pubs are a fundamental part of the British social scene, and whether you're a tee-totaler or a beer guzzler, they should be a part of your travel here. Smart travelers use pubs to eat, drink, get out of the rain, watch sporting events, and make new friends.

Though hours vary, pubs generally serve beer daily from 11:00 to 23:00, though many are open later, particularly on Friday and Saturday. (Children are served food and soft drinks in pubs, but you must be 18 to order a beer.)

A cup of darts is free for the asking. People go to a public house to be social. They want to talk. Get vocal with a local. The pub is the next best thing to having relatives in town. Cheers!

Pub Grub: For £8-15, you'll get a basic budget hot lunch or dinner in friendly surroundings. In high-priced London, this is your best indoor eating value. (For something more refined, try a **gastropub,** which serves higher-quality meals for £12-20.) The *Good Pub Guide* is an excellent resource (www.thegoodpubguide.co.uk).

Pubs generally serve traditional dishes, such as fish-and-chips, roast beef with Yorkshire pudding (batter-baked in the oven), and assorted meat pies, such as steak-and-kidney pie or shepherd's pie (stewed lamb topped with mashed potatoes) with cooked vegetables. Side dishes include salads, vegetables, and—invariably—"chips" (French fries). "Crisps" are potato chips. A "jacket potato" (baked potato stuffed with fillings of your choice) can almost be a meal in itself. A "plough-man's lunch" is a traditional British meal of bread, cheese, and sweet pickles. These days, you'll likely find more pasta, curried dishes, and quiche on the menu than traditional fare. Meals are usually served from 12:00 to 14:00 and again from 18:00 to 20:00—with a break in the middle. Order at the bar, and then take a seat. It's not necessary to tip unless it's a place with full table service. For details on ordering beer and other drinks, see the "Beverages" section, later.

Good Chain Restaurants

I know—you're going to Britain to enjoy characteristic little hole-in-the-wall pubs, so mass-produced food is the furthest thing from your mind. But several excellent chains with branches across the UK offer long hours, reasonable prices, reliable quality, and a nice break from pub grub. My favorites are Pret (a.k.a. Pret à Manger), Wasabi, and Eat; other dependable chains include Le Pain Quotidien, Wagamama Noodle Bar, Loch Fyne Fish Restaurant, Busaba Eathai, and Thai Square.

Carry-Out Chains: Major supermarket chains have smaller, offshoot branches that specialize in sandwiches, salads, and other prepared foods to go. These can be a picnicker's dream come true. Some shops are stand-alone, while others are located inside a larger store. The most prevalent—and best—is M&S Simply Food (there's one in every major train station). Sainsbury's Local grocery stores also offer decent prepared food; Tesco Express and Tesco Metro run a distant third.

Indian Cuisine

Eating Indian food is "going local" in cosmopolitan, multiethnic Britain. You'll find Indian restaurants in most cities, and even in small towns. Take the opportunity to sample food from Britain's former colony. Indian cuisine is as varied as the country itself. In general, it uses more exotic spices than British or American cuisine—some hot, some sweet. Indian food is very vegetarian-friendly, offering many meatless dishes.

An easy way to taste a variety of dishes is to order a *thali*—a sampler plate of various specialties.

Afternoon Tea

Once the sole province of genteel ladies in fancy hats, afternoon tea has become more democratic in the 21st century. These days, people of leisure punctuate their day with an afternoon tea at a tearoom. Tearooms, which often serve appealing light meals, are usually open for lunch and close at about 17:00, just before dinner.

The cheapest "tea" on the menu is generally a "cream tea"; the most expensive is the "champagne tea." **Cream tea** is simply a pot of tea and a homemade scone or two with jam and thick clotted cream. **Afternoon tea**—what many Americans would call "high tea"—is a pot of tea, small finger foods (such as sandwiches with the crusts cut off), scones, an assortment of small pastries, jam, and thick clotted cream. **Champagne tea** includes all of the goodies, plus a glass of bubbly. **High tea** to the English generally means a more substantial late afternoon or early evening meal, often served with meat or eggs.

Desserts (Sweets)

To the British, the traditional word for dessert is "pudding," although it's also referred to as "sweets" these days.

Trifle is the best-known British concoction, consisting of sponge cake soaked in brandy or sherry (or orange juice for children), then covered with jam and/or fruit and custard cream. Whipped cream can sometimes put the final touch on this "light" treat.

The British version of custard is a smooth, yellow liquid. Cream tops most everything that custard does not. There's single cream for coffee. Double cream is really thick. Clotted cream is the consistency of whipped butter.

Fool is a dessert with sweetened

pureed fruit (such as rhubarb, gooseberries, or black currants) mixed with cream or custard and chilled.

Flapjacks here aren't pancakes, but are dense, sweet oatmeal cakes (a little like a cross between a granola bar and a brownie). They come with toppings such as toffee and chocolate.

Beverages

Beer: The British take great pride in their beer. Many locals think that drinking beer cold and carbonated, as Americans do, ruins the taste. Most pubs will have **lagers** (cold, refreshing, American-style beer), **ales** (amber-colored, cellar-temperature beer), **bitters** (hop-flavored ale, perhaps the most typical British beer), and **stouts** (dark and somewhat bitter, like Guinness).

At pubs, long-handled pulls (or taps) are used to draw the traditional, rich-flavored "real ales" up from the cellar. Served straight from the brewer's cask at cellar temperature, real ales finish fermenting naturally and are not pasteurized or filtered, so they must be consumed within two or three days after the cask is tapped. Naturally carbonated, real ales vary from sweet to bitter, often with a hoppy or nutty flavor.

Short-handled pulls mean colder, fizzier, mass-produced, and less interesting keg beers. Mild beers are sweeter, with a creamy malt flavoring. Irish cream ale is a smooth, sweet experience. Try the draft cider (sweet or dry)...carefully.

Order your beer at the bar and pay as you go, with no need to tip. An average beer costs about £4. Part of the experience is standing before a line of hand pulls, and wondering which beer to choose.

As dictated by British law, draft beer and cider are served by the pint (20-ounce imperial size) or the half-pint (9.6 ounces). In 2011, the government sanctioned an in-between serving size—the

The British Accent

In the olden days, a British person's accent indicated his or her social standing. Eliza Doolittle had the right idea—elocution could make or break you. Wealthier families would send their kids to fancy private schools to learn proper pronunciation. But these days, in a sort of reverse snobbery that has gripped the nation, accents are back. Politicians, newscasters, and movie stars are favoring deep accents over the Queen's English. While it's hard for American ears to pick out the variations, most Brits can determine where a person is from based on their accent... not just the region, but often the village, and even the part of town.

schooner, or two-thirds pint (it's become a popular size for higher alcohol-content craft beers). A popular summer drink is a **shandy** (half beer and half British "lemonade," similar to 7-Up).

Other Alcoholic Drinks: Many pubs also have a good selection of wines by the glass and a fully stocked bar for the gentleman's "G and T" (gin and tonic). **Pimm's** is a refreshing and fruity summer liqueur, traditionally popular during Wimbledon. It's an upper-class drink—a rough bloke might insult a pub by claiming it sells more Pimm's than beer.

Non-alcoholic Drinks: Teetotalers can order from a wide variety of soft drinks—both the predictable American sodas and other more interesting bottled drinks, such as ginger beer (similar to ginger ale but with more bite), root beers, or other flavors (Fentimans brews some unusual options that are stocked in many pubs).

How to Dial

To make an international call, follow the dialing instructions below. Drop an initial zero, if present, when dialing a European phone number—except when calling Italy. I've used the telephone number of one of my recommended London hotels as an example (tel. 020/7730-8191).

From a Mobile Phone

It's easy to dial with a mobile phone. Whether calling from the US to Europe, country to country within Europe, or from Europe to the US—it's all the same. Press zero until you get a + sign, enter the country code (44 for Britain), then dial the phone number.

► To call the London hotel from any location, dial +44 20/7730-8191.

From a US Landline to Europe

Dial 011 (US/Canada access code), country code (44 for Britain), and phone number.

► To call the London hotel from your home phone, dial 011 44 20/7730-8191.

From a European Landline to the US or Europe

Dial 00 (Europe access code), country code (1 for the US, 44 for Britain), and phone number.

► To call my US office from Britain, dial 00 1 425 771 8303.
► To call the London hotel from Germany, dial 00 44 20/7730-8191.

For a complete list of European country codes and more phoning help, see www.howtocallabroad.com.

STAYING CONNECTED

One of the most common questions I hear from travelers is, "How can I stay connected in Europe?" The short answer is: more easily and cheaply than you might think.

The simplest solution is to bring your own device—mobile phone, tablet, or laptop—and use it just as you would at home (following the money-saving tips later). For more details, see RickSteves.com/phoning. For a practical one-hour talk covering tech issues for travelers, see RickSteves.com/mobile-travel-skills.

Using A Mobile Phone in Europe

Sign up for an international plan. To stay connected at a lower cost, sign up for an international service plan through your carrier. Most providers offer a simple bundle that includes calling, messaging, and data. Your normal plan may already include international coverage (T-Mobile's does).

Use free Wi-Fi whenever possible. Unless you have an unlimited-data plan, you're best off saving most of your online tasks for Wi-Fi. You can access the internet, send texts, and even make voice calls over Wi-Fi.

Minimize the use of your cellular network. The best way to make sure you're not accidentally burning through data is to

Tips on Internet Security

Make sure that your device is running the latest versions of its operating system, security software, and apps. Next, ensure that your device and key programs (like email) are password-protected. On the road, use only secure, password-protected Wi-Fi. Ask the hotel or café staff for the specific name of their network, and make sure you log on to that exact one.

If you must access your financial info online, use a banking app rather than accessing your account via a browser, and use a cellular connection, not Wi-Fi. Never log on to personal finance sites on a public computer. If you're very concerned, consider subscribing to a VPN (virtual private network).

put your device in "airplane" mode (which also disables phone calls and texts), turn your Wi-Fi back on, and connect to networks as needed. When you need to get online but can't find Wi-Fi, simply turn on your cellular network (or turn off airplane mode) just long enough for the task at hand.

Disable automatic updates so your apps will update only when you're on Wi-Fi.

Use Wi-Fi calling and messaging apps. Skype, WhatsApp, FaceTime, and Google Hangouts are great for making free or low-cost calls or sending texts over

Wi-Fi worldwide. Just log on to a Wi-Fi network, then connect with any of your friends or family members who use the same service.

Buy a European SIM card. If you anticipate making a lot of local calls or need a local phone number, or if your provider's international data rates are expensive, consider buying a SIM card in Europe to replace the one in your (unlocked) US phone or tablet. SIM cards are sold at department-store electronics counters, some newsstands, and vending machines. If you need help setting it up, buy one at a mobile-phone shop (you may need to show your passport).

There are no roaming charges when using a European SIM card in other EU countries, though to be sure you get this "roam-like-at-home" pricing, buy your SIM card at a mobile-phone shop and ask if this feature is included.

TRANSPORTATION

Figuring out how to get around in Europe is one of your biggest trip decisions. **Cars** work well for two or more traveling together (especially families with small kids), those packing heavy, and those delving into the countryside. **Trains** and **buses** are best for solo travelers, blitz tourists, city-to-city travelers, and those who want to leave the driving to others.

Smart travelers can use short hop **flights** within Europe to creatively connect the dots on their itineraries.

If your itinerary mixes cities and countryside, connect cities by train (or bus) and explore rural areas by rental car. Arrange to pick up your car in the last big city you'll visit, then use it to lace together small towns and explore the countryside. For more detailed information on transportation throughout Europe, see RickSteves.com/transportation.

Trains

Regular tickets on Britain's great train system (15,000 departures from 2,400 stations daily) are the most expensive per mile in all of Europe. For the greatest savings, book online in advance and leave after rush hour (after 9:30 weekdays).

Since Britain's railways have been privatized, a single train route can be operated by multiple companies. However, one website covers all train lines (www.nationalrail.co.uk), and another covers all bus and train routes (www.traveline.org.uk for information, not ticket sales). Another good resource, which also has schedules for trains throughout Europe,

is German Rail's timetable (www.bahn.com).

While generally not required, reservations are free and can normally be made well in advance. They are an especially good idea for long journeys or for travel on Sundays or holidays. Make reservations at any train station, by phone, or online when you buy your ticket. With a point-to-point ticket, you can reserve as late as two hours before train time, but rail-pass holders should book seats at least 24 hours in advance (see later for more on rail passes). You must reserve in advance for Caledonian Sleeper overnight trains between London and Scotland (www.sleeper.scot).

Rail Passes

Since Britain's pay-as-you-go train tickets are some of the most expensive in Europe, BritRail passes can pay for themselves quickly, especially if you ride a long-distance train (for example, between London and Scotland). A rail pass offers hop-on flexibility and no need to lock in reservations, except for overnight sleeper cars.

BritRail passes cannot be purchased

Rail Pass or Point-to-Point Tickets?

Will you be better off buying a rail pass or point-to-point tickets? It pays to know your options and choose what's best for your itinerary.

Rail Passes

A BritRail Pass lets you travel by train in Scotland, England, and Wales for two to eight days within a one-month period, 15 days within two months, or for continuous periods of up to one month. In addition, BritRail sells England-only and other regional passes. Britain is also covered (along with most of Europe) by the classic Eurail Global Pass. Discounted rates are offered for children, youths, and seniors.

Rail passes are best purchased outside Europe (through travel agents or Rick Steves' Europe). For more on rail passes, including current prices, visit RickSteves.com/rail.

Point-to-Point Tickets

If you're taking just a couple of train rides, buying individual point-to-point train tickets may save you money over a pass. Use this map to add up approximate pay-as-you-go fares for your itinerary, and compare that to the price of a rail pass. Keep in mind that significant discounts on point-to-point tickets may be available with advance purchase.

Map shows approximate costs, in US dollars, for one-way, second-class tickets at off-peak rates.

locally; buy your pass through an agent before leaving the US. Make sleeper reservations in advance; you can also make optional, free seat reservations (recommended for busy weekends) at staffed train stations.

For more detailed advice on figuring out the smartest rail-pass options for your train trip, visit www.ricksteves.com/rail.

Buying Tickets

In Advance: The best fares go to those who book their trips well in advance of their journey.

To book ahead, go in person to any station, look online at www.nationalrail.co.uk, or call 0345-748-4950 (from the US, dial 011-44-20-7278-5240, phone answered 24 hours) to find out the schedule and best fare for your journey; you'll then be referred to the appropriate vendor—depending on the particular rail company—to book your ticket. You'll pick up your ticket at the station, or you may be able to print it at home.

Buying Train Tickets as You Travel: If you'd rather have the flexibility of booking tickets as you go, you can save a few pounds by buying a round-trip ticket, called a "return ticket" (a same-day round-trip, called a "day return," is particularly cheap for short excursions); buying before 18:00 the day before you depart; traveling after the morning rush hour (this usually means after 9:30 Mon-Fri); and going standard class instead of first class. Preview your options at www.nationalrail.co.uk.

Senior, Youth, Partner, and Family Deals: To get a third off the price of most point-to-point rail tickets, seniors can buy a Senior Railcard (ages 60 and up), younger travelers can buy a 16-25 Railcard (ages 16-25, or full-time students 26 and older), and two people traveling together can buy a Two Together Railcard (ages 16 and over). A Family and Friends Railcard gives adults about 33 percent off for most trips and 60 percent off for their kids age 5 to 15 (maximum 4 adults and 4 kids). Each Railcard costs £30; for non-UK citizens, it's best to purchase the pass at a staffed rail station in England, Scotland, or Wales upon arrival as you need a UK delivery address to buy it online (pass also sold at some London airports; some passes require passport-type photo; passport needed for proof of age; see www.railcard.co.uk).

Buses

Most domestic buses are operated by **National Express** (www.nationalexpress.com); their international departures are called **Eurolines** (www.eurolines.co.uk). A smaller company called **Megabus** undersells National Express with deeply discounted promotional fares—the further ahead you buy, the less you pay (some

trips for just £1.50, tel. 0141/352-4444, www.megabus.com). While Megabus can be much cheaper than National Express, they tend to be slower than their competitor and their routes mainly connect cities, not smaller towns. They also sell discounted train tickets on selected routes.

Try to avoid bus travel on Friday and Sunday evenings, when weekend travelers are more likely to make buses sell out.

To ensure getting a ticket—and to save money with special promotions—book your ticket in advance online or over the phone. The cheapest prepurchased tickets usually cannot be changed or refunded; other fare types charge a change fee. Check if the ticket is only "amendable" or also "refundable" when you buy. Round-trip bus tickets usually cost less than two one-way fares.

Taxis and Ride-Booking Services

Most British taxis are reliable and cheap. In many cities, two people can travel short distances by cab for little more than the cost of bus or subway tickets. If you like ride-booking services such as Uber, their apps usually work in Britain just like they do in the US. London's Uber is facing a legal challenge; check ahead to confirm it is operating.

Renting a Car

It's cheaper to arrange most car rentals from the US, so research and compare rates before you go. Most of the major US rental agencies (including Avis, Budget, Enterprise, Hertz, and Thrifty) have offices throughout Europe. Also consider the two major Europe-based agencies, Europcar and Sixt. Consolidators such as Auto Europe (www.autoeurope.com—or the sometimes cheaper www.autoeurope.eu) compare rates at several companies to get you the best deal.

Rental Costs and Considerations

Figure on paying roughly $250 for a one-

Great Britain's Public Transportation

Rail
Eurostar
Bus
Ferry with
(8H) crossing time

Orkney
Islands
Stromness
Scrabster Gill John O' Groats
Thurso

Lewis

Skye
Portree Inverness Elgin
Kyle Culloden
Mallaig Loch Aviemore Aberdeen
Ness
Fort William SCOTLAND

Mull Pitlochry
Iona Oban Dundee
Perth Leuchars
St. Andrews

Stirling Edinburgh North
Glasgow Sea
Berwick
Holy
Island

Cairnryan Hexham
(2H) Carlisle Newcastle To Amsterdam
Larne Stranraer Penrith Durham (15H)
(2.5H)
N. Belfast Keswick Whitby
IRE. Windermere Settle Danby Scarborough
Isle ENGLAND
of Man York Hull
Irish To Zeebrugge
Sea Blackpool Preston Leeds (10H)
Dublin (7H) Liverpool Grimsby
Holyhead Conwy Manchester
(2-3H) Bangor Chester Lincoln
REP. Caernarfon Betws- Stoke Peter- King's
OF Bed y-Coed Derby borough Lynn Norwich
IRE. Pwllheli Blaenau Telford Wolv.
Harlech Ffest. Birmingham Ely
Aberystwyth Ironbridge Coventry Cambridge
Rosslare Gorge Warwick Harwich
Stratford To Hoek
(3.5H) WALES Chelt. Moreton Ebbs- (6H)
Carmarthen Stow Oxford fleet
Fishguard Newport London Canter-
Swansea Windsor bury
Cardiff Bath Reading Dover
Bristol STONE- Ashford
Atlantic Wells HENGE 1.5H
Ocean West- Salisbury To
Glastonbury bury Calais
Exeter EUROSTAR
Dartmoor Southampton Brighton Newhaven (2.5H)
Portsmouth To
St. Ives Truro Dieppe
Penzance Falmouth Plymouth English Channel To Paris,
Brussels &
To Roscoff To St-Malo Amsterdam
(6H) (11H) To Caen FRANCE
(Ouistreham)

week rental for a basic compact car. Allow extra for supplemental insurance, fuel, tolls, and parking.

Manual vs. Automatic: Almost all rental cars in Europe are manual by default—and cars with a stick shift are generally cheaper. If you need an automatic, request one in advance. An automatic makes sense for most American drivers: With a manual transmission in Britain, you'll be sitting on the right side of the car and shifting with your left hand... while driving on the left side of the road.

Age Restrictions: Rental companies in Britain require you to be at least 21 years old and to have held your license for one year. Drivers under the age of 25 may incur a young-driver surcharge, and some rental companies will not rent to anyone 75 or older.

Choosing Pick-up/Drop-off Locations: Always check the hours of the locations you choose: Many rental offices close from midday Saturday until Monday morning and, in smaller towns, at lunchtime. When selecting an office, plug the addresses into a mapping website to confirm the location. A downtown site is generally cheaper—and might seem more convenient than the airport. But pedestrianized and one-way streets can make navigation tricky when returning a car at a big-city office or urban train station. Wherever you select, get precise details on the location and allow ample time to find it.

Picking Up Your Car: Before driving off in your rental car, check it thoroughly and make sure any damage is noted on your rental agreement. Rental agencies in Europe tend to charge for even minor damage, so be sure to mark everything. Find out how your car's gearshift, lights, turn signals, wipers, radio, and fuel cap function, and know what kind of fuel the car takes (diesel vs. unleaded). When you return the car, make sure the agent verifies its condition with you. Some drivers take pictures of the returned vehicle as proof of its condition.

Be aware that Brits call it "hiring a car," and directional signs at airports and train stations will read *Car Hire*.

The AA: The services of Britain's Automobile Association are included with most rentals (www.theaa.com), but check for this when booking to be sure you understand its towing and emergency road-service benefits.

Car Insurance Options

When you rent a car in Europe, the price typically includes liability insurance, which covers harm to other cars or motorists—but not the rental car itself. To limit your financial risk in case of damage to the rental, choose one of these three options: Buy a Collision Damage Waiver (CDW) with a low or zero deductible from the car-rental company (roughly 30-40 percent extra), get coverage through your credit card (free, but more complicated), or get collision insurance as part of a larger travel-insurance policy.

If you're already purchasing a **travel-insurance policy** for your trip, adding collision coverage can be an economical option. For example, Travel Guard (www.travelguard.com) sells affordable renter's collision insurance as an add-on to its other policies; it's valid everywhere in Europe except the Republic of Ireland, and some Italian car-rental companies refuse to honor it, as it doesn't cover you in case of theft.

For more on car-rental insurance, see RickSteves.com/cdw.

Navigation Options

Your Mobile Phone: If you'll be navigating using your phone, remember to bring a car charger and device mount.

Driving all day can burn through a lot of very expensive data. The economical work-around is to use map apps that work offline. By downloading in advance from Google Maps, City Maps 2Go, Apple Maps, Here WeGo, or Navmii, you can

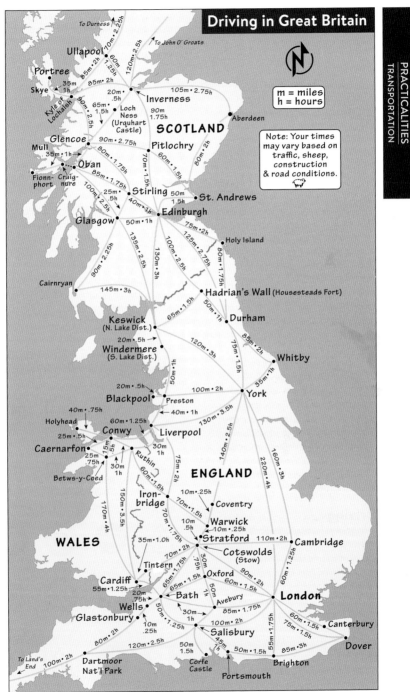

Driving in Great Britain

m = miles
h = hours

Note: Your times may vary based on traffic, sheep, construction & road conditions.

To Durness
To John O' Groats

Ullapool
70m · 2.25h
120m · 2.5h
Portree
35m · 2h
60m · 1.25h
Skye
85m · 2h
85m · 2h
105m · 2.75h
Kyle of Lochalsh
1h
20m · .5h
Inverness
Aberdeen
30m · 1h
65m · 1.5h
90m · 1.75h
Loch Ness (Urquhart Castle)
SCOTLAND
Glencoe
90m · 2.75h
Pitlochry
80m · 2h
Mull
80m · 1.75h
70m · 1.5h
60m · 1.5h
35m · 1h
Oban
85m · 1.75h
Fionn-phort
Craig-nure
100m · 2.5h
25m · .5h
Stirling
50m · 1.5h
St. Andrews
40m · 1h
Edinburgh
Glasgow
50m · 1h
75m · 2h
Holy Island
135m · 2.25h
100m · 2.5h
125m · 2.75h
80m · 1.75h
90m · 2.25h
130m · 3h
Cairnryan
145m · 3h
Hadrian's Wall (Housesteads Fort)
65m · 1.5h
50m · 1h
Durham
Keswick (N. Lake Dist.)
120m · 3h
85m · 2h
20m · .5h
75m · 1.5h
Windermere (S. Lake Dist.)
Whitby
50m · 1h
100m · 2h
35m · 1h
20m · .5h
York
Blackpool
Preston
40m · 1h
130m · 3.5h
40m · .75h
Holyhead
60m · 1.25h
Liverpool
140m · 2.5h
160m · 3h
25m · .5h
Conwy
30m · 1h
75m · 2h
220m · 4h
Caernarfon
15m · .5h
Ruthin
25m · .75h
30m · 1h
60m · 1.5h
ENGLAND
Betws-y-Coed
Iron-bridge
10m · .25h
Coventry
150m · 3.5h
70m · 1.5h
Warwick
170m · 4h
10m · .5h
10m · .25h
Stratford
110m · 2h
Cambridge
WALES
35m · 1.0h
Cotswolds (Stow)
70m · 2h
30m · 1h
90m · 2h
60m · 1.25h
Tintern
75m · 1.75h
Oxford
60m · 1.5h
65m · 1.5h
60m · 2h
Cardiff
20m · .75h
Bath
50m · 1h
Avebury
London
55m · 1.25h
50m · 1h
85m · 1.75h
55m · 1.75h
Wells
30m · 1h
60m · 1.5h
Glastonbury
100m · 2h
75m · 1.5h
Canterbury
10m · .25h
Salisbury
80m · 2h
120m · 2.5h
50m · 1.5h
45m · 1h
85m · 3h
To Land's End
100m · 2h
Dartmoor Nat'l Park
Corfe Castle
50m · 1.5h
Dover
Brighton
Portsmouth

still have turn-by-turn voice directions and maps that recalibrate even though they're offline.

You must download your maps before you go offline—and it's smart to select large regions. Then turn off your data connection so you're not charged for roaming. This option is great for navigating in areas with poor connectivity.

GPS Devices: If you want the convenience of a dedicated GPS unit, known as a "satnav" in Britain, consider renting one with your car ($10-30/day). These units offer real-time turn-by-turn directions and traffic without the data requirements of an app.

Paper Maps and Atlases: Even when navigating primarily with a mobile app or GPS, I always make it a point to have a paper map, ideally a big, detailed regional road map (easy to buy locally at bookstores or gas stations). It's invaluable for getting the big picture, understanding alternate routes, and filling in if my phone runs out of juice.

Several good road atlases cover all of Britain. Ordnance Survey, Collins, AA, and Bartholomew editions are all available at tourist information offices, gas stations, and bookstores. The tourist-oriented Collins Touring maps do a good job of highlighting the many roadside attractions you might otherwise drive right past. Before you buy a map, look at it to be sure it has the level of detail you want.

Driving

Driving here is basically wonderful—once you remember to stay on the left and after you've mastered the roundabouts. Every year, however, I get a few notes from traveling readers advising me that, for them, trying to drive in Britain was a nerve-racking and regrettable mistake.

Many Yankee drivers find the hardest part isn't driving on the left, but steering from the right. Your instinct is to put yourself on the left side of your lane, which means you may spend your first day or two drifting into the left shoulder or curb. It helps to remember that the driver always stays close to the center line.

Road Rules: Be aware of Britain's rules of the road. Seat belts are mandatory for all, and kids under age 12 (or less than about 4.5 feet tall) must ride in an appropriate child-safety seat. It's illegal to use a mobile phone while driving. In Britain, you're not allowed to turn left on a red light unless a sign or signal specifically authorizes it, and on motorways it's illegal to pass drivers on the left. Ask your car-rental company about these rules, or check the "International Travel" section of the US State Department website (www.travel.state.gov, search for your country in the "Learn About Your Destination" box, then click "Travel and Transportation").

Speed Limits: Speed limits are in miles per hour: 30 mph in town, 70 mph on the motorways, and 60 or 70 mph elsewhere.

STOP AND LEARN THESE ROAD SIGNS

Speed Limit (mph) · Yield · No Passing · End of No Passing Zone

One Way · Intersection · Roundabout Ahead · Expressway

Danger · No Entry · Cars Prohibited · All Vehicles Prohibited

No Through Road · Restrictions No Longer Apply · Yield to Oncoming Traffic · No Stopping

Parking · No Parking · Road Narrows · Peace

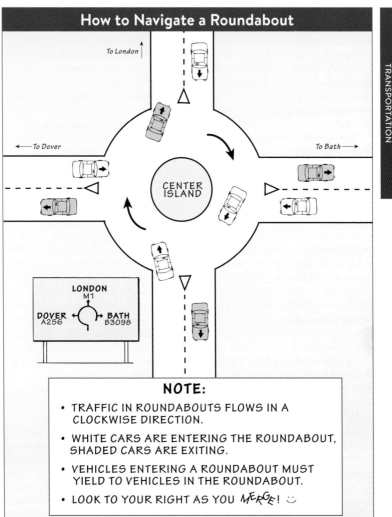

The national sign for the maximum speed is a white circle with a black slash. Motorways have electronic speed limit signs; posted speeds can change depending on traffic or the weather.

Note that road-surveillance cameras strictly enforce speed limits. Any driver (including foreigners renting cars) photographed speeding will get a nasty bill in the mail. Signs (an image of an old-fashioned camera) alert you when you're

entering a zone that may be monitored by these "camera cops." Heed them.

Roundabouts: Don't let a roundabout spook you. After all, you routinely merge into much faster traffic on American highways back home. Traffic flows clockwise, and cars already in the roundabout have the right-of-way; entering traffic yields (look to your right as you merge). You'll probably encounter "double-roundabouts"—figure-eights where you'll slingshot from one roundabout directly into another. Just go with the flow and track signs carefully. When approaching an especially complex roundabout, you'll first pass a diagram showing the layout and the various exits. And in many cases, the pavement is painted to indicate the lane you should be in for a particular road or town.

Freeways (Motorways): The shortest distance between any two points is usually the motorway (what we'd call a "freeway"). In Britain, the smaller the number, the bigger the road. For example, the M-4 is a freeway, while the B-4494 is a country road.

Motorway road signs can be confusing, too few, and too late. Miss a motorway exit and you can lose 30 minutes. Study your map before taking off. Know the cities you'll be lacing together, since road numbers are inconsistent. British road signs are never marked with compass directions (e.g., A-4 West); instead, you need to know what major town or city you're heading for (A-4 Bath). The driving directions in this book are intended to be used with a good map.

Unless you're passing, always drive in the "slow" lane on motorways (the lane farthest to the left). Remember to pass on the right, not the left.

Rest areas are called "services" and often have a number of useful amenities, such as restaurants, cafeterias, gas stations, shops, and motels.

Fuel: Gas (petrol) costs about $5.50 per gallon and is self-serve. Pump first and then pay. Diesel costs about the same. Diesel rental cars are common; make sure you know what kind of fuel your car takes before you fill up. Unleaded pumps are green and labeled "E," while diesel pumps (often yellow or black) are labeled "B."

Note that self-service gas pumps and automated tollbooths and parking garages often accept only a chip-and-PIN credit card or cash. It might help if you know the PIN for your US credit and debit cards,

but just in case a machine rejects them, be sure to carry sufficient cash.

Driving in Cities: Whenever possible, avoid driving in cities. Be warned that London assesses a congestion charge. Most cities have modern ring roads to skirt the congestion. Follow signs to the parking lots outside the city core—most are a 5- to 10-minute walk to the center—and avoid what can be an unpleasant grid of one-way streets (as in Bath) or roads that are only available to public transportation during the day (as in Oxford).

Driving in Rural Areas: Outside the big cities and except for the motorways, British roads tend to be narrow. Adjust your perceptions of personal space: It's not "my side of the road" or "your side of the road," it's just "the road"—and it's shared as a cooperative adventure. If the road's wide enough, traffic in both directions can pass parked cars simultaneously, but frequently you'll have to take turns—follow the locals' lead and drive defensively.

Narrow country lanes are often lined with stone walls or woody hedges—and no shoulders. Some are barely wide enough for one car (one-lane roads are often referred to as "single-track" roads). Go slowly, and if you encounter an oncoming car, look for the nearest pullout (or "passing place")—the driver who's closest to one is expected to use it, even if it means backing up to reach it. If another car pulls over and blinks its headlights, that means, "Go ahead; I'll wait to let you pass."

Parking: Pay attention to pavement markings to figure out where to park. One yellow line marked on the pavement means no parking Monday through Saturday during work hours. Double yellow lines mean no parking at any time. Broken yellow lines mean short stops are OK, but you should always look for explicit signs or ask a passerby. White lines mean you're free to park.

In towns, rather than look for street parking, I generally just pull into the most

It's cheaper to fly to England in winter, and London makes the season fun.

central and handy pay-and-display parking lot I can find. To pay and display, feed change into a machine, receive a timed ticket, and display it on the dashboard or stick it to the driver's-side window. Most machines in larger towns accept credit cards with a chip, but it's smart to keep coins handy for machines that don't.

In some municipalities, drivers will see signs for "disc zone" parking. This is free, time-limited parking. But to use it, you must obtain a clock parking disc from a shop and display it on the dashboard (set the clock to show your time of arrival). Return within the signed time limit to avoid being ticketed.

Some parking garages (a.k.a. car parks) are automated and record your license plate with a camera when you enter. The Brits call a license plate a "number plate" or just "vehicle registration." The payment machine will use these terms when you pay before exiting.

Flights

To compare flight costs and times, begin with an online travel search engine: Kayak is the top site for flights to and within

Europe, easy-to-use Google Flights has price alerts, and Skyscanner includes many inexpensive flights within Europe. To avoid unpleasant surprises, before you book be sure to read the small print about refunds, changes, and the costs for "extras" such as reserving a seat, checking a bag, or printing a boarding pass.

Flights to Europe: Start looking for international flights about four to six months before your trip, especially for peak-season travel. Depending on your itinerary, it can be efficient and no more expensive to fly into one city and out of another. If your flight requires a connection in Europe, see my hints on navigating Europe's top hub airports at www. ricksteves.com/hub-airports.

Flights Within Europe: Flying between European cities is surprisingly affordable. Before buying a long-distance train or bus ticket, check the cost of a flight on one of Europe's airlines, whether a major carrier or a no-frills outfit like **EasyJet** or **Ryanair.** Other airlines to consider include **CityJet** (based at London City Airport, www. cityjet.com), **TUI Airways** (www.tui. co.uk), **Flybe** (www.flybe.com), and **Brussels Airlines** (with frequent connections from Heathrow to its Brussels hub, www. brusselsairlines.com).

Be aware that flying with a discount airline can have drawbacks, such as minimal customer service and time-consuming treks to secondary airports.

Flying to the US and Canada: Because security is extra tight for flights to the US, be sure to give yourself plenty of time at the airport. Charge your electronic devices before you board in case security checks require you to turn them on (see www.tsa.gov for the latest rules).

Resources from Rick Steves

Begin Your Trip at RickSteves.com

My mobile-friendly website is the place to explore Europe in preparation for your trip. You'll find thousands of fun articles, videos, and radio interviews; a wealth of money-saving tips for planning your dream trip; travel news dispatches; a video library of my travel talks; my travel blog; tips on finding the right rail pass for your itinerary and budget, and our latest guidebook updates (www.ricksteves.com/update).

Our **Travel Forum** is a well-groomed collection of message boards where our travel-savvy community answers questions and shares personal travel experiences —and our well-traveled staff chimes in when they can be helpful.

Our **online Travel Store** offers bags and accessories designed to help you travel smarter and lighter. These include my popular carry-on bags (which I live out of four months a year), money belts, totes, toiletries kits, adapters, and guidebooks.

Rick Steves' Tours, Guidebooks, TV Shows, and More

Small Group Tours: We offer more than 40 itineraries reaching the best destinations in this book...and beyond. You'll enjoy great guides and a fun bunch of travel partners. For all the details and to get a tour catalog, visit RickSteves.com/tours or call us at 425/608-4217.

Books: This book is just one of many in my series on European travel, which includes country and city guidebooks, Snapshots (excerpted chapters from bigger guides), Pocket guides (full-color little books on big cities), and my budget-travel skills handbook, *Rick Steves Europe Through the Back Door*. A complete list of titles appears near the end of this book.

TV Shows and Travel Talks: My public television series, *Rick Steves' Europe,* covers Europe from top to bottom with over 100 half-hour episodes (watch them at the website). My free online video library, Rick Steves Classroom Europe, offers a searchable database of short video clips on European history, culture, and geography. And, to raise your travel I.Q., check out the video versions of our popular classes (covering most European countries as well as travel skills).

Audio Tours on My Free App: I've produced dozens of free, self-guided audio tours of the top sights in Europe. For those tours and other audio content, get my free **Rick Steves Audio Europe app,** an extensive online library organized by destination. For more on the app, see page 29.

Radio: My weekly public radio show, *Travel with Rick Steves,* features interviews with travel experts from around the world. It airs on 400 public radio stations across the US, or you can hear it as a podcast. A complete archive of programs is available on my website.

Podcasts: You can enjoy my travel content via several free podcasts, including my radio show, clips from my public television show, my audio tours of Europe's top sights, and my travel classes.

HOLIDAYS AND FESTIVALS

This list includes selected festivals in England plus national holidays observed throughout Britain (when many sights and banks close). Before planning a trip around a festival, verify the dates with the festival website, the Visit Britain website (www.visitbritain.com), or RickSteves.com.

Jan 1	New Year's Day
Mid-Feb	London Fashion Week (www.londonfashionweek.co.uk)
Mid-Feb	Jorvik Viking Festival, York (www.jorvik-viking-festival.co.uk)
May	Early May Bank Holiday (first Mon); Spring Bank Holiday (last Mon)
Early-mid-May	Jazz Festival, Keswick (www.keswickjazzfestival.co.uk)
Late May	Chelsea Flower Show, London (www.rhs.org.uk/chelsea)
Late May-early June	Bath Festival (www.bathfestivals.org.uk)
Late May-early June	Fringe Festival, Bath (www.bathfringe.co.uk)
Early June	Beer Festival, Keswick (www.keswickbeerfestival.co.uk)
Early-mid June	Trooping the Colour, London (www.qbp.army.mod.uk)
Late June	Royal Ascot Horse Race, Ascot (near Windsor; www.ascot.co.uk)
Late June-mid-July	Wimbledon Tennis Championship, London (www.wimbledon.org)
Mid-July	Early Music Festival, York (www.ncem.co.uk)
Late Aug	Notting Hill Carnival, London (www.thelondonnottinghillcarnival.com)
Late Aug	Bank Holiday (last Mon)
Mid-Sept	London Fashion Week (www.londonfashionweek.co.uk)
Late Sept	Jane Austen Festival, Bath (www.janeausten.co.uk)
Late Sept	York Food and Drink Festival (www.yorkfoodfestival.com)
Nov 5	Bonfire Night (bonfires, fireworks, effigy burning of 1605 traitor Guy Fawkes)
Dec 24-26	Christmas holidays

CONVERSIONS AND CLIMATE

Numbers and Stumblers

- Some British people write a few of their numbers differently than we do: 1 = 1, 4 = 4, 7 = 7.
- In Europe, dates appear as day/month/year, so Christmas 2022 is 25/12/22.
- What Americans call the second floor of a building is the first floor in Britain.
- On escalators and moving sidewalks, Brits keep the left "lane" open for passing. Keep to the right.
- To avoid the British version of giving someone "the finger," don't hold up the first two fingers of your hand with your palm facing you. (It looks like a reversed victory sign.)

Weights and Measures

Britain uses the metric system for nearly everything, including most weight and volume measurements. A **kilogram** equals 1,000 grams (about 2.2 pounds). One hundred **grams** (a common unit at markets) is about a quarter-pound. One **liter** is about a quart, or almost four to a gallon.

However, Britain still uses some imperial measurements. Driving distances and speed limits are measured in miles. Beer is sold as **pints**—a British pint equals 1.2 US pints (milk can be measured in pints or liters). An imperial **gallon** is 1.2 US gallons (about 4.5 liters). A person's weight is calculated in **stones** (1 stone equals 14 pounds).

Clothing Sizes

Women: For pants and dresses, add 4 (US 10 = UK 14). For blouses and sweaters, add 2. For shoes, subtract 2½ (US size 8 = UK size 5½).

Men: For clothing, US and UK sizes are the same. For shoes, subtract about ½ (US size 9 = UK size 8½).

Children: Clothing is sized similarly to the US. UK kids' shoe sizes are about one size smaller (US size 6 = UK size 5).

Britain's Climate

First line, average daily high; second line, average low; third line, average days without rain. For more detailed weather statistics for destinations in this book (and elsewhere), check www.wunderground.com.

London

J	F	M	A	M	J	J	A	S	O	N	D
43°	44°	50°	56°	62°	69°	71°	71°	65°	58°	50°	45°
36°	36°	38°	42°	47°	53°	56°	56°	52°	46°	42°	38°
16	15	20	18	19	19	19	20	17	18	15	16

York

J	F	M	A	M	J	J	A	S	O	N	D
43°	44°	49°	55°	61°	67°	70°	69°	64°	57°	49°	45°
33°	34°	36°	40°	44°	50°	54°	53°	50°	44°	39°	36°
14	13	18	17	18	16	16	17	16	16	13	14

Packing Checklist

Whether you're traveling for five days or five weeks, you won't need more than this. Pack light to enjoy the sweet freedom of true mobility.

Clothing

- ❑ 5 shirts: long- & short-sleeve
- ❑ 2 pairs pants (or skirts/capris)
- ❑ 1 pair shorts
- ❑ 5 pairs underwear & socks
- ❑ 1 pair walking shoes
- ❑ Sweater or warm layer
- ❑ Rainproof jacket with hood
- ❑ Tie, scarf, belt, and/or hat
- ❑ Swimsuit
- ❑ Sleepwear/loungewear

Money

- ❑ Debit card(s)
- ❑ Credit card(s)
- ❑ Hard cash (US $100-200)
- ❑ Money belt

Documents

- ❑ Passport
- ❑ Tickets & confirmations: flights, hotels, trains, rail pass, car rental, sight entries
- ❑ Driver's license
- ❑ Student ID, hostel card, etc.
- ❑ Photocopies of important documents
- ❑ Insurance details
- ❑ Guidebooks & maps

Toiletries Kit

- ❑ Basics: soap, shampoo, toothbrush, toothpaste, floss, deodorant, sunscreen, brush/comb, etc.
- ❑ Medicines & vitamins
- ❑ First-aid kit
- ❑ Glasses/contacts/sunglasses
- ❑ Sewing kit
- ❑ Packet of tissues (for WC)
- ❑ Earplugs

Electronics

- ❑ Mobile phone
- ❑ Camera & related gear
- ❑ Tablet/ebook reader/laptop
- ❑ Headphones/earbuds
- ❑ Chargers & batteries
- ❑ Phone car charger & mount (or GPS device)
- ❑ Plug adapters

Miscellaneous

- ❑ Daypack
- ❑ Sealable plastic baggies
- ❑ Laundry supplies: soap, laundry bag, clothesline, spot remover
- ❑ Small umbrella
- ❑ Travel alarm/watch
- ❑ Notepad & pen
- ❑ Journal

Optional Extras

- ❑ Second pair of shoes (flip-flops, sandals, tennis shoes, boots)
- ❑ Travel hairdryer
- ❑ Picnic supplies
- ❑ Water bottle
- ❑ Fold-up tote bag
- ❑ Small flashlight
- ❑ Mini binoculars
- ❑ Small towel or washcloth
- ❑ Inflatable pillow/neck rest
- ❑ Tiny lock
- ❑ Address list (to mail postcards)
- ❑ Extra passport photos

INDEX

MAP INDEX

Start your trip at

Our website enhances this book and turns

Explore Europe

At ricksteves.com you can browse through thousands of articles, videos, photos and radio interviews, plus find a wealth of money-saving travel tips for planning your dream trip. And with our mobile-friendly website, you can easily access all this great travel information anywhere you go.

TV Shows

Preview the places you'll visit by watching entire half-hour episodes of *Rick Steves' Europe* (choose from all 100 shows) on-demand, for free.

ricksteves.com

your travel dreams into affordable reality

Radio Interviews

Enjoy ready access to Rick's vast library of radio interviews covering travel tips and cultural insights that relate specifically to your Europe travel plans.

Travel Forums

Learn, ask, share! Our online community of savvy travelers is a great resource for first-time travelers to Europe, as well as seasoned pros.

Travel News

Subscribe to our free Travel News e-newsletter, and get monthly updates from Rick on what's happening in Europe.

Classroom Europe

Check out our free resource for educators with 400+ short video clips from the *Rick Steves' Europe* TV show.

Audio Europe™

Rick's Free Travel App

Get your FREE Rick Steves Audio Europe™ app to enjoy...

- Dozens of self-guided tours of Europe's top museums, sights and historic walks
- Hundreds of tracks filled with cultural insights and sightseeing tips from Rick's radio interviews
- All organized into handy geographic playlists
- For Apple and Android

With Rick whispering in your ear, Europe gets even better.

Find out more at ricksteves.com

Pack Light and Right

Gear up for your next adventure at ricksteves.com

Light Luggage

Pack light and right with Rick Steves' affordable, custom-designed rolling carry-on bags, backpacks, day packs and shoulder bags.

Accessories

From packing cubes to moneybelts and beyond, Rick has personally selected the travel goodies that will help your trip go smoother.

Rick Steves has

Experience maximum Europe

Save time and energy

This guidebook is your independent-travel toolkit. But for all it delivers, it's still up to you to devote the time and energy it takes to manage the preparation and logistics that are essential for a happy trip. If that's a hassle, there's a solution.

Rick Steves Tours

A Rick Steves tour takes you to Europe's most

great tours, too!

with minimum stress

interesting places with great guides and small groups of 28 or less. We follow Rick's favorite itineraries, ride in comfy buses, stay in family-run hotels, and bring you intimately close to the Europe you've traveled so far to see. Most importantly, we take away the logistical headaches so you can focus on the fun.

nearly half of them repeat customers—along with us on four dozen different itineraries, from Ireland to Italy to Athens.

Is a Rick Steves tour the right fit for your travel dreams? Find out at ricksteves.com, where you can also request Rick's latest tour catalog.

Europe is best experienced with happy travel partners. We hope you can join us.

Join the fun

This year we'll take 33,000 free-spirited travelers—

See our itineraries at ricksteves.com

A Guide for Every Trip

BEST OF GUIDES

Full color easy-to-scan format, focusing on Europe's most popular destinations and sights

Best of England
Best of Europe
Best of France
Best of Germany
Best of Ireland
Best of Italy
Best of Scotland
Best of Spain

COMPREHENSIVE GUIDES

City, country, and regional guides with detailed coverage for a multi-week trip exploring the most iconic sights and venturing off the beaten track

Amsterdam & the Netherlands
Barcelona
Belgium: Bruges, Brussels, Antwerp & Ghent
Berlin
Budapest
Croatia & Slovenia
Eastern Europe
England
Florence & Tuscany
France
Germany
Great Britain
Greece: Athens & the Peloponnese
Iceland
Ireland
Istanbul
Italy
London
Paris
Portugal
Prague & the Czech Republic
Provence & the French Riviera
Rome
Scandinavia
Scotland
Sicily
Spain
Switzerland
Venice
Vienna, Salzburg & Tirol

THE BEST OF ROME

Rome, Italy's capital, is studded with Roman remnants and floodlit-fountain squares. From the Vatican to the Colosseum, with crazy traffic in between, Rome is wonderful, huge, and exhausting. The crowds, the heat, and the weighty history of the Eternal City where Caesars walked can make tourists wilt. Recharge by taking siestas, gelato breaks, and after-dark walks, strolling from one atmospheric square to another in the refreshing evening air.

...ired **Pantheon**—which ...rgest dome until the ...early 2,000 years old ...a day over 1,500).

...ol of Athens in the **Vat-** ...bodies the humanistic ...sance.

...h, gladiators fought ...e another, entertaining ...0.

POCKET GUIDES

Compact, full color city guides with the essentials for shorter trips

SNAPSHOT GUIDES

Focused single-destination coverage

Rick Steves books are available from your favorite bookseller. Many guides are available as ebooks.

CRUISE PORTS GUIDES

Reference for cruise ports of call

Complete your library with...

TRAVEL SKILLS & CULTURE

PHRASE BOOKS & DICTIONARIES

PLANNING MAPS

Be creative! You c "Two, please," "Please, where any language, especial want, such as the bil please).

HELLOS A

Pleasantries

Hello.
Do you speak English?
Yes. / No.
I don't speak French.
I'm sorry.
Please.
Thank you (v much).
Excuse me attention!
Excuse m
OK?
OK. (two say it)
Good.

ACKNOWLEDGMENTS

Thank you to Risa Laib for her 25-plus years of dedication to the Rick Steves guidebook series.

PHOTO CREDITS

Avalon Travel
Hachette Book Group
1700 Fourth Street
Berkeley, CA 94710

Printed in China by RR Donnelley
Third Edition
First printing January 2021

ISBN: 978-1-64171-306-1

For the latest on Rick's talks, guidebooks, tours, public television series, and public radio show, contact Rick Steves' Europe, 130 Fourth Avenue North, Edmonds, WA 98020, 425/771-8303, www.ricksteves.com, rick@ricksteves.com.

RICK STEVES' EUROPE
Managing Editor: Jennifer Madison Davis
Assistant Managing Editor: Cathy Lu
Special Publications Manager: Risa Laib
Editors: Glenn Eriksen, Tom Griffin, Suzanne Kotz, Rosie Leutzinger, Teresa Nemeth, Jessica Shaw, Carrie Shepherd, Meg Sneeringer
Editorial & Production Assistant: Megan Simms
Graphic Content Director: Sandra Hundacker
Maps & Graphics: David C. Hoerlein, Lauren Mills, Mary Rostad
Digital Asset Coordinator: Orin Dubrow

AVALON TRAVEL
Senior Editor and Series Manager: Maddy Prasher
Associate Managing Editors: Jamie Andrade, Sierra Machado
Copy Editor: Kelly Lydick
Indexer: Stephen Callahan
Production: Rue Flaherty, Jane Musser, Ravina Schneider
Cover Design: Kimberly Glyder Design
Maps & Graphics: Kat Bennett, Mike Morgenfeld

Although every effort was made to ensure that the information was correct at the time of going to press, the author and publisher do not assume and hereby disclaim any liability to any party for any loss or damage caused by errors, omissions, mushy peas, or any potential travel disruption due to labor or financial difficulty, whether such errors or omissions result from negligence, accident, or any other cause.

Let's Keep on Travelin'

Your trip doesn't need to end.

Follow Rick on social media!